WITHOUT HONOR

WITHOUT HOPE

WITHOUT HONOR

Defeat in Vietnam and Cambodia

Arnold R. Isaacs

THE JOHNS HOPKINS UNIVERSITY PRESS

Baltimore and London

© 1983 by THE JOHNS HOPKINS UNIVERSITY PRESS

All rights reserved

Printed in the United States of America on acid-free paper

Johns Hopkins Paperbacks edition, 1999
9 8 7 6 5 4 3 2 1

The Johns Hopkins University Press
2715 North Charles Street
Baltimore, Maryland 21218-4363
www.press.jhu.edu

The Library of Congress has cataloged the hardcover edition as follows:

Isaacs, Arnold R.
  Without honor.

  Bibliography: p. 535
  Includes index.
    1. Vietnamese Conflict, 1961–1975.   2. Indochina—
History—1945-   I. Title.
DS557.7.I82   1983   959.704´3   83-48054
ISBN 0-8018-3060-5
ISBN 0-8018-6107-1 (pbk.)

A catalog record for this book is available from the British Library.

for
H. R. I. and V. R. I.

Contents

vii

Illustrations and Maps

Preface

The years 1972 to 1975 saw the conclusion of America's military effort in Vietnam, the failure of an illusory peace agreement, and finally the collapse of the U.S.-backed armies in South Vietnam and Cambodia and the Communist conquest of all of Indochina, amid scenes of terror and suffering that will forever sear the memories of those who were there. This book is an account of what happened in those years. Though it is not a personal memoir, I was present during most of the major events of the period. I arrived in Vietnam for the first time in June 1972 and served as Saigon correspondent for the Baltimore *Sun* until July 1973, traveling during that time throughout South Vietnam and also in Laos and Cambodia. During 1974 I returned to Indochina periodically from my new base in Hong Kong, again traveling widely through the Vietnamese countryside. In 1975 I spent the entire last three months of the war in Vietnam and Cambodia, reporting on the unfolding military and human disasters in both countries. I left Vietnam for the last time aboard a U.S. evacuation helicopter on the afternoon of April 29, 1975, the final day before Saigon's surrender to the Communists.

That first-hand experience, I believe, is useful chiefly in lending this book something of the *feel* of the history it describes. In writing it, I have tried not just to retell events but also to give the reader some sense of their mood and texture and setting; a sense, I hope, of the nature of the societies and the war and how it looked and sounded and felt to be there in that time, especially in the last grim months before the Communist victory. As to the events themselves, a working correspondent's perceptions, though vivid, are also hurried and episodic and incomplete, particularly in tumultuous or dangerous situations. For that reason, though I have drawn some vignettes and other material directly from my notebooks and dispatches of the period, I have tried wherever possible to verify and expand that material from documentary sources. My research turned up an unexpected wealth of government and military records, official and quasi-official reports, and unpublished personal narratives. Together with the memoirs of key officials and other published material, these make possible a far more comprehensive and authoritative account than any single reporter could have compiled at the time the events were taking place.

In this account, I have to the limits of my ability remained scrupulously faithful to the facts as I was able to determine them. Where the evidence is elusive or ambiguous or incomplete, I have attempted to make that clear to the reader; where I have stated suppositions or opinions, I have tried in every case to label them as such, while also explaining the basis for them. The sources for all quotations or factual statements that are not based on my own reports from Indochina are given in the notes that follow the text; the only exceptions are a small number of statements from informants who wished to remain unnamed. No individual mentioned in the book is imaginary or a composite. In two cases I have used pseudonyms, which are identified as such in the text. All other names are genuine. I have not made up or reconstructed any direct quotations, or relied on my own or anyone else's memory for the words. All quotations appear here exactly as they occur in my own notebooks or in the documentary materials I have used. The personal judgments and conclusions expressed here are of course fallible and subject to dispute, and many readers, I am sure, will disagree with them. I can only hope that they will nonetheless perceive my effort to derive those judgments from a fair and careful examination of the facts.

In general, I think my views will be sufficiently clear to any reader and need not be detailed here. But one point does need to be made. This book is strongly, even passionately, critical of American decisions in the last three years of the war. I believe those decisions were for the most part callous, cynical, and wrong, and that more humane possibilities existed. Yet I also believe that there were no longer any good choices for the United States to make, only choices of evils, and my judgments should be viewed in that context. The basic moral decisions of the war were not those that prohibited a last few weeks of bombing or denied a last few hundred million dollars of aid in the final months of the conflict, as Richard Nixon and Henry Kissinger and their apologists argue. The crucial American choice was made much earlier, when virtually all institutions of American public life and all segments of American opinion concluded that the goals of our intervention were unattainable and that extrication from the war had become imperative. I too held that view at the time, and I still believe that choice was unavoidable. But I also came to understand that it represented a broken promise to millions of Vietnamese—not just a few corrupt generals—who depended on American protection against a ruthless and determined enemy. Abandoning our Vietnam effort was a necessary act, in terms of our own needs, but it was also an act of betrayal, for which the overwhelming majority of Americans, including both our leaders and their critics, share the responsibility. By the time of the events described in this book, that betrayal was an irreversible fact, part of a tragic set of circumstances that arose from our earlier errors, and in which any possible American decision at the end of the war would be, in some measure, wrong.

No one could witness these events without strong emotions. Mine, I think, will be evident to any reader of this book. When I left Vietnam, I was full of an anguished rage at all who had caused and sustained the many years of butchery there. All of the warring parties, I felt, were careless of the human cost of their decisions. None of them, not the Vietnamese Communists, nor the military rulers of South Vietnam, nor the leaders of the United States, were motivated by any decent concern for the millions of people caught up in the conflict, or represented any cause that seemed to me to justify the violence and suffering they all inflicted. All of them, I believed, shared the blame for a war of immense and needless cruelty. That remains my conviction today; my anguish, too, remains. Along with all I learned in Indochina about venality and violence and despair, I also remember countless humbling lessons, taught to me by ordinary Cambodians and Lao and Vietnamese, about bravery and endurance and dignity under terrible hardship. I only wish those men and women had had a cause or a leadership worthy of their sacrifices.

This book contains a great deal that is critical, and little in praise, of American and South Vietnamese officials. Therefore it is all the more necessary to acknowledge here that a great many of those same officials, both military and civilian, generously shared their knowledge and understanding with me during my years of reporting in Indochina. They did so with remarkable patience and cordiality, even though many of them must have felt that the American press was no friend of their cause. I am grateful to them all, as I am to the many soldiers, peasants, and other Vietnamese, Lao, and Cambodians who answered my questions and tried to help me understand their lives and their countries. I owe thanks also to the editors of the Baltimore *Sun*, particularly Paul Banker, who allowed me an extraordinary degree of freedom not only during my six years in Asia but through my entire career on the staff of that newspaper. I am thankful to Edward K. Wu, my colleague in the *Sun*'s Hong Kong bureau, whose comprehensive and well-organized files of Communist news agency reports and other material were an indispensable aid in my research.

To my fellow correspondents in Southeast Asia I am indebted for kindnesses at many times and in many places. I thank Dan Southerland, Barry Hillenbrand, Mal and Le Lieu Browne, Neal Ulevich, George Esper, Dick Pyle, Denis Gray, Dick Blystone, Bob and Civia Tamarkin, Sydney Schanberg, Tiziano Terzani, Bud Pratt, Arnie Abrams, John Schulz, and Ann Mariano for their many acts of friendship and assistance. Don Oberdorfer, one of the best and wisest of all American reporters, lent me a bulky file of his notes and other material, including his historic photographs of Hue just before it fell to the Communists in March 1975. Paul Brinkley-Rogers allowed me to use his notes on the final days of the Khmer Republic. Brian Barron replayed tape recordings and showed me his films of Da Nang just before its fall, and Roy Rowan—who was the very first to suggest that I write this book—let me use his tapes of radio conversations at sea during the Saigon evacuation. Brian Ellis helped me to reunite three families that would otherwise have been broken apart in the chaos of South Vietnam's collapse, and for that he has my admiration, respect, and thanks—as well as those of the hundreds of others he managed to help in those last weeks of the war. I owe a very special debt of gratitude to Larry Green and Lien Huong, whose friendship in the midst of so much misery sustained me more than they can possibly know.

For assistance during my research in the U.S., I have to thank that most unusual general, John E. Murray, former U.S. Defense Attache in Saigon, who not only searched his own records but made numerous inquiries on my behalf to help clarify several important points. I am all the more grateful because he helped me knowing that he would probably disapprove of many of the judgments in this book. Representative Paul N. McCloskey, Jr., one of the more serious congressional students of the war and a frequent visitor to Indochina, allowed me access to his personal files, which provided a mass of invaluable material. I was also allowed to use the private files of Representative Millicent Fenwick, a member of the congressional delegation to Vietnam in early 1975; Donald I. Berney, former head of the Saigon office of the Military Sealift Command; and John H. Sullivan, formerly of the House Foreign Affairs Committee staff. Robert L. Burke, former chief of information for the American military command in Vietnam, lent me several significant documents from his personal records. Charles Whitehouse and Bui Diem shared their recollections and insights in two long and useful conversations, and Donald M. Fraser took the time to write a letter clearing up a minor but troublesome mystery. William E. Le Gro, Charles R. Timmes, Chhang Song, Spencer M. King, Thomas C. Thayer, Willard Webb, Peter Arnett, and Frank Snepp answered telephone inquiries.

I received invaluable assistance from Richard Hunt, Vince Demma, and Jeff Powell at the U.S. Army Center of Military History; from Edward Marolda at the Operational Archives Branch of the Naval Historical Center; from Ben Frank and Joyce Bonnett at the Marine Corps Historical Center; and from Lou Granger at the Military Sealift Command Headquarters. Thomas Ainsworth of the State Department and Lt. Col. Kerry J. Crane of the Air Force helped clear the way for my access to certain restricted materials; their attitude of helpful common sense saved me what could otherwise have been months of bureaucratic haggling. I am particularly grateful to Cathy Lawson of the State Department for tracking down the memorable photograph by David Hume Kennerly that appears on the jacket. I am thankful also to the staffs of the Enoch Pratt Free Library of the City of Baltimore, the Milton S. Eisenhower Library of the Johns Hopkins University, the Albert S. Cook Library of Towson State University, and the Albin O. Kuhn Library of the University of Maryland Baltimore County.

Brad Jacobs was instrumental in reviving this project when it seemed to have no future, and John Woodruff, Peter Jay, and Steve Broening read and commented usefully on all or parts of the manuscript. Dave McElroy and Edie Foley helped prepare the maps. At the Johns Hopkins University Press, I am grateful to Jack Goellner, Carol Ehrlich, Barbara Lamb, Gerry Valerio, Nancy Essig, and especially Anders Richter, for their help and support. None of those named here can be held responsible for the judgments expressed in this book; for any errors of fact or interpretation, I alone am to blame.

To this list I have finally to add the names of Jenny, Katy, and Robert, for enlivening my life and for teaching me the real secret of being a successful parent—which is to have nice children. To my wife, Kathy, I give thanks for countless reasons, of which I will mention only one: her instant and unswerving support for my decision to give up fulltime employment in order to write this book. My last acknowledgment is to my parents, Harold and Viola Isaacs, married 50 years, for the first and most enduring lessons in the telling of truth and the meaning of love. It is to them that this book is dedicated.

ARNOLD R. ISAACS

PART I

The
Peace

Chronology

1972

JANUARY

25   President Nixon discloses that Henry Kissinger has been secretly negotiating with the North Vietnamese since 1969.

FEBRUARY

21–28   President Nixon visits China.

MARCH

30   The North Vietnamese open a major offensive in South Vietnam.

APRIL

4   U.S. resumes bombing North Vietnam after a three-and-one-half-year halt.

MAY

1   Quang Tri Province capital falls to the Communists.

8   Nixon orders mining of North Vietnamese ports and waterways.

22–30   Nixon visits the Soviet Union.

JULY

19   Henry Kissinger and North Vietnam's Le Duc Tho resume peace talks in Paris.

SEPTEMBER

15   South Vietnamese marines recapture Quang Tri City.

OCTOBER

8–12   In Paris, Le Duc Tho proposes a new peace plan, for the first time offering a settlement without the removal of South Vietnam's President Nguyen Van Thieu. After reaching agreement on all but a few details, he and Kissinger also agree that the pact will be signed October 31, following a secret journey by Kissinger to Hanoi.

18–23   In a final exchange of messages with Hanoi, Nixon affirms that the agreement is "complete." But in Saigon, during five days of talks with Kissinger, President Thieu rejects the agreement.

26   Radio Hanoi broadcasts the agreement and accuses the U.S. of reneging. A few hours later, Kissinger announces that "peace is at hand."

NOVEMBER

7   Nixon is reelected by a landslide over Sen. George McGovern.

20   Kissinger and Tho resume negotiations in Paris.

DECEMBER

12   Thieu announces that he still opposes the "false peace."

16   Kissinger announces that the talks are deadlocked. He blames Hanoi.

18–30   Heavy air raids by B-52s and tactical aircraft are carried out on Hanoi, Haiphong, and other North Vietnamese targets.

30   The "Christmas bombing" ends, but raids continue in southern North Vietnam.

1973

JANUARY

8–13   Kissinger and Tho meet in Paris and again agree on a settlement. The principal features are the same that were drafted in October, though some minor changes have been made.

15   All remaining bombing in North Vietnam is halted.

21   After the last of a series of warnings from Nixon that U.S. aid will be cut off if Saigon continues to block an agreement, Thieu agrees to sign.

23 Kissinger and Tho initial the agreement.

26–27 Communist forces attack hundreds of villages in South Vietnam.

27 The agreement is formally signed in Paris.

28 Saigon time (January 27, Washington time) The agreement takes effect, calling for a ceasefire. But South Vietnamese troops keep fighting to recapture villages seized by the Communists just before the truce.

F E B R U A R Y

9 With nearly all the contested villages recaptured, government forces do not stop attacking but remain on the offensive.

9 U.S. bombing resumes in Cambodia, where no ceasefire exists. Many of the strikes are against North Vietnamese bases and supply routes in Cambodia. Bombing continues until halted by Congress on August 15.

M A R C H

15 The U.S. announces that it has protested to Hanoi about illegal infiltration of North Vietnamese troops and weapons into South Vietnam. Nixon warns Hanoi that it should not "lightly disregard" the protest. Kissinger urges Nixon to approve renewed air strikes on North Vietnam.

15 U.S.–North Vietnamese Joint Economic Commission begins meeting in Paris to arrange U.S. postwar reconstruction aid, promised in the agreement.

29 The last U.S. troops are airlifted out of South Vietnam, and the release of 595 American war prisoners is completed in Hanoi.

A P R I L

3 Nixon and Thieu meet in California. Nixon promises "adequate" aid and "vigorous reactions" if the Communists violate the agreement.

17 The U.S. breaks off talks on economic aid to Hanoi and withdraws its minesweeping task force from North Vietnam. The reasons given are ceasefire violations by the Communists and the lack of progress on military withdrawal from Cambodia.

25 Saigon and the Communists exchange proposals in Paris for a political settlement. Saigon demands withdrawal of all North Vietnamese forces followed by elections, while the Viet Cong want "democratic liberties" restored before any other action is taken. With only slight changes, each side will maintain the same position throughout the talks.

M A Y

17 Kissinger and Tho open new talks in Paris.

J U N E

13 The signers of the agreement issue a joint communique reaffirming its provisions, but providing no new enforcement measures. Fighting falls off, but only briefly. No settlement is reached on Cambodia.

J U L Y

19 The minesweeping force is again recalled from North Vietnam.

23 The talks on postwar U.S. reconstruction aid to Hanoi are suspended again.

A U G U S T

15 A congressional ban on all bombing or other U.S. military action in Southeast Asia takes effect.

O C T O B E R

 North Vietnam's leadership resolves that the struggle in the South must proceed along "the path of revolutionary violence."

16 The Nobel Peace Prize is awarded jointly to Kissinger and Le Duc Tho. Kissinger accepts, but Tho, saying that peace has not been established, declines.

Chapter 1

"This war will never end": January 28, 1973

As on every other morning, Saigon began to come awake before dawn. At five-thirty the sky was still black except for the glowing asterisks of parachute flares falling slowly toward the horizon, miles away. The nightly curfew would not legally end until six, but as usual was not being strictly enforced in its final half hour. Under dim streetlights yawning policemen, some in the gray civil police uniforms and others in the mottled brown fatigues of the paramilitary Field Police, slumped over their rifles after the nighttime vigil.

Trucks and jeeps loaded with troops or with supplies from the Saigon docks rolled past the steel-and-barbed-wire stanchions that stood in front of still-silent government ministries. The vehicles rumbled along boulevards whose names evoked almost 2,000 years of heroic memories: Hai Ba Trung, named after the two Trung sisters who led a Vietnamese uprising against Chinese occupiers in the first century A.D. and then drowned themselves rather than surrender when their rebellion failed; Le Loi, after the emperor who led another revolt against Chinese rule 1,400 years later; Nguyen Hue, after the warrior who reunified the country for the first time in 150 years at the end of the eighteenth century. Now, at the sound of the motors, murmured coos came from under the fluted-tile eaves of the old French-style buildings, where pigeons dozed and fidgeted through the darkness. In the doorways where the city's flotsam of homeless refugees spent their nights, families began to stir, rolling up the thin straw mats or army ponchos on which they had slept. Mothers huddled over small charcoal cooking fires

Fireworks in Hanoi in celebration of the Paris peace agreement
(*VNA/courtesy of Southeast Asia Resource Center*).

while their children wandered off to relieve themselves into gutters where packs of thin, snapping dogs argued morosely with the rats over piles of rotting garbage. Overhead, the night sky vibrated with the sound of blacked-out helicopters crossing over the city. Higher and farther sounded the motors of a patrolling gunship.

In the maze of alleys and lanes near the central market, a few shopowners were already taking down the wooden shutters from in front of their stalls as the dawn lightened. Some stalls were already decorated with sprays of brightly colored paper blossoms for the coming Tet festival: the lunar new year, gayest and best loved of Vietnamese holidays.

All the stalls bore another decoration: newly painted South Vietnamese flags, three horizontal red stripes across a saffron yellow field. By government order the flags had been painted on virtually every wall in the country, symbolizing the territorial control of the Republic of Vietnam.

At sidewalk soup kitchens, early risers hunched on low wooden stools, heads bent, chopsticks darting in bowls of steaming noodles flavored with pungent greens, hot red peppers, and spicy fish sauce. Food venders leaned over their braziers, the light of charcoal or kerosene fires reflecting on brown peasant faces under polished-straw conical hats. The singsong of Vietnamese voices sounded in the cool, smoky air, blending with the clink of tools wielded by streetcorner mechanics, with the scratchy wail of a tune from a cheap radio, with the splutter of traffic—the beginnings of the normal din of an Asian city, swelling quickly but not yet loud enough to smother the sound, louder these last few mornings than for many months past, of bombing and artillery out past the city's edge.

At six o'clock on the morning of January 28, 1973, there were still two hours to wait before the guns were supposed to be silenced by the cumbersomely titled Agreement on Ending the War and Restoring Peace in Vietnam, the result of more than four years of public and private peace negotiations. Proclaimed "peace with honor" by the president of the United States, greeted in the rest of the world with grateful relief, the agreement had brought no outpouring of joy in Saigon when it was announced four days earlier. Peace was an idea as remote as the legend of the Trung sisters; years of conflict had produced a terrible, sad numbness. "We have waited for this too long," a Vietnamese friend said to me after the peace agreement was announced. "Now we don't feel anything."

Midnight, Greenwich Mean Time, was the hour fixed in Article Two of the agreement for "the complete cessation of hostilities" throughout South Vietnam. That would be 8 A.M. in Saigon. In Hanoi, which would not agree with its southern adversary even on the time of day, the clocks would say 7 A.M. It would be one o'clock in the morning in Paris, where America's Henry Kissinger and North Vietnam's Le Duc Tho drafted and initialed the agreement and where, in the ballroom of the Hotel Majestic, it had been formally signed by the foreign ministers of the four warring governments: William P. Rogers for the United States, Nguyen Duy Trinh for North Vietnam, Mrs. Nguyen Thi Binh for the South Vietnamese Provisional Revolutionary Government, and, representing an unwilling and suspicious President Nguyen Van Thieu, Tran Van Lam for the Republic of Vietnam. The ceremonies, even the language of the agreement, reflected the undiminished hostility and mistrust and the unresolved disputes that still characterized the war. Because South Vietnam considered the Provisional Revolutionary Government illegal, while the Communists viewed the Saigon-based Republic of Vietnam as a puppet of the Americans with no legitimacy of its own, neither name appeared anywhere in the 23 articles of the treaty, which referred only to "the Vietnamese parties." Nor would Lam and Mrs. Binh consent to sign the same copy. Instead, they signed on separate pages. It was left to the American and North Vietnamese representatives alone to sign still a third copy with a slightly different text spelling out that Washington and Hanoi, "with the concurrence" of Saigon and the P.R.G., had agreed on the treaty's terms.

In Washington, where President Richard Nixon waited to proclaim a day of prayer and thanksgiving, it would still be Saturday evening—7 P.M., thirteen hours earlier than Saigon time—when the agreement took effect, ending America's involvement in the longest, least popular, and least understood war in its history.

As it always does in the tropics, day broke swiftly. By the time we had driven past the city's northern edge and turned onto Highway 13, a road of many bloody battles in the past ten months, the sky had lightened to a pale blue, the high wispy clouds touched with lavender where they were brushed by the slanting early rays of the sun. Above them, three luminous white contrails marked the soundless passage of a flight of U.S. B-52 heavy bombers; the planes themselves, as usual, were too high to be seen or heard. "Certainly the last trip for those crews, maybe one of the last for any American airmen over Vietnam," I wrote later that day, not knowing then that the bombers would fly for nearly another month over Laos and for more than half a year, in one of the heaviest, cruellest, and morally most questionable bombing campaigns of the whole war, over Cambodia.

Along the roadside, straggling columns of People's Self Defense Force volunteers—South Vietnam's home guard, over-aged men and youngsters barely into their teens, dressed in unmatching bits of uniforms and carrying outdated World War II carbines—trudged past, heading back home after night guard duty. Beyond them, the highway stretched away across the gently rolling, scrub-covered land toward the pounding of the guns. Farther on, past a stretch still held by the Communists despite a months-long, prodigiously costly South Vietnamese operation to clear it, the same road reached the shattered city of An Loc, where Lt. Col. William B. Nolde, the senior American adviser to the Binh Long Province chief, had been killed by a North Vietnamese shell at nine o'clock the night before. Nolde, 43 years old and the father of five children, had written a friend when the ceasefire was announced, "We tend to think only in terms of what this war has cost us, the United States, but by comparison to what it has cost so many Vietnamese, our price pales." He was the 46,941st American killed in action in the war—and, though not the last American to die in Vietnam, the last officially listed casualty of America's war there.

Fifteen minutes before the ceasefire, the rhythmic chug of a machinegun sounded from just beyond the palm-shaded houses and open-fronted shops of a hamlet called Chanh Hiep, which sat on the shoulder of the highway eighteen miles north of Saigon. Over the sound of machinegun fire came the higher-pitched, more rapid bursts of the government militia's American-supplied M-16 rifles and the answering slap of Communist AK-47s from farther out across the village rice fields. From the sound of the firing, the attacking force was small—no more than a squad, perhaps. The Communist command, as it had also done when a ceasefire was anticipated the previous October, had split its army into small bands and ordered them to penetrate all the villages they could reach, in the hope they could remain until their presence was legalized by international truce-observer teams.

The battle of Chanh Hiep had begun at three o'clock that morning, when a Communist loudspeaker called out of the darkness advising the hamlet's defenders to put down their weapons rather than risk dying in the war's last hours. Instead, the militiamen opened fire and traded shots for the rest of the night with the attackers. Now, the villagers stood or crouched in their doorways. They were afraid, with the fighting so near. But to leave would risk having their homes looted by government soldiers: they would not do so unless the hamlet itself came under fire. As eight o'clock approached, those who wore watches kept glancing at their wrists. Not much showed in their faces. It was as if they were wondering, but not really able to believe the firing would actually stop.

For one of them, a middle-aged office worker named Duong, the truce was already too late. He had driven from Saigon on his motorbike for his customary Sunday visit with his eighteen-year-old son, a member of the local militia unit. But he had not found the boy. Instead, he was told by a neighbor that the youngster was missing, believed captured by the Communists in a savage battle a few days earlier on one of Vietnam's perennial battlegrounds, the old Michelin rubber plantation that lay to the west, near the Cambodian border. Until that moment, Duong hadn't even known his son's unit had been sent to the plantation. "He is lost now," he said despairingly over the gunfire. "There is one chance in a million of finding him. If the Viet Cong have him I will never see him again."

Groups of soldiers stood in the village street: not infantry, but cadets from the South Vietnamese army's engineering school. Like many thousands of others plucked from noncombat duties that weekend, they had been handed rifles instead of textbooks and sent to the field, where the Saigon command wanted every available soldier to meet the expected pre-ceasefire attacks.

You could tell, looking at them, that the cadets were inexperienced and frightened. They kept looking anxiously toward the firing, where combat soldiers would have hardly turned their heads. One of them had a cheap portable radio and as the ceasefire hour neared, the others clustered around him, waiting for the time signal.

When it came, there was no pause in the rifle and machinegun fire nearby. The farther-away thump of artillery did not stop either.

Precisely at the stroke of eight o'clock the radio began broadcasting a speech by Nguyen Van Thieu, South Vietnam's wartime president, to whom the Paris agreement meant not peace for Vietnam but only abandonment by the United States. For three months he had resisted signing, until his American ally threatened to sign without him and to shut off the aid that kept his army in the field. But though he had finally consented to the agreement, none of Thieu's misgivings had truly been allayed. Just because "peace" is mentioned in the agreement, he was saying now on the radio, it does not mean that Vietnam will really have peace.

We stood in the dusty street and listened to Thieu's voice and to the undiminished gunfire and watched the hands of our watches crawl past one minute after another. Remember the Geneva agreements of 1954 and 1962, the president said, the Communists broke those treaties and they would also break this one. "We should not believe the Communists will respect the ceasefire. Believing this is a naive and erroneous attitude." Some of the listening cadets giggled, a Vietnamese way of showing not amusement but anxiety.

Other radios were on in the houses. Thieu's familiar high-pitched voice echoed in the street. In it was the same message that was also in the sound of rifle shots near the village. A ceasefire was not peace. The Communists could remain where their soldiers were at this hour, but, Thieu said, "this ceasefire does not mean the Communists will be able to go to the Saigon market and have beef noodles. Nor will they be allowed to return to the hamlets allegedly to visit their wives, parents, and brothers and sisters. . . . Any Communists who penetrate into the hamlets and villages must be shot dead on the spot." It was true, Thieu admitted, that no Tet had passed in peace for many years. But for this Tet too, wartime conditions would remain in force. Soldiers would stay with their units; leave would be granted later.

More minutes went by. A sergeant, not one of the cadets but an infantryman who paused on his way to rejoin his own unit farther on up the road, turned abruptly away from the radio and looked across the street, where the villagers now stood unsmiling and tense. No one was looking at watches any more. "The president can say anything," the sergeant said bitterly, "but this war will never end."

An hour later, South Vietnamese 105-mm howitzer shells were falling every ten seconds into another roadside hamlet named Tuong Hoa, a few miles past Chanh Hiep. The rounds passed overhead with the sound of sand sliding down a chute, followed an instant later by the dull, metallic splat of the explosion. Just out of sight in the jumble of houses on a shallow slope falling away to the east of the road, the sound of rifle fire and grenades resounded off masonry walls. Dust danced in the road every time a shell landed. Denser clouds of dust and smoke swirled over the village.

When the firing slackened for a moment, a woman appeared at the edge of the hamlet, jogging clumsily with a wailing child clinging to her back. The child was bleeding from shrapnel wounds in both buttocks. Raw, glistening red flesh showed through the flayed skin. Behind them came the rest of the villagers, using the brief lull to run for safety after having been trapped in their houses when the fighting began. Running at first, they slowed into a long, plodding line as they passed around a wide, shallow bend in the road. In their arms or on their heads they carried cooking pots or hurriedly done-up cloth parcels of possessions. Most walked silently, but one, a girl of ten or eleven, was sobbing hysterically, indicating with gestures that someone—her mother?—had been shot.

A moment later two infantrymen emerged from among the houses carrying a third, dead or badly wounded, his uniform soaked in blood from chest to knees. Then came an entire company, running half-crouched, each man stamped into the same classic image of fear and flight, rifle gripped in one hand, helmet clamped on with the other. A flurry of Communist rifle shots popped the air over our heads, and we too jogged back down the road.

As were its first hours, the rest of Ceasefire Day was also filled not with peace but with more images of suffering and death and violence: the ceaseless booming of artillery; the swallow-swoop of planes diving toward the horizon and then rising just ahead of black clouds of napalm, which sprouted soundlessly into the sky seconds before the sound of the explosions reached our ears; the winking headlights of jeeps racing past with casualties on stretchers that jutted over the rear seats, bouncing on the rough roads. At the Bien Hoa military cemetery I counted 56 new coffins stacked up awaiting burial, with red-and-yellow government flags draped over the cheap wood. Rows of empty graves stood open, waiting for more dead and headstones with names or simply the word "Unknown."

Back on the highway we were stopped at a roadblock in front of a village where angry flames rushed through shell-struck houses. An old peasant was arguing frantically but unsuccessfully with the soldiers at the barricade, pleading for permission to go back into the burning village to search for his wife. Two hours earlier she had been wounded—by a South Vietnamese artillery shell, he thought, although there had been no Communist troops in the village at the time. Not unkindly, but unyielding, the soldiers refused to allow him through the barricade. Finally he turned and walked back toward us, saying despairingly, "I don't believe in anybody or anything any more."

The fighting that day was extremely heavy everywhere in South Vietnam. The ceasefire "appeared to have initiated a new war, more intense and more brutal than the last," an American pacification official reported to his superiors from Lam Dong Province, at the southern end of the Annamite Hills. A major battle was being fought at Tay Ninh, a province capital northwest of Saigon. Correspondents who tried to make the 55-mile journey to Tay Ninh from Saigon on the morning of the ceasefire were able to get no farther than a place called Trang Bang, about halfway there, where Communist troops had cut the road and were engaged in a furious firefight with government forces trying to clear it. One carload of reporters waiting at Trang Bang tuned their radio to the American armed forces station, which began broadcasting President Nixon's ceasefire proclamation at exactly eight o'clock. Nixon had just reached the words "a new era of peace and understanding for all mankind" when a South Vietnamese fighter-bomber suddenly roared overhead and dropped its bombs with a tremendous clap only 100 yards or so from the road.

More than 400 miles north of Saigon, an artillery battle had raged all night over the wrecked city of Quang Tri, where South Vietnamese marines faced North Vietnamese infantry across lines that had not changed for months despite fighting that cost thousands of casualties on both sides. Craig Whitney, a *New York Times* reporter who had spent the night in one of the marines' bunkers, listened as the shelling kept on for a few minutes past eight o'clock. Then he saw an officer speak into a field phone, and the barrage stopped. The men in the bunker listened for incoming rounds, but the Communists had stopped firing too.

Peering over the rubble at enemy positions on the far bank of the Thach Han River, the marines suddenly saw a huge gold-starred red-and-blue Liberation flag rise into the quiet air. Then, amazingly, a few green-clad Communist soldiers stood up. A handful of marines cautiously climbed out of their burrows and waved tentatively; the waves were returned. To Whitney it was a moving scene, reminding him, he told friends later, of descriptions he had read of the Armistice in World War I. Whitney's mood was shattered just a few hours later, though, when he and his companions, driving back to Hue, ran into a savage battle among the burned-out villages lining the road south.

Here and there were a few other glimpses of a peace that might have been.

Not far from Saigon, Bill Stewart of *Time* magazine reached a village where government soldiers had been fighting in the darkness against 30 or so Viet Cong raiders. About fifteen minutes before the ceasefire, the South Vietnamese commander, a major, told them to cease firing. The Viet Cong stopped shooting too. One dead Communist soldier lay in the village street, but "the war appeared to have ended," Stewart reported, "and there were smiles everywhere." Often, government troops left enemy corpses on display for days, to discourage local peasants from joining the guerrillas. But with the mood of peace on them, the soldiers allowed the unknown Viet Cong to be buried right away, an act of respect. He was laid to rest "in a fallow field," Stewart wrote, "beside beds of marigolds."

Such moments were rare, however. At the end of the day, it was clear that of the four signers of the Paris accords, only the United States had fully observed the ceasefire hour.

The end of the war was proclaimed to correspondents in Saigon at the daily press briefing that had been long ago nicknamed the Five O'Clock Follies, though for years the actual starting time was four-fifteen. The Follies, too, were coming to an end. Today's performance, the 2,950th, would also be the last.

The briefing was held in the dim, cavernlike ground floor of a dingy office building on Lam Son Square, in use since plusher American-run facilities had been closed as part of the American troop withdrawal program. Well before the starting time, the room was packed with correspondents and cameramen. A forest of microphones sprouted in front of the still-empty podium, while technicians at their rank of tripod-mounted television cameras fiddled with lights and exposure meters and rolls of tape. Spools of wire trailed over the peeling linoleum floor.

Major Jere K. Forbus, the briefing officer, arrived at the usual time. Pushing his way through the jostling correspondents, he passed out copies of the last daily U.S. military communique. Mimeographed as usual on white paper that also bore the insignia of all five U.S. armed services, the communique's first sentence was one millions of Americans had awaited for many years. It said, "All offensive military operations by U.S. forces in the Republic of Vietnam ended at 0800 today."

Unlike the Geneva agreement of 1954, which had given Vietnam an interval of relative peace, the Paris agreement of 1973 did not stop the fighting for a single hour.

At the time of the failed ceasefire, the Vietnam conflict was—though one could give various dates for its beginning—already the longest major war of the twentieth century. More than 27 years had passed since Ho Chi Minh proclaimed independence from French colonial rule on September 2, 1945; the intermittent fighting already occurring would erupt into full-scale war against the French in December of the following year, after various attempted compromises collapsed. The Paris agreement of 1973 came nearly nineteen years after the vanquishing of the French and the division of the country; twelve years after the founding of the National Liberation Front to complete the revolution in non-Communist South Vietnam; almost eight years after the Americans, when their more limited advisory effort failed to halt the Liberation Front's growing successes or end the political paralysis in Saigon, intervened with their own bomber fleet and combat divisions to try to prevent a Communist victory.

Now, leaving behind a well-armed but burdensomely expensive South Vietnamese army—and a society controlled by a military-bureaucratic elite that had become psychologically and materially dependent on American support—the Americans were departing, not defeated, exactly, but certainly not victorious, either. To Ho Chi Minh's successors, the American exit was proof of another triumph of their movement against great odds. The U.S. "war of aggression" had ended, boasted the Liberation Front and the Provisional Revolutionary Government in their ceasefire proclamation. "Our entire nation is the victor. Anyone carrying the Vietnamese blood in his being, who really loves the country and the people, has the right to be proud."

Between the revolutionaries and their decades-old dream of a united Communist Vietnam, there now stood only one enemy: their own countrymen in the South. Political leaders are seldom entirely immune to their own propaganda, and the Communists, after telling themselves and their followers for so many years that the Saigon regime was merely a puppet of the Americans with no popular following, may have overestimated their own support and underestimated the strength and resilience of anti-Communism in South Vietnam. But they had an unshakable confidence in their own. The Vietnamese Communists were not gentle or humanitarian. They were the masters of a totalitarian system who had inflicted great violence in the implacable pursuit of their goal. Their struggle had exacted a terrible price from their own people. But one did not have to admire their system to acknowledge that they had written one of history's most extraordinary sagas of heroic, determined, and skillful struggle against superior military force. "Our children will keep on fighting if need be" to secure Vietnamese independence, Ho Chi Minh had said all the way back in 1945, and so they had. No one who knew their history could believe that in 1973 they had given up that goal. Within the framework of the Paris agreement or outside it, whichever better suited their purpose, they would continue their struggle.

Like the war, the peace negotiations too had a long history. Between the first meeting of American and North Vietnamese representatives and the

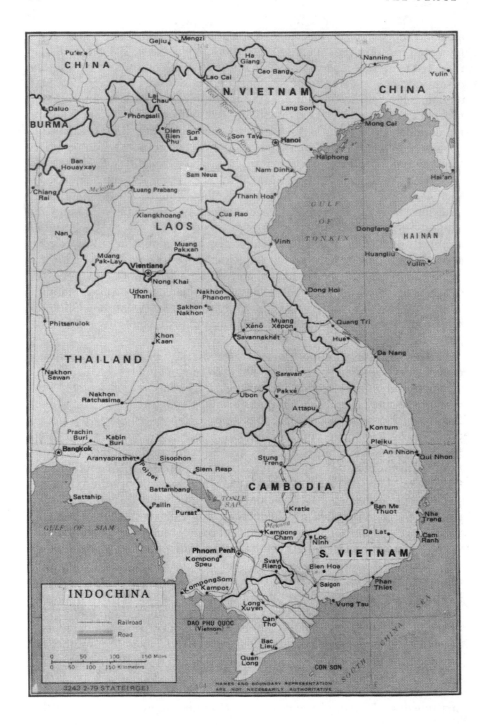

signing ceremony in the Hotel Majestic, exactly four years, seven months, and seventeen days had passed, while perhaps three-quarters of a million Vietnamese human beings were killed.

The events that really produced the agreement occurred not in Paris, however, but on the battlegrounds of Vietnam; in the rival capitals, Saigon and Hanoi; and in Washington, Peking, and Moscow during the year 1972. Numerologists in the South Vietnamese capital had forecast an important development that year, remembering that momentous events in modern Vietnam had a pattern of occurring in a nine-year cycle in years whose last two digits also added up to nine: in 1945, the end of the Japanese occupation and the start of the war against the French; in 1954, the Geneva agreement, the end of French rule, and the division of the country; in 1963, the overthrow and murder of the Republic of Vietnam's first president, Ngo Dinh Diem, whose fall started the chain of events that led to full-scale American intervention. 1972 would surely bring another historic event to continue the cycle, many Vietnamese believed, and what could it be but a peace agreement?

As it happened, though the accords were not completed until 27 days into the following year, the numerologists were right. For Vietnam, whose history intersected that year with a dramatic rearrangement of relations among the United States, China, and the Soviet Union, 1972 was the watershed.

Chapter 2

The Paris Agreement

At midsummer of 1972, seven months before the peace agreement, Vietnam's warring armies lay battered and exhausted across the land.

A powerful Communist offensive which had thundered over the country since the last day of March had been blunted. War still flamed on battlefields from one end of South Vietnam to the other: on the sandy, ribbonlike plain that followed the curve of the northern coast; in the boulder-strewn, bomb-scarred hills of the central highlands; on the red-earth plains stretching away from Saigon; in mud-brick villages under the palm groves that grew along the numberless waterways veining the shimmering green ricelands of the Mekong Delta. But everywhere, after months of savage fighting, the war had settled into a murderous stalemate. Both sides had spent prodigiously in blood, in war materiel, and in nerve, and neither had come within reach of victory. There hung over the land, like the clouds of the summer monsoon, a deepening sense that unless some solution could be found, the war that had ravaged Vietnam's people for nearly three decades would go on and on forever.

The nations directly or indirectly involved in the conflict—North Vietnam and its supporters, China and the Soviet Union; South Vietnam and its ally, the United States—were all being propelled by the events of 1972 to reexamine the policies that had led them to deadlock both on the battleground and in the peace negotiations. In each of those countries, that reexamination was beginning, almost invisibly, to thaw long-frozen assumptions and attitudes.

The North. The leaders of North Vietnam, four months after launching

their Easter offensive, had little cause for self-congratulation. Their investment had been heavy. A dozen infantry divisions and hundreds of tanks and
heavy guns had been committed to the attack. Plans for industrial and
economic reconstruction had to be set aside, while past accomplishments
were put in danger of destruction by renewed American bombing. "Our
northern armed forces and people, while striving to build socialism and
consolidate the North in all aspects, must thoroughly understand that to
fight the Americans for national salvation is a primary task," said a Communist party document explaining the decision to start the offensive.

To man the attacking units, previously exempt classes of young men were
called up for military service, including those regarded as future state and
party leaders: skilled workers, technicians, university students. Also drafted
were the sixth and seventh sons in families that had already given five to the
revolutionary struggle.

Yet the offensive was halted well short of the major triumphs its planners
must have hoped for—though not before jolting the South Vietnamese as
never before. In its first days the attack stunned defenders just below the
Demilitarized Zone. An entire 1,500-man regiment surrendered on April 2;
with it were lost 22 artillery pieces. An intrepid pilot flying a twin-rotor
Chinook helicopter picked up the regiment's team of American advisers
only minutes before the surrender. Four weeks later, the rest of the 3rd
ARVN (Army of the Republic of Vietnam) Division and other defending
units yielded all of Quang Tri Province. After overrunning Quang Tri,
however, the North Vietnamese inexplicably paused instead of driving on to
Hue, the gracious capital of the Vietnamese emperors. For a few days Hue
had seemed theirs for the taking. But instead they allowed the South
Vietnamese time to set up a defense line on the My Chanh River, which
formed the southern boundary of Quang Tri Province; the new line was
never breached.

Farther to the south, other Communist divisions attacking out of the
mountains had also been stopped, in battles that cost thousands of casualties
on both sides, in front of the province capitals of Kontum in the central
highlands and An Loc north of Saigon. Massed Communist forces suffered
terrible losses under U.S. bombing.

By midyear the ARVN was no longer falling back anywhere and had
retaken the offensive on the northern front, where the marine and airborne
divisions, regarded as South Vietnam's best, counterattacked across the My
Chanh in late June. By then, the North Vietnamese themselves admitted, the
offensive was "no longer developing in a spectacular way." Several years
later a leading Hanoi propagandist admitted the offensive "fell short of
expectations."

If their military accomplishments were disappointing, the offensive's
political consequences were perhaps even more so. Having halted U.S.

escalation with their last major attack, the Tet offensive of 1968, the Hanoi leadership in 1972 hoped that at best they might complete the work of Tet and knock the U.S. out of the war altogether, or at least might force Washington to further concessions in the long-stalled peace talks. Nearly a year later, possibly with the benefit of hindsight, North Vietnam's Lt. Gen. Tran Van Tra, commander of the Tet attack on Saigon and in 1973 head of the P.R.G.'s military delegation there (still later he would become the first Communist chief of the city after its surrender) remarked that "the aim of the 1972 offensive was to force the U.S. to sign a peace agreement."

Nixon, however, was more inclined to strike back than to negotiate. In a series of orders during the first two weeks of April, he progressively removed the bombing restrictions that had been in effect since November 1968.* B-52s made their first raids on the North April 10, and five days later struck the Hanoi-Haiphong area. On May 8, when Quang Tri had been lost and Hue seemed in danger, Nixon ordered a step that military planners had advocated for years but that had never before been authorized: the mining of Haiphong and other North Vietnamese ports. For Nixon, it was a gamble that the bombs falling on North Vietnam would neither damage his seemingly easy march to reelection nor explode his diplomatic maneuvers with the two Communist superpowers: the People's Republic of China, where he had made a triumphal peacemaker's journey in February, and the Soviet Union, where he was scheduled to journey only sixteen days after the mining began.

The American president won both bets. China ritually denounced the bombing but said not a word to revoke its newborn rapprochement with Washington. The Russians hesitated for three days, during which Nixon first considered calling off the summit but then decided to let the Russians bear the responsibility. Then Soviet foreign trade minister Nikolai S. Patolichev, who was then visiting Washington, signaled that the visit was still on.

In the U.S., the renewal of the air war brought only feeble ghosts of the

---

* U.S. aircraft bombed the North during the halt but under rules permitting only "protective reaction" if U.S. reconnaissance planes were fired on. 285 sorties were flown against targets in the North in 1969, 1,003 in 1970, and 1,705 in 1971. Between November 1971 and March 1972, officers under Gen. John D. Lavelle, the 7th Air Force commander, deliberately fabricated hostile-fire reports to justify additional raids, at a time when American commanders were concerned about an apparent Communist military buildup. In a congressional inquiry, Lavelle took responsibility for the false reports. He was relieved of his command and demoted one rank, to lieutenant general. The House Armed Services investigating subcommittee that examined the affair was clearly unconvinced that Lavelle deserved all the blame, however. The investigation, it said, left "questions which cannot be ignored" about possibilities that "extend from possible tacit approval of General Lavelle's actions by his superiors, to possible civilian direction of the bombings." Documentary evidence to support the "vigorous denials by those who possibly were involved" was withheld by the Defense Department, the committee said, adding that "the incredible secrecy" surrounding the case ". . . suggests that the files may have been thoroughly sanitized by this time."

protests that had riven the country in past years. With more than four-fifths of the half-million-man army already home, with draft calls declining and American losses down to fewer than ten men killed each week, the peace movement, apparently, had run out of zeal. The public would stand for anything but the reintroduction of American ground forces, the Nixon administration believed, and the president had already moved to assure the country that no such action was contemplated. On April 20 he had announced a further cut in authorized U.S. troop strength from 69,000 to 49,000, to be reached by July 1. For any practical purpose, the announcement was a smokescreen, because the number of Americans involved in the war was actually rising. Of the 20,000 men to be withdrawn, many were Air Force flight and ground crewmen who simply moved from Vietnam to bases in neighboring Thailand without missing a day of combat. Some crews actually carried out missions while on their way to their new duty stations: "They pack up, throw their suitcases in the plane, make their strike and then just fly on to Takhli," an officer with the 366th Tactical Fighter Wing told me as its three squadrons of F-4 Phantoms were in the process of shifting from Da Nang to Takhli air base in Thailand.

Air power in Thailand was being reinforced from elsewhere as well. Altogether, during April and May, at least fifteen squadrons of Air Force and Marine strike planes were added to land-based air strength in Southeast Asia, approximately doubling the number of tactical aircraft. Troop strength in Thailand rose from 32,000 to 45,000. Off the Vietnamese coast, four more carriers and additional gunfire support ships augmented the U.S. naval force involved in the war. The new carriers added another 360 strike aircraft to the tactical force, while the number of men in the fleet rose to 39,000, nearly double the number at the start of the year. And the Southeast Asia B-52 fleet, based at U Tapao air base in Thailand and on Guam, was increased from slightly more than 50 aircraft in January to more than 200 by the end of May. Personnel at Guam's Andersen Air Force Base were increased from 4,000 to 12,000. The increases in Thailand, in the fleet, and on Guam more than offset the 20,000 who were transferred out of Vietnam.

U.S. air power was employed not just in the North but also on the battlegrounds in the South, where it was widely credited with saving the South Vietnamese defenders of An Loc and Kontum. Had a similar intensification of the American war occurred on the ground, Nixon could have faced a huge domestic blow-up. But the response to the air offensive was surprisingly tepid. As long as the American war was kept in the air, fought by professionals and not by draftees, the electorate seemed willing to let him fight it.

If the North Vietnamese were disheartened at the feeble response of the American antiwar movement, they were openly furious at their allies, China and the Soviet Union, for treating with the American president while his bombs were falling on their country.

The bombing itself did not come as a surprise: "air defense tasks and the evacuation and dispersion" of urban populations were listed by the party leadership early in 1972 among the "important tasks" for the year. But what Hanoi may not have expected, as a scholar sympathetic to North Vietnam's view pointed out, "was a serious American escalation *without* major diplomatic and political setbacks for Nixon"—some action by Peking and Moscow to "make it clear there could be no detente while the United States continued its intervention in South Vietnam and carried out a war of destruction against North Vietnam." When no such actions occurred, the official Hanoi press began to bristle with suggestions that those negotiating with Nixon were playing the imperialists's game.

"Nixon has . . . raved about a switch from an 'era of confrontation' to an 'era of negotiations,' " said the party newspaper, *Nhan Dan*, ten days after the mining began. " 'Negotiations' in Nixon's way, however, mean the recourse to a position of strength, the use of armed might to impose arrogant U.S. terms and U.S. rule on other nations." All right-thinking people, declared another commentary a few days later, would condemn Nixon: "an extremely bellicose aggressor, an international pirate, a loathsome bloodthirsty man and a dangerous plotter." It was left to the reader to draw the appropriate conclusion about the Soviet and Chinese leaders who received the "pirate" in their capitals with full state honors.

Three days after Nixon left the Soviet Union, *Nhan Dan* scornfully cited several passages from his statements there and, in unmistakable outrage at its fraternal Soviet ally, added: "Nixon may make as many discourses as he likes, what he says is being drowned in the explosions of the bombs and shells the U.S. is raining day and night on Vietnam. . . . How can Nixon speak of good faith, peace and freedom when he is feverishly intensifying his war of aggression against Vietnam and the other Indochinese countries? . . . Men of conscience must know how to live, how to distinguish right from wrong, must know what is good and what is bad and who is one's friend and who is one's foe."

Eleven weeks later, the North Vietnamese showed the depth of their anger and discouragement in still another *Nhan Dan* editorial complaining that Nixon's policies were abetted by "those who are departing from the great, invincible revolutionary thoughts of the time and are pitifully mired on the dark and muddy road of unprincipled compromise."* The editorial continued with an extraordinarily blunt diatribe.

---

* 1972 was hardly the first time the Vietnamese revolutionaries felt betrayed by the major Communist powers. When Ho Chi Minh's uprising against France began in 1945, it received virtually no backing from the Soviet Union, which then hoped for a possible Communist seizure of power in France itself. Moscow would not embarrass the French Communists by

What is the fundamental situation in the world today? . . . Unhealthy trends have thrown everything into confusion and the crafty imperialists have also interfered to blur the line between right and wrong, between black and white. . . . The imperialists pursue a policy of *detente* with some big countries in order to have a free hand to consolidate their forces, oppose the revolutionary movement in the world, repress the revolution in their own countries, bully the small countries and stamp out the national-liberation movement. . . .

With regard to the socialist countries, the defence of peace and peaceful coexistence cannot be dissociated from the movement for independence, democracy and socialism in the world. For a country to care for its immediate and narrow interests while shirking its lofty internationalist duties not only is detrimental to the revolutionary movement in the world but will also bring unfathomable harm to itself in the end. . . . if in order to serve one's narrow national interests, one is to help the most reactionary forces stave off dangerous blows, one is indeed throwing a life-buoy to a drowning pirate; this is a harmful compromise advantageous to the enemy, and disadvantageous to the revolution. . . . Proletarian internationalism towers above bourgeois nationalism and national egoism. The revolution is a path strewn with fragrant flowers. Opportunism is a fetid quagmire. We Communists must persevere in the revolution and not compromise with our adversaries.

In such a mood, North Vietnam's leaders considered the results of the Easter offensive. There was little that was encouraging. They had not broken the battlefield stalemate or smashed the South Vietnamese army. They had

---

supporting the Viet Minh. In the French National Assembly, Communist members never opposed military budgets for the Indochina War. Soviet restraint was duly acknowledged: "In the Indochina question," a French premier told the Assembly in 1947, "we have always noted to this day the correct attitude of the Soviet government." At the Geneva conference in 1954, the Russians and Chinese both pressured Ho to offer major concessions. Among them were division of the country at the 17th parallel instead of more than 250 miles farther south, and an agreement to wait two years, instead of six months, for the national elections the Viet Minh were confident they would win. "I don't know how we are going to explain this to our comrades in the South," Pham Van Dong, the chief Communist negotiator, is said to have sighed. If the Geneva settlement did not reflect the Viet Minh's true military and political strength at the time, wrote the authors of the *Pentagon Papers* in their study of the period, "their interests were compromised by their own Communist allies, not the West. . . . The two big Communist powers did not hesitate in asserting the paramountcy of their interests over those of the Viet Minh." Russian and Chinese motives were complex. China, which had just fought American forces in Korea, was apparently anxious to avoid another U.S. military intervention close to its borders. The Soviet Union's main interest was thought to be to block the proposed European Defense Community. Soviet leaders helped arrange an Indochina settlement, it was widely supposed, in return for French rejection of the EDC. Whether there was an explicit deal or not, that was how it worked out. Seven weeks after the Geneva accords were completed, the French National Assembly refused to ratify the EDC by a 55-vote margin. Geneva left Ho Chi Minh and his successors with an enduring distrust not just of diplomatic agreements but of the value of Soviet and Chinese "friendship."

SOUTH VIETNAM
Provinces and Military Regions

suffered fearful losses in their own. Far from driving the United States out of the war, they had brought down a new rain of American bombs on their own country. Their allies, in what to Hanoi seemed acts of outright betrayal, had demonstrated that the new relationships both wanted with the United States ranked far ahead of solidarity with the Vietnamese. Over the summer, an important decision began to crystallize in Hanoi. A new effort would be made to break the deadlock in the peace negotiations—and it would be made before the American election, when Hanoi apparently believed the pressure on U.S. negotiators would be strongest. To achieve a settlement, the North Vietnamese now considered a major concession: dropping the demand, to which they had clung through four years of public and private talks, that South Vietnam's President Thieu must be removed before the fighting could stop.

The South. Paradoxically, North Vietnam's difficulties produced no corresponding optimism in Saigon. Instead, on South Vietnam's side of the battle lines the mood was just as bleak—and for some of the same reasons.

Like Hanoi, Saigon was unsure of its powerful ally. Though grateful for the U.S. air support that had saved them from worse defeats, and elated by the decision to mine North Vietnamese ports, the South Vietnamese leaders knew there was no assurance that the Americans would keep supporting them indefinitely. President Thieu watched Nixon's summitry in Peking and Moscow with exactly the same misgivings as his North Vietnamese enemies. Like them, he too feared his patron would arrange an unfavorable settlement behind his back.

Thieu could claim a defensive victory in the offensive, but that was all. The major towns had been held; of 44 province capitals, only Quang Tri was temporarily lost. Yet the government's strategic position was clearly weakened. Below the Demilitarized Zone and down 500 miles of South Vietnam's western edge, nearly all the outlying bases in the thinly populated mountains had fallen, leaving the Communist army emplaced closer than before to the populous, prosperous coastal lowlands.

Not for the first time, Vietnamese and American perceptions of the situation appeared different. After the successful defense of An Loc and Kontum and after Hue avoided attack, a good many U.S. officers concluded that the offensive had ended in a significant success, a test met and mastered. The outcome "was ample evidence that the U.S. effort had not failed," an American army historian wrote in a passage that was representative of the views held by many others. "The Vietnamese army withstood and repelled the vicious onslaught of the enemy, and its success instilled a new sense of esprit and national unity throughout the country."

That impression lingered into the post-ceasefire period, contributing to later exaggerated estimates of Saigon's staying power. The image of success was created while the government army still enjoyed "the protective umbrella of a powerful U.S. air arm, superior artillery, and a functioning, efficient and sufficient U.S.-run logistics system," an American intelligence officer told congressional investigators after the war, and though the U.S. withdrawal after the ceasefire erased most of those advantages, "we did not change our views of the South Vietnamese . . . [as] an efficient, aggressive military force." As a result, he added, Washington was lulled "into a false sense of security concerning Vietnam."

The Vietnamese reaction to the offensive, if a reporter's random glimpses were any guide, was markedly less hopeful. The offensive reversed a slowly growing sense of hope that had accompanied apparent battlefield gains during the previous three years. It confirmed what most Vietnamese had always sensed, that the Communists would always meet reverses by expending more of their own resources. The Easter attack was in its way a delayed answer to a question President Johnson once asked his generals: "When we add divisions can't the enemy add divisions? If so, where does it all end?"

To most Vietnamese it mattered little, though it was true, that village security even at the height of the offensive was somewhat better than it had been four or five years before. The lesson they had learned was that the future, like the past, held only more war and bloodshed.

The murderous battle that summer in Quang Tri was, in one sense, not at all typical of the fluid, small-unit Vietnam war. It began as a World War II-style engagement of massed divisions; after a few weeks Quang Tri began to evoke the memory of an even earlier model of warfare: the static, trench-bound slaughter of World War I. In another sense, though, the battle there was a wholly accurate image of the Vietnam War in 1972, the symbol of the hopeless, endless, bloodsoaked stalemate that the war had become.

The South Vietnamese counterattack began at the end of June, with the Marine Division advancing into the sand-duned coastal strip between Highway One* and the sea, while the Airborne Division, after building a pontoon bridge across the My Chanh to replace the permanent span that had been wrecked during the retreat in May, drove straight up the highway toward the province capital. At the very start of their advance the paratroopers met one of the most appalling scenes of the entire war: the burned, blasted remains of a huge convoy of soldiers and refugees that had been trapped on the wrong side of the blown bridge and destroyed during the

---

* Vietnam's Highway One—which actually begins in Cambodia—is something like America's U.S. Route One, which runs along the American East Coast. After reaching Saigon from the Cambodian border, the Vietnamese Highway One bends eastward to reach the South China Sea, then follows the entire length of the coast—in peacetime, all the way to Hanoi.

flight out of the province. For miles, smashed vehicles lay in an almost unbroken line on both sides of the road. Driving north with a jeepload of other correspondents a couple of days after the paratroopers recrossed the river, I counted more than 400 wrecks in the first two miles, and I stopped counting long before we reached the end of the destruction. Army trucks, their canvas sides burned or shot away, lay with their ribs sticking up like the skeletons of dinosaurs. Slewed among them were scores of civilian vehicles: buses with their side panels shredded by shrapnel and bullet holes; bent, broken motorbikes; shattered scooter-buses; burned, blackened cars with shot-out headlights staring like the eye sockets of a skull.

Although government soldiers had already removed hundreds of bodies, many of the wrecked vehicles still contained a grisly cargo of corpses, shriveled, blackened mummies after two months under the beating Vietnamese sun. No one ever reliably counted the dead; estimates ranged into the thousands.

The paratroopers' advance moved swiftly past the slaughtered convoy to the edge of Quang Tri city, which, Saigon's planners estimated, could be retaken by the ninth day of the counteroffensive. Instead, it took two and a half terrible months, while one of the heaviest air and artillery bombardments since World War II leveled not just the city but nearly every building in the entire province. As August began, artillery was being fired at the incredible rate of 25,000 rounds a day, while U.S. and South Vietnamese fighter-bombers flew dozens of missions and as many as 40 B-52s, each carrying up to 30 tons of bombs, also struck the province every day.

The heavy bombers usually flew in cells of three, too high to be seen, their presence announced only by the shuddering triple thunder-roll of their bombloads. "Arc Light" strikes, they were called, after the military code name for the strategic bombing campaign. A three-plane raid saturated a "box" nearly two miles long and more than a half-mile wide. Even from three or four miles away, the effect was volcanic, as if the earth itself were exploding. The shock wave, outreaching the sound, could be felt over 30 or more miles. In the nights in my room at the dilapidated Huong Giang hotel in Hue, distant B-52 bombing would set the windows vibrating in their casements, as if three sets of unseen fists were beating rapidly on the glass.

Under the air and artillery bombardment, Quang Tri was literally being obliterated. "My god," said an awed American one day, "there's been so much lead thrown in here that if somebody flew over with a big magnet the whole goddamn province would just rise up in the air."

Tactically the city was not a significant objective. The Marine Division, which relieved the exhausted paratroopers in front of the city in July, was not at all anxious to assault it directly. "We'd like to pound the place until there's nothing standing and we can walk in without a fight," an American marine officer, one of the division's advisory team, said one day as we crouched to watch U.S. Phantom jets scream overhead to bomb Communist bunkers barely 500 yards away—so close that earlier, a brick-sized hunk of shrapnel from a "friendly" artillery shell had whizzed all the way to the marine lines and sliced off the top of a palm tree just twenty feet over our heads. But President Thieu would not leave a province capital in Communist hands. "It had become a symbol and a major challenge," wrote Lt. Gen. Ngo Quang Truong, Saigon's commander in the northern region; to withdraw again would admit defeat.

When the North Vietnamese could not be forced out by air strikes and shelling, Thieu ordered the marines to assault their positions. In the attack, which began early in September, the marines suffered 150 men killed or wounded every day. In six days more than 200 fighter-bombers struck the citadel, which measured only a little more than 500 square yards. Yet it still took five days for the marines to clear the last few hundred feet of rubble. The last assault began at dawn on September 15, and at five o'clock that afternoon, the saffron-and-red government flag was finally raised over the citadel's ruins.

Since the end of June, Saigon announced, the campaign had cost 2,000 government soldiers killed and 9,000 wounded, half the original strength of the two attacking divisions. Communist casualties were said to have been 19,000 dead. Both sides would suffer many more losses, though there would be no more significant changes in the battle lines, in the four months remaining before the ceasefire.

When it was finally recaptured, Quang Tri was no longer a city but a lake of shattered masonry. Even the thick citadel walls were so thoroughly smashed one could no longer see where they had stood. The destruction was equally complete elsewhere. In the southeastern quadrant of the province that was now back in South Vietnamese hands, it was estimated that 98 or 99 percent of all buildings had been destroyed. Only charred skeletons remained of the villages that had once stood on the sandy land. Traditionally Quang Tri was so poor that as a Vietnamese saying put it, "Dogs ate pebbles and chickens fed on salt." In its fields now were not just pebbles and salt but a deadly litter of unexploded shells and bombs, waiting to kill and maim for years to come.

President Thieu, on a visit to the ruined citadel after its recapture, proclaimed the battle a great victory. But if it was, it was another case—on a larger scale than ever before—of destroying Vietnam to save it. Closer to the surface than ever, a sense of war-weary despair began to show in South Vietnamese society. Desertions from the army and militia rose to a record rate of more than 20,000 men a month, the equivalent of two full divisions, and many more than were being killed or wounded in battle. More than a million refugees waited in squalid camps, mourning their shattered homes. Casualties were unprecedented. Nearly 150,000 men were killed or wounded in 1972, two-thirds more than in the previous year, leaving a burden of grief beyond anything South Vietnam had experienced earlier in the war.*

"If this were truly a patriotic war," said a young navy officer I met one day in a Saigon bookstore, "everybody would be willing to fight. But we do not want to kill other Vietnamese. We do not want victory. We only want peace." And a businessman in a cafe on busy Tu Do Street, lowering his voice, whispered: "The people will not tell you this because they are afraid to say it. But we want peace, peace at any cost, peace with Communist rule if necessary."

There had always been such voices. But now, with the hope of peace as battered as the shell-blasted villages across the land, they seemed more numerous and more insistent. South Vietnam had survived the offensive. Its army, though tired, was still in the field. Its government still stood. Its reserves of will and endurance, however, were depleted. President Thieu remained unrelentingly suspicious of any negotiations with the Communists, as he would demonstrate in the coming months. But to an extent he and his generals could not entirely ignore, his country's thoughts were turning to the miracle of peace and the one place it might possibly be achieved: the conference rooms in Paris.

The Powers. History seldom provides precise starting points. But if there was a single moment at which the Vietnam War became an anachronism in global politics, it was on July 15, 1971—the day President Nixon disclosed that he would visit the People's Republic of China "at an appropriate date." That announcement, like the first great guncrack of pack ice beginning to break up, not only revealed but further liberated the slowly warming currents that had begun flowing beneath the frozen surface of superpower relationships. In the next ten months, as Nixon's blue-and-silver presidential jet journeyed to China in February 1972, and then to the Soviet Union in

---

* High desertions were endemic in the Vietnamese armed forces for many reasons. It was politically impossible for the government to discipline deserters more harshly than it treated Communist "ralliers," who were freed after relatively brief indoctrination in Chieu Hoi (Open Arms) centers. Thus, penalties were light. In addition, because of a chronic need for manpower, amnesties were periodically declared during which deserters could return to their units without being punished. While the amnesties brought some men back, they also left the soldiers believing there would always be another, so they could keep right on deserting with the expectation of avoiding punishment. In addition, the South Vietnamese public, or large segments of it, did not look down on deserters. Families, employers, and pagodas were typically willing to harbor them, or at least unwilling to assist government recruiters who were trying to recapture them. Throughout the war, desertion consistently outweighed battle casualties as a drain on South Vietnam's military manpower.

May, the three-cornered world order that had lasted more than a decade began to shiver and break apart, heaving and sliding into new shapes and patterns.

While reaching new perceptions of each other, the big powers also turned new lenses on Vietnam. Through them, the image of their own vital interests and fundamental philosophies clashing on the Indochina battleground now seemed greatly diminished. Instead, in Moscow and Peking as well as in Washington, the war began to seem an irrelevant, troublesome historical leftover that might endanger the new relationships each was trying to achieve.

China, when the war was escalating in the 1960s, looked on the United States as its chief enemy. But by 1972 the Soviet Union was cast in that role. Reentering diplomatic interchange after its self-ostracism during Mao Tse-tung's Great Proletarian Cultural Revolution, China was ready to seek what Henry Kissinger later called a "tacit nonaggression treaty" with Washington. Though doctrinally in favor of Vietnamese liberation, China was deeply suspicious of Hanoi's ties with Moscow. The North Vietnamese, understandably, still wanted a quick and humiliating expulsion of American power from the Indochina peninsula. Peking wanted a more gradual exit, one that would preserve some American influence in Southeast Asia to counterbalance the Soviet menace to China's north and west.

As they prepared to receive President Nixon in Peking, the Chinese leaders reassured Hanoi they would do nothing against North Vietnam's interests; to the Americans they insisted they would not act as a go-between or be "enmeshed" in the Vietnam problem in any way. But all the logic of China's concerns now put it on the side of a negotiated settlement there, even—or perhaps preferably—one that fell well short of completing South Vietnam's "liberation" and reunification with the North.

The Soviet Union, too, had developed interests that would be served by a Vietnam peace agreement. The leaders in the Kremlin could not have been thrilled by the actions of their North Vietnamese allies in the spring of 1972. Far too many of the tanks and heavy guns they had sent were rusting in the Quang Tri dunes or among the rubber groves near An Loc, without much military success to show for the Soviet investment. Hanoi was the cause of deep embarrassment in May, when the Russian leaders had to choose between calling off the summit or receiving Nixon while his bombs were still falling around their freighters in Haiphong Harbor. Moscow was all the more furious, no doubt, because the Chinese had not had to endure any comparable humiliation while conducting their own summit with the American president.

Too, the Kremlin had specific goals on matters ranging from arms limitation to liberalized trade. Agreement on those issues involved not only Soviet national interests but those of the Communist party chief, Leonid

Brezhnev, who was identified with the policy of detente. Success would enhance his authority, while failure would threaten it. Such interests far outweighed solidarity with the Vietnamese. Even when Soviet ships were struck in Haiphong and Russian crewmen killed, hardly more than a pro forma complaint was made to Washington. When a plane landed in Moscow during Nixon's visit carrying two dead and twenty wounded seamen, not a word appeared in the Soviet press.

In their talks with Nixon, the Soviet leaders insisted they did not control events in Vietnam. For the record, they espoused Hanoi's negotiating proposals. But they did not dispute that they would find a settlement convenient, and in numerous if not entirely explicit ways they indicated they wanted to be helpful. Barely two weeks after Nixon's departure from Moscow, Soviet President Nikolai Podgorny traveled to Hanoi. In his briefcase, the Americans were confident, was Moscow's message that it was time for the North Vietnamese to seek a negotiated settlement of the war.

Leonid Brezhnev and Mao Tse-tung and their associates did not have to consider public opinion. Nixon and Kissinger did, and in that sense, the fundamental decision for an American exit from the war was made for them before they took office. Whatever outcome they privately expected or hoped for from a settlement—and that was not easy to discern, then or later—their actions were circumscribed by the political imperative to end direct U.S. military engagement.

As 1972 passed the halfway mark, peace before the November election must have seemed not only a desirable but a realistic goal. North Vietnam, Nixon reasoned, had enjoyed a free ride for the first three years of his administration. Immune from direct American pressure on their homeland, the North Vietnamese had been able to wait without offering any concessions of their own, while U.S. troops were withdrawn at the dictate of American political realities. Now, all that was changed. Every day that Hanoi refused to settle, it would be further punished by American bombs. In addition, the two major Communist powers at last seemed ready to assist U.S. efforts—if not by direct diplomatic intervention, at least by acquiescence to American actions. Hanoi, Nixon and Kissinger believed, was now isolated in its stubbornness. Washington and Moscow each "has its own point of view and its own approach," Nixon told Congress after his return from the Soviet summit. ". . . But at the same time, both the United States and the Soviet Union share an overriding desire to achieve a more stable peace in the world." Kissinger, after revisiting Peking in June, declared, "We do not believe there is any major country in the world today that wants the war to continue."

Historically, the Vietnamese Communists had maintained a bristling independence on decisions of war and peace, skillfully manipulating the

Soviet-Chinese rivalry for their own ends. But they could not completely disregard the changed world environment. No diplomatic notes or fraternal advice were needed to tell Hanoi that the United States now had a freer hand than ever before, at least in its international relations, to apply military pressure without worrying about the Russian or Chinese response. Whatever their rage and resentment, the North Vietnamese leaders still had to weigh their allies' actions while deciding on their own. In the flurry of messages flashing around the world came one from Brezhnev to Nixon: the Vietnamese had listened with "an attentive attitude" to Podgorny's transmittal of American proposals and were ready to resume secret meetings with Henry Kissinger. An exchange of cables with Hanoi fixed the date: July 19, 1972, in Paris.

Breakthrough and Breakdown

The secret Paris negotiations were started by Nixon and Kissinger in August 1969, barely six months after they took office. They hoped to open a private forum that might be more useful than the propaganda-laden formal peace talks—semipublic in that each session was publicly announced and both sides customarily issued statements afterward—that were held every Thursday in the Hotel Majestic. Kissinger's first private meeting was with Xuan Thuy, head of the North Vietnamese delegation to the official talks. Six months later, Hanoi sent Le Duc Tho, one of the half-dozen top North Vietnamese leaders, to a second secret rendezvous.

When he wished, the silver-haired Tho could convey a quality of relaxed charm. "He does not seem, at least in private conversation, to make any effort to mask his thoughts with stiffened facial muscles or a controlled emptiness in his eyes," wrote one journalist, obviously remembering more typically robotic Communist functionaries. Tho laughed easily, giving the impression "of a basically amiable man, easy to talk with." Yet his life bespoke different qualities, chiefly a granite commitment to the revolutionary cause for which he had endured eleven years in French prisons and many years of war.

A Politburo member since 1955, or possibly even earlier, Tho had served as secretary of the Communist party Central Committee and as a member of its military commission—a sign of true inner-circle status. In Paris his only title was "special adviser" to the peace talks delegation, but in fact he was the senior negotiator. At his initial meetings with Kissinger he did nothing but restate known Communist positions; still, the presence of such a senior official gave some hope that Hanoi was not entirely indifferent to the negotiating process.

Nixon and Kissinger had come to the White House believing they could settle the war in relatively short order. The war would be over in a year, Nixon predicted to his cabinet during his second month in office. Like other American strategists before them, however, Nixon and Kissinger saw the Vietnamese Communists through the prisms of their American political values and an American sense of time. Nothing had prepared them, though the lesson was there to be read in the life of the man sitting opposite Kissinger in their secret meeting place, for the stubborn passion of an Asian revolutionary movement that had already fought against superior force for many years and, though it had suffered appalling losses, was still prepared to fight for many more.

In his memoirs, Kissinger's favorite word for Le Duc Tho and the North Vietnamese is "insolent." Even allowing for the frustrations of their talks, which were obviously monumental, it is a curious word to choose—and one revealing of Kissinger's attitudes. "Insolent" suggests something more than stubborn, bloody-minded, or uncooperative. It is a word customarily used about persons in unequal relationships: a child to a parent, a student to a teacher, a soldier to an officer. The word suggests defiance of rightful authority. Kissinger's repeated use of it carries a suggestion that the North Vietnamese somehow had an obligation not to frustrate American purposes—a view also conveyed by his comment that they were "too egotistical to think of foreign policy in terms of an international system." As the weaker of the two warring parties and as a country that did not share responsibility for the worldwide strategic balance and nuclear peace, he seems to have felt, North Vietnam owed it to the United States to be more submissive—or if not to the United States, certainly to the Communist superpowers, whose obligations, in Kissinger's mind, included making their lesser allies behave.

Henry Kissinger does not seem to have easily conceded that any interests could be "vital" except those of the nations wielding power in the international arena. The concerns of lesser countries deserved consideration only to the extent that they affected the nuclear balance. If dangerous to the grand designs of superpower arrangements, they had to be squelched. Kissinger's concepts of the proper workings of the world did not encompass the thwarting of the United States by what he contemptuously called "a miserable little country" or, on another occasion, "a third-class Communist peasant state."

By mid-1972, the peasants' stubborn refusal to meet minimum American terms for a Vietnam peace agreement seems to have produced a sense of rising fury in Washington. The events of that year and the statements of

American leaders and their later recollections would come together to leave an impression that is unprovable but hard to avoid: that among the judgments, emotions, calculations, and impulses running within the Nixon administration was a half-buried wish for the negotiations not to succeed until an opportunity had been found or made to punish the North Vietnamese with heavier, angrier military blows than ever before. Both Nixon and Kissinger indicate in their memoirs that such a strategy was considered, but each ascribes it to the other. Kissinger describes Nixon as favoring at one point a settlement only after a "dramatic show of force." In Nixon's version it was Kissinger, at a somewhat later stage, who wanted to break off the talks and drastically intensify American bombing.

Possibly not even Nixon or Kissinger themselves could now state with absolute accuracy what mix of impulses and reasoning led to their decisions in 1972—but it does not seem unlikely that on some level, and to some unmeasurable extent, one of the influences was their sense of vengeful rage at an opponent that had defied American power so long and so obstinately.

In July 1972, as Kissinger and Le Duc Tho prepared to resume their talks, an enormous gap still lay between the American and Communist negotiating positions. The Americans had offered various formulas for a ceasefire that would stop the killing while South Vietnam's political future was settled by an election or through further negotiations. The Communists, however, insisted not only that Nguyen Van Thieu must be removed but that the Saigon regime must be effectively disarmed at the same time, *before* a ceasefire and before negotiations could begin for a permanent political settlement. Hanoi's terms were no secret; they were stated often, publicly, and in detail, as in a speech by Prime Minister Pham Van Dong on February 4, 1972:

> Nguyen Van Thieu and his machine of oppression . . . constitute the main obstacle to the settlement of the political problem in South Vietnam. Therefore, Nguyen Van Thieu must resign immediately, the Saigon administration must end its warlike policy, disband at once its machine of oppression and constraint against the people, stop its "pacification" policy, disband the concentration camps, set free those persons arrested on political grounds and guarantee . . . democratic liberties. . . . After the above has been achieved, the Provisional Revolutionary Government of the Republic of South Vietnam will discuss with the Saigon administration the formation of a three-segment government of national concord with a view to organizing general elections [for] the definitive government of South Vietnam.

To collaborate in that procedure, Nixon said in his May 8 speech, would cross the line "from generosity to treachery." Under public and congressional pressure he had withdrawn most of the half-million-man U.S.

expeditionary force; he had offered to remove all the remaining troops in return for a ceasefire and the release of American prisoners. But he would not agree to topple his ally's president and dismantle its army in advance of a truce, as the Communists demanded.

The administration's domestic critics, whether out of confusion or impatience or plain intellectual dishonesty, habitually ignored the implications of the Communist position, enraging Nixon. His response to criticism was seldom generous, sometimes pathological; but on the matter of the Vietnam negotiations his anger was understandable. He was offering basically what the doves favored—a simple deal to stop shooting, pull out U.S. troops, and exchange prisoners. And in return he was regularly pilloried by opponents who remained silent on Hanoi's refusal to settle on those terms.

Kissinger and Le Duc Tho met for six and a half hours on July 19, the longest meeting they had ever had. Kissinger sensed a new mood: "They were about as positive in this first session," he informed Nixon, "as we would expect if they do want to settle." At subsequent meetings on August 1 and August 14, the atmosphere continued to seem encouraging. And then came a major shift of signals from Hanoi—literally overnight. On the last day of August, *Nhan Dan* repeated the customary argument that "the military and political aspects of the issue . . . are inseparable," since "the underlying cause of the Vietnam war is the American imposition of a stooge administration on the South Vietnamese people." Thus, it was the U.S. responsibility to assure that Thieu would resign and Saigon would "give up its war-seeking policy" before any other issues could be resolved. The very next day, however, in a speech marking the 27th anniversary of the Viet Minh uprising against France, Pham Van Dong significantly changed the formula. The U.S. must stop supporting the Thieu administration and agree to a coalition, he said, but without specific mention of Thieu's removal. Nor did he speak of dismantling Saigon's army and administrative structure. Instead, the North Vietnamese prime minister said the three political forces to be included in a coalition—Saigon, the Communists, and a supposedly neutral "third segment"—would be "even and on the same footing with regard to their status, competence and responsibility."

Ten days later the Provisional Revolutionary Government, in what Hanoi called "an important statement," seemed to retreat even farther. Thieu's removal was mentioned, but only once and so fleetingly as to be a very strong hint that the matter was now negotiable. The demand that the U.S. stop supporting the "stooge administration" was similarly reduced to a single perfunctory sentence. If that too was negotiable, it meant a possible agreement that would permit the U.S. to keep aiding the Saigon government after a ceasefire—always before categorically refused by the Communists.

Another apparent concession had to do with the selection of Third Force representatives in a coalition. Previously, Hanoi and the Viet Cong had always implied that such members would have to meet Communist standards of neutrality and devotion to independence and peace, meaning in effect that the Communists would control the nomination of both their own *and* the supposed neutral bloc, thus dominating two-thirds of the resulting government. But now the P.R.G. said the Third Force group should be chosen "through consultations" in which it and Saigon would have an equal voice. Perhaps most importantly, the P.R.G. declared that a political solution should "proceed from the actual situation that there exist in South Vietnam two administrations, two armies, and other political forces."

The inference was the same as in Pham Van Dong's speech but even plainer: instead of having to disband, as all previous Communist peace plans had demanded, the Saigon administration and armed forces could remain in being while political matters were being negotiated.

In two private meetings with Kissinger during September, Le Duc Tho stated the Communists' political proposals so ambiguously that Kissinger was convinced he was genuinely eager, at last, for a settlement. When the two parted on September 27, Tho left with a promise: the next meeting would be "decisive." Three days later, a note from Hanoi promised that its delegation would return to Paris "in a constructive spirit and a serious attitude, in a last effort at arriving at an agreement of the essentials with the American side."

In Saigon, the signals from Hanoi generated an immediate and acute anxiety attack. On September 28, the government seized that day's editions of two Vietnamese newspapers for reporting that a settlement was imminent, and that it would involve Thieu's resignation. The next day, Thieu denied that progress was being made in Paris. Instead, he insisted, the Communists were being "more stubborn than ever." On October 2, while Kissinger's deputy, Alexander Haig, was in Saigon, Thieu told the South Vietnamese National Assembly: "A political solution is a domestic affair of the South. It is a right and responsibility of the southern people to settle it among themselves. No one is allowed to interfere. . . . Only the present Republic of Vietnam government is competent to discuss and approve any domestic political solution for the South, and no one has the right to do it in its place."

Three days later, an army broadcast declared that South Vietnam "will reject any solution agreed upon by outsiders," while *Tin Song*, a newspaper reflecting the views of Thieu's press secretary and kinsman, Hoang Duc Nha, proclaimed: "It is time that South Vietnam puts much more emphasis on self-determination than ever before. Self-determination means any response to the situation must be based on the interests of South Vietnam without pressure from anywhere."

Saigon's misgivings had already been expressed directly to the U.S. government. As early as July, Thieu privately informed Washington that a ceasefire would be acceptable only if followed by withdrawal of North Vietnamese troops. The demand was "unfulfillable," Kissinger felt. But, he wrote later, the U.S. "did not pursue the disagreement . . . since it seemed irrelevant to the deadlocked negotiations."

In August, on a visit to the South Vietnamese capital, Kissinger listened to further objections from Thieu but concealed his own growing expectation that an agreement was near. Instead, he engaged Thieu in fanciful pipe-dreaming about possible ARVN amphibious landings in the North. In his memoirs, Kissinger attributes his later collisions with Thieu in part to the latter's "infuriating negotiating style" and his "characteristic Vietnamese opaqueness"; no national origin is assigned to his own dissembling.

Whoever was being opaque, Kissinger certainly understood by the end of his Saigon visit that the South Vietnamese leader was fundamentally opposed to the direction of American policy—an impression that was later confirmed, if any confirmation was needed, when General Haig traveled to Saigon at the beginning of October to encounter, as he reported back to Washington, "solid, unified . . . opposition" by the South Vietnamese government to U.S. peace terms. By then, though, the breakthrough Kissinger was expecting was imminent. When it came, though Saigon's objections were no longer irrelevant, Kissinger chose not to consider them.

The "last effort" Hanoi had promised began at ten-thirty on the morning of October 8, a bright autumn Sunday in Paris. Kissinger and Tho and their aides met in a suburban villa owned by the French Communist party and sparred for just over two hours over familiar formulas. Then Tho asked for a recess. When the meeting resumed at 4 P.M., Tho announced that his government had a new proposal, and handed Kissinger the text of a nine-point draft agreement—in English—which he said Hanoi would sign. Under the draft, the U.S. would guarantee to respect Vietnam's "national rights" (independence, sovereignty, unity, and territorial integrity) while an internationally supervised ceasefire would begin 24 hours after the signing of an agreement. During the next 60 days, all U.S. and other foreign troops on the South Vietnamese side would be withdrawn and all prisoners exchanged. There would be no restriction on U.S. aid to South Vietnam for civilian purposes; military aid would also be permitted, but only to replace weapons or supplies used up or worn out after the ceasefire.

Following the truce, Saigon and the Communists would open negotiations to arrange "genuinely free and democratic elections" under the supervision of a Council of National Reconciliation and Concord. The members of the council would form three equal segments representing Saigon, the Provisional Revolutionary Government, and a neutral Third

Force. The matter of "Vietnamese armed forces in South Vietnam"—that is, North Vietnamese troops—was also to be settled by negotiations after the ceasefire "in a spirit of national reconciliation."

Other points in the draft called for eventual reunification of Vietnam "through peaceful means," a U.S. contribution "to healing the wounds of war and to post-war reconstruction" in North Vietnam and the rest of Indochina, and a commitment by the U.S. and the Vietnamese on both sides to withdraw military forces from Laos and Cambodia and stop military actions there.

Thus, as Hanoi declared in a subsequent broadcast, its proposal was for a settlement "in two stages in accordance with the oft-expressed desire of the American side"—a ceasefire first, with a U.S. withdrawal and the return of its prisoners, to be followed by negotiations on South Vietnam's political future. In the meantime the North Vietnamese agreed that "the two present administrations in South Vietnam will remain in existence with their respective domestic and external functions." That meant President Thieu could stay in office while his army and police continued to administer the territory under their control. That concession, never before offered by the Communists, was what the American negotiators had been waiting for. In a recess after Tho's presentation, Kissinger exulted to his aide, Winston Lord, "We have done it."

The day after receiving the nine points, even before beginning to refine their wording, Kissinger agreed with Tho on a timetable. The U.S. would stop all bombing and mining of North Vietnam on October 18, Kissinger would fly to Hanoi to initial the agreement on the 19th, and the formal signing by the American secretary of state and North Vietnam's foreign minister would take place in Paris October 26. As they began to go over the textual details, however, the American delegation realized a little more time would be needed. On the fourth day of their meeting Kissinger suggested a new schedule: the bombing halt to start on the 21st, the initialing the following day, and the formal signing on the 30th. The North Vietnamese agreed.

While the drafting continued in Paris, nothing of the breakthrough was disclosed to President Thieu in Saigon except for cryptic messages, relayed through U.S. Ambassador Ellsworth Bunker, that a ceasefire might be near. Thieu should order his military commanders, Kissinger advised in repeated cables, to seize as much territory as possible, especially around Saigon, in advance of a possible truce. (That advice did not deter the Americans from subsequently expressing huge indignation at the Communists for issuing exactly the same instructions to *their* units. In fact, Kissinger later cited the dangers of a ceasefire-eve "land-grab" as one of his pretexts for refusing to complete the agreement on schedule.)

When Kissinger and Tho completed a final sixteen-hour session at two o'clock on the morning of October 12, only two matters of any substance remained unresolved. One was the exact wording of a provision permitting continued resupply of arms and war materiel from outside South Vietnam. The second was the matter of civilian prisoners held by Saigon for Communist activity. Hanoi wanted the release of those prisoners to be part of the general exchange of "captured personnel" that would also free American prisoners of war. But the U.S. would not mortgage the release of captured Americans to any decision by Saigon. It would tie the P.O.W. release only to the withdrawal of American troops.

These were not trivial matters, but it was clear they would not prevent conclusion of an agreement that was now so nearly complete. On October 12, when Kissinger flew to Washington to give President Nixon his first full report, his schedule called for a final drafting session with Xuan Thuy in Paris on the 17th, departure for Saigon that evening, and meetings with President Thieu beginning on the 19th—time, Kissinger was confident, to win South Vietnam's approval and allow him to meet the schedule for initialing the agreement in Hanoi.

When he kept his date with Thuy in Paris, the two met for twelve hours but were unable to finish agreement on all the disputed points. He could not go to Hanoi until every issue was settled, Kissinger warned, cautioning also that he could not proceed either until Saigon had accepted the agreement. Yet his arrangements with the North Vietnamese negotiators had left no loopholes. The need for Saigon's approval was mentioned not as a condition but as an American undertaking; by Hanoi's account, never disputed by Kissinger or other U.S. negotiators, both sides "agreed to be responsible for the concurrence of their respective allies." Neither the terms of the agreement nor the timetable for signing it were made contingent on decisions in Saigon.

From his plane, after leaving Paris, Kissinger transmitted proposed texts for the few clauses that were still in dispute. With all that had already been achieved, he did not believe that such last-minute details would be allowed to block the agreement. Nor did he anticipate problems in Saigon. Most of his aides were similarly hopeful. All of them were wrong. Kissinger's improvisational style—like a lumberjack leaping from log to log across a stream, one writer said—contributed to the crisis that was about to confront him. So did his habitual condescension toward the Vietnamese, both enemy and ally. Nearly two decades earlier, the Communist general and military theorist Vo Nguyen Giap remarked that "the basic error committed by the imperialists had been . . . to neglect the effort of which a people fighting for its independence is capable." In October of 1972, Henry Kissinger fell into that error about not just one, but both Vietnams.

With what would seem uncanny prophecy, Kissinger himself, nearly four years before, had outlined the events that overtook him at the threshold of what was to be his greatest triumph. "Clashes with our allies in which both sides claim to be deceived," he wrote in a *Foreign Affairs* article published just before he joined the Nixon White House,

> happen so frequently as to suggest structural causes. . . . When an issue is fairly abstract—before there is a prospect for agreement—our diplomats tend to present our view in a bland, relaxed fashion to the ally whose interests are involved but who is not present at the negotiations. The ally responds equally vaguely for three reasons: (a) he may be misled into believing that no decision is imminent and therefore sees no purpose in making an issue; (b) he is afraid that if he forces the issue the decision will go against him; (c) he hopes the problem will go away because agreement will prove impossible. When agreement seems imminent, American diplomats suddenly go into high gear to gain the acquiescence of the ally. He in turn feels tricked by the very intensity and suddenness of the pressure while we are outraged to learn of objections heretofore not made explicit. This almost guarantees that the ensuing controversy will take place under the most difficult circumstances.

That passage described, with astonishing exactness, the collision that was about to take place between the United States and its South Vietnamese ally. Just how difficult the "difficult circumstances" would be, not even Kissinger could have guessed.

By the time Kissinger's blue-and-silver Air Force jet touched down at Tansonnhut Airport on the evening of October 18, Saigon time, the South Vietnamese capital was feverish with speculation. By insisting so vehemently that nothing was happening in Paris, the government had succeeded only in convincing the Saigonese that exactly the opposite was true.

Overnight, banners blossomed throughout the city proclaiming Thieu's terms: no ceasefire unless all North Vietnamese troops were withdrawn from the South, and no coalition under any guise. On the morning of the 19th, in a fleet of limousines escorted by jeeps that bristled with the rifles of Vietnamese and American security guards, Kissinger and his entourage drove the four blocks from the American embassy on Thong Nhut Boulevard to the Doc Lap Palace. In the American party, beside Kissinger, were Gen. Creighton Abrams, the Army chief of staff; William H. Sullivan, assistant secretary of state for the Far East; Ambassador Bunker; and Bunker's deputy, Charles Whitehouse. Waiting for them were Thieu; Vice-president Tran Van Huong; Foreign Minister Tran Van Lam; Pham Dang Lam, the head of Saigon's delegation to the formal Paris peace talks; Tran Kim Phuong, the South Vietnamese ambassador to Washington; Nguyen Phu Duc, Thieu's foreign affairs adviser; and Hoang Duc Nha, his press secretary and confidant.

At the start of the meeting Kissinger produced an English copy—but none in Vietnamese—of the draft agreement. It was the first time the South Vietnamese were told, in any detail, of the nine points that had been negotiated more than a week before in Paris. Kissinger did not mention the timetable for signing that had been agreed on with the North Vietnamese. For the next three and a half hours, he outlined the agreement's provisions "like a professor defending a thesis," one Vietnamese official later recalled. Thieu asked some carefully noncommittal questions, then asked for some time to study the draft. The talks recessed until early evening.

Behind their bland expressions the South Vietnamese were apprehensive about the terms they had just been given, and they were outraged by the high-handed American attitude. A treaty that affected them more vitally than it did the United States had been negotiated without their presence. "We are consulted," Foreign Minister Lam complained to a reporter, "but we cannot participate in these meetings." And now they were under humiliating pressure to approve it in only two or three days after seeing it for the first time—and not even in their own language.

Thieu had to ask Kissinger and Bunker, when they returned that evening, for a Vietnamese translation, which still had not been furnished. In the meantime he had asked Nha, who had been educated in the U.S. and whose English was fluent and idiomatic, to study the text they had been given that morning. This meant the first South Vietnamese reaction would be influenced principally by the man in Thieu's entourage who was the most mistrustful of American motives. Perhaps his wider American experience had given Nha a better sense of how remote Vietnam was to most Americans and how disinclined they were to keep making major sacrifices for Vietnam's sake. Too, as the Vietnamese official responsible for dealing with the American press, Nha may have realized more fully than his colleagues the extent of unsympathetic American opinion toward the Thieu government. Whatever the reasons, Nha—incurring Henry Kissinger's lasting dislike—was among Thieu's aides the one who most strongly advocated rejection of the American plan.

Thieu's feelings about his powerful sponsor cannot have been improved when he was shown a typewritten document that had been captured from a Viet Cong district political officer, describing the peace agreement in great detail. The comparison was painful: the Communists were distributing and explaining it even to their low-level cadres in the field, while the Americans refused the same confidence to the president of the allied country whose survival was at issue.

The American negotiators, meanwhile, had received a message from Hanoi accepting the exact wording Kissinger had suggested from his plane on the last two unresolved clauses: replacement of war materiel, and the matter of civilian prisoners held by South Vietnam. The U.S. reply was in the form of a personal message from President Nixon to Prime Minister Pham

Van Dong, agreeing that the text of the agreement could be considered complete. However, Nixon asked for clarifications of certain "understandings" that were not to be part of the treaty text. These were an assurance that American P.O.W.'s in Laos and Cambodia would be freed with those in Vietnam, an assurance from North Vietnam that a Laos ceasefire would be concluded shortly after the Vietnam truce, and confirmation of much vaguer statements concerning Cambodia. Nixon also proposed still a third postponement of the signing schedule, putting the first two steps back for another 48 hours: the bombing halt on October 23 and the initialing in Hanoi on the 24th. The formal signing was still to be on the 31st. If the "understandings" were resolved satisfactorily, Nixon added, no further delays would be needed: the U.S. could be counted on to meet the new timetable.

Hanoi, which was now in a position to use the agreement as a wedge to split the U.S. from its South Vietnamese ally, quickly accepted the American formulations on every single one of the points raised in Nixon's message. When Nixon agreed in a last communication that Hanoi had "satisfied all his points," no more disputes remained. The American commitment to sign the nine points on the last day of October was not "hypothetical" or "conditional," as Kissinger would subsequently assert. It had been expressed to Hanoi unequivocally and unconditionally in the name of the president of the United States.

Thieu and his advisors raised scores of objections to the proposed agreement, but three were paramount. First, Saigon could not accept a ceasefire that did not also require the withdrawal of North Vietnamese troops from the South.* Second, the Council of National Reconciliation was a disguised coalition government, or the seedling of one, and thus impermissible. The Vietnamese text used words suggesting it would have "governmental" status, Thieu and his associates claimed, not just "administrative" responsibilities as stated in the English version. The inference was that the Americans had been tricked. And third, Thieu would not tolerate the agreement's implied acceptance of the Communist view that Vietnam was one country, temporarily divided. The text's references to "three Indochinese countries" instead of four and to Vietnam's "unity and territorial integrity" seemed to Thieu to deny South Vietnam's independence and sovereignty. Both must

---

* Thieu invariably said there were 300,000 North Vietnamese soldiers in the South, while U.S. order-of-battle estimates listed fewer than half that many: about 145,000. The discrepancy arose, apparently, because Thieu for political reasons would not acknowledge that any indigenous South Vietnamese Communist movement existed. (The P.R.G. was dismissed in Saigon's propaganda as a "ghost.") Thieu's 300,000 "North Vietnamese aggressors" included some 70,000 southern guerrillas and support troops and about the same number of political cadre, sympathizers, and agents. These last U.S. intelligence did not list as armed troops at all.

be explicitly recognized, he demanded, and the Demilitarized Zone acknowledged as a true international boundary, to make it clear that North Vietnam was a foreign country with no legal right to keep its army in the South.

As the meetings continued with Kissinger, Thieu also staged a series of "consultations" with National Assembly members, province and village officials, and other groups. After each such session, unspecific but obviously authorized leaks carried the message that Thieu was holding firm against American pressure. Along with the leaked accounts, malicious remarks about Kissinger, obviously inspired by members of Thieu's inner circle, began to appear in Saigon newspapers and float through the Tu Do Street coffee shops where politicians, journalists, and intellectuals congregated. Some of the comments had a flavor of anti-Semitism, a prejudice many in Vietnam's heavily Catholic elite had acquired from the French. It was said, for example, that because Kissinger was a Jew he wanted to stop aiding South Vietnam in order to make funds available for more aid to Israel. Another widely repeated story had Nha charging Kissinger—to his face—that he was not really concerned about the Vietnamese cause, but only with winning a Nobel Peace Prize for himself.

In one sense the American negotiators were entitled to feel that they had been misled, that Thieu had previously agreed to proposals he was now rejecting. On the matter of North Vietnamese troops, for more than two years no American plan had explicitly required their removal from the South. Thieu had consented to Nixon's ambiguous offer of a "ceasefire-in-place" in the fall of 1970 and to subsequent private peace proposals in May and October of 1971 that specifically left the question of "other outside forces" to subsequent negotiations after a ceasefire and an American withdrawal. The same principle was contained in Nixon's speeches of January 25 and May 8, 1972, to which Thieu had not objected. The South Vietnamese leader had assented also to the creation of an "independent body representing all political forces in South Vietnam" to organize and administer elections, a concept also stated in American peace proposals since 1971. To the Americans there was no apparent difference between such a body and the Council of National Reconciliation, which Thieu was now denouncing as a coalition government in disguise.

If Thieu had acquiesced in those earlier American proposals, however, it was also clear that they did not reflect his own convictions. His assent was an expedient that appeared to involve no risk, as long as there seemed no possibility that the Communists would meet American terms. Thieu's reluctant concurrence with American initiatives was forced on him by the political and psychological circumstances of his own presidency and the regime he led. More was involved than just dependence on American material support: Thieu's link with the Americans was also a crucial aspect of his own power. It may have cost him respect, even self-respect, but the perception that he was the American choice was an important source of his control over ambitious fellow generals whose habits of political conspiracy, formed in the early and mid-1960s when coups occurred every few months, were not entirely forgotten. While the risks remained abstract, South Vietnam's and Thieu's own interests dictated compliance with American wishes; any other course, indeed, seemed inconceivable.

Underlying past South Vietnamese acquiescence, too, was a wider pattern of passivity that grew out of the entire Vietnamese relationship with the United States. Few Vietnamese believed their own actions would decide their country's future. Military and government leaders guarded their personal and bureaucratic interests, so American pressure for reforms was, generally, unavailing. But the Vietnamese did not really have a strategy or doctrine of their own. They depended on their ally for policies, just as for airplanes, tanks, rifles, canteens, boots, and mosquito nets, not out of trust but from an inability to believe that they could form policies of their own—or that it would make any difference if they did.

The Vietnamese government had no strategy derived from South Vietnamese conditions and needs, one Vietnamese general wrote after the war: "It was dependent on the U.S. for major policies and military strategy." And another memoir by Vietnamese military leaders commented:

> No matter how well-intentioned and dedicated Americans had proved to be, the Vietnamese always felt that their friends were playing the leading role in all fields of endeavor. . . . In its haste to achieve quick success and a military victory, the United States had been too eager to take everything upon itself and allowed itself to control almost every facet of the [Republic of Vietnam's] effort in the process. So encompassing and visible was this control that it left the RVN utterly passive, dependent, subservient, and unable to make decisions for its own sake. . . . The towering and conspicuous role of the U.S. as a "big brother" gave the impression that everything had been preordained by the U.S.

In this climate, and in a state of complete dependence on the Americans for military support, only the most dire extremity would have led Thieu to the great risk of opposing his sponsor's diplomacy. No such extremity existed while the U.S. and North Vietnam were still far from agreement; but when the Communists suddenly appeared ready to accept American terms, the combination of forces acting on Thieu and his associates changed. Now, abruptly, the risk of rejecting American wishes seemed far less than the danger of accepting them.

On the morning of Sunday, October 22, the day Kissinger had hoped to journey to Hanoi, he handed Thieu a letter from Nixon. It contained a grave warning: "Were you to find the agreement to be unacceptable at this point and the other side were to reveal the extraordinary lengths to which it has gone in meeting demands put upon them," the American president had written, "it is my judgment that your decision would have the most serious effects upon my ability to continue to provide support for you and for the government of South Vietnam."

In the immediate context, the threat was a bluff. Nixon had already instructed Kissinger that if Thieu remained unyielding, the agreement should not be signed. Any North Vietnamese charges of bad faith would simply have to be faced down for a while longer. In the longer run, though, Nixon's letter stated an obvious truth: If Thieu were seen to be blocking a settlement, American support would not last long. The threat was one to which Thieu would ultimately have to yield. Yet he was also prepared to go quite a long way in risking American patronage, for his objections to the agreement went beyond the specific points on which he had lectured Kissinger and which were lettered on propaganda banners all over Saigon. Thieu's resistance was rooted in the essence of his regime. At some bedrock level where the true possibilities of men and societies are determined, it seemed to me that Thieu and his generals could not find the self-confidence to face the end of American participation in the war. Further, the agreement could only appear to Thieu as a threat to his own power. By his own lights Nguyen Van Thieu was a patriot, and his concern for his country was genuine. But at the same time he was a man who was always very, very careful of his own political position. From that viewpoint he had no reason at all to endorse the agreement that had been concluded, he felt, behind his back.

"Everyone is tired of an endless and fruitless war," one of South Vietnam's Buddhist intellectuals had written months earlier, "but no one is prepared to call a halt to it. The blood and suffering of the hundreds of thousands of lives thrown into battle have to be justified by some concrete results, however meager." The nine points offered no concrete results to Thieu. The agreement could be justified to his people only if it really brought peace, and the South Vietnamese leaders did not believe it would. The treaty would leave South Vietnam, without the ally whose presence had become its leaders' indispensable crutch, facing an implacable enemy. It would give the Communists a status that Kissinger called harmless but that mocked everything Thieu had told the South Vietnamese public for many years. It would leave the Communist army intact and in place, when the only vindication for Thieu's years of leadership would have been some demonstrable military success. And it would expose him as no longer able to command and distribute the tokens of American power, which had been the foundation of his own.

To Kissinger, Thieu restated his objections to the settlement, but he did not reject it. Before replying to Nixon's message he wanted to confer again with his advisers and with National Assembly leaders, he said; he asked Kissinger to return late that afternoon. Kissinger used the interval for a quick four-and-a-half-hour side trip to Phnom Penh—the only time he would ever see Cambodia—arriving back at the palace, with Ambassador Bunker, at 5 P.M.

Though he spoke English fairly well, on this occasion Thieu would not do so. With Nha translating, he announced to Kissinger that he could not accept the treaty. The United States, he suggested, was conniving with China and the Soviet Union to sell out South Vietnam; he listened, unmoved, to Kissinger's indignant answer that President Nixon had risked "his whole political future" in reescalating the air war and mining North Vietnam's ports less than six months earlier. At one point Thieu turned his back on Kissinger and gazed at a map on the wall, then commented bitterly that compared to the United States, South Vietnam was no more than a dot. Its loss would mean little to America, he said, which had its strategies to pursue with Moscow and Peking. But for South Vietnam the nature of the agreement was a matter of survival. The bargain that had been made with Hanoi was "tantamount to surrender" and rather than accept it, South Vietnam would simply have to fight on, without American support if necessary. As he spoke Thieu frequently wept. Nha was also in tears.

Kissinger, in reply, declared that neither the president nor the American public would easily understand the charge that the nine points were a sellout. Urging Thieu to avoid public statements that would turn their dispute into an open breach, Kissinger returned to Ambassador Bunker's residence to arrange for transmission of a message to Hanoi in Nixon's name, explaining that because "difficulties in Saigon have proved somewhat more complex than originally anticipated," the agreed-on schedule for concluding the settlement could not be met after all. The message told the North Vietnamese that Kissinger would be returning to Washington to consult on "what further steps to take," and asked them to withhold any public reaction until the U.S. could send a fuller explanation, which it promised within the next 24 hours. "The U.S. side," the message concluded, "reaffirms its commitment to the substance and basic principles of the draft agreement."

From Saigon, Kissinger also proposed to the White House that if it was not going to meet the rest of the schedule, the U.S. could at least carry out its promise to stop the bombing of North Vietnam. Nixon refused. One of his strongest convictions about Vietnam was that Lyndon Johnson had blundered monumentally in ending the bombing in 1968 without obtaining adequate concessions in return. Nixon would not repeat that mistake. The most he would do was order the bombers, without announcement, to keep below the 20th parallel, about 70 miles south of Hanoi.

The following morning, after a last 45-minute meeting in which he and a much calmer Thieu failed again to break their impasse but agreed not to engage in any public debate, Kissinger left Saigon—not, as he had hoped, to surface in Hanoi for the most thrilling of the diplomatic spectaculars he and Nixon so relished, with flashbulbs popping while he and Le Duc Tho smiled out at an astonished and grateful world, but instead to return to Washington to try to salvage his agreement if he could. The American embassy in Saigon issued a terse statement that said, in its entirety: "We have made progress. Talks will continue between us and the government of Vietnam. It is not in the interests of the negotiations to be more specific at this time."

The next evening Thieu delivered a rambling, two-hour televised speech in which he all but confirmed that a deal had been made between Washington and Hanoi, but that it was unacceptable to Saigon. The details were still hinted at, however, not stated. Then, suddenly and from the most unexpected source of all, came verification of the rumors that had seethed for so many days. On October 26, toward the end of a hot, drowsy Thursday lunch hour in Saigon, news agency monitors began picking up a broadcast from Hanoi. Nine months earlier, when President Nixon disclosed the secret negotiations for the first time, the North Vietnamese were outraged.* Now it was their turn, at a time and in circumstances that could only embarrass the United States. Not only had an agreement been reached in Paris, Radio Hanoi's announcer said, but the United States had agreed three times on a date for signing it and had reneged each time. North Vietnam was still ready to proceed if the U.S. would meet the October 31 deadline, the last one agreed to. But the Americans' attempt to delay still again "has brought about a very serious situation" that could risk the entire agreement, the broadcast warned. "The Nixon administration," it added, "must bear before the people of the United States and the world responsibility for delaying the signing of the agreement, and thus prolonging the war in Vietnam."

Less than twelve hours later, Henry Kissinger faced hundreds of reporters and cameramen in the White House briefing room. He acknowledged that Hanoi's statement, in its essentials, was correct. But "certain concerns and ambiguities" had arisen, he went on, that would require "one more negotiating meeting with the North Vietnamese negotiators lasting, I would think, not more than three or four days."

The press conference lasted for an hour. Its transcript filled eighteen closely typed pages. But its message came in the first minute or two and was contained in just four words: "Peace is at hand." That electrifying phrase would bedevil Henry Kissinger for the next three months.

---

* For 29 months after the first secret session, the talks had remained one of the world's best-kept diplomatic secrets. But on January 25, 1972, with the negotiations deadlocked and intelligence reports warning of a major Communist offensive, and while antiwar critics were blaming him for the impasse, Nixon revealed the negotiations in a televised speech, disclosing the latest American peace plan and seeking to show that the Vietnamese Communists, not the Americans, were responsible for the continuing war.

As was so often true in Vietnam, where events ran in grooves that seemed never to lead anywhere new but forever looped around to meet their own earlier traces, what was happening seemed a repetition of the past. October 1972 was an echo of October 1968, when Thieu first tried to resist President Johnson's election-eve bombing halt and then stalled for weeks before finally agreeing to send a South Vietnamese delegation to the Paris peace talks. The American dilemma was even older. It had been expressed as early as 1963 by Ambassador Henry Cabot Lodge, in reply to orders that he should threaten to slow or suspend American aid in order to force President Ngo Dinh Diem and his brother Ngo Dinh Nhu to reform their autocratic regime. He would like to know, Lodge cabled back, how "to apply sanctions in a way which will really affect Diem and Nhu without precipitating an economic collapse and without impeding the war effort. We are studying this here and have not found a solution." If an answer could be found, he added sardonically, "it would be one of the greatest discoveries since the enactment of the Marshall Plan."

The question in Lodge's cable had been raised innumerable times since, but no one had yet satisfactorily answered it. Like Diem, Thieu made an advantage of his own weakness. His regime would collapse if American support ended. But that would also mean the defeat of every American objective in Indochina, for which so many lives and dollars had been spent and on which so many reputations depended. Unless Washington was willing to face that prospect, it must keep underwriting Saigon. And so its threats were empty and Thieu could remain defiant, a puppet pulling his own strings.

In Saigon, after Hanoi revealed the nine points, Thieu kept proclaiming his opposition. "Peace will come when I sign the agreement. . . . Any signature, even ten signatures, without mine will be completely of no value," he told a meeting of provincial and national legislators on October 27. In a National Day broadcast on November 1, he denounced the draft treaty as "humiliating . . . a surrender," and demanded that the U.S. step aside and let him negotiate with the Communists directly. The government arranged for resolutions endorsing its stand to be approved by both houses of the National Assembly, the Supreme Court, the provincial councillors' convention, and other political and civic organizations. This procedure Thieu called another "Dien Hong," after a famous conclave of the Vietnamese kingdom's elders in the thirteenth century to decide whether to submit to or resist Mongol invaders.

In the U.S., meanwhile, Kissinger was under criticism for his premature declaration of peace. Yet the phrase "peace is at hand" succeeded, where less dramatic words might not have, in turning attention away from the broken American promise. Having raised a flood of hope that an agreement was near, Kissinger was questioned only perfunctorily about the exact nature of his commitments to Hanoi. The fact that the U.S. reneged on its promise, while not completely disguised, was sufficiently obscured for Kissinger's purposes. He retained his extraordinary dominance over American foreign policy, losing no ground in his obsessive bureaucratic combat against the State Department or rivals on the White House staff. His reputation as a superdiplomat was damaged only superficially and, it turned out, temporarily. If he was not wholly unscathed, Kissinger still emerged from the crisis in pretty good shape for a man who had just deceived both his enemy and his ally and had led the United States into an act of bad faith that can have few parallels in its diplomatic history.

Hanoi's fury was as great as Saigon's. The North Vietnamese leaders were skeptical of diplomacy to begin with, and they were now quick to suspect that they had been made the victims of premeditated, deliberate deception. Their forces in the South, which had been dispersed under orders to seize as much territory as possible before a truce, were suffering heavy losses in South Vietnamese counterattacks. The Communists' ideology did not permit them to acknowledge, or perhaps even to perceive, that Saigon was defying American wishes. Instead, their conclusion was that Nixon had never intended to go through with the agreement at all. "Thieu owes his existence to U.S. dollars and bombs," shrilled Radio Hanoi. "Thieu cannot survive if he does not receive U.S. backing. He cannot on his own oppose the policies and decisions of the United States." His opposition to the peace agreement "is only a behind-the-scenes manipulation by the U.S.," the broadcast added. "In an attempt to evade its responsibility in the settlement of the Vietnam question, the Nixon administration is using Thieu as a mouthpiece."

Hanoi's suspicions could only have deepened when, within a few days of Kissinger's departure from Saigon, a massive American airlift began pouring new weaponry and equipment into South Vietnam.

Long convoys of brand-new trucks, tanks, and armored personnel carriers, with shipping labels still hanging from bumpers or gunports, wound out of the gates of Tansonnhut Air Base. Towed behind them were scores of new 105-mm and 155-mm howitzers. At Tansonnhut and at the huge Bien Hoa Air Base not far away, workmen wrestled huge crates carrying disassembled helicopters and fighter aircraft out of the bellies of American transport planes. Alongside the twin-engined C-123s that were up to then the largest transports in the Vietnamese air force, there appeared in the revetments at Tansonnhut two full squadrons of four-engined C-130s, their U.S. Air Force tail numbers still faintly outlined under fresh coats of olive-drab paint.

According to U.S. records, 266 fighters and transports and 277 helicopters were shipped in the airlift, which was codenamed Enhance Plus. In the earlier Operation Enhance, ordered to replace the abnormal losses in the Easter offensive and carried out mainly by sea, another 155 fixed-wing aircraft and 69 helicopters had been provided. Besides aircraft, Enhance and Enhance Plus supplied 222 tanks, 117 armored personnel carriers, more than 1,700 trucks, seven new Navy craft, and 95 artillery pieces, including 39 long-range 175-mm guns. In equipment costs alone the shipments represented more than three-quarters of a billion dollars.

Additional material was turned over by departing U.S. and Allied units, including all or most of the equipment of two full South Korean divisions—38,000 men. Meanwhile, to avoid the stricture that American installations must be dismantled following a ceasefire, the U.S. also began signing over to the South Vietnamese not only its bases but items of equipment ranging down to the chairs and typewriters in American offices. "It's not mine any more," an American officer grinned one day when I asked to use his desk for a moment. "It belongs to the Vietnamese government now." The transfer was accomplished by a "Memorandum of Understanding" between the U.S. command and the South Vietnamese Joint General Staff, signed on November 2. (The North Vietnamese and Viet Cong were formally notified of the transfers after the ceasefire by American military representatives to the truce commission in Saigon. The American negotiators, according to the U.S. delegation's official historian, regarded the memorandum as a "subterfuge" violating the spirit and possibly the letter of the Paris agreement, and they were worried that the Communist delegates might contest the transfers once they realized that no bases were being dismantled. Somewhat to the Americans' surprise, the Communist representatives simply asked to inspect the memorandum and other relevant documents, and never raised the issue again.)

The Enhance and Enhance Plus shipments gave an impression of formidable military power. "If we had been giving this aid to the North Vietnamese," an American general was reported to have said, "they could have fought us for the rest of the century." The sight of the new weaponry was no doubt reassuring to the Vietnamese soldiers and civilians who saw the convoys, and the arms swelled the inventories that would become the benchmark for replacements after a settlement. They may also have helped reconcile Thieu to the departure of the U.S. forces.

Yet it was not at all clear that the shipments really responded to South Vietnam's military needs. The Enhance Plus airlift was hurriedly ordered by the White House without any recommendation by the Joint Chiefs of Staff, who had not previously indicated that any such buildup was needed. By imposing burdens of management and maintenance far beyond South Vietnam's ability to carry, the Enhance programs mortgaged the Vietnamese military machine even more heavily to continued high levels of U.S. military aid funds. Nor was the new equipment very effectively used. Much of it stayed in storage right up until South Vietnam's defeat two and a half years later. The buildup, commented Bui Diem, the former South Vietnamese ambassador to Washington and later Thieu's diplomatic adviser, had political value: "Practically everything which could be construed as a form of guarantee from the U.S. not to abandon South Vietnam was welcomed by Mr. Thieu. But it was hastily and ill-conceived, and the whole program had little military value."

This was especially true of the aircraft buildup. From 1,397 aircraft in June of 1972, the Vietnamese air force inventory shot up to 2,075 only six months later. This number was "completely beyond their ability to maintain," a U.S. Air Force study later declared. The Vietnamese already had more planes than trained pilots, as was explained to me once by an air force colonel with, I thought, remarkable delicacy: there were, he said, "some aircraft available for attrition." After the ceasefire the air force was the largest, though not the only, user of the thousands of American civilians employed by the U.S. Defense Department to work in Vietnam. With overtime these Americans sometimes earned up to $1,000 a week, twice as much in a single day as a Vietnamese mechanic earned in an entire month. These salaries were charged to American military aid budgets.

Aimed at bolstering South Vietnam's military strength and confidence, the Enhance buildup also began to evoke an image that was distinctly unmilitary: of the placid white ducks nestling in their straw baskets on sidewalks outside shops and restaurants in Saigon's Chinese quarter, fattened for Peking-style feasts by being force-fed until they could not even waddle and were fit only to be devoured.

"Your target is Hanoi"

Soon after President Nixon's expected landslide reelection victory over Senator George S. McGovern, diplomacy resumed with both Vietnams.

To President Thieu, Nixon promised that the U.S. would try to revise the agreement to meet South Vietnam's objections, though he warned that not all the changes sought by Saigon could be obtained. "Far more important than what we say in the agreement . . . is what we do in the event the enemy renews its aggression," he told the South Vietnamese leader in a secret message on November 14. "You have my absolute assurance that if Hanoi fails to abide by the terms of this agreement it is my intention to take swift and severe retaliatory action." It was a strong promise, stepping close to or perhaps even beyond the constitutional powers of an American president. But Thieu was unmoved. On November 18, the day before Kissinger was to fly to Paris to resume negotiations, the South Vietnamese presented a list of 69 amendments to the draft treaty—a proposal Kissinger himself later called "preposterous."

North Vietnam, meanwhile, continued to insist that the U.S. sign the agreement that had already been negotiated. If Washington really wanted a settlement, Le Duc Tho declared on his arrival in Paris, it should "abide by the provisions agreed upon between the two parties." Otherwise, "the Vietnamese people will have no other way than resolutely carrying on their fight."

In their first meeting on the morning of November 20, Kissinger handed Tho the entire list of Saigon's demands. The gesture may have demonstrated American conscientiousness in representing an ally's interests. But it also put the U.S. at a disadvantage in the ensuing debate over which side was acting in bad faith. Hanoi's spokesman, Nguyen Thanh Le, did not sound entirely unreasonable when he later explained that North Vietnam's position "is that the text of the agreement agreed upon on October 20, 1972, should be maintained. But if the U.S. side insists on changing it, our side will have also to propose necessary changes."

Kissinger and Tho continued meeting until November 25, recessed until December 4, and met again almost daily until December 13, but without concluding the agreement that had seemed so close. Outside, reporters and cameramen waited in the cold and searched unavailingly for clues in the demeanor of the negotiators as they came and went. One wire service report devoted several excited sentences to the possible significance of Kissinger's parting handshake with a butler. Inside, he and the North Vietnamese wrangled, sometimes drawing farther apart and sometimes closer together, but never quite resolving all their differences.

Nor could Washington overcome its disputes with Saigon. On November 29, Thieu's aide Nguyen Phu Duc arrived at the White House to deliver a 14-page letter from the South Vietnamese leader—drafted by Nha— restating all his objections to the draft treaty and also asking for a Thieu-Nixon summit conference before any agreement was concluded with Hanoi. Nixon received Duc in the Oval Office but refused Thieu's appeal for a summit. Though the U.S. would seek improvements in the peace agreement, Nixon told Duc, the time had come for Saigon to "face the reality" that Congress would quickly cut off all funds for the war if Thieu were perceived as preventing a settlement. Not even his administration's firmest congressional supporters, Nixon declared, would keep supporting South Vietnam under those circumstances.

Thieu remained unyielding. He was still rejecting the "false peace," he told the National Assembly in Saigon on December 12, while offering his own plan for direct talks between North and South Vietnam. His speech betrayed self-doubt as well as stubbornness. If North Vietnamese troops remained in the South while a disguised coalition government was formed and Hanoi could still receive aid from its Communist allies, "the annexation of South Vietnam through military and political means will only be a question of time." The Republic of Vietnam "does not hesitate to continue the struggle," Thieu added, "but it needs assistance." The presence of North Vietnamese troops was still a crucial issue; "the simplest way to achieve peace," Thieu said, "is to make North Vietnam end its war of aggression in the South. We do not demand that the war end with a victory . . . only in justice and with minimum righteousness, that is, that the invaded must cease to be invaded and that the aggressor must go home."

Meanwhile, as Kissinger and the Communist negotiators continued sparring in Paris, Hanoi seemed to be subtly turning American tactics back on the U.S. by allowing suggestions to appear that *its* southern ally was unhappy with the agreement. Statements carefully attributed to the Provisional Revolutionary Government or to other specifically southern organizations revived the old demand for dissolving the Thieu government—reversing what was, in U.S. eyes, the fundamental Communist concession.

Thus, on November 5, the National Liberation Front Central Committee and one of its front groups, the Vietnam Alliance of National Democratic and Peace Forces, jointly declared that the Saigon government must rescind all "coercive laws and regulations" and that the people must demand Thieu's resignation. Two weeks later, the Giai Phong (Liberation) Press Agency— the P.R.G.'s voice, not North Vietnam's—declared: "Nguyen Van Thieu is an obstacle to peace and national concord. The pressing demand at present is his removal." North Vietnam approvingly noted the demands for abolishing the "stooge administration" but did not explicitly endorse them, commenting instead in the party newspaper, *Nhan Dan*, "That is the legitimate demand which the South Vietnamese people and the P.R.G. are fully entitled to raise."

Such nuances may have reflected genuine disagreements by the P.R.G. with the terms negotiated by Hanoi. But the statements were primarily a ploy, positioning the North Vietnamese to tell the U.S., in effect, that if the Americans were going to challenge basic aspects of the agreement because of their ally's objections, the Communists could play exactly the same game. At any rate, no more was heard of any dissenting P.R.G. views after the agreement was completed.

Throughout the November and December meetings, the North Vietnamese continued to offer an alternative to renegotiation: signing the October draft "without delay and without any change." But this Nixon and Kissinger would not do. Though they thought the agreement itself was acceptable, to sign it without any modification would be to humiliate the

South Vietnamese government beyond endurance. Thieu would be left with two choices, equally bad: to defy the U.S. and attempt to withstand the Communists on his own, while Congress would almost certainly shut off all American aid, or to swallow the agreement and lose all face not just before his people but before the military and bureaucratic elite that kept him in power. To avoid that choice the Americans needed some change, however cosmetic, in the original treaty.

Two issues proved major problems in the Paris meetings: the question of civilian prisoners held by the South Vietnamese and the status of the Demilitarized Zone. On the prisoner issue, the North Vietnamese had agreed in October to condition the release of American prisoners only on the simultaneous withdrawal of U.S. troops. Now, however, Tho proposed again that civilian detainees in the South be made part of an overall prisoner exchange. This was, as the American negotiators charged, backtracking on an agreement already made.

Hanoi had not revived the issue without some provocation, however. For after the nine points were broadcast, the South Vietnamese authorities not only ordered the arrest of thousands of suspected Communists and other dissidents but also prepared a new law, issued as Decree Law 020 on November 25, 1972, allowing detention without trial not just in wartime, as previous laws stipulated, but "until order and security are completely restored"—wording that could plainly let the government keep holding Viet Cong detainees after a ceasefire. The government also began placing criminal charges against detainees in the "A" and "B" categories: those who "held important positions in the Viet Cong infrastructure down to the hamlet level." The customary charges were draft dodging or violating identity-card laws. After conviction on those or other counts, the detainees were classed as common criminals, not political prisoners, and thus in Saigon's view were not eligible for exchange. All these circumstances could hardly help suggesting to the Communists that the rules were being changed *after* the terms of the October agreement were drafted.

Throughout December, P.R.G. propaganda complained of a "white terror campaign" in which, the Communists charged, "tens of thousands" were arrested and more than a thousand killed. A wave of arrests clearly occurred—though as usual, the numbers were disputed. One news account said 20,000 persons were arrested in the last three months of 1972. At the end of the year, an American embassy officer reported, there were 9,316 "A" and "B" detainees being held without trial, while several thousand more civilians were in prison after being sentenced by military courts for Communist activity or other political offenses. In the prisoner exchanges that eventually were carried out in 1973 and 1974, the South Vietnamese handed 5,081 civilian detainees back to the Communists.

The dispute over the Demilitarized Zone was of less practical importance, since the territory on both sides of the zone was firmly under Communist control. Yet matters of basic principle were involved for both Hanoi and Saigon. To the Thieu government, recognition of the DMZ as a true international boundary would uphold South Vietnam's claim to sovereignty. The Communists were just as fiercely committed to the opposing principle that "Vietnam is one. The Vietnamese people are one." The only definition of the partition line they would accept was that written in the Geneva conference declaration: "The military demarcation line is provisional and should not in any way be interpreted as constituting a political or territorial boundary." To all other formulations, Hanoi responded with outrage. Demands for the DMZ to be recognized as an international boundary represented "a mere scheme to turn the two halves of Vietnam into two separate states," declared the controlled party press. "This is to perpetuate the partition of Vietnam and put South Vietnam under . . . U.S. domination." To Hanoi, American recognition of Vietnam's "national rights" was, along with the removal of U.S. troops, the central accomplishment of the peace settlement, for which the Communists had made important concessions of their own. That recognition could not now be withdrawn or qualified.

Other matters in dispute at different times included the status of American civilian technicians working with South Vietnam's armed forces, whom Hanoi tried to insist must be withdrawn with U.S. troops, and the troublesome Vietnamese-language description that Saigon said gave governmental, and not just "administrative," status to the Council of National Reconciliation.

As Kissinger and Tho continued their meetings, agreement emerged now and then on one or another issue, but never on all at the same time. The North Vietnamese, Kissinger concluded, were deliberately stalling, perhaps believing that the U.S. "dare not continue the war because of domestic and international expectations." Delay held for Hanoi the prospect of an open split between Washington and Saigon—a windfall they may not have expected when they first offered the nine points to Kissinger, but which subsequent events had made appear temptingly possible.

On December 13, Kissinger left Paris for Washington; three days later, he again stepped into the White House press room to announce that the peace talks were at an impasse. Blaming Hanoi for the deadlock, he also issued a warning to Saigon: "We are not continuing a war to give total victory to our allies." Though the U.S. sympathized with South Vietnam's concerns, it would not indefinitely give Thieu a veto over American decisions. "If we can get an agreement that the president considers just," Kissinger said, "we will proceed with it." His tone was still hopeful. With the text of an agreement 99 percent complete, he told the packed press room, "we believe that it would be a relatively simple matter to conclude the agreement." Privately, however, he and Nixon had already reached a crucial decision: unless Hanoi met American terms in a space of hours, there would have to be another spasm of war.

For eight weeks, no American bombers had struck north of the 20th parallel in North Vietnam. Then, at 7:43 P.M. Hanoi time, December 18, bombs began falling on the runways and buildings of Hoa Lac airfield, fifteen miles west of the North Vietnamese capital.

The Vietnamese were not caught unprepared. Additional evacuations of civilians from Hanoi had been announced on December 7, and the city authorities had ordered schools to remain closed, with children directed to enroll in the villages to which they had been moved earlier. When the Paris negotiations were suspended on the 13th, thousands more persons spontaneously left the capital. Hanoi city buses transported those who wanted to leave. About 200,000 of the city's one million residents left before the bombing began. Another 300,000 followed in the coming days.

The first bombs to fall were dropped by three B-52s from U Tapao air base in Thailand, using the call-signs "Snow-1," "Snow-2," and "Snow-3." Two minutes behind the "Snow" cell came three more bombers of the "Brown" cell. Nine others—"Maple," "Gold," and "Green"—were approaching Kep airfield northeast of Hanoi. Their strike was to start just four minutes after the first bombs dropped at Hoa Lac. After them, high in the night sky, more aircraft streamed toward North Vietnamese targets: 129 B-52s in all, divided into three waves that were timed to reach the Hanoi area at intervals of four to five hours. The bombs of the leading "Snow" aircraft were the first of an eleven-day blitz the Air Force called Linebacker II, but which the rest of the world would give a more emotion-laden name: the Christmas Bombing.

Planning orders for the Linebacker raids had been flashed to Andersen Air Force Base on Guam late on December 15. Among the 12,000 officers and airmen there—"Andy," they called it, or simply "The Rock"—many were still hoping that peace-at-hand would also mean home-for-Christmas. But on the morning of the 18th, air crews were told what some of them had already grown to suspect. Colonel James R. McCarthy, commander of the 43rd Strategic Wing, was the briefing officer for the 27 crews who would join 21 Thai-based bombers to form the first wave. "Gentlemen," he began, "your target for tonight is Hanoi."

For the rest of the briefing, McCarthy recalled later, "you could have heard a pin drop."

The lead Guam-based ship, "Rose-1," began its takeoff roll at nine minutes to three in the afternoon, Guam time. From the balconies of crew billets, crowds of airmen watched as more planes took off in a steady stream. Lieutenant Colonel George Allison, a B-52 navigator who would later fly two Linebacker missions, found his eyes drawn to an even more striking sight, he thought: the line of taxiing aircraft lumbering toward the runways. From his vantage point, he could not see the planes themselves, only the 48-foot-high tail fins moving slowly past long rows of revetments. The procession of fins suggested an image Allison did not like but which was "too vivid to dismiss"—they reminded him, he said, of "moving targets in a shooting gallery."

That night, three B-52s were shot down by surface-to-air missiles. Two fell over Hanoi, and the third, with Maj. Cliff Ashley at the controls, struggled toward Thailand with flames streaming from its port wing. Ashley hoped to fly all the way to U Tapao, but 30 minutes after he crossed the Thai border, with the fire looking to the men inside "like a wall of red flame," the pilot of an escorting F-4 Phantom radioed, "I don't think you're going to make it." The six crewmen and the deputy mission commander, Lt. Col. Hendsley R. Connor, baled out, watching the huge plane wheel over to the left and plunge toward the ground, the whole fuselage now ablaze. All seven men landed safely and were rescued.

In the subsequent Linebacker raids, twelve more B-52s were shot down, all by missiles, while five other Air Force planes and six Navy aircraft were lost as well. Nearly 100 American airmen were killed, missing or captured.*

"War by tantrum," a columnist called it. Altogether during Linebacker II, 729 B-52 sorties were flown, all at night. On some nights the raids were spread over many hours, on some they were compressed into much shorter periods. On the night of December 29, 72 bombers approaching Hanoi from four different directions struck targets just a few miles apart within a single fifteen-minute interval. At exactly the same time another 30 aircraft struck Haiphong and eighteen more hit Thai Nguyen, a rail center north of Hanoi. During daylight hours, fighter-bombers flew another 1,000 sorties, nearly all of them radar-directed through heavy clouds. During the entire campaign there were only twelve hours clear enough for visual bombing.

Never before in the history of air warfare, American officers insisted, had such care been taken to hit only designated military targets. At first, B-52

---

* For nearly seven and a half years after they were first used in combat in Southeast Asia, no B-52s were lost to enemy fire. The first and only B-52 combat loss before Linebacker II came just a month earlier, on the night of November 22, when a ship piloted by Capt. N. J. Ostrozny was struck by a missile near the North Vietnamese city of Vinh. The plane, though burning, managed to reach Thailand before crashing, and the pilot and crew parachuted safely. Until just two weeks previously, normal orders for B-52 crews were to break off a mission or divert to alternate targets if the threat of missiles or enemy interceptors appeared too dangerous. These "no sweat" orders, as the aircrews called them, were changed in the second week of November, because too many targets were thought to be escaping attack. Under the new orders, crews on most missions were supposed to "press on" to their assigned targets despite missile or fighter threats. Beside Captain Ostrozny's aircraft and the fifteen lost in the Linebacker II raids, one more B-52 was shot down in a raid south of the 20th parallel after Linebacker was ended, bringing the total lost in combat to seventeen during the entire war. The first B-52 mission was flown June 18, 1965, in Binh Duong Province of South Vietnam; the last on August 15, 1973, in Cambodia.

pilots were briefed to fly straight and level for four full minutes before releasing their loads. No maneuvering was allowed, even to evade missiles or fighters, in order to make sure the bombs would fall in exactly the right spot. The bomb run, the campaign's historians later noted tartly, was "a long four minutes" for the crews. Radar navigators were told that if they weren't completely certain they were at the correct aiming points, "don't drop; bring the bombs back."

Though the straight-and-level orders were subsequently eased to permit some evasive maneuvers, crews still took great risks in trying to bomb accurately. But a three-plane cell of B-52s released as many as 200 or more bombs from altitudes as high as seven miles, and absolute precision was impossible. In heavily populated zones such as Hanoi and Haiphong, civilian areas could not be entirely avoided. Egypt and India protested damage to their embassies, while a Polish freighter in Haiphong Harbor, the 5,720-ton *Josef Conrad*, was hit by bombs that killed three of its crew and mortally wounded a fourth. In Hanoi, the 1,200-bed Bach Mai hospital, North Vietnam's largest and best equipped, was bombed twice, once in a fighter-bomber strike and then more seriously with a string of bombs from a B-52 mission that was meant, U.S. officials later said, for targets "several thousand feet" away. Though all patients had been taken to shelters and were safe, according to North Vietnamese accounts, two doctors and 26 other people, including two children of hospital staff, were killed.

Schools, pagodas, markets, shops, and homes were all targets of the "barbarous" and "criminal" bombing, Hanoi charged, with more than 1,300 civilians killed in the capital and another 300 deaths in Haiphong. The Americans, comparing those losses with the much higher ones of Dresden, Tokyo, and other air-raid targets in World War II, replied that if they had been trying to terrorize civilians, the casualties would have been far higher. If the U.S. had chosen to destroy Hanoi, Adm. Thomas H. Moorer, chairman of the Joint Chiefs of Staff, told a congressional inquiry, "there would not be any Hanoi today." North Vietnam's own casualty reports, U.S. officers said, proved American restraint and the accuracy of American bombing.

Perhaps because it came just as peace had seemed so near, the Christmas bombing brought a torrent of international denunciation that outdid anything heard earlier in the war.

Sweden's Prime Minister, Olaf Palme, compared it to Nazi atrocities, opening a breach in Swedish-American relations that would take years to heal. Roy Jenkins, the normally pro-American leader of the British Labor party, called the raids a "wave of terror," and his party's executive committee declared, "This continued slaughter of the Vietnamese people is a complete contradiction of the statements made by both Mr. Nixon and Dr. Kissinger." Pope Paul VI called the bombing "the object of daily grief" and wondered publicly if the reasons for breaking off the negotiations had been "sufficient."

Nixon's and Kissinger's new friends the Chinese reacted much more strongly than they had to the earlier air offensive—Linebacker I—of the previous May. A rally of 10,000 people in Peking's Great Hall of the People was held to protest the bombing, with virtually the entire Chinese leadership in attendance. The aging Mao Tse-tung demonstratively granted an audience at his Forbidden City residence to Nguyen Thi Binh, the Provisional Revolutionary Government's foreign minister. The meeting, Mrs. Binh declared, would greatly encourage her people.

In Paris, *Le Monde* likened the Hanoi raids to the terror-bombing of Guernica in the Spanish civil war. The London *Daily Mirror* said they had "made the world recoil in revulsion." In Hamburg—where nearly 50,000 people died and four-fifths of the city was flattened in a single week of Allied air raids in World War II—*Die Zeit* editorialized, "Even allies must call this a crime against humanity."

Outrage at home was equally intense. Much of it came from Congress, where not only long-time doves but members who had always supported the administration were appalled by the bombing and also by the manner in which it was ordered: in sullen, stubborn silence, without a word from the president to the people and with few of the customary courtesies of "consultation" with legislative leaders. Proposals proliferated to end the war by denying the funds to pay for it. It would be "difficult to get any Vietnam legislation" passed, warned Hugh Scott of Pennsylvania, leader of the president's party in the Senate, if no peace agreement were obtained by Inauguration Day.

Nixon refused even to answer. His spokesman announced tersely that the bombing would go on "until such time as a settlement is carried out." With only a 36-hour pause across Christmas Day, the blitz continued. Instead of being home for the holiday, American P.O.W.'s awaited another New Year's Day—the ninth, for the oldest prisoners—behind North Vietnamese barbed wire. 1972, the year that was supposed to bring peace, was ending instead in another blind, brutal paroxysm of war.

"Peace with honor"

At a few minutes after nine o'clock on the bright, springlike morning of January 16, 1973, yet another blue-and-silver White House jet, with bold letters spelling out "United States of America" on both sides of the fuselage, shrieked down onto the runway at Tansonnhut and braked to a stop in front of the military VIP terminal.

When the boarding stair had been rolled into position, the doors opened and brisk aides, with well-pressed faces and suits, trotted crisply down the steps. Behind them the presidential emissary emerged and descended. A handshake with Ambassador Bunker, waiting at planeside; another with Gen. Frederick C. Weyand, the U.S. military commander—then into the ambassador's armor-plated black limousine for the imperiously swift, siren-led drive to the American embassy downtown.

The scene had become familiar. This was the sixth high-level mission to South Vietnam in as many months, and all had begun with the same airport ritual. But this one had a discernibly different mood. The Christmas bombing had ended December 30, as abruptly as it had started. With American air strikes again restricted to the area south of the 20th parallel, Henry Kissinger and Le Duc Tho met again in Paris from January 8 to January 13. On January 15, the White House announced that the remaining bombing of North Vietnam would be stopped as a result, the spokesman said, of "the progress made in the negotiations." Nothing was officially known yet. But in the atmosphere was a certainty: a peace agreement was again at hand, and this time would not be allowed to slip away.

The visitor to Saigon was Alexander Haig, now a full general and the Army vice-chief of staff. He conferred with Thieu on January 16 and again the next day without any obbligato, this time, of angry leaks from the palace. Thursday morning, January 18, Haig left for hurried consultations in Cambodia, Laos, and Thailand. And Friday, South Vietnam's Foreign Minister, Tran Van Lam, confirmed what everyone believed. Though Saigon was still seeking "clarifications" on a few points, Lam told reporters, "we are quite close to a conclusion. It is quite true."

Thieu's doubts about the agreement were no fewer in January than they had been in October. His obduracy had won time and the Enhance arms shipments. The Christmas bombing, as a sort of farewell gift of destruction from his American protectors, had presumably shifted the military balance farther in Saigon's favor. (North Vietnam's warmaking ability after the bombing, Admiral Moorer claimed, was "less than one-half" what it had been before its ports were mined in May 1972.) Yet Thieu had also been subject to steadily growing American pressure to accept the peace agreement. On December 19, just hours after the Hanoi raids began, Nixon warned him that the U.S. would proceed with negotiations "preferably with your cooperation, but, if necessary, alone." On January 5, after the bombing ended and as the Kissinger-Tho talks were about to resume, Nixon told the South Vietnamese leader in another letter that though the U.S. would again present Saigon's views to the North Vietnamese, he neither expected nor would require Hanoi to accept them. "The result," Nixon wrote, "is certain to be once more the rejection of our position." The problem of North Vietnamese troops would be "manageable" in the American view, he added, and if U.S. terms were met on the remaining issues, "we will proceed to conclude the settlement. The gravest consequences would then ensue if your government chose to reject the agreement and split off from the United States."

The same day—January 5—Thieu's ambassador-at-large, Bui Diem, arrived in Washington to be given the same message, in varying accents of firmness, by Kissinger and other administration officials. The mood in Congress and the public demanded the agreement, Kissinger said in their meeting. The success or failure of America's entire foreign policy depended on it. South Vietnamese worries were exaggerated: with the agreement, there would be a new basis for continuing U.S. aid for Saigon, and Washington would not tolerate Communist violations. Two days later, Secretary of State Rogers told Diem that Nixon had taken as many risks as he could for Vietnam and could go no further to satisfy Saigon's views. Alexander Haig was the bluntest of all. If an acceptable agreement were offered, he warned, "I have no doubt about the determination of our president to proceed. . . . If your president decides to reject it, it will be the end of everything—in other words, the abandoment of South Vietnam."

After cabling back to Saigon that in his opinion only trivial changes in the agreement were possible—and none at all on Thieu's "life-and-death" issue of North Vietnamese troops in the South—Diem left Washington for Paris on January 10. There, two days after his arrival, he saw Kissinger again. But the American negotiator offered no new encouragement. "Your overwhelming and urgent requirement," he lectured Diem, "is . . . continued U.S. support."

When Haig returned to Saigon on January 16, he carried with him still another Nixon letter to Thieu, the severest so far. Plans for completing the agreement were now irreversible, Nixon wrote. Should Saigon still refuse to sign, "I shall have to explain publicly that your government obstructs peace. The result will be an inevitable and immediate termination of U.S. economic and military assistance." Nor would the United States tolerate a demonstrative resignation by Thieu. An aid cutoff, Nixon said, could not be "forestalled by a change of personnel in your government."

Even now Thieu did not capitulate easily, but he was running out of maneuvering room. After several further exchanges, and after the administration arranged for two of Saigon's firmest Senate supporters, Barry Goldwater of Arizona and John Stennis of Mississippi, to warn publicly against continued recalcitrance, Nixon issued an ultimatum. If he had no "positive" answer from Thieu by noon, Washington time, on January 21, he would tell Kissinger to initial the agreement without South Vietnam's concurrence. At that, Thieu yielded at last.

American diplomacy did not consist only of threats, however. Nixon's messages to Thieu were also full of assurances of political, economic, and military support, as well as promises—which critics later charged stepped past the limits of American presidential authority—to retaliate for any Communist violations of the ceasefire.

"The United States recognizes your government as the only legal government of South Vietnam," said Nixon's January 16 letter, an assurance that would later also be given publicly. ". . . I want to emphasize my continued commitment to the freedom and progress of the Republic of Vietnam. It is my firm intention to continue full economic and military aid." Repeatedly, American representatives sought to persuade Thieu that with U.S. help, he and his regime could withstand any political challenge from the Communists. As additional reassurance, Kissinger claimed to have promises from the Soviet Union and China that they would impose restraint on the North Vietnamese. "Dr. Kissinger promised me this before and after the signing of the agreement. . . . He said that Russia and China promised to be cooperative with the United States," Thieu revealed in 1975. Tran Van Lam recalled being told by Kissinger: "Don't worry. I have a deal with the Soviet Union and China. From now on they will stop supplying all offensive arms to North Vietnam." And promises to retaliate against the Communists were reaffirmed. "We will respond with full force," said Nixon's January 5 message, "should the settlement be violated by North Vietnam." All this, if Thieu would just sign the agreement.

In the available record of these exchanges, there is a remarkable omission. Nowhere in any of the letters or other documents that have been published, nor in any other accounts that I was able to find, was there a single hint that Thieu's obligations *after* a ceasefire were ever mentioned at all. Sign, he was told repeatedly—even brutally; but nothing more. The U.S. might have counseled him that while South Vietnam certainly had a right to defend itself against flagrant violations, a policy of self-restraint and a somewhat more conciliatory public posture after a ceasefire might be useful, for reasons not just of generosity and good will but of self-interest. For it took no great foresight to see that especially after he had acted for three months as the spoiler of a settlement most Americans wanted, Thieu would quickly lose American support if he appeared too belligerent or intransigent after the settlement finally took effect.

If any such advice was ever given, not a syllable of it shows in the available evidence. Thieu accepted the agreement because he had to and because he was promised continued support, not because he had any trust either in its terms or in the intentions of his enemy. Nor did he believe his ally had acted wisely or honorably. He acted only under the most extreme pressure, and the circumstances of his acquiescence did not promise any generosity of spirit or any willingness to take risks in carrying out terms he did not, and never would, believe in.

On Saturday, January 20, the day President Nixon was inaugurated for his second term, General Haig returned briefly to Saigon for a last meeting with Thieu, then flew to South Korea to inform the government in Seoul and, it was presumed, to arrange for the pullout of the 38,000 Republic of Korea troops still in South Vietnam. After that, the countdown moved swiftly. On Sunday, Foreign Minister Lam left Saigon for Paris. Monday, Kissinger flew out of Washington, also heading for the French capital. And on Tuesday, at 12:45 P.M. Paris time, while photographers waited in a cold drizzle outside, he and Le Duc Tho initialed the "Agreement on Ending the War and Restoring Peace in Vietnam."

President Nixon announced the settlement in a televised speech that evening from the White House. "We today have concluded an agreement to end the war and bring peace with honor in Vietnam," he began, "and in Southeast Asia." The last four words were untrue: a weakness of the Paris pact was that it did *not* conclude the wars in Vietnam's neighboring countries. Le Duc Tho had given written, but private, assurances of a truce in Laos, but only vague expressions of hope about Cambodia. ". . . All parties must now see to it," Nixon's speech went on, "that this is a peace that lasts, and also a peace that heals, and a peace that not only ends the war in Southeast Asia but contributes to the prospects of peace in the whole world."

At precisely the same hour—Wednesday morning in Saigon—President Thieu was also on the air. But his words were more somber. "The signing of the agreement means the beginning of peace," he said. "But it does not mean peace." Not for the first or last time, Thieu was more realistic than his American patron.

Before the agreement was even signed, the legend began to be created: the bombing had done it.

Kissinger was arch. "There was a deadlock which we described in December," he said, "and there was a rapid movement when negotiations were resumed. . . . These facts have to be analyzed by each person for himself." Subsequently, the image of a recalcitrant Hanoi forced to capitulate under the B-52 raids became enshrined in the memories of a good many senior military leaders and other Americans, who argued that the Christmas bombing was not only decisive in achieving a settlement but also showed that the war could have been won years earlier if only all-out air war had been authorized.

Yet the events did not really show that the bombing forced the North Vietnamese to any new decisions on war or peace. The terms obtained in January differed only very slightly from those that Hanoi had offered three months before. There were a few minor changes, which saved some face for

President Thieu. The Vietnamese phrase that troubled him by seeming to give governmental status to the National Council of Reconciliation was dropped, and the council's name now appeared without benefit of any adjectives at all. Its makeup, however, to which Thieu objected far more strongly, was unchanged. As to the legal status of the two Vietnams, Kissinger was able to secure a clause stating that both "shall respect the Demilitarized Zone on either side of the Provisional Military Demarcation Line." That sentence, however, was placed immediately after a re-affirmation of the Communist view that the line was "only provisional and not a political or territorial boundary."

Because the same article declared that "modalities of civilian movement" across the demarcation line would be one of the issues to be negotiated after the truce, Kissinger argued that military movement was implicitly pro-hibited. But such legalisms hardly constituted an unequivocal affirmation of South Vietnam's sovereignty. The question of whether North Vietnam was a foreign country with respect to the South—a crucial point for Saigon—was, Kissinger acknowledged, "an issue which we have avoided making explicit in the agreement."

A few other concessions were represented in the protocols and "under-standings" that were completed along with the final version of the agree-ment. A somewhat earlier date was set for the promised Laos ceasefire, and the international truce-observer force, which Hanoi wanted limited to only 250 men, was expanded to 1,160. (At whatever strength, though, the international commission could hardly play any but a symbolic role. "If the idea is to keep soldiers from the peacekeeping force standing between all the hostile units," a diplomat in Saigon commented, "you couldn't do that with 50,000 men. If the idea is a symbolic presence, then 500 will do just as well.")

On virtually all other points, however, including Thieu's vital issues of North Vietnamese troops and the composition of the National Council of Reconciliation, the agreement in January was the same that had been negotiated in October. Whatever marginal face-saving had been accom-plished, no Vietnamese, Communist or non-Communist, and whether wearing general's stars or peasant's pajamas, could fail to see that Nguyen Van Thieu and the South Vietnamese government had been forced to accept a settlement they did not want.

The three months that had given time for Thieu's acquiescence had achieved something else as well. To an extent that remains unmeasured and intangible, they must have deepened the chasms of hostility and mistrust that already lay between Hanoi and Washington and between Hanoi and Saigon. By any fair standard, Nixon and Kissinger had treated their Viet-namese ally with contemptuous disregard, and their Vietnamese enemy with bad faith and brutality. In doing so, they had almost certainly magnified the enormous difficulties of enforcing the peace they had finally succeeded in negotiating.

News of the ceasefire brought no outpouring of joy or relief in South Vietnam.

"After these long years I hope to be discharged and return to civilian life," said a sergeant named Xay, the leader of a 23-man militia platoon at a dusty outpost near Cu Chi, northwest of Saigon. Now 34, he had been a soldier ten years. Pointing to the edge of the jungle, perhaps a thousand yards past the jumble of barbed-wire and bamboo defenses outside his platoon's position, Xay said: "The enemy still controls the jungle over there. . . . Our orders are to keep vigilant, to keep our men here and our supplies full so we will be ready for anything." Even the prospect of a discharge, remote as it seemed, was not completely appealing. "I will not stay here," Xay said, staring out over the dry fields, "even though my wife has a business here. . . . They may try to take some revenge for what we have done here. For that reason, if I am discharged I will go to Saigon and try to find a job where it will be safe. . . . We do not know what will happen."

We do not know—that was what you heard everyplace. In Saigon's central market, brightly decorated with Tet flowers, a medical corps sergeant named Hien, strolling with his wife and young child, told me: "We ordinary people are very, very glad about the ceasefire, but we are all concerned about the future, too. We do not know if there will really be peace." "We cannot predict the future," said the wife of a disabled veteran; if there really was peace, she wanted to return to her family's home in My Tho, but if not they would have to stay in Saigon. "We cannot make any plans." A high school teacher worried because even after a ceasefire, the two sides would still be in conflict over who was to rule the South: "I am afraid if we do not solve our political problems, war will break out again."

In the spate of government announcements, none spoke of repairing the wounds in Vietnam's land and spirit. Instead, the regime spoke only of staying alert against the Communist enemy. Lieutenant General Nguyen Van Minh, commander of the region encompassing the provinces around Saigon, gave a lunch for a group of foreign correspondents a few days before the ceasefire; when one of them asked what the government would now do to repay the soldiers who had fought so long, Minh first looked surprised, then shook his head impatiently. "We have had no time to think about that," he snapped. "That question you will have to ask me later."

Underlying Vietnamese doubts was an understanding of what many Americans failed to see—that the Paris agreement was flawed at its core because it did not resolve the issue over which the war had been fought. Le Duc Tho had stated it succinctly months before: "The most arduous problem now existing between the two sides is the problem of power in South

Vietnam." Who would rule: that was what all the killing was about. And it was not decided, just deferred to negotiations between two sides whose perceptions contained no visible basis for compromise. To negotiate a settlement would require bridging a gulf of hate and suspicion that was as wide as a million graves. Few Vietnamese believed that gulf could be crossed, and in the end it was not.

Of the nine chapters and 23 articles in the treaty, few were carried out:

Chapter 1 (Article 1): **"The United States and all other countries respect the independence, sovereignty, unity and territorial integrity of Vietnam as recognized by the 1954 Geneva agreements."** This was a statement of principle without practical effect. The pro-Communist Australian writer Wilfred Burchett reported, presumably from North Vietnamese sources, that Kissinger tried to have this article "buried much farther down in the agreement," on the grounds that ". . . it was not 'convenient' for U.S. public opinion" to give such prominence to a statement of Vietnam's national rights. Placing it first could cause problems in securing congressional approval for aid to North Vietnam, Kissinger is described as having told Le Duc Tho, but if it were "de-emphasized," he could "guarantee that the billions would be forthcoming." Tho would not be bribed, however, Burchett's account continued. "First things came first and Vietnam's independence, sovereignty, unity and territorial integrity were . . . what 30 years of wars of national liberation had been all about."

Chapter 2 (Articles 2–7): **"A ceasefire shall be observed throughout South Vietnam as of 2400 hours GMT on January 27, 1973."** This proved to be effective, at most, only for brief periods in a few parts of the country.

"The United States will stop all its military activities" against the North. This was accomplished.

"The armed forces of the two South Vietnamese parties shall remain in place. The Two-Party Joint Military Commission . . . shall determine the areas controlled by each party and the modalities of stationing." This provision was never carried out.

"The United States will not continue its military involvement or intervene in the internal affairs of South Vietnam." In the direct sense of American armed action, this was observed. The U.S. did continue supplying arms and other resources to the Saigon government, and publicly backed it as the only legitimate authority in South Vietnam.

"Within 60 days of the signing of this agreement, there will be a total withdrawal from South Vietnam" of U.S. and all other Allied troops. This was accomplished.

"The two South Vietnamese parties shall not accept the introduction of troops, military advisers, and military per-

sonnel including technical military personnel, armaments, munitions and war materials" into the South, except for "periodic replacements of armaments, munitions and war material which have been destroyed, damaged, worn out or used up after the ceasefire, on the basis of piece-for-piece, of the same characteristics and properties." This provision was ignored by North Vietnam, which continued to send fresh troops and weaponry to the South; it was initially observed by the U.S. with respect to its arms shipments, but was interpreted more and more loosely as the fighting continued. (For example, propeller-driven A-1 Skyraiders were replaced by A-37 jet bombers, which hardly had the "same characteristics or properties." Since A-1s were no longer being built, the Pentagon said the A-37s were the "closest available approximation.") During the negotiations, the U.S. promised Hanoi that all its civilian personnel "working with the armed forces of the Republic of Vietnam" would be withdrawn in twelve months—this was not included in the agreement but was one of the accompanying written "understandings." It clearly applied to all U.S. government employees, the State Department's legal adviser acknowledged; it was unclear whether employees of private American firms under contract to the American or South Vietnamese government were covered as well. In any event the promise was not kept.

Chapter 3 (Article 8): "The return of captured military personnel and foreign civilians . . . shall be carried out simultaneously with and completed not later than the same day as the troop withdrawal mentioned in Article 5." As far as is known, all U.S. P.O.W.'s were freed. An exchange of Vietnamese military prisoners was carried out, though long after the deadline and with complaints from each side that not all its prisoners were returned.

"The parties shall help each other to get information about those military personnel and foreign civilians of the parties missing in action, to determine the location and take care of the graves of the dead so as to facilitate the exhumation and repatriation of the remains." This point became the source of years of embittered controversy between the U.S. and Hanoi. Between 1972 and 1981, according to a member of a congressional task force, North Vietnam handed over to the U.S. the remains of 74 American dead, mainly pilots shot down over the north; the Americans sought information on some 2,500 men who were listed as missing or who were known dead but whose bodies had never been recovered. As late as mid-1981 the Pentagon accused Hanoi of deliberately withholding information on as many as 160 of these cases.

"The question of the return of Vietnamese civilian personnel captured and detained in South Vietnam will be resolved by the two South Vietnamese parties. . . . [They] will do their utmost to resolve this question within 90 days." In exchanges that were not completed in 90 days but dragged on for more than a year, South Vietnam returned 5,081 civilian prisoners and the Communists released 606. Each side accused the other of failing to account for much larger numbers of detained civilians. South Vietnam listed 70,255 civilians missing, while the Communists insisted that the Saigon regime was holding 200,000 political prisoners—a charge that was later repeated incessantly by many activists in the international antiwar movement. The Paris protocol on the prisoner exchanges specified that "the detaining parties shall not deny or delay" the return of civilian prisoners ". . . for any reason, including the fact that they may, on any grounds, have been pros- ecuted or sentenced." The U.S. State Department's legal interpretation was that while ordinary criminals did not have to be freed, "a person who is detained because of his participation in the conflict must be returned even if he has also been convicted of a crime . . . the intent of the negotiators was that where the primary or main reason [for detention] was involvement in the armed struggle, incidental criminal charges or convictions would not justify denial or delay of return." The South Vietnamese did not operate on that principle, however. Before and after the ceasefire, the Saigon authorities tried a large number of Communist detainees for criminal offenses and then classed them, after conviction, as common criminals. Despite the clear wording of the protocol, few if any of these prisoners were later exchanged.

Chapter 4 (Articles 9–14): **"The South Vietnamese people shall decide themselves the political future of South Vietnam through genuinely free and democratic general elections under international supervision."** No elections were held.

"The two South Vietnamese parties undertake to respect the ceasefire . . . settle all matters of contention through negotiations, and avoid all armed conflict." This was never carried out; each side blamed the other for regularly breaking the ceasefire.

"The two South Vietnamese parties will: achieve national reconciliation and concord, end hatred and enmity, prohibit all acts of reprisal and discrimination . . . [and] ensure the democratic liberties of the people: personal freedom, freedom of speech, freedom of the press, freedom of meeting, freedom of organization, freedom of political activities, freedom of belief, freedom of movement, freedom of residence, freedom of work, right to property ownership, and right to free enter- prise." Reconciliation was not achieved; none of the restrictions on personal freedom in either the Communist or Saigon-controlled zones were ever lifted.

"The two South Vietnamese parties shall hold con- sultations . . . to set up a National Council of National Rec- onciliation and Concord of three equal segments. . . . The two South Vietnamese parties shall sign an agreement on the

internal matters of South Vietnam and do their utmost to accomplish this within 90 days after the ceasefire comes into effect." The council was never established, and no political agreement was ever concluded.

"The question of Vietnamese armed forces in South Vietnam shall be settled by the two Vietnamese parties." This, too, was never carried out.

Chapter 5 (Article 15): **The reunification of Vietnam shall be carried out step by step through peaceful means on the basis of discussions and agreements between North and South Vietnam, without coercion or annexation by either party."** Reunification was achieved not through "peaceful means" but when Hanoi's tanks smashed onto the grounds of the Independence Palace in Saigon on April 30, 1975. Legal reunification was completed July 2, 1976.

Chapter 6 (Articles 16–19): Establishment of various truce-supervisory bodies, including a Four-Party Joint Military Commission (the U.S., North and South Vietnam, and the P.R.G.), a Two-Party Joint Military Commission (South Vietnam and the P.R.G. alone), and an International Commission of Control and Supervision. Though these bodies were formed, except for supervising the P.O.W. exchanges and the U.S. withdrawal they carried out none of the other tasks assigned to them.

"The parties agree on the convening of an International Conference within 30 days." The conference was held, in Paris; but its resolutions did not make the peace accords effective.

Chapter 7 (Article 20): **"The parties . . . shall strictly respect the 1954 Geneva Agreements on Cambodia and the 1962 Geneva Agreements on Laos, which recognized the Cambodian and the Lao peoples' fundamental national rights. . . . The parties shall respect the neutrality of Cambodia and Laos . . . [and] refrain from using the territory of Cambodia and the territory of Laos to encroach on the sovereignty and security of one another and of other countries. . . . Foreign countries shall put an end to all military activities in Cambodia and Laos, totally withdraw from and refrain from reintroducing into these two countries troops, military advisers and military personnel, armaments, munitions and war material."** Since no deadline was established for these obligations to become effective, the U.S. continued bombing in Laos until a ceasefire was signed there and in Cambodia until Congress prohibited further U.S. military action in Southeast Asia. American aid and arms shipments supported the weak Cambodian government until it fell to the Communists in April 1975. The North Vietnamese continued to maintain troops in both countries and to equip and train Lao and Cambodian

Communist forces. The U.S. legal interpretation of Article 20 was that it was "an agreement in principle" and that the ban on foreign military activities was not legally binding until made so by ceasefire agreements in Laos and Cambodia.

Chapter 8 (Articles 21 and 22): **"In pursuance of its traditional policy, the United States will contribute to healing the wounds of war and to postwar reconstruction of the Democratic Republic of Vietnam and throughout Indochina."** No U.S. aid to the D.R.V.N. (North Vietnam) was ever given; for years, Hanoi insisted that U.S. compliance with Article 21 was the price for its own cooperation on the matter of missing-in-action American servicemen.

Chapter 9 (Article 23): **"This agreement shall enter into force upon signature. . . . All the parties concerned shall strictly implement this agreement and its protocols."** Neither agreement nor protocols accomplished their stated purpose.

The treaty was negotiated by North Vietnam and the United States, and, as this list has shown, only North Vietnam and the U.S. derived anything from it. Washington got its troops out and its prisoners back; Hanoi won an end to the bombing and an American withdrawal from the war in the South. South Vietnam, as Nguyen Van Thieu had seen, received nothing: neither a political settlement nor a peace.

There was, before and after the Paris agreement was signed, a paradoxical twist to the U.S.-North Vietnamese relationship. North Vietnam was thought of, and was, a secretive, closed, tightly controlled Asian Communist state, run by men who submerged their personalities and their disagreements, if any, in the shadows they had inhabited for many years as members of a conspiratorial underground movement. The United States was a free, democratic society where policy was supposed to be fashioned in the sunlight of open debate. Yet in the peace talks and afterward, North Vietnam's objective was plain; the American goal was inscrutable.

To Le Duc Tho and his Politburo colleagues, the Paris agreement was only a stop along the way to their ultimate goal. Both Marxist theory and Vietnamese history taught, as the Communist party first secretary Le Duan once wrote, that "the revolution in South Vietnam has to pass through several transitional phases prior to advancing toward national reunification and socialism." In November, during the Kissinger-Tho talks, the party's theoretical journal, *Hoc Tap*, rationalized a settlement that fell short of final victory: "There is a time for us to advance, but there is also a time for us to step backward temporarily in order to advance more steadily later. We cannot exterminate imperialism at one time and in a single battle. We drive it back step by step and destroy it part by part." A peace agreement accomplishing the end of U.S. intervention was, clearly, one of Le Duan's transitional events, in no way altering the Vietnamese Communists' conviction that in the end they would see all Vietnam unified under the gold-starred flag of the revolution they had launched almost three decades before.

But what did the U.S. leadership really want? A disengagement of American troops from the shooting war, of course, and the return of American prisoners; and beyond that, only some form of honorable compromise that would not represent a visible, humiliating defeat of American objectives. But did honorable mean only a "decent interval" for an American exit, after which the U.S. would not interfere while the Vietnamese adversaries played out the end of their long conflict? Or did it require the indefinite survival of a non-Communist, U.S.-backed regime in the South? When Kissinger negotiated an agreement full of provisions that would almost certainly prove unworkable in Vietnamese conditions, did he and Nixon believe against all logic that its terms would be observed and that it was within America's ability to enforce them? Or were they only erecting a screen to cover an American withdrawal?

No certain answers to these questions ever emerged; perhaps there were none. Nixon, by one insider's account, "vacillated between a strong impulse to get out of Vietnam at almost any price and an equally strong impulse to 'bomb North Vietnam back to the Stone Age.' " Before the Paris agreement was many months old, Nixon's attention was turned elsewhere: As the Watergate crisis overtook his administration, whatever concern he may have had for Nguyen Van Thieu's survival was consumed—permanently—in concern for his own.

As for Kissinger, during the negotiating phase he had made ambiguity one of his servants. There is strong reason to think he left North Vietnam, China, and Russia believing that a "decent interval" was all the Americans expected or hoped for. That was certainly his message in an unpublicized meeting in October 1971 with Wilfred Burchett, whom Kissinger evidently regarded as a possible emissary to Hanoi. Inviting Burchett to "communicate my views to your Vietnamese friends," Kissinger confided, according to Burchett's account: "Our policy . . . is to disengage. But we can't do it all at once. Hanoi does nothing to help. They want everything right now. . . . The trouble is that Hanoi is not willing to wait for the political processes to work themselves out after we have completed our disengagement. . . . We want to get it all over with." The same message was conveyed through Chou En-lai in June 1972. Hanoi was greedy and wanted everything at once, Kissinger reportedly told the Chinese prime minister. It should see the historical process in two stages, not just one. The American withdrawal would be the first; then history would take its course.

Kissinger often suggested the same beliefs to American war critics, implying that he was a reluctant advocate of force and that without him, Nixon would receive only the wild-eyed advice of the real warmongers. But in the domestic debate, Kissinger was a chameleon. To liberal audiences, including influential newspaper and television journalists whom he cultivated more industriously and skillfully than anyone else in American public life, he frequently sought to appear a dove-at-heart. In the administration's inner councils, however, he was customarily among those advocating the harshest possible military actions. To Saigon, and to those in the American military and civilian bureaucracies who were committed to the war's purposes, Kissinger stressed that the terms he had negotiated in Paris would allow Thieu to remain strong and in power indefinitely. To the Communists he hinted that all he wanted was for the U.S. to escape with a cover of dignity. Thus, all who dealt with Kissinger were led to view American aims in the aspect most encouraging to them.

Much later, in his memoirs, Kissinger would declare that he and Nixon did not "go through the agony of four years of war and searing negotiations simply to achieve a 'decent interval' for our withdrawal. . . . We sought not an interval before collapse, but lasting peace with honor." Perhaps. Still, for Kissinger to say anything else would be to admit a cynicism that would shock even a much-calloused public. His real expectations remained hidden, for Henry Kissinger was a man who wore so many masks it was impossible to tell when, if ever, his real face was showing.

Across South Vietnam, the approaching truce was heralded not with celebration but with the heaviest warfare in many months.

On January 26 and 27, Viet Cong and North Vietnamese units attacked hundreds of villages, hoping to plant their flag before the ceasefire took effect. Heavy rockets hit the Bien Hoa Air Base, killing a U.S. marine and wounding twelve American civilian aircraft technicians. To the north, shelling at Da Nang killed another American soldier. Altogether, four U.S. servicemen died and four air crewmen were reported missing between the ceasefire announcement and the time for it to take effect: eight o'clock Sunday morning, Saigon time, January 28. Vietnamese casualties were in the thousands on both sides.

In the air, American bombers flew their heaviest raids over the South since May: over 900 fighter-bomber sorties and more than 50 three-plane B-52 missions in the final 48 hours. On the eve of the ceasefire, Saigon slept to the occasional crackle of rifle fire as jittery patrols warned curfew violators with bursts into the sky. The air trembled with distant artillery and bombing. Gun-flashes lit up the horizon with the sheet-lightning of war.

Chapter 3

Ceasefire

A swath of shattered, burned houses showed the course of the ceasefire fighting in Tay Ninh.

"The Viet Cong came here on Saturday," said a farmer sadly standing in front of his damaged home on Tuesday, January 30—the third day of the truce. "They put up their flag in front of my house, and their soldiers patrolled over there." He pointed to a long, low embankment alongside the road that led to the main temple of the Cao Dai religious sect—the "Holy See," it was called, Tay Ninh's best-known landmark. A few feathers of smoke still trembled upward from the charred beams and timbers in the wreckage around us.

"The government troops came back the next morning," the farmer continued. First, though, South Vietnamese artillery shelled the area, riddling his home with shrapnel holes and blasting most of the neighboring houses into blackened ruins. Then the troops moved in, finally clearing the cluster of houses about nightfall. Four government soldiers were killed, an infantryman resting nearby told us, and four others were wounded. He was untroubled by the fact that the fighting took place after the ceasefire hour. "We could not let them remain here," he explained. "We are supposed to provide security for the people and not allow the Communists to stay."

If the fighting had ended as many Americans may have imagined, with both sides freezing in position at eight o'clock Sunday morning as if at a referee's whistle, the Viet Cong flag would still have been flying in front of the farmer's home, in place of the South Vietnamese banner that now fluttered there. The liberation colors would also have been raised over perhaps a third of the city, which had been invaded by about a thousand Communist troops the night before the ceasefire. By pushing them back out after the truce was to have taken effect—in fighting that killed about 50 civilians and destroyed 3,000 to 5,000 houses—government forces were

ENEMIES *Above,* South Vietnamese soldiers on the march in the Mekong Delta *(photo by Dan Southerland); facing page, top,* National Liberation Front guerrillas in Tay Ninh Province *(photographer unknown, courtesy of Dan Southerland).*

DEVASTATION *Facing page, bottom,* Quang Tri City was reduced to a lake of rubble after it was lost to the Communists and then recaptured in 1972 *(photo by Larry Green).*

CEASEFIRE *Facing page,* villagers flee fighting in their hamlet on Cease-fire Day (*photo by Larry Green*); *below,* Henry Kissinger and Le Duc Tho, flanked by aides, initial the Paris peace agreement (*White House photo*); *immediate left,* North Vietnam's Prime Minister Pham Van Dong (*courtesy of Southeast Asia Resource Center*).

ALLIES *Above,* Richard Nixon and Nguyen Van Thieu stroll on the grounds of the Western White House in San Clemente, California (*White House photo*).

PRISONERS *Facing page, top,* American prisoners of war under guard at Gia Lam Airport in Hanoi, awaiting release (*U.S. Navy photo*); *bottom,* Communist prisoners, in prison garb and guarded by South Vietnamese military police, wait to be exchanged at the Tay Ninh airfield in South Vietnam (*photo by Larry Green*).

unquestionably violating the peace agreement and its ceasefire protocol, which declared that "at the exact time stipulated . . . all ground, river, sea and air combat forces of the parties in South Vietnam shall remain in place." Yet to have stopped firing in Tay Ninh at 8 A.M. Sunday, leaving part of the city occupied by Communist troops, would have been a travesty of the agreement's intent. If the basis of the settlement was to reflect the existing battleground balance, the South Vietnamese really had no choice but to keep fighting until the city was cleared.

"This is government controlled territory," said a major wearing the shoulder patch of the 25th ARVN Division. "There are no Communists here." By any fair standard, he was right. Capital of a province of more than 400,000 people that jutted like a fist into Cambodia, Tay Ninh lay in the midst of contested territory and not far from unchallenged Communist base areas straddling the Vietnamese-Cambodian border. But the city itself, like South Vietnam's other major towns, was securely under Saigon's authority. On any normal day, government officials and soldiers moved without danger in the city and its nearby surroundings. So did Americans, many of whom journeyed there by car or bus to see the Cao Dai temple with its garish wall murals depicting the sect's eccentric variety of saints—among them the Chinese revolutionary Sun Yat-sen and the French novelist Victor Hugo.

Intelligence officers believed that if the Communists had succeeded in seizing the city, it was to be declared the P.R.G.'s provisional capital. If that gave Tay Ninh a political significance that other ceasefire objectives lacked, however, the pattern of the fighting there was identical to that in hundreds of other battles: technically legal Communist assaults just before the truce, answered by technically illegal government counterattacks after the guns were supposed to stop.

Favored by the 8 A.M. truce hour, since their units traditionally moved and attacked at night, the Communists seized numerous positions they had never historically controlled. If the lines had actually frozen at the time set in the agreement, for example, all major highways radiating out from Saigon would have been blocked. Highway One would have been cut both east and west of the capital within 30 miles and at many other points along its route up the coast: north and south of Da Nang, and also in the extreme south of Quang Ngai Province, where two North Vietnamese battalions seized a little fishing and salt-making village called Sa Huynh—apparently planned to be a P.R.G. seaport, where supplies could be transported by shallow-draft coastal vessels from North Vietnam. The fighting there cost hundreds of casualties on both sides and continued until February 16, when the 2nd ARVN Division finally succeeded in driving out the attacking force.

Altogether, Communist troops occupied more than 400 hamlets just before the ceasefire, 144 of them in the provinces around Saigon. Some of these were traditionally contested. But many, especially those that lay on major highways, were normally government-controlled. (Not all the "land grabbing," as the ceasefire attacks came to be called, was by the Communists. In some places the South Vietnamese also attempted to seize traditional Communist positions. The most significant such attempt was in the far north, just below the DMZ, where government marines tried to recapture positions on both banks of the Cua Viet River from North Vietnamese troops who had been entrenched at the river's mouth since the Easter offensive. The Communists, defending "their" territory just as the South Vietnamese defended theirs, inflicted heavy losses on the marines before driving them out.) The post-ceasefire battles, without exception and regardless of the circumstances, were all described in official Saigon handouts as Communist ceasefire violations. But with hundreds of correspondents and cameramen in Vietnam to cover the truce, the government's violations could not be concealed. They were too widespread and too obvious, and were carried out without restraint on weaponry or expenditure of munitions. Anyone traveling in the countryside could see that the South Vietnamese were heavily bombing and shelling Communist positions. Situation reports from American advisers in the provinces were sprinkled with observations such as these:

"Ceasefire or no, operations are continuing much as before."

"With the support of daily air strikes and heavy artillery barrages . . . they have finally begun to roll the VC back."

"More VNAF [Vietnamese air force] tacair strikes were flown in Lam Dong in the three days after the ceasefire than had been flown in the previous six months."

"An unprecedented volume of artillery plus more VNAF support [than] ever witnessed in this area. . . . "

Artillery expenditures and air strikes after the ceasefire, reported the U.S. Defense Attache Office, were actually "higher than during the 1972 spring offensive."

Yet, though they may have been technically violating the ceasefire, by any but the most narrowly legalistic standard the South Vietnamese were justified, and the Communists had to bear a heavy responsibility for much of the continued fighting. In sending squads of men to raise their flag just before the ceasefire in hundreds of places to which they had no historic claim, they may have acted within the letter of the peace agreement. But they grossly violated its spirit.

Exactly the reverse was true on the matter of arms and equipment. Since no agreement had yet been signed, the Enhance and Enhance Plus shipments of late 1972 were legal, as were the transfers of U.S. and other allies' materiel and bases to Vietnamese control. But if the settlement was meant to reflect the existing balance, the U.S. and Saigon were evading that intent, just as the Communists did in their eleventh-hour flag raising. And, just as the Saigon command felt justified in technically violating the ceasefire in order to recapture territory it regarded as rightfully under its control, the North Vietnamese may have felt that their buildup of men and supplies after the truce was also legitimate, since it restored the intended battlefield equilibrium. "They're just doing the same thing we did," an American officer admitted one day. "Only they don't have C-5s, so they couldn't quite meet the deadline."

Nonetheless, the U.S. regarded Hanoi's infiltration as a serious violation of the agreement. After stories were leaked to reporters in Washington and Saigon that more than 300 tanks, 150 or so artillery pieces, an equal number of antiaircraft guns, and 30,000 or more fresh North Vietnamese troops were heading over the infiltration routes to the South, President Nixon announced March 15 that the U.S. "had informed the North Vietnamese of our concern. . . . I would only suggest that based on my actions over the past four years, that the North Vietnamese should not lightly disregard such expressions of concern."

Not all of the reported infiltration took place after the ceasefire, however. One of the most widely publicized "violations," in fact, may not have been a violation at all. This was the emplacement of SA-2 SAMs—surface-to-air missiles—at the former U.S. Marine base at Khe Sanh, just below the Demilitarized Zone. Late in February the U.S. formally protested the missiles to the international truce supervisors, demanding their removal. But years later a quasi-official history of the ceasefire, based on American military records, admitted that the missiles and their launchers had been moved into South Vietnam "sometime in January 1973 and probably not later than the 27th"—which would have made them legal under the peace agreement.

Nor, for that matter, was U.S. replenishment of supplies for South Vietnam carried out quite as scrupulously as American officials claimed. U.S. practice generally was to supply whatever the South Vietnamese said they had lost, without verifying that the replacements were sanctioned under the peace agreement. Sometimes they weren't. The U.S. replaced three tanks and four armored personnel carriers which Saigon claimed were lost after the ceasefire but which were actually destroyed earlier, according to a classified report by U.S. government investigators. In subsequent months, the same report found, nine more tanks were reported to the Americans as combat losses, but in fact were recovered from the battlefield.

The political provisions of the agreement were even less effective, if possible, than the ceasefire clauses. "Only a miracle" would produce national reconciliation, said the Saigon newspaper *Dai Dan Toc*. In the floods of recriminatory invective issuing from both sides, that hardly seemed an overstatement. "Because of the Communists' blind and mad ambitions and dishonest and villainous nature," said a fairly representative broadcast over the official Saigon radio station, the road to peace was "studded with dangerous roadblocks." The Communists, for their part, complained unceasingly that Saigon was wrecking the truce. "The fascist militarist forces, the tools of neo-colonialism, running counter to our nation's desires, are seeking to sabotage the agreement, peace and national concord," Gen. Vo Nguyen Giap declared at a Hanoi meeting, "in order to perpetuate the partition of our country and maintain neo-colonialism in South Vietnam."

With these and similar accusations filling the press and airwaves, the promised political negotiations between Saigon and the Provisional Revolutionary Government opened in the Paris suburb of La Celle St. Cloud. Eight meetings were held during the 90 days during which an agreement was supposed to be concluded. At the last of these, only three days before the deadline, the delegations at last exchanged draft proposals for a settlement, "not so much to break the deadlock," as one experienced observer commented, "as to place the blame for it on each other."

Saigon's plan made both elections and the restoration of full democratic freedoms contingent on the removal of North Vietnamese troops from the South, though the peace agreement itself did not state any such condition. As the North Vietnamese withdrew, the South would demobilize an equal number of men in its own armed forces. The Council of National Reconciliation would be established, also in stages as the North Vietnamese withdrawal was accomplished. Within 30 days after the last North Vietnamese soldier was out of the South, elections would be held.

The Communists' proposal contained no timetable for an election but demanded instead that other provisions of the agreement must be complied with first, chiefly the clauses having to do with democratic freedoms, formation of the Council of National Reconciliation, exchange of civilian detainees, and demarcation of zones of control. Their rationale for refusing to set an election date, as stated early in 1974, was that the fighting had not stopped and "the people in areas under the Saigon administration's control have been deprived of their democratic freedoms. Hundreds of thousands of political prisoners of various political and religious tendencies are still under detention. The opposition forces continue to be repressed and terrorized. Holding the general elections under these conditions would only mean an election farce . . . with the aim of legalizing the dictatorial Nguyen Van Thieu regime."

With only marginal changes, both sides clung to the same proposals for the remainder of the La Celle St. Cloud talks, which would continue fitfully until mid-1974 without ever approaching the state of a genuine negotiation.

As the two sides sparred in Paris and at the Joint Military Commission headquarters in Saigon, fighting continued on South Vietnam's many battlefields. The "land-grabbing" campaign was over, for practical purposes, by the second week in February, when the South Vietnamese had regained control of all but a handful of the positions they lost just before or immediately after the ceasefire. If there was ever a chance to lessen the violence, it might have come then, at a moment when the pre-truce battle lines were roughly restored. But it did not happen that way.

The Communists, after their flag-raising offensive, seemed ready for a time to seek a lower level of combat, in anticipation that their political agents would be able to function more freely in contested or Saigon-controlled zones. A directive issued just before the ceasefire by COSVN (the "Central Office for South Vietnam," which actually served as Communist head-quarters only for the Saigon region and the Mekong Delta) called on party and military leaders to recruit, rearm, and resupply, but put the main emphasis on organizing demonstrations to exploit South Vietnamese war-weariness. Terror would be used, where needed, to kill "cruel tyrants" and other oppressors. But the directive's authors clearly had in mind something resembling the peace movement in other countries, which could gradually be turned to Communist purposes. The central issue was to be the Paris agreement itself. As soon as the ceasefire was in effect, the directive said,

> We must timely seize this opportunity and do our utmost to turn this situation into a high, broad movement in which the people will ac-claim peace and discuss the agreement, for the purpose of demanding its implementation, in the streets, in their homes, at bus terminals, in the markets, restaurants, factories, classrooms, on the ricefields, and so on. . . . If the puppet troops, police or government personnel interfere with these gatherings, we must strive to get them interested in the discussions. By so doing we will divide them, neutralize the majority of them and isolate the most obdurate element. . . . We must be able to turn the broad movement of people acclaiming peace and discussing the agreement into a broad movement of revolutionary actions by the masses.

"Forms of struggle," the directive added, would include not just meetings, but strikes, market shutdowns, and the like. Specific slogans would demand freedom of movement and appeal to government soldiers to desert. The intent, plainly, was to identify the Communists with peace, for which mil-lions of Vietnamese were assumed to yearn, while the Saigon government would be identified with continuing repression and war.

In North Vietnam, meanwhile, public statements following the ceasefire seemed to give priority to economic reconstruction. This was "the most striking thing" U.S. analysts perceived in Pham Van Dong's major policy statement to the National Assembly in Hanoi on February 20. Though he reaffirmed the Communists' resolve to complete the "national and demo-cratic revolution" in the South, after which Vietnam could be reunified,

Dong also declared that the peace agreement "created ever more favorable conditions for building socialism in the North, building the socialist economy, the socialist culture and the socialist man." Addressing a populace that had been called on to make immense sacrifice, Dong promised that an "immediate task" for the Communist leadership was to "stabilize and improve step by step the living conditions of the people."

None of this meant, of course, that Hanoi regarded the peace agreement as anything but a temporary truce. Building up their armed strength, if not using it, remained a top-priority goal for the Communists. They strongly defended what they regarded as their zone, and were certainly guilty of outright violations of their own on occasion, such as when they shelled the town of Hong Ngu, in the upper delta near the Cambodian border, killing 80 civilians during March and April.

In the first weeks and months of the ceasefire, however, and despite American and South Vietnamese statements to the contrary, such flagrant violations were the exception, not the rule. In most battles, including those publicized by Saigon as major Communist violations, the circumstances were actually ambiguous. Each side took the view that if a clash occurred anywhere, it had the right to retaliate against the other side's bases, not just against its troops who were actually in violation of the truce. Thus, the South Vietnamese felt bombing of Communist zones was legal retaliation for an attack on one of their outposts; the Communists, if a government patrol penetrated territory they believed was theirs, held it was justifiable to shell a district headquarters or some other fixed government position. As the fighting continued, and every action was related to some past event in an ever-lengthening chain of alleged cause and effect, the whole concept of ceasefire violations became, in essence, meaningless.

Nonetheless, Communist tactics continued to suggest that for a time, at least, they genuinely meant to subordinate warfare to political action. Armed force would be kept to the level needed to protect political and administrative agents and activities, said a directive from the Communist command in one delta province, and would not be used in a manner that "clearly violated" the peace agreement. As even the quasi-official American ceasefire history acknowledged, in the months after the ceasefire "Communist activities in the delta generally followed the patterns suggested by this directive."

By the second month of the truce, however, the Communists were admitting in internal party documents that their political action was less effective than they had hoped. "We had not fully assessed the obstinacy of the U.S. and its puppet," COSVN admitted in a March directive, which also indicated that though the leaders still hoped the Paris agreement would serve Communist purposes, some of their agents and field commanders had evidently begun to doubt it. "Holding that the enemy has so seriously broken the agreement that it is no longer is valid and has no value, [and] feeling that the current situation is 'a return to normal war' as before," COSVN admonished, "is the main mistaken attitude at this time."

If Communist strategy was to give primacy to the political offensive, Communist access to the population was exactly what the South Vietnamese authorities were determined not to allow. All wartime prohibitions against Communist activity remained in force. The agreement's guarantee of full democratic liberties, Saigon maintained, could be put in effect only as part of an overall political settlement. Until then, since the South Vietnamese regime remained in control of its own territory, its laws would continue to apply.

Thieu's suspicions of Communist intentions had all been confirmed by the flag-raising campaign at the very start of the ceasefire, and now that his generals seemed to have the upper hand again, he was not going to prevent them from pursuing and further battering an enemy they believed was seriously weakened. With the "land-grab" campaign over, the South Vietnamese took the offensive. The ceasefire battles, instead of being a last spasm of violence before a truce took hold, were only a transition from one stage of conflict to another. They represented, wrote an American officer, "the end of the second Indochina war and the beginning of the third."

Traveling that spring over nearly the entire length of South Vietnam, I was seldom beyond the sound of gunfire. From February to June, major battles were fought in the hills around Hue, along the principal highways through the central highland region, in much-fought-over Binh Dinh and Kontum provinces, in traditional battlegrounds northwest of Saigon, and in Chuong Thien and Dinh Tuong provinces in the delta.

In these and in numberless smaller battles, both sides suffered severe losses. The 1st ARVN Division, already worn by heavy casualties in its campaign in Laos in 1971 and in the 1972 Easter offensive, lost almost 1,200 men killed or wounded in their positions near Hue during the first four months of the truce. The South Vietnamese took nearly 500 casualties, I was told by II Corps staff officers in Pleiku, in a single operation to clear the road between there and the most important town in the southern highlands, Ban Me Thuot. Altogether, according to official statistics, more than 6,600 South Vietnamese soldiers were killed in the first three months of the truce—a rate as high as in all but the very worst months of the war.

To find anything resembling a truce that spring, you had to travel more than 400 miles north from Saigon to Quang Tri. Almost alone among Vietnam's battlegrounds, Quang Tri had fallen quiet. Only minor skirmishes and occasional shelling were occurring on what had been the most blood-soaked battlefield of the war. In the ruins of the province capital, South Vietnamese marines sunned on the roofs of their bunkers and watched

Communist soldiers doing the same on the far bank of the Thach Han River. It was not unusual to see soldiers from both sides on opposite riverbanks at the same time, washing clothes and exchanging occasional waves or insults. A monstrous South Vietnamese flag and dozens of smaller ones flew over the rubble on the south bank, while on the Communists' side was an answering display of Liberation Front banners. Except when the two sides blared propaganda songs or slogans at each other through high-powered loudspeakers, the air was lazily still.

To understand why Quang Tri was nearly at peace, however, was also to understand why the rest of South Vietnam was still at war. In Quang Tri, the two armies faced each other across well-defined, if not completely continuous, fronts. There was no doubt about where each side belonged. More important, though, was that there were no people, except soldiers, in the battle area. Thus, the war lacked the political component it had everywhere else. Where there were villages, there were political and economic targets for the Communists to attack and the government to defend. All through the war, the Communists fought not only to inflict damage on the government forces, but also for access to the population to tax, to propagandize, to obtain supplies and information, and above all to show they would outfight or outlast any attempts to keep them away. The Communists believed that their right to conduct such activities had been guaranteed by the Paris agreement, and that the South Vietnamese were illegally preventing them. Thus, in their own eyes, their attacks after the ceasefire were meant to enforce the agreement, not to violate it. Saigon was just as adamant that Communist political action remained illegal until both sides had agreed on a political settlement. Thus, on every day of the truce, both sides proved again what the Communists had long argued in the negotiations: that the military aspects of the war could not be separated from its political aspects. Its effort to do so was the Paris agreement's fatal flaw. In Quang Tri, however, all that could be won or lost by more fighting was a few hundred yards of rubble. There were no people, only ruins. And in the ruins, for a time, there was peace.

On their side of the lines, in Quang Tri and the other four coastal provinces that formed South Vietnam's Military Region I, the Communists were rebuilding. From their bunkers, government soldiers could see white smoke rising like spindrift, showing where farmers were burning the stubble in long-untilled fields to prepare for replanting. Sometimes there would be enormous booms as the fires reached unexploded bombs or shells lying in the dry rice stalks. The smoke symbolized the major strategic change in the war—the end of American bombing, which once made it impossible for any civilian life to exist in Communist-held zones, at least in daytime. Now, civilian and military trucks carrying construction crews could be seen even in daylight, jouncing over cratered roads. Here and there the sunlight winked from new tin roofs on rebuilt houses.

The Communists were refurbishing not only villages but roads, airfields, pipelines, and other supply installations. As usual in periods when they were resupplying and reinforcing, they kept military action to a low level, giving something of a respite to the three million people of the five northern provinces. For the first time since before the 1972 Easter offensive, Highway One was safe enough for civilian traffic to come all the way from the southern parts of the country. Buses, trucks, and occasional private cars with Saigon registration plates rolled past the scarred villages of Quang Ngai and Quang Nam, threaded the refuse-choked streets of Da Nang, labored up the hairpin turns leading to the lovely Hai Van Pass, and descended the opposite slope toward Hue. Alongside the road, farmers on the government side of the lines, too, were beginning to return, at least in daytime, to homes and ricefields they had abandoned many months earlier.

Except in Quang Tri, however, there was little rest for the soldiers. In the contested fringes of the government-held zone, which away from the major towns extended only a few hundred yards to each side of the highway, the Military Region I command was on the offensive. Despite Saigon's claims that the ceasefire was being observed, officers in the field spoke freely of their continuing "pacification" drives against the Communists' enclaves along the coast and against enemy positions on the nearer slopes of the Truong Son range to the west. On the road from Da Nang south to the shattered town of Sa Huynh, the guns could always be heard, day and night. The U.S. Defense Attache Office acknowledged in a secret report to Washington that the principal cause of the fighting was not Communist ceasefire violations, as Saigon insisted, but the government army's "attempts to eliminate spheres of Communist influence." The Communists, though reacting sharply to government attacks, were carrying out very few attacks of their own.

In these battles the South Vietnamese temporarily improved security in their slender ribbon of territory along Highway One. But there was nothing they could do about the evident Communist build-up deeper in the mountains. The five regular ARVN divisions in the region were tired, stretched thinly over its many battlefronts, and still weakened by the unprecedented casualties of the past year's fighting.* The Vietnamese air force was being forced out of the sky over the Communist zone by ever more dangerous

---

* The 1st Division, for example, lost an estimated 50 percent of its company grade officers and senior noncommissioned officers during 1971 and 1972. Despite its reputation as ARVN's best, American military analysts described it in mid-1973 as "far from . . . combat effective." Another supposed elite unit that suffered heavy losses was the Airborne Division, which had 2,900 men killed and 12,000 wounded in 1972 and 1973, with 300 more missing in action—a number equivalent to more than its entire assigned strength.

antiaircraft defenses. Though large, the air force had been designed for a "relatively permissive air environment" by American advisers who assumed U.S. planes would continue to be available to strike heavily defended areas. With the Americans gone, Vietnamese pilots continued to bomb in close support of their troops on the ground. But they had no ability to face the missiles and other weapons protecting the Communist logistical zones. Despite their temporary successes and the lull in Communist-initiated activity, government commanders in the northern region were worried men as 1973 reached its midpoint. The enemy buildup meant major blows were going to fall soon, they were sure, and their own forces seemed dangerously vulnerable.

In the central Vietnamese highlands, the post-ceasefire war shifted back and forth, as always, across the forested ridges that marched away in jagged ranks toward South Vietnam's western border. During February and March, bloody battles were fought to clear the only two overland routes to Pleiku, the Military Region II headquarters: Highway 14, which led south to Ban Me Thuot, and Highway 19, which ran east across the mountains to reach the coast at Qui Nhon, capital of Binh Dinh Province. When the road-clearing operations were finished, ARVN turned to another series of battles to try to expand their few remaining enclaves in northern Binh Dinh. Then, in June, a major clash erupted in two villages called Trung Nghia and Polei Krong, which lay on the Dak Bla River west of Kontum.

From the residents of the two villages, 4,000 of whom were waiting out the battle in a drab, muddy camp that had been named Mary Lou by the American Green Berets who once served there, I learned something of the history of Trung Nghia and Polei Krong. The story stretched back over a decade. It was not a particularly unusual one, but in it lay a capsule of the Vietnamese people's long tragedy. For the families in the Mary Lou camp were victims not only of Communist attacks but also of a conscious South Vietnamese policy to push civilians out to the edge of the contested zones, as a means of extending Saigon's control. As it happened, both villages came into existence in the first place as the result of forced movement of populations for political-military reasons. Polei Krong's inhabitants, all members of hill tribes, had been rounded up in their new village in the mid-1960s when the South Vietnamese government was trying to group everyone in western Kontum and Pleiku provinces into settlements nearer to the government-held towns. And Trung Nghia was born as a "strategic hamlet" during the Diem years: its people, ethnic Vietnamese, had been more or less forcibly transplanted from their former homes in Communist-threatened areas of coastal Quang Ngai and Binh Dinh.

Both villages were evacuated in April 1972, during the Easter offensive. With tens of thousands of others, the villagers were taken south to camps in

Pleiku. But in September, the Kontum province chief ordered that all Kontum refugees must be brought back to their own province, even though many still could not return home and there was a serious shortage of refugee accommodation. The reason, apparently, was the province chief's desire to capture a larger share of relief funds, which offered numerous opportunities for graft.

Late in 1972, the people of Polei Krong and Trung Nghia returned home to start rebuilding. But the villages were attacked again at the time of the ceasefire, and they had to flee again. When government troops retook the villages, the people were ordered back, against their own will and against the advice of the U.S. refugee-affairs adviser in the province, because of Saigon's view that the government flag must be planted in all contested zones. As the villagers feared, the Communists—who claimed to have been in possession of both on Ceasefire Day—attacked again on June 7. For the third time in little over a year, the residents fled, stumbling for three days across the densely wooded ridges to government lines near Kontum. This time, they had had enough. "This is the third time we have had to leave our homes," said one of them, standing inside the garlands of barbed wire ringing the Mary Lou camp while in the distance there was the periodic crash of heavy 175-mm guns firing out toward the west. "Now we no longer want to return. We want to be resettled somewhere else where it will be safe."

Far to the south in the flat green ricelands of the Mekong Delta, the war had changed least of all. The delta war was "a war of nameless little battles that make no headlines but have cost more lives over the years than all the fighting in the rest of Vietnam," I wrote after a trip through the region in May, the fourth month of the ceasefire. That dispatch was datelined from Vinh Tuong, a large, fairly prosperous village on the main highway traversing Chuong Thien Province in the heart of the delta. In Vinh Tuong, as elsewhere, I found that the wary hopes of the first days of the truce had quickly given way to a resigned realization that the war was not over, after all. For more than a month, no one had gone to tend the village orchards, though the groves of mango trees and coconut palms were just a ten-minute walk from the sandbagged militia outpost on the highway. "The Viet Cong have put mines out there," explained a local cabinetmaker, which had killed or wounded several civilians. Now no one tried to go at all. That evening in Vi Thanh, the province capital, a silky twilight was suddenly shattered by a barrage of more than 100 rounds from government artillery positions on the outskirts of the town. The batteries had been firing at that rate, I was told, every night for weeks.

The delta war went on for many reasons. The region was a rich prize: South Vietnam's agricultural heartland. The native Viet Cong insurgency, though weaker than in the early 1960s, was still strong, and the peculiar intimacy of the guerrilla war carried with it a burden of hatred and personal scores to settle that could not be resolved by faraway diplomacy. And the Paris agreement simply did not apply to the peculiarities of the delta. It seemed meant to end some other war on some other planet, as I came to understand one warm afternoon in a place called Chan Mat.

"I beg you to understand," the young widow said, looking down at the clumsy, old-fashioned sewing machine on the table in front of her, "here we are controlled by the government by day and the Viet Cong by night, and it is very difficult for us."

Outside the little tailor shop, nothing suggested a battlefield. The hamlet of Chan Mat had no wrecked homes, no sandbagged gun emplacements, no heaps of rusting barbed wire or blackened gun pits with their litter of expended shell casings. It looked like a thousand other Mekong Delta villages, a pleasant cluster of a few dozen homes and shops, shaded by palms and fruit trees, strung out along a single dusty street. In the fields stretching away toward the South China Sea, the early summer rains had just begun to touch the brown earth with the lemony green of young rice shoots. Here and there, farmers bent over rows of seedlings, their straw hats catching the sun to form small cones of light, bobbing under the May sky. Smaller figures, village children, danced after flocks of ducks that looked, from a distance, like white quilts fluttering across the ground.

Yet the appearance of peace was an illusion. Chan Mat was a casebook example of a contested village, claimed by both sides, warred on by both armies, loyal probably more to its own survival than to either the Saigon government or the liberation forces. Trying to "determine the areas con-trolled by each party," as required in Article 3 of the Paris agreement, perhaps sounded straightforward enough in Paris, or even in Saigon. In Chan Mat, though, it was like telling someone to label the whites and yolks in a dish of scrambled eggs.

Straddling the main highway that crossed Vinh Binh Province toward the sea, Chan Mat was classed in the records at the province headquarters as government-controlled. The villagers knew better. "There are always men with guns," said an old man with a wispy Ho Chi Minh beard who was repairing a bicycle outside a little garage. "Sometimes they are the govern-ment, sometimes they are the Viet Cong. The Viet Cong always know when the government is not here, because every family has someone working for them." Across Vietnam, there were thousands of other hamlets similarly situated, forming a sort of dispersed no-man's-land in which millions of people tried to survive by doing whatever had to be done to get along with both sides.

Chan Mat, the day I visited, was still shocked and frightened by an incident two days before, when a Viet Cong squad walked into the village in the middle of the afternoon and headed straight for a house where an off-duty government policeman was visiting his brother. In a sudden burst of firing the intruders shot down the policeman, the brother, and another man who happened to be in the house. Then they withdrew. "The family and everyone else knows who did the killing," one woman admitted, "but everybody is too afraid to identify them."

If the village was frightened and angry at the Communist killers, however, it was almost equally angry at the government soldiers from the militia post a mile away. The militiamen had come slowly and reluctantly when someone ran to tell them about the killings, and then refused to follow the Viet Cong into the forest on the far side of the village rice fields. But in order not to return to their outpost empty-handed, they grabbed a 14-year-old boy who was tending ducks in the field and dragged him back with them. Two days later, the boy was still being held.

"I am sure he is innocent," his older sister protested. Like so many in the delta and elsewhere in Vietnam, she had suffered at the hands of both sides. Her husband, a government militiaman, had been killed in battle two years before, and now her brother was under arrest as a suspected guerrilla. She had heard that he was beaten after his arrest but hoped he was not badly hurt; though she had been allowed to leave some food for him at the village police station, she had not yet been permitted to see him.

As usual, in such glimpses of Vietnam's numberless private tragedies, I never learned the end of the story. With luck, the youngster might have been back with his family in another day or so, but if unlucky he might have remained in prison for months or years. Police procedures in such cases were erratic. A suspected Communist might or might not be brutalized for a confession. He might be brought before a military court, or simply held for many months without trial on the decision of a "province security committee" headed by the province chief. If tried, he might be allowed to try to produce evidence of his innocence, or he might be kept completely incommunicado, unable to contact anybody who might testify for him. The circumstances varied, seemingly, with the whim or corruptibility of the local police chief, or with the pressure from higher up at any given time for better arrest statistics. Actual guilt or innocence often had very little to do with the outcome.

The assassination squads were one face of the Viet Cong; propaganda agents were the other. Since the ceasefire, villagers said, the Communist political agents had been giving special attention to families with relatives in the government armed forces. Their sons, husbands, brothers, and fathers should desert, these families were told. To be killed now that the ceasefire was in effect would be needless. Deserters could come over to the liberation side without fearing any reprisals for their previous service to the "puppets."

If the Viet Cong appeal was coming through, the government's was not—and in this fact lay a significant truth about the contested zones, which was that the balance of political strength did not necessarily correspond with military strength. On the flip-charts in the province headquarters five miles away, numerous programs were listed to win the "hearts and minds" of the villages: health services, public works, economic development, propaganda, and information. But the officials in charge of carrying these programs out preferred to do so in less dangerous places than Chan Mat. The government-appointed hamlet chief visited only occasionally and always during the day, spending most of his time and every night without fail at the militia outpost. Higher authorities from the village, district, or province headquarters were almost never seen. Chan Mat saw nothing of the Saigon government except its soldiers and police, who were frightened and unwilling defenders, better at casual theft and brutality toward civilians than at protecting them from acts of terror.

The question with no answer was that with which American and Vietnamese strategists wrestled inconclusively for many years: which side were the people in a place like Chan Mat really on? Of the villagers I spoke to that afternoon, only one gave the hint of an answer—an elderly stonemason, who had been watching us for hours while consuming enough beer to drown his discretion. Finally, facing us in a shabby but well-stocked little shop on the village street, he said loudly—obviously remembering the killing of the policeman—"Nobody likes these people who go around killing other people." Everyone else in the shop worriedly signaled him to be quiet. Perhaps they disagreed; perhaps they were afraid the Viet Cong would hear of his comment and take vengeance. No outsider, probably, would ever find out which was the case. No doubt the village had its Viet Cong families and its pro-government families, and even among these there had to be some accommodation, some arrangements to live and let live while what passed for normal life went on.

Probably, I thought, the majority were for neither side. "Most of them do not like the Viet Cong because they know life under the Communists is very hard," an army captain had said in the province headquarters, speaking of the peasants in the contested villages. "But"—he tapped the rank-badge pinned to his collar—"they do not like us, either."

It seemed plausible that what the people of Chan Mat really wanted was just to be let alone, to live and tend their rice fields without either the government and its police or the Viet Cong with their constant demands for food, labor, information, and attendance at propaganda meetings. Like millions of other Vietnamese in thousands of other hamlets, Chan Mat's inhabitants had wondered briefly what the Paris agreement would mean. Now, they said, they did not think about it all. It had changed nothing. As for so many terrible years before, all that was real was the daily struggle to survive.

The Peacekeepers

Singly and in groups of two or three, the women stepped timidly into the Tay Ninh province headquarters. Some walked quickly across the open courtyard, glancing about nervously like sparrows. Others moved hesitantly. All had the same anxious eyes, and each clutched a photograph.

When no one ordered them away, the women began moving toward a banquet table inside, where twelve thin, pale South Vietnamese officers, freed from Communist prison camps earlier that day, were sitting down to a welcome-home lunch given by the province chief. One by one, the women shyly approached the returned prisoners, showed their photos, murmured their request. The pictures showed sons, husbands, brothers, fathers, all missing in the war. Perhaps one of the newly released officers knew or had seen them in the camps, or knew someone from the same units, or had some news, however vague. It was a sad, frail hope. You could tell, looking at them, that the women expected disappointment. The twelve officers studied the photographs, shook their heads and gently handed them back, then turned to their meal while the women padded away.

Only a few lucky Vietnamese families were to find vanished loved ones after the ceasefire. The Paris agreement called for a complete exchange of prisoners of war and an accounting of those who had died in captivity, all to take place within the first 60 days. But fewer than half the soldiers listed as missing by both sides were ever returned. South Vietnam returned 26,880 P.O.W.'s but were accused by the Communists of illegally continuing to hold another 15,000 military prisoners. For its part, the Provisional Revolutionary Government handed over only 5,336 of the 31,981 South Vietnamese servicemen listed by Saigon as missing in action. In addition to these were the civilian detainees held by both sides, whose release had not been guaranteed by the agreement but was left to later negotiations between Saigon and the P.R.G. Eventually, South Vietnam freed 5,081 civilians and the Communists released 606. The Communists attributed the small number of military and civilian prisoners to their "humane and lenient policy" under which they said they had "released on-the-spot many captured Saigon officers and soldiers and also set free those detainees who . . . realized the right path."

The majority of the Vietnamese prisoner exchanges were completed within the 60-day limit, though the last few batches were held up for months longer in a series of disputes over the protocol and mechanics of the exchange. Several hundred of those held by the South Vietnamese refused release at the last minute and, over Communist protests, were sent to Chieu Hoi (Open Arms) centers to go through the same indoctrination that was given to battlefield defectors. Any P.O.W.'s held by the Communist side who might have voluntarily joined their captors were simply kept off the list for exchange in the first place.

For the South Vietnamese soldiers who came back ill and hungry from stockades in the Communist-held jungles, release was a miracle. It was like coming back from the dead.

"This is the first time I have seen sunlight in eleven months," said a newly freed lieutenant named Duong. His comment seemed metaphorical as well as literal. The returned prisoners told of hunger, malaria, hard labor, and constant fear. For many there was the added danger of American bombing, especially in the Parrot's Beak region of Cambodia, where many prisoners captured in the Saigon region were held.

There was hint of a much worse tragedy in the fact that except for a handful of high-ranking officers, nearly all of those freed by the Communists had been captured in the 1972 Easter offensive or later. Of the many thousands missing in previous years, there was barely a trace, nor any way of knowing how many might have been executed, died of illness or starvation or mistreatment, taken north, enlisted on the Communist side, or simply kept in captivity despite the peace accords, perhaps so they could not testify on their treatment.

The exchange of Vietnamese P.O.W.'s, like other ceasefire procedures, was administered by the Joint Military Commission, the centerpiece of the intricate peacekeeping structure created by the Paris agreement. Initially, the commission's members were the four signers of the agreement: North and South Vietnam, the United States, and the P.R.G. After 60 days, the four-party commission would be superseded by a new body consisting of just the two South Vietnamese members. The delegates' responsibilities were numerous. They were to investigate reported truce violations and issue instructions to prevent recurrence. They were to agree on entry points through which both sides would replenish their supplies, and they were to supervise arms shipments to assure that they conformed to the limits imposed by the agreement. They were to oversee removal of mines and other obstacles to civilian travel. And they were to "determine the areas controlled by each party and the modalities of stationing."

That last task, of course, was the crucial one for maintaining a ceasefire. Unfortunately it was also primarily a political and not a military matter, as American military officers had warned since well before the agreement took effect. As far back as November 5, 1972—ten days after Kissinger's "peace is at hand" press conference—Gen. Frederick C. Weyand, the U.S. commander in Vietnam, warned at an embassy planning meeting that if the negotiators in Paris could not agree on which side controlled which territory, military delegates in Saigon could hardly be expected to do so. Handing that crucial political question to the truce commission, Weyand predicted, would only jeopardize its ability to achieve the more limited aim of stopping the fighting.

In the following weeks, Weyand and his small ceasefire planning staff tried vainly to persuade Kissinger and the rest of the U.S. negotiating team that if the ceasefire were to have any chance of succeeding, the procedures would have to be established beforehand and not left to the uncertainty of later negotiations by the military delegates. Weyand proposed that the two sides exchange lists of military units and describe their strength and locations, so that when a ceasefire went into effect it would be known where all units were supposed to be—a procedure that might also have helped avoid the last-minute land-grabbing campaigns. No such plan was ever seriously offered in Paris, however, and the results were exactly as Weyand predicted.

When the Joint Military Commission began operating after the ceasefire, the American delegates found themselves contending not just with a continuing war and a suspicious enemy but with a stubbornly obstructive ally as well. The South Vietnamese had previously acknowledged their responsibilities as host member, but their actions verged on sabotage. The sites they proposed for the Communist delegations in the Saigon region ranged from "a few shells of buildings with concrete floors" to "an open field surrounded by mines," said one official U.S. report. The South Vietnamese authorities would neither supply food to the Communist teams nor allow them to buy food in local markets. The Americans unilaterally took over most of the basic housekeeping tasks, but had little success in resolving the endless quarrels about the delegates' "privileges and immunities" that soon began consuming most of the commission's time and energy.

To American eyes, the disputes often seemed preposterously trivial. "I sometimes think these guys have a school somewhere where they just study how to be petty," an exasperated American officer said to me one day. But to the Vietnamese on both sides the issues were not minor at all. For the Communists, recognition of the Provisional Revolutionary Government as an equal claimant to power in the South was—along with the U.S. withdrawal—the heart of the Paris agreement. The P.R.G. representatives were in Saigon not so much to administer the truce as to demonstrate to the South Vietnamese public, to the world, and, I sometimes thought, to themselves, that they had won a legal status equal to that of the Saigon government. Any infringement of their rights threatened that recognition and thus a fundamental principle of the peace agreement.

The South Vietnamese, for their part, had no intention of granting any appearance of legality either to the P.R.G. or to the North Vietnamese. Nothing would be allowed to impair the image of Saigon's control in its own zone. Communist delegates might be stationed there but they would be seen, if at all, under the rifles of ARVN military guards.

While doing their best to make the Communist representatives appear as prisoners, not truce delegates, the Saigon authorities also inspired hostile public demonstrations. In Ban Me Thuot, one of 26 designated local truce observation sites, a crowd stoned and beat up the arriving North Vietnamese delegates, slightly injuring six of them. The incident, the chief American delegate on the scene reported to his superiors, appeared to have been planned by South Vietnamese government officials and assisted by local police commanders. A similar incident occurred at Da Nang, and the Communists subsequently refused to send teams to any of the local sites. Eventually they withdrew from the seven regional headquarters as well, stationing their representatives only in Saigon.

In its 60-day lifetime, the Four-Party Joint Military Commission's only complete success was in overseeing the withdrawal of U.S. troops and the release of American P.O.W.'s. These were not accomplished without disputes: on several occasions, the Communists sought to hold up the prisoner release in return for action on other unrelated clauses of the agreement, and in late March, during the final phase, there was a tense ten-day confrontation over the status of ten prisoners—seven U.S. airmen, two American civilians, and a Canadian missionary—who had been captured in Laos. In the end, though, the Communists lived up to their commitment in Paris that the release of U.S. P.O.W.'s would be linked only to the troop withdrawal and not to any other matters. The ten Laos prisoners were freed as well, as had also been privately promised in Paris but not publicly stated because of the fiction that the Lao Communists were independent of Hanoi's control. A face-saving declaration was issued by the Lao, calling the release a gesture of good will.

The U.S. withdrawal and the return of American prisoners were accomplished because American disengagement was the one clear, solid commitment of the Paris agreement. On all matters involving the disputes between the Vietnamese sides, the agreement was vaguer and the good faith of the negotiators more questionable—and, as General Weyand had foreseen, what had not been fully resolved in Paris could not be settled by the military truce delegates. The exchange of Vietnamese military prisoners, though incomplete and disputed, was the only Vietnamese issue even partly resolved by the Joint Military Commission. On all other matters it remained paralyzed—a result that was almost guaranteed by the unanimity principle, established in the Paris protocols, barring any action unless all members agreed.

Though they recognized that the effort was almost hopeless, the American delegates offered several proposals to try to make the ceasefire more effective. On one occasion the U.S. proposed to Saigon that the use of artillery, mortars, and fighter aircraft should be temporarily suspended, unless authorized by a corps or higher command in response to a specific attack, to see if the Communists would reciprocate. American officials also tried to persuade President Thieu to authorize meetings between unit commanders in the field to arrange local implementation of the ceasefire. Both proposals were rejected. Saigon's representatives on the truce commission were given virtually no negotiating power and thus could not settle even the most trivial issues without instructions—which they rarely obtained.

American complaints to the Communists about ceasefire violations and illegal infiltration of troops and supplies were just as unavailing. Both sides, the Americans concluded, were to blame for the continuing war. "Implementing the ceasefire," wrote the official historian of the U.S. delegation, "was an impossible task from the beginning—none of the Vietnamese parties were willing to stop fighting. The Americans did not fail from lack of effort; no amount of effort could have succeeded."

The other half of the peacekeeping structure was the International Commission of Control and Supervision, a successor to the similarly named International Control Commission that had existed since 1954. The new body had two of the same members, Canada and Poland. But India, the third member of the old commission, was dropped, along with the concept of a neutral member. Instead, Indonesia and Hungary were added, thus giving the new body two Communist and two pro-Western members.

The ICCS was to observe the truce, investigate and report on violations, monitor the prisoner exchanges and supply shipments, and later to help supervise the national elections. Like the Joint Military Commission it was to operate on the unanimity principle—and like the Joint Military Commission, too, it was paralyzed from the start. The atmosphere was a bit more polite, perhaps. But the impasse was the same. The Polish and Hungarian delegations, it quickly became apparent, were there not to foster conciliation but to protect the interests of the Vietnamese Communists in every way possible. After the first couple of weeks, the two Communist delegations normally refused even to authorize investigations of reported Viet Cong or North Vietnamese violations. Since the unanimity rule prohibited any action without the consent of all four members, that left the Indonesians and Canadians able to make only their own unilateral "observations," without any official standing under the agreement.

Some had theorized that even if the ICCS was deadlocked at the political level, the presence of its teams around the country might deter flagrant breaches of the ceasefire. But it did not work out that way. The observers watched from their compounds as South Vietnamese aircraft divebombed Communist positions. They were kept awake at night by artillery. They were taken to see blown bridges, mined roads, destroyed villages. On occasion they interviewed witnesses, took photographs, and dug about for shell fragments in the earth. But they never had any apparent influence on either Vietnamese side. I went one day with an ICCS team to an ARVN regimental headquarters in the Mekong Delta where, the South Vietnamese complained, three Communist rockets had landed a day or so before. A good-sized battle was going on a few miles to the west, and every few minutes we heard the boom of a government howitzer.

"Listen to that," said a beefy Polish officer, looking disdainfully at the mud caked on his cavalry-style boots. "All day long, boom, boom, boom. And we come out here for three rockets. It is ridiculous."

An atmosphere of futility began to pervade the ICCS headquarters in Saigon, which occupied the same bedraggled compound that had housed the old control commission. The letters ICCS, said the Saigonese, really stood for the Vietnamese words "im cho coi sao," meaning "wait quietly and watch how things turn out." The Americans had an earthier version: the real meaning of the initials, they said, was "I Can't Control Shit." The new tenants put gardeners to work to cut down the weeds that had overgrown the grounds and hired painters to touch up the cracked, flaking walls of the old ICC villas. But no remodeling could brighten the image of ineffectiveness. Since the warring sides never made the basic decision to try to make the ceasefire work, the international peacekeepers never had a chance.

"We have asked for greater freedom of movement," said Capt. Klaus Bartels, one of two Canadian officers on the first ICCS team established in Communist-held territory. "But when we ask to go somewhere, they always explain that this is a newly liberated area and they haven't cleared all the mines yet, so they can't guarantee our safety."

In ten days, Captain Bartels and his fellow observers had only once been allowed to leave the thatched barracks built for them by Viet Cong troops. On that occasion, which was recreational rather than in the line of peace-keeping duty, they had been permitted to stroll the mile or so to the bomb-pitted Ben Het airstrip. The rest of the time the ICCS officers had been politely but firmly confined to their camp.

Ben Het lay in a fold in the bony hills not far from where Vietnam, Cambodia, and Laos come together. American Green Berets served there first, followed by Vietnamese rangers, during years in which the base was repeatedly surrounded and attacked but never captured until October 1972, when it was finally overrun. Craters everywhere marked the passage of B-52s that had bombed the base after its fall. A smashed helicopter lay near the airstrip, and the bones of another were strewn among the wrecked buildings nearby. Several burned tanks crouched on the red earth. Torn strips of steel runway matting twisted up out of the strip like great metal claws. On the surrounding hillsides the vegetation was thin and gauzy and large patches were completely bare, the result of repeated sprayings with chemical defoliants.

The eight ICCS officers there, two from each of the four delegations, were supposed to monitor shipments of military supplies, but so far they had seen nothing at all. "They told us they have enough supplies on hand," Captain Bartels said, and thus were not receiving replacements. Obviously, the team would see only what its hosts meant it to see. Scores of thousands of American and South Vietnamese soldiers had ranged these hills for a decade, trying to find and check the flow of men and supplies to the Communists on the battlefield. Where they had failed, it was hardly conceivable that eight immobilized foreigners could succeed. They were there, really, because establishing a team on Communist territory was supposed to enhance the ICCS's image of even-handedness. Shortly after the Ben Het detachment moved into its thatched compound, another team was sent to Duc Co, also in the Communist zone farther south in the highlands. Both sites were abandoned after a few months because of malaria, however; most of the other designated ICCS posts in Communist territory were never manned at all.

In Saigon-held territory, life for the truce teams was more comfortable but no less frustrating. "We have a pair of eyes but no hands," was the way one officer put it. Canada, which had been considerably soured by its long and futile membership on the old ICC, joined the new commission more because it did not want to embarrass the U.S. than out of any belief that it would be effective. The results more than confirmed its doubts. After visiting Indochina in March, Canada's External Affairs Minister Mitchell Sharp announced that his country would withdraw from the commission in 60 days "unless there has been some substantial improvement or distinct progress has been made toward a political settlement. . . . Canadians should not take part in a charade in which they will be required to supervise not a ceasefire but continuing and possibly escalating hostilities."

In Saigon, the head of the Canadian delegation, Ambassador Michel Gauvin, declared the commission was "not performing adequately the tasks assigned to it." If the two Vietnamese sides did not adhere to the agreement, he said, Canada could certainly not take responsibility for enforcing it. When the 60 days were up, though it agreed to remain on the commission temporarily to avoid any adverse effect on talks then being held by Kissinger and Le Duc Tho in Paris, Canada announced its decision to withdraw. On July 31 it did so, to be replaced, after several months, by Iran.

The compound that housed the Communist delegations at Tansonnhut for more than two years continued to be called Camp Davis, the name it had been given by the U.S. command in memory of the very first American soldier to die in Vietnam—Specialist 4th Class James Davis, killed in December 1961.

For weeks after the ceasefire, ARVN guards kept American and other foreign reporters away from the compound. Several correspondents had their credentials suspended for trying to enter, and one or two were even detained for several hours. The Communists argued vainly in the Joint Military Commission that their "privileges and immunities"—supposed to be the same as those granted to foreign diplomats in the South Vietnamese capital—entitled them to invite anyone they wished to their headquarters. But the South Vietnamese, invoking the unanimity rule, insisted that until all delegations had agreed on procedures for dealing with the press, they had no obligation to give access to the Communist delegates.

Even to the correspondents clamoring to meet the compound's exotic new residents, this hardly seemed a momentous matter compared to the major problems of the failed ceasefire. But it was not trivial to the Communists. Having won the right to be in their enemy's capital, they wanted to demonstrate their achievement on the world's magazine covers and television screens. The American embassy, sensitive to the influence of the press and television at home, intervened and finally prevailed on the South Vietnamese to change their policy—one of the few times U.S. pressure was successful. Eventually, the Saigon government spokesman announced that foreign journalists would be allowed to visit the Communist delegations every Saturday morning. (A few months later, when the irrelevance of the truce commissions and the Paris agreement had been established beyond all doubt, Vietnamese reporters were permitted to attend as well.) The Saturday press conferences would continue until the very last week of the war. They quickly became known as the "P.R.G. Follies"—counterpart to the daily "Five O'Clock Follies" offered by Saigon spokesmen downtown.

Camp Davis looked, as we rolled up in two olive-drab army buses for the first Saturday performance, more like a prison barracks than anything else. Doubtless that was exactly what the South Vietnamese intended. Double rolls of barbed wire ringed the compound, and military police stood guard outside. Our escort, a pompous little major from ARVN's public relations staff, ostentatiously remained outside the barriers. As the rest of us walked through into the compound, cameramen and photographers had their cameras already aimed and shooting. The P.R.G. and North Vietnamese delegates inside, equally determined to record the triumphant moment on film, aimed dozens of cameras at us, too, and for a while the scene looked like some mad parody of photojournalism, with everyone in sight frenziedly taking pictures of each other.

Inside, in meeting rooms decked with huge North Vietnamese and Liberation Front flags and portraits of Ho Chi Minh and other senior Communist leaders, we were served soft drinks and offered harsh Hanoi-made cigarettes in packages that pictured the Viet Minh flag-raising at Dien Bien Phu. Lt. Gen. Tran Van Tra, head of the P.R.G. delegation, and Lt. Col. Bui Tin, the North Vietnamese spokesman, congratulated themselves and us on our

historic encounter. "I hope," said General Tra, "we will have more opportunities to meet with the distinguished representatives of the press, opportunities for you to get impartial information." Bui Tin reminded us that we
owed the meeting to the "struggle of the Democratic Republic of Vietnam
and the Provisional Revolutionary Government"—and, he added gra-
ciously, the Foreign Correspondents Association of Saigon.

Afterward, we were invited to stroll through the compound. The Communist soldiers, obviously under orders to be friendly, answered our questions with smiles, though without departing very far from the stilted phrases
of official propaganda. They were all inexpressibly glad to be in Saigon to
implement the agreement and foster national reconciliation; they hoped,
one said, that we would now "illuminate the truth for the people of the
world." But, it seemed, boredom was beginning to set in—a quality that
must have become the dominant aspect of life at Camp Davis in the months
to come. "We would play volleyball," one young North Vietnamese officer
said wistfully when someone asked how he was spending his time, "but we
don't have a ball."

Chapter **4**

"An army with a country": Thieu's Vietnam

When he yielded to American pressure and accepted the Paris agreement, the shrewd, stubborn, suspicious soldier who ruled South Vietnam was in as strong a position as his own talents and the aid of his American ally could arrange.

Nguyen Van Thieu's authority ran, if tenuously in places, to perhaps 90 percent of his country's nineteen million people. No rival challenged his sway over the 1.1-million-man armed forces. Except for the illegal Communist underground, no civilian political force of any significance existed to express or energize opposition to his rule. The Enhance and Enhance Plus arms shipments had given him not just ample weaponry and supplies for the ceasefire battles but a huge stockpile for the future. Whatever his inner doubts, he had President Nixon's public and private assurances that the United States was not abandoning its ally and that American military force would be used to enforce the peace agreement if needed.

Utterly distrustful of the agreement and of the Communists, certain that any conciliatory actions would weaken his regime, Thieu apparently saw his military advantage as large but temporary, an asset that must be used before it evaporated. His objective after the Paris agreement was exactly what it had been before: the destruction of his Communist enemy. In his decisions after the ceasefire and for two more years, he would to the limit of the choices available to him countenance no concessions and no compromise.

Nguyen Van Thieu's talents as a leader were manipulative, not inspirational. With his power resting on the twin pillars of the army and his

101

alliance with the Americans, he saw little need for personal popularity and showed little interest in courting it. His personality left a surprisingly slight imprint in the minds of his countrymen. The word they most often used about him was "clever." For a people with two thousand years of experience in maneuvering against superior force, this implied grudging praise. If Thieu was ruthless enough and cunning enough to outplot the chronic plotters among his generals, and if he could win and keep the support of the Americans, he was thereby entitled to his office.

By repression and guile, Thieu ended the political turbulence that had plagued South Vietnam for years before his presidency. In restoring stability, however, he also erased whatever political alternative might have existed to either the Viet Cong or his anti-Communist militarism. The Communists, of course, had done the same. There was no evidence, in 1973 or later, that their definition of the Third Force ever included anyone who would not willingly comply with their demands. Nor, of course, in North Vietnam or in the areas under their control in the South, did they tolerate dissent from *their* military crusade.

The war served as Thieu's ally in stifling most normal political activity. His non-Communist opponents were paralyzed by the risk that in challenging him, they might also undermine the war. Many South Vietnamese disliked the inefficiency, corruption, and authoritarianism of their regime but feared a Viet Cong victory even more. There was in the land a vast sickness of the war, a loathing of the army and its rule, and a thirst for peace, but no political force existed to give such feelings a voice.

Few governments have been as thoroughly militarized as Thieu's. As an American officer once commented, South Vietnam was "not a country with an army but an army with a country." The officer corps was Thieu's power base and also his governing apparatus. Military men were the administrators in all provinces and all districts and had authority over virtually all civil matters. The system carried with it serious political liabilities. Armies are not often popular with the civilians among whom they live and move, and South Vietnam's was no exception. Its soldiers were unwilling draftees, trapped in a seemingly endless war, poorly paid and victimized by a system of entrenched corruption and favoritism. It was not surprising that they in turn victimized unarmed civilians. Soldiers stole, fought, and raped, as in all armies. Having learned from the Americans a style of war relying on huge amounts of firepower, the Vietnamese followed their mentors in preferring to flatten any number of villages with artillery or bombs rather than use infantry—perhaps saving some military casualties, but hardly endearing the army to the villagers whose homes were blown apart.

Battles in populated areas were inevitably followed by looting of civilian homes. Even worse was the casual violence, no less shocking even if you understood some of the reasons for it. "Soldiers in the ARVN are the most depressed South Vietnamese," an American medical relief worker wrote.

They are automatic soldiers . . . from age 18 to age 45. For many this means an almost unavoidable violent death, and they therefore lose their conscience when it comes to robbery or shooting people. One paraplegic girl patient of ours was shot in her rice field at 2 P.M. The bullet settled in her spinal cord. Two soldiers were walking along the road a few feet from her and just shot her. This is more common than [you] can imagine. One old woman patient of ours right now was told by ARVN soldiers to come out of her shelter. She came out feet first, and as she did, they shot her in the leg. Her leg had to be amputated. Had she come out head first, she said, the "children" as she calls them, would have shot her in the head.

What made the army's depredations worse was that civilians seldom had any recourse. Civil police lived in "mortal fear of military offenders," because soldiers were better armed and more numerous, reported an American adviser. "The police habitually look the other way whenever an ARVN soldier breaks the law. The ARVN military police, who have jurisdiction, are not concerned with the type of incidents that plague the civilian community such as mugging and traffic violations, and these crimes are largely overlooked."

If there was a gap between villagers and soldiers, there was perhaps an even wider one between the villagers and the officers who represented not just the army but the civil administration. ARVN officers were chosen on the basis of education, and thus came almost without exception from the urban elite, since only in the most extraordinary circumstances did peasant boys have a chance to go past a few years of primary school.

Only a minority of officers were dependent on their military salaries, according to American surveys. Their origins were in one of three groups: "the old aristocracy, the officer group created by the French, and the rising commercial/business classes from the major cities," an American general reported, adding—in tones of injured wonderment—that many of them preferred rear-area assignments to combat commands and sought appointment as province or district chiefs "so that they could avoid the rigors, boredom and dangers of training and combat." Officers represented a class, too, that was compromised in many Vietnamese eyes for its collaboration with the French. Villagers who were not necessarily Communist sympathizers still did not find it hard to agree with the liberation line that Thieu's army and administration were commanded not by patriotic Vietnamese, but by puppets of foreign rulers.

With the huge social and cultural distances separating South Vietnam's officers from the villagers whose affairs they governed, the regime appeared to the peasants, as an experienced American official wrote, "a government of 'them,' remote, arbitrary, and often abusive." Another U.S. consular officer commented in an official assessment on the "traditional remote superior attitude" of Vietnamese government officials. "Those seeking government services come as supplicants," her report added, "and it is expected that they do so."

If the militarization of government institutions weakened the regime's political base, the military also suffered from being politicized. Douglas Blaufarb, a long-time Central Intelligence Agency official with years of experience in the Vietnam pacification program, pointed out in a little-noticed but well-reasoned 1977 book called *The Counterinsurgency Era*, "in addition to being a national defense force, ARVN was also a political cabal whose first priorities were to perpetuate the system and to protect the safety, livelihood and future prospects of those who controlled it." Thieu could not challenge the system except at the risk of a coup d'état against himself, while the Americans, in Blaufarb's view, "were convinced that stability was the first requirement for progress in any other field and therefore refrained from a persistent and determined attempt to force the Thieu regime in the desired direction."

Thus, the entwining of political and military power in wartime Vietnam resulted in a regime that was effective neither politically nor militarily. In Blaufarb's analysis,

> When a regime relies for its continued survival upon powerful sub-ordinates whose support has to be purchased and who have to be carefully balanced in order to prevent combinations that might be tempted to reach for power themselves . . . the effect upon the government's services [is] highly destructive of performance standards and of the relationship with the public, particularly in the armed forces and police, the two services which are closest to the leadership of a military regime and whose support is essential to any regime. At the top of any given service and filling the key posts are men who know that they enjoy their positions as a result of political loyalty and have been given within broad limits a free hand to make of it what they will. The quality of their performance has little to do with their continuance in office, and exploitation of their position for financial gain, if appearances are preserved, is expected rather than otherwise.
>
> Once the top leadership of a service is of this character, it follows . . . that the entire service will be permeated with the same attitudes. Subordinates down to the lower ranks are chosen to build a structure which will serve the private needs of their superiors. Their loyalties are purchased, too. . . . Part of the political bargain between superior and subordinate is the promise of prestige and ease of life, which reverses the normal order of the military in which the prestige is supposed to reward such qualities as courage, leadership, and competence in an arduous profession. When personal loyalty is offered in exchange for office, the martial qualities are the first to suffer. It is no part of the political bargain by which an officer obtains and keeps his job that he should take risks with his life, that he should work long

and late, that he should put the comfort of his troops before his own, and that the demands of duty, in other words, shall have first call on his time and energies. As a result, a political army—an army whose leaders play a critical role in keeping an existing regime afloat—is often a very poor army indeed.

If militarization flawed Thieu's leadership even while keeping him in power, so did his alliance with the Americans. This cost Thieu the respect of many Vietnamese, not just leftists or Liberation Front sympathizers but rightists or the utterly nonpolitical as well, who saw him as a creature of the United States. "He is like Bao Dai," a Saigon politician once said, comparing Thieu to the last of the Vietnamese emperors, who dutifully served French interests and retired to France after 1954. "He confers decorations and buries the dead." Yet for Thieu, the army and the Americans were allies enough. Never in his years in power did he seek associates with a different perspective from his own, who might have given his regime and the nation a stronger sense of common purpose. "His regime is like a planet of five moons," is the way one Vietnamese described it. "He is of course the planet. Around him gravitate four moons, the commanders of the four military regions. The fifth moon is his nephew, Hoang Duc Nha. The planet gets its light from the sun, which is Washington. As long as the sun gives its light, the planet and the moons will turn."

During 1972, while his army with American help fought off the Easter offensive, Thieu sharply curtailed the limited freedoms that had been allowed during his first five years in office. Martial law was proclaimed in mid-May and Thieu assumed the power to rule by decree, which was later ratified by a ramrodded vote in the National Assembly. With these powers Thieu proceeded to curb the press, the country's array of political parties, and laws governing the limited local elections permitted under the 1967 constitution.

The press law stiffened penalties for publishing material thought to endanger national security and also set a punitively high schedule of "security bonds" that would be forfeited for any of a large variety of offenses. The law eventually drove most of Saigon's opposition dailies out of business, while forcing the survivors to be far more circumspect than in the past. With similar bureaucratic requirements, the new political party law effectively wiped out all but Thieu's own Dan Chu (Democracy) party.* Hamlet elec-

* The Dan Chu party was never a mass organization. Its members were the same army officers and civil servants who already ran the country. Formed only in late 1972, the party was organized on a semiclandestine basis—its leadership was known, but members did not normally announce their affiliation—and appeared to have as its purpose helping Thieu tighten his grip on his administrative apparatus. Except in that one sense, the party played no significant role in South Vietnamese political life.

tions were abolished, and elected chiefs replaced by appointees. Only powerless village councils continued to be elected.

While institutionalizing these changes, the regime also arrested thousands of known or suspected dissidents during 1972, and thereafter Thieu created what a journalist perceptively described as "not a massive, ever-present police operation comparable to that of the Soviet Union . . . [but] a mosaic of free expression and fear, of political opposition and political conformity, of gentle interference and harsh punishment."

Opponents who lived in Saigon under the eyes of American and other foreign reporters could and did publicly denounce the regime, hold meetings, even circulate petitions. But their lesser-known supporters would be arrested or intimidated into silence, especially in the provinces, where publicity was less likely. Thus, the legal opposition became a collection of heads with no bodies. In the National Assembly and the Senate, speakers could denounce the government—but they were prevented, effectively, from seeking to organize a following.

The matter of political repression, and particularly of political prisoners, became perhaps the most sharply debated issue of all, in the international arena, during the last years of the Republic. Neither South Vietnam's critics nor its partisans could be accused of contributing to public enlightenment on this issue. The standard Communist charge was that more than 200,000 political prisoners were held by the Thieu government, a statistic first publicized by the Reverend Chan Tin, a left-wing Catholic priest in Saigon who operated somewhere in the hazy boundary zone between the overt dissident movement and the revolutionary underground. Though the figure of 200,000 prisoners was never verified by any meaningful investigation, it was nonetheless parroted by Amnesty International and other well-meaning human rights and antiwar groups in the U.S. and Europe. On the opposing side of the debate, Graham A. Martin, the U.S. ambassador in Saigon from mid-1973 to the end of the war and a frequent and passionate defender of the Thieu government against its critics, insisted just as unconvincingly that the embassy staff could not document any political prisoners in South Vietnam at all.

Early in Martin's ambassadorship, however, and relying on an embassy estimate that was reported before Martin arrived in Saigon, the State Department did acknowledge that "there are political prisoners in South Vietnamese jails and cases of abuse and mistreatment do occur." Its estimate was that 500 to 1,000 political prisoners, defined as persons jailed for "non-violent, non-Communist opposition to the present government," were in South Vietnamese prisons. That careful definition almost certainly reduced the true number, since the Saigon authorities classed nearly everyone they arrested as a Communist. The law against "pro-Communist neutralism," for example, banned "acts of propaganda for and incitement of neutralism," since these were "assimilated to acts of jeopardizing public safety." Thus, in theory, a person could be imprisoned for advocating neutralism but would not be considered by American officials to be a political prisoner.

A procedure called "An Tri," or "security placement," was used to hold suspected Communists or anyone else considered "dangerous to the national defense, national security and public order." An Tri was used when there was not enough evidence to try a suspect for terrorism or some other proscribed Communist activity. A detainee could be held for a maximum term of two years, without trial, under the An Tri decree, but since additional two-year detentions could be ordered when the original terms expired, there was no effective limit at all. An Tri cases were decided by Province Security Committees, headed by province chiefs—all military officers. Judges served, but only as advisers. The committees met in secret. Defendants were supposed to have the right to submit written statements in their defense, but were not necessarily allowed to appear before the committee, which in An Tri cases was authorized to order not only detention but also confiscation of property.

The American attitude toward this procedure was expressed in an "Analysis of Province Security Committees" that was prepared in the U.S. mission, evidently for the guidance of advisers on police and security matters. The committees, this document said frankly, were "extra-constitutional and non-judicial, based on the right of the state to survive." The detention process reflected "the political 'facts-of-life' in a country at war," the U.S. analysis continued; "the nature of these committees, and their strictly political function, dictate a 'hands-off' policy by all U.S. personnel and agencies."

Military courts were only slightly less arbitrary in their procedures than were the province security committees. A defendant had no right to call witnesses or examine his accusers. Though the charge against him would be read, he was not allowed to see the complete dossier on which it was based. A defense lawyer could not even question the defendant to elicit additional detail or explanation. All that was permitted was a summary statement of defense before the court pronounced its verdict. "Trials were far from fair," admitted the ARVN intelligence chief after the war, "because they were conducted in haste and because witnesses gave secret testimony. . . . Long detention and unfair trials gave rise to considerable popular grievances. . . . There is no doubt that many suspects were victims of circumstance rather than committed and active enemies of the state."

Because prosecutors and military judges put great store in confessions, prisoners were at times tortured into admitting Communist activity—just as the Viet Cong and North Vietnamese tortured many of the Americans they captured to extort admissions of war crimes. "There is no doubt that torture was employed," declared Douglas Blaufarb, in the interrogation centers that the CIA funded and advised in each province. In coastal Quang Ngai, American Quaker medical relief workers reported treating prisoners who had been severely beaten or forced to drink whitewash. In the prison ward of the province hospital, they saw three prisoners who spent eleven, thirteen, and fifteen months, respectively, handcuffed to their beds. They complained to both South Vietnamese officials and the American province advisers, only to be told a short while later they would no longer be allowed to see patients who were prisoners. Some accounts of torture, no doubt, were planted by the Communist underground. But there were too many such stories for all of them to be false.

Though it was certainly repressive and sometimes brutal, the South Vietnamese system was also inefficient. To the real subversives, the Communist underground, Thieu's police and counterintelligence agencies seem to have been no more than an occasional inconvenience. The police, like other government agencies, were poorly administered and often corrupt. Intelligence files were badly compiled and out of date. Different agencies refused to cooperate with each other. And a crude ideological standard by which dissent of any kind was called "Communist" left the police often unable to discern who the real Communist activists were. "The security forces are penetrated by Communist agents; and Communists when apprehended, all too often go free by reason of carelessness or venality," lamented a CIA assessment. The Phoenix program, designed to identify and capture or kill Communist political agents and organizers, horrified antiwar Americans when its existence was disclosed. Official statements that more than 20,000 "eliminations" were achieved by Phoenix—Phung Hoang, in Vietnamese—raised the image of an indiscriminate CIA-controlled Murder, Inc., in Vietnam.

According to many who were associated with the program, though, it more closely resembled the Keystone Kops. "Thought of by geniuses and implemented by idiots," was the way one ex-CIA man put it. A Pentagon study in 1971 called Phoenix "only marginally effective . . . a fragmented effort, lacking central direction, control and priority." Most of those who were "neutralized" by the Phoenix program were low-level village or hamlet agents who were not even Communist party members, the Pentagon study found. The program had no real backing from the Saigon government, which would not even give it a budget. A State Department officer, after working in the Phoenix program in the delta, wrote that Phoenix was unpopular with the villagers and that its intelligence was so poor it normally captured Viet Cong activists by accident, not intentionally. Often those who were taken prisoner were able to conceal their true identities. Few were held for long. "Perhaps 90 percent of the VCI [Viet Cong Infrastructure] suspects captured are free within 90 days of capture," the State Department official wrote. "Various reasons come to mind: insufficient evidence, third party assurances, holiday releases, bribery, inertia, intimidation and influence."

The claimed 20,000 eliminations made Phoenix sound very efficient or very sinister, depending on your viewpoint, but in fact, about 90 percent of them were actually casualties in normal battlefield combat. After the fact, and on the flimsiest evidence or sometimes on none at all, bodies were declared to be Viet Cong agents and labeled as Phoenix "kills" in order to meet the quotas assigned to province and district officials.

Phoenix was part of a system of repression that was never effective enough to suppress Nguyen Van Thieu's real enemies but must have made enemies of many who passed through its jails and interrogation cells. It could not stifle dangerous ideas of peace or compromise with the Viet Cong, but it could cause those ideas to be identified exclusively with the Communists, while reinforcing the conviction that the Thieu regime offered only endless war.

If the government had a fatal flaw it was not authoritarianism, but corruption. Graft pervaded the regime, from the military police corporal at a highway checkpoint all the way up to the gold-braided generals at the Joint General Staff's mustard-colored compound next to Tansonnhut Air Base. Corruption's effects reached more deeply into South Vietnamese society than did restraints on the press or political liberty. Corruption touched every poor farm family that saw its sons drafted while the children of the elite stayed home with purchased exemptions. Corruption sapped the army itself, where soldiers without money or influence remained in combat assignments while others with the means to do so bribed their superiors for safe jobs at headquarters.

My much-admired acquaintance Nguyen Van Huyen, who as president of the South Vietnamese Senate raised one of the last voices opposing Thieu's march to dictatorship and who later resigned his seat to protest the strong-arm tactics by which a constitutional amendment was passed to permit Thieu a third term, compared corruption to a cancer. "The whole body is sick. The whole system is involved in corruption," he said, "from top to bottom. All the chiefs of province, all the big civil servants, all the high-ranking members of the executive. How in this condition can we suppress this sickness?" To an American adviser in the delta, corruption was "the most fundamental problem facing Vietnam. Corruption is the principal reason that military units do not fight well, that police operations are ineffective and that the ordinary person has a hard time when he tries to conduct simple transactions at government offices."

Money could buy anything. It could, as in one case I knew of, buy a soldier a false death certificate and an illegal exit from the country. At times such departures were said to begin aboard Vietnamese navy ships which, with the connivance of bribed officers, carried deserters and draft evaders to sea to rendezvous with Hong Kong fishing junks. The system was paid for by and largely benefited the young men of South Vietnam's Chinese minority. It continued to operate in somewhat the same fashion long after the Communist victory in 1975.

The customs operation at Saigon's Tansonnhut Airport was described in a U.S. congressional report as a "cesspool of corruption" where as much as a billion piastres—anywhere from $3.6 to $8.5 million, depending on which of several exchange rates you used—was diverted from government revenues.

The draft system was another source of enormous corruption. In villages in the Mekong Delta, American officials estimated in 1972, the going rate for "documentation for the purpose of avoiding the draft" was 10,000 to 20,000 piastres, or between 20 and 40 U.S. dollars. In Can Tho, the Military Region IV headquarters, even if a person legitimately qualified for a draft exemption, the proper papers still cost him 30,000 piastres; and for false documents, the bribe could reach as much as 100,000 piastres or more.

In Vinh Binh, admittedly one of the worst-administered provinces in the country, the senior American adviser disgustedly reported that corruption was "so far-reaching that the beginning and ending become lost." He appended a price list for safe or lucrative government and military positions:

. . . For young man to join PF*—10,000 piastres.
. . . For job as national policeman—30,000–50,000 piastres.
. . . Buying position of hamlet chief—depends on size, location and wealth of hamlet. In some cases 150,000 piastres.
. . . Positions of village and district chiefs depend upon wealth of the area. Long Toan district 250,000 piastres up to Chau Thanh district for 1,000,000 piastres per annum.
. . . The price for a province chief job also varies, however, it was reported that ten million piastres was involved in the last change of province chief in Vinh Binh and that this money went to the ministry of interior in Saigon.

Corruption not only wrecked soldiers' morale but at times endangered their lives. Pilots sometimes demanded bribes to fly missions in support of ground troops, especially hazardous ones such as medical evacuation. "Helicopter pilots are robbers," complained a South Vietnamese officer in 1974, "since each time they transport supplies to this unit they request some rice, or a portion of dry rations, or some money as a bribe. If their request is

* Popular Forces: the local militia, whose members were customarily assigned to duty within their home districts. PF assignments were prized because militiamen could ordinarily keep working their farms or at their civilian jobs.

not satisfied they refuse to unload the supplies with the excuse that their aircraft are out of order or that the landing zone is not secure."

Trade with the Viet Cong, an enormously profitable business, was a widespread scandal. An American intelligence officer I knew, who served in Tay Ninh Province on the Cambodian border, was convinced by the time his tour ended in mid-1972 that the war in the entire Saigon region could have been stopped for a year, if not longer, if the flow of supplies to the Communists from government-held areas could be checked. The Viet Cong and North Vietnamese units in the region depended on North Vietnam for almost nothing except their weapons and ammunition. Everything else they acquired, illegally, from the government zone. Food, fuel, medicines, sampan motors, mosquito netting, radios, batteries, bicycle and motorbike parts, uniform cloth—all were sold, in large quantities, across the invisible front lines.

Some contraband was sold by individual villagers, perhaps Liberation Front sympathizers or agents or perhaps not, who carried a basket or two to the edge of their rice fields or loaded a three-wheeled scooterbus with cans of gasoline to be exchanged at some roadside rendezvous. But much more was sold, with profit as the sole motive, by the truck or even convoy load, with the connivance of officers up to the rank of division commander or higher. Profits were enormous. A liter of gasoline purchased for 80 or 90 piastres in 1972 could bring three or four times as much from middlemen who purchased it for the Viet Cong in their base areas near the border. The return on other goods was as high, or nearly so. The profits financed protection, which was paid richly enough to guarantee complete immunity for the bigger traders. At a local billiard parlor my American acquaintance introduced me to the Tay Ninh police chief, who admitted after some prodding that he simply could not control trading with the enemy. Sometimes his men would arrest a small trader, who would be held for a few weeks and then usually released, if no other charges were placed against him. The biggest dealers were too well protected, he said with visible embarrassment. About them he could do nothing.

Vietnamese investigators also found trading with the enemy prevalent in the border region. The Military Security Service, ARVN's counter-intelligence branch, reported that officers—including field-grade officers—"enthusiastically engage in activities or support merchants who sell essential supplies to the Communists. They even use manpower and facilities of their units in their personal activities in order to make more money." The MSS report was leaked to American officials, apparently because its authors believed it would just be buried if it remained in South Vietnamese channels.

U.S. officers documented similar cases involving the Vietnamese navy. In one instance, provincial militia troops in a fishing village in the lower delta sank a patrol boat, wounding three sailors, after the navy crews refused to share the profit from diesel fuel they were selling to local fishermen—including Viet Cong agents. They could not pay the provincial troops the proposed 1,000 piastres for each 55-gallon drum, the navy men were said to have explained, because all the proceeds went straight to navy headquarters in Saigon. The sinking of the boat was officially reported as a Viet Cong ambush.

Soldiers and civilians could perhaps sympathize with a poor farmer, or an enlisted serviceman who could not support his family on his military pay, who earned a few extra piastres by delivering a few bottles of gasoline or some antimalaria drugs to the Viet Cong. But that did not mean ordinary Vietnamese forgave the high-ranking officers who were earning not just a bit of extra rice and fish but huge fortunes from a trade that could one day cost the lives of their own soldiers. Most Vietnamese I met made a clear distinction between small and large corruption. They did not like paying "tea money" to a minor civil servant for some routine service, but they understood that it was a matter of survival. For the higher-ups who became rich on corruption, the Vietnamese had nothing but contempt.

In the army, favoritism and bribery, rather than competence, governed promotions. "The selling of command/political positions is commonplace," said a secret assessment prepared by the U.S. Defense Attache Office. Another secret report declared, "Cronyism, purchase of promotions and bribes for good duty locations still are prevalent throughout ARVN."

On military payrolls were thousands of "ghost soldiers," men whose death or desertion had never been reported and whose commanders pocketed their pay. Probably more numerous were "flower soldiers," who worked at civilian jobs and, instead of reporting for duty, turned their military pay over to the officers who allowed them to stay home. A cautious American estimate was that as many as 20,000 soldiers—equivalent to nearly two divisions—were paying bribes to escape military duties. "Obviously," the analyst added, "the fighting spirit of the remaining personnel, unwilling or unable to pay, is adversely affected." Other estimates were much higher. U.S. Senate investigators early in 1974 cited reports of as many as 100,000 nonexistent soldiers on the South Vietnamese payroll. A high-ranking ARVN officer, after the war, recalled an investigation later that year which found there were 30,000 "flower soldiers" in the delta region alone, representing somewhere between seven and nine million piastres in monthly salaries that went to corrupt officers.

Corruption, nearly all Vietnamese believed, reached into the highest levels of the regime. "The house leaks from the roof down," the Saigonese said. Wives of high-ranking generals and palace confidants made ostentatious shows of wealth. The wife of Gen. Dang Van Quang—Thieu's military affairs adviser and one of the most powerful men in Saigon—was recalled by Gen. William Westmoreland as "a flashily beautiful woman who appeared at formal events literally dripping with jewels." Another who flaunted wealth was Mrs. Cao Van Vien, whose husband was chief of the Joint General Staff and whose riches flowed from G.I. bars and from hotels she rented to the U.S. government to billet servicemen.

Punishment for corruption was so rare it caused amazement even when it was mild. A colonel commanding a major training center was found to have used draftee labor and army materials to build an ice-making plant—on army property—which he ran for his own profit. He was demoted one rank and sentenced to 60 days' confinement, not in prison but in his own quarters. This light penalty, a Vietnamese general later recalled, caused "quite a sensation" in the armed forces.

Many Americans in Vietnam were sickened by the corruption; others joined it. Most, though, tried to brush it off. It was the Asian way of life, American officials often said. Vietnamese were used to it, even expected it, since the prestige of their leaders required conspicuous consumption of wealth. But that, I came to think, was defensive poppycock. The Vietnamese weren't tolerant of corruption. If you asked them, they would tell you they hated it. Even those involved in it were often covered with shame. Corruption exacted its highest price, perhaps, in demoralizing men who might have been able to give their country better leadership—officers and government officials who tried, in the swamp of graft and favoritism and influence peddling, to do their jobs honestly and competently, or even just to fight the war with a sense of honest patriotism.

There were many such officers, but the one I remember most vividly was a paratroop major I met in a rest camp north of Hue, the commander of a battalion that had just suffered fearful losses in the battle to recapture Quang Tri city.

He had been a combat officer for nine years, the major said. He had no powerful friends and no money and did not expect ever to sit behind a desk—or to be promoted, for that matter, unless a superior was killed or disabled. For anyone used to the American army's system of rotating assignments and scheduled promotions, this business of men serving in combat jobs for years and years, with no respite, took some getting used to. But that was how the South Vietnamese army worked. Sitting in a field tent and nipping stronger and stronger slugs of brandy, the major spoke on into the evening about the government whose uniform he wore. As he talked, his face hardened in the flickering light of the lantern hanging from the tent-pole. In it was something far deeper than the combat soldier's dislike of the rear echelon. It was an unspeakable, angry, corroded bitterness that seemed to come from some unreachable depth in his soul. My notes of that evening's talk were lost—washed into illegibility when that notebook was soaked in a rainstorm up across the My Chanh a day or so later. But I needed no notes to remember the major's summation of his own life. "I do not fight for the government," he said, gesturing at what was left of his battalion—only 150 men or so, fewer than half the number he had led into the battle. "I do not fight for my commanders. I only fight because I am a soldier, because it is my destiny. And I fight for my men. That is all."

The question of Thieu's personal corruption was argued for years. Some who were by no means his admirers still did not think he himself profited, though he clearly tolerated corrupt subordinates. Others were just as sure that he shared in the booty. In 1974 the People's Anti-Corruption Movement, one of a number of protest organizations that sprang into existence as the regime slid into its last decline, charged Thieu and several of his relatives with specific acts of corruption in a document called "Indictment No. 1." It catalogued the Thieu family's properties, which included, besides his residence in the Joint General Staff compound, two other houses in Saigon, a villa in Switzerland, and hundreds of acres of profitable farmland in various parts of the country. No such property could have been amassed, the anti-corruption leaders insisted, without illegal profits from corruption.

The evidence was circumstantial and Thieu denied the charges. In the end it hardly mattered. Whether he himself was corrupt or not, the sickness was imbedded in his regime; he was unwilling or unable to suppress it, and ultimately it was a major reason for the collapse of his army and government.

If his regime had grave defects, Thieu could not have governed South Vietnam for eight difficult years without considerable talents as well. He was a capable organizer and a shrewd tactician, particularly where his own survival was concerned. Critics sometimes compared Thieu with Ngo Dinh Diem, the autocratic mandarin who was South Vietnam's first president before he was overthrown and murdered in 1963. But though there were some similarities, the comparison was inapt. Diem, who spent years in exile rather than serve the French, had a prestige Thieu never attained. Yet Thieu was the more flexible man, a better planner, better informed and usually more realistic. A more accurate comparison perhaps would have been with his admirer Richard Nixon, whom Thieu resembled in his inner lack of self-belief, in an obstinate conviction that he alone knew what was best for his country, and in his inability to trust or confide in anyone except a small group of associates whom he chose for their loyalty rather than for any qualifications for high office. Preternaturally suspicious of all outside his inner circle, Thieu would resemble Nixon, too, in his last crisis: clinging to his office for too long, unable to see or acknowledge his own errors that were bringing him down.

Nguyen Van Thieu reached South Vietnam's presidency from modest beginnings in a village called Tri Thuy, near the town of Phan Rang on the central coast, where he was born April 5, 1923. His father and grandfather were fishermen and farmers. In later life, Thieu sometimes portrayed his origins as very poor. "My mother supported the family by bringing baskets of rice and coconuts to the village market," he told one interviewer. But in fact the family seems to have been modestly prosperous. When Thieu was born they owned twelve acres of land, and there was money enough to send him and his brothers away to school. Thieu's choice of a career, however, was interrupted by the Japanese occupation of Indochina in the summer of his eighteenth year. Returning home, he spent the war years in his village. In the turbulence following the Japanese surrender in 1945, he flirted briefly with the local branch of the Viet Minh, but soon turned against them. After first studying to become a merchant marine officer, Thieu entered the French-founded Dalat Military Academy, graduating in 1948.

Following a year of further training in France, he returned to Vietnam as an infantry lieutenant. His military service lasted all through France's unsuccessful war against the Viet Minh. If he felt any ambivalence about fighting against his own country's independence, it does not show in the public record of his life. By 1954, Thieu had reached the rank of major and commanded a battalion. When South Vietnam achieved independence that year, he transferred to the army of the new republic. And as the United States replaced France as Saigon's patron, Thieu traveled twice to the U.S., in 1957 and 1960, for training.

Born a Buddhist, Thieu married into a Catholic family and in 1958 converted to Catholicism himself—a convenient decision under the Diem regime, in which Catholics were consistently favored in promotions. But when restive officers overthrew Diem, Thieu, then commander of the 5th ARVN Division, joined the revolt, which installed Gen. Duong Van Minh as president. In later years, when Thieu and Minh had become political enemies, Minh accused Thieu of having delayed his assault on Diem's palace guards until after the success of the coup was assured. If true, it would not have been the first time or the last that Nguyen Van Thieu refused to move until he could see clearly in which direction his own interests lay.

Thieu stepped adroitly through the succession of coups and reshuffles that followed the overthrow of Diem. In June 1965 he joined what would be the last of the military regimes, a junta that went under the name of the National Leadership Committee. Thieu, by now a lieutenant general, was its chairman and for protocol purposes the head of state, although the real authority was held by Prime Minister Nguyen Cao Ky, the flamboyant, mustachioed commander of the South Vietnamese air force.

The United States, which had begun bombing North Vietnam in February of that year and introduced its first ground combat units the next month, welcomed the military takeover. The generals represented Vietnam's "most important single institution of national cohesion" if they could remain united, Ambassador Maxwell Taylor cabled Washington, and thus their control "responds to the reality of the situation. . . . It also appears probable to us that the generals are less likely than any purely civilian government to panic and abandon the war effort in favor of negotiations and neutralism." On that score, at least, Nguyen Van Thieu would not disappoint his American backers; in return, their support for him would be constant and unswerving for nearly a decade.

In the next two years, while a new constitution was adopted that set presidential elections for September 1967, Thieu worked quietly to solidify his alliances within the military hierarchy. When the generals gathered to pick the "official" candidate, he, not Ky, was selected; Ky was forced to withdraw his already-declared candidacy and join Thieu as vice-presidential nominee. The election, when it was held, was the only one in modern Vietnamese history to offer a semblance of a true contest. Eleven candidates, of eighteen who sought to run, qualified for places on the ballot. Thieu and Ky won with 1.6 million votes, just over one-third of the total. Truong Dinh Dzu, a "peace candidate" who campaigned for prompt peace negotiations and reconciliation with the Liberation Front, was a surprise second-place finisher, with 817,120 votes. Dzu's campaign, however, marked the last time such views would be permitted in a political contest in South Vietnam. He himself was arrested the following February and convicted by a military court of "conduct detrimental to the anti-Communist spirit of the people and the armed forces." He served five years in a series of prisons, including Saigon's Chi Hoa jail and the well-known Con Son island prison colony, before being released in March 1973.

As president, Thieu consolidated his control of the military leadership, isolating his rivals, dispersing potential plotters, and awarding key commands to generals whose loyalty he could depend on. At the same time he nursed the army through successive nervous crises as the Americans withdrew between 1969 and 1972. With the help of numerous American and other foreign experts, he instituted extensive land reforms—probably his administration's single most popular program, and his most important attempt to match the Communists in offering social change to Vietnam's peasants.

For a time, in the late 1960s and until the 1972 Easter offensive, the Thieu government gave the appearance of success. The destructive Tet offensive of 1968 had turned many Vietnamese against the Viet Cong, whom they blamed for bringing war to their towns and villages, while the Communists lost many of their most experienced political agents and guerrilla commanders. The general mobilization that was declared after Tet also tended to bind more people to the government side, since from 1968 on, few families did not have some member serving in the government army or militia. The "thousands of farm boys who have been churned through the military machine have perhaps become no more pro-government," a journalist observed, "but they have definitely become more anti-Viet Cong. It is immensely easy to dislike someone who is trying to kill you." With every draftee, parents, wives, children, sisters, and brothers all acquired an instant sympathetic concern, if not for the success of the government army, at least for the safety of whatever unit their men were in.

Mobilization had its dark side too. "A young man entering ARVN at present," a perceptive American official noted, "may well be entering for life. He is leaving normal society and will probably never be able to return during his useful life. He thus feels alienated and loses interest in that society." Ultimately that alienation would become a grave peril. But in Thieu's first term in office, the danger was not yet apparent.

The shift in loyalty from the Viet Cong to the government also reflected the greatly increased violence that was made possible by American firepower and that was turned more and more on the rural areas whose "pacification" was now the chief U.S.-South Vietnamese objective. In areas that had been historically under Viet Cong control and where people gave allegiance to the Liberation Front as a matter of course, "suddenly, bombing, defoliation, Phoenix raids and forays by American and government troops became a daily occurrence," wrote one long-time observer. "And as a result supporting the Viet Cong turned from being an almost mindless act to something that was very dangerous. . . . whatever valid revolutionary ideas had been transmitted from the Viet Cong cadres to the peasants and urban dwellers of South Vietnam had been deadened in favor of an overpowering concern for their personal welfare."

Another American reported the same conclusion after surveying attitudes in Binh Duong Province north of Saigon during 1970. In contrast to the mid-1960s, living under the Viet Cong now meant "minimal supplies of rice, constant fear of sudden death and no chance to make a living," he found. In 1970 and 1971 more than 50,000 Communists were reported to have "rallied" to the government side. Dramatic increases were recorded in rural security: in mid-1971, official statistics showed 85 percent of the population living in areas that were virtually free of Communist activity, compared with only 50 percent in mid-1969. In the Saigon region and the Mekong Delta, U.S. Defense Department analyses showed, enemy attacks by battalion-sized or larger units "virtually disappeared" by 1971, "except near remote base areas or in Cambodia." One could be skeptical about the statistics, perhaps. Yet the evidence was there to see. Civilian traffic moved on roads where none had traveled a few years before; unarmed American aid workers and correspondents went about freely in hundreds of villages where once they would have dared go only with military escort, or not at all.

The apparent success of pacification led to some exuberant claims. "The military threat is now containable," declared Sir Robert Thompson, the

British antiguerrilla expert who became a frequent consultant to President Nixon. In a paragraph he might not have cared to reread when North Vietnamese tanks drove across the Demilitarized Zone a year later, Sir Robert wrote in 1971 that without the support of the local guerillas the North Vietnamese army could muster "little more than raiding parties" in the South, and that if perfect peace had not been achieved, the Vietnamese were within sight of "a degree of security which they have not enjoyed for the past 25 years." A well-known military affairs writer, retired Marine Col. Robert D. Heinl, Jr., exulted in the *Armed Forces Journal:* "If successful pacification is the yardstick, the war in Vietnam is already settled. We have won."

But pacification was not the yardstick, and its apparent success was not victory. To a large extent it reflected only a strategic retreat, not a surrender or the extinction of the Viet Cong. The heart of "protracted war" strategy, after all, was to avoid combat when conditions were unfavorable. The Communist apparatus, though hurt, was far from destroyed. "Lower level VC suffer while the instigators and organizers of the insurgency continue to operate," reported a Vietnamese-speaking American official from Vinh Binh. The Viet Cong, he added, "still seem to have the same access to the populace that they always possessed. They collect taxes at a better rate than does the government. The enemy is still able to propagandize easily."

American military intelligence specialists surveying two other provinces, Chuong Thien and Binh Duong, found that while the Viet Cong's infrastructure had "suffered numerical losses, their presence and influence in the countryside has not correspondingly diminished." Tax collection, propaganda, and procurement of food were continuing "without serious interruption" by government forces despite the pacification program, and the Communists, the intelligence teams concluded, were "still a strong and feared force in the village. . . . they still have a strong psychological grip on the people."

A study by the CIA's Office of National Estimates about the same time concluded that a substantial proportion of pacification successes occurred "because the Communists, concerned about their manpower losses, chose not to contest pacification as vigorously as in the past. . . . The Communists appear willing to let the present situation prevail and perhaps get a little worse, while they strengthen their apparatus in the expectation that at a later date the [government] gains will be easily reversed."

The Communists, in other words, were able to keep waging political struggle even when their military fortunes were at an ebb—a point many Americans, especially those in senior military positions, were never able to grasp.

These same Americans often failed to see, too, that fear or rejection of the Viet Cong did not necessarily mean approval or support for the Thieu government. Partly, rural loyalties were based on a perception that the Americans and Saigon were becoming stronger than the Communists. Partly they were based on material gain: on the difference between a Japanese-built motorbike and a bicycle; between factory-made shoes and a pair of straw or homemade rubber sandals; between a gasoline-powered pump to lift water from the canals to the rice fields and the old-style earthen jar on the end of a rope. All this spelled an expedient, not a principled, commitment. "Such a political world where all act from self-interest is a topsy-turvy community in constant flux," wrote the author of the Binh Duong survey, adding:

> Today's arrangements will change as people strive to better their position. No one can be relied on; no loyalties are fixed. The man who helped you today may betray you tomorrow. Therefore, gloomy VC prospects at present [1970] do not indicate a secure following for the GVN [Government of Vietnam]. The VC's loss has not been the GVN's permanent gain. People follow the GVN because it is strong and offers a chance to make a living. Should it be unable to maintain both security and a reasonable livelihood for individuals, it will be deserted as was Macbeth by his thanes. . . . Villagers all readily acknowledged that if the VC came back in force, recalculation of behavior would be in order. In fact, the GVN is surrounded by fair-weather friends.

The truth was that the Thieu government offered little except self-interest to command the support of rural Vietnamese. Its officers and officials often refused to share the dangers and hardships of those they sought to lead, unlike the Communist cadres. The regime was tainted with the anti-nationalist past of its president and most of its officers. Officers came from the elite; enlisted soldiers, from the peasantry. The war made rich men of colonels, generals, bureaucrats, and entrepreneurs; it made refugees of the farmers and unwilling draftees of the sons of the common people in the towns and villages. Falling somewhere between democracy and dictatorship, the regime had the disadvantages of both: it was authoritarian enough to be unpopular, democratic enough to be inefficient. Rather than motivating the army or the society to strive to meet national goals, the South Vietnamese system provided haven for opportunists who used privilege and power for their own gain. From the top down, few of its leaders ever seemed to have any real goal other than to perpetuate their own power.

Ostensibly, South Vietnam possessed the trappings of democratic insitutions: elections and a National Assembly in which various parties and political groupings were represented. But these were widely regarded even by those who participated in them as a sham, a false front erected to appease, or deceive, the Americans. "It was a half-hearted democracy whose true nature was autocracy," two of Thieu's generals wrote after the war. "But under pressure from U.S. public opinion . . . this turned out to be a weak and trembling autocracy."

From time to time, Thieu and his American sponsors acknowledged some of the regime's problems, but they invariably shrank from any drastic attempts at reform. Instability and change were more to be feared than any existing weaknesses. And the system stifled change. Under CIA tutelage, the government tried to adapt the Communist concept of political cadres to its own purposes. But it could not supply the unity of purpose that would make its political agents an effective extension of its authority, as the Communists were able to do. And the circumstances of the war made it impossible for any authentic political leadership to emerge in the villages and towns. The government was a military organization preoccupied with military matters. It was not designed to respond to popular sentiment, and the social makeup of its leaders almost assured that it would not. In the countryside, if non-Communist spokesmen for village aspirations appeared, they would be terrorized by the Viet Cong and forced into silence or away to the cities; or the same would be done by those in Saigon government's apparatus who saw their position and its benefits endangered. In South Vietnam's villages, the only contestants for power were the Viet Cong on one side and the bureaucrats and soldiers of the Saigon regime on the other, who controlled, as a Saigon politician once said, "the bodies of the people but not the soul."

In winning and wielding power, Thieu was at once greatly aided and greatly damaged by his association with the Americans. In him, Washington had at last found a leader who could end the disastrous cycle of instability that followed the overthrow of Diem. The Americans had seen him installed at the head of a constitutionally based, elected government that would be easier to defend, in the growing American debate on the war, than the military juntas that had preceded it. It was understood in Saigon that the Americans wanted no more coups d'état. Ambitious generals and politicians all saw that Thieu was the anointed of the distant American president, from whom flowed not just the planeloads of soldiers and weapons and munitions but also the motorbikes, air conditioners, television sets, and other goods flooding into Vietnam on the tide of the artificial American-dollar boom.

These symbols of American wealth and power were, for Thieu, the modern version of the heavenly mandate of the Vietnamese emperors. If they confirmed his power, however, they also branded him a vassal of the foreigners. The common view, indeed, ascribed a degree of American control far beyond any that the U.S. could actually exercise. "The Vietnamese in the street is firmly convinced that the U.S. totally dominates the GVN and dictates exactly what course shall be followed," an American adviser once wrote, lamenting that in reality the Vietnamese were impervious to nearly all American suggestions for reform.

In fact, just as the Thieu regime seemed to combine the worst effects of democracy and dictatorship, the Americans seemed to reap all the disadvantages of both intervention and nonintervention in Vietnamese affairs. The U.S. could not really dictate events, certainly where the personal interests of members of the Vietnamese power structure were concerned. But the Americans did often make Vietnamese decisions meaningless. The sheer weight of the U.S. presence overwhelmed the Vietnamese capacity for organization and leadership, so the result of the alliance in the end was a kind of paralysis. In South Vietnam, during Thieu's years, a fatal passivity ran from the president's office to the village street. Among all but a tiny handful of Vietnamese, the Americans were deemed responsible for Vietnam's fate. Neither in the leadership nor in the population at large—except for the Communists—was there any conviction that the future could be grasped in their own hands. But the Americans, imprisoned in their own faulty doctrines and their ignorance of Vietnamese realities, never found a way to influence the ruling system either. Through the entire war, power in South Vietnam was used only for the personal ends of those who held it.

By the time of the peace agreement, Thieu's relations with his ally had become schizophrenic. Believing he had been sold out at Paris, Thieu became more and more mistrustful of American intentions, worrying constantly, according to some of his associates, that the Americans would engineer his overthrow and perhaps even his murder, as many Vietnamese believed they had been responsible for the assassinations of Ngo Dinh Diem and his brother. Yet Thieu also remained convinced that the Americans would never allow South Vietnam to be defeated by the Communists. As a result, no policy change reflected his changed circumstances. A half-million American soldiers and the enormous weight of U.S. air and firepower had been removed, but Thieu's strategy was still exactly the same as in 1969: "not giving up any real estate," an American military historian wrote, "and trying to keep the North Vietnamese off balance by extensive use of artillery and airpower, with troops being used cautiously. The leadership didn't really believe that the U.S. wouldn't come in with its air and naval power if South Vietnam was about to go under."

In that hope, Thieu clung to the narrowest and most ungenerous interpretations of the Paris agreement. Though there were concessions that did not seem to represent serious risk—creation of the National Council of Reconciliation, for example—Thieu offered none. A different policy in Saigon would not necessarily have made the ceasefire effective. Certainly the Viet Cong, no less than Thieu, remained determined to destroy their enemy. Just as certainly they had not permanently given up the use of military force, whatever temporary tactical compromises they might observe.

Between them Thieu and the Viet Cong had long ago cut away whatever political middle ground might once have existed on which to seek a genuine settlement. They now represented the only choices available to a population that disliked both and was desperately tired of the war. No non-Communist political force in the South had the stature or organization to challenge Thieu. However unloved, he would continue to dominate South Vietnam for two more years after the Paris agreement, until he was overtaken by the sicknesses of his regime, the failures of his policies, and the dimming of the Washington sun.

Chapter **5**

The Americans Leave (1)

The calendar said March 29, 1973. But the last few thousand American soldiers in Vietnam called it "X plus 60"—the 60th day of the truce, and the deadline for the last U.S. troops to go home.

It was, when it came, a day with an overwhelming sense of anticlimax. Camp Alpha, the processing barracks for departing GIs at Saigon's Tansonnhut Air Base ("It's Camp Omega today," someone murmured as we drove through the gate), gave the impression not of a war zone but of a second-rate hotel lobby at the end of a salesmen's convention. In the lines of men coiling out of the gymnasium-like staging area onto buses that would take them to the flight line, you saw none of the teenaged grunts or fresh-faced platoon leaders who actually fought the battles. The last soldiers of America's war in Vietnam were captains and majors and senior sergeants, middle-aged men with thinning hair and thickening waists. Looking at them, you remembered not battle but the beery haze of officers' and NCO clubs. Many of them had seen combat in earlier tours, of course. But they were leaving now from offices, not foxholes, where with typewriters and duplicating fluid they had carried out the necessary but hardly glorious tasks of shutting down the American war machine.

At mid-afternoon, about 50 of them attended a forlorn little ceremony that was the last formation of the Military Assistance Command Vietnam—always called by its acronym, "Mack-Vee"—once an army of a half-million men. In a courtyard outside the huge headquarters building everyone in the little group stood at attention while a terse general order was read: "Head-

123

quarters Military Assistance Command Vietnam is inactivated this date and its mission and functions reassigned." Then an honor guard marched briskly forward carrying the MAC-V flag with its insignia of an upward-pointing sword. Facing Ambassador Bunker and General Weyand, the last MAC-V commander, the flag-bearer dipped the banner, then furled and encased it in an olive-drab bag resembling a golf bag, in which it was to be flown out of the country.

A few hours later, Weyand attended a second ceremony with the chief of the South Vietnamese Joint General Staff, the ineffectual Cao Van Vien. "Our mission has been accomplished," the lanky Weyand pronounced haltingly in Vietnamese from a phonetic script. Then he boarded a special Air Force flight and was gone.

Not many hundred yards away, Vietnamese workers celebrated the historic day by busily and thoroughly looting Camp Alpha's billets and storerooms. Lines of "hooch maids" streamed through the gate carrying electric fans, clothing, lamps, stacks of old magazines and paperbacks, and other booty that could be used or sold in the Saigon market. Another group, including off-duty Vietnamese soldiers and airmen in civilian clothes, ripped away a section of chicken-wire fence to break into the mess hall, which was supposed to be turned over to the international truce observers. Ignoring the curses of a few furious Americans who had worked past midnight to tidy up for the new tenants, the intruders carried off tables, chairs, and crates of food. Even ceiling fans were ripped from their fixtures. The crowd turned unruly, though still good-natured, and began smashing what could not be carried away. In less than fifteen minutes, the formerly immaculate dining room was a shambles of broken bottles, spilled food, and upturned furniture—a tiny but telling metaphor, I thought, for the country we had thought to save with American technology and wealth but had never fully understood.

The three-day airlift removing the last American troops had been carefully calibrated to coincide with the release of the last group of U.S. war prisoners. On March 27, 32 men were handed over to U.S. representatives in Hanoi and flown aboard U.S. Air Force hospital planes to Clark air base in the Philippines. On the 28th, 50 more were released, including ten captured in Laos whose status had been the subject of a tense ten-day dispute in the Joint Military Commission. And on the 29th, another 67 prisoners, the last of a total of 595 freed in the exchanges, were flown to freedom. In Saigon, the last 5,200 U.S. servicemen were flown out at a rate roughly matching the repatriation of the prisoners. Another 825 American military delegates to the truce commission were to leave in the two days following the deadline, leaving 159 Marine embassy guards and 50 military members of the Defense Attache Office as the only uniformed Americans remaining in Vietnam.

By the time the last flight of the 29th was ready to load, a slanting afternoon sun was casting long bars of shadow across the tarmac. Communist truce delegates in baggy green uniforms clustered about the plane, aiming cameras at the departing Americans as they compiled a copious photographic record of what was, to them, a triumphant occasion. A few dozen American and European reporters and cameramen also recorded the scene. Not far away but unnoticed was a flatbed truck loaded with twenty coffins: South Vietnamese dead, flown back from the north to be buried.

At planeside a Communist colonel named Bui Tin, the spokesman for the North Vietnamese truce delegation, was carrying a gift: a straw-mat painting of a Hanoi street scene, which he planned to present as a memento to the last departing American. When Master Sgt. Max Beilke of Alexandria, Minnesota, stepped onto the boarding stairs, Colonel Tin hurried forward and thrust the package at him. But the gesture was too early. A few minutes later, while Tin watched empty-handed, two more Americans boarded the plane, Col. David Odel of Crystal Lake, Illinois, the Tansonnhut base commander, and Chief Master Sgt. Vincent R. Jacobucci of Forest Hills, New York, his senior noncommissioned officer.

Odel and Jacobucci paused for a moment at the top of the boarding steps, waved back to the truce observers and cameramen on the ground, then disappeared inside. The doors slid closed and the huge C-141 transport swerved toward the taxiway. At 6 P.M., 60 days and ten hours after the failed truce, it lumbered off the ground into an orange sunset that silhouetted the watchtowers out on the airport perimeter. For the first time in over eleven years—it seemed longer—there was no significant American military presence in Vietnam.

The United States was not beaten: that was, and has remained, an article of faith for most American military professionals.

In the narrow sense that major U.S. units were never overwhelmed in battle, it is true. Yet on that day in March of 1973, if you looked on military order-of-battle maps for the place names that had appeared in America's newspaper headlines or flashed across its television screens, you would find nearly all of them in Communist-held zones. The Ia Drang valley, Dak To, Con Thien, Khe Sanh, the Parrot's Beak, the nameless ridge somebody called Hamburger Hill—not one of them remained in friendly hands. U.S. commanders never stopped explaining that the war was not fought to hold territory. But to a confused and increasingly skeptical public at home and to many of the soldiers themselves, the pattern of bloody battles followed by abandonment of the battlefields came to symbolize the futility of an ill-conceived war. "UUUU," some GIs scrawled on their helmet covers, standing for "the unwilling, led by the unqualified, doing the unnecessary for the ungrateful."

Those soldiers and their comrades fought bravely, on the whole, if often cynically. They surely deserved better than the indifference or contempt many of them met when they returned home; whoever was to blame for the war's mistakes, it was certainly not the young men who were sent to fight in it.

It was also true, though, that what was achieved by American arms hardly seemed commensurate with the effort that had been made or the resources that had been expended—which were vastly greater than those available to the enemy. The American expeditionary force in Vietnam, said one army study, enjoyed "a degree of tactical mobility and devastating conventional firepower unparalleled in military history. . . . The logistics scene was characterized by almost unlimited supply, remarkable [sic] high operational readiness rates as applied to equipment, a seemingly endless flow of ammunition and petroleum and immunity for the most part from external fiscal restraints." In contrast to past wars, commanders were not subject to rationing of weapons, ammunition, or fuel. Whatever they said they needed, in most cases, they got.

In firepower, the disparity between the two sides was so enormous as to make the war seem hardly a contest at all. According to Pentagon records, U.S. forces during 1969 used 128,400 tons of munitions a month: 75,600 tons of bombs and the rest in ground munitions.* The highest Communist expenditure of the war, not reached until 1972, was only about 1,000 tons a month—*less than 1 percent* of what the Americans used. As late as 1974, when South Vietnamese commanders were bewailing severe shortages and when their forces were losing positions all over the country, the government was still using 56 tons of ammunition for every ton used by the Communists.

The American army and its supplies were flown about in more than 3,000 helicopters. It was supported by hundreds of fighters and bombers. It had every manner of military gadgetry, it seemed, ever devised by man. It was facing an opponent, as the former pacification chief Robert Komer once wrote, "that walked, that used mortars as its chief form of artillery, that used

---

* A large percentage of this colossal firepower was expended in empty jungles. At some stages of the war, nearly two-thirds of all shells and bombs were aimed at "places where the enemy *might* be, but without reliable information that he *was* there," according to Pentagon systems analysts. A 1966 study, though based on fragmentary evidence, suggested among other conclusions that fewer than 100 Communist soldiers were killed in the entire year by such "harassment and interdiction" firing—which cost, incidentally, two billion dollars—but that it did supply the enemy with 27,000 tons of dud bombs and shells that could be turned into mines and booby traps, which caused over 1,000 American deaths in that year. Even among American commanders there were some who were skeptical of harassing tactics. No less than Lt. Gen. Frank Mildren, the army's deputy commander in Vietnam, declared, "In my estimation, pure H & I fires in the Vietnam environment have little, if any, value while doing practically no damage to the enemy." The army's own study of artillery use in Vietnam observed neutrally, "There were many who agreed with General Mildren, but there were many who did not."

almost no armor until 1972, and that was near-totally lacking in air support." Yet what was achieved was no better than an ambiguous standoff.

Many, perhaps most, military men blamed political limitations for the war's disappointing result. But there was another view: that U.S. military commanders massively misunderstood and mismanaged the conflict. "The military disaster in Vietnam grew out of ineptitude at the top," charged "Cincinnatus," the author of an angry, pseudonymous book he titled *Self-Destruction: The Disintegration and Decay of the United States Army During the Vietnam Era.* The Americans had no strategy except to inflict casualties they hoped would break the Communists' will to continue the war. They did kill appalling numbers, but their calculus proved incorrect; throughout the war, the Communists proved able to absorb their losses without either altering their long-range objective or losing discipline in their army or population. And they were able to control the rate of attrition by avoiding battle whenever it suited their purposes.

Compounding the errors of the attrition policy, the Americans falsely reported and evaluated their progress. Military commanders have exaggerated enemy casualties, as Cincinnatus observed, ever since Samson reported slaying a thousand foes with the jawbone of an ass. But in Vietnam, the "body count" became the *only* standard of battlefield achievement, and thus of the success and future promotion of field commanders. The result was intense pressure to report huge numbers of enemy deaths, whether the figures were reliable or not. When Vietnam-era generals were polled after the war, 61 percent said they believed the body counts were inflated. "The immensity of the false reporting," wrote one of the respondents, "is a blot on the honor of the army."

Claims from the field were further padded as the reports went up the chain of command. "Battalions raised the figures coming in from the companies, and brigades raised the figures coming in from the battalions," admitted one former Pentagon official. "In addition, something had to be (and was) put in for all the artillery and air support . . . to give the supporting arms their share of the 'kill.' "

South Vietnamese body counts, which may have been even less trustworthy than American reports, were also given a spurious credibility by being reproduced, without any disclaimers, in official reports that were distributed in the U.S. defense and foreign affairs bureaucracies and to Congress.

Not content with the reported body counts, in fact, American analysts increased ARVN's claim of enemy deaths by 35 percent, an arbitrary estimate of the number of Communist soldiers who died of wounds or were permanently disabled. In 1972 this method produced an astonishing estimate of 180,000 enemy troops permanently put out of action, or more than half the entire Communist combat force. If only one man were wounded for each one killed, that would mean the entire Communist army had become casualties. Yet despite its obvious absurdity, the statistic was enshrined in official reports, no doubt contributing to the Nixon administration's optimistic assessments of the battlefield balance at the time of the ceasefire.

By the time it flew out of Vietnam in March of 1973, the American army was full of moral and professional confusion that could not be easily suppressed. Much of its doctrine had been disproven or put in question. Many of its units had declined in morale and discipline. The traditional military values seemed to be eroding. Though the results of their efforts steadily proved disappointing, American commanders retained a fatuous optimism about the future, always promising that success was not far off if only the public and the political leadership would be patient and keep supporting them. They grumbled about politically imposed restraints, but no responsible commander ever told his civilian superiors that the mission could not be accomplished under the conditions established for the war. Nor did senior commanders welcome such news from their subordinates. When the shortcomings of their strategy became apparent, American military leaders never seemed to have anything to propose but more of the same. They were less callous, no doubt, but seemed no more imaginative than the World War I generals who, after wasting whole armies in the dreadful slaughter of that war's trenches, could think of nothing except to send more armies to die in the same seas of mud.

It was left to an enemy to pronounce verdict on the American war in Vietnam. Just before Saigon surrendered to the Communists in 1975, an American colonel burst out to a North Vietnamese liaison officer, "You know you never defeated us on the battlefield." The Communist officer considered for a moment. "That may be so," he replied, "but it is also irrelevant."

Whatever damage it did to itself, the U.S. military leadership's worst blunder may have been to create and perpetuate a South Vietnamese army that became, Cincinnatus wrote, "a mirror image of the American military system with all its blindnesses."

At its inception in the 1950s, the U.S. military aid program in Vietnam was designed to meet a North Vietnamese invasion, not a guerrilla threat. The model was the Korean War, still fresh in the minds of the American officers who were assigned to Saigon in the early years of the Republic. Under their tutelage, South Vietnam's army was formed as a highly conventional force, top-heavily organized into corps and divisions—a "road-bound, over-motorized, hard-to-supply force," wrote Bernard Fall, that was grotesquely unsuited for the conditions in which it would have to fight. "It was not until 1959," U.S. army historians acknowledged years later, "that the internal subversion and insurgency openly supported by the North was recognized as the major threat."

American advice was damaging for more reasons than just a strategic miscalculation. It also stifled Vietnamese leadership and creativity. The South Vietnamese officer corps was accustomed to taking French orders; it now invariably accepted American suggestions. Training materials were word-for-word translations of American manuals, without even a paragraph tailored for Vietnamese circumstances. Because of their experience and understanding of their own society, the Vietnamese should have been more knowledgeable and creative than the Americans in such areas as antiguerrilla techniques. But their military leaders, through the entire war, developed no doctrine or strategies of their own. "The fact that they have no leadership is largely our fault," an American official would lament as the government army was collapsing in 1975; "we made them followers. . . . the North Vietnamese have succeeded because their generals and their officers are leaders."

What the South Vietnamese did have was a force that "acquired the habits of a rich man's army," two of its generals wrote later. When U.S. air and artillery support were available, many ARVN units didn't even bother to carry their mortars into battle with them. Following the example set by U.S. officers, Vietnamese commanders customarily pulled back as soon as their troops contacted enemy forces and called in air strikes, even against no more significant opposition than a few snipers. While they could, it was inevitable that the Vietnamese would keep fighting in the American style. No commander in any army is going to turn down fire support that is there for him to use. But the habit was hard to break. After the ceasefire, when the South Vietnamese army was suddenly faced with the loss of American firepower, not only were its self-confidence and morale shaken but its very ability to survive was put in doubt.

"We have created an army in our own image that depends on massive firepower and mobility. When these assets are removed, operational paralysis sets in," warned an American army officer in a 1972 paper that thoughtfully but futilely suggested an advisory program aimed at teaching tactics that could be sustained after a U.S. withdrawal. Instead, the U.S. gave the impression, with the Enhance and Enhance Plus buildup, that American resources would be available indefinitely and in unlimited quantity. And so the South Vietnamese believed. No adjustments in ARVN's training or doctrine followed the ceasefire. It was more than a year before it was even put under orders to conserve ammunition, and even then, the orders were not rigidly observed, for fear that cutting back too sharply would wreck the soldiers' morale.

In the period leading up to the ceasefire, and in the months that followed, American policymakers do not seem to have addressed very seriously the question of whether ARVN could continue fighting with the methods Americans had taught. The assumption was that Congress would provide the necessary aid. But that was far from certain: lawmakers who had clearly run out of patience with supporting their own country's war effort were not likely to be generous for very long in aiding a Vietnamese regime that was widely seen in the U.S. as ineffective and unpopular.

The cost of the war as ARVN fought it, moreover, was beyond South Vietnam's means not just in money but in men, which the Americans could not provide. Deaths and desertions, especially from 1972 on, outnumbered the approximately 150,000 young men who theoretically became available for conscription each year—of whom only about 90,000 actually entered the armed forces. Even before the heavy losses of the 1972 offensive, Pentagon systems analysts had concluded that South Vietnam "cannot continue with over one million men in the armed forces." The same study estimated that if Saigon's military doctrines and tactics remained unchanged, it would require a minimum of $3 billion a year in U.S. military and economic aid on into the indefinite future. "Even this level," the study added, "may not be enough to provide adequate military security. . . . The Vietnamese are at present hard pressed to accommodate the war cost even with such a U.S. support level." That estimate was made in 1971, when the war was at its lowest level in years and before the worldwide inflationary surge later in the decade; in any event, no aid bill after the 1973 ceasefire ever came close to the $3 billion mark.

A few analysts tried to suggest means of forming a "people's army" trained to wage a less expensive war after the Americans withdrew. One such study by the Rand Corporation's Brian Jenkins commented in 1971 that without some move in that direction, South Vietnam's economic problems "could produce popular unrest, political agitation, and government instability, which ultimately would be reflected in weakness on the battlefield." Those problems included inflation, unemployment resulting from the U.S. withdrawal, and "the plight of South Vietnam's soldiers, who find themselves impoverished by low salaries and soaring costs"—problems which would quickly prove after the ceasefire to be even graver than anyone could have predicted in 1971. Jenkins's conclusion was that "the South Vietnamese have no choice but to try to develop a cheaper way to defend their country, and to do so before reductions in foreign aid immobilize the army they have now, and before the country collapses while trying to support and man it."

Whether there was any means of following that advice will never be known, because it was never tried. Instead, while the U.S. administration mortgaged Saigon's future with new arms that were costly to maintain and use, Congress did reduce aid, in part because of misleadingly optimistic assessments given to it by the executive branch. South Vietnam's economy and its leadership weakened drastically in the two years after the ceasefire, and when its army crumbled in 1975, a major reason would be the American decisions that had formed, equipped, trained, and indoctrinated it in accord with American, and not Vietnamese, realities.

The completion of the U.S. troop withdrawal and of Operation Homecoming—the recovery of the P.O.W.'s—were the last unequivocal achievements of American diplomacy in Vietnam. Within a few weeks, all the rest of the arrangements set out in the Paris agreement began to evaporate. Though the U.S. administration continued to claim a fictitious peace, its actions and those of both Vietnamese sides quickly grew to be predicated on a continuing war. For the remaining two years of the conflict, no U.S. dealings either with the Communists or with Saigon accomplished any American purpose. Nor were any of them free of ambiguities and distortions that would lead to accusations of American bad faith both from its enemy and its ally.

Between the United States and North Vietnam, two significant matters remained to be settled. One was the accounting for missing-in-action servicemen and repatriation of the remains, if they could be recovered. The other was the promise that the U.S. would "contribute to healing the wounds of war" in North Vietnam as well as elsewhere in Indochina. The disputes over these matters lingered long after the war ended and involved a succession of the same misunderstandings and mutual misperceptions that had beset America's confrontation with the Vietnamese from its very beginnings. The Communists supplied information on only a small fraction of missing Americans while leaving an ugly impression that they were bargaining for aid with the bones of dead Americans and the feelings of their families; for their part, they felt they were promised postwar aid without conditions, and regarded its denial as an act of outright duplicity.

The American negotiators assigned to the Four-Party Joint Military Team to deal with missing-in-action matters (not to be confused with the Joint Military Commission) were hopeful at first. An atmosphere of "friendly cooperation" marked their first meetings, an official chronology reported, leaving the U.S. delegation hopeful that the task of accounting for the missing could be substantially completed in a matter of weeks, or perhaps a few months at most. The North Vietnamese delegates promised to meet their obligations "scrupulously." A campaign was already beginning throughout the North to collect information about downed pilots and air crewmen, they told the Americans. But then they began stalling. A U.S. proposal for sending teams to investigate known crash sites was rejected. Though American delegates were allowed to visit a cemetery near Hanoi where 24 Americans were buried, it took another ten months before any remains were handed over. Even then one body was withheld, on the technicality that he had not died while a prisoner but when his plane crashed.

A formal protest by the U.S. to Hanoi declared that "the accounting for the missing and the repatriation of the remains are purely humanitarian obligations unrelated to other issues," a position also taken by American delegates in the Joint Military Team sessions every Tuesday and Thursday in a conference room at Tansonnhut. The North Vietnamese, however, argued that the MIA search must be related to progress on other matters, especially economic aid. Off the record, they were rather candid. "Of course we have information on many of your MIA personnel, and in some cases even the remains of your pilots we shot down," a North Vietnamese delegate told one of the American officers during a coffee break one day. He added bluntly:

> And you must know that we do not like to keep them. Their graves defile our ancestral soil, and are ugly reminders of the horrors of the bombing. . . . So we want to give them back. But why should we give them to you for nothing? Your government has done so much damage to our people and our land that it must pay. That is your obligation, and even your president committed himself to this. So we will not give you what you want just because you ask for it or demand it.

American teams were able to conduct a few investigations within South Vietnamese-controlled territory. Eighteen searches between May and December 1973 recovered the remains of nine previously missing Americans—seven of these at a single site in dense jungle near Nha Trang, where local hunters found the wreck of a U.S. helicopter that had vanished in 1969. Because the P.R.G. had once warned U.S. investigators that a prospective search area was insecure, the Americans felt a precedent was set for notification of unsafe zones. But on December 15, when three unarmed helicopters marked with the bright orange stripes and initials of the Joint Military Commission landed a search team at a place called Binh Chanh, just ten miles southwest of Saigon, Communist troops opened fire moments after the searchers stepped onto the ground. A rocket grenade landed squarely on one of the helicopters, blowing it up and killing the Vietnamese pilot. The other two quickly took off, leaving the American team on the ground. One of them, 32-year-old Capt. Richard M. Rees of Kent, Ohio, stood and raised his hands over his head. Like the others, he wore an orange armband identifying him as a member of the truce team, and he carried no weapon. As he stood he tried to shout something over the sound of the gunfire, but his comrades couldn't make out what he was saying. Then he crumpled back to the ground, dead.

Blandly, the Communist delegates insisted they were never told of the planned search at Binh Chanh. The U.S., however, declared that proper and detailed notification had been given to both the P.R.G. and the North Vietnamese a full week earlier. Maj. Richard Laritz, the American team's operations officer, was blunt and furious. Captain Rees, he said, was "murdered in cold blood."

The Binh Chanh incident ended all searches and left the Americans embittered not only at the death of an unarmed U.S. officer but at the Communists' callous refusal to ease the feelings of American MIA families. The

North Vietnamese, however, were no less outraged at the United States for backing down on the promised postwar aid—which, from Hanoi's view, was presumably a "humanitarian" issue as well.

The U.S. commitment was embodied not only in the vaguely-worded Article 21 of the Paris agreement but in a secret personal message from President Nixon to Prime Minister Pham Van Dong, delivered four days after the agreement was signed. Its wording was carefully negotiated in advance by Henry Kissinger and Le Duc Tho, and listed these among the "principles" under which Article 21 was to be carried out:

> 1) The Government of the United States of America will contribute to the postwar reconstruction in North Vietnam without any political conditions.
>
> 2) Preliminary United States studies indicate that the appropriate programs for the United States contribution . . . will fall in the range of 3.25 billion dollars of grant aid over five years. Other forms of aid will be agreed upon between the two parties. This estimate is subject to revision and to detailed discussion between the Government of the United States and the Government of the Democratic Republic of Vietnam.

At Hanoi's insistence, the text nowhere made the aid conditional on Congress's approval. There was, however, a separate one-paragraph "addendum" saying that both countries would implement the agreement in accordance with their "constitutional provisions." Kissinger, during his four-day visit to Hanoi shortly after the Paris accords were signed, handed his hosts a document stating more explicitly, "In matters of economic assistance [the president] can only recommend to the Congress. . . . the president may not expend funds except those which are authorized and appropriated by the Congress."

Details of the aid program were to be worked out by a U.S.-North Vietnamese Joint Economic Commission, the Nixon message said, if possible within 60 days. The commission's establishment was announced, though without mention of the proposed $3.25 billion funding or the timetable, at the end of Kissinger's Hanoi visit. Subsequently Pham Van Dong replied to Nixon with a letter of his own, repeating all of Nixon's points and adding several additional ones, which like Nixon's had been agreed on in advance: that the commission would be established on March 1, with three members from each side, and would be headquartered in Paris.

To the North Vietnamese the exchange of messages constituted a binding codicil to the peace agreement. Relying on the phrase "without any political conditions" that occurred in Nixon's letter, they insisted that reconstruction aid was an absolute U.S. obligation not connected with any other issues—the same claim the Americans made with respect to the missing-in-action search. Nixon and Kissinger, however, took the position that aid was not only subject to congressional approval but also that it depended on substantial compliance by the Communists with the rest of the Paris agreement.

Two weeks after the Joint Economic Commission began meeting in mid-March, it concluded a basic agreement on "principles, functions, organization and working procedures" for the aid program—an agreement that repeated Nixon's message that aid would be provided with no political conditions. At that point, there seemed no obstacle to a final agreement. Within a few days, however, and almost immediately after the last American prisoners had been freed, the U.S. position began to change. Just as the Communist delegates had done with respect to the missing-in-action search, the Americans now demanded progress on other, unrelated issues as a condition for completing the aid agreement.

These matters included not just the MIA question and North Vietnam's infiltration of fresh troops and supplies into the South, but—prominently— the crisis in Cambodia, where a weak U.S.-sponsored government was under grave threat from Communist insurgents armed by Hanoi and where heavy American bombing was continuing. The problem of Cambodia was one of many ambiguities in the Paris agreement. Article 20 required withdrawal of foreign troops and an end to military actions in Cambodia and Laos by the Americans and both Vietnamese sides, which would appear to demand both that the North Vietnamese remove their troops *and* that the Americans stop bombing. The article set no deadline and provided no enforcement procedure, however, and the State Department's legal interpretation, at least when the agreement was drafted, was that it stated "objectives, not present obligations," which would become binding only when included in separate Laos or Cambodian settlements.

In the written understandings exchanged by Kissinger and Le Duc Tho, the Vietnamese had privately assured arrangement of a ceasefire in Laos, and an agreement between the American-backed Lao government and the Lao Communists was duly signed, though somewhat later than Hanoi had promised. But the Vietnamese refused to be made responsible for a ceasefire in Cambodia. Hanoi, Tho repeatedly told Kissinger, did not control the Cambodian insurgent movement.

During the post-ceasefire negotiations, however, Nixon and Kissinger began to set progress in Cambodia as the price for completing the economic aid agreement. While insisting that U.S. bombing there was justified until the Cambodian sides reached a ceasefire, the U.S. leaders demanded that North Vietnam withdraw its troops immediately, thus seeming to assert one interpretation for themselves and another for Hanoi, even though the obligations of both under the Paris agreement were identical. Nor, apparently, was a withdrawal under Article 20 the only demand. "Another condition for economic aid," a congressional committee investigating the

MIA issue reported being told by Kissinger, ". . . was an armistice in Laos and Cambodia"—even though the Paris agreement set no such requirement and the North Vietnamese had repeatedly insisted they could not guarantee that a Cambodian settlement would be arranged.

Cambodia was also a major reason for a series of other American actions in mid-April which, in Communist eyes, jeopardized the Vietnam peace agreement. One signal was in Laos, where B-52s and fighter-bombers carried out two days of strikes April 16 and 17 at a place called Tha Vieng, where Washington charged the Communists were attacking in violation of the Laos truce. Presumably this was true; yet there was no evidence of any general offensive threatening the Laos agreement, and the renewed raids could only be interpreted as a warning that more serious bombing might follow, perhaps on North Vietnam itself. Also on April 17, the U.S. naval task force that was clearing mines in North Vietnamese waters—another obligation under the Paris ceasefire—was abruptly recalled, "because of difficulties in Laos and Cambodia," according to its commander. Within a day or so U.S. reconnaissance flights resumed over North Vietnam for the first time since the ceasefire, another obvious warning. And simultaneously with these warnings, the U.S. broke off the Joint Economic Commission talks, recalling the head of its delegation, Maurice Williams, back to Washington.

Within the administration, proposals for resuming the bombing of North Vietnam were being debated during March and April. Henry Kissinger, believing that such a display of force could intimidate Hanoi into complying with American interpretations of the peace agreement, urged Nixon repeatedly for more than a month to order a new series of strikes. But Kissinger was by now almost the only one seriously arguing in favor of such a move. With the Watergate cover-up beginning to come apart, Nixon temporized. And even without Watergate, it was hard to believe that bombing would be politically sustainable. The American public welcomed disengagement from a frustrating war; it could hardly be expected to share Kissinger's concern for the course of future events in Vietnam.

The mood was evident in Congress. "I guess I have been about as regular a Republican, about as loyal an administration Republican as there is in the whole Senate," Sen. Norris Cotton of New Hampshire told Defense Secretary Elliot Richardson during a committee hearing. While U.S. soldiers were still in combat, Cotton felt congressional dissent might encourage the enemy. But now that the Americans were out of Vietnam, he said,

> Speaking as a dyed-in-the-wool, moss-backed administration Republican, I do not want to go on record to authorize one red cent to continue hostilities in Southeast Asia. . . . I think perhaps it has a little more significance for me to say it than for some of my friends

who have been fighting the battle all back through the years. They have been doves all the time. I have just been a dove since we got our prisoners back. . . . I recognize the moral obligation that you and the president and the administration feel, having made these agreements, to enforce them. . . . On the other hand, some of us may feel rather strongly that no matter what have been the terms of these agreements, Congress wasn't party to them, they weren't a treaty of peace, they were executive agreements. The only thing that can possibly happen if we stay over there, whether we fly or whether we just keep our forces there to try to unilaterally. . . . enforce the terms of the agreement, we are just getting back into another conflict over there. I cannot see it any other way. . . . I think the time has come now when we are free, each of us, to vote our will.

Even the Pentagon, which raised a series of budgetary and technical objections to Kissinger's plans, seemed less than wholeheartedly eager to get back into the war. Vaguely menacing statements came almost daily from administration spokesmen, but there was no real will to act, and on April 17, the same day the two-day series of strikes in Laos ended, Kissinger drew back, proposing now to wait until there was a "clear-cut provocation" from Hanoi. As the Nixon presidency slid deeper into the scandal that finally destroyed it, the bombing plans were shelved, not to be seriously considered again. And by forcing a test with Congress over the peripheral issue of bombing Cambodia, the administration shut the door on its own options: by midsummer, bombing and all other military actions in Indochina were legally forbidden.

While publicly swapping accusations, Washington and Hanoi also agreed in private diplomatic exchanges to resume negotiations. On April 27, William Sullivan opened preparatory talks in Paris with North Vietnam's deputy foreign minister, Nguyen Co Thach, and on May 17, Kissinger and Le Duc Tho began a last effort to rescue the crumbling peace agreement. Once again, American officials pressed for a commitment to arrange a ceasefire in Cambodia; and once again, the Vietnamese denied they were in a position to do so. On June 13, four weeks after they began, the Kissinger-Tho talks produced a joint communique that simply reaffirmed the terms of the original Paris accords. "Ceasefire II," it was called in Saigon, or more derisively, "Son of Ceasefire."

There was no last-minute land grabbing, as in January, and for a few days after the new communique was issued the fighting, except for some sharp battles in the central highlands, fell off dramatically. But the lull did not last long. In an apparent effort to solve the key problem of establishing zones of control, the joint communique called for opposing commanders to meet within 24 hours to arrange means of putting the ceasefire into effect. But this provision was immediately repudiated by the South Vietnamese. No matter what the communique said, the Saigon command announced, its commanders were not authorized to engage in any such meetings until the Joint Military Commission had agreed on procedures. The commission remained paralyzed, the fighting soon resumed at its old intensity, and Son of Ceasefire was proven as fictitious as its parent.

Other provisions of the communique called for resumption of the economic aid talks and the minesweeping. Though all mines should have become inactive anyway, the American task force returned to North Vietnam June 18 to carry out test sweeps. By early July it notified Hanoi that Haiphong and other coastal ports were safe for shipping. The Vietnamese refused to allow American ships or men to sweep inland waterways, however, asking instead for equipment and training so its own forces could do the job. Some help was given, and desultory negotiations on further Vietnamese requests were still going on when U.S. authorities ordered the task force to leave Vietnamese waters again on July 18, for what would turn out to be the last time.

The economic talks, meanwhile, also resumed on June 18, five days after the joint communique was issued, with the chief American negotiator declaring to the North Vietnamese that "their performance on Laos and Cambodia under Article 20 was essential" before the commission's work could reach "a fruitful conclusion." In the next five weeks, the two delegations again agreed on nearly all the matters before them. But instead of completing the agreement the U.S. broke off the negotiations, on the grounds that the North Vietnamese were still violating the peace agreement. The suspension was announced July 23 and described as temporary, but the commission never reconvened.

In Saigon, the Joint Military Team on missing-in-action matters continued to meet until June 1974, when both Communist delegations—the P.R.G.'s and North Vietnam's—announced they would boycott all future sessions. During that time the team accomplished, though only after months of delay, the recovery of the bodies of the 23 Americans officially reported to have died in North Vietnamese prison camps. The P.R.G. acknowledged that 47 more Americans died in captivity in the South, but those bodies were never returned. Otherwise, no progress had been made. The Communist boycott arose from disputes similar to those that paralyzed the Joint Military Commission, issues having to do with their delegates' "privileges and immunities." Some contacts continued with American negotiators, by letter and informally during the liaison flights flown by U.S. Air Force planes to Hanoi, but the boycott of the formal meetings was never lifted.

The failure of Ceasefire II represented the end of the last effort by the United States and North Vietnam to rescue the failed peace. Instead of the "era of reconciliation" promised in the Paris agreement, the post-ceasefire negotiations, both on the missing-in-action issue and on postwar reconstruction aid, left only an increased and enduring mistrustful bitterness in Washington and Hanoi alike.

Toward South Vietnam, the United States behaved not as if carrying out a peace treaty or disengaging, but as if reconfirming a military alliance.

"You can be sure that we stand with you," President Nixon told Thieu as the South Vietnamese leader boarded a helicopter to leave Nixon's compound at San Clemente, California. The date was April 3, 1973—the last time the two men would meet. In the formal joint statement issued after their talks, Nixon pledged to seek "adequate and substantial economic assistance" for South Vietnam, an unspecific but encouraging answer to ambitious plans Thieu had presented for modernizing the armed forces and rebuilding the economy. Denouncing the Communist buildup in the South since the ceasefire, the two presidents declared that "actions which would threaten the basis of the agreement would call for appropriate vigorous reactions." In private, Nixon's reassurances were blunter. Reaffirming promises made while the agreement was being negotiated, he now told Thieu again that the United States "will meet all contingencies in case the agreement is grossly violated."

Thieu's resentment at the terms of the Paris accords was undiminished. But he was profoundly relieved at Nixon's statements, and his doubts about U.S. support, said one member of his party, seemed to be forgotten. He was so encouraged, indeed, that a champagne celebration was held on his plane as he flew away from California.

Within the U.S. government, in fact, there was clearly no desire to return to military force in Vietnam. But in South Vietnam the U.S. went to extraordinary, if secret, lengths to foster Saigon's belief that American air power would be available to retaliate against Communist violations of the truce. The four ARVN corps commanders were flown to the new U.S. Southeast Asia headquarters at Nakhon Phanom in Thailand and given procedures for requesting air strikes. Secret communications equipment was installed linking the South Vietnamese Joint General Staff, the Vietnamese air force headquarters, and the four military region commands with the U.S. command at Nakhon Phanom. ARVN contingency plans all assumed that U.S. air support, particularly from B-52s, would be available against strong enemy attacks; no one discouraged such planning. Vietnamese commanders routinely submitted target lists to the Defense Attaché Office in Saigon for transmittal to the U.S. 7th Air Force. By one account, target information was updated daily.

None of these arrangements were altered, even after the U.S. Congress voted to ban all bombing after August 15, 1973. The hotlines to the 7th Air Force remained in operation, target lists kept on being compiled and updated, and senior Vietnamese officers continued to be flown to Nakhon

Phanom periodically to review plans for American re-intervention. With nothing in their own tradition or experience that equipped them to understand the American constitutional process or the limits of presidential authority, the Vietnamese commanders and planners continued to believe they could rely on American air power in any military emergency. The briefings, contingency plans, hotlines, and all the rest of it, they assumed, reflected the real policy of the American government.

"Our leaders continued to believe in U.S. air intervention even after the U.S. Congress had expressly forbidden it," wrote the ARVN chief of staff after the war. "They deluded themselves into thinking that perhaps this simply meant that U.S. intervention would take a longer time to come because of the complex procedures involved." It was a delusion that would last until the final hours of the war.

To Thieu and his generals, the expectation of U.S. air power involved more than simply rescue if they were threatened with defeat. It also helped confirm them in a military policy that would eventually cause their downfall: a policy requiring defense of all South Vietnamese territory, everywhere in the country, whether feasibly defensible or not. Thieu's belief, as described by one of his advisers, was that "the integrity of the South Vietnamese territory had to be defended at all costs, and that consequently, everywhere there was a Communist attack or infiltration, the South Vietnamese forces must respond immediately." The reason was political: "Mr. Thieu foresaw too the possibility of a political settlement being forced on him and tried, through his 'hold on' policy, to prevent the Communists from claiming that they controlled territory and population inside South Vietnam. So the flag of South Vietnam should be everywhere, even over the remotest outpost of the country."

Clearly, South Vietnam lacked the means to carry out such a policy. It, too, was a delusion.

Diplomatically, U.S. policy after the ceasefire was to extend complete support to the South Vietnamese, no matter what the circumstances. President Thieu's longstanding "Four No's" policy—no negotiating with the enemy, no Communist activity in the South, no coalition government, and no surrender of territory—stood in obvious contradiction to important principles of the Paris agreement. But Washington ignored the contradiction, and Thieu's policy remained unaltered. The U.S. associated itself with all of South Vietnam's complaints about Communist violations but had no criticism of Saigon, even when South Vietnamese actions clearly violated the agreement or when Thieu interpreted it in ways that would hardly contribute to its success.

The public posture evidently reflected the nature of private American diplomacy as well. During the first 60 days of the truce, while a breakdown might have threatened the U.S. withdrawal and the release of American prisoners, U.S. officers on the Joint Military Commission did on occasion remonstrate with their counterparts or other Saigon officials about South Vietnamese obstructionism. At one meeting in mid-February, the deputy chief of the U.S. delegation bluntly told Prime Minister Khiem and several other senior commanders that if South Vietnam's policies were not changed, other countries might conclude that neither Saigon nor the U.S. was sincere about carrying out the agreement. A week later, Maj. Gen. Gilbert H. Woodward, chief of the American delegation, declared to his South Vietnamese counterparts that they were not exempt from compliance just because they were America's allies. Saigon's performance, Woodward said, had not been acceptable.

Such exchanges produced a few minor improvements but no significant change. U.S. officers in Saigon had no sense that their efforts were being assisted at higher levels. "More active support from Kissinger or Haig, representing the President," commented the U.S. delegation's official historian, "would have been more effective in overcoming South Vietnamese foot-dragging."

After the 60-day withdrawal and prisoner exchange were completed and the U.S. was no longer a member of the truce commission, American concern about South Vietnamese actions seems to have diminished even more. The U.S. did put some restrictions on ammunition shipments, especially artillery shells. This apparently reflected not an effort to end the fighting, however, but a belief by American military specialists that munitions were being wasted. In the first months of the ceasefire, in fact, ARVN's gunners were firing 105-mm howitzer rounds faster than American munitions plants could manufacture them. U.S. officers formally notified the South Vietnamese command that it must bring ammunition usage "down to a reasonable defensive expenditure level," and in April 1973, allocations of 105-mm shells to ARVN were reduced by more than two-thirds.

On fundamental issues of observing the ceasefire or striving for any sort of genuine political compromise, there was no sense in Saigon of any serious U.S. effort to change South Vietnamese policies—certainly not after American prisoners had been returned. "We could detect no evidence in Saigon of active policy initiatives emanating from Washington directed at a solution to the problems left unresolved by the Paris agreement," Senate Foreign Relations Committee investigators would report early in 1974. "What we saw and heard, including conversations with senior officials, suggested to us that our present policy toward Vietnam is directed to the maintenance of the status quo at a time when Washington's attention is directed elsewhere."

Without evident concern that he might be risking American support or approval, Thieu kept his army heavily on the offensive from early spring to the end of 1973. It could be argued, perhaps, that his policy was justified by previous Communist violations. But it was indisputable that justified or not, government forces encroached deeply upon territory that was Communist-held at the time of the ceasefire, and to which the Viet Cong presumably had a legal claim. Even while the U.S. government maintained in public that Saigon was substantially complying with the ceasefire, its own internal reports contained plentiful evidence that major South Vietnamese offensive operations were under way.

"Generally speaking," reported a Defense Attache Office assessment soon after Ceasefire II, "enemy actions in the past month have been defensive, designed to hold and improve P.R.G. control. . . . [The Communists] apparently do not plan to initiate offensive action at this time, but generally plan, at least temporarily, to adhere to the ceasefire in regards to main force warfare." But the government army, though nowhere characterized as violating the ceasefire, was described as having been "able to expand its control in several key areas, such as the lowlands of Quang Tin, Quang Ngai and Binh Dinh provinces," while in the Mekong Delta, DAO said, "aggressive ARVN actions against Communist strongholds have continued following Ceasefire II."

In a major operation that lasted from July to October, ten battalions of South Vietnamese rangers supported by armored units pushed the Communists out of the region known as the Seven Mountains in the western delta. In the provinces around Saigon, government units suffered heavy casualties, though without making much progress, in a series of attempts to clear roads that had been blocked by Communist forces since the 1972 Easter offensive or before. In mid-October, heavy air strikes were ordered on Communist bases north of Saigon, aimed, the Saigon command said, at storage areas where ammunition, fuel, and other supplies were stockpiled. Hundreds of sorties were flown in November and December, including one series of missions against Loc Ninh, the most important P.R.G.-held town in the region. The effectiveness of these strikes was questionable. Most of the bombs landed miles from their targets, a Vietnamese air force general confided, because pilots remained at high altitudes to avoid antiaircraft fire. "Poor targeting, poor execution and low VNAF morale" were to blame for the results, he added. According to an agent report that reached DAO, even the Communist gunners groused that VNAF planes were flying higher than their 37-mm guns could reach.

Communist attacks during the summer and fall of 1973 were primarily aimed at protecting their logistical buildup, and were most intense in the western highlands. Though directives and party resolutions circulated to their troops continued to emphasize defensive warfare, the Communist command did not let the ceasefire keep them from assaulting government-held positions if they threatened its road-building and other resupply activities. Beginning in June west of Kontum, their attacks rippled south-ward. In September a ranger camp called Plei Djereng, west of Pleiku, came under attack and fell, even though it had been warned by a Communist defector to expect the assault. 200 of the camp's 293 defenders were killed or captured. Six weeks later, two more border defense bases were overrun in Quang Duc Province in the southern highlands, opening more than a month of extremely heavy combat there.

The Communists also continued to harass isolated government enclaves in other regions. The most publicized battle was at a surrounded ranger base called Tong Le Chan in northern Tay Ninh Province, which was made a major symbol of Communist villainy and ARVN valor. There was nothing symbolic about the cost to the South Vietnamese of its defense, however. During the Tong Le Chan siege, which would last more than a year, enormous quantities of fuel were spent in air resupply missions; inaccurate parachute drops resulted in large quantities of supplies falling into North Vietnamese hands. A special company was formed to collect the errant chutes and their loads, a defecting Communist platoon leader told ARVN intelligence. There was even a deal, he claimed, whereby the Communists agreed not to shoot down the supply planes if the rangers in the base would not fire on their troops collecting supplies outside the perimeter. (There was no such immunity for helicopters, however. At least three were destroyed and a number of others damaged while attempting to land replacements and evacuate the wounded.) Whatever propaganda advantage was secured by its defense, when Tong Le Chan was finally abandoned, precious supplies had been squandered there for little military purpose.

1973 ended with combat still unabated. "Fighting continues," the U.S. Defense Attache Office reported at the close of the year, "with little adher-ence to the accords by either signatory."

On October 16, the Nobel Committee of the Norwegian Parliament announced that the 1973 Peace Prize would be awarded jointly to Henry Kissinger and Le Duc Tho, whose peace agreement, the committee said, "brought a wave of joy and hope for peace over the entire world."

The award was one of the most controversial in the history of the Nobel prizes. Two members of the committee resigned in protest; the next Nobel for literature, it was sardonically speculated in Stockholm, would surely go to Walt Disney. Kissinger was appreciative: "Nothing that has happened to me in public life," he said, "has moved me more than this award." Le Duc Tho, after waiting a week, declined the honor. "Peace has not yet really been established in South Vietnam," he wrote Mrs. Aase Lionaes, president of the Norwegian Nobel committee. "In these circumstances it is impossible for me to accept."

Whether the awards were merited, and if Kissinger's or Tho's were the more appropriate response, might perhaps be debated. But there could surely be no argument that no Peace Prize in history was ever more grotesquely mistimed. For October was the month when, far from heeding the Nobel committee's exhortation to take "moral responsibility for lasting peace for the war-stricken peoples of Indochina," the signers of the Paris agreement let it become a forgotten irrelevancy: "like a dictionary," as one observer memorably put it, "for a language that nobody speaks."

The agreement's only true achievement, the extrication of American forces from the war, had been confirmed and completed, in a sense, by the congressional action ending the bombing of Cambodia on August 15 and barring all U.S. military action in Indochina thereafter. But it was in October, after the beginnings of the constitutional crisis over the Watergate tapes, that the disengagement was made irreversible. From then on the Nixon presidency would remain on the defensive, with little attention to spare for Indochina and no inclination or ability to challenge its domestic adversaries by reintervening there. Increasingly U.S. policy on the war was simply to speak of it in the past tense while hoping that the Thieu regime would survive without trying to redeem Nixon's pledges to enforce the agreement.

It was also in October that the Vietnamese Communists made the first of the crucial decisions that would lead them to their unexpectedly swift victory only a year and a half later. Early that month, the 21st plenum of the Communist party Central Committee convened in Hanoi and approved a resolution declaring that "the path of the revolution in the South is the path of revolutionary violence." Though they would continue for another year to demand a political settlement along the lines specified in the Paris agreement, the Communists' new policy effectively made the ceasefire a dead letter.

The new line was made public in a general order to Communist units issued October 15 and disclosed at the regular Viet Cong press conference in Saigon six days later. Because the U.S. and South Vietnam had "thoroughly, systematically and gravely violated and sabotaged the most essential provisions" of the agreement, the order announced, Communist units were now directed to "strike back at the Saigon administration as long as it has not discontinued its war acts, any place and in appropriate forms and places"—which meant the Communists no longer accepted any obligation at all to recognize government-held territory anywhere in the country. After a second general order November 4 repeating the same points, the Viet Cong announced their policy change in rather more dramatic fashion with a heavy shelling attack on Bien Hoa Air Base near Saigon, destroying three fighters. The attack was justified, the P.R.G. delegation at Tansonnhut declared, because "it is from this airfield that the Saigon administration has sent its aircraft to bomb and strafe liberated zones."

The South Vietnamese had taken the same attitude from the start of the truce, holding that attacking Communist bases was legitimate retaliation for violations elsewhere. Their policy was now stated in more and more aggressive tones, and was also successively broadened to justify attacking wherever and whenever military commanders wanted. By the time the ceasefire's first anniversary approached, there was no discernible difference between the stated "ceasefire policy" and an unqualified state of war. "We will not allow the Communists to enjoy stable security in their staging areas from which they will harass us, attack our posts, destroy our infrastructure bases, sabotage our roads and bridges and seize our rice," President Thieu declared in a speech to officers of the Mekong Delta command early in January 1974. "Appropriate punitive actions" would be taken "not only right in our zone of control, but also right in the areas in which the North Vietnamese Communist troops are still stationed." Nor would the government act only in answer to Communist attacks. "These appropriate punitive actions must be taken beforehand," Thieu explained, "because otherwise, the lives of the compatriots and the troops and their families will be unjustly lost." Under that doctrine, obviously, there was no offensive operation that would not be justified, anywhere and in any circumstances.

The effects of Saigon's military policies were clearly reflected in its own and in American official reporting. The computerized Hamlet Evaluation System, by which U.S. officials monitored the progress of the war, showed that nearly a million more people—6 percent of the population—were brought under government control during 1973. According to official statistics, more than 700 hamlets were wrested from the Viet Cong. The area of Communist-held territory in the South, American officials believed, was reduced by 15 to 20 percent.

These statistics were not considered by the U.S. to be evidence of ceasefire violations, however, even though they represented substantial shifts in the balance that was supposed to have been accepted by both sides under the Paris agreement. Instead, Washington regarded Saigon's actions as taken in legitimate self-defense and in the exercise of its sovereignty. It even welcomed South Vietnamese battlefield successes as testimony of its ally's strength and staying power. The post-ceasefire situation was reported by the administration to Congress in this light, too, so that in the same Senate hearing, while one Pentagon official testified that an additional million people had come under Saigon's control, another Defense Department witness declared, "The South Vietnamese, by comparison with the North Vietnamese, have been exemplary in adhering to the ceasefire agreement."

The American perspective, viewing the 1973 fighting in the context of South Vietnamese successes rather than of a breakdown of the Paris accords, was displayed in a cable sent by Ambassador Martin to Washington the day after Christmas, 1973. Reporting that "the highest officials of the Polish and Hungarian ICCS Delegation have privately informed us that they estimate the NVN/VC forces control 20 per cent less territory than on January 28, 1973," Martin explained that "the joint GVN and U.S. actions in publicizing massive North Vietnamese violations of the Paris agreements has suc- cessfully conditioned world reaction to accept the strong GVN reactions to these . . . violations as quite proper and natural responses to North Viet- namese aggression." Referring approvingly to the "increasingly evident self-confidence and up-beat morale of the GVN and the ARVN," Martin cited South Vietnam's battlefield gains as an argument in favor of continued U.S. support: "The ARVN has not only held well, but has up to now kept the other side off balance. If we remain constant in our support, and determined to carry out the commitments we have made at the highest level"—a reference to Nixon's pledges to Thieu—"we have every right to confidently expect that the GVN can hold without the necessity of U.S. armed intervention."

All was not optimism as 1973 drew to a close. The Defense Attache Office in Saigon expressed growing concern at the Communist buildup, even while ARVN was making gains on the ground. "Hanoi," the DAO declared in a secret assessment at the end of October, "has developed its strongest military position in the history of the war." Three months later, the DAO chief, Maj. Gen. John Murray, gave Washington his appraisal: "The dominant fact is the enemy's strength. Positioned better. Structured better. Unharassed by U.S. air. Supported with: better roads, longer pipelines, larger stockpiles, more guns and tanks and sophisticated equipment." (With what sounded almost like a touch of professional sympathy for his opposite numbers in the enemy command, Murray, a logistics specialist, added, "Vanishing is the enviable logistic simplicity of a bag of rice and a bandolier of bullets.") With the improved road network the Communists had built since the ceasefire, Murray warned, the six divisions poised in the North could "ride quickly, not walk slowly" to the battlefields whenever Hanoi chose to employ them.

In late 1973, too, Murray and his colleagues were also becoming alarmed at growing evidence that U.S. aid was not going to continue at levels required by the scale of war that the South Vietnamese were waging. Congress—which had, after all, been told for months that "peace with honor" had been achieved—was considering cutbacks in the military aid program. Further uncertainties arose even in connection with funds already appropriated, because of vastly complex bookkeeping changes as aid for ARVN was disentangled from funds that had supported the U.S. military effort. So great was the confusion that early in January 1974, in one of the countless messages that hummed between Saigon and various Defense Department headquarters, an exasperated Murray complained, "Cannot determine whether funds here have been cut, or if so, from what to what."

Adding to Murray's difficulties was an order from Ambassador Graham

Martin not to explain the developing aid problem to the ARVN command. The Vietnamese would be too demoralized, Martin told Murray. Evidently convinced that with his own fervent support, and because of the president's pledged word, the necessary funds would be provided in the end, he simply refused to listen to Murray's anguished explanations that because of the months-long lag between orders and deliveries, the Vietnamese had to be told to start economizing right away in order to avoid a crisis later. "They can't stand the shock," he told Murray. The "near disastrous" consequence, as one of Murray's staff later termed it, was that the Vietnamese blithely kept requisitioning and expending supplies at their normal profligate rate—with the result that when reductions were finally imposed, the shock that Martin had sought to avoid would be doubly devastating.

If there was concern about these matters as 1974 began, however, there was not yet any sense of crisis. Within the American government, the dominant note was still one of complete confidence in South Vietnam's future. News from the battle zones still seemed encouraging. In the upper delta, the government remained on the offensive. Soldiers from the 7th and 9th ARVN divisions carried out a major and successful attack in February into a swampy area called Tri Phap at the juncture of Dinh Tuong, Kien Phong, and Kien Tuong provinces, a region that had been a major Communist base since the French Indochina war. ARVN planners were also readying an offensive into Cambodia's Svay Rieng Province—the "Parrot's Beak." But, like the Americans before them, the South Vietnamese were only winning battles and not the war. Their gains at the end of the year, like the promise of peace at its beginning, were an illusion.

PART II

The
Pawns

Chronology

1. L A O S (1972–1975)

1 9 7 2

J U L Y

1   Prime Minister Souvanna Phouma writes to his half-brother Prince Souphanouvong, chairman of the Lao Patriotic Front, proposing a new effort at peace negotiations.

O C T O B E R

17   Peace talks begin in Vientiane.

1 9 7 3

J A N U A R Y

28   Laos time (January 27, Washington time) The Vietnam peace agreement takes effect.

F E B R U A R Y

21   A peace agreement is signed in Vientiane, providing for a ceasefire, an immediate end to U.S. bombing, and formation of a new coalition.

S E P T E M B E R

14   The Vientiane government and the Pathet Lao sign a protocol to the peace agreement, assigning ministries in the coalition and spelling out ceasefire and other administrative procedures.

1 9 7 4

A P R I L

5   The new coalition government is formed.

1 9 7 5

M A R C H – A P R I L

While Communist forces mount their final offensives in Vietnam and Cambodia, Pathet Lao troops seize government-held positions north of Vientiane.

A P R I L

30   South Vietnam's government surrenders to the Communists.

M A Y – J U N E

Pathet Lao forces begin to occupy government-held towns, while Souvanna orders government units not to resist. Communist-inspired demonstrations break out against pro-Vientiane administrators and military commanders, and many rightist officials resign.

A U G U S T

18   Pathet Lao administrators take over Luang Prabang.

23   The Pathet Lao takes control of Vientiane, staging a huge rally to welcome the new administration. Communist troops enter the city.

D E C E M B E R

3   The Lao monarchy is abolished and the People's Democratic Republic of Laos is proclaimed.

2. C A M B O D I A (1969–1975)

1 9 6 9

M A R C H

18   The U.S. begins "Operation Menu," secret bombing of Vietnamese Communist bases inside Cambodia.

A P R I L

16   Prince Norodom Sihanouk, Cambodian head of state, reestablishes diplomatic relations with the U.S. after a four-year break.

26   Sihanouk orders the Cambodian army to adopt an "offensive spirit" against Vietnamese Communist intruders in the border region.

A U G U S T

14   Gen. Lon Nol, the army commander, is named prime minister, and Sisowath Sirik Matak becomes deputy prime minister in a new right-wing cabinet.

N O V E M B E R

      Cambodian army units in the border region are reinforced and ordered to challenge Vietnamese-occupied "sanctuaries."

1 9 7 0

F E B R U A R Y

4   The U.S. Joint Chiefs of Staff report that "Menu operations may have contributed" to more aggressive policy by the Sihaunouk government against the Vietnamese sanctuaries.

M A R C H

      While Sihanouk is abroad, violent demonstrations inspired by Lon Nol and Sirik Matak break out in Phnom Penh against Vietnamese intrusions.

18   The National Assembly deposes Sihanouk as head of state.

23   Sihanouk, in Peking, announces formation of a national united front and a liberation army to fight against the Lon Nol government.

27–28 South Vietnamese army units carry out raids in Cambodia.

29   The Vietnamese Communists attack Cambodian government outposts.

A P R I L

      The U.S. begins bombing in direct support of Cambodian troops. Larger South Vietnamese operations take place in Cambodia April 14–16, with U.S. logistical and air support, though no Americans cross the border. U.S. begins secret arms shipments to Phnom Penh.

24–25 At a "Summit Conference of the Indochinese Peoples" in southern China, Sihanouk aligns with the Vietnamese and Lao Communist movements.

30   U.S. forces enter Cambodia to disrupt Vietnamese bases and to capture COSVN, the Communist headquarters for southern Vietnam.

M A Y

5   Sihanouk announces formation of a government in exile, to be based in Peking.

J U N E

30   The last U.S. troops are withdrawn. President Nixon proclaims the Cambodia operation a success.

J U L Y

      Communist forces have occupied most of eastern Cambodia, threaten all routes to Phnom Penh, and have inflicted heavy losses on the inexperienced Cambodian army, while beginning to form and train a Cambodian liberation movement.

OCTOBER
9   The Khmer Republic is proclaimed in Phnom Penh.
DECEMBER
22   Congress prohibits U.S. combat forces or advisers in Cambodia and Laos.
1971
FEBRUARY
         U.S. intelligence estimates that 10,000 Cambodians have been organized to fight on the
         Communist side.
OCTOBER–DECEMBER
         The Cambodian army suffers disastrous losses in the Operation Chenla II campaign.
1972
MARCH
10   Lon Nol is named President.
OCTOBER
8   In the Paris peace talks, Le Duc Tho predicts that "the question of Cambodia certainly
         will be settled" after a Vietnam agreement. But Hanoi will not take the responsibility
         for arranging a Cambodian ceasefire.
26   Henry Kissinger announces that "peace is at hand" in Vietnam.
28   Prince Sihanouk and North Vietnamese leaders issue a joint statement declaring that
         "the problem of each Indochinese country must be settled by its own people."
1973
JANUARY
1   Sihanouk and Penn Nouth, prime minister of the exile government, denounce "the
         maneuver for a 'ceasefire in Cambodia' " and call for "total and definitive liberation of
         our beloved country."
8   Lon Nol declares that Sihanouk has been "ousted by the Cambodian people for good."
20   Khmer Republic Prime Minister Hang Thun Hak says Sihanouk is "formally excluded"
         from any peace negotiations.
28   Phnom Penh time (January 27, Washington time) The Vietnam peace agreement takes
         effect.
28   Lon Nol, in a qualified ceasefire offer, says Vietnamese Communists must "lay down
         their weapons" and leave Cambodia, and government units will "suspend all offen-
         sives" while reoccupying Communist territory.
29   Sihanouk's exile government says "no compromise is possible" with the Lon Nol
         regime.
31   The insurgents reject Lon Nol's ceasefire proposal as a "conjurer's trick."
FEBRUARY
9   The U.S. resumes bombing in Cambodia after an eleven-day halt.
APRIL
13   Sihanouk, after visiting the "liberated zone," says in Peking he will negotiate with the
         U.S. but only on "the question of ending U.S. interference . . . not the question of a
         ceasefire."
MAY
27   Kissinger tells China's U.N. ambassador that the U.S. will stop bombing and will
         arrange Lon Nol's departure in return for a ceasefire and talks between the "Sihanouk
         group" and Lon Nol's associates. After "some months" the U.S. will "not oppose"
         Sihanouk's return to Cambodia to head a coalition government.

JUNE

4   The Chinese agree to pass on the U.S. offer after Sihanouk returns from a long trip abroad.

JULY

1   The U.S. Congress votes to end all bombing in Cambodia after August 15.

5   Sihanouk returns to Peking.

6   Foreign Minister Long Boret announces that Khmer Republic representatives are prepared to meet "Cambodians from the other side" as part of a process that would also involve a ceasefire and withdrawal of all Vietnamese Communists. The Khmer Rouge quickly reject the proposal.

18   The Chinese inform Kissinger that they will not pass on his peace offer to Sihanouk after all. Kissinger blames the congressionally imposed bombing halt.

19–21   The insurgents' "national congress" vows that the "traitorous Phnom Penh gang" will be overthrown and replaced by the United Front.

AUGUST

6   An accidental B-52 strike kills 137 people in the Mekong River town of Neak Luong.

15   U.S. bombing ends. Nixon promises that military and economic aid to Cambodia will continue.

1974

JULY

9   At the recommendation of U.S. Ambassador John Gunther Dean, the Phnom Penh government says for the first time that it will negotiate "without preconditions" with the Khmer Rouge.

1975

JANUARY

1   Khmer Rouge troops assault Phnom Penh's defenses.

         Khmer Rouge attacks halt supply convoys on the Mekong River. The U.S. begins airlifting ammunition and fuel to the Cambodian capital.

28   President Ford requests a $222 million military aid supplement for Cambodia.

FEBRUARY

         The U.S. airlift expands. The U.S. embassy calculates that without a supplement, all U.S. aid funds supporting the government army will be used up in April.

MARCH

17   The Senate Foreign Relations Committee endorses $82.5 million in additional military aid on condition that a settlement be reached and all military support end on June 30. No other Cambodia aid proposal receives committee approval in either house, but President Ford rejects the compromise.

APRIL

1   Lon Nol leaves Cambodia for Indonesia. Neak Luong falls.

10   President Ford tells Congress that "it may be too late" for additional aid to Cambodia.

11   The U.S. asks Sihanouk to return to Phnom Penh to take over the government and arrange a ceasefire. Sihanouk refuses.

12   U.S. Marine helicopters evacuate U.S. embassy staff and other foreigners from Phnom Penh. Cambodian government leaders are offered evacuation, but only acting president Saukham Khoy accepts.

17   Khmer Rouge troops enter Phnom Penh and government forces surrender.

Chapter 6

Laos:
The Kingdom
of Lane-xang

America . . . has ended its suffering, but it cannot forget that in international morality, peace has the same value for all people, small or large."

That plaintive observation, in an editorial in the daily mimeographed bulletin of the official news agency, Lao Presse, greeted Henry Kissinger as he arrived in the Lao capital of Vientiane on his way to Hanoi, thirteen days after the Paris agreement was signed. It accurately reflected the feelings of Vietnam's two weaker neighbors about the agreement. For years, the American-sponsored regimes in Laos and Cambodia had lived with the fear that their interests would be sacrificed to America's anxiety for a quick exit from the war. That was exactly what now seemed to have happened in Paris, where the United States had quickly dropped its longstanding demand for an Indochina-wide truce as soon as a settlement became possible for Vietnam alone. For most Americans, in the euphoria surrounding the achievement of the ceasefire, the omission of Laos and Cambodia seemed no more than a minor detail—if it was thought of at all. But America's allies in Phnom Penh and Vientiane were shocked and dismayed.

Article 20, to be sure, pledged the U.S. and both Vietnamese sides to respect Lao and Cambodian neutrality and to end military intervention. But Article 20 was plainly little more than a diplomatic ornament. Only 185 words long, it contained no deadline for intervention to end. Nor did it create any mechanism for enforcement. It was simply a promise—one that

Two Cambodian children in a refugee center, 1975
(*David Hume Kennerly/The White House*).

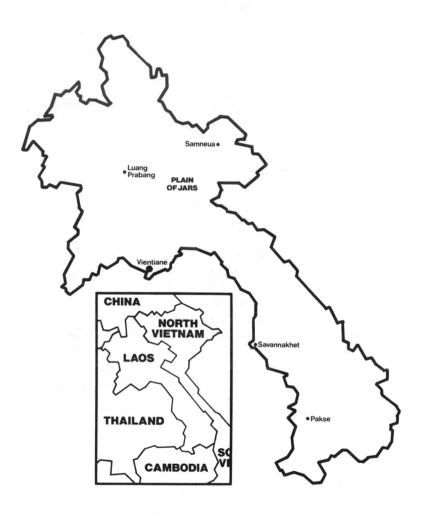

LAOS

had been made in two earlier peace treaties in the preceding nineteen years, only to be broken both times.

Like South Vietnam, Laos and Cambodia had been excluded from the crucial negotiations in Paris. Although both of the two lesser allies would be left at severe military disadvantage, they would have to try to make their own political arrangements after the Vietnam agreement was concluded. Fearful of leaks and diplomatic complications, Kissinger and his emissaries gave only vague messages of reassurance to Prime Minister Souvanna Phouma in Vientiane and President Lon Nol in Phnom Penh while the talks with Le Duc Tho reached the climactic stage.

Nearly a dozen years before, on the eve of the 1962 Geneva conference that was supposed to end the conflict in Laos, King Savang Vatthana had told his subjects bitterly, "Foreign countries do not care either about our interests or about peace; they are concerned only with their own interests." The events that followed the Geneva conference only confirmed that warning. When the Paris agreement of 1973 was revealed, the king's words once again appeared prophetic.

The war that ebbed and flowed across the inaccessible ridges of the Lao hinterland always seemed distant from Vientiane.

The smallest and least war-marked of the four Indochinese capitals baked drowsily on the north bank of the Mekong, midway along the wide eastward bend the river follows after descending out of the knobby mountains of northern Laos onto the great Indochina plain. When swollen by the summer rains, the river swam close by under the sentry-rank of palms that stood along Vientiane's diked waterfront; tumbling in the silt-brown waters were tree-stumps and branches torn from the walls of the steep gorges along its course. In the dry winter months the water receded, exposing sandbars from which fitful breezes stirred up feathers of sand and wafted them ashore to leave a gritty coating on the city's potholed streets, walled pagodas, and lowslung French buildings with their overgrown, vine-tangled gardens. Thailand, on the opposite bank, was a hazy smear across the horizon. In the shrunken channel far from the city's edge, long-prowed dugouts of traders and fishermen plied back and forth, made into painted miniatures by the slanting afternoon sun.

Modern war had not overcome the lassitude into which Laos had settled after a brief moment of imperial glory nearly six centuries before under the early kings of Lane-xang—"Land of a million elephants." The poorest, least populous, and least developed of the Southeast Asian nations, Laos was colonized almost absent-mindedly by the French at the very end of the nineteenth century as a sort of afterthought to their conquest of Vietnam.

Seven decades later, it was still a remote, sleepy place. "It . . . is difficult to convey to the casual reader," wrote one journalist after visiting Laos, "the profound insignificance of this country." And a scholar observed that Laos was "neither a geographic nor an ethnic unit, and it does not constitute a viable economic entity." If the attributes of a modern national state include such features as shared traditions, effective administration, and the "positive support" of its inhabitants, he added, "it must be said that Laos lacks most of these characteristics."

In an area the size of Great Britain, Laos had only 470 miles of paved roads in 1970. Its legal exports, chiefly tin and timber, never exceeded $3 million a year in value. Opium, exported illegally, was probably more valuable. The 1972 U.S. aid program of $350 million was twice the entire Lao gross national product and ten times the national budget. In the entire country in 1970 there were only eighteen high schools, with an enrollment of fewer than 7,000 students.

The population was roughly estimated at about three million. Of these, approximately half were ethnic Lao—racially, culturally, and linguistically akin to the Thai and living in the fertile plains of the Mekong and its tributaries. The rest of the population were tribal people belonging to a variety of racial and language groups, who inhabited the mountainous interior of the country. In 1972, somewhere between 1.7 and two million people lived in areas claimed by the American-backed Royal Lao Government, and perhaps a million under a Communist movement called the Neo Lao Hak Sat, or Lao Patriotic Front. The Communists were commonly called the Pathet Lao—"Land of the Lao."

Buddhism was the kingdom's official religion, practiced by the Lao and by some of the hill tribes. More pervasive, however, was an animistic belief in spirits called *phi*, which existed in innumerable varieties. There were *phi* representing the elements of earth, air, fire, and water; others representing the vital organs of man; and still others for villages, households, roads, streams, trees, and animals. Rice, a sacred substance, had its own guardian *phi*. These spirits determined the course of virtually all events, and no important decision was ever made without consulting their wishes and ritually propitiating them, often with animal sacrifice.

It was the hill people, rather than the Lao, who bore the brunt of the war in Laos: this was one of the reasons the conflict seemed so remote from the capital. A city of perhaps 170,000 in the early 1970s, Vientiane had no sandbagged guard posts or barbed-wire barricades in front of government buildings, no checkpoints on the roads out of town or at Wattay Airport. There was a curfew, theoretically, but on most nights indolent police patrols preferred to snooze in their jeeps without interrupting their slumbers to pursue curfew breakers.

Though it had been at war with the Pathet Lao and the North Vietnamese for nearly a decade, Prince Souvanna Phouma's government still considered itself neutralist. It preserved the name given to it by the 1962 Geneva accords: Provisional Government of National Union. Souvanna kept open the four ministries awarded to the Pathet Lao under that agreement, even though their occupants had left many years earlier for Sam Neua, the Pathet Lao "capital" in the far northeast of the country near North Vietnam. Souvanna maintained diplomatic relations with the Soviet Union, China, and North Vietnam.

The Pathet Lao—who, unlike the Communists in South Vietnam or Cambodia, never formed a rival government—kept a military delegation in Vientiane, a remnant, like the government's name, of the failed 1962 truce.

The delegation was housed in two dilapidated villas adjoining the main post office and the central market, in the heart of the city. Inside their compound, the green-uniformed Pathet Lao soldiers spent their time at badminton or volleyball or tended small plots of vegetables. Each morning a few of them walked out through the green wooden gate to do their marketing under the eyes of a lackadaisical police escort. At night, rumor had it, the police, believing like all Lao that no man was intended to live celibately, sometimes accompanied their charges to one of Vientiane's numerous brothels. The ordinary citizens of Vientiane hardly regarded the Pathet Lao delegation as enemies. Instead they were, most people in the city believed, a guarantee against attack—and in fact, Vientiane heard no shots in anger for many years.

The lazy pace and tolerant atmosphere of the capital made it easy—too easy—to view Laos as farce rather than tragedy. "The land of a million irrelevants," ran a popular wisecrack among resident foreigners. The war was often pictured as a harmless if incomprehensible affair, something out of a noisy Chinese opera with rival princes whose names all sounded alike and with battles in which everyone blazed away furiously but no one was hurt because the soldiers, devout Buddhists on both sides, purposely aimed too high to kill anyone.

It is quite true that by custom and culture, the Lao are one of Asia's least warlike peoples. They had "not learned to kill each other like the civilized nations," John Kenneth Galbraith once observed. Sexually free, the Lao practiced make-love-not-war long before the phrase was invented by the youth rebellion in the West. ("How the hell," an American official once remarked to me, half in exasperation and half in admiration, "can you fight a war in a country where the gross national product is measured in orgasms?") To the foreigners who came there, the Lao exhibited "delightful and admirable qualities of warmth, easy hospitality and friendliness. There seems to be a harmony to life in Laos: strife has been low and tolerance for deviance high."

Had only the competing Lao factions been involved, the comic-opera image of the war might well have been accurate. But geography determined that the Lao would not be left to fight or finish their war according to their own pacific inclinations. Laos was a battleground in the larger war, and there was nothing at all harmless or comic about the devastation wrought there by the clash of American and Vietnamese Communist power.

In that contest, the Americans and North Vietnamese gave their respective Lao proxies enough support to keep from losing, but not enough to win. There was a sense that the ultimate advantage lay with the Communist side, because the North Vietnamese were closer and more numerous than the Americans and because a friendly Laos was of prime importance to Hanoi and only a convenience to Washington. Still, the matter of who ruled Laos was secondary. The main issue for both Americans and North Vietnamese lay in the jungle-cloaked ridges and steep-sided valleys of eastern Laos along the border with Vietnam, where men and arms moved from North Vietnam to the battlefields in the South along a complex of roads and tracks nick-named the Ho Chi Minh trail. America's purpose in Laos was to stem or slow that traffic. North Vietnam's was to keep it flowing.

In violation of the 1962 Geneva accords, Hanoi kept a substantial army in Laos. Its strength fluctuated with the demands put on it by the war in Vietnam. American intelligence estimated that there were 67,000 North Vietnamese troops in Laos early in 1970, 100,000 in the spring of 1971, and 80,000 late in 1972. Early in 1973, Sisouk Na Champassak, the Lao defense minister, gave a figure of 56,000—a decrease that may have reflected the assignment of additional troops to the ceasefire battles on the Vietnamese side of the border.

Most of the North Vietnamese in Laos were service or supply troops stationed along the Ho Chi Minh trail in logistics bases called "binh trams." These troops had no effect on the battles in Laos. But about 20,000 North Vietnamese were thought to be in combat units fighting alongside the somewhat larger but less effective Pathet Lao army. Many of the 35,000 Pathet Lao troops served as porters and laborers for the Vietnamese units. The Lao Communist forces were accompanied by North Vietnamese advisers, who exhibited a dedication and discipline seldom matched by Lao officers. The more easygoing Lao looked upon the "puritanism of the Vietnamese cadres," wrote one analyst, "with respectful amazement." (The American advisers who served with government units no doubt evoked equal amazement at times—though seldom, one can safely assume, for reasons of puritanism.)

Had they wished to spend the manpower and resources, the North Vietnamese certainly had the ability to overrun all of Laos. But as long as they were still heavily engaged in South Vietnam, garrisoning Laos would have been more burdensome than it was worth, and would have risked as well another active front or perhaps open hostilities with Thailand, which sat nervously on the far side of the Mekong, clandestinely supporting the

Lao war effort but not openly confronting the Vietnamese. Thus, Hanoi was content to maintain a stalemate. Communist forces advanced each dry season and fell back when the rains turned their trails into mud. The pattern seemed to reflect a Lao proverb about the cyclical nature of life: "When the water rises, the fish eat the ants. When the water falls, the ants eat the fish."

The North Vietnamese fought to sustain the Lao Communists and to keep the government army occupied safely away from the trail region. The ultimate conquest of Laos could wait. "The Communists believe that when they attain their objectives in South Vietnam, Laos will fall in their hands," a CIA study concluded in 1970. "But as long as they have been able to use Laotian territory to support the war in South Vietnam, they have not been willing to pay the costs or run the risks of decisive action in Laos."

The United States, in the 1950s, made Laos its first test of strength in Southeast Asia, investing nearly a half-billion dollars in support of a series of inept right-wing leaders before accepting the 1962 Geneva compromise and the resulting coalition regime under Souvanna Phouma. The experience of trying to make Laos an anti-Communist bastion had not exactly been encouraging. The U.S. financed an army of 25,000 men, which proved able to create no end of mischief in domestic affairs without being much use against the Communists. The Joint Chiefs of Staff, indeed, recommended against such a force; it was created at the urging of the State Department under John Foster Dulles, for whom the symbolism of ringing Communist China with anti-Communist armed forces apparently outweighed military advice.

By the time the Kennedy administration decided to support a neutralized Laos, Washington's focus was already beginning to shift toward Vietnam. And when the Geneva accords broke down and the U.S. expanded clandestine support of Lao military actions, propping up the Lao government was subordinate to the main goal of waging war against the North Vietnamese, and particularly against the Ho Chi Minh trail. To that end the U.S. carried on the longest sustained bombing campaign of the war—the longest, indeed, in military history. To bomb in Lao territory the Americans needed, or if they did not need at least found useful, the acquiescence of something that could be called the government of Laos. Souvanna offered that acquiescence, receiving in return the support he needed to keep his forces in the field. Like Hanoi, Washington did not really need victory in Laos, only a regime that would not demand an end to the bombing.

Laos's future, indeed, was a subject that seems not to have figured very often in American official thinking, probably because no one had any very useful thoughts about it. To the extent that it was considered at all, it was conceived as a problem that would somehow be resolved as part of a broader Vietnam settlement. "In their most optimistic moments," congressional observers wrote in 1971, "Lao and Americans . . . expressed a guarded belief that the Lao will be able to cling to their territory until the war ends in Vietnam," when "an agreed settlement in which the great powers will participate . . . will lead to a similar resolution of the situation in Laos." With such vague hopes the politicians, the generals, and the ordinary Lao had to be content while their country was used and misused by the North Vietnamese on the ground and by the Americans from the air. And in the end, of course, the "great powers" did not resolve the conflict in Laos but left it to find its own level—an outcome that could only favor the Communist side.

The air war in Laos began in the early 1960s, when Thai mercenary pilots, recruited and paid by the CIA—then and later the most active U.S. agency in the Laos war—flew obsolete T-28 fighter-bombers painted with Lao Air Force markings to strike targets in Lao territory. Then in May 1964, three months before the Tonkin Gulf incident led to the first U.S. raids on North Vietnam, American jets were secretly authorized to fly "armed reconnaissance" in support of the "Lao" T-28s—and to drop their bombs if they were fired on. The first strikes occurred June 9, after two U.S. planes had been lost to antiaircraft fire. Under the code name Yankee Team, the bombing started at a relatively low level of about five missions a week, but gradually intensified while the Johnson administration also moved toward full-scale air war on North Vietnam. Prince Souvanna did not protest the trail bombing but asked, and was given, air support for government forces in northern Laos.

The Laos air war underwent two more drastic escalations, in 1968 and again in 1969. These were related to the curtailment and then to the complete halt of bombing in North Vietnam. "Air power now used north of the 20th"—that is, above the 20th parallel in North Vietnam, the line fixed by President Johnson for the partial bombing halt of March 31, 1968—"can probably be used in Laos (where no policy change planned)," the State Department advised U.S. embassies in Asia in a message explaining the new situation. When bombing stopped in the rest of North Vietnam seven months later, the rate of strikes in Laos took another corresponding jump. The use of air power was later described in a remarkable classified study by a Pentagon systems analyst, who wrote: "In a war without fronts there is a temptation to use all the air power available to the government forces for strikes at the hundreds of fleeting targets offered by the insurgents. And in such operations, the amount of air power employed will depend primarily on the number of aircraft ready to fly." Thus, raids shifted between North Vietnam and Laos not for military but for political reasons: "When political decisions allowed North Vietnam to be bombed, most of the sorties went there, but when they didn't the sorties shifted to Laos. . . . When bombing in North Vietnam was permitted again in 1972, the sorties shifted back into that area." Still later, when both countries were off limits following the Vietnam and Laos ceasefire agreements, "the available sorties simply swung into Cambodia," the analyst wrote, "until there, too, the bombing was halted."

So consistent was this pattern that it seemed little consideration was given to the possibility that the different targets available might have dictated different levels of bombing in the various areas under attack. "The distribution and rates of . . . sorties apparently depended more on the number of sorties available with the aircraft in the theater," the Pentagon study concluded, "than on strategy or considerations of the relative effectiveness of the sorties among the target areas. Probably the best analogy would be the use of a fire hose, running under full pressure most of the time and pointed with the same intensity at whichever area is allowed, regardless of its relative importance."

In 1969, under a new president who evidently sought to use air power to replace the ground forces he was under great political pressure to withdraw, sorties over Laos doubled and redoubled. At times, 700 to 800 raids were flown in a single day. For the full year of 1969, the daily average of fighter-bomber sorties was nearly 400; two years earlier, it had been only about 120. B-52 bombing climbed from 93,199 tons in 1968 to 218,250 tons two years later, according to Defense Department records. In all the bombing before 1969, 454,998 tons had fallen on Laos. In the Nixon administration, more than that was dropped each year. The total tonnages for the war would be staggering. When air raids finally ended in 1973, U.S. aircraft had dropped 2,092,900 tons of bombs on Laos, three-quarters of that after President Nixon's inauguration. This was approximately the tonnage dropped by U.S. air forces in all of World War II in both the European and Pacific theaters of war. It amounted to two-thirds of a ton of bombs for every single man, woman, and child in Laos; fully two tons for every person thought to be living in the Pathet Lao zone.

Until well into the Nixon administration, this massive campaign was still euphemistically called "armed reconnaissance." And even after the bombing was announced, many details—including its scope—continued to be withheld. Secrecy muffled, if it could not completely silence, public debate. But the expanding devastation could not be entirely hidden. "Black is the predominant color of the northern and eastern reaches of the plain," wrote one reporter after flying over the Plain of Jars, a grassy plateau east of the royal capital, Luang Prabang, named for the giant pottery urns found there. "Napalm is dropped regularly to burn off the grass and undergrowth that covers the plain and fills its many narrow ravines. The fires seem to burn constantly, creating rectangles of black. . . . The craters are countless. . . .

In many places it is difficult to distinguish individual craters; the area has been bombed so repeatedly that the land resembles the pocked, churned desert in storm-hit areas of the North African desert."

Of about 9,400 villages in Laos, 3,500 were in territory held by the Pathet Lao after 1962. In the ensuing decade most of these were obliterated by bombing. "There just aren't any villages in northern Laos any more," said an Air Force officer. A sergeant at Udorn air base in Thailand, after helping burn classified reconnaissance photographs, wrote in his diary, "The countryside in the photographs . . . looked like a bombers' test range."

The Plain of Jars supported a population of about 150,000 people in 1960; a decade later, after mass evacuations, fewer than 9,000 were left, and none of its villages were still standing. Refugees among the tens of thousands who trekked out of the plain after government forces briefly recaptured it in 1970 told terrible stories. "There wasn't a night when we went to sleep that we thought we'd live to see the morning," one of them said. Under the bombing, whole villages moved underground. "We never saw the sun," said another refugee. "Our hair was falling out."

Reports cited by U.S. Senate investigators told of daily raids with napalm, phosphorus, and antipersonnel bombs. "They say the jets bombed both villages and forest. . . . Everything was fired on, buffalos, cows, ricefields, schools, temples, tiny shelters outside the village. . . ." In Xieng Khouang Province, which encompassed the Plain of Jars, Communist authorities after the war estimated fully five-eighths of all the draft animals in the province—50,000 of about 83,000 buffalo—were killed in the bombing. "We could work in the fields only at night; by day we slept underground in the bunkers," said an old woman after reaching a refugee camp near Vientiane. "Everything that moved was bombed. Our village was bombed three times. The second time my daughter was killed. Then we left and went to live in the forest. It's very difficult to live there. There's not enough to eat." Another refugee remembered, "The planes came like birds and the bombs fell like rain."

People died not only under the bombs but of disease or exhaustion along the evacuation trails that led away from the Plain of Jars and from other areas in the way of the intensified conflict. "Every time the war forced a move," said Dr. Patricia McCreedy Weldon of the U.S. aid mission, "as many as ten per cent of the people died. The majority were already weakened by diseases, and the exertion killed them." On some of the more arduous evacuation marches, U.S. officials guessed, the death rate was higher: perhaps one person of every five. At one time or another, about three-quarters of a million people—one of every four in Laos—were forced from their homes by the war.

The bombing did not improve the Lao government's position on the ground. In the early 1970s, each swing of the pendulum left the Communist forces slightly ahead of where they had started and the government forces with somewhat less ground. After nearly twenty years of American aid, the Royal Lao Army remained poorly trained, badly led, and by widespread consensus hardly fit to face the enemy at all. "The principal military shortcoming in Laos," Ambassador William Sullivan acknowledged in 1969, "is leadership." The command still seemed to warrant the verdict of a former American ambassador who told one of the CIA-sponsored rightist leaders of the 1950s, "Your chief of staff couldn't lead a platoon around the corner to buy a newspaper." ("I know," the rightist chieftain reportedly replied, "but he's loyal.")

The conscription system, American officials admitted, was no more than "impressment." As many as 30 percent of all recruits deserted at the first opportunity. Regional commanders were in effect warlords who felt quite free to ignore orders from Vientiane, and frequently did. Corruption was pervasive. Many units, full-strength by the payroll records, were far under strength in fact, with their commanders pocketing the pay of the missing men. The Pathet Lao army was hardly a model of skill or battlefield aggressiveness either, but was still regarded as much better than the government's. The prevailing view was stated by Rand Corporation analysts who wrote that the Royal Armed Forces "outclass the LPLA [Lao Peoples Liberation Army] in firepower, mobility, technical equipment and clothing, indeed in almost all material ways. The LPLA, on the other hand, seem to have a more effective organization, better leadership, especially at the middle and lower levels, and a stronger will to fight."

Political weakness mirrored military weakness. Souvanna Phouma admitted in 1967 that the Pathet Lao were "more effective in political organization" than his government. Popular dissatisfaction was reflected in the National Assembly elections of January 1972, in which only eighteen incumbents were reelected from among the 59 assembly members. The new assemblymen represented no coherent party or philosophy. But the voting still "reflected the decay of the old established forces," as one experienced observer commented, adding, "The voters also seemed to be showing a great fatigue for the war, choosing new faces unconnected with those groups seen as responsible for sustaining it."

Increasing the sense of political fragility was the fact that there was no apparent successor to the aging Souvanna. It was not easy to imagine a satisfactory Lao settlement, even with Souvanna. Without him, one appeared impossible. Both the Communist powers and the U.S. accepted the fact that he was the only leader capable of bringing the country to any stage of reconciliation, and shared a desire that he should remain in office. It was American support, however, that kept him there, a relationship that perhaps assured the survival of a non-Communist regime but which also misshaped Laos's political institutions. For the American purpose was not really to strengthen the Lao government or social system. As one scholar shrewdly wrote:

> U.S. strategic aims are not so much concerned with the autonomous development of an allied territory—particularly if the consequences upset security—as with the compliance of indigenous political and military leaders with America's objectives. "Established" local leaders are most likely to go along with these policies, if only because U.S. assistance renders it unnecessary for them to endanger their own privileges by having to seek more broadly-based support. . . .
> . . . The terms of the bargain become evident when the interests of the two parties start to diverge. For example, Hanoi's use of the Ho Chi Minh trails deeply disturbs Washington, although it is hardly a matter of grave concern to the Lao people or even to the Lao government, since the trails run through remote, mountainous, tribal country far from Vientiane's writ. Why then should the latter provoke North Vietnamese hostility by allowing the Americans to attack this area? The answer is that the Lao government, narrowly-based, faction-ridden and lacking rural support, has little or no alternative. Deprived of U.S. backing the regime would disintegrate into separate and perhaps conflicting regional warlord and "family" groups which would be no match for the more disciplined, organized and motivated Pathet Lao.

While continuing to arm and equip the regular armed forces, the U.S. relied more heavily on irregular units of hill tribesmen that were formed, trained, paid, and often for all practical purposes commanded by the CIA. First called the "Armee Clandestine," these units were later known as "SGU" (Special Guerrilla Units) and finally as "BGs," for the French term "battaillons guerriers." Hmong, or Meo, units under General Vang Pao became the best-known guerrillas, though Lao Theung and other tribesmen were also recruited.

The irregulars fought from isolated mountain bases in country so remote and rugged that it seemed the far side of the moon. They were supplied and supported by a CIA air effort that had an exotic flavor all its own. Once, at an airstrip north of Vientiane, I heard an unidentifiable but ear-splitting bellow over the noise of aircraft motors. When I went to investigate, I found, off to one side of the runway, a half-dozen water buffalo lying on their sides, tightly strapped to cargo pallets. Even their horns were tied down to immobilize their heads. Their eyes bulging like baseballs, the terrified beasts were producing an astonishing din of roars, groans, moos, and yowls. A grinning American crewman explained: up-country somewhere, at one of the Meos' nameless little hilltop bases, a guerrilla unit was planning a feast, and the buffalo were on the menu. They would travel the same way as replacements, ammunition, rice, and other necessities: on a transport flown by the CIA's airline, Air America.

Carrying water buffalo as passengers might have dismayed other airlines, but the mission didn't surprise the Air America crews. Not much did. The loadmaster had flown with buffalo before, he confided. "Had one of them get loose one time," he drawled. "Like to kicked the sides of the plane out before we got him strapped down again."

No flying could have contrasted more sharply with the air war on the Ho Chi Minh trail, a futuristic and eerily impersonal campaign of electronics and exotic weaponry that was directed by men and computers hundreds of miles from the battlefield. The "electronic war," designed largely by a Pentagon agency innocuously named the Defense Communications Planning Group, involved sowing hundreds of thousands of sensors to detect troop or truck movements—a $2 billion program codenamed Igloo White. (The sensor war made at least one notable contribution to the annals of military euphemisms. When a Senate aide asked if there were many false alarms, his respondent, a Marine Corps major, answered: "That word has been stricken from the vocabulary. That is now a nontargetable activation.") The sensors' signals, activated by sound or vibration, were relayed by drone aircraft to a huge computer installation in Thailand called the Infiltration Surveillance Center, housed in what was said to be the largest building in Southeast Asia. There, Air Force technicians plotted targets and selected weaponry. Computerized instructions were radioed to bombers and gunships through on-board "black boxes" that automatically navigated the planes to their targets and released bombs. Air crews, on missions over the trail, were often little more than passengers.

The weaponry was as unusual as the means used to deliver it. From small antipersonnel mines called Dragonteeth and Gravel—the latter resembling large green teabags—weapons used on the trail ranged all the way up to a 2,500-pound propane bomb called Pave Pat II. Dropped by parachute, this device was detonated just above the treetops. It blew down several acres of jungle to expose suspected truck routes or other targets beneath the trees.

If the war on the Ho Chi Minh trail seemed something from the twenty-first century, the war the Americans supported on the ground in northern Laos was in many respects—though not in the destructiveness of the weapons involved—something from the Middle Ages.

The Hmong and the other tribal people who fought that war were among the most isolated in Asia. The Hmong, or Meo as they were commonly called by Americans, were fairly recent migrants from southwestern China, distinct from the Lao in appearance as well as in their warlike tradition. They were "comparable to the Gurkhas of Nepal" as a warrior tribe, one writer noted: "Indefatigable walkers and horsemen, they range the upper mountain slopes for days, hunting with their long, homemade flintlock rifles." The Hmong were frequently regarded by the Lao and by other tribes as being troublesome and belligerent—though one of them, after a bloody tribal uprising against the French in 1921 against a proposed opium tax, offered this defense: "They say we are a people who like to fight, a cruel people, enemy of everybody, always changing our region and being happy nowhere. If you want to know the truth about our people, go ask the bear who is hurt why he defends himself, ask the dog who is kicked why he barks, ask the deer who is chased why he changes mountains."

In Laos, caught up in a war they did not understand until far too late to escape it and that was fought with weapons too powerful for their traditional way of life to withstand, the Hmong would finally run out of mountains. On the long, long list of victims of the Indochina war, the Hmong, along with the Cambodians, would be perhaps the saddest of all.

The Secret Army

There were 23 of them, boys no older than their middle teens, waiting on a nameless hill at a place called Ban Long Pot.

A few soldiers had come from the secret CIA-built base at Long Cheng to teach them their new trade. The last of the few training sessions was ending as John Everingham, an adventurous young Australian who had learned fluent Lao and was willing, unlike most foreigners in Vientiane, to spend the days of trekking to reach the mountain villages, walked into Long Pot. "The boys could service their own M-2 carbines, hit the dirt when the bullets began to fly," Everingham wrote, "little more. The bombs rumbled in Muong Soui. The helicopter was almost there. They waited, terrified. Several mothers had come up from their villages to sob, and stuffed small charms into the pockets of their soldier sons' new U.S. Army uniforms. An Air America helicopter whooped in, made three trips to Muong Soui, leaving only crying mothers atop the hill."

That was the "secret war" in 1970: a war that was devouring not men, but children. During the previous year 60 boys were taken from Long Pot and the surrounding villages, all those from the district who reached fifteen. "I put them in the helicopter myself," Gair Su Yarng, the district headman, said remorsefully. By the end of the year, twelve of them had already been killed. "Of the first eighteen men sent out of this village," Gair Su said, "only one was still alive then, just one. If Vang Pao stays leader of the Meo, we will all be dead soon."

Gair Su, a clan leader who ruled an area he described as stretching over "two days' walk," had joined the secret war years before when he was offered a brutal choice by one of Vang Pao's officers: he could send soldiers for the CIA-run guerrillas, or the village would be regarded as Pathet Lao territory and bombed. After that Gair Su enforced the levy on the district's sons—until he was told that instead of fifteen-year-olds, he must start sending every boy who reached fourteen. That he would not do. "After I sent those 60 men last year to Vang Pao, we could not cut forest to make fresh rice fields," he told Everingham. "Not enough men. We didn't grow enough rice, and the Americans stopped dropping the rice in the third month this year. Most families have only their pigs' corn to eat."

U.S. rice supplies had been cut off, Gair Su believed, to punish the village for refusing to send its fourteen-year-olds to the guerrillas. (This was a well-documented practice of Vang Pao's, confirmed both by Lao officials and by CIA officers who worked with the Meo.) He still wanted to stay in Long Pot and try to defend it, Gair Su said; he could not try to reach an accommodation with the Pathet Lao because the village would then be bombed out of existence. His eyes filled with tears. "If they didn't drop the bombs," he said, "we wouldn't have to fight the Pathet Lao. . . . If they didn't drop the bombs we could stay here at Long Pot. Maybe there would be peace. But if the Pathet Lao come to our village now, we will be bombed. . . ."

The Hmong's misfortune was to occupy the land that lay between Communist North Vietnam and the Mekong plain—a location that made them so valuable an ally, and so threatening as a possible enemy, that neither side in the war could risk leaving them to their traditional way of life. The hill tribes, in fact, were in a position analogous to that of Laos itself. Just as Laos was embroiled in the war because of a conflict among stronger foreign powers, who armed the Lao factions with the means to inflict far worse damage than they could have with their own resources, so the tribes were caught up in the conflict between the warring Lao sides. Tribal people died not just in a war that served no purpose of their own, but because to fight that war, they were given weapons far more destructive than any they possessed in their own culture.

The exact origins of the Meo clandestine army remained, even after more than twenty years, somewhat obscure. Some of the irregular battalions were evidently formed by U.S. Special Forces "White Star" training teams, which were assigned to Laos in mid-1959. CIA arms shipments seem to have begun in 1960 or very early in 1961, and were then sharply expanded in the early months of the Kennedy administration. By mid-1961, one of the new president's guerrilla war experts reported, 9,000 of these "splendid fighting men" had been armed and equipped for combat. Kennedy and his associates, who were fascinated by theories of unconventional warfare, may even have believed their own romantic fantasies of the Lao tribesmen as backward but brave fighters, defending their mountains with the help of dedicated and resourceful Americans. In retrospect, though, U.S. actions in Laos in the early 1960s look less like a thrilling adventure and more like the cruel exploitation—no less so even if the cruelty was unintended—of a remote, preliterate people who were certainly brave, but who had no experience to prepare them for twentieth-century war or power politics.

The Hmong warrior tradition was created in tribal conflicts that were fought without highly destructive weapons and that were usually settled rather quickly. These limitations were cast aside when the Americans enlisted them in a modern, highly lethal war against a relentless enemy. The power of American arms made the authority of the Hmong leaders over their own people more brutal as well. And the Hmong were terribly vulnerable, in ways their American sponsors did not heed until far too late, to Communist counteraction against their lands and livelihoods.

As Hmong losses grew, American officials in Laos often told visitors that they had made the initial request for arms and advisers to defend themselves—as if that relieved the United States of responsibility for all the suffering its proxy warriors would endure. Other Americans took little comfort in that argument. One drew a mordant but apt analogy. "It's no help to your case," he commented to my colleague John Woodruff, "if you tell the judge the twelve-year-old girl invited you into her bedroom."

The American responsibility for the Meo was not made to smell any sweeter because it was kept secret and thus, in intelligence jargon, "deniable," meaning that the U.S. was not openly committed to the guerrillas even after they had served American purposes at such cruel cost. "Do you see any obligation on the part of the United States," Ambassador Sullivan was asked in Senate hearings in 1969, "for the safety or well being of General Vang Pao and his people?" Sullivan—with what inner emotion can only be guessed—had to reply at the dictates of American political realism. "No formal obligation of the United States," he told the committee. "No."

By then, the escalation of the war had stretched the Hmong beyond the limits of their endurance. Early in 1970, the CIA reported that the guerrilla army's "losses over the past year or so have exceeded their capability to replace them." Foreigners working with the Hmong saw almost no young men any more in the villages. "Most of the young men between the ages of 15 and 25 are either dead, permanently maimed, or . . . smart enough to take off some place and never be found," one aid worker concluded. "Vang Pao is no longer the great messiah," an embassy officer acknowledged to a congressional visitor. ". . . Many Meo have walked away from the war."

At Long Cheng, when the tide of battle lapped close as in the 1970–1971 dry season, most of the hundred or so Americans from the CIA, Air Force, and Army who were stationed there flew out each night for the safety of Vientiane or Udorn air base in Thailand—which "shows something about our 'commitment' to our hilltribe allies," wrote a disgusted aid official. Vang Pao began to talk openly of resettling his surviving followers somewhere out of the war, perhaps in western Laos. Each time, U.S. officials talked him out of it. Everyone was sorry for the Hmong. But the war had to come first.

Vang Pao was not a heartless man. His anguish at his people's losses was patently sincere. But in a society that was still feudal in outlook and organization, he had been able to supplant the traditional clan leaders by his control of American riches to reward those who followed him and American bombs to punish those who refused. American power made Vang Pao not only the military but also the political chief of the Hmong. It was not in the nature of his circumstances or culture that he would walk away from the source of his authority. Sorrowfully, perhaps, but inevitably, Vang Pao would continue waging war as long as his American patrons demanded it.

The Hmong's tragedy in any case had become irreversible well before either they or their American sponsors realized it. The lands that supported them belonged to the Communists, leaving them dependent on American supply drops to their hilltop redoubts. Their traditions of clan organization and leadership, which were among the qualities that recommended them to the Americans to begin with, were largely destroyed. And the cost in blood was, by the 1970s, devastating. From a peak of nearly 40,000 men in 1967, the irregular units' strength dropped to only about 27,000 in early 1972. In 1971 alone, their casualties of 2,259 killed and 5,775 wounded represented 30 percent of the entire irregular force—nearly half of its infantry strength. And those were just the military casualties. The full tally of deaths in the remote hills of Laos would probably never be known. The prewar Hmong population was roughly estimated at somewhere between 150,000 and 300,000. Of these, nearly all were driven from their homes. The most conservative reports listed 18,000 to 20,000 killed in combat between 1963 and 1971. Many more died after fleeing the battle zones; Hmong refugees were decimated by malaria, which was almost unknown in their tribal homelands but was "hyperendemic," U.S. Senate consultants reported, in the region to which they were driven.

By the time Henry Kissinger and Le Duc Tho initialed the Vietnam peace agreement, the Hmong of Laos had virtually been destroyed as a people, and in their future lay not peace, but further devastation as the Communist conquest of Laos two years later scattered them in a diaspora ending either in death or in years in squalid refugee camps in Thailand.

To replace the depleted irregular units, the U.S. arranged in the early 1970s for Thai "volunteers" to take over more and more of the war on the Lao battlefields. The Thai were recruited from the Thai army and "sheep-dipped," with Lao identity cards substituted for their own documents. Like the Hmong and other Lao tribal guerrillas, the Thai were paid by the CIA with Defense Department funds. By late 1972, about 21,000 Thai troops were in Laos, more than triple the number a year before. Though they helped maintain some semblance of a battlefield defense, they also represented an increased dependence on foreign military force which, like the U.S. bombing that was the only other military asset the Royal Lao army had, would presumably no longer be available after a peace agreement.

Over the years, the two Lao factions had intermittently exchanged peace offers; and on July 1, 1972, Prince Souvanna wrote his half-brother, the Lao Patriotic Front chairman Prince Souphanouvong, proposing a new effort at negotiations. Changes in the world climate, Souvanna wrote, indicated that "reason and good sense seem at last to prevail, while it has become apparent that strength cannot be the ultimate solution for the Indochina problem."

In reply, Souphanouvong reiterated the customary Pathet Lao demand for a complete end to U.S. bombing as a precondition for peace talks to start. But he also agreed to send an envoy, Prince Souk Vongsak, to Vientiane. Souk Vongsak arrived July 15, and nine days later, Souvanna proposed a ceasefire to be followed by political discussions which, he said, could be based on the Pathet Lao's five-point program, which had been announced two years before. The five points were: (1) an end to U.S. bombing and withdrawal of U.S. advisers and military equipment; (2) a Lao foreign policy of "peace and neutrality"; (3) election of a new National Assembly that would be "truly representative of the Lao people of all nationalities"; (4) establishment of a provisional coalition, physically based in a neutralized zone, to administer the country until new elections; and (5) unification of Laos "through consultations . . . on the principle of equality and national concord." The fifth point also called for "pro-American forces [to] . . . withdraw forthwith" from "illegally occupied" areas and the resettlement of people who had been "forcibly removed" from their native places—in other words, the forced return of the Hmong and other tribal people to areas under Communist control.

Even after Souvanna accepted the five points as the "basis for discussion"—a major concession—Souphanouvong initially continued to demand a bombing halt. On August 13, he chided Souvanna for failing to mention

> the question of prime urgency—the total cessation by the United States of aerial bombardments on the whole Lao territory, with no conditions attached. This entirely runs contrary to the spirit of the five points of the L.P.F. [Lao Patriotic Front] which you have accepted. I hope that Your Royal Highness will think it over and rid yourself of all pressure and categorically urge the U.S. to put an immediate halt to the bombing . . . in order to create conditions in which we could seriously engage in exchanges of views on the basis of the five points of the L.P.F. . . . and find together an adequate solution to normalizing the situation in our kingdom.

The following month, however, tacitly giving up its demand for a bombing halt, the Pathet Lao notified Souvanna that they would send a delegation to Vientiane to open negotiations. The talks began October 17. Heading the Pathet Lao delegation was Phoun Sipraseuth, a Politburo member who was believed to rank fourth among the leaders of the clandestine Lao Peoples Revolutionary Party. The negotiations continued each Tuesday in a conference room on the fourth floor of the education ministry.

The meetings had none of the pomp or supercharged atmosphere of the Vietnam negotiations. No silver jets hurtled envoys across the world. No black limousines sped past popping flashbulbs through high steel gates. Instead, in keeping with Vientiane's relaxed, rustic atmosphere, the two Lao delegations drove to their rendezvous each week in modest convoys of Mercedes and Toyotas, stepped out with no particular protocol in the dusty ministry courtyard and, in a hubbub of small talk, trooped up the three flights of steps to the conference room. Newsmen and foreign diplomats congregated comfortably on the airy balcony just outside the meeting room. In front of the doors, government and Pathet Lao guards lounged, murmuring softly together and occasionally, in Lao fashion, clasping hands.

Unlike the warrring Vietnamese, the Lao seemed to have a fairly promising basis for compromise. Both sides recognized the 600-year-old monarchy. (The Pathet Lao would later abolish it and unseat Savang Vatthana, but all during the war they professed to respect him as the "Supreme Power" in the country.) Personal ties of friendship and kinship had endured, despite the war and the division of the country. Both sides knew that Laos's fate would be decided by events in other countries and would not be significantly affected by any more bloodshed in their own. In Souvanna Phouma, too, Laos had a leader who, unlike Nguyen Van Thieu in Vietnam, was genuinely committed to conciliation.

Souvanna, who kept a collection of Mahatma Gandhi's works on display in his study along with signed photographs of Presidents Kennedy, Johnson, and Nixon, seemed almost desperately anxious for an agreement as the 1972 negotiations began. Souvanna believed, one of his top military commanders later recalled, "in the fundamental honesty of his half-brother, Prince Souphanouvong, and that under his leadership, the Neo Lao Hak Sat would negotiate in good faith. Furthermore, he believed that any agreement was better than none and that we should not be overly concerned with the content; we could work it all out later after the new coalition government took control."

The two Lao sides both advocated neutralism, a coalition government, and an end to foreign intervention. The disputes were about the definitions of those terms. On the matter of intervention, Souvanna insisted on a North Vietnamese withdrawal; the Pathet Lao, having never acknowledged North Vietnam's presence in the first place, interpreted "non-interference" to mean the end of American bombing, dissolution of American-led special units, and removal of the Thai forces. With respect to a coalition, Souvanna proposed that the Pathet Lao should reoccupy the four cabinet seats they had been awarded in the 1962 Geneva settlement. The Pathet Lao, however, had demanded for several years that the coalition formula be revised to reflect "present-day realities." In their view, Souvanna and his associates, having accepted U.S. assistance to wage war against the Communists, could no longer be considered neutral, and their majority in the coalition should be eliminated. Their places would be taken, under the Pathet Lao plan, by "patriotic neutralists"—so defined, evidently, on the basis of demonstrated agreement with Pathet Lao policies.

Two days after Hanoi's October 26 broadcast of the draft Vietnam agreement and Henry Kissinger's "peace is at hand" press conference, Phoumi Vongvichit, secretary general of the Lao Patriotic Front and one of Souphanouvong's senior associates, arrived in Vientiane as "special adviser" to the Pathet Lao delegation—the same title used by Le Duc Tho in Paris. "We come to Vientiane," Phoumi declared at Wattay Airport, "with a good faith to contribute our best to the progress of the negotiations, to find an adequate solution responding to our Lao people's urgent aspiration for independence, sovereignty, peace and national reconciliation." But the negotiations still faced the fundamental difficulty that had always blocked a Lao settlement: the necessity, as one writer put it, "to guarantee the foreign supporters of the Lao factions . . . that their vital interests will not be compromised."

The United States, though publicly in favor of a negotiated Lao peace, actually wanted one only if the talks there remained "parallel with the Vietnam negotiations," so that it could keep bombing the Ho Chi Minh trail until a Vietnam ceasefire was reached. (For exactly the same reason, eight years earlier, when Souvanna, Souphanouvong, and the rightist Prince Boun Oum attempted to negotiate, secret guidance given to American officials informed them that U.S. policy was not to encourage agreement but to "slow down any progress"; negotiating tactics were suggested to Souvanna purposely to keep the talks bogged down.) Thus, as the Paris talks stalled after Kissinger's failure to win Thieu's agreement, so did the negotiations in Vientiane.

In the talks, government negotiators—rather perfunctorily and seemingly without much hope—proposed a return to the 1962 ceasefire lines, which gave the Pathet Lao significantly less territory than they occupied in 1972. Not surprisingly, the plan was summarily rejected. Any truce, the Pathet Lao insisted, must be a ceasefire in place, with no "regroupment zones" or exchanges of territory. On political issues, the Pathet Lao allowed the impression to exist that Souvanna Phouma would be acceptable to them as head of a new coalition. But they were also able to establish quite swiftly that what was being negotiated was a new coalition, not the reconstitution of the

1962 settlement. This meant, as one experienced observer commented, that the two delegations met "as equals rather than as a constitutional government delegation and a penitent splinter group"—a psychological point of no small importance to either side.

The actual meetings were spent for the most part on matters of much less substance, however. Once the basic positions had been stated, the formulas were repeated week after week, with hardly the change of a syllable. Endless hours were consumed in trivial disputes, such as that over the placement of the red Lao flag with its three-headed elephant symbol. (The Pathet Lao did not object to the flag, which they too accepted as the national emblem. But they were furious because it had been placed in the meeting room without their consent.) With such arguments going on inside, the mood among spectators on the balcony turned listless. "All we are doing," shrugged a diplomat one Tuesday, "is waiting for the rest of the world to decide what to do about Laos."

"See you next war"

The announcement of the Paris agreement restored a sense of urgency to the Laos peace talks—but with the psychological balance tipping sharply toward the Pathet Lao. The Royal Lao government, which had publicly asked the United States to conclude a Laos ceasefire as part of the Vietnam settlement, found itself rebuffed. From then on, Prince Souvanna seems to have decided that his freedom of action had run out and that his only course was to offer whatever concessions had to be made to get an agreement.

In early February the Pathet Lao and North Vietnamese increased the pressure not only at the conference table but also on the battlefield, temporarily capturing Paksong, on the Bolovens plateau in southern Laos, and threatening other government-held towns. There were no massive North Vietnamese reinforcements, however, as some on the government side had feared. The United States continued heavy bombing in support of government forces. Between January 27 and February 22 nearly 8,900 sorties were flown in Laos, an average of nearly 350 a day. Souvanna apparently felt, however, that he could not count on such support for much longer. A form of psychological deadline was set when the international Vietnam peace conference was scheduled to start February 26 in Paris. Though the conference was not directly connected with Laos, it was widely felt in Vientiane that the U.S. wanted a settlement by that date, and some Lao firmly believed that Washington had given Souvanna a virtual ultimatum to reach the best agreement he could.

What actually passed between the Lao prime minister and U.S. representatives has not been fully disclosed. Sisouk Na Champassak, the Lao defense minister, said at the time that the U.S. had not explicitly warned that the bombers would be grounded. But his perception, like that of other officials, was that the Americans wanted a settlement and would not provide air support indefinitely.

Major General Oudone Sananikone, the army chief of staff, wrote in a postwar memoir that John Gunther Dean of the U.S. embassy and his staff "frequently urged members of the government to make more concessions. . . . Some of these urgings took the form of thinly veiled threats of cuts in American assistance." The Pathet Lao negotiators, Sananikone added,

> were well aware of what was going on. They already knew that Souvanna Phouma would agree to almost anything; now they knew that the Americans were, in effect, in their corner. Armed with these advantages, they became even more obdurate. . . . each time an impasse occurred, Souvanna Phouma ordered his delegation to concede. On the worst of these occasions, the right wing members would threaten to resign. This put Souvanna Phouma in a difficult position which was ameliorated by pressure from the American embassy. We would find that the weekly shipments of American supplied rice for the army would not arrive, or that the American supplied money to pay the army would be delayed, or that only part of the fuel needed to run the army's vehicles would be delivered. Capitulation by the right wing was essential to maintain the NLA [National Lao Army]. The American military attaches made this very clear to all senior officers. . . . The right wing leadership—which essentially was the leadership of the NLA—was being rendered impotent by American pressure.

In this atmosphere, Phoumi Vongvichit returned to the Lao capital on February 3 from Sam Neua, where he had gone for consultations. Two days later, he and Souvanna met for the first of a two-week series of private meetings in which, while the official delegations marked time, the two men concluded the terms of the Laos settlement. On point after point, in matters of both style and substance, Souvanna yielded. His concessions apparently went beyond any that might have been recommended by his American ally; when the agreement was completed, a number of its provisions were, congressional inquirers later reported, "received as unpleasant surprises in Washington," even though the U.S. recognized that Souvanna's bargaining position had been weak to begin with. The fifteen-day period agreed on in the U.S.-North Vietnamese discussions passed without an agreement. But on the night of February 20, 1973, finally, the official Vientiane Radio newscast announced that an agreement had been completed.

The following morning, the two delegations assembled at Prince Souvanna's modest villa on the bank of the Mekong, a few miles from the center of Vientiane. Five copies of the peace agreement had been prepared, typed in Lao script. One was for the king, one for each of the two sides, and one for each of the two new political entities that were to be created: the new coalition government and a body called the National Political Consultative Council. The ceremony did not last long. Phoumi Vongvichit signed the five copies for the Patriotic Front. Pheng Phongsavan, the public works minister and Souvanna's close confidant who had headed the official government negotiating team, signed for what was now to be called, somewhat derogatorily, the "Vientiane administration." In the audience, along with Lao officials of both sides and a few dozen foreign newsmen, were diplomats representing Great Britain and the Soviet Union, as cochairmen of the 1962 Geneva meeting, and Canada, India, and Poland, the three members of the moribund International Control Commission. The signing completed, Pheng and Phoumi stood, smiled broadly, and reached across the small table where the pile of documents rested to shake hands.

There were few smiles among Vientiane officials, however, as the terms of the agreement became known. Souvanna's concessions had been even broader than the most worried anti-Communists had feared. In its final form, the agreement reflected nearly every Pathet Lao demand except that which would have given outright control of the new coalition to their own and "patriotic neutralist" ministers. Instead, seats in the new government were to be shared equally between the two sides, under a prime minister and "two personalities who stand for peace, independence, neutrality and democracy and who will be chosen by the two sides by common agreement."

In every other respect, the Pathet Lao were definitely more equal than their adversaries. Their terminology was accepted, denying Vientiane the status of a legitimate national government; it was referred to only as the Vientiane administration or the "Vientiane government side," while the Communists were called, somewhat more grandly, the "Patriotic Forces side." The agreement also reflected the Pathet Lao view of foreign intervention in Laos. Chapter I, a statement of "general principles" which recognized "the present realities of Laos where there are two zones separately controlled by the two sides," also demanded that Lao neutrality be respected by "the Lao parties concerned, the United States of America, Thailand, and the other foreign countries." Thus the U.S. and Thailand were specifically obligated to end military action in Laos, while North Vietnam

was nowhere mentioned—enabling the Communist fiction to be preserved
that foreigners had intervened only on the anti-Communist side.

In its remaining chapters, the agreement provided:

> An in-place ceasefire to take effect at noon, Vientiane time, on the
> day after the signing, February 22.

The very first sentence of the ceasefire article, even before it declared an end to hostilities between the two Lao armies, stipulated
that at the ceasefire hour, "foreign countries end completely and
definitively all their bombardments on the whole Lao territory"—that
is, an immediate halt to U.S. bombing. The ceasefire terms were
markedly favorable to the Pathet Lao. The government was not even
assured that it would be able to supply its troops in outposts encircled
by Communist forces. Instead, arrangements for resupply in such
situations were left to be decided by "common agreement" in a bi-
lateral truce commission that was to administer the ceasefire. Also left
to later unanimous agreement was the problem of replacement of
damaged or worn-out military equipment. While not even admitting
the existence of its own ally and supplier, the Pathet Lao had thus
obtained a legal veto over all military aid to its opponent's army.

About the only issue on which the Vientiane government's position
prevailed was the repatriation of refugees, which was to be voluntary
and not forced, as the Pathet Lao's Five Points had demanded.

> Formation of a new coalition cabinet within 30 days of the signing of
> the agreement.

Each side would have half the seats, under a prime minister and
two "personalities" who ostensibly stood above factional divisions. It
was assumed that Prince Souvanna would remain prime minister and
that each side would name one of the two mutually chosen "personalities." That is what happened, although it took far longer than
the 30 days allowed for the arrangements to be completed.

To be formed at the same time as the government was the new
National Political Consultative Council, which was to oversee the
peace agreement and arrange the "genuinely free and democratic
elections" that would choose a permanent government.

The creation of the council represented another of Souvanna's
concessions. The government had opposed the idea as, in the words
of a well-informed Asian diplomat, "unconstitutional, unneeded, and
dangerous." But to the Pathet Lao, whose experience in two earlier
coalitions had not left them with an abiding trust in power sharing,
the council was a necessary safeguard for the principles of the agreement. Because the Vientiane side was expected to have a slight numerical edge in the cabinet, with Souvanna remaining prime minister,
it was assumed that the Pathet Lao would have an equivalent supe-
riority in the council. Both bodies were to act "in accordance with the

principle of unanimity," which meant that the Pathet Lao had veto power, if they wished to exercise it, over any government decision.

Withdrawal of all foreign forces within 60 days after formation of the provisional government.

Like the opening statement of "general principles," this chapter made no mention of North Vietnamese. It did specify the CIA-controlled irregulars, requiring the disbanding of foreign-organized "special forces"—a requirement avoided by integrating the guerrillas into the regular army as the truce went into effect.

Reactivation of the International Control Commission, but without any powers beyond those that had already proven inadequate after the 1954 and 1962 Geneva agreements.

"Neutralization" of Vientiane and the royal capital Luang Prabang.

This meant that the two cities would not be considered part of the Vientiane-controlled zone, even while the provisional government was being formed. Neutral status for both cities was even more than the Pathet Lao originally sought in the negotiations, it was later disclosed. "The PL proposed neutralization of Vientiane to assure the security of the coalition government," two experienced observers reported, "and when the government countered by proposing it for the royal capital at Luang Prabang, the PL insisted upon both, and won."

The Pathet Lao representatives, understandably, were jubilant at the ceasefire agreement. For the first time in many years, they invited correspondents to a full-dress press conference at their headquarters, where a beaming Phoumi Vongvichit declared that the agreement "responds to the supreme and authentic aspirations of our Lao people."

As we sipped soft drinks, Phoumi answered questions in a gentle but professorial manner, obviously relishing his appearance before the reporters and cameramen of the West at an hour the Pathet Lao believed was triumphant. At one point, when no one raised a hand from the wooden chairs set out on the plank floor of the tin-roofed building, Phoumi smilingly solicited more questions, as if unwilling to let the conference end. When someone asked if he had had any contact with U.S. Ambassador G. McMurtrie Godley—who was often called "the air marshal" for his reputed enthusiastic direction of the U.S. bombing in Laos—Phoumi replied with delicate irony. "This morning we met with the U.S. Ambassador after the signing," he said. "He congratulated us, and we thanked him for all he had done to help us reach this accord."

On the government side the agreement was greeted with deep dismay. The arrangement whereby the Pathet Lao retained complete control of their own zone while gaining a half-share in the national government seemed a case of "what's mine is mine and what's yours is half mine, too." Also disturbing was the delay in withdrawal of foreign troops until after formation of the new government. This meant that through the political phase of the settlement the Pathet Lao would still hold its military trump, the North Vietnamese army, while Souvanna would have given up his with the cessation of U.S. air support. "This means the government will be formed under pressure from the North Vietnamese," complained Sisouk Na Champassak, "because . . . there will be no American bombing. How can you freely form a government if you have foreign forces remaining here for 60 days afterward?" Another senior Lao official put it more succinctly and more grimly. "This," he said disconsolately, "is the worst defeat we have suffered."

In its first hours, the Laos truce looked not only like a severe political setback, it also looked like the same sort of failure the Vietnam ceasefire had been.

Attempting to grab additional territory just as the battle lines were frozen, the North Vietnamese and Pathet Lao attacked in every part of the kingdom in the hours before the truce. As in South Vietnam four weeks earlier, only the United States strictly observed the timetable. As noon approached on February 22, American bombers dropped their last loads and headed for their bases in Thailand. So did the "ABCCC's"—Airborne Control and Command Centers, C-130 aircraft loaded with radar and other gear which directed the bombing strikes while orbiting in the skies over Laos. As one of the ABCCC's left Lao airspace, its pilot radioed back a last message.

"Goodby," he said, "and see you next war."

A distraught Prince Sisouk flew that day to inspect military positions and confer with unit commanders north of Vientiane. With a handful of other European and American correspondents, I hitchhiked on a Lao Air Force C-47 that accompanied the defense minister's plane. From the big American-run logistics base at Vang Vieng, headquarters for air supply to the guerrilla army, we flew to Sala Phou Koun, which overlooked the highway between Vientiane and Luang Prabang. Artillery was booming as our party landed, hours after the truce was supposed to take effect. Later we landed at the CIA base at Long Cheng, a small valley set among improbable spirelike mountains resembling those on a Chinese scroll painting. The other chief feature of the scenery at Long Cheng was the forest of radio masts sprouting from the buildings that surrounded the airstrip.

It was late afternoon by now, but Lao Air Force T-28s were still rumbling off the perilously short runway, their wing-racks fully loaded with bombs. They were supporting Vang Pao troops who were under attack in positions as close as nine miles away. We could hear the deep crunch of the bombs falling in the hills. After his meeting with Sisouk, Vang Pao came out to show us an unsigned, typed communication he had received a few hours earlier—a document that conveyed something of the anonymity in which the Americans had cloaked the war they were now walking away from. I copied the message in my notebook:

> To: Major General Vang Pao, commanding general, Military Region 2.
> From: Chief of unit, SKY, Long Tieng.
> Subject: Cease-fire agreement.
>
> 1. In accord with the terms of the cease-fire agreement between the Royal Lao Government and the Neo Lao Hak Sat that established 1200 22 February as the time armed action between those forces would cease, the United States is honoring this agreement.
>
> 2. As we discussed previously, USAF air support would cease as of 1200, 22 February. I confirmed this prior to attending your lunch in honor of your distinguished visitors today by talking with CRICKET, the ABCCC in this area. USAF were under instructions to clear Lao air space by 1200 this date.

SKY, presumably, was a code name having to do with the ground control center at Long Cheng, manned, as were other such units around Laos, by American Air Force officers in civilian clothes who worked with CIA advisers and communicators directing the secret war.

Shaking his head, Vang Pao said he did not see how his positions could be held without American air support. One of his outposts, part of a string screening Long Cheng from Communist-held territory on the Plain of Jars, had fallen at 2:30 that afternoon, and others were under heavy shelling. "We are not like South Vietnam," he said, standing at the side of the runway and speaking over the engines of fighters and transports that shrieked in the crisp, clear afternoon air, "South Vietnam, the Americans have given all means, thousands of tanks, trucks, airplanes. . . ." The rest of the sentence did not need to be spoken. America was leaving Laos with no such military machine, but with an army of teen-aged boys belonging to a people that had already lost its spirit, to face a stronger enemy.

In Vientiane the next morning, Prince Souvanna called reporters back to his villa to charge that instead of honoring the ceasefire, the Communists had planned all along to mount a "general offensive" and seize additional territory as soon as the skies were clear of American bombers.

"We had faith in this agreement," Souvanna said, his usual composure utterly gone, "and we have been tricked. Our faith has been violated." If the Communist attacks continued, he said, he would ask for renewed U.S. air strikes. The request was made that day and quickly complied with; nine B-52s struck targets that night near Paksong. The Pathet Lao were unapologetic and, to all appearances, unimpressed with the post-truce air raids. "We have fought the American bombers up until Wednesday," said their spokesman, Soth Phetrasi, "and can do so again if we have to."

In contrast to Vietnam, however, the post-ceasefire fighting turned out to be no more than a spasm. In a few days the level of combat had significantly lessened, though some fighting continued. Casualties in March dropped to eighteen government troops killed a week, about one-fourth the weekly average before the truce. Of the clashes that did occur, many were of the sort described in one account as "meeting engagements by patrols producing excited shots in the air and rapid departure." One more round of American B-52 air attacks came April 16 and 17, after a Communist assault overran a town called Tha Vieng south of the Plain of Jars. But there was no fullscale resumption of the war, even when the political discussions dragged on far behind the schedule set by the agreement.

The pace of the political talks was torpid even by the undemanding standards of Laos. Instead of 30 days to form the new government, it took seven months to draft a protocol on how to proceed, and even that was not successfully completed until the suppression of an attempted coup in August 1973 by Thailand-based rightist exiles. During the coup John Gunther Dean, the U.S. chargé d'affaires, raced around Vientiane—at some physical risk—in an unusual display of personal diplomacy aimed at persuading both the rightists and the Communists that the U.S. was firm in its support of Souvanna and would not countenance any sabotage of the agreement. Dean's demonstration seemed finally to convince the Lao rightists that they had no hope of resuming the war. The Communists, too, though their propaganda continued to denounce American "interference," seemed to accept U.S. sincerity in backing the agreement. When it was finally signed in September 1973, three and a half weeks after the coup attempt, the protocol assigned cabinet ministries and arranged for the demarcation of a new ceasefire line, while also specifying the composition of the Consultative Council, spelling out the details of neutralizing Vientiane and Luang Prabang, reaffirming the timetable for withdrawing foreign troops, and outlining procedures for the exchange of prisoners and the repatriation of refugees who wished to return to their home villages.

Following the protocol, more months were consumed in further dickering. Foreigners in Vientiane stopped even trying to guess when the new government would actually be established: it turned out to be in April of 1974, a full thirteen months and fourteen days after the ceasefire agreement was signed.

In all these tortuous negotiations, Laos remained placid, and a spirit of accommodation survived. Communist members of the coalition professed deep suspicion of the Americans and the Lao rightists, and incessantly raised alarms of supposed plots. But in fact the anti-Communists seemed resigned. The war was over, and if coalition was only a stop on the path to full Communist control, as many of the rightists feared, there was nothing further to be done about it. In the end, just as in a quarter-century of conflict,

Laos's fate was decided not by any actions of its own but by developments outside. Communist rule was established after the Communist armies in South Vietnam and Cambodia won their unexpected victories in the spring of 1975.

After their takeover, the Pathet Lao made little pretense at being anything but obedient vassals of the North Vietnamese. They abolished the monarchy, fulfilling a prediction Savang Vatthana had voiced years earlier that he was "doomed to be the last king of Laos." With the Communist seizure of power, the grim drabness of an alien totalitarianism settled over a land that should have had a gentler destiny. Communist rule turned out harshly for some 20,000 Vientiane-side officials who were reported incarcerated in "reeducation camps" in the malaria-ridden hinterland. The tragedy of the Hmong continued, as the tribe's remnants fought on hopelessly and were reportedly attacked with poison gas weapons by Vietnamese Communist troops trying to subdue them. Those Hmong who could do so fled to Thailand. Some 40,000 of them were in squalid camps there in the late 1970s, of whom only a few could realistically hope for resettlement.

Even so, Laos's fall was still a less bloody affair than that of the other Indochinese nations. The Lao spirit of pacifism did, after all, spare many of its people the events that would, after the Paris agreement, engulf Vietnam and Cambodia in savagery and terror.

VICTIMS *Above,* boy soldiers in Laos are hardly taller than their rifles (*Wide World Photos*); *facing page,* Hmong women and babies at a Lao refugee camp. Relief workers seldom saw any but women, the aged, or the very young; nearly all Hmong men and boys were fighting or fleeing the war (*photo by John Woodruff/courtesy of Baltimore Sunpapers*); *right,* the cartoon by Khut Khun, Cambodia's most popular cartoonist, shows the weariness of the fifth year of war. Khut Khun died during the Khmer Rouge rule.

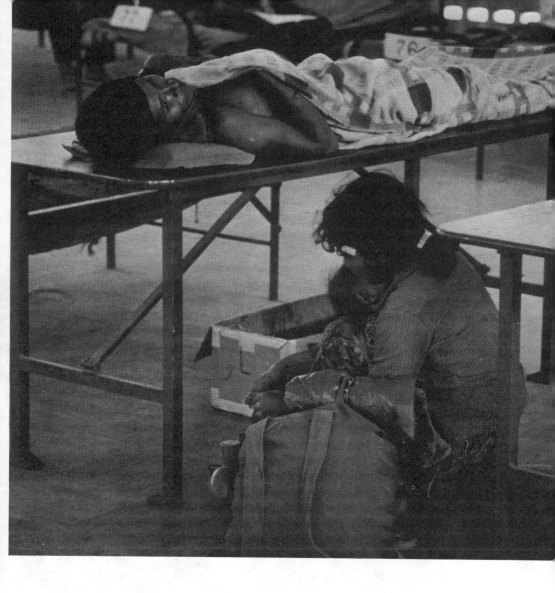

CAMBODIA *Above,* a soldier's wife waits by her wounded husband's bed in a makeshift Phnom Penh hospital (*David Hume Kennerly/The White House*); *facing page, top left,* Prince Norodom Sihanouk (*Francolon/Gamma-Liaison*); *top right,* a teenaged Khmer Rouge soldier after his capture (*photo by Dan Southerland*); *bottom,* the story of the siege of Phnom Penh is written on the faces of children waiting for meals served by relief agency worker (*courtesy of Catholic Relief Services*).

EVACUATION *Facing page,* a U.S. Marine helicopter loads during the evacuation of Phnom Penh (*USMC photo*); *left,* Ambassador John Gunther Dean (*State Department photo*); *below,* Cambodia's President Lon Nol, a few weeks before he left the country. The author, in white shirt and holding a notebook, is at right (*author's collection*).

Chapter 7

Cambodia: "The land is broken"

The Paris agreement did not bring even a fictitious peace to Cambodia. Instead, it brought a new paroxysm of violence and devastation.

In part this was because Cambodian events had acquired their own dynamic. Like Laos, though much later, Cambodia had been drawn into the war not through its own actions but by those of the conflicting sides in Vietnam. But by the end of 1972 the war was also a bloody contest for power in Cambodia itself, whose outcome could no longer be wholly decided by Hanoi, Saigon, or Washington. The sense of shared identity that somehow survived across the battle lines in Laos did not exist in Cambodia. Nor were the Khmer Communists dutiful satellites of the North Vietnamese, as were the Pathet Lao. The Paris agreement did not mean to them that they should end their own war. Instead, though this was not yet fully realized in Phnom Penh or Washington, the Khmer insurgents believed that they had been betrayed by their Vietnamese ally. The conclusion they drew from the Paris agreement was that they must intensify their assault, in the apparent fear that they would be cheated of victory unless they won it quickly.

Cambodia had no one comparable to Souvanna Phouma who might have been accepted by both sides as a symbol of national unity. Ruling in Phnom Penh was the ailing, ineffective, and enigmatic Lon Nol, whose army had suffered an unrelieved string of defeats since the first year of the war and whose deservedly unpopular government was kept afloat only by United States aid. The insurgent movement was nominally led by Prince Norodom

Sihanouk, head of the Peking-based Royal Government of National Union of Cambodia (often called GRUNK, from its French initials).

Sihanouk, Cambodia's chief of state until he was overthrown and exiled in March 1970, was still the only Cambodian leader with international standing. But he had no meaningful authority. The men who actually commanded the insurgents were mysterious, shadowy figures who were thought to represent a number of factions, whose objectives and philosophies differed and whose relative strengths were hard to discern, leaving the entire movement the hostage of its most militant segment. Who really held the power to decide matters of war and peace remained, in early 1973, a complete enigma to the rest of the world. Thus, not only were there no peace negotiations taking place, there was no contact between the two sides at all. There was not even a door to knock on.

In any case, the announced peace terms of both sides appeared to leave no room for negotiating. Each demanded, in effect, the unconditional surrender of the other; the opposing leaders, indeed, had condemned each other to death. The impasse reflected a war that had been fought with terrible brutality. Its first weeks in 1970 had seen the mass murder of thousands of unarmed Vietnamese civilians who had been living peacefully in Cambodia for many years. In the conflict that followed, execution of prisoners, cannibalism, torture, and mutilation of the dead were practiced by both sides.

The growing tragedy in Cambodia arose, too, from American decisions early in 1973 that have never been convincingly explained and that left, even years afterward, some of the most troubling memories of the entire American effort in Indochina.

The story of what Cambodia had become in three years of war was written on the faces of six or seven soldiers' wives standing at a roadblock near a place called Prek Ho, ten miles or so south or Phnom Penh. They were listening intently to the sound of rifle and machinegun fire coming from a few hundred yards down the road, on the far side of a bridge that arched over a small stream. Each of the women clutched a parcel of food. It was for their husbands, they said, who had been in battle for two days with nothing to eat. One showed me the contents of her small shopping bag. It contained a few loaves of bread, some vegetables, and four or five small tins of food, provisions that did not have to be cooked and could sustain a soldier in combat. For that she had spent a thousand riels in the market. Her husband, a sergeant, earned only 7,000 riels a month.

The women knew their husbands had not eaten because the truck with the unit's rations was still parked at headquarters. Khmer soldiers did not have a regular ration system, but were supposed to receive field rations when actually in combat. Often, as now, they did not, with the result that the government army could not operate for long away from village markets

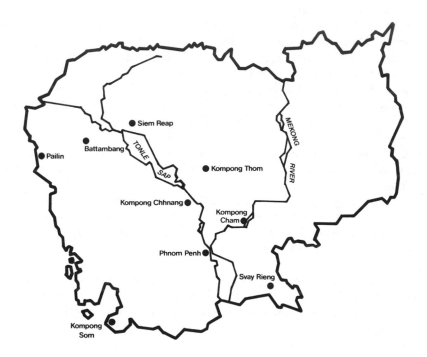

CAMBODIA

and was thus unable to patrol for more than a day or so against an enemy that moved freely through the countryside.

When they saw the ration truck still parked on the second day, the women at the Prek Ho bridge said, they had gone to the market and had now come to find their husbands' unit. But a guard at the roadblock refused to let them go on because of the heavy fighting ahead. Patiently, the women waited several hours for the firing to lessen. But then they advanced on the guard again.

"Our husbands are out there," one of them wailed. She shook her shopping bag in the guard's face; it trembled in her hand. She waved toward the sound of the gunfire. "Why don't you let us go to them? Why don't you just kill us right here?" She began to weep. The other women edged closer. The guard smiled, not in amusement but in nervousness, and cradled his rifle uneasily in his arms. Plainly he didn't want to shoot. But he didn't want to let the women walk into the midst of a battle, either.

The women's cries grew louder and wilder. Most of them were sobbing now, and for a moment it looked as if they were going to walk right past the guard, daring him to shoot. But before they did, another soldier drew up to the roadblock on a motorbike. He dismounted and walked over to the women and the unhappy guard, speaking softly to them. The wailing quieted. The soldier was from the same unit as the women's husbands, and after a moment's clearly painful uncertainty, they handed him their parcels. He tied them carefully onto the rack behind his seat and drove on, toward the battle. The women looked after him until he disappeared past the first bend in the road; then, backs hunched under their thin sarongs like little punctuation marks of sorrow and despair, they turned to trudge back toward Prek Ho.

Fighting without food was nothing unusual for a soldier of the Cambodian government. Most of the time he also fought without adequate medical treatment for his wounds, without drugs for malaria or other illness, without honest or competent officers, without any provision for allotments to his family. His pay was always inadequate, often late, and not infrequently stolen by corrupt commanders. And almost always, from the very first weeks of the war, he fought without victory.

"I am sure that in any country, in your country, if soldiers received the same conditions as our soldiers, they probably would not fight ever," Lt. Gen. Sosthene Fernandez, the army commander, told a group of correspondents not long before the Lon Nol regime's defeat. Long before that it was already hard to see why Cambodia's army fought—or to what purpose.

Prewar Cambodia, if not the paradise it was sometimes sentimentally remembered to be, was still a peaceful, fertile place that offered its seven million people not great material well-being but the psychic security of tradition, religion, and a village life as tranquil and slow as the flow of the numberless muddy streams that nourished the great rivers: the Mekong, the Bassac, and the Tonle Sap. "Living standards are relatively low," wrote one scholar just as the war began that would destroy prewar Cambodian life forever, "but there is little dire poverty and no starvation. An estimated 90 per cent of the farmers own the land they till." Theravada Buddhism, the state religion, permeated village life, its rituals marking the seasons as surely as the rhythms of planting, transplanting, and harvesting rice.

Cambodian agriculture was primitive and yields were low, but enough rice was grown to feed the population well and leave a large surplus for export. Cambodia also had Asia's lushest supply of fresh-water fish, a rich source of protein. Visiting the great Tonle Sap Lake region in 1860, the French explorer Henri Mouhot—European discoverer of the great ruins at Angkor Wat—was astounded at the teeming fish life. Fish "are so incredibly abundant," he recorded wonderingly, "that when the water is high they are actually crushed under the boats, and the play of the oars is frequently impeded by them." An American aid officer during the war, after interviewing numerous refugees, reported: "Most Khmer farmers ate well before the war. Fish was plentiful. The average farm house was usually made from wood, in many cases had a tile roof, and also appears to have been quite comfortable. The constant and pervasive influence of the local Buddhist pagodas also added to the sense of well-being. . . . While talking about the war or their present condition," he added, "most refugees will repeat over and over again how nice it was on their farms before the war and how much they want to return."

Not only Buddhism and a peasant timelessness pervaded Cambodia, however. It was also a land that lived with an ingrained pessimism, a sense of a civilization long past its flowering and threatened by more vigorous, more powerful, and more populous neighbors.

Khmer civilization reached its zenith in the Angkor, or Kambuja, era, from the ninth to the fifteenth centuries A.D. For a time Khmer emperors ruled not just the area of modern Cambodia but parts of Vietnam, Laos, Thailand, and the Malay Peninsula. But since then the Khmer had been in retreat. Angkor fell to Thai invaders in 1431; for the next four centuries, Cambodians were pressed by the Thai from one side and the Vietnamese from the other—"eaters of Khmer earth," Sihanouk once called them—into an ever-shrinking and less important pocket of the Southeast Asian mainland. In the nineteenth century Cambodia was on the verge of disappearing entirely as an independent nation. Like an Asian Poland it faced partition between two expanding neighbors. Only the intervention of France, which established a protectorate keeping the Cambodian monarchs on the throne, though without much real power, preserved the Khmer national identity. Cambodia remained a civilization that feared the future. When it looked ahead it saw not hope but extinction—a fate that would come perilously close in the 1970s.

Until the start of that decade, while the rest of Indochina was at war, Cambodia managed to remain neutral. Preserving that neutrality was the obsession and only constant aim of its ruler, Prince Sihanouk, who maneuvered between appeasing the Vietnamese—whom he saw always as the chief threat to Cambodia's independence and indeed to its very survival—and seeking the protection of other, stronger powers. Sihanouk's frequent diplomatic reversals won him a reputation for inconstancy; and his vain, flamboyant, whimsical style of governing prevented him from being taken entirely seriously in the West. In the 1960s, he reminded one writer of "some middle-aged gossiping dandy in a Sheridan play or a Mozart opera." One of his foreign advisers, summing up the many contradictions of his character, described Sihanouk as

> both a prince charming and a prince of darkness. He . . . always tacitly connived in the corrupt practices of his entourage, his family, the armed services and the administrative services in general. . . . He can be ruthless and even ferocious to his enemies, including those whom he senses are latently critical of his rule. Hypersensitive to criticism of any sort, egocentric and extremely aggressive, he has a capacity for enthusiasm of so incandescent a nature that its duration is perforce brief. He is endowed with phenomenal energy, childlike lucidity, and some talent for the arts. Histrionic and indiscreet . . . [Sihanouk was] persuaded of his ability to outwit all comers, and to perform brilliantly upon the international stage.

Vice-president Richard Nixon, who met him in 1953, thought the prince "an intelligent man but vain and flighty. . . . He appeared to me," Nixon added in his memoirs, "totally unrealistic about the problems his country faced." But Sihanouk was more constant and above all more realistic than Nixon or his many other critics realized. He was not blameless in the catastrophe that overtook his people. While in power, he was careless of domestic abuses; and after he was overthrown, he lent his name and prestige much too easily to a Communist movement that would produce, in his own later words, "the incorrigible assassins of the Khmer people, nation and race." Yet whatever his faults, Sihanouk's responsibility was light compared with that of the men on both sides who fought over Cambodia after his rule ended.

Even Sihanouk's agility did not keep the war away entirely. From the mid-1960s on, North Vietnamese and Viet Cong forces freely used the regions bordering South Vietnam to rest, resupply, and train their troops. Substantial amounts of supplies for the Vietnamese Communists were allowed to be landed at Cambodia's American-built port, Sihanoukville (later renamed Kompong Som), and trucked overland to the sanctuary areas. Sihanouk entered into these arrangements at a time when he believed that the Communists were going to win the war in fairly short order and that

Cambodia must accommodate them, in the hope that when the war was over, the Vietnamese revolutionaries would be grateful enough to leave Cambodian territory. Sihanouk had expressed this quite bluntly in 1964. "Our interests," he said then, "are served by dealing with the camp that one day will dominate the whole of Asia—and by coming to terms before its victory—in order to obtain the best terms possible."

His calculations were upset, however, by the U.S. intervention that denied the Vietnamese Communists a quick victory. The war was prolonged and Sihanouk found himself the unwilling host to a seemingly permanent Vietnamese occupation of parts of his country.

Under Lyndon Johnson, U.S. policies toward the Cambodian sanctuaries were relatively cautious. From 1966 on, U.S. forces in South Vietnam were authorized to direct artillery or air strikes into Cambodia in answer to fire from over the border. Beginning in October 1967, the U.S. also mounted secret intelligence raids into Cambodia. American commanders from time to time proposed air and ground attacks on the sanctuaries. Under the Johnson administration, all those proposals were turned down. But that restraint lessened sharply with the change of administrations in Washington. President Nixon, in one of his first acts after taking office, asked Gen. Creighton Abrams, the new U.S. commander in Vietnam, for a new assessment of the war. In his reply, dated February 11, 1969. Abrams proposed—among other new tactics—B-52 raids on Cambodian territory. The White House did not reply immediately, but the idea remained very much alive. On March 13, the Joint Chiefs of Staff handed a specific proposal to the secretary of defense, suggesting a single "short-duration, concentrated" attack of 42 B-52s on a spot on the map known as Base Area 353. The target area, said the Chiefs, was the site of the mobile Communist military headquarters called the Central Office for South Vietnam: COSVN.

COSVN was to occupy a bizarre place in the evolution of America's Cambodia strategy. It was offered, like Eve's apple, every time the military leadership sought to expand American actions there; in 1970 it became a famous, if chimerical, objective when Nixon himself called it one of the targets of the U.S. "incursion" into the Cambodian sanctuaries. The Joint Chiefs' March 13 proposal described COSVN as occupying "a tract of land approximately 9 square kilometers in size," which contained "COSVN headquarters and support elements, consisting of an estimated 1,600 enemy personnel. A successful strike on the COSVN headquarters," the Chiefs added, "would produce a degradation in the command, control and coordination of the VC/NVA effort in III and IV Corps."

Nixon agreed to the proposal, though not primarily for military reasons. In February, the Communists had mounted an offensive in South Vietnam which Nixon believed was a "deliberate test" of his intentions, and the

Cambodia air strike would be his signal to Hanoi that the new American president was a dangerous opponent. The strike was carried out March 18, 1969, the first of 3,695 B-52 raids that were flown in extreme secrecy over the Cambodian sanctuaries before the overt U.S. intervention there more than a year later. The raids were given the code name Menu; specific target areas, all within a few miles of the Vietnamese border, were called Breakfast, Lunch, Dinner, Supper, Snack, and Dessert. The bombing was kept secret from Congress and the press, and even military records were falsified to show that the missions were not over Cambodia but over South Vietnam.

Three weeks after the first Menu strike—which caused no noticeable "degradation" of the Communist command—the Joint Chiefs proposed another. Again, COSVN was the enticement. After listing the numerous Communist military and political headquarters thought to be in the area, the Chiefs' memorandum added, "Neutralization of this complex probably would have a most immediate effect upon the conflict, certainly in III Corps." In drafting that and subsequent similar proposals, the Chiefs seemed undismayed that somehow COSVN was never "neutralized." Reading the sequence of Menu memoranda, indeed, almost suggests they preferred an undestroyed COSVN to a destroyed one—at least, whenever further U.S. military action in Cambodia was being considered.

The second series of raids took place April 24 and 25. In the following months, the Cambodia strikes steadily increased in frequency and intensity until they represented 16 percent of all B-52 missions in Southeast Asia. COSVN aside, American commanders were delighted with the results. Menu "has been one of the most effective campaigns of the war," Adm. Thomas Moorer reported to Defense Secretary Melvin Laird in October 1969. Four months later, Gen. Earle K. Wheeler told Laird, "Menu operations have been effective and can continue to be so with acceptable risks." Wheeler was referring to risks that the bombing would be revealed. But there were other risks, which neither U.S. military commanders nor the administration gave much consideration. Menu, not alone but in conjunction with other forces, was upsetting the delicate balance on which peace in Cambodia rested.

It was the Cambodians, the weakest of the conflicting parties, who first tried to force the issue. Sihanouk, after earlier complaining that the Vietnamese were trying to detach Cambodia's Rattanakiri Province and were inspiring uprising by local tribesmen, announced in April 1969—just weeks after the Menu bombing began—that he had ordered the Cambodian army to adopt an "offensive spirit" against intruders in the border region. A month later it was announced that Cambodian MIG jets had bombed and strafed Vietnamese base areas. The arrangement for Vietnamese use of Sihanoukville was quietly suspended; there were "no confirmed arms or

munitions shipments into Sihanoukville" after July 1969, a top-secret U.S.
report later stated. In November, under a new, rightist-dominated cabinet,
reinforcements were sent to the border area to attack North Vietnamese and
Viet Cong bases.

The Cambodians had unchallengeable justice on their side. The Vietnamese were, after all, flagrantly abusing Cambodian territory. But whether
the new policy was prudent was a different matter. The Cambodian army
may not have merited quite the scornful description given it by one visitor:
"a few thousand stumbling well-fed peasants to provide an excuse for
distributing generalships to the royal houses." But it was clearly no match
for the Vietnamese. The Cambodian force—then called FARK, for Force
Armee Royale Khmere—numbered only a few more than 30,000 men with
a mismatched arsenal of obsolete weapons. Its probes against the sanctuaries had no possibility of expelling the Vietnamese; all they could do was
help provoke a crisis Cambodia was completely unprepared to meet.

American military leaders speculated that Cambodian decisions may have
been inspired, in part, by the secret U.S. bombing. "It appears that the
Cambodian government's attitude has recently hardened against the VC/
NVA presence in Cambodia," the Joint Chiefs reported to Laird in February
1970. "Menu operations may have contributed to this. . . . Prior to Menu,
the Cambodians had no help against the enemy." A later report, stamped
"Top Secret—Sensitive—Noforn—Eyes Only—Absolutely for Eyes of Ad-
dressee Only," passed on this appraisal from General Abrams:

> Something appears to have been giving the Cambodians the courage
> to openly change their attitude, and to take action against the VC/
> NVA. . . . Cambodian government policy appears to have gradually
> shifted from one of cooperation to one of applying graduated pressure
> against VC/NVA troops in order to control their activities in Cambodia
> and to extract a guarantee of their eventual withdrawal. . . . The
> Royal Cambodian Government has directed movements by the Cam-
> bodian armed forces (FARK) against VC/NVA. During the past year,
> FARK contacts with VC/NVA have increased in frequency and inten-
> sity. Additional restrictions, such as prohibiting new base areas and
> installing a pass system, have been implemented to directly control
> VC/NVA activity. Tactical operations are being conducted along the
> border in an effort to reassert Cambodian sovereignty. . . . As the
> overall picture is fitted together, it appears that Menu operations may
> have played a significant, if not a decisive, part in this Cambodian
> change.

Abrams's comments, the Chiefs recommended, "should be forwarded to the
President."

The North Vietnamese reaction to the Cambodian raids showed that they
wanted to preserve the existing arrangements, not open a new war against

Cambodian government forces. "The VC/NVA units were under orders at that time, and for political reasons, to refuse direct combat with the FARK," wrote Sak Sutsakhan, who commanded Cambodian operations in the border regions from November 1969 to March 1970. (Then a colonel, Sak later became the Lon Nol government's military commander and then the last chief of state of the disintegrating Khmer Republic.) To help protect their bases, the Vietnamese did begin providing some arms and tactical advice to insurgent Cambodian hill tribesmen—"Khmer Loeu," or "Highland Khmer"—who opposed the Cambodian authorities for their own reasons. This was a significant shift in Vietnamese policy. Previously, in order not to endanger their arrangments with Sihanouk, the Vietnamese had given no support either to tribal rebellions or to the tiny Khmer Rouge ("Red Khmer") guerrilla uprising—which in any case operated far from the border region. Now, however, faced with growing hostility from the Cambodian regime, the Victnamese were willing to begin aiding a Khmer liberation war. The dissident tribesmen—in revolt against forced labor and other oppressive practices imposed by the Sihanouk regime—would later become one nucleus of the Khmer Rouge movement.

As armed conflict gradually spread in the Cambodian sanctuaries, American commanders tended to welcome it as a help to U.S. forces on the Vietnamese side of the border. That was, certainly, an appropriate focus for U.S. military officers. American political leaders, on the other hand, had some responsibility to consider the broader consequences, for the United States as well as Cambodia, if the Cambodian authorities invited a war they could not hope to win. But the evidence doesn't indicate that Washington gave much thought to Cambodian realities, either in early 1970 or later.

From the earliest beginnings of U.S. involvement, American policy makers perceived Cambodia only through lenses that were focused on Vietnam. Cambodia, however, was not Vietnam. Its culture, politics, history, and needs were different. Its war was a different war with different military, political, and moral circumstances—none of which seem to have been weighed very carefully, if at all, when the United States chose to wage war on Cambodian territory. Possibly for that reason, American actions there were enveloped from the start in ambiguity of purpose, official untruths, confusion, and controversy. In a sense, the act of deceit that began the American war in Cambodia—the secret B-52 bombing—set the pattern for everything that would follow.

The Cambodian army's campaign in the border regions was inconclusive. But the growing conflict awakened the virulent anti-Vietnamese prejudice that always simmered just beneath the smiling surface of Khmer life. Unhappily for Sihanouk, this historic hatred was revived at exactly the time when his enemies needed an issue to exploit. At the start of the 1970s,

Sihanouk was no longer the dominant leader he had once been. Cambodia's economy had stagnated after he spurned U.S. aid in the early 1960s. Peasants still revered him, but among the urban, educated Cambodians, many had begun to feel suffocated by his one-man rule, which they came to view as outdated and feudal. Many were also offended by the nepotism and corruption he tolerated. Frustration was high among military officers, who resented Sihanouk's cancellation of U.S. military aid in 1963; discontent also seethed among the "educated unemployed," graduates of a rapidly expanding university system who then found no jobs in a still-backward social, economic, and administrative structure.

These domestic issues, not matters of war and peace, were the root causes of Sihanouk's political decline. But the Vietnamese presence became the issue that united all his opponents, from conservative nationalists to extreme leftists. Sihanouk was as anti-Vietnamese as any of his opponents, but he understood the limits of Cambodia's ability to confront the intruders, and they did not. In that difference lay the seeds of his downfall—and Cambodia's.

General Lon Nol, whom Sihanouk appointed prime minister in August 1969, subscribed to a misty Khmer nationalism that seemed oblivious to inconvenient realities. He once speculated that with help from the Americans and from ethnic Khmer living in South Vietnam, Cambodia "could make quick work of recapturing" its lost provinces from the Vietnamese—a territory encompassing not only the whole Mekong Delta, but also the city of Saigon. If he had any reasons why the Americans would assist in such a venture while they were allied with the South Vietnamese, they were not recorded.

As a police official and then army commander, Lon Nol had worked closely with Sihanouk for many years. But in early 1970 he seemed to be carried away by his own anti-Vietnamese passion, which was also being reinforced by his deputy prime minister, the ambitious, intelligent Sisowath Sirik Matak. It was Sirik Matak—a member of a noble Cambodian family that had long been the chief rival of the Norodom clan, to which Sihanouk belonged—who was thought to be behind the more aggressive military policy in the border regions. The two men grew more and more restive under Sihanouk's rule, and in March 1970, while the prince was in Moscow asking Soviet leaders to help him put pressure on the Vietnamese Communists, they first organized violent anti-Vietnamese demonstrations in Phnom Penh and then issued a ludicrously impractical demand for all Vietnamese troops to leave Cambodia in 72 hours. From abroad, Sihanouk denounced their actions, but instead of changing course, on March 18, while soldiers surrounded the National Assembly and the ministries, Lon Nol and Sirik Matak obtained a unanimous assembly vote to depose him as chief of state.

Instead of coming home to confront his usurpers, Sihanouk flew on to

Peking, where five days later he announced the formation of the National United Front of Cambodia (FUNK, from its French initials) and a liberation army to fight the "reactionary and pro-imperialist" Lon Nol and the "U.S. imperialists." A month later, he formally allied with the Vietnamese and Lao Communists. He did so, clearly, not for ideological reasons but from wounded pride and a thirst for revenge. "I am not and will not become a Communist," he wrote shortly afterward in an article that revealed how thoroughly his personal and political responses were mingled,

> for I disavow nothing of my religious beliefs or of my nationalism. . . . If I am fighting in the camp of the Indochinese and Asian revolutionaries, it is because on a personal level, I want to see justice done me some day after having been odiously calumniated and dishonored by the Lon Nol group; and because, on the national level, I must fulfill my duty as a patriot, a Khmer—and an Asian. With Lon Nol and the armed intervention of the foreign powers that support him, my homeland and my people have lost everything—peace, dignity, independence, territorial integrity—and are immersed in the worst sufferings, the worst misfortunes and the worst catastrophe of their history. In these circumstances I can only hope for the total victory of the revolution, in which I shall certainly not have any place but which cannot but save my homeland and serve the deepest interests of the mass of the "little" Khmer people.

From that pledge, Sihanouk would not retreat for many years. He was far too clear-eyed not to have realized, even in those earliest weeks, that he had tied himself to interests that were mortally dangerous to Cambodia's survival. But he was too proud and vindictive, too, ever to consider rejoining the men who he considered had betrayed him and the nation which, in his own mind, he embodied.

With Sihanouk's fall, the Vietnam War fell on his helpless country like a collapsing brick wall.

In Henry Kissinger's later retelling, the United States "barely lifted a finger" after Sihanouk was overthrown and for many days afterward, while, "weeks before *any* American action," the Vietnamese Communists "broke out of the sanctuaries and began plunging deep into Cambodia with the obvious purpose of overthrowing the government." Washington began considering military aid for the new Phnom Penh government, according to Kissinger, only as it "gradually and reluctantly perceived the impossibility of Cambodia's neutrality, due to Hanoi's insistence on Communist domination of *all* of Cambodia."

The available evidence, however, indicates that the U.S. was not as passive as Kissinger suggests. Nor was Hanoi nearly as quick or decisive in assaulting the new Cambodian regime. Rather than North Vietnamese military action followed after an interval by an American response, there seems actually to have been a rather symmetrical reaction by both sides to the March 18 events. Both the U.S. and North Vietnam paused briefly, unsure what the new situation would mean. Both then expanded military activities during the last days of March and the first few days of April. Further escalation by both sides occurred in mid-month until finally, with the decision to send U.S. troops over the border on April 30, the Vietnam war spilled openly and uncontainably into Cambodia for good.

The first significant foreign military actions in Cambodia after Sihanouk's overthrow were not by North Vietnam but by America's ally, South Vietnam. Air strikes by the South Vietnamese air force began as early as March 20, and fairly large ground probes, involving at least a battalion of infantry with armored vehicles and air and artillery support, occurred March 27 and 28. The North Vietnamese were still under orders to avoid combat if possible: "Our purpose," said a directive to Communist units, "is to conserve forces as much as we can." Hanoi certainly wanted to defend the illegal sanctuaries, but it wanted to do so without fighting the Cambodians, if possible. The Vietnamese began attacking Cambodian army outposts only on March 29, not, apparently, with the intention of defeating the new Phnom Penh government but to eliminate possible threats in their rear before the attack they now felt certain would be made by American and South Vietnamese forces from across the border.

The Cambodia working group on Kissinger's own National Security Council staff did not conclude that the North Vietnamese wanted to overthrow Lon Nol. They reached exactly the opposite conclusion, in fact: that "the North Vietnamese would be reluctant to occupy Phnom Penh or permit the Viet Cong to do so while the internal political situation still did not rule out the return of Sihanouk and in view of the obvious opposition of the Cambodian people to such a prospect." As late as mid-April, according to a classified Pentagon study, U.S. intelligence assessments still did not support Kissinger's later assertion that the Vietnamese were trying to conquer all of Cambodia. "The intelligence community had identified three enemy strategic goals in Cambodia," the Pentagon study reported. "These were:

"—The isolation of Cambodia by sealing the border area from South Vietnam.

"—The isolation of Phnom Penh from the countryside.

"—The organization of a Cambodian liberation army."

Directives to North Vietnamese commanders stressed that they should disperse and protect their rear bases, but that fighting in Cambodia should be conducted as far as possible by Cambodians, with guidance and moral support from the Vietnamese but only a necessary minimum of materiel, training, and manpower. These directives reflected the ideology of "people's war" and also, according to most intelligence reports, the actual conduct of the Vietnamese in Cambodia.

Hanoi's real preference, almost certainly, would have been to renew their lease on the sanctuaries with the new landlord, so to speak, recreating the same accommodation they had with Sihanouk. Such an arrangement was proposed quite explicitly to the new Phnom Penh government by Chinese emissaries, it was later confirmed by Gen. Sak Sutsakhan. The Chinese, Sak disclosed, were "sent from Peking for the express purpose" of arranging matters between Lon Nol and the Vietnamese Communists. China could consider that "the matter between Sihanouk and the Khmer government was nothing more than an internal problem" with which Peking would not concern itself, the Chinese envoys told the Cambodians, if the new Phnom Penh authorities would permit China to continue supplying the Vietnamese Communists on Cambodian territory, allow the Vietnamese to keep using the sanctuaries, and give propaganda support to Vietnam's "liberation."

This was no trivial offer. It meant that China would not sponsor Sihanouk as head of a rival Khmer government or support a Cambodian liberation war. Lon Nol and his associates would have to swallow a continued illegal Vietnamese occupation of parts of Cambodia—but distant and lightly populated parts. In return, they could remain in power while their most feared and formidable enemy, who still commanded strong support in the countryside, would be left with no base, no international backing, and no source of arms. It was a bargain that might have saved enormous suffering, as it turned out. But the new Cambodian leaders, swept up in the anti-Vietnamese emotions they had inflamed for their own purposes and naively expecting unlimited military assistance from the United States, turned it down.

The Chinese persisted for weeks, indicating how strongly Peking and possibly Hanoi preferred the old arrangements to the uncertainties of a new war. The Chinese effort, in fact, was still under way when Hanoi, at the "Summit Conference of the Indochinese Peoples" that met April 24 and 25 in southern China (but with no offical Chinese presence), appeared to cast its lot with Sihanouk and the new National United Front of Cambodia. Even then the Chinese delegation remained in Phnom Penh, leaving only after the U.S.-South Vietnamese invasion of the sanctuary areas on April 30. Peking did not break relations with Lon Nol until May 4. The next day Sihanouk announced the formation of his exile government, which would be based in the Chinese capital for the rest of the war.

The Americans, meanwhile, were quickly moving toward a relationship with the new Cambodian leaders based on an evident assumption that they were now joined in a fight against a common enemy. Among other actions, that assumption led to a redirection of the still secret B-52 raids—after a week's halt—to give direct tactical support to Cambodian government forces. An April 2 strike proposal from the Joint Chiefs of Staff listed targets only 1.8 miles from the closest Cambodian army positions, so close that the targets could not have been chosen without liaison between U.S. officials and Cambodian field commanders. (The Chiefs did not neglect their old stand-by COSVN, however. The target area, their proposal said, "has historically served as a base area for headquarters elements of the COSVN and it is estimated that there are presently approximately eight COSVN terminals"—radio installations—"located in or near the target area.")

Four days before the strike request, the North Vietnamese had begun attacking Cambodian outposts in the sanctuaries. But at that stage they were hardly "plunging deep into Cambodia," and the change in bombing policy was a U.S. response in far less time than the "weeks" Henry Kissinger claimed were allowed to pass.

The policy change became clearer in subsequent Menu planning. On April 7, the Chiefs pointed out that the B-52 strikes "will . . . indicate a clear resolve on our part and may constitute an inhibiting influence on enemy initiatives westward into Cambodia and into South Vietnam." A week later, they wrote that bombing would "provide tangible evidence of U.S. support for the efforts of the new Cambodian government to resist the incursions and pressures of the VC/NVA."

In Phnom Penh, meanwhile, the U.S. embassy began to receive and consider Cambodian proposals for air strikes and military aid within days of Sihanouk's overthrow—beginning even before the first Vietnamese attack on Cambodian forces. Senior Khmer commanders approached embassy officers as early as March 25 to ask for military aid; and "shortly," according to a quasi-official account of the first months of the U.S. Defense Attache Office in Cambodia, "requests for air strikes on Communist positions began to pour into DAO and the embassy." Some of the strike proposals were made personally by Lon Nol to Lloyd Rives, the U.S. chargé d'affaires. All the requests were passed onto U.S. headquarters in Vietnam, and some of the proposed targets were struck, though officials in Phnom Penh never knew if that was in response to Cambodian requests or on the basis of other intelligence.

While thus establishing a military relationship with the United States in the very first weeks of the war, the new Cambodian leaders also rather quickly arranged military cooperation with the South Vietnamese. Following two secret nighttime flights to Phnom Penh in early April by Vice-President Ky, President Thieu secretly authorized his corps commanders to "conduct offensive operations" in a zone running the whole length of the Cambodian border and from 24 to 36 miles deep on the Cambodian side. The first significant penetration began April 14 and involved two regiment-sized task forces that remained in Cambodia for three days. The operation was called Toan Thang ("Total Victory") 41—a code name presaging the U.S.-South Vietnamese incursion at the end of the month, which would be called Toan Thang 43.

The U.S. had publicly distanced itself from the earlier South Vietnamese attacks in late March, but it gave an unmistakable endorsement to those of mid-April. American units provided a screening force on the Vietnamese side of the border, while U.S. engineers supplied pontoons and other equipment to be used in the operation. The Americans repaired armored vehicles for use in Cambodia and in some cases swapped their operating tanks for ARVN's out-of-service ones so that armor units would cross the border at full strength. American command helicopters and gunships flew support missions, though without landing in Cambodia. All these actions left no doubt, as a South Vietnamese general later asserted, "that not only had the U.S. consented" to cross-border operations by the Vietnamese, but it "was also fully backing them to the extent permitted by its policies."

In mid-April, also, the first American assistance began to flow to the Cambodian army—arranged by intelligence agencies, instead of through normal military assistance procedures, to preserve secrecy. 6,000 captured Communist AK-47 rifles and a slightly larger number of American M-2 carbines, along with stores of ammunition, were flown to Phnom Penh. Also airlifted to the Cambodian capital were 3,000 to 4,000 Khmer Krom— ethnic Khmer from South Vietnam. (The term is a short form of "Khmer Kampuchea Krom," or "Khmer of Lower Cambodia.") These were soldiers who had been serving not under Vietnamese but under direct U.S. command in units called Civilian Irregular Defense Groups, controlled by American Special Forces.

These early aid measures were carried out in extreme secrecy. Messages on the subject were given a special classification, "Nodis Khmer," which gave access to only a handful of named officials. So tight was the secrecy that on one occasion an officer assigned to draft the Joint Chiefs' reply to a query on some supply matter went to find the incoming message he was ordered to answer—and was told he wasn't allowed to see it.

Every one of these events—the start of significant South Vietnamese operations across the border with U.S. support, the use of American B-52s in direct support of Cambodian troops, the covert aid and liaison between American officials and Cambodian commanders—occurred while, according to Nixon and Kissinger, the U.S. was still passively awaiting developments. They also occurred, apparently, without much thought about the nature of the American obligation that was being created to a weak, naive new client. In the National Security Council working group, during its deliberations on Lon Nol's early requests for military aid, civilian members warned against actions that would "propel Cambodia into the war at a time when the Khmer should be trying to regain their neutrality." But the administration was swayed more by the views of military leaders, who focused on the tactical opportunities for the United States and not on any possible consequences for the Cambodians.

American decisions, sliding down a slope of logic from that fundamental perception, led inexorably to the orders that sent 32,000 Americans and 48,000 South Vietnamese troops into Cambodia in what the Nixon administration insisted on calling an "incursion" into North Vietnamese-occupied zones, rather than an invasion of neutral territory. In announcing that action of the last day of April, President Nixon, whose private judgment of the Lon Nol regime at the time was that "I do not believe he is going to survive," gave reasons pertinent only to American and Vietnamese needs: the offensive was "to protect our men who are in Vietnam and to guarantee the continued success of our withdrawal and Vietnamization programs." (And—of course—to capture COSVN, which however once again proved elusive. The Communist headquarters suffered "some temporary disruption" at the start of the campaign, the CIA later concluded, but was "quickly restored to almost normal efficiency.")

What was disrupted somewhat more thoroughly was the mood of the United States. Facing an uproar of domestic opposition, Nixon set a June 30 deadline for the use of American ground forces in Cambodia and imposed an arbitrary 30-kilometer limit on their penetration. These decisions were taken for political reasons, without military advice; the last thing to be considered, clearly, was what would happen to Cambodia and its people as the result of the American intervention. In its public statements the administration sought only to reassure Americans that the U.S. had taken on no new military commitments in Asia. Nor did the White House or cabinet officers predict a massive military aid program for Cambodia. "Mr. Secretary," Rep. George Mahon of Texas asked Defense Secretary Laird in a congressional hearing, "we are committed in South Vietnam. Are we committed to prevent a Communist takeover of Cambodia and Laos?" "No we are not, Mr. Chairman," Laird replied, "except that as far as Laos is concerned we are committed to uphold the 1962 Geneva accords. . . . As far as Cambodia is concerned, we have no treaty commitment to Cambodia." Support for the Cambodian government, Laird added, was "not the reason" for the incursion. Nixon himself, as U.S. troops were being pulled out on June 30, explained that "to get drawn into the permanent direct defense of Cambodia . . . would have been inconsistent with the basic premises of our foreign policy."

This, of course, was at a time when Cambodian popular support for the war was still strong. By the time it was publicly avowed that the United States was, after all, committed to the survival of an anti-Communist Cambodian government, that support had almost completely evaporated.

If the new Khmer leaders were naive about the danger they had brought on their country, the people whose anti-Vietnamese prejudices they had inflamed and exploited were even more so. In its first few months, the war was a popular crusade. Young men and women volunteered for the army by the thousands to fight the "Yuon"—the pejorative Khmer term for the

Vietnamese. With only a few hours of training or perhaps none at all, clutching outdated weapons and Buddhist amulets, they sang patriotic songs as they set out for the war on commandeered civilian trucks. The dark side of the outburst of patriotism was the killing of thousands of helpless Vietnamese civilians. Many more were rounded up and forced out of their homes, and about 200,000, half of the entire Vietnamese minority, fled the country.

If fervor could win wars by itself, the Cambodians would have expelled the Vietnamese as easily as Lon Nol imagined they could march to restore the "lost provinces." But while they were deadly enough at shooting down unarmed Vietnamese civilians, the Cambodians' spirit was no match for the weaponry and battle experience of their real enemy. "The new government in Cambodia is weak, uncertain and apparently ineffectual," the *Washington Post*'s Robert Kaiser reported at the end of May. He added, "The same adjectives would flatter the Cambodian army."

The Vietnamese Communists still seemed more concerned with restoring and defending their logistical bases and supply routes to South Vietnam than with overrunning Phnom Penh. "The bulk of the Communist forces have not moved great distances from the border," a CIA assessment reported late in June, adding, "We doubt that Hanoi sees an early effort to eliminate the Lon Nol regime by a direct military assault on Phnom Penh as worth the probable military and political costs." Douglas Pike, the American government's most prominent Hanoi-watcher, concluded that the Vietnamese were carrying out " 'spoiling operations' against the Cambodian army, but not at the price of high casualties or expensive logistical outlays." It was "a sort of war-on-the-cheap," Pike believed, with "the immediate and short-run objective of putting the Cambodian government so much on the defensive that the Communist base system in Cambodia would be protected." The implication of those tactics was clear: Cambodia remained subordinate to Hanoi's purposes in Vietnam. "The liberation of Cambodia," said an official North Vietnamese declaration, "is the work of the Khmer people."

Even if Cambodia was not their chief objective, though, the Vietnamese Communists easily defeated the Cambodian government units—now called FANK (for Force Armee Nationale Khmere)—wherever they met. The last few government outposts in the border region were lost late in June, and the rest of Cambodia east of the Mekong, except for a few besieged pockets, was quickly yielded too. "Within four months," said a classified Pentagon appraisal, "the Communists had overrun half of Cambodia, taken or threatened sixteen of its nineteen provincial capitals and interdicted—for varying periods—all road and rail links to the capital. VC/NVA forces in the countryside appeared able to move at will. A series of small unit contacts with FANK had decimated about eighteen FANK battalions, killed at least 800 FANK soldiers and resulted in 3,100 FANK desertions and missing in action. These results were produced by as few as 10,000 enemy troops."

A major Vietnamese effort, meanwhile, was devoted to organizing a Khmer liberation movement, which would not only help tie down Cambodian government forces but would also legitimize continued Vietnamese use of Cambodian territory. Soon after Sihanouk's overthrow, Vietnamese "armed action teams" of propaganda and administrative agents were sent to villages in the Communist-held zone to create an administration under Sihanouk's National United Front of Cambodia (FUNK). The teams emphasized the themes of loyalty to Prince Sihanouk, protection of Khmer lives and civilization from American and South Vietnamese invaders, and the overthrow of local tyrants. The Vietnamese agents were under orders to keep as low a profile as possible, in order not to have anti-Vietnamese feelings turned on them. Their success in organizing Cambodian adherents appears to have been considerable. By late summer, the Vietnamese were said to be amazed at the "phenomenal" growth of the FUNK apparatus.

By November 1970, as the first rainy season of the war came to its end, the Communists appeared to have reached all the objectives that had become imperative for them when the war spread to Cambodia. Their supply system in the border area survived, and a force of 12,000 to 15,000 Cambodian insurgents had been organized to fight the Phnom Penh government under Vietnamese guidance. That force would reach 18,000 to 25,000 men by the end of 1971; it would be ready to assume virtually the entire burden of combat in another year after that.

As they marched into their hopeless war, Cambodia's new leaders were sure the rest of the world would see Cambodia as they did: a peaceful, law-abiding state, threatening no one, that had been plunged into war by no fault of its own and that now in simple justice deserved help—particularly from the United States, which had so often proclaimed itself the ally of those resisting Communist aggression in Southeast Asia.

Their perception of Cambodia's plight was accurate enough, but the Cambodians were sadly ignorant of the international facts of life. Not understanding that by 1970 the United States was on the way out of Indochina, not in, the Cambodians were alarmed and baffled by American hesitancy to come to their aid. The prevailing attitude was summed up in a plaintive article by Sim Var, a member of Cambodia's National Assembly, who wrote in the fall of 1970:

> It is normal for the United States to have been guided in its action above all by the concern for the security of its soldiers and not with the aim of helping Cambodia defend itself against aggression. We must nevertheless recognize that Cambodia suffers the consequences

of the limited American intervention. . . . In these conditions, we believe that the American government ought to assume its responsibilities concerning Cambodia. . . . the reservations of the United States on this subject seem to us incomprehensible since, if ever a country has a just cause, it is Cambodia.

The Nixon administration was not opposed to helping Cambodia, but for domestic political reasons felt it could not seem to be committing itself to the new Phnom Penh government, and it did not muster the imagination or courage to see that long-range American interests—and certainly the Cambodians'—might be better served by searching for a way to return to the previous equilibrium. Instead, Nixon and Kissinger adopted the narrow perspective of their military commanders, which was that American military aims could now be pursued on Cambodian territory. Their focus remained on the Vietnamese battlefields, and Americans tended to treat their new ally in remarkably demeaning fashion. The offical cable telling Lon Nol about the U.S. incursion was not delivered until the Cambodian leader had already heard the news on a local radio broadcast; during or after the invasion, no details—not even the size of the forces involved or anything of its results— were ever communicated to the Cambodian government or military command.

In the early months of the war, the U.S. was no more straightforward in discussions of military aid. "Because no one really knew, and because no one wanted to commit the U.S. in advance, it was the practice not to tell or try to tell the Khmer exactly what the extent of the U.S. assistance program would be," says the quasi-official Defense Attache Office history. A different sort of leader might have seen this American vagueness as reason for caution. But Lon Nol's mystical confidence was unshakable. He would not even believe, according to one of the Americans who worked most closely with him at the start of the war, that President Nixon would really withdraw U.S. troops from Cambodia at the June 30 deadline.

In that, Lon Nol was deluded. But the graver delusion was not his but Nixon's, in failing to see that in return for a tactical advantage that could be no more than temporary, he had made vastly more complicated the task of extricating the United States from the war.

The military accomplishments of the American invasion could not be consolidated, because political pressures at home made it impossible for U.S. troops to remain in the sanctuaries and the Cambodian army was completely incapable of doing so. The Communists, who had lost substantial but not irreplaceable amounts of material and who had conserved nearly all their troops, were soon able to resume using Cambodian bases for the same purposes as before. Cambodian morale, meanwhile, nosedived when June 30 came and U.S. forces pulled back across the border—turning their backs, as the Cambodians saw it, on the war that had suddenly begun to ravage Khmer territory.

If the American withdrawal after the invasion was the first blow, the government army's offensive spirit was destroyed forever in the fall of 1971, when a major government force trying to relieve the besieged town of Kompong Thom—the campaign was called Chenla II, after one of the pre-Angkor Cambodian empires—was attacked and virtually wiped out along Highway 6, leading northwest from Phnom Penh. Nearly 3,000 government soldiers were killed or disappeared in the disaster, and it was estimated that the equipment of a full twenty battalions was lost. Few offensives were attempted after that.

By mid-1972, American aid to the Cambodian army had reached a total of about $400 million—$2,000 for every soldier, if the official strength figures could be believed. But it had not done much apparent good. The army was still roadbound because it had no ration system and could not operate away from village markets. It was under strength because commanders listed "ghost soldiers" on their rosters and pocketed their pay. Its leadership was flagrantly incompetent. Its tactics usually consisted of lining soldiers and vehicles up along a road, as if on parade, and ordering them to advance, without flank security and without the slightest idea where the enemy was. The result, not surprisingly, was that units frequently kept marching until the road was cut behind them, trapping them under Communist guns.

Because there was no allotment system, soldiers' wives and children had to accompany them in order not to starve. This meant that soldiers on the march were held to the pace of the smallest, weakest child, while their positions, even at the front line under fire, were always encumbered with soldiers' families. Dependents often became casualties. Not many Khmer officers were patrolling into enemy territory in 1972, but I met one lieutenant who was taking his company out every day. Not for any military objective, however; he was only trying to recover the body of his wife.

While the army lurched from one defeat to another, the political leadership quickly and irrevocably squandered the popular support it had enjoyed in 1970. Bickering and backbiting were endless. Corruption became endemic and was never brought under control. Lon Nol's collaborators in the 1970 movement were driven out of the government one by one, often by the machinations of his detested younger brother, Lon Non—"petit frère," he was scornfully called. Lon Nol, who made himself a marshal and then president and stayed in office through one of the most blatantly rigged elections in Southeast Asian history, turned more mystical than ever and seemed increasingly deaf to what little bad news his courtiers allowed him to hear. U.S. aid, meanwhile, was largely dissipated through inefficiency and graft. "The government of the Khmer Republic, and especially the Khmer military," a delegation of U.S. senators reported, "has taken advantage of United States assistance over a sustained period of time, substantially subverting the intended purpose of that assistance. The situation which the delegation found is wholly unacceptable."

Disruption of civilian life was virtually complete. Civilian travel was possible only for 20 or 30 miles or so outside Phnom Penh and for shorter distances around the other besieged towns. A new Khmer expression came into use: "The land is broken."

An example of the war's impact was its effect on the educational system. At the start of the last prewar school year, official statistics showed, Cambodia had 5,275 primary schools with nearly a million pupils. A year later, only 1,064 schools were open and the number of pupils enrolled dropped by nearly two-thirds, to 322,933.

Of 29 civilian public hospitals when the war began, only thirteen were still operating a year later. The rest were destroyed. Phnom Penh's population grew from 600,000 to over a million as refugees fled to the city from battles in the countryside. They huddled in pagodas and schoolyards with little or no help from anyone while corrupt army officers built handsome villas with the proceeds of embezzled payrolls and black-marketing of supplies. There were so many villas that one disgusted American diplomat began speaking of U.S. military aid as "the world's largest upper-income housing program." The regime, said another diplomat flatly, "doesn't give anyone in the country any reason to fight for it."

The limits of Cambodia's abilities and of the American public's tolerance assured that no victory over Communist forces was possible. A victory in Cambodia in any case was not the central American goal. "The mission over there," Brig. Gen. Theodore C. Mataxis, first commander of the military aid team in Phnom Penh, recalled years afterward, "was, help Vietnam all you can." That the Cambodian people were thus condemned to permanent, inconclusive warfare did not seem to affect the calculations of American policy makers. Nor did the problem of how America could extract itself from Cambodia, or Cambodia from the conflict, if a negotiated settlement in Vietnam became possible. Cambodia had now joined Laos in the terrible bind fashioned by geography and by the contest among the more powerful nations that chose Cambodia and Laos as battlegrounds. That bind was perceptively described by James G. Lowenstein and Richard Moose of the Senate Foreign Relations Committee staff, the authors of a series of reports on Indochina events. Both Laos and Cambodia, they wrote in 1972,

> are victims of the North Vietnamese, of course, because North Vietnam uses their territory to move supplies and men, as a base of operations and to promote local Communist movements. But they are also victims of the continuing American defense of South Vietnam. . . .

Though the United States disavows any formal commitment
to the defense of Laos and Cambodia, our present strategy requires
that these two countries be supported and kept in the war. . . .
    Fate has thus forced a cruel bargain on Laos and Cambodia. On the
one hand, American assistance sustains them for without it they
would literally be at the mercy of the North Vietnamese. . . . On the
other hand, their reliance on continuous American assistance prevents
them from agreeing to the kind of compromise that would offer them
an alternative to continued fighting but would, in return, require
them to permit the unopposed use of their territory by the North
Vietnamese.

When a negotiated Vietnam settlement suddenly began to seem possible
in the fall of 1972, it became apparent that the anti-Communist Lao and
Cambodian governments were in a political and military trap even worse
than Lowenstein and Moose described. For while their relationship with the
U.S. precluded their settling on the best terms they could get by accommo-
dating the Vietnamese Communists, that same relationship gave them no
assurance that the United States, in *its* dealings with Hanoi, would protect
Lao or Cambodian interests. And by 1972, the direction of American
diplomacy was deeply threatening to the two weaker Indochinese states.
Since Phnom Penh and Vientiane had no hope of withstanding the North
Vietnamese without direct American military support, they needed settlements that redressed an unfavorable military balance—that is, in which the
U.S. would be able to compel North Vietnam to surrender positions it had
won on the battlefield. But by 1972 the U.S. had accepted the existing
battlefield situation in South Vietnam, its primary area of interest; if it had
not been able to force the North Vietnamese to withdraw there, it clearly had
even less prospect of forcing them to give up Lao and Cambodian territory
that Hanoi found it essential to control.
    South Vietnam, American negotiators believed, had a reasonable chance
to survive after an American exit that left the conflicting Vietnamese forces
in place. But the same principle represented a far worse danger for U.S.
clients in Laos and Cambodia. Moreover, the political logic that was pro-
pelling American leaders toward a peace agreement left almost no room to
protect peripheral interests. The American public clearly wanted a settlement on almost any grounds that would not be an immediate, humiliating
defeat. Just as clearly, it would not tolerate blocking a Vietnam agreement
just because it did not meet Lao or Cambodian needs.
    In the end, the United States did sacrifice the interests of its two smaller
allies. For years Washington called for an Indochina-wide truce, but it did
not stand by that demand once its minimum conditions for a Vietnam
agreement were met. Probably American negotiators had no choice. But
from the standpoint of two weak, helpless countries that had paid a fearful

cost in a war serving American interests better than their own, the U.S. actions could not seem anything but an act of brutal cynicism.

In Laos, where the difficulties of arranging a peace agreement were significantly less than in the other warring states, the U.S. acquiesced in, if it did not encourage, a settlement that was obviously adverse to its client regime. The Laos ceasefire put in jeopardy those Lao who had fought at American urging and who felt entitled to American protection. In accepting it, the U.S. may not have acted in a wholly honorable manner. But the Laos ceasefire at least reflected the military and political realities, and it achieved, or held the hope of achieving, two aims: to extricate the United States from its commitment, and to stop or at least slow the killing on Lao battlefields.

In Cambodia the American choice was different. The chances of a negotiated peace were infinitesimal, perhaps nonexistent. But the U.S. never took even the same risks it took in Laos. It fostered, instead of squelching, the wildly exaggerated beliefs of Lon Nol and his few confidants in their ability to withstand the Communists. It promised open-ended military support, a promise the Cambodians believed but which the Nixon administration should have known it could not keep. The U.S. never advocated any form of compromise peace that had not already been unequivocally rejected by one, or usually both, sides. The United States was not the first of the warring powers to violate Cambodia; the Vietnamese Communists started the process by which Cambodia was dragged into the war it skirted for so long. But the U.S. did use Cambodia for its own purposes at a very heavy cost in Cambodian suffering. American actions from 1969 on helped turn Cambodia into a slaughterhouse, in which teen-aged peasant boys on both sides now murdered each other mindlessly and died in the mud, almost without memory of why they fought. The land lay slathered in blood, but neither in early 1973 nor later did the United States offer any plan or policy that promised anything but more fear, pain, and butchery.

The Bombing

If it gave little thought to Cambodia's needs in deciding to make war there, the United States was no more mindful of Cambodia when it sought to achieve peace.

In Paris, during the October 1972 exchanges and again when the Vietnam agreement was concluded in January 1973, Henry Kissinger pressed Le Duc

Tho to assure a settlement for Cambodia as well as for Laos. Tho was willing to guarantee a Lao ceasefire, but on Cambodia he was more cautious. An end to the Vietnam war would "certainly" lead to a Cambodian settlement, he told Kissinger in October—but the statement was framed as a prediction, not as an undertaking by the North Vietnamese. In January, Tho again refused to commit Hanoi to take responsibility for a Cambodian ceasefire, explaining that Hanoi had less influence with the Cambodians than with the Pathet Lao. "Practically speaking, when discussing with our allies in Cambodia it is not as easy as when we discuss with our allies in Laos," he explained. "But I am firmly convinced that the restoration of peace in Vietnam will create favorable conditions for the restoration of peace in Cambodia. . . . When we have a peace in Vietnam and when our allies in Laos have peace in their country, it is illogical that we still want war in another place."

When it was clear that no firmer commitment could be obtained, the U.S. negotiators read a unilateral statement into the record, telling the North Vietnamese that the Lon Nol government would halt offensive operations as soon as a Vietnam ceasefire took effect and that a *de facto* truce could result if the insurgents reciprocated. If the Communists continued to attack, however, government forces and U.S. air forces would take "necessary counter-measures," thé statement continued, and the U.S. "would continue to carry out air strikes in Cambodia as necessary until such time as a ceasefire could be brought into effect."

On its face, that declaration seemed to conflict with Article 20 of the Vietnam agreement, which simply required an end to foreign military actions in Cambodia and Laos and made no mention at all of ceasefires there. The legal rationale for U.S. bombing, stated in a long briefing paper by George Aldrich, the State Department's legal adviser, was that because Article 20 had no specified time at which it would become effective, its provisions "should be understood as agreements in principle" which the U.S. and North Vietnam would then try to include "in ceasefire or other settlement agreements in Laos and Cambodia. Only when such agreements are concluded will the obligation to withdraw become operational." Under that reasoning, continued U.S. bombing was legal—but so, apparently, was the continued presence of North Vietnamese troops. Nonetheless Washington kept demanding that Hanoi withdraw its forces from Cambodia immediately; the legal contradiction was simply ignored.

On January 24, after the Vietnam agreement was announced, Kissinger declared to reporters in Washington, "We can say about Cambodia that it is our expectation that a *de facto* ceasefire will come into being within the period of time relevant to the execution of the agreement." Whether that expectation was really warranted by Le Duc Tho's careful statements in Paris

was debatable. And so was the subsequent American assertion that Cambodia's President Lon Nol, acting on the American promise to Hanoi, really
declared a "unilateral ceasefire" that could have led to peace if only the
insurgents had reciprocated.

What the Cambodian leader actually said, in a speech to the National
Assembly that was also broadcast to the nation, was this:

> We Cambodian people request that the North Vietnamese aggressors
> and their Viet Cong lackeys lay down their weapons and immediately
> pull out of Cambodian territory. We forbid all arms caches and sanc-
> tuaries and all military bases or other strategic installations on our
> land. By virtue of the 1954 Geneva agreement, we are legitimately
> and entirely entitled to reoccupy our territory which has been illegally
> controlled by the North Vietnamese and the Viet Cong. Therefore in
> order to permit the North Vietnamese and Viet Cong troops to with-
> draw from our territory with the shortest delay, we affirm that as of
> Monday, 29 January 1973 at 0700 Phnom Penh time all units of the
> National Cambodian Armed Forces will suspend all offensives and
> transform these war activities into a drive to contact the people and
> assure their security. Any impediment against this move of our armed
> forces can occur only from infringements upon these rules. Whoso-
> ever does so must bear complete responsibility for all consequences.
> We will always maintain the rights of legal self-defense by continuing
> our self-defense operations across the country.

"Friendly countries," the marshal added, should help supervise the Paris
agreement "by forcing the parties concerned to strictly respect it, and especially should keep enough troops in this region to prevent any aggressors
from nurturing an attempt to fight."

In other words, Lon Nol was not offering a ceasefire in place, as had been
conceded to the Communists in South Vietnam, but demanding that they
give up their weapons and allow government forces to reoccupy
Communist-held territory, while the government also asserted the right to
begin shooting again if its advancing troops met any resistance. What was
more, the Cambodia president seemed to be appealing also for the continued
presence of American forces in Indochina or in neighboring countries,
despite the fact that a U.S. withdrawal was a centerpiece of the agreement
both for Washington and for Hanoi.

If this was a ceasefire offer in any sense, it was so qualified that a
suspicious enemy could hardly be expected to embrace it. Even in the U.S.
government, there were doubts that Lon Nol had really fulfilled Kissinger's
promise to the North Vietnamese. Moose and Lowenstein of the Senate
Foreign Relations Committee staff were told by American officials, they
wrote in one of their reports, "that it was not the kind of offer which the
United States had wanted or expected Lon Nol to make."

As was also true of his 1969–1970 campaigns against the sanctuaries, Lon Nol's position contained undeniable justice, but little realism. To insist that the Vietnamese Communists leave occupied territory defied the reality, accepted by both sides in Paris, that a peace agreement could not revise the actual battlefield balance. To speak of suspending offensive operations was meaningless: there had hardly been any since the Chenla II debacle. The suggestion that U.S. troops remain to "force" observance of the accords was simply fanciful. And, most significantly, Lon Nol ignored the fact that he faced not just Vietnamese but formidable Cambodian enemies as well—who had, well before the Paris agreement was signed, rejected negotiations in the most categorical fashion and in language strongly suggesting that they would not be bidden in such matters by Hanoi or anyone else.

The Cambodian insurgents, indeed, had begun to assert their view almost as soon as it became known that the U.S. and North Vietnam were close to a settlement. On October 28, 1972, just two days after Hanoi broadcast the nine-point draft agreement, Prince Sihanouk paid a "friendship visit" to the North Vietnamese capital and secured from his hosts a joint statement affirming that "the problem of each Indochinese country must be settled by its own people. That is a sacred and inalienable right." In the following weeks, Khmer Rouge leaders continued to proclaim that on matters of war and peace they were not following Hanoi's policies but their own. The Cambodian people would "never compromise, hold talks or accept any ceasefire with U.S. imperialism and its allies," said the insurgent radio late in December. Instead, the broadcast declared, the insurgents would launch stronger attacks against Lon Nol and his associates—"the evil souls" of President Nixon's "foul doctrine"—and "trample them underfoot."

Sihanouk and Penn Nouth, prime minister of the exile government, angrily derided the idea of a compromise peace in their "New Year's message to the Cambodian people" of January 1, 1973. "The U.S. imperialist aggressors and their lackeys . . . have been feverishly plotting to divide the Cambodian, Vietnamese and Lao peoples and to divide the Cambodian and Chinese peoples," they declared, adding that "the maneuver for a 'ceasefire in Cambodia' " was only a trick to get the insurgents to stop fighting.

To anyone experienced in reading Communist rhetoric, the references to "imperialist plots" to divide the Cambodians and Vietnamese were unmistakable signs that the two revolutionary movements were in serious conflict. The shrill tone of the Cambodian broadcasts, in fact, was much like that of Hanoi's the previous spring and summer when the Vietnamese believed they were being let down by *their* allies.

When the Paris agreement was concluded, Sihanouk fleetingly expressed a more flexible attitude—at the urging, he seemed to be saying, of Hanoi. "Our friends told us," he told an interviewer, "that our adversaries are accusing us of bellicosity at a time when peace is being built and—should our motives be misinterpreted—we could find ourselves isolated." The Khmer insurgents, he said, did "not want to be considered as warmongers." But in the same interview he acknowledged that decisions on such matters were not up to him but to the leaders of the Khmer Rouge resistance inside Cambodia. And comments from that leadership indicated no flexibility at all. Lon Nol's "so-called ceasefire proclamation," proclaimed the clandestine insurgent radio, was a "most despicable conjurer's trick intended to mislead national and international public opinion. . . . This is only a deception engineered by the U.S. imperialists and their lackeys."

In Peking, the government-in-exile proclaimed on January 29 that "no compromise is possible" between the Cambodian factions. The insurgents' terms were stated as "the total, definitive, unconditional cessation of bombing and strafing by U.S. aircraft and all other acts of aggression, the withdrawal from Cambodia of all military and civilian personnel of the U.S. and its satellite, the cessation of all U.S. support and aid to the fascist Phnom Penh regime, and the total elimination of the entire traitors' clique of Lon Nol [and] Sirik Matak."

Sihanouk quickly stepped back into line. There was "no question," he cabled the Hong Kong-based *Far Eastern Economic Review*, of his government's "signing joint military and political ceasefire and peace agreements with the Washington and Phnom Penh governments" as the Vietnamese Communists had done. Presumably with the approval of the Khmer resistance leaders, he did indicate willingness to negotiate with U.S. representatives. Through Chou En-lai and North Vietnam's Pham Van Dong, he offered to meet Kissinger during the latter's visit to Peking in February, but was snubbed. Similar proposals were transmitted as late as May, when Sihanouk, during a tour of Africa, asked the presidents of Guinea and Senegal and the king of Morocco to relay his overtures directly to President Nixon. Only after those approaches were similarly rebuffed did the prince reverse himself and announce that he would not meet Kissinger after all.

It did not seem likely at the time, and does not now, that talks between Sihanouk and the Americans would have produced a settlement. Probably, nothing more would have happened in any such talks than a nonnegotiable Khmer demand for an end to American bombing and military aid to Phnom Penh. ("When we speak of negotiating with the U.S.A.," Sihanouk said in Peking April 13, after returning from a month-long visit to the Cambodian "liberated" zone, "we mean to negotiate the question of ending U.S. interference in Cambodia, not the question of a ceasefire. They are two different questions. . . . If the U.S.A. ceases its interference in Cambodia, the traitorous Lon Nol regime will quickly collapse. Then, the Cambodian question will be easily solved.") Yet it remains somewhat puzzling why Sihanouk's overtures in the spring of 1973 were so peremptorily rejected.

The U.S. may have felt that the Lon Nol regime's morale would have collapsed completely if there were any American dealings with its mortal enemy. Henry Kissinger would later claim that the United States all along regarded Sihanouk as the key to a settlement. But American statements and actions at the time were directed instead at North Vietnam, which the U.S. continued to insist must somehow end the Cambodian fighting. While putting futile pressure on Hanoi, the U.S.—just as futilely—also kept supporting Lon Nol's hopeless war.

If they really believed that North Vietnam could compel the Khmer Rouge to compromise, the Americans were profoundly wrong. The rift between the two Communist forces had widened with amazing swiftness as the Vietnamese prepared to reach a settlement with the U.S.; soon after that settlement was concluded, Vietnamese influence on the Cambodian insurgents appeared to have evaporated almost completely. Insurgent cadres in Cambodia were being told that their movement "is absolutely not under the guidance of the Vietnamese Communist party," reported Ith Sarin, a left-wing former school administrator who rejoined the government side early in 1973 after spending most of the previous year in training as a Communist official. The Cambodian movement, Ith Sarin said, "seems to have control over all activities in its zones. The VC/NVA are far from being the masters."

At the end of 1972, American intelligence reported no Vietnamese infantry units still in action against the Phnom Penh government, though U.S. estimates were that 10,000 or so Vietnamese were supporting the approximately 40,000 Khmer Rouge insurgents as tactical advisers or in specialized detachments such as artillery, engineer, or sapper units. Much of that support ended after the Paris agreement.

Hanoi still proclaimed loyalty to the three-year-old declaration of the Indochinese Peoples Summit Conference at which the alliance with Sihanouk was concluded. But in the Cambodian view, the Vietnamese had now betrayed the joint cause. Khieu Samphan and other Khmer resistance commanders complained to Sihanouk that the Vietnamese were seizing arms and supplies being sent by China for the Cambodians' use. The Khmer Communist leaders believed Hanoi wanted to "sabotage . . . the development of the Khmer Rouge armed forces," Sihanouk disclosed years later, in order to "nip Khmer Rouge power in the bud so as to prepare for the coming to power (after a foreseeable victory over the U.S. and Lon Nol) of a government that would be Cambodian in appearance only and in reality Vietnam's servant."

Shortly after the Paris agreement was signed, according to Sihanouk, the Khmer Rouge demanded that the Vietnamese Communists "purely and simply clear out of Cambodian territory." The Vietnamese did not comply. They held their bases in eastern Cambodia to support their operations in

South Vietnam, just as in the years before 1970. But in early 1973 Hanoi was no longer controlling the struggle for power in Cambodia. Primitively armed and organized but driven by an equally primitive fanaticism, the Khmer Rouge had seized their own destiny. Their view of their struggle was absolute. To their "mortal hate" of the Phnom Penh government, as Ith Sarin wrote, was mated an equal hate of the Vietnamese and other foreign Communists who might try to cheat them of the triumph they believed they could win. Their fearful intensity gave no place for thoughts of bargaining with their enemies; it drove them instead through deeper and deeper layers of savagery to the final, futile conquest of a ruined land.

For eleven days after the Paris agreement, no American bombers struck Cambodia. But on February 9 strikes resumed, and for the next six months the air war was waged with unprecedented fury. More than 250,000 tons of bombs were dropped in the 1973 campaign—more in half a year than fell on Japan in all of World War II. Not only was the bombing many times heavier than any previously carried out in Cambodia; it also struck the populous heartland west of the Mekong and not just the almost-empty eastern region, code-named Freedom Deal by the Air Force, where most U.S. air action had been concentrated in the past.

U.S. military and civilian officials who controlled the bombing insisted civilian casualties were minimal. But they often relied on the assurances of Cambodian commanders—and no one who ever saw the Cambodian military in action could fail to see its officers' notorious unconcern about civilian losses in their operations. Cambodian officers frequently had little idea where their own troops were, let alone the enemy's. Bombing indisputably occurred in regions that had been thickly settled. A B-52 "box"—the area covered by the bombs from a three-plane cell—was almost two miles long and more than a half-mile wide. In many parts of central Cambodia, there was no stetch of land that size that did not contain some human habitation.

Because the dispirited Cambodian army so seldom recaptured lost ground, it was normally impossible for diplomats or journalists to get first-hand information from bombed areas, and thus the dispute over the extent of civilian casualties remained unresolved. Critics of American policy suspected, or feared, that the casualties were enormous, while officials in the U.S. military command and the embassy felt the criticisms were exaggerated. Yet the embassy's claim that almost no civilian casualties were caused by the bombing lacked credibility too. The *New York Times*'s Sydney Schanberg spent a half-hour in a Phnom Penh hospital and found three patients, one a fifteen-year-old boy, who were victims of American bombs. In bombed areas south of the capital, Schanberg saw villages reduced to "ashes, broken cooking pots, shattered banana and mango trees, twisted corrugated iron roofing and sometimes the concrete stilts of a house reaching toward nothingness— that is all that is left."

Some months after the bombing ended, I was able to drive one day over a stretch of road west of Phnom Penh that had been temporarily retaken by government troops. Once, pleasant villages had stood almost shoulder-to-shoulder on that highway. Now they were not just ruined, but obliterated. For five miles, not a house still stood on either side of the road, or as far away as one could see across the fields. No trees were left, just broken stumps. In a few places grass had begun to grow again, but most of the land was blackened and dead. It was as if the bombers had sought to destroy the earth itself.

There was no evidence that American bombing was helping the Cambodian government win the war, or even hold its ground. The government army was perhaps losing more slowly, but that was the most that could be said. Despite the very heavy bombing, said one account of the 1973 campaign, the Khmer Communists "seized considerable territory in southern and northeastern Cambodia. FANK [Force Armee Nationale Khmere] overall response to these initiatives was grossly inadequate." The account continued:

> FANK combat performance was characterized by poor leadership, low morale, and the refusal of units to advance against enemy resistance. Despite heavy U.S. air support, FANK abandoned their positions to K.C. units with increasing frequency between February and July withdrawing into urban enclaves and positions along primary lines of communication leaving the population in the countryside largely to the K.C. . . . FANK grew to rely almost exclusively on U.S. air strikes for fire support. . . . The K.C., on the other hand, became increasingly adept at concentrating multi-battalion forces for attacks against FANK and took full advantage of the almost unrestricted movement afforded them throughout the country by FANK's defensive posture and lack of aggressiveness.

That appraisal was not from a querulous journalist or critical congressional staffer, but from the Defense Department itself.

As the Cambodians kept losing ground, even the units that were supposed to be the best proved unreliable. U.S. military aid specialists had lavished considerable attention on the government's 7th Division. But early in April the division's troops, ambushed near the province capital of Takeo, panicked and abandoned five of their eight 105-mm howitzers to the enemy, along with 40 truckloads of shells.

Incidents of "mass indiscipline" multiplied, usually arising from the government's failure to pay the troops. In mid-May, hundreds of infantrymen left the lines northwest of Phnom Penh and marched into the heart of the city to demand their pay. Firing automatic rifle bursts into the air, they scattered frightened pedestrians as they advanced down the broad boulevard toward the general staff headquarters. Not only had they received no pay; they had been without food, they said, for three days. Frightened staff officers promised to pay them immediately at the Olympic Stadium grounds. A sympathetic colonel met them there with a jeepload of sacks of bread he had bought with his own money. "As soon as the sacks left the army jeep," wrote a witness, "the men pounced in hordes, grabbing loaves and chewing them in seconds." A Cambodian lieutenant watched the scene. "You say there is a new government?" he asked, referring to the recently appointed High Political Council, which had been formed at American urging. "I wish they were here now. . . ."

The officer corps was as inept as ever, and as corrupt. There were, by various estimates, somewhere between 40,000 and 80,000 "phantoms" on military payrolls, two full years after the Khmer government had acknowledged in a formal written agreement with the U.S. government that as "a matter of the highest urgency" it would seek "to effectively suppress and prevent the illegal diversion of payroll funds." The phantom soldiers represented up to $2 million a month that ended up in the pockets of corrupt officers. The FANK command was taking "some first steps toward eliminating corruption," a Pentagon general lamely told Senate critics in May 1973, "but . . . your allegations of corruption, padding of payroll, ineffectiveness in combat, are true."

The American bombing may have made matters worse. When one of Lon Nol's associates urged him to take action against corrupt officers, reported William Harben, head of the American embassy's political section, the marshal responded that there was no reason to get excited. "The American B-52s are killing a thousand enemy every day," he said, "and the war will soon be over."

Early in 1973, the U.S. withheld a $4 million exchange support payment to force the Cambodians to reduce their military payroll from about 300,000 to 252,000, which was done in March. About the same time, six officers were reportedly reprimanded for payroll abuses: the highest ranking a lieutenant colonel and the lowest a second lieutenant. The severest penalty imposed for such offenses, reported the American embassy, was 60 days' house arrest. In September 1973, FANK strength was supposed to be 235,000. But in the following nine months, according to Pentagon officials, another 65,000 "nonexistent personnel" were purged from the rolls; 20,000 more "ghosts," the FANK command admitted, were removed toward the end of 1974.

Debilitated and dispirited, the government army by the spring of 1973 had lost control of most of the Cambodian countryside. All roads leading from the capital were blocked, including Highway 4, which ran to the port of Kompong Som; supplies could reach Phnom Penh only by air or by barge up the Mekong from South Vietnam. Steadily, during the stifling, dusty dry-season months of late spring, government forces fell back toward the capital, often abandoning positions even when there was no strong enemy pressure. By early summer, the battle fronts lay no more than ten to twenty miles from the city's edge in all directions. The Khmer Rouge, meanwhile, was growing rapidly in size, capability, and independence from its North Vietnamese sponsors. Only a few thousand Vietnamese specialists and advisers still remained with the Khmer Communist army, which numbered from 40,000 to 50,000 men early in 1973—well over double its size a year before.

As the army gave up more territory, tens of thousands more refugees crowded into Phnom Penh. Outside pagodas and schools where refugees were housed, tents of flimsy blue plastic sheeting began to sprout, as new arrivals overflowed the available space. While many thousands of people were without livelihoods, prices soared out of reach. The average Cambodian's income in April of 1973 represented only one-third to one-half of his prewar purchasing power, according to American estimates.

Inflation and corruption together affected the most vital commodity of all. Rice was supposed to be sold through a government monopoly at a controlled price of about $8 for a 220-pound sack. But corrupt officials siphoned off so much from government stocks to black-market dealers that for weeks at a time, no rice at all could be found in the state shops. Instead, buyers had to go to the illegal traders, whose prices had doubled in six months and were now nearly three times the official price.

Hunger was new to Cambodia. Before the war, the average Cambodian was considerably better fed than most other Asians, consuming about one and a half pounds of rice and nearly half a pound of fish every day. Now, for the first time, a substantial part of the population—not just homeless and jobless refugees from the countryside, but the urban poor as well—was finding it hard to get enough to eat.

Of all America's deeds in Indochina, its neglect of Cambodian war victims was surely among the most shameful.

Long after it was apparent to everyone else that civilian suffering was acute and growing worse, and that the Khmer government was neither competent enough nor concerned enough to do anything about it, American officials continued to deny any need for a major relief effort. From the start of the war almost to its end, instead of food and medicine the U.S. government supplied only a long list of statements declaring, in absolute contradiction to all the evidence, that Cambodia's refugees were being adequately cared for.

"The performance of the government of the Khmer Republic and of individual Cambodians in caring for war victims has been impressive," said the State Department's William Sullivan in April 1971. "Our assistance has not been sought, and there has been no need of it." By the fall of that year, a half-million Cambodians had already fled into Phnom Penh and an unknown number were refugees in outlying province capitals, but Ambassador Emory C. Swank told investigators from the U.S. General Accounting Office that it was "the policy of the United States not to become involved with the problem of civilian war victims." Since the U.S. was providing military and economic aid to Cambodia, the GAO reported Swank as saying, U.S. policy was to encourage "other countries—which could not provide military assistance because of their own internal political situations—to assist Cambodia with its humanitarian needs." Even if the refugee problem became "much more severe," Swank believed, Cambodia was not likely to ask for U.S. help because the Khmer priority was military aid: "Cambodian government officials . . . desire that any assistance obtained from the United States be channeled toward the advancement of the war effort."

In the spring of 1972, Phnom Penh's refugee population had passed three-quarters of a million, more than the city's entire prewar population. But the U.S. government was not notably concerned. The "vast majority" of Cambodian refugees, Roderic L. O'Connor of the Agency for International Development told Sen. Edward Kennedy's refugee subcommittee, "are said to be self-sufficient within ten days." What this meant was that ten days' food supply was the maximum given—when any help was given at all, which was seldom—by the Cambodian government's Directorate for War Victims. William Sullivan was again on hand, contributing his view that "the Khmer government takes considerable pride in attempting to cope" with the refugee problem "through its own institutions and its own organization."

The efforts of which the Khmer government was said to be so proud included bugeting a grand total of $324,000 for the Commissioner General for War Victims for the first year and a half of the war—an allocation that was later reduced to a bit over $250,000 "because of the higher priority afforded the military effort." By the end of the war's first year the Commissioner General had actually succeeded in spending the sum of $28,515 in government funds for food and other refugee relief.

American officials did display concern for the well-being of Cambodian civilians in one respect. The U.S. government was quite anxious, said AID's O'Connor in the Kennedy subcommittee's 1972 hearings, to make sure that pharmaceutical supplies did not find their way into the hands of "people that don't know how to use them or don't even need them," which could cause "a serious medical problem." To protect Cambodians against this danger, and also because drugs might be captured or illegally sold to the enemy, pharmaceuticals were not only not given to Cambodia but were kept off the list of commodities Cambodians could buy under the U.S. import subsidy program.

On this matter, the usual claim that no request had been received from the Khmer authorities could not be made. The Cambodian government's health ministry, through the finance minister, formally asked the U.S. to include $3 million worth of drugs in the 1972 import program; the request was denied. And when the health ministry's representative in the Khmer Red Cross approached the U.S. embassy for help in obtaining medicines from the American Red Cross, embassy officials simply referred him to the Red Cross's international service, without endorsing his request or even bothering to inquire later on what had become of it. The request was for "such drugs as antibiotics, vitamins, antimalaria etc. . . . and such medical articles as dressing materials, surgery equipment, clothing and food." It took six months for U.S. Red Cross officials to send their reply: "We have on hand in our warehouse a stock of 6,433 bottles of vitamin tablets called 'CHOCKS.' The total is about 385,900 units. Before these can be shipped . . . we must have your Society's acceptance of the shipment, with a statement regarding duty-free entry. If you feel these vitamins would be of use to you in your medical program, please let us know."

By then the shortage of medicines had already become, in the words of the General Accounting Office report, "extreme." At government hospitals and clinics where refugees were supposed to receive free care, they were given no medicines, just prescriptions with which to buy their own drugs from privately owned pharmacies. "Because the refugees had no money," the GAO found, "they usually went without medicines." At one hospital, investigators were told that a 15 percent mortality rate among small children with gastric disorders could easily be reduced with the proper drugs—but none were available.

Through the whole war, Cambodians remained very well protected from the danger of having drugs they might not know how to use. Only a few months before Phnom Penh's surrender, an official U.S. government report told of "patients with traumatic blast injuries writhing in pain because of an inadequate supply of painkilling drugs."

In the spring of 1973, following another year of defeat and growing misery in Cambodia, AID's Robert H. Nooter professed encouragement at the fact that only about 10,000 Cambodians were in officially designated refugee camps. "Thus," Nooter declared, "out of a total refugee population of approximately 700,000, less than 10,000 have failed to make some accommodation with their new situation. . . . The camp system of treating refugees has a lot of defects which we became aware of in Vietnam, and where these people who are displaced can be assimilated into the general economy and find work and earn their own way, that is by far the best way all around." In fact, the economy was not absorbing refugees but was being destroyed. The distinction between the 10,000 in "camps" and the hundreds of thousands of other homeless Cambodians living in schools or pagodas or empty fields was no distinction at all, but a bureaucratic abstraction. Yet AID favored only "relatively small amounts of assistance to those refugee families living in camps," nothing for the others. Pressed to explain why the U.S. was not making a greater effort, Nooter said the problem was "how to organize the program so that material that is put in for refugee purposes will arrive at the end point. A program that doesn't have some well thought out control system simply wouldn't be effective." (This was at a time when hand grenades, M-16 rifles, and just about any other piece of military gear imaginable could be purchased in the Phnom Penh black market. A brand-new M-16 was said to go for about $50. But the absence of "well thought out controls" did not prevent the American government from continuing to supply the Cambodian army.) After a ceasefire, AID promised, refugee relief would have "first priority." Its vision of postwar conditions seemed to lack a certain realism, however. "Tourism to Angkor Wat should again become an important source of foreign exchange," the agency told Congress—breezily ignoring not only that no ceasefire seemed possible, but also that the great Angkor ruins had been occupied by Communist forces since the first year of the war.

The first U.S. refugee relief grant—the only one in the first three years of the conflict—was a munificent $50,000 to the International Red Cross in December 1972. That was followed in the spring of 1973 by another $100,000 to the Red Cross and two additional grants of a half-million dollars each to CARE and Catholic Relief Services. With the total number of refugees estimated by AID's own specialists to be about twice as many as the 600,000 to 700,000 who had registered with the government, this three-year grand total of $1.15 million for "humanitarian" needs represented something less than one dollar for every Cambodian uprooted by the war. It was also less than two-thirds of what was being spent that spring for a single day's American bombing.

There was, of course, something called "economic aid," which over the entire course of the war amounted to slightly more than $750 million. More than 95 percent of this money, however, went to underwrite the Khmer government's budget, not to help refugees or the needy. About $270 million was spent for import subsidies, another $52 million went to a special fund for foreign exchange support, and $385 million was designated for food imports. Under the import subsidy, the U.S. supplied dollars for import purchases and accepted Cambodian riels which were then turned back to the government as "counterpart funds." Those riels, and the money derived from the exchange support program, were then used to pay soldiers and civil servants and for other government expenditures. Similarly, U.S.-supplied food was shipped to the government, and except for very small amounts doled out to refugees, was either reserved for the army and civil service or sold on the open market, also generating counterpart accounts of Cambodian currency. The only meaningful humanitarian use of economic aid funds came in 1974 and 1975, when about $27 million in counterpart funds was used for relief purposes—about 5 percent of the aid funds for those years. Otherwise, except very marginally through the Khmer government's own meager and often misspent relief programs, U.S. economic aid did not help those who lost homes and livelihoods in the war.

The miserly American relief effort coincided with the utter devastation of Cambodia's economy. Rice harvests in the 1960s had averaged nearly three million metric tons a year, with an exceptionally good crop of 3.8 million tons in the last prewar year, 1969–70. In 1972–73, the harvest was only about one-fourth as large, 953,000 tons. The following year it was halved again, to 493,000 tons. It was estimated that half of all the country's livestock, including draft animals, was slaughtered by 1973. The fresh-water fish supply, a major protein source, was sharply reduced because more than half the fishing area was under Communist occupation or in a combat zone.

A third of all Cambodia's bridges were destroyed, two-fifths of the road network made unusable, the railroad put out of operation. Much of the country's industry, including its lone oil refinery near Kompong Som, had stopped functioning. Only 300 of 1,400 rice mills and 60 of 240 sawmills were still operating in 1973. Timber and rubber, the major commercial products, had each declined to only one-fifth of prewar production levels.

Because of shortages the economy was not just inflationary but hyperinflationary. The U.S. aid mission reported that from the start of the war to February 1974, a price index based on "working class" consumption rose more than twelve times. Food prices were more than eighteen times higher than before the war. No one tried to measure unemployment, but it was obvious that the overwhelming majority of the Cambodians forced off the land into Phnom Penh or the province capitals would find no jobs except for casual labor, which soon did not pay enough even for food.

As early as 1971, public health specialists and relief agencies began to report rising malnutrition and vitamin deficiency, not because there wasn't enough food but because prices were climbing out of reach of more and more families. Similar reports and warnings of worse hunger ahead multiplied in the following years, but with almost no American response. Until February of 1974, of the 200 military and civilian officials in the American embassy, only one was assigned to refugee matters. And as late as March of 1975, six weeks before the end of the war and while Cambodian children were starving to death in the pagodas, the embassy officer in charge of economic assistance programs could say of malnutrition and disease among the refugees: "We're trying to assess the magnitude of the problem. None of the agencies with which we're working has a definite fix. . . . We'll have a better feel for it in a couple of weeks."

The decay of the Khmer Republic's economy and of its army was matched by the decay of its political institutions. Lon Nol and Lon Non were visibly more isolated, unpopular, and unresponsive than ever. American exhortations to reform invariably resulted in shadow plays in which appearances changed, but the reality did not. In the late spring of 1973, after a visit by Alexander Haig, Lon Non was persuaded to leave the country while Lon Nol, at American urging, invited the men who helped him take power in 1970 back into the government to form a new High Political Council that was empowered to rule by decree, bypassing the ineffective National Assembly. Its members, in addition to Lon Nol, were Sirik Matak; the former assembly leader In Tam, who was also named prime minister; and Cheng Heng, who had succeeded Sihanouk as head of state.

The Americans hoped the council would assume effective governing power and that the other members would neutralize Lon Nol. Nothing of the sort happened, and the council soon lapsed into inactivity. In Tam was never permitted any real power. By October he was publicly complaining that the marshal's constant interference undermined his authority; in December, he resigned. Even with military disaster at their throats, sighed an exasperated U.S. embassy officer, "it seems too much to expect any three Cambodians to cooperate with each other."

Yet American support for Lon Nol remained unwavering. If American actions produced any change, the feeling seemed to be, then the U.S. would be responsible for the results, which might be even worse than the existing situation. In Khmer eyes, however, the Americans were already responsible, especially after the formation of the High Political Council. The U.S. had thus made the worst of all its alternatives. It paid the price of interfering in Cambodian affairs but was still stuck with the inept leadership that was responsible for Cambodia's weakness to begin with. If the disillusioned Khmers blamed the Americans for anything, it seemed to me, it was not for meddling in Khmer politics, but for failing to get rid of Lon Nol.

Through it all, as if the U.S. could think of nothing else to do, the bombing grew in fury. Sortie rates and bomb tonnages climbed each month. In May, the tonnage was almost equal to the total for the whole year of 1972. Skirting the congressional ban on American military presence in Cambodia, U.S. Air Force "FACs"—Forward Air Controllers—landed a dozen or more times a day to refuel their twin-engined OV-10 spotter aircraft at Phnom Penh's Pochentong Airport. As government troops kept giving ground, the sounds of the bombing drew closer to the capital. On days and nights when action was heavy on one or another of the fronts around the city, the drumroll of B-52 bombloads erupting on the torn earth seemed never to stop.

The bombing was not only troubling. It seemed inexplicable. Among non-American diplomats in the Cambodian capital, among the journalists who were assigned there or visited frequently from Saigon, and among some civilian and military officers in the American embassy itself, few could see any purpose in the air offensive. There was a growing feeling that Washington had gone crazy. No American objective seemed within reach, or even within sight. It did not take an expert to see that Lon Nol was still losing the war, or to reason that if air power over much longer periods had not beaten the Communists in Laos or Vietnam, it was not going to expel them from Cambodia either. Nor did one have to be privy to the secret diplomatic cables to realize that the ceasefire the Nixon administration kept talking about was a mirage. "Frankly," said a European diplomat, "we don't see what the Americans are trying to accomplish."

The United States in fact had no good choices left in Cambodia. More and more, the bombing seemed to take on a quality of rage, as if pure violence could succeed in achieving American goals when nothing else could.

For three years, the Nixon administration's announced rationale for air strikes in Cambodia was the president's "inherent right" to use military force to protect American troops in South Vietnam. When the U.S. withdrawal from Vietnam was completed, the administration's critics quickly pointed out, that argument became invalid. It took the government a month to formulate a new legal basis for its actions, but on April 30—three years to the day after the American incursion—Secretary of State Rogers presented to the Senate Foreign Relations Committee a legal memorandum declaring that the president was constitutionally empowered to bomb Cambodia for the purpose of bringing about compliance with the Paris peace agreement.

The logic of this document was, to put it mildly, difficult to follow. Asserting that the wars in Cambodia, Vietnam, and Laos were "so inter-related as to be considered parts of a single conflict," the memorandum then detoured to suggest that the bombing in Cambodia was somehow made legal by the fact that it was already taking place. The question, it said, "is not whether the president may do something new, but rather whether what he has been doing must automatically stop, without regard to the consequences even though the [Paris] agreement is not being implemented by the other side."

The continued fighting and the presence of North Vietnamese troops in Cambodia, the document continued, threatened "the right of self-determination of the South Vietnamese people, which is guaranteed by the agreement." This seemed to say it was South Vietnam that had to be defended against violations, not Cambodia, where no ceasefire existed and where the U.S. always denied any formal obligation to the defense of the Phnom Penh government. But then the memorandum declared that the administration did have the right to bomb in support of Cambodian forces: "Under present circumstances, United States air support and material assistance are needed to support the armed forces of the Khmer Republic and thereby to render more likely the early conclusion of a ceasefire and the implementation of Article 20 of the agreement." The memorandum explicitly rejected an American commitment to the Lon Nol government, however. "U.S. air strikes in Cambodia," it said, "do not represent a commitment to the defense of Cambodia itself but instead represent a meaningful interim action to bring about compliance with this critical provision of the Vietnam agreement."

Subsequent variations on the theme were no less confusing. Secretary Rogers, asked in a Senate hearing if North Vietnamese violation of Article 20 was the basis for the U.S. bombing, lapsed into near-incomprehensibility: "If you look at Article 20 strictly as a lawyer, you can say maybe they didn't, but it was in our discussions with them that we would both seek a ceasefire in Cambodia. . . . It was clear in the discussions that each side would make a good faith effort to see that a ceasefire was brought about and that foreign troops would be withdrawn. That is what has not happened." Defense Secretary Elliot Richardson declared that because implementation of the Paris agreement had "not yet been accomplished in full . . . it follows that the president's authority to use military, political and diplomatic means to fully terminate the conflict must also continue." And Fred Buzhardt, the Pentagon's general counsel, told the House Armed Services Committee that since the president had "used military means as well as diplomatic means" in Indochina in the past, the Paris agreement "could not have the legal effect of terminating the president's authority to continue the means he was using previously to terminate the war."

In addition to questions about the president's constitutional powers, the administration also faced—but never convincingly addressed—an essential contradiction in its interpretation of the Paris agreement itself. Either military action in Cambodia was legal, in the absence of a ceasefire, or it was not. If it was, *both* U.S. bombing and North Vietnamese troops were permissible under the agreement. If military action was not allowed, then the United States was in violation, just as North Vietnam was. And if the purpose of the strikes was to enforce the agreement, it was not clear why Cambodians were being bombed, as New York Rep. Otis Pike pointed out: "We keep justifying this bombing because the North Vietnamese are not supporting the treaty. We haven't any treaty with the Khmer. They didn't agree to anything with us and we didn't agree to do anything with them." Why, Pike asked the Pentagon's Fred Buzhardt, if North Vietnam was breaking its treaty commitments, did the United States not bomb North Vietnam?

"I think it is not a question of what people do we have the legal authority to bomb," Buzhardt replied lamely. "It is a question of the purposes. We have the legal authority to bomb for the purposes of terminating the war. And the conflict that is going on is in Cambodia and not in North Vietnam."

Not just the legality but the military purpose of the bombing remained obscure. It was aimed not only at forces opposing the Phnom Penh regime but also at the Vietnamese Communists in the traditional sanctuary regions, far from the Cambodian battlegrounds. In February and March, according to 7th Air Force commanders, four-fifths of American strikes in Cambodia were flown against "North Vietnamese lines of communication into South Vietnam," *not* Cambodia. Targets included "North Vietnamese base camps, bivouac and storage areas and truck parks." South Vietnamese war prisoners returned from camps in the Parrot's Beak region verified that strategic bombing there was extremely heavy. "We were threatened by B-52s from late February through all of March," a newly freed captain told me, and another ex-prisoner called the B-52 raids the "first fear" of all the men in his camp.

Though a greater proportion of the raids was later shifted to direct support of Cambodian troops, significant numbers of strikes were still flown over targets relevant to the war in Vietnam, rather than Cambodia. "As far as the B-52 efforts are concerned," a Defense Department witness told the Senate Appropriations Committee early in May, "approximately 35 per cent is up in the northeast quadrant." A month later, the department informed Congress that one of the objectives of the bombing was still "to interdict the massive flow of men and material from North Vietnam destined for ultimate employment against friendly forces in Cambodia *and South Vietnam*" (emphasis added).

What effect this had on Hanoi's perceptions can only be guessed. It is not likely that the bombing supported any impulse, if there was one at all on the Communist side, to act in good faith to carry out all the unfulfilled provisions of the Paris agreement.

Whatever its purpose, the bombing in Cambodia, as the months lengthened with no sign of either military success on the Cambodian battlefield or of the beginning of peace talks, looked less and less like a temporary remnant of the war, and more and more like another commitment that could keep America engaged in Southeast Asia indefinitely. Anti-bombing proposals in various forms began moving through both houses of Congress, and now—with no more American soldiers in combat and no more prisoners awaiting return—there was no doubt that they would pass. On June 26, a supplemental appropriations bill was sent to Nixon with a rider denying all funds for U.S. air operations in Cambodia. Nixon vetoed it, declaring that a halt would "undercut ongoing diplomatic efforts to achieve a ceasefire" and "reverse the momentum toward lasting peace in Indochina." But Congress's willingness to accept American war in Asia was at an end, while Nixon's influence was being dissipated in the growing Watergate investigation.

After his initial veto, Nixon chose not to resist any longer. Reluctantly, he agreed not to veto a revised amendment that would allow six weeks of bombing and then end it for good on August 15, 1973.

Congress fixed a date nine days and six hours too late for Neak Luong. Between four-thirty and five o'clock on the morning of August 6, a B-52 crewman forgot to flip a switch that would direct the aircraft to its bomb-release point. The error caused the huge plane to home in instead on the ground-based radar beacon that was supposed to give it the target coordinates. The device—no larger than a woman's handbag—should have been put "a mile or so away in the boondocks," an Air Force officer later admitted. But it was suspended from a pole, five or six feet off the ground, smack in the middle of Neak Luong, a ferry port and garrison town on the Mekong, 38 miles downriver from Phnom Penh. The errant bomber's load of bombs fell in a line more than a mile long through the middle of the town. Much of the central market was smashed. Part of the city hospital was destroyed and the rest heavily damaged. The bombs demolished hundreds of huts that housed government soldiers and their families. 137 people died, including 56 soldiers, and another 268 were wounded; the accident was believed the worst of the entire war.

Clumsily, the Americans tried to minimize it at first. "It was no great disaster," said a hapless Air Force colonel at the embassy in Phnom Penh—the same officer who once upbraided correspondents: "You always write it's bombing, bombing, bombing. It's not bombing. It's air support." Neak Luong, though, was too large a tragedy to hide for long. Reporters saw and interviewed wounded victims who were brought to Phnom Penh in Cambodian navy patrol boats. The *Times*'s Sydney Schanberg managed to make his way to Neak Luong despite an effort by the U.S. air attache's office to keep him from going. Schanberg found "trees for acres around are stripped of leaves and charred, with sheets of tin from soldiers' huts hanging from some of the high branches. . . . A woman's scalp sways on a clump of tall grass. A bloody pillow here, a shred of sarong caught on barbed wire there. A large bloodstain on the brown earth. . . ."

Schanberg counted 30 bomb craters through the center of the town, and also found a weeping 48-year-old soldier named Keo Chan, who survived because he was on duty several miles from his home when the bombs fell out of the darkness. His wife and ten of his eleven children—all but the youngest—had been killed. "All my family is dead! All my family is dead!" he shrieked at the shaken Schanberg. "Take my picture! Take my picture! Let the Americans see me!"

The disaster at Neak Luong seemed to validate the sense of unraveling that enveloped Cambodia as the date for the bombing halt approached. The government had two or three times as many troops as its enemy and many more heavy weapons, but it began to appear conceivable that it might simply give up as soon as American air support ended. U.S. planners hurriedly updated plans for evacuating the embassy staff and other Americans. Early in August, the marine colonel who was designated to lead the evacuation landing force, Col. S. G. Olmstead, secretly flew to Phnom Penh to reconnoiter helicopter landing sites. The embassy's mood, recalled a later Marine Corps account, "fluctuated from 'never-go' to 'maybe tomorrow' on almost a daily basis."

Cambodian leaders, meanwhile, seemed to realize for the very first time that they might actually lose the war. The first draft law since the war began had been passed by the National Assembly earlier in the year, and in July the authorities tried to put it into operation, with results about on a par with other accomplishments of the Cambodian military command. Military police roamed through the streets rounding up frightened young men for conscription. Those with money were able to buy their way out of the induction centers, while the rest remained there, in conditions resembling a prisoner-of-war camp. Outside the centers, crowds of sobbing women milled about, trying to pass packages of food and wads of money into the camps for their husbands or sons. So overwhelming was popular opposition that inductions were abruptly halted. The draft laws, admitted the High Political Council, had been "very badly applied." In the uproar few were conscripted, but the army's losses were climbing. In July, the equivalent of a 500-man battalion was killed or wounded every week.

As its forces kept losing ground, the badly frightened Khmer command at last began relieving incompetent officers—including at least one division commander—for failures on the battlefield. The pay system improved slightly. But it was late—very late—for any reforms to save the hapless government army. In the end it was not any decision in Phnom Penh that saved the Khmer Republic to fight on for another twenty months; it was the suicidal fanaticism of the Khmer Rouge.

In its final weeks, the rage of American bombing was met by an equal madness, it seemed, on the land beneath. Under the bombs the Khmer Rouge pressed toward Phnom Penh that summer with a profligate, disastrous disregard for their own losses. They did not disperse, they did not dig in, they did not shift their offensive away from the capital to other objectives, even when a date for the bombing to stop was fixed. Instead, the Communists massed their battalions and sent them forward again and again over fields that were made killing grounds for the planes that swooped like fistfuls of hardflung knives above the monsoon clouds.

How many died, perhaps not even the Khmer Rouge knew. More than two months before it ended, American officials asserted the bombing had killed 10,000 insurgent troops and wounded 10,000 more. The figure may have been exaggerated; Air Force claims often were. But the estimate was made, on the other hand, with weeks of the heaviest bombing yet to come. Whatever the numbers, the losses were clearly terrible. In the war-ringed capital we listened to the bombs lash the earth and wondered incredulously why, when they knew the raids would stop in a few more weeks, the Khmer Rouge did not just go to earth and wait for them to be over, then rise up to take the city that seemed ready to fall into their hands. But they fought on with a fury that could only be called demented. Their assault on the capital faltered with only a few days left before the bombing halt, and when they did not after all break through and capture Phnom Penh, it seemed certain that their casualties must have been a major cause for their failure.

The reasons can only be guessed. The Khmer Rouge leaders' suspicions of Hanoi may have become so acute by the summer of 1973 that they felt they could not delay their offensive by a single hour, bombs or no bombs, lest their ally somehow contrive to steal their victory from them. It is possible, too, though this is only supposition, that they simply did not believe the bombing was really going to end. The capacity for crazed violence that had lain behind Cambodia's smiling face was now in command, it seemed to me, and perhaps the hate it generated left no room to conceive that an enemy who possessed such a powerful means of destruction would stop using it.

That hate was expended not only on the battlefield, but also on the people in the Communist zone. Khmer Rouge fanaticism sprang from several roots. The ideology of their leaders, the backwardness and ignorance of those they had trained as cadres, the youth and inexperience and perceived friendlessness of their movement among the Indochinese revolutionaries, all contributed to the barbarism that began to characterize their rule. But so too, I believe, did the shattering of all normalcy in Cambodian life, to which American bombs contributed. Khmer culture is one of those that traditionally permits little outward expression of hostility, and thus does not teach its people to control aggressive drives when customary restraints are loosened. It is for that reason, perhaps, that "smiling peoples" like the Khmer often turn savagely cruel when they do become violent. The phrase "running amok" was contributed to our language by the Malays, a people culturally akin to the Khmer and similarly nonaggressive: "amok" is a Malay word for someone in the grip of uncontrollable bloodlust.

A Cambodian acquaintance compared the violence in his formerly gentle country with that which overtook another traditionally peaceful, passive people: the Balinese, who in 1965 and 1966 in the upheavals that swept Indonesia after the crushing of an attempted pro-Communist revolt, "slashed and clubbed and chopped to death" as many as 40,000 people on their idyllic island who were real or suspected Communists or who had the misfortune to be alien Chinese or Japanese. A Balinese said of that slaughter that the killers acted "as if they were ridding the soil and their souls of evil and purifying themselves." That characterization seemed completely plausible when applied to the Cambodian Communists a decade later.

The Khmer capacity for violence did not appear newborn in the 1970s. Like some red-tinged, iridescent underwater creature flickering in dark pools, it can be glimpsed swimming in the flow of Cambodian history and legend back into antiquity. "Traditional Cambodian literature and folk tales abound with accounts of grisly executions and mutilations of enemies," one scholar noted, and Wilfred Burchett found a consciousness of great cruelty even among the great temples of Angkor Wat, on whose stone friezes

> battle scenes are not shown in glamorized heroic form but realistically, with all the horror and suffering that war brings. There is no glorification of even military successes. Cambodian troops are shown marching over a battlefield thick with their own dead. In the naval battles which took place on the Great Lake between multi-oared galleys laden with opposing troops—the Cham always recognized by lotus-shaped headdresses—one sees the wounded toppling overboard to be seized by crocodiles. The lake bottom is piled high with bodies, Cambodian and Cham, intertwined in death, prey for giant turtles, crocodiles and huge fish. The land battles are directed by generals on elephants armed with javelins, while the infantry fight with pikes and crossbows. Grim scenes show the fate of Cambodians taken prisoner, hung by the wrists on racks while spikes are driven into their bodies, then thrown into the flames, their bodies still bristling with spikes.

From 1973 on, Cambodia seemed an entire country gone amok. All its psychological anchors were ripped loose in the hurricane of violence that had fallen on it. American decisions and American bombs had helped destroy peacetime Cambodian life, and it is in that sense that some connection can be said to exist between American actions and the savagery of the Khmer Rouge.

Certainly, Khmer Rouge fury grew with that of the bombing. Early in the war, when the Vietnamese were still to a large extent in control, the regimen in the insurgent areas was commonly reported to be quite mild—much more so, for example, than in Communist-held zones of South Vietnam. In the summer of 1970, a Cambodian military intelligence report, based on information from prisoners and refugees, remarked that villagers under Communist rule "appreciated not being submitted to taxation and excesses by the invaders who, for propaganda purposes, are well-behaved and respectful of the needs and cares of the population." In mid-1972, I was told by refugees from Svay Rieng Province that they could move quite freely from their farms in the insurgent zone to the government-held towns, where they could sell their crops and buy kerosene and other goods not available in the villages. No such movement, except by trusted agents, would have been permitted by the Viet Cong in Vietnam.

As the Khmer Communists took over administrative control from the Vietnamese, they imposed an Orwellian rigor on their cadres, who were required to assume new names to symbolize the surrender of all individual consciousness and were trained in a blind submissiveness to the orders of the

"Angkar"—"organization"—while being constantly criticized for any assertion of personal views or feelings. No such extreme measures, however, were yet turned on the ordinary people. On the contrary, the "most important" object of Angkar discipline, reported Ith Sarin, was "not to disturb "the ways of the people'. . . . The farming people of the base area who knew nothing of socialist revolution quickly began to love and support the Angkar because of its sentiments of openness and friendliness." If the Communists in those early stages intimidated the easygoing Khmer, it was not by cruelty but by virtue. He could never be a "progressive," one farmer admitted, because he didn't want to work that hard!

An American foreign service officer, Kenneth Quinn, exhaustively interviewed refugees from areas adjoining the South Vietnamese delta and concluded that during 1971 and 1972, Khmer Rouge administration was "characterized by a tightening of political control and the beginning of the process of changing political values, myths and institutions, but not total revolution." Brutality existed but was still "quite limited," Quinn found. Among both Cambodians and foreigners, the common perception even after several years of war was that reported by Henry Kamm of the *New York Times*, one of the most knowledgeable and experienced American journalists in Asia, who wrote early in 1973 that in Cambodia "there are no real hatreds among the population" and that if the war in Vietnam could be ended, Cambodia should easily achieve reconciliation.

That perception would not last many more months. Sometime in 1973 the Khmer Rouge leadership "apparently decided to accelerate its program to alter Khmer society," said a study by another American diplomat, Timothy Carney. In the spring of that year, at the same time U.S. bombing was intensifying, refugee accounts of life in the Communist zones suddenly became much grimmer. Local leaders who had originally been chosen and trained by the Vietnamese, or whose primary loyalty was thought to be to Prince Sihanouk, were purged and replaced by Khmer Rouge cadres who seemed as implacably hostile to the Vietnamese as to the Phnom Penh government.

Under the Khmer Rouge, forced relocations of entire villages became a widespread practice. "In the process," Kenneth Quinn reported, "all vestiges of the past, including religious and private property, were left behind." The relocations were carried out with deadly brutality. One refugee who escaped from the insurgent zone early in the summer of 1973 told a European friend in Phnom Penh: "They rounded up all the people and forced them to march out of the village; it was at night and cold, and one woman tried to go back for a blanket; they shot her on the spot, just like that. Then they burned down all the houses. No one was allowed to save anything." Buddhist practice was now forbidden along with all other traditional folk customs, holidays, and songs. Bright clothes, even pinned-up hairdos for women, were banned. Monks were made to work in the fields with everyone else. Any defiance of the new order was punished swiftly and savagely.

"Beginning in early 1973," Quinn's interviews indicated, ". . . the use of terror escalated sharply. Refugees from all the areas stated that the older local cadres were replaced by younger men whom they had never seen before. These new cadres were described as 'fanatics' who would allow no dissent or even questioning of their directives.

"From this point on, according to the refugees, anyone who spoke out or refused to comply was arrested and never seen or heard from again."

On the battlefronts around Phnom Penh, the lightening of enemy pressure was sensed as a sailor senses the first breaths of a shift in the wind.

After capturing important positions on the capital's perimeter early in July, the Khmer Rouge then gradually began to seem a shade less determined. By August, government troops on the highways leading out from Phnom Penh were able to advance a few hundred or a few thousand yards, finding only one or two enemy corpses along their line of march. Phnom Penh's crisis of nerves was by no means over when, at eleven o'clock on the morning of August 15, the last American bombers shrieked away. ("It was quiet enough around Phnom Penh today," Sydney Schanberg began his dispatch the next day, "to hear an artillery shell drop.") But, though the frightened capital did not yet fully realize it, the danger of a frontal Communist assault had passed.

If the prospect of defeat was receding, however, there was still none of peace. The Nixon administration, trying strenuously but vainly to persuade Congress not to stop the bombing, kept hinting that its diplomacy was about to achieve some unspecified breakthrough. Having successfully achieved a Vietnam settlement, Nixon told Congress in his veto of the first bombing-halt measure, "we are now involved in concluding the last element of that settlement, a Cambodian settlement." A subsequent message alleged that "delicate negotiations are still under way." Henry Kissinger later charged that "major efforts toward negotiation" in 1973 ". . . were thwarted by the forced bombing halt in August of that year."

For nearly nine years, those assertions remained unexplained and unproven, until Henry Kissinger finally provided an account in the second volume of his memoirs. The "major effort," according to Kissinger, was an American proposal given on May 27, 1973, not to any Cambodian faction, but to China's United Nations ambassador, Huang Hua. In it, the U.S. offered to stop bombing Cambodia and to arrange for Lon Nol to leave the country for "medical treatment," if the insurgent side would agree to a temporary ceasefire and talks "between the Sihanouk group and the remainder of the Lon Nol group." U.S. discussions with Sihanouk in Peking would also be authorized. After "some months," the United States "would not oppose the return of Prince Sihanouk" as the head of a new Cambodian regime that would include Khmer Rouge representatives but would also preserve what Kissinger called "key elements of the Lon Nol structure."

Before making this proposal, the Americans had "learned," Kissinger also disclosed—without further explaining the nature of the information or its source—that in the spring, the Khmer Communist leadership had not irrevocably decided against negotiations, but planned instead to evaluate the military situation later in the year. "In the event that military victory was out of reach and a stalemate emerged," Kissinger wrote, "the Khmer Rouge would negotiate for the best conditions obtainable. If, on the other hand, the military situation was favorable, negotiations would be avoided and total victory sought." The purpose of the intensified bombing was to produce that stalemate.

Other administration officials were far from sure that any American action was able to achieve that aim. "The resources . . . are adequate," Defense Secretary James Schlesinger told Congress. "The survival of the Cambodian regime is less dependent on military resources than on the cohesion of the government leadership, morale, and discipline of their troops, and similar issues which we have very limited ability to influence." But Kissinger's faith in the ability of U.S. air power to achieve a political end was, as usual, unquenchable.

On June 4, eight days after receiving the American proposal, Huang Hua informed Kissinger that China was willing to "communicate the U.S. tentative thinking to the Cambodian side," although not immediately since Sihanouk was then still traveling away from Asia.

Kissinger took the view that by agreeing to pass on the proposal, the Chinese—and specifically Chou En-lai—also committed themselves to it, though no such endorsement was made explicit in Peking's messages. Kissinger also assumed, he wrote in his memoirs, that because the Chinese "would never offer to pass on a message that they thought would be turned down," they had checked with the Khmer Rouge and were given reason to expect that the American plan would be successful. Believing, accordingly, that the pieces were finally being put into place for a settlement, awaiting only Sihanouk's return from his travels, Kissinger met several more times with Chinese representatives during June, concluding again that the Chinese understood and would meet America's needs—particularly for a decent interval before Sihanouk's return, to save American face. He also discussed plans for traveling to Peking early in August to open talks with Sihanouk, if a ceasefire had been arranged by then. But Congress intervened. By imposing a halt to the bombing it undercut Kissinger's diplomacy, removing the military pressure he regarded as essential. The bombing, in Kissinger's view, was China's tool as well as America's. Chou En-lai "needed to be able to argue to the Khmer Rouge that he had brought them the end of our bombing" in order to obtain Cambodian assent to the rest of the deal. And thus, he believed, "the legislated end of military activity destroyed all possibility of a neutral free Cambodia."

Sihanouk returned to Peking, finally, on July 5, but declared that the time for negotiations with the United States had passed. "It is too late now," he said. "It is useless." The Chinese did not pass on the American proposal after all, and on the 18th, in a note to Kissinger from their liaison office in Washington, told him they no longer intended to do so. Instead, they now counseled the U.S. to accept Khmer Rouge terms. Kissinger's visit to Peking was postponed; his planned meeting with Sihanouk never took place.

"We nearly made it," was Kissinger's conclusion. ". . . This was the most promising negotiating opportunity if not the only one—with the Chinese and us working actively in parallel—and it was torpedoed by the United States Congress and our domestic turmoil."

Perhaps. But all of Kissinger's conclusions were subject to serious question. His assertions that the Chinese adopted his proposal by agreeing to pass it on, and that they thought it would be accepted by the Khmer Rouge, remain no more than suppositions, unsupported by any evidence either in his own account or from elsewhere. His belief that the Khmer Rouge were prepared to negotiate, if a battlefield stalemate were established, contradicts all their public statements and all other evidence that has since become available. And in any case no such stalemate existed in June or early July, when the demoralized government forces were falling back on all sides of Phnom Penh. The Khmer Rouge offensive faltered only at the very end of July, weeks after the bombing halt was written into U.S. law. Neither Kissinger's account nor any other shows there was ever the slightest hint from Sihanouk or any of the Khmer leaders that the American plan, or any version of it, might be acceptable. Indeed, Sihanouk's character and everything he ever said or wrote about his own role make it seem extremely unlikely he would ever have consented to join with his usurpers.*

Nor, for that matter, was the proposal consistent with the policies of the Phnom Penh government, which apparently was never told about the American initiative at all. During the period of Kissinger's discussions with the Chinese, the Phnom Penh leaders had not yet agreed to negotiate with their Khmer Rouge opponents. They did so for the first time only on July 6, when Foreign Minister Long Boret announced that upon declaration of an immediate ceasefire, and as part of a process that also included the withdrawal of all Vietnamese Communist troops, Khmer Republic represen-

---

* In January 1973, Sihanouk told guests at his Peking home that a similar U.S. offer had been relayed to him by the Chinese sometime in 1972, proposing that he head a "government of reconciliation" in Phnom Penh. He refused, the prince said, because the plan would have required dissolving his own Cambodian Royal Government of National Union.

tatives would meet with "a delegation of Cambodians from the other side." The offer was far from unconditional, and it was left unclear whether Phnom Penh would deal with Sihanouk, who was, after all, under a death sentence for treason and whom government spokesmen had previously declared "formally excluded" from any possible peace talks.

Of all possible settlements, in fact, a "Sihanouk solution" would have been the hardest for Lon Nol and his associates to accept. They feared his vengeance, and they may have sensed that once back in Phnom Penh, the prince might have attracted popular support that their own decrepit and unpopular regime would not be able to withstand. Allowing Sihanouk to return would undermine the foundation of their own power: the principle, as Lon Nol once said, that "Sihanouk has been ousted by the Cambodian people for good."

Thus Henry Kissinger's claim that a Cambodian settlement was within reach, only to be obstructed by the American Congress, is based on a proposal that was never presented to any Cambodian on either side, that was premised on a military stalemate that did not exist, that led to no negotiations of any kind, and whose principles were violently rejected then and later not just by one but by both Cambodian sides—hardly, it seems, a plan that would warrant any description of American diplomacy as "promising."

There was a possible alternative course for the United States in 1973: to reduce support for the Phnom Penh government, detach itself from Lon Nol, and try to allow the two sides to seek their own level. No such admission of the weakness of the American position was acceptable to the administration in Washington, however. Kissinger would not even consider easing Lon Nol out of power to try to get negotiations started, though others in the American government thought that might be a useful first step. Instead, Kissinger insisted that Lon Nol must be kept in office as a chip to be bargained away for Khmer Rouge concessions. Kissinger seemed not to recognize that Lon Nol was an asset that was losing its value the longer it was hoarded. Since no concessions were ever offered, Lon Nol remained in power, allowing the Khmer Communists' stubbornness to serve them better than they perhaps knew, because it left U.S. interests in the hands of a feeble, incompetent leader whose rule would be a misfortune for his American sponsors—and for his own people, a catastrophe.

Whatever the United States did or did not do, nothing that has been learned of the character and motives of the Khmer Rouge makes it seem possible that they would ever have abandoned their war in return for Prince Sihanouk's participation in some form of coalition.

Not a syllable of any Khmer Rouge statement before, during, or after the U.S. initiative indicated the slightest willingness to negotiate. Long Boret's

July 6 proposal was quickly rejected—"mean and despicable," Sihanouk
called it—and later that month, at a "national congress" held in the liberated
zone from July 19 to 21, the insurgents issued a definitive statement of their
war aims:

> First: to force U.S. imperialism and all its foreign lackeys to stop the
> aggression against and bombing of Cambodia, withdraw their troops
> and military personnel . . . and let the Cambodian people settle their
> own internal affairs without any foreign interference—
> Second: with regard to the traitorous Phnom Penh gang headed by
> arch-antipeople, extreme fascist and most corrupt gangsters Lon Nol,
> Sirik Matak, Son Ngoc Thanh, In Tam, Cheng Heng and Sosthene
> Fernandez, the Cambodian nation and people will seal their fate and
> overthrow them under the circumstances of no foreign interference—
> Third: the [National United Front of Cambodia] with Head of State
> Samdech Norodom Sihanouk and the [Royal Government of National
> Union of Cambodia] with Samdech Penn Nouth as prime minister
> and Mr. Khieu Samphan as deputy prime minister will control Phnom
> Penh and lead the genuinely independent, peaceful, neutral, sovereign
> and democratic state of Cambodia on the basis of territorial integrity.

Far from being receptive to a "Sihanouk solution," the Khmer Rouge by
now were brutally purging the prince's remaining loyalists among their
cadre inside Cambodia. As titular head of their movement, Sihanouk in
Peking was still useful to the insurgents in their relations with the rest of the
world. But he was no longer their device for holding the support of the
Cambodians under their control. Harsher, more direct methods were now
meeting that purpose. "We do not need him any more," party workers
bluntly explained. The revolutionaries no longer proclaimed in Cambodia
that their fight was to restore Sihanouk; after the spring of 1973, advocating
that policy became perilous. "If you still use his name and support Sihanouk," said a village chief who reached government lines at Kompong
Thom after fleeing the Khmer Rouge zone, "then you will be sent away and
you will never return."

Sihanouk, in Peking, appealed to foreign powers to "give up completely
and forever . . . meddling with Cambodian affairs," though just before the
bombing ended, in an act that seemed to suggest some desperation, he
cabled U.S. Sen. Mike Mansfield, one of his admirers, offering to forget the
"painful past" if Washington would shut off military aid to the Lon Nol
government. The Americans could evacuate their high-level "collaborators" if they wished, he said, presumably meaning those the Khmer
Rouge threatened to execute. The U.S. had no reply other than to state that
the Cambodians should negotiate on their differences themselves—the one
route to peace that appeared, and was, utterly impassable. The Khmer

Rouge leaders remained completely adamant against peace talks as the bombing stopped. The Cambodian people, proclaimed the movement's secretary-general, Ieng Sary, "are perfectly aware that these maneuvers, conceived and executed by the Nixon administration and its lackeys, seek only to get them to lay down their arms and go to a negotiating table and rob them of the fruits of total victory."

With respect to his own role, Sihanouk displayed his customary relentless realism. "The Khmer Rouge do not love me at all," he told the writer Oriana Fallaci. "I know it! I understand very well they keep me with them because they stand to gain by it, because I am useful to them. . . . I understand very well that when I shall no longer be useful to them they'll spit me out like a cherry pit." The future did not belong to him or to the "traitors" in Phnom Penh, he had said on another occasion, but to the revolutionaries who, regardless of all other values, represented true Khmer patriotism. "They are pure patriots, not puppets of the Soviet Union, China or North Vietnam and they are honest and able. Though I am a Buddhist, I prefer a Red Cambodia which is honest and patriotic than a Buddhist Cambodia under Lon Nol which is corrupt and a puppet of the Americans."

The trap into which Sihanouk's patriotism, stubbornness, and injured pride had led him in 1970 was now closed completely. He was given no room to maneuver for a negotiated peace even if he wanted to; nor could he mitigate the actions of the revolutionaries toward their own people, which had now fallen into a pattern of incomprehensible brutality. "They kill people who do not follow their instructions or ideology," said a farmer named Nou Seng, who broke out of a Khmer Rouge prison with about 150 others and was one of five or six who made their way on foot all the way to Phnom Penh. The killings, he said, did not begin until about 1974, but then they became frightful. "They accuse the people of betraying their program, and then they kill them. They asked five people to carry a boat, and if the five could not lift up the boat, they asked three people to do it, and when the three could not do it, they killed them. There was no explanation."

These and other accounts reflected a terrifying mindlessness in the killing. When the Communists captured the old royal capital of Oudong in the spring of 1974, they murdered about a hundred captured civilians, said a girl who had been a cook for one of their units. "Some they shot, and some they beat with sticks." Among the victims many had already been wounded in the fighting and were killed, apparently, because the Khmer Rouge soldiers did not want to waste time or medicine taking care of them.

Buddhism, once such a vital strand of Cambodian life (and publicly praised by the revolutionaries as late as mid-1973 as "a traditional and state religion which is profoundly attached to peace") was a particular target.

Religious books were burned in the temples at Oudong, and when a number of monks refused to leave the monastery there, they were summarily shot.

Cambodia's conflict had plunged past the universal careless cruelty of modern war and weaponry; it had become an affair of deliberate, senseless terror. Not only was there no negotiated peace within sight; Cambodians had begun to fear that even a peace agreement would not stop the butchery. Violence was like a living thing gone mad. As it entered its final phase the war had mutilated not only Cambodia's land, but its soul.

Chapter 8

Fall of the Khmer Republic

Under Siege

The 107-mm rocket is a terror weapon. Ineffective against dug-in troops and too inaccurate for use against specific targets, it has only one purpose: to kill or maim at random over a large area, such as a city.

Fired from a simple launching tube set up on metal or bamboo stakes, the Chinese-made projectile is 33 inches long and weighs 42 pounds. Its maximum range is 8,300 meters, a shade under five miles. In flight, it does not swoosh like an artillery shell or whir like a mortar. It travels with a distinctive piercing whistle, like that of a faulty microphone. If it is coming down nearby you can hear it for about two seconds before it lands, the whistle rising to a sudden exclamation point just before the metallic whumpf of the explosion.

The fuse mechanism detonates the warhead instantly on impact. Even the branch of a tree will set it off. Thus, the rocket will not penetrate anything more solid than a thatched roof. The high-explosive blast tears apart the missile's nose, peeling back the metal jacket in strips like the skin of a banana and spraying out a deadly fan of shrapnel. Usually the last foot or so of the tube remains unfragmented, looking like an evil misshapen flower with splayed, jagged petals of steel. Because the rockets do not crater the ground or pierce walls or roofs, they cause little physical damage. Even after weeks of rocketing, a city can look surprisingly intact. And thus Phnom Penh in March of 1975 looked much as it always had, despite the rocketing that had killed or wounded hundreds of civilians since New Year's Day.

241

Along the Cambodian capital's wide boulevards, bougainvillea, frangipani, and other flowering trees were in bloom—bursts of scarlet, lavender, and white among the low mustard-colored buildings. The streets were a hive of cars, motorbikes, pedal-rickshaws, pushcarts, and bicycles. The central market with its filigreed iron roof still bustled, though if you watched the crowd for a while you would see that many of the men, women, and children moving among the vegetable and fish stalls were not buyers but penniless refugees, hoping to sell a few peppers or a squash or perhaps a small bundle of firewood they had carried from the city's outskirts.

The throb of artillery was hardly heeded, and even the sporadic incoming rockets, three or four or a dozen every day, drew little attention. If the whistle-crash was nearby, people would scurry into doorways for cover from a possible second round. But if the explosion was more than a few blocks away, most would scarcely glance up. Only in the still, sweltering nights, when the stutter of machinegun fire floated over from the far bank of the Mekong, did the siege of the city seem close.

Yet despite the surface normalcy, as it neared the end of its fifth year of war, Phnom Penh was a city in torment. The rockets, a form of horror encompassed in a few seconds of time and a few square yards of space, were the least of it. Far worse was the permanent and crushing poverty, hunger, disease, and despair. Being there was like watching someone die, too slowly and in terrible pain.

The final siege began at one o'clock on the morning of New Year's Day, when mortar shells and rockets rained out of the darkness onto government positions on all sides of the capital. Troops holding the east bank of the Mekong directly opposite Phnom Penh quickly gave up all but one small position; by dawn, more than 200 soldiers had swum back across the river to safety. In villages around the perimeter, residents stopped, when they could, to cremate their dead and to dig in the debris to rescue precious jars or sacks of rice before joining the flow of refugees that streamed on foot and in creaking oxcarts back toward the city. Several rockets lanced over the refugee-filled roads into the downtown district, the first of the shelling attacks that would continue every day for the next three and a half months.

Between 80 and 100 Khmer Rouge battalions, with 25,000 to 30,000 men, were committed to the offensive. The understrength government units had only about the same number of soldiers to oppose them. The battle lines around the Phnom Penh enclave resembled a four-fingered hand, with the palm representing the capital and its suburbs and the fingers pointing along the principal highways. The longest fingers, to the southeast and the west, extended fifteen to seventeen miles. The shortest, to the northwest, reached only five miles past the city's edge. Between the fingers, however, Communist units could approach much closer, through marshes and abandoned rice fields, and no part of the city was beyond range of their rockets.

More vulnerable than Phnom Penh, however, was the Mekong. For more than a year, with all land routes blocked, the river had been the city's only supply line, over which 60,000 tons of civilian and military supplies were shipped every month on barges and shallow-draft freighters. Much of the 60-mile route from the Vietnamese border to Phnom Penh passed through Communist-held territory. In 1973 and 1974, the insurgents had not made any serious effort to attack the river convoys, to the puzzled relief of American intelligence analysts. In the very first days of their 1975 offensive, however, they seized a number of positions on both banks and several mid-channel islands, while other insurgent forces blocked Highway One to cut off Phnom Penh from Neak Luong, the chief garrison along the river's course toward South Vietnam.

Using antishipping mines for the first time—primitive but effective devices, placed in the channel with wires leading to hand-operated detonators on the bank—the insurgents sank more than a dozen freighters, tankers, tugs, and barges on the river in January, more than were lost in all of 1974. Only bits of three convoys reached Phnom Penh that month, with far less than the normal monthly supply shipments. The last vessels arrived January 30. It would be four to five more months before the summer rains began, and another two or three months after that before the water would rise and widen the river enough so supply ships could again dodge Khmer Rouge ambushes on the banks. In the meantime, unless some of the chokepoints could be retaken by government forces, no more convoys could get through.

The Cambodian generals dithered. "We must open the Mekong in the very near future," proclaimed the armed forces commander, Lt. Gen. Sosthene Fernandez. U.S. officials, optimistic as usual, suggested that the clearing operation could be carried out, at least if the Cambodians were given the supplemental military aid President Ford requested at the end of January. "We believe the government will be able to keep the Mekong open," Lt. Gen. Daniel Graham, head of the Defense Intelligence Agency, told Congress on the very day the last ships made it to Phnom Penh. His Pentagon colleague and chief of the military assistance program, Lt. Gen. Howard Fish, in one of the year's most breathtakingly ill-advised predictions, declared a few days later: "Overall, the military prognosis for Cambodia is promising. . . . While the situation on the Mekong is extremely serious, the Cambodian armed forces appear capable of dealing with it, given adequate logistic support."

The Cambodians' problem was not arms or dollars, however, but men. An offensive on the river would, as one foreign military attache in Phnom Penh observed, absorb "not battalions or brigades, but divisions." None of the units defending Phnom Penh could be spared. The garrison at Neak Luong, 38 miles downriver, was fighting for its life, compressed into a shrinking pocket along with 60,000 helpless and hungry civilians under a constant rain of rocket and mortar fire. A few small units were sacrificed in hopeless assaults on Communist riverbank positions, but no major clearing operation was ever launched. After a few weeks, talk of reopening the convoy route faded away.

To keep Phnom Penh supplied until the rainy season, a major U.S. airlift began. Fuel and ammunition were transported from U Tapao air base in Thailand by a civilian airline called Bird Air, whose crews, mostly ex-Air Force men, flew C-130 transports "borrowed" from the U.S. Air Force without charge and with their markings painted out. During January, Bird Air flights to Phnom Penh's Pochentong Airport were stepped up from three or four a day to ten and then to twenty, while the Air Force turned over another seven C-130s to make the additional flights. On February 14 three chartered DC-8 cargo jets, each capable of carrying 45 tons of freight—three times the capacity of the C-130s—joined the munitions lift. Twelve days later, the jets began hauling rice from Saigon as well. By March, Phnom Penh was living and fighting on the 1,000 to 1,500 tons a day being landed at Pochentong under sporadic rocket and artillery fire.

Despite the blockade, most commodities were still available in the Cambodian capital for those with the money to buy them.

Officially, gasoline for civilian use was strictly rationed. But on every street corner children waved at passing cars, offering fuel from bottles that were set out in rows on the sidewalks. Most of the gasoline was from military stocks and had been stolen from military depots or siphoned out of army vehicles and sold by hungry soldiers. Restaurants were supposed to be shut on Mondays and Thursdays, but the regulation only closed the front doors. Anyone could go around through a side or back entrance and order soufflés or fancy French pastries. For the privileged elite there were still tennis matches, nightclubs, expensive French meals, and opulent, brandy-drenched dinner parties.

But Phnom Penh was running down like an unwound clock. Because of shelling at the airport, all international airline flights were cancelled except those of Air Cambodge's lone Caravelle, which had no schedule but darted in every couple of days when the airport authorities judged the shellfire was not too dangerous and when the increasingly reluctant Taiwanese pilots could be persuaded to make the run. There were very few arriving passengers, but every outgoing flight was jammed with passengers, many having paid huge bribes for passports and exit permits. Customs and immigration checks no longer took place at the airport terminal, which stood empty and unattended with most of its windows blown out. Instead, passengers were hustled onto buses at planeside and driven past the wreckage of the Pochentong village market, right outside the airport gates, to complete entrance formalities at the airline office downtown.

Electric power was cut and then cut again, until civilian homes and businesses had electricity for only one five-hour interval every two days.

After seven o'clock, when the hot nights darkened, the city looked lifeless and dead. Because there was not enough fuel to charge the ancient storage batteries that powered the telephone system, line after line went out. Eventually fewer than half the 5,000 or so phones in Phnom Penh were working at all, and those only fitfully.

The city had become a sink of desperate poverty. It seemed to have more beggars than Calcutta: children, women, maimed soldiers being pushed in crude wheelchairs or huddling on the sidewalks. In Khmer fashion they were less aggressive or insistent than beggars in Saigon. A few pursued, but most just stared with shamed, pleading eyes. The looks followed you everywhere: around the central market; across the tree-shaded square in front of the central post office where foreigners and well-off Cambodians lounged over croissants and café au lait every morning at the popular Taverne de la Poste; under the brightly flowering bougainvillea trees in front of the Hotel Le Phnom where pedicab drivers waited for fares. Along Monivong Boulevard at night, every darkened doorway had its cluster of prostitutes, hissing like so many bats in a cave to draw the attention of passers-by. They were not just professional whores, as in the old days, but penniless refugee women, many of them, selling themselves for a few nearly worthless riels to buy food.

At the Phnom Penh docks, before the supply barges stopped coming, dock workers sewed oversize pockets inside their ragged clothes to try to hide some of the grain that dropped from the sacks of rice and corn they were unloading. The *Times's* Sydney Schanberg watched them try to smuggle the food home. "As they leave work through a narrow opening in the steel gate," he wrote, "military policemen whap at the workers' pregnant bulges with their hands and nightsticks, until the corn and rice spills on the ground."

For the wounded or sick, the nightmare of the siege was blacker. Hospitals, dreadfully overcrowded even before the offensive, were now collapsing under the load of fresh casualties. At the health ministry's 600-bed Preah Keth Maelea hospital, parts of which dated back to the nineteenth century, 6,000 wounded patients were treated in January alone, a third of them civilians, including many children. Families of wounded soldiers or other patients moved into the wards because they had nowhere else to go, making the hospital, in effect, a refugee camp for military dependents and other homeless people. Thousands slept at night in the buildings or on the grounds, with devastating effects on sanitation. The staff was helpless. "They have the guns," the director said of his military patients. "If I tried to put out their dependents, they would shoot me or my staff."

Most of the hospital's equipment was not working. Three of its four sterilizers were broken beyond repair, a visiting AID doctor reported to the U.S. embassy in 1974, and there was no running water above the first floor because the electric pumps were out of order.

Because of filth and a terrible shortage of medicines, serious infection was almost certain. The high infection rate also meant patients stayed sick much longer, making the overcrowding even worse. Major surgery was performed "in crude circumstances, often with insufficient drugs and without whole blood or serums," said a report by U.S. government inspectors, in operating rooms that were "crudely furnished, unclean and totally without sterile precautions." Outside Phnom Penh conditions were worse. The inspectors found one province hospital at Takeo that was completely out of water because its well had gone dry. Operating rooms were often "a single room in a dilapidated building, furnished with a bloodstained wooden table and a few surgical instruments. Bloody remnants of previous surgical cases were left on the floor."

Most hospital services were available only to patients who could pay. The "non-payants," who were the great majority, received almost no attention. International Red Cross surgical teams reported a "widespread system of gouging patients," with doctors, nurses, and orderlies exacting bribes before they would perform even the most routine service.

Poverty seemed to have deadened anger. In past years, students, soldiers, market vendors, and other Cambodians had been quickly voluble on the corruption and incompetence of their government. But now you seldom found anything but dull resignation. "There's not a damn thing they can do about anything," a diplomat said, "except keep their heads down and try to survive." The daily struggle to live also submerged fear of the shelling. "I am not afraid," said a disabled soldier selling parking tokens outside the central market. "With my physical condition and the hardships of my family, I don't think about the rockets."

The soldier's name was Chau, and his story was typical of the thousands of Cambodian lives that had been ruined in the last five years.

When the war began, Chau was living in South Vietnam's Chau Doc Province, whose large Khmer community supplied many of the early volunteers for the Cambodian army. Recruited by agents of Son Ngoc Thanh, a Khmer-Vietnamese political leader who helped the U.S. organize clandestine cross-border missions in the 1960s, Chau went with about 200 other volunteers to Kompong Cham and enlisted. After a few months' training he was assigned to an infantry brigade in Prey Veng, east of the Mekong, the first of many battlegrounds he would fight on in the next two years. He served in Takeo in the south, in Kompong Cham again, in Neak Luong on the Mekong, and in all his months in combat was never issued a pair of boots nor any food except for pebble-hard, ancient rice that had to be soaked for two or three hours before the soldiers could cook it.

He was wounded twice, once in the arm by a grenade and once in the leg by a fragment from a B-40 rocket. After his unit was cut off south of Neak Luong—and, as was normal, ran out of supplies and went without food for three days before straggling back to government lines—his arm wound began ulcerating. He developed a fever and became "very weak." Ever since, he had been in and out of military hospitals. Always he had to buy his own medicines; of the drugs that were delivered to the army medical service, nearly all were diverted to the black market. Seldom was there any left for wounded or sick soldiers.

By 1975, Chau estimated, of the 200 men he had enlisted with, more than half had died or disappeared in the war. Most of the rest, he believed, had left the army and gone back to Vietnam, either discharged or as deserters. He himself, though relieved from active duty, was still receiving a salary of 12,000 riels a month—about six U.S. dollars. With that and with the 600 riels a day he earned selling parking tokens at the market, he had to buy food for his family as well as medicine for himself. Like most soldiers' families, Chau's wife and three children were, for any practical purpose, indistinguishable from refugees. They had no home and were living in a make-shift shelter in a Phnom Penh schoolyard.

"I have heard that some houses will be built for ex-servicemen," Chau said, but without hope in his voice. "But I haven't seen anybody get a house. . . . Every soldier faces hardship in getting food to eat."

After five years, a billion dollars of American aid, and the efforts of more than a hundred U.S. military officers attached to the American embassy, the Cambodian army had still remedied none of its fundamental weaknesses.

Its tactics had improved a bit, and its logistics and transportation systems seemed a little less hopeless than two or three years earlier—though this may have been mainly because it had so much less territory to defend. It still had no supply system worth the name, however. It almost never issued any field rations except uncooked rice, so that units still could not operate more than a day or so away from village markets and cut-off troops invariably ran out of food. Before operations, soldiers had learned to buy a fish or a bit of meat and dry it themselves, so they would have some food to carry into battle. There was still no pay allotment system for most units, so a soldier's wife and children had to move when he did, remaining with him even at forward positions under fire, in order not to starve.

The officer corps was as corrupt and incompetent as ever. High-ranking commanders could usually be found in Phnom Penh's villas or nightclubs, seldom or never in the field where the troops were. Graft and payroll padding with nonexistent "ghost soldiers" were still prevalent. "There's a lot of room for improvement," admitted the affable information minister, Chhang Song. "Anything you do is an improvement." He paused, then shrugged. "But when you do reduce corruption," he added, "it is just a drop of water out of a glassful."

The men themselves were angriest about the lack of medicine and treatment for the wounded. "It is zero. If a soldier has money he can get medicine," an infantryman told me bitterly one day just behind the front northwest of Phnom Penh. "But if he has no money, he will die." In military hospitals the wounded had to pay to have their litters kept clean and their bandages changed. Otherwise they lay in their own blood and filth, depending on relatives or comrades to bring them food.

Because of casualties, desertions, and "ghosts," manpower shortages quickly became critical as losses climbed in the New Year offensive. By late February most of the battalions in the Phnom Penh defense lines had fewer than 100 men, instead of the 300 they were supposed to have. The conscription system was still a bad joke: in the year and a half since it was introduced, it was variously reported that somewhere between 20,000 and 30,000 men were drafted. Nearly that many were killed or wounded in the first ten weeks of 1975. During the offensive, only one replacement was recruited for every three men lost through death, wounds, or desertion.

In January, the panicked government ordered police to press-gang men on the streets, reminding witnesses of Kuomintang China in World War II. But most of those rounded up got no farther than the recruiting stations, where they handed over whatever money they had or which could be brought by their families and were allowed to go home. Student deferments were handed out liberally, protecting the sons of the elite. Other methods of draft evasion were rife. One young man showed Sydney Schanberg a paper certifying him to be mentally disturbed and ineligible for military service. This "lop-lop" certificate, named for the Khmer term for "crazy," cost him the equivalent of 31 American dollars.

The press-ganging stopped when it dawned on government officials that they were causing immense ill will without solving their recruitment problem—which from then on would be met, like so much else in Cambodia's endless catalogue of ailments, by simply being blotted out of mind, a form of denial that was the Khmer Republic's trademarked answer to any crisis. Commanders spoke of their problems with a sort of pathetic helplessness. "We have not yet organized," one general explained, as if the war had been going on five months rather than five years. "It takes much time to organize an army."

How many were actually fighting on the government side no one, possibly not even the army command itself, was sure. On paper the government had 240,000 men under arms, more than three times as many as the Khmer Rouge army. Of these, one general estimated, perhaps 150,000 were available for duty. Some foreign attaches thought that no more than 75,000 were actually on combat assignment, only slightly more than the 70,000 believed to be the Communists' combat strength. General Fernandez, in a conversation with a few correspondents a couple of weeks before he was sacked by Lon Nol in yet another useless command shakeup, acknowledged that 20,000 "ghosts" were taken off the army's rolls in the last few months of 1974—this nearly two years after U.S. officials had assured congressional and journalistic critics that the problem was under control and no longer represented a significant diversion of U.S. funds.

"I tell you frankly," General Fernandez went on, "our army is the poorest in the world—poorly fed, poorly clothed, poorly paid." He spoke with the air of a sympathetic, but uninvolved, onlooker. "A simple worker at your embassy gets three times more than a soldier. A general gets paid less than a coolie in your country. In spite of this our soldiers are not discouraged. All the hospitals are full of wounded, this proves our fighting spirit. . . .

"I ask you not to attack us for corruption, et cetera, because it demoralizes our soldiers. We have done what is possible to make our army like other armies of the world."

It was still fighting, that much was true. In their foxholes, with their families next to them and no place else to go, Cambodian soldiers often displayed an astonishing heroism, despite the dreadful conditions under which they fought and although their bravery was usually wasted by the venality or incompetence of their commanders. Many others, though, chose not to fight any longer. More than 3,500 front-line soldiers, equal to a dozen full-strength battalions, deserted in January and February.

The army was like a corpse twitching, its spirit gone while the muscles still somehow functioned. Its condition was summed up by a captain I met one day not far from where the disabled Chau was selling his parking tokens. Tall and tough-looking, with close-shaven hair, neat camouflage fatigues, and sunglasses, he looked anything but an artist. But it turned out that before the war he had taught Khmer classical dance on the fine arts faculty of Phnom Penh University. He had enlisted in the army "in March," he told me. That meant 1970; few Cambodians bothered to mention the year when they spoke of that fateful month. Everyone knew which March they meant.

"There are great hardships in the army," the captain said. "Because we are lacking medicines, and because most of the time we are fighting in the open without shelter, many are getting sick. Some never get any proper clothing, they make shirts out of ponchos. In some areas the soldiers only get a half-kilo of rice every five days. It is impossible. . . .

"According to my opinion, the spirit of the Khmer soldier could still be high if he had enough clothing, enough food, a proper camp to live in, his wife and children taken care of. Before the soldier had one mind, to fight the enemy. Now he has five minds. Instead of thinking only of one thing, he thinks about his family, his children, food.

"Most of the time when our soldiers are getting defeated or retreat, it is because of this lower morale. As a Cambodian I suffer from this very much, but I don't know what to do. I resent very much seeing the refugees, the small children begging. We Cambodians never had beggars like this. . . .

"Many soldiers have decided not to resist any longer. Some continue to resist, but some flee and hide. If they are caught they are sent back to the battlefront. As a soldier, I don't feel angry, I have compassion. In my own opinion, I am glad they are deserting. . . . All the officers spend many hours discussing this and we are very sad, but we don't know what to do about it.

"I also was a writer and I used to write what I had seen, but now I can't do anything. . . . Everybody is just trying to live. Nobody has any ideas for reform or something new."

Now that it was too late for more than a fraction of the help that was needed, there was a visible refugee relief effort in Phnom Penh for the first time in the war.

More than a hundred foreign relief workers, nearly all of them having arrived only in the last few months, were in the besieged Cambodian capital. They drove about in cars and vans, conferred busily with each other over walkie-talkies, papered their offices with charts and graphs showing programs that were finally going to begin after nearly five years of inaction. Most of these programs would hardly get under way before the war ended. In any case, Cambodia's tragedy had reached such dimensions that no eleventh-hour effort would make much difference.

American policy had become somewhat less grudging, though hardly generous. At the end of 1973, a decision was at last made to support a larger relief effort. In February of 1974, the embassy's refugee staff was increased from one to seven, though the main responsibility for expanded relief programs was given to the international voluntary agencies, primarily CARE, Catholic Relief Services, the International Red Cross, and World Vision, Inc. Funds came principally from the "counterpart" account of Cambodian riels generated by other U.S. economic aid programs.

It took most of 1974 to get the program started, and even then the increased effort was far less than was needed. According to AID records, 551,000 refugees received some assistance in December 1974, compared to 272,000 the previous January. But there were still four times as many who received no help at all. About 1.2 million refugees were registered with the Khmer refugee ministry. Another 900,000 to one million, by U.S. estimates, were unregistered. To these had to be added another half-million military dependents, since the wives and children who left their homes to follow husbands or fathers from front to front were indistinguishable in their needs and lack of resources from the mass of refugees who fled the fighting or the Communists. The total of 2.7 million displaced persons represented about half the entire population living in the shrunken government-held portion of Cambodia. Nor were the refugees the only ones to suffer. "The general level of health of almost the entire Cambodian population . . . has deteriorated rapidly," reported State Department inspectors after touring Cambodia in February 1975. "Malnutrition, including the advanced stages of kwashiorkor and marasmus, has increased dramatically over the last several months."

Children suffered the most. Comparing age-weight statistics for 2,000 children in January 1975 with pre-1970 records kept by the Cambodian National Nutritional Service, the U.S. inspectors found that the average two-year-old now weighed nearly one-third less than two-year-olds before the war. The data, they concluded, "confirm the universal medical impression given us by those involved in Cambodian health and nutrition that children are starving to death."

How many died, in clinics or pagodas or untended in the dusty, rutted streets, no one would ever know. At a 60-bed child nutrition center run by World Vision in a converted private home on the capital's outskirts, 49 children died of the 137 admitted during January. Hundreds more had to be turned away. On some mornings, as many as a thousand starving and desperate patients were waiting outside when the staff came to work. Most were from military families; usually the fathers had been killed or were missing, and the children were starving because the families had no money. Doctors walked among them, using marking pens to mark the arms of the 200 who seemed the worst cases. These would be examined; the rest were sent away.

Starvation was occurring not because of an overall food shortage but because the distribution system created by the U.S. and Khmer governments put the helpless poor at the very end of the food line.

All through the final blockade, adequate if not ample stocks of rice were for sale in the market. Food stocks, replenished by the American airlift, were sufficient, admitted Assistant Secretary of State Philip Habib, "but rice is too costly for the poor to buy, and to some extent there is a maldistribution of supplies." This was at a time when the United States was providing four-fifths of the entire Cambodian rice supply. Almost every grain, however, went to the Khmer government; and the Cambodian leaders decided how to allocate it. The needs of the army, civil service, and commercial market all came before those of the starving poor. In mid-February 1975, of a daily distribution through official channels of 545 tons, only *eighteen tons* were made available for free distribution through the relief agencies—this in a city where more than half the population could not afford to buy enough food.

Even that scant allotment was often delayed or reduced. Officials of the voluntary agencies spent hours and days haggling with Khmer bureaucrats for the release of a few tons that were already supposed to be earmarked for them. Relief allowances were only about 200 grams of rice a day per person, less than one-fourth of the amount a Cambodian would normally eat. A family's monthly allotment usually lasted only six or seven days, even when the rice was cooked into watery gruel to make it last longer.

Not until six weeks before the war's end did the U.S. adopt a system under which American and not Khmer officials would decide how much rice would flow to the refugees. Before March 3, 1975, U.S. rice was shipped exclusively under the "Food for Peace" law's Title I, which permitted shipments to foreign governments but not to private agencies. The Khmer government reimbursed the U.S. with riels that were then turned back to the Cambodian treasury as counterpart funds. To obtain rice for the refugees, the relief agencies used other counterpart riels to buy the same rice back from the Cambodian government or, in some cases, from the commercial market. This procedure, acknowledged by Philip Habib to be "complicated and ridiculous," made the agencies completely dependent on Cambodian decisions as to how the rice should be allocated.

One possible reason for this procedure may have been that it had the effect of evading amendments passed by Congress more than a year earlier, in December 1973, that were supposed to prohibit Food for Peace counterpart funds from being used for military purposes. Once counterpart riels passed through the relief agencies and were then handed back to the government in payment for U.S.-supplied rice, the riels were considered "free" and no longer subject to U.S. legal restrictions on their use. Thus, they could be used to pay soldiers' salaries or for other military budget items. (Not that anyone was really trying to make the Cambodians observe the new Food for Peace law anyhow. More than a year after the amendments were adopted, the Khmer government had still not instituted accounting and reporting procedures to assure that the funds were not put to military use. A plan had been devised, an AID official told the Senate at the end of February 1975, and AID was "optimistic that it would be operational not long thereafter." That was fairly typical of Cambodia aid bookkeeping.)

Under Title II of the Food for Peace act, the U.S. could have shipped rice directly to the relief agencies, bypassing the Khmer authorities, but proposals to shift from Title I to Title II were caught in a wrangle among various U.S. agencies. AID was finally in favor by 1975, but the State, Agriculture, and Treasury departments, and the Office of Management and Budget at the White House, were all opposed, for various petty bureaucratic reasons that did no credit to any of the agencies involved. Only when a congressional delegation visiting Phnom Penh expressed outrage at the workings of the relief program was it finally changed. The administration, now desperately courting House and Senate votes for increased military aid, finally authorized Title II rice shipments on March 3, the day the delegation returned to Washington, and the first sacks were given out four days later. Even the new program, however, furnished only enough rice to feed fewer than two of every five registered refugees in the stricken Cambodian capital. For those who were unregistered, for reasons of ignorance or bureaucratic inefficiency, there were no relief allowances at all.

All hope of making refugees self-sufficient had evaporated. In the belatedly expanded U.S. relief program, $8 million, of a total of $20 million dedicated to "humanitarian" efforts, was supposed to be used for resettling refugees on land where they could grow their own food. Only a handful of families were ever actually relocated, and they were driven off their new land a few months later by the New Year offensive. With the war-ruined economy providing no jobs except for casual labor that earned only a few hundred almost valueless riels a day, and with practically no land to farm that was not either in Khmer Rouge hands or a battlefield, the vast majority of refugees faced only permanent homelessness and want.

The Cambodiana, for example, the unfinished shell of a luxury-class hotel that was started under the Sihanouk regime, was never intended to be a permanent camp, only a temporary haven for refugees coming in from the villages. But of more than 3,600 people in its buildings and grounds in February 1975, more than half had been living there for more than two years. It looked like a medieval plague-house. On clammy cement floors or on bare earth among the foundation walls, families huddled on wood pallets or on straw mats stained with rivulets of urine and the filth of diarrhea. Clouds of mosquitoes swarmed up from the brown, foul-smelling mud along the riverbank. Every few steps someone, usually a child or an old person, lay gaunt and gray-faced with fever.

Among the sick was the husband of a 47-year-old woman named Sunn Leng, who had lived with her family in the Cambodiana ever since fleeing the besieged town of Takeo more than a year earlier.

"I am the only one who can work," Mrs. Sunn said. "I try to gather a few vegetables to sell in the market, but I earn only about 1,000 riels a day"—the equivalent, in early 1975, of 50 U.S. cents—"and it is not enough." For herself, her sick husband, five children, and her aging mother-in-law, she received a monthly relief ration of 22 pounds of rice and a few pounds of fish, enough to last only about five days. In addition, most days the children were given a bowl of thin soup. Before the offensive she used to send the older children out to the edge of the city to gather firewood to sell, but now she would not let them go any more because of the rockets. "We cannot go anyplace," she sobbed. "My husband is too sick, my mother is too old, we have many children. There is no place to go."

On a pallet nearby in the gloomy concrete cavern was a woman named Nenn. Originally from Takeo, like Mrs. Sunn, she had left her home three years before to accompany her husband, a soldier, to Kompong Speu, west of Phnom Penh. He was killed there in mid-1974, and four of their seven children disappeared—whether killed or captured Mrs. Nenn was never able to find out—in the same attack. The rest of her relatives had long since died or vanished, so with her three remaining children she made her way to the capital. Somehow she never registered as a refugee and thus received no relief rations at all in the nine months she had spent at the Cambodiana. "There is no one to help," she said. "I get nothing from the government because I have no number." By gathering and selling vegetables and by begging in the market, she earned about 500 riels a day. But there were days when she and her children did not eat at all.

The refugees knew the government army was usually defeated, but of the dozens I interviewed during February and March, most knew little more than that of the war. None had heard of the U.S. airlift that was keeping the city alive. Even after months or years in the capital their horizons, unlike those of the more sophisticated Vietnamese, were still those of the villages from which they came, and the daily struggle to survive consumed all their energy and attention. Some had seen or heard of Khmer Rouge atrocities and were afraid of a rebel victory, but there were also many who didn't care. "We keep praying every day for the war to end," said one woman. "But we don't know. Whichever side wins, we don't care. We just want to live in peace."

Peace. Everyone, not just the desperate refugees, wanted peace. But short of surrendering, no one knew how peace could be achieved. From Washington there came only the familiar formulas, now more threadbare than ever. "Our immediate goal in Cambodia," President Ford declared in his January 28 message to Congress requesting an additional $222 million for military aid, "is to facilitate an early negotiated settlement. . . . Once the insurgents realize that they cannot win by force of arms, I believe they will look to negotiations rather than to war."

The Khmer Communists, however, did not realize any such thing, for the excellent reason that a victory by force of arms was becoming increasingly likely. They now held more than four-fifths of Cambodian territory, compressing government forces into Phnom Penh, a half-dozen surrounded province capitals, the threatened Neak Luong pocket on the Mekong, and a few swatches of land along the Thai border and on the Gulf of Thailand coast. Numerically the insurgent army was probably equal to the fighting strength of the Khmer Republic forces. Though more lightly armed than their opponents—besides the inaccurate rockets, their only heavy weapons were mortars and about a dozen U.S.-made 105-mm howitzers they had captured in the course of the war—the insurgents appeared to have all the ammunition they needed.

Their casualties were heavy, but they inflicted serious losses as well. 4,260 government soldiers were killed and more than 10,000 wounded in the first seven weeks after New Year's Day, according to figures compiled by the American embassy, with hundreds more missing. The total casualties were the equivalent of a full-strength battalion every day. Because soldiers' families lived in the front lines and because of the random shelling of the capital, civilian casualties were also high: 7,000 a month, the health ministry estimated.

Having choked off the Mekong and blocked all other supply routes, and with the airport within range of their rocket-launchers and artillery, the insurgents had every reason to think they could force Phnom Penh to capitulate for lack of supplies, if the tired and demoralized troops defending it did not collapse first. "The enemy is writhing in death-throes," boasted the Khmer Rouge leader Khieu Samphan, in a speech predicting that time would soon run out for the "flesh-eating, bone-gnawing and blood-sucking . . . traitorous clique" in the Cambodian capital.

The Lon Nol government also faced defeat because U.S. aid, which provided all its supplies, was running out. In December, nearly halfway through the fiscal year, Congress enacted an effective ceiling of $275 million on military aid in 1975, which included $200 million in appropriated funds and authority to use up to $75 million worth of materiel already in Defense Department stocks. This represented about $75 million less than the previous year's program. While awaiting the new appropriation, however, the Pentagon had kept spending at the same rate as under the more generous 1974 budget, so that long before a new fiscal year was to start, nearly all available money was used up. At the beginning of February, the Pentagon informed Congress, only $86 million was left: $29 million in supplies already stockpiled in Cambodia, another $42 million in materiel that was being delivered, and only $15 million in unspent funds. To make matters worse, the money was being spent faster than ever because of the airlift. Funds to keep the planes flying would run out in mid-April, the American embassy calculated; and very quickly after that, by April 25 at the latest, the government army would be completely out of ammunition.

No one tried to deny that the Cambodians wasted ammunition. They fired about as much artillery ammunition as the entire South Vietnamese army, which was at least five times as large and was defending a much larger territory against an enemy that was also better armed and several times bigger than the Khmer Communist army. Even an inexpert correspondent could see that Cambodian commanders habitually used firepower to compensate for their own poor tactics and execrable leadership. U.S. files were full of reports declaring that the Cambodians should practice better conservation. But not much was achieved. "The Khmer Armed Forces (FANK) depend on firepower to win," said an official assessment by American officers in Phnom Penh early in 1975. "Seldom have the FANK outmaneuvered the enemy; instead they have outgunned him." However much waste there was, though, obviously it was too late now for significant changes in Cambodian tactics. The argument to Congress was not theoretical, as were similar disputes about aid to South Vietnam, but concrete and exact. Unless more funds were authorized and appropriated, Cambodian soldiers in a matter of weeks would have nothing left to fight with.

What no one could tell, however, was whether the Phnom Penh government could survive even with more aid. Many congressmen had compassion for the Cambodians. But they wondered too if more aid would accomplish anything but the waste of another few thousand lives before a defeat that seemed inevitable.

Not quite five weeks after President Ford's aid request reached Congress, Rep. Bill Chappell of Florida stood in the middle of a dusty street in a village called Koki, a dozen miles southeast of Phnom Penh. In front of him stood six Cambodian soldiers. Only one had combat boots; the others wore flimsy rubber sandals. But Chappell wasn't looking at their feet. "Did you fire any shots at the enemy yesterday?" he asked heartily. A shy, bespectacled Cambodian major translated the question into Khmer. The soldiers looked utterly puzzled for a moment, and then one answered that he had fired about 500 rounds of ammunition.

Chappell, looking pleased, asked all the others the same question. In turn, they all assured him that they too had fired 500 rounds.

"Did any of you kill any of the enemy?" The Communists were in bunkers, a soldier said, so it was hard to see if any of them were hit. But when Chappell's face dropped, another soldier interrupted. He had seen a few enemy soldiers fall, he thought. Chappell brightened again. "Ask 'em if they whipped hell out of 'em yesterday," he bellowed at the interpreter. The major, apparently having reached the limits of his mastery of English colloquialisms, stared uncomprehendingly, and for a moment the conversation stopped dead. Then an American reporter who had been listening to the exchange called out, "Congressman, are you going to ask these guys if they have boots?"

For the first time, Chappell glanced down at the feet of the men in front of him and saw the sandals. He turned back somewhat indignantly to the questioner. "They don't fight in those," he announced.

"Ask 'em," the reporter persisted, and Chappell nodded to the interpreter. No, the men answered after the question was translated, they had no boots. They fought as they were dressed, in sandals and ragged bits of uniform. One of them gestured at the only man in the group who had on a presentable fatigue shirt. It wasn't issued, he explained, but purchased in the black market.

Chappell himself was wearing crisply pressed fatigue pants he had borrowed from one of the U.S. officers on the army attache staff in Phnom Penh. His congressional colleague John Murtha of Pennsylvania, a marine reserve officer who had once volunteered for active service in Vietnam, borrowed not just pants but boots as well. And one of their escorts, the Defense

Department's logistics specialist Erich Von Marbod, had amazed his fellow passengers on the flight from Saigon that morning by appearing in a brand-new steel helmet and an equally new, personally tailored set of camouflage fatigues, with his name sewn over the pocket.

Thus garbed, the three were driven from the embassy demanding vociferously and at length to be taken "right to the front." Their escort and driver, a soft-spoken major named Lally from the attache's office, made a valiant and for the most part successful effort to maintain his poise. His composure faltered only once, after he tried diplomatically to remind his distinguished charges that they were expected at lunch with Prime Minister Long Boret. An excited Von Marbod demanded to continue toward the front line instead. "Screw the lunch!" he kept shouting, as Major Lally looked stricken and Cambodian officers who had just briefed the visitors stared in slightly alarmed incomprehension. Von Marbod was dissuaded from plunging on toward the guns only when it was explained to him that the local division commander might lose his job if he allowed two valuable American congressmen to travel into danger. Von Marbod did eventually make it to Long Boret's lunch—still in his camouflage costume.

After their briefing at the division headquarters, the party proceeded to Koki, where Chappell encountered the five sandaled soldiers. After they told him about the lack of boots, the reporter asked, "Congressman, are you going to ask them how much they're paid?"

28,000 riels, a sergeant replied, a little less than fifteen dollars a month. The reporter asked if that was enough to feed their families, and the interpreter translated the question directly this time, not waiting for Chappell. The soldiers turned voluble for the first time. Amid an angry chorus of no's, one of them protested, "Our families are hungry." But the congressman no longer seemed interested in the conversation. Turning away, he commented that he had been in military service himself and knew about soldiers' griping. "I've never met a soldier," he said tolerantly, "who thought he was paid enough."

Representative Chappell's anti-Communist opinions were clearly not burdened by an excessive accumulation of facts. "Where is the Khmer Republic?" he had demanded of a government witness a few months earlier in a hearing at which he also sought a broader grasp of Asian geography by inquiring, "Is Indonesia an island nation?" Not unexpectedly, he announced on the flight back to Saigon that on the basis of his eight-hour investigation in Cambodia, he had "pretty much come to the conclusion" that he would support the administration's supplemental aid request. Even Chappell, however, seemed to have derived some chastening sense of a tragedy for which simple anti-Communism, however heartfelt, was not an adequate answer. There was "no good solution," he acknowledged, to the Cambodian crisis.

None of his colleagues dissented from that view, though they agreed on little else. In the group were four other House members and one senator, Dewey Bartlett of Oklahoma, who had interrupted a longer mission to South Vietnam for the brief journey to Phnom Penh. (Besides Chappell and Murtha, the House members were the dovish Paul N. McCloskey, Jr., of California, Bella Abzug of New York, and New Jersey's aristocratically eccentric, pipe-smoking Millicent Fenwick.) Arriving on the morning of March 1, after a brief session with Ambassador John Gunther Dean and before Chappell and Murtha set out for their adventures at the front, the group was received by Lon Nol in the Chamcar Mon Palace, in a plushly carpeted room decorated with chandeliers and scenes of Angkor Wat. The war was not being fought to achieve victory but only to hold out until peace talks could be arranged, the Cambodian leader assured his visitors, adding: "If peace cannot be achieved, I would like to assure you that this is not our fault. The other side is at fault. . . . I would like to urge you not to abandon us, not to abandon seven million Cambodian people who have suffered so much for a peaceful cause."

Ambassador Dean, however, called the congressional visitors' attention to another of Lon Nol's remarks: that though he had reached office through constitutional procedures, he "would do whatever is possible and necessary so that peace and the welfare of my people can be achieved." At those words, Dean leaned over to Senator Bartlett and whispered excitedly that Lon Nol meant he would step down, if that were a precondition for negotiations. As the group was leaving the palace, Dean gave the same interpretation to other members, telling them he read the president's vague remark as a "very strong suggestion" Lon Nol was prepared to resign.

Stepping very close to the limits of ambassadorial propriety, Dean arranged for a translation of the Cambodian leader's statement to be distributed and encouraged Bartlett and the others to pass on his own reaction to the press. The result, as Dean intended, was that within hours, news agency wires around the world were announcing that the American ambassador to Cambodia was predicting the resignation of the president to whom he was accredited.

Lon Nol, however, had no intention of resigning. At most, a senior aide explained later, he might consider stepping down if he were "assured" that peace talks would follow, a condition unlikely to be met by the adamant Khmer Rouge. His remarks to the congressional delegation were similar to many vague statements he had made in the past and represented no change in policy. The episode, it soon became evident, told more about Ambassador Dean's preoccupations than about Lon Nol's plans.

Dean, who passed his 49th birthday three days before the congressional visit, had been ambassador to Cambodia for exactly eleven months. Arriving from Laos, where he had been an energetic middleman in the negotiations between the Vientiane authorities and the Pathet Lao, he hoped to contribute to "some kind of a nonmilitary solution" for Cambodia as well. Sharing something of the same background as Henry Kissinger—Dean too was German-born and had emigrated to the U.S. while in his teens, in the 1930s—he was also, like Kissinger, a man of strong ego and was not bashful about claiming a share of credit for the Laos settlement. In Cambodia, however, he faced obstacles he had not met in his previous assignment. Not only was the Cambodian conflict far more intractable, but his own government, to Dean's continuing frustration and eventually to his anguish, seemed to lack both urgency and realism in thinking about a Cambodian peace agreement.

When Dean took up his post at the end of March 1974, there had been no American diplomatic efforts to arrange peace talks on Cambodia for at least seven months, following the collapse of Kissinger's initiative with the Chinese. In his first month as ambassador, Dean proposed to Washington that an approach be made to the Khmer Rouge leader Khieu Samphan, who was then on a long tour of several Communist and neutral nations. The suggestion was turned down. In June, as the rainy season was about to offer the customary respite from Communist military pressure, Dean told his superiors in a long assessment that time was not on Phnom Penh's side and that "steps must be taken to find . . . a compromise settlement." He evidently conveyed the same views to Congress; it was certainly Dean's appraisal that was reflected in one congressional report stating that the U.S. objective in Cambodia was to produce a stalemate leading to a " 'Laos-type' solution featuring a coalition government in which the Communists undoubtedly would play a major role."

Dean received support from an unlikely source: Graham Martin, the superhawkish ambassador to Saigon. Martin thought Cambodia was draining away resources that could be better used in Vietnam, which was, after all, the central American interest in the region. Even if Cambodia came under Communist rule or under a regime sympathetic to the Communists, Martin didn't believe that would be disastrous for the Vietnamese; what mattered strategically to Vietnam were the sanctuary areas near the border, and those were under unchallenged Communist control anyway. He therefore advocated disengaging from the Lon Nol government while seeking to arrange a ceasefire, possibly while returning Prince Sihanouk to Phnom Penh. Neither Martin nor Dean could persuade Kissinger to withdraw support from Lon Nol, however. To Kissinger, the marshal still represented a bargaining chip that should only be away in return for significant concessions. His ambassador's job was to make Lon Nol's rule more effective, Kissinger seems to have thought, and not to pepper Washington with annoying suggestions for a difficult and risky change of course.

During the summer of 1974, while Washington was convulsed in the end of the Watergate crisis and President Nixon's resignation, there was no change in its Cambodia policy—although in Phnom Penh, Dean did at last persuade Lon Nol to do what the U.S. administration had falsely claimed for many months had already been done: extend a realistic offer for unconditional peace talks. On July 9, at Dean's recommendation, the Cambodian leader proposed negotiations "without preconditions" at which "all problems dividing Cambodians can be brought up for discussion"—the first time in more than four years that the regime had agreed to talks without demanding impossible conditions. The Khmer Rouge, however, rejected the proposal as quickly and unequivocally as it had all others.

In September, a month after President Ford took office, Dean traveled to Washington to urge a more forthcoming policy. In the following months, the Ford administration did float several proposals through third parties, advocating on one occasion an international conference on Cambodia and also indicating that the U.S. would accept a coalition "in which all elements could play a role." In December 1974 and early January 1975, the State Department subsequently disclosed, the administration "concurred in an initiative to open a dialogue with Sihanouk." All these overtures, however, produced no result. In Phnom Penh, with another dry season at hand and with the government and its army seeming more decrepit than ever, Dean began talking about a "controlled solution" in Cambodia, meaning, he later explained, "a nonmilitary solution which would take into account the realities." By early 1975, it was quite clear he did not hope for much more than a negotiated transfer of power to the Khmer Rouge.

Dean also began saying more and more openly that "personalities"—obviously meaning Lon Nol—should not become obstacles to a settlement. Speaking as an anonymous "diplomatic source," he made it undiplomatically clear that in his view it was time for Lon Nol to leave. Additional aid, he told visiting reporters in February, was needed to gain time, "not for the other side to negotiate with Lon Nol—I don't think that would be the case—but to keep together the armed forces, institutions that could be viable elements in a compromise settlement. I don't think Lon Nol is in a position to work that out."

Washington, however, was not ready to reach that view. After Dean's comments during the congressional visit were publicized, he was instructed not to try to influence the Cambodian president's decision in any way. U.S. policy remained that negotiations should take place between the Khmer Rouge and Phnom Penh—a legally punctilious view, perhaps, but hardly a realistic one. Representative Fenwick, who did not claim or display any great store of sophisticated knowledge about the war but whose intuitions were strikingly acute, posed the difficulty squarely while testifying in the Senate Foreign Relations Committee a few days after the delegation returned to Washington. U.S. efforts had been futile because they sought talks between the Communists and Lon Nol, she said, adding: "I think the only way that is realistic is to realize that Lon Nol's government is through, and not to try to negotiate on that basis. . . . We have tried to get a coalition of some kind using Lon Nol as a part of the equations. He does not belong in the equation, and as long as he stays there we are not going to get anything better than what we have got."

By March of 1975, it probably made no difference whether Lon Nol remained in power or not. The Khmer Rouge were so close to victory that they were unlikely to consider negotiations or compromise no matter who was in the presidential palace. It is also true that forcing Lon Nol out was never as simple a matter as it was sometimes made to sound, if only because no possible successor among the squabbling ranks of Cambodian politicians looked much better. Just the same, the fact that he was still president after five such disastrous years was evidence of Kissinger's misplaced belief in him as a bargaining asset and, more broadly, of a baffling American paralysis, an inabilty to use power in its own interest even on as utterly dependent a client as the government of the Khmer Republic. Unlike President Thieu in South Vietnam, Lon Nol had no admirers, as far as I know, among the Americans who dealt with him. He had squandered the loyalty of his own people, and out of incompetence or unconcern he had frustrated countless American efforts to reform his regime, which largely as a result of his failures of leadership now stood on the threshold of defeat at the hands of a barbarous enemy. Yet no serious American effort was ever made to find or impose leadership that might have served not just Cambodian but American interests more effectively.

After Dean's remarks to the congressional delegation, rumors flew through Phnom Penh that the marshal was leaving. To disprove them, the government a few days later invited a small group of American and European newsmen to his villa inside the Chamcar Mon Palace grounds—not to question him but simply to report that he was still in Cambodia. Another wartime chief might have tried to appear in a pose suggesting active command. But Lon Nol chose to greet the seven invited reporters and photographers in a small garden where he kept ducks, geese, peahens, some large tortoises, a pair of pet monkeys, and three young ocelots in cages. Slowly and painfully, leaning heavily on a cane, he shook hands and mumbled a greeting to each of us, then hobbled back inside. As I watched him go, I wondered how the United States, while expending so much power in Cambodia to display the firmness of American will, had been so unable to find the firmness to fashion a better instrument for its policy.

Nearly another month would pass before Lon Nol finally left Cambodia, and by then there would no longer be even a pretense of reviving his moribund government or opening the way for peace talks. It would just be a matter of saving him from the Khmer Rouge executioners at the city's gates.

Not just for Ambassador Dean but for most other Americans in the

Cambodian capital—diplomats, military officers, relief agency workers, and journalists—the last months of the sieg᠆ were a time of moral anguish. No one wanted to see the war go on. But as long as the government and army wanted to try to hold out, many Americans argued passionately, it would be an unforgivable act of treachery to deny the means to do so by shutting off aid. If it was to end in defeat, it should be for the Cambodians, not for the Americans, to decide when to give up.

Yet the battlefield situation seemed so hopeless, the chance of a peace agreement so remote, and the country's suffering so awful that it also seemed the only meaningful moral obligation that remained was to let the slaughter end as quickly as possible. No illusion could still survive about the Khmer Rouge. Evidence was unarguable that they were murdering captured soldiers, civil servants, teachers, and others considered counterrevolutionary for any of a vast range of reasons. Senseless destruction of villages and brutal forced evacuations were reported to be common practice everywhere the insurgents occupied. No one could yet know how extreme was the cruelty that would come, but we knew enough to see that the Communist victory was going to be a murderous affair. Those who opposed military aid could only argue, with heavy hearts, that the war was already lost; whatever bloodbath was going to occur would not be avoided by prolonging Phnom Penh's resistance for a few more weeks or months.

While struggling with such moral dilemmas, the Americans still had an army to supply and a city to feed. At Pochentong, after the airlift was in full swing, flights landed approximately every fifteen minutes during daylight hours under gradually intensifying rocket and artillery fire. The unloading was supervised by a dozen or so U.S. Air Force officers, who flew over each morning on the first flight from U Tapao and left on the last flight before dark. Wearing helmets and flak jackets over civilian sport shirts, they worked out of a heavily sandbagged bunker in the middle of the loading area. Under American prodding, Cambodian commanders tried to ease the threat to the airfield by occupying the "rocket belt" to the north. After suffering heavy losses, government troops reached their objective, the shattered village of Tuol Leap, on March 15. Though they held it for the next ten days, however, they did not succeed in clearing the surrounding area— the "principal problems" were "lack of coordination and aggressiveness among the commanders concerned, as well as insufficient troops," according to a confidential embassy report—and Communist crews continued to rocket the field from launchers in the forested fields.

A warning system was set up, consisting of a Cambodian spotter in a foxhole a couple of miles north of the runway. When he heard the thunk of a rocket leaving its launcher, he pressed a button that set off a siren back at the field. The warning time was about fifteen seconds—enough, usually, for those in the loading area to take cover. Feelings about the system were mixed. It was nice to have the extra time to get to a bunker. But the siren didn't say where the round was headed, so that often you would spend those fifteen seconds scared to death—it felt longer, especially if there were pallets of munitions around—of a round that might land as much as a half-mile away.

Pochentong was a busy place. Beside receiving the airlift flights, the field housed the Khmer air force's small fleet of obsolete T-28 fighter-bombers and C-123 transports. Several dozen even more antiquated C-46s, C-47s and other craft belonged to a profusion of small one- or two-plane charter companies, mostly owned by adventurous American civilian pilots, which contracted with the Khmer government to fly food and supplies from Phnom Penh to other surrounded enclaves around the country. From first light until dark, the sound of aircraft motors was seldom stilled. Several of the charter planes, wrecked in the shelling, stood about the field like dinosaur skeletons in a museum; most of the rest would keep flying until the last week of the war.

During the first month of the airlift, a few airlift planes were lightly damaged by shelling, and several times flights were suspended for a few hours. No aircraft were made unflyable, though, until a salvo of rockets whistled into the loading area just before seven o'clock on the morning of March 22. One shredded the tires and ruptured the steering hydraulics of a Bird Air C-130. Another round, bursting just off the port wing of a chartered Trans-International Airline DC-8, set fire to one of its engines and damaged the flight controls. Following previously ordered emergency procedures, the crews of both planes raced aboard other C-130s, which took off immediately without waiting to unload. Three hours later, just as the American controllers were calling for flights to resume, another rocket wounded fourteen Cambodian cargo handlers, and the airlift was grounded for the rest of the day. It was the grimmest reminder yet that Phnom Penh's lifeline was growing more vulnerable.

That afternoon I left Cambodia for the last time, flying with a half-dozen other American and British correspondents to Saigon on an embassy-controlled Air America C-47. These flights were normally for U.S. government personnel only. But because the embassy wanted nonessential foreigners out of the country, the rules had been waived. Since the airport was still being shelled, we hoped to arrive there just in time for the plane, but through a mixup we were 45 minutes early. After taking cover twice from rocket blasts we finally saw our plane dropping toward the runway. Another rocket burst narrowly missed its wingtip just as its wheels touched the ground.

The near-miss left the pilots in no mood to linger. They were already gunning the motors as we ran out to board, the propwash trying to blow the aft door shut in our faces. Before everyone was aboard, someone removed the wheel chocks and the plane began to roll forward. But somehow we all scrambled on. In a few more minutes we were circling up through a hazy sky. As we leveled off at 8,000 feet and turned eastward, we could see below the twin X-shapes of the two crippled airlift planes, one olive-drab and one silver with a torn wing, nose-to-nose on the runway. Beyond, the untilled powder-dry rice fields followed the great shallow bend of the shrunken Mekong toward the sudden military disaster that had begun to overtake South Vietnam.

Among the memories of Cambodia were a few bright ones—but just a few. The war had already begun to devastate its land and spirit when I first came there in mid-1972, but a few glimpses of prewar charm were still possible then. There was the national ballet school, which rehearsed in an open pavilion on the grounds of the old royal palace: with a permit from the authorities you could go to the rehearsals to be entranced by gleaming-eyed boys and girls, as young as six years old and ranging up to sixteen, ornately costumed and performing with breathtaking precision the intricate classical Khmer dances retelling the stories of the Ramayana and other legends.

I was glad too to be able to remember the light-hearted Cambodian New Year celebrations which, even in the grim spring of 1973 with American bombs falling only a few miles away, were still a poignant moment in which the war could be briefly forgotten and beloved folkways revived. For the Khmer, the new year—falling in April—was traditionally a time for games and street shows, and even in that fourth wartime spring, gay crowds filled the grassy malls along Phnom Penh's wide boulevards and the slopes of the Phnom itself—the knobby, steep hill in the city's center that gave it its name. At the top was a huge monastery, where hundreds of people climbed to make good-luck offerings to the orange-robed monks who sat in the pungent fumes of thousands of burning incense sticks. Down below, jugglers, magicians, tightrope walkers, and fortunetellers mingled with laughing young men and women playing at various forms of lawn bowls or beanbag games.

Those memories now belonged to the past. The ballet classes on the palace grounds were suspended soon after I had first seen them; another new year was approaching, but this year there would be no festivities. The dark memories were dominant: of refugees beyond hope and beyond counting, of suffering beyond my imagining, of defeat and despair—and of shame for my own country, which had contributed to such vast misery and was so unforgivably indifferent to the victims of its policies. Like most of my colleagues, remembering Phnom Penh's survival against all expectation in the past, I had been unwilling to state in print that the war was finished. "It seems impossible for the city to hold out much longer; it seems equally impossible that it will fall," I had written in a long dispatch a few days earlier that attempted to describe the eerie blend of normalcy and hopelessness in the blockaded capital.

There could still be some miraculous survival. We all remembered how the Khmer Rouge faded away in 1973 after many thought they had victory in their grasp. Still, looking down at the sere fields from the windows of the Air America plane, I was sure I would not see Cambodia again, and I was right. That day Cambodia's war—though not its agony—had less than four weeks to run.

Calvary

The wind from three whirling rotor blades scooped up puffs of dust and leaves and bits of grass and lashed them toward the white-helmeted military bandsmen drawn up on the Chamcar Mon Palace grounds. The helicopter motors, as if warning that little time was left for ceremony, screamed an impatient accompaniment to the Khmer national anthem, while the man for whom it was being played stood silently at attention, his face showing nothing of his thoughts.

Lon Nol, preparing to leave Cambodia at last, wore a neatly knotted black tie and a dark gray business suit that wilted slightly in the steamy heat. At the last notes of the anthem, he limped slowly and painfully, using his cane, to inspect an honor guard. Then, lifting the cane in fleeting salute to the officials and aides who had come to see him off, he turned toward one of the helicopters, his weeping wife walking next to him. Aides helped the couple aboard and a moment later the craft lifted into the air, followed shortly afterward by the other two carrying the rest of the kinsmen and associates who would follow him out of the country. It was five minutes past noon on the first day of April 1975, five years and two weeks, exactly, after Lon Nol overthrew Prince Sihanouk.

From Chamcar Mon, the flight to Pochentong took only a few minutes. Air Cambodge's lone jet stood fueled and ready for a flight to U Tapao, where it would meet a plane sent by Indonesia's President Suharto. The Indonesian leader had invited Lon Nol to vacation on Bali, thus allowing a face-saving, if transparent, excuse for his departure from Phnom Penh.

As Lon Nol stepped down from his helicopter at Pochentong, two Communist rockets whistled down to explode a couple of hundred yards away. Ambassador Dean, along with a few other dignitaries who were waiting to bid him a planeside farewell, ducked behind the wall of sandbags that stood in front of the empty, damaged terminal building. But Lon Nol scarcely seemed to notice the explosions. Wavering ever so slightly on his cane, he kept walking slowly toward the plane. Minutes later he and his party, 29 passengers in all, were in the air. After his takeoff, the government radio station broadcast an eleven-minute recorded statement in which the marshal insisted that he did not intend to remain permanently in exile. While abroad, he would consult with other world leaders about a peaceful solution to the war, he said, but "when my health improves or whenever our brothers indicate to me that our national problem requires my presence, I shall promptly return to our homeland to continue the struggle for national freedom."

Even with his regime in its final extremity, persuading the enfeebled marshal to leave the country had not been an easy matter. Outside the palace, no one could fail to see that his popular support had completely vanished, and many of his associates in the army and the government no longer believed he could continue as president. But Lon Nol showed no sign of reaching the same conclusion, and in the moral and political wreckage of the Khmer Republic, no individual or group seemed to have the will or ability to convince him to step down. Those who might have done so remained snared in the atmosphere of petty intrigue and pointless bickering that had characterized the Republic's entire political life and was still as bad as ever, or worse, in its last weeks.

The Cambodians might have drifted indefinitely had not a group of Asian ambassadors stepped in to try to precipitate a decision. The four envoys— representing Japan, Malaysia, Singapore, and Thailand—met with Prime Minister Long Boret on March 18 and told him Lon Nol must leave for two reasons: first, to seize whatever slim chance might still exist for peace talks, and second, because his departure might win some additional votes in the American Congress for the Ford administration's aid request.

The ambassadors' approach at last pushed the Cambodians into action. For the next two days, Long Boret conferred with various military and civilian leaders, including Lt. Gen. Sak Sutsakhan, who had been named armed forces commander a week earlier, and Saukham Khoy, a retired general who, as president of the Senate, was Lon Nol's constitutional successor. The next step was to circulate formal resolutions among senior army commanders, the National Assembly, and the leadership of the president's own Socio-Republican party, calling on him to leave the country "on a temporary basis, while the terms of a ceasefire were worked out."

With the resolutions approved, and shortly after the March 21 announcement of still another cabinet change in which General Sak was named defense minister and deputy prime minister, he and about a dozen other leaders went as a formal delegation to call on the president and present the resolutions to him. Lon Nol was "shocked that the country would thus turn its back on him," General Sak later recalled, and asked for time to consider the proposal. He spent several days meeting with the delegation members separately, evidently hoping to find that they were not as united as they claimed. None urged him to stay, however. Briefly, at the urging of his brother Lon Non, the president seemed ready to defy the resolution, and though he finally agreed to leave, it was not without conditions. He would not give up the title of president, and demanded that his successors must not capitulate to the Communists but seek an "honorable peace" or, failing that, continue the struggle.

Lon Nol had one other condition to impose: all his money was invested in Cambodia, he told his ministers, and he needed funds for himself and his family to go abroad. Having paid a far more fearful price for his leadership, the cabinet agreed to pay a price for his departure too. A half-million dollars was promised, according to later congressional testimony by Ambassador Dean, of which at least $200,000 was actually paid.*

Any thought that Lon Nol's exit would soften the Khmer Rouge policy against negotiations was quickly smashed. Prince Sihanouk—whose own maneuvering room was cut away by Khmer Rouge battlefield successes just as was the Republic's—immediately declared in Peking that the marshal's departure was no more than a "dirty and vulgar trap" arranged by the United States. Lon Nol's successor, Saukham Khoy, was branded a "big war criminal and executioner," no more acceptable than the rest of the Phnom Penh leadership.

Speaking explicitly in the name of the Khmer Rouge leadership, Sihanouk categorically rejected negotiations. Washington might believe, he said,

that the temporary retreat of Quisling Lon Nol and his replacement by other super-traitors, mortal enemies of the Cambodian people, will save the skin of its neo-colonialist system established in Phnom Penh. . . . In the name of the FUNC (National United Front of Cambodia], RGNUC [Royal Government of National Union of Cambodia] and CPNLAF [Cambodian Peoples National Liberation Armed Forces], I proclaim openly again that on no account, under no circumstances, neither in the near future nor in the more remote future, will the Cambodian resistance agree to be reconciled with the traitors. . . . The

* The amount may have been larger. Two days before Phnom Penh fell to the Khmer Rouge, Sydney Schanberg reported in the *New York Times*, the National Bank of Cambodia cabled the Irving Trust Company of New York to ask if an earlier instruction was being carried out to pay Lon Nol not $200,000 or $500,000, but one million dollars. Irving Trust refused comment on Schanberg's report.

FUNC, RGNUC and CPNLAF will always fight U.S. imperialism and its valets in the spirit of no retreat or compromise until they are eliminated totally, definitively and irreversibly from the sacred soil of Cambodia.

In Phnom Penh, the 60-year-old Saukham Khoy seemed to address the crisis with little more realism than his predecessor. "First of all, I want the Khmer people to help me fight corruption," he told one American reporter. "After that I would like to ask all my commanders to help me recruit new men for the military. And then when we improve the military situation we can talk to the other side—we can negotiate." To the suggestion that it had grown very late for talk of improving the situation, he responded that America would surely save the Republic in the end: "President Ford will send troops to Phnom Penh and resign. If I were president of the United States, I'd do that to save American honor."

Hopes of improving the battlefield balance were as fanciful as his hope of rescue by American troops. Less than eight hours after the Air Cambodge Caravelle carrying Lon Nol circled up from the Pochentong runway, the government suffered its worst defeat so far in the offensive: the loss of Neak Luong, which after enduring months of shelling and starvation now fell in a final flaming house-to-house battle. Of its 4,500 defenders, nearly all were killed or captured. A week later, only 160 men had made their way to government-held territory. Neak Luong's capture freed about 5,000 Khmer Rouge troops to join the assault on the capital. Even more frightening, a half-dozen U.S.-supplied 105-mm howitzers had fallen into Communist hands, along with sizable stocks of shells, significantly augmenting the destructive firepower that could now be aimed at Phnom Penh and its airport.

The next day, while the country's new leaders prepared a series of orders closing theaters and dance halls, forbidding the traditional Khmer New Year celebrations that were due to start on April 13, and tightening curfew hours, they also decided to give up some of the surrounded enclaves elsewhere in Cambodia and bring the troops back to reinforce the desperately depleted units around Phnom Penh. Among the positions to be yielded was a town called Kompong Seila, 70 miles southwest of the capital. About 1,300 soldiers and 2,000 dependents, who had been besieged there for almost a year, were airlifted back to Phnom Penh. As if to prove that even after five such terrible years the Cambodian war could still find new depths of horror, the Kompong Seila troops came back amid dreadful whispers of cannibalism during the siege—rumors that some of the soldiers promptly verified, in grotesquely vivid fashion. When a paymaster ordered them to move to another and more dangerous position before being paid, they refused, then killed him and calmly cooked and ate his flesh.

Other reinforcements were flown to the capital from Takeo in the south and from the long-encircled enclave at Svay Rieng, near the Vietnamese border. But the Communists were reinforcing too. From Neak Luong their units moved up Highway One and in sampans on the Mekong, driving toward Phnom Penh's southeastern defense line.

Elsewhere, other Khmer Rouge forces began threatening the remaining enclaves. Prey Veng, east of the capital, came under attack in the first days of April, as did Kompong Speu to the west. In Battambang Province in the far northwest, adjacent to Thailand and the country's richest rice-growing region, insurgent troops began advancing to within mortar range of the province capital, driving before them an estimated quarter of a million frightened refugees. Battambang had seen relatively little fighting in the past, partly, it was said, because the province governor accommodatingly sold the Khmer Rouge supplies for their campaigns elsewhere. The province had long been notorious, too, for the large numbers of nonexistent ghost soldiers on its garrison's payroll. Now the reckoning was paid. Battambang's defenses, it was reported during the war's last weeks, consisted of "empty holes and no soldiers to fill them."

As the Republic's battle lines crumbled, so did John Gunther Dean's hopes for a controlled end to the fighting. On April 3, acting president Saukham Khoy asked the superpowers to help arrange peace negotiations and also promised that his government would "try to make contact with the Cambodian brothers of the other side," but without result. Dean proposed to Washington that the embassy staff and other foreigners be evacuated by helicopter on April 5, before the defense of Phnom Penh deteriorated further. But Kissinger would not hear of it. In a phone call to the embassy and a subsequent "flash" message, he refused to authorize evacuation; all Kissinger would allow was a further reduction of the embassy staff to no more than 50 people.

The embassy's military attaches continued to visit the battered govern- ments units at the front, not because there was anything very useful to say or do any more but only because morale would have plunged even further if they stopped coming. Airlift flights still landed at Pochentong with loads of rice, fuel, and ammunition, under shelling that gradually intensified to 80 or 90 rounds a day. But no one in the embassy seriously tried to pretend any longer that the Republic could be saved. For Dean and his staff, only one meaningful task was left: to arrange the evacuation of the remaining Americans, along with those other foreigners and Cambodians for whose safety the U.S. was willing to take responsibility.

At the end of its war, as at the beginning, it was Cambodia's fate to depend on American decisions that were not based on Cambodian needs or cir- cumstances or even on consideration of American moral responsibilities there. Instead Cambodia remained peripheral, as it always had been, to the larger American concerns with Vietnam. "I think it is in the national interest of the United States that South Vietnam survive," Defense Secretary James Schlesinger once said, "and the value of Cambodia's survival derives from its importance to the survival of South Vietnam." It was Vietnam, not Cambodia, that had used up the store of America's patience for underwriting a remote and seemingly endless conflict. And it was a last cruelty of history that in the very last American debate on the war, Cambodia's crisis was obscured by the sudden collapse of the South Vietnamese army.

However uselessly, Cambodian soldiers were fighting and dying bravely as the siege tightened around their capital in 1975. Almost certainly they fought only from some dark desperate drive of fear and hatred, not for their moribund regime, but their heroism was undeniable. Yet from mid-March on, the dominant image on American television screens was of the panicky rout of Saigon's divisions: an image that must have reinforced the perception in the public and in Congress that any further U.S. efforts in Indochina would be futile. Whatever the decision on last-minute aid for Cambodia (and there were morally troubling questions on both sides of that argument), it seemed that after all they had endured, the Cambodians were at least entitled to have their case judged on its own circumstances, without the burden of Vietnam's faults and failures added to their own. But even that was denied. In the atmosphere that surrounded and conditioned the aid debate, little attention was given to Cambodian imperatives. Like a dying child struck by a speeding fire truck, Cambodia would come to the end of the war as it did to the start: a victim of blind forces it had not created or controlled or even understood.

When debate began in February on President Ford's proposed $222 million supplement, it was evident from the first day that little support survived in Congress or the public for the administration's Cambodia policy. Opinion polls showed that Americans overwhelmingly wanted no more to do with the Indochina war for any reason. "It saddens all responsible Americans to see Cambodia collapse," said George Mahon, the conservative Texas Democrat who headed the House Appropriations Committee. "But it is just almost impossible to convince rank-and-file Americans that there is any end to this." It was hard to believe a few hundred million more dollars could save the ruined Khmer Republic anyway. Intelligence estimates made available to Congress indicated that Phnom Penh was almost certain to fall whether it received the supplement or not.

There was even less reason to think negotiations would materialize even if by some unexpected chance the Cambodian regime did survive until summer. Two years of hints by Kissinger had come to nothing. The Khmer Rouge, who had consistently and unequivocally refused to negotiate, now seemed to have a decisive military advantage.

So unconvincing was the administration's case that some in Congress began to believe it had no serious hope of saving Cambodia at all, but was just positioning itself to put the blame on the Democratic majority in Congress, rather than on the executive, when Phnom Penh fell. Possibly even more cynical was the view expressed by certain officials who speculated that losing the Cambodia supplement might help the administration win other additional funds requested for Vietnam, since Congress might be more reluctant to hand the president two rebuffs in a row. "We were not making Cambodia the sacrificial lamb," one official told the *New York Times;* "we want that aid, but it is a political fact of life that Congress would be more wary to try the cutoff act twice."

As an alternative to the administration's plans, committees in both the House and Senate began considering compromises that would keep the Cambodians from running out of ammunition but would also require the administration to find a way of ending the fighting by June 30, when all U.S. military support would end. An author of the compromise was Representative McCloskey, who had gone to Phnom Penh "with the belief that I would never vote another nickel for Cambodia" but returned feeling that because American actions had such a major responsibility for the crisis, the Cambodians should be given a last chance to keep from being overrun while a hopeless and misconceived war was brought to an end.

"I can only tell you my emotional reaction, getting into that country," McCloskey burst out in a Senate hearing; "if I could have found the military or State Department leader who has been the architect of this policy, my instinct would be to string him up." American actions in Cambodia represented "greater evil than we have done to any country in the world," he added, "and wholly without reason, except for our benefit to fight against the Vietnamese." It was not just war critics like McCloskey who were chastened at the tragic shambles Cambodia had become. "I have not supported a dollar of this war without feeling guilty," Senate Republican leader Hugh Scott admitted at the same hearing, "and I might as well say so."

In the House, amendments based on McCloskey's proposal failed in committee, but a similar plan was approved, by a single vote, in the Senate Foreign Relations Committee. The Senate version was sponsored by two members who, like McCloskey, were liberal Republicans: Jacob Javits of New York and Charles Percy of Illinois. Their proposal, which turned out to be the only Cambodia aid measure to advance as far as full committee endorsement, would have provided $82.5 million in additional military aid, along with $72.9 million for economic and humanitarian assistance, until June 30, after which all military aid would be prohibited. The president, meanwhile, would have to certify to Congress periodically that the U.S. and Khmer governments were actively seeking an "orderly conclusion" to the conflict. Those favoring the compromise declared in the committee's majority report that it would avoid the "chaotic, uncontrolled situation" that would occur if funds were simply allowed to run out in the next few weeks, while avoiding "perpetuation of the fighting without hope of a solution."

The opposing view was stated in a minority report signed by Sen. Hubert Humphrey and three other committee Democrats—Stuart Symington, George McGovern, and Dick Clark—that responded to the administration's arguments this way:

> The administration would have us believe that supplemental military assistance will enable the Lon Nol government to stagger through to the rainy season and possibly produce a stalemate. Should that occur, the administration then hopes the insurgents will tire of fighting and decide to talk. . . . Everything about the course of this struggle and everything we know about the insurgents indicates that the administration's reasoning is dead wrong. There is not a stalemate now in Cambodia and there never has been: since late 1971 we have seen the relentless attrition of the Cambodian army, the steady decimation of its civilian population, and the spreading control of the insurgents. Today, the Phnom Penh government is clearly unable to produce a stalemate. Intelligence estimates indicate that even with additional aid the odds against its survival are almost prohibitive. . . . The insurgents, or the Royal Government of National Union (GRUNC), seem well aware, perhaps better than the executive branch, of the weakness of the Phnom Penh position. Unlike the administration, they understand that the longer the war lasts the more helpless will be the forces of the government. . . . We should not wish to prolong the present military struggle to the point where the weary Phnom Penh forces finally collapse or are overwhelmed. Out of a hopeless last ditch defense might well come the bitter bloodshed which even the proponents of the committee recommendation seek to avoid. It would be far better for us to work for a humane transfer of power—an honorable surrender, if need be. Indeed, there appears to be no rational alternative.

The argument that the U.S. should continue aid to show it was a reliable ally, even if defeat could not be avoided, was a "cynical approach," Humphrey and his colleagues wrote, "and we reject it. . . . It is a cruel hoax to lead the Cambodians on in order to maintain our image providing only enough support to sustain their misery because, although we know that more aid will not help, we lack the political courage to end it."

It was not Humphrey or the antiwar minority that assured the defeat of the committee compromise, however, but the administration itself. Even his own party's congressional leaders told Ford that unless he agreed to the June 30 cutoff there was no possibility of any aid for Cambodia at all. But Ford refused. His reason was the same that had been advanced for years against congressional attempts to end the war by legislation: if a deadline were set, the Communists would have no reason to negotiate. Since the Khmer Rouge showed absolutely no interest in negotiating anyway, and since a quick capitulation was inevitable if the aid were denied, the administration's logic seemed to be based on a chimera—or, as congressional Democrats suspected, a crass effort to shift the blame. From whatever motive, the White House was adamant, leaving Congress to conclude that rather than accept a congressional mandate to end the war, the administration would rather have no aid at all.

Faced with this unyielding attitude, Congress deferred a vote until after an Easter recess. By the time it reconvened April 7, further decay on the Cambodian battlefields had, for all practical purposes, ended the debate. Three days later, addressing a joint session to deliver his "State of the World" address, Ford read his former congressional colleagues a pleading letter from Saukham Khoy asking for continued American support. But he did not renew the request in his own name. Asking for action only on the funds sought for South Vietnam, the president mentioned the Cambodia proposal only in the past tense. "In January, I requested food and ammunition for the brave Cambodians," he reminded his audience. "I regret to say that as of this evening, it may be too late."

In Phnom Penh, which had lived in a state of misty unrealism for so long, Ford's speech shattered the last naive expectations of an American rescue.

"The United States led Cambodia into this war," said a tearful Saukham Khoy after Ford's speech was broadcast. "But when the war became difficult the United States pulled out." Perhaps, he added desperately, Cambodia could declare itself socialist and seek help from the Soviet Union. But the Republic was fast slipping beyond anyone's help. Its soldiers were now yielding as much as a half-mile a day to the advancing enemy on the Phnom Penh perimeter. On the northwest front, which guarded Pochentong and the vital airlift, Khmer Rouge units were within mortar range of the runways. The government's artillery was pulled back to firing positions within the city limits, and the crash of outgoing rounds rumbled through ministry offices and across crowded refugee encampments.

Because of the twelve-hour time difference, when President Ford finished speaking to Congress it was already Friday morning, the 11th, in the Cambodian capital. Within a few hours a message reached the Navy helicopter carrier USS *Okinawa*, standing off the Cambodian coast in the Gulf of Thailand: the evacuation plan, under the somewhat transparent code name Eagle Pull, was to be carried out.

Aboard the *Okinawa* were the 800 or so men of the 2nd Battalion, 4th Marine Regiment, now designated the 31st Marine Amphibious Unit, and two dozen huge CH-53 helicopters. With the escort and support vessels that made up the rest of "Amphibious Ready Group Alfa," the *Okinawa* had been on station since March 2, awaiting the order to execute what was known in military planners' files as "CONPLAN 5060C—Noncombatant Emergency and Evacuation—Cambodia." Steaming toward the group, and scheduled to join it later on the evening of April 11, was another carrier, the USS *Hancock,* with twelve more helicopters. In order to have her aircraft available, as well as the *Okinawa*'s, it was decided to put the evacuation off until the next morning. L-hour, the time the first marine helicopter would land in the Cambodian capital, was set for nine o'clock on the morning of the 12th, Phnom Penh time.

It was now, with only hours to go before the United States physically abandoned the regime it had supported for five disastrous years, that Henry Kissinger finally reached for a solution that might once have offered a better end, but which he had always before refused. On his orders, George Bush, chief of the U.S. liaison office in Peking, was instructed to make a peace offer directly to Prince Sihanouk, inviting him to return to Phnom Penh not to negotiate or share power with the leaders of the Republic, as was always U.S. policy in the past, but to take over the government.

Whether Kissinger seriously thought any such arrangement could still be made, or whether he ordered the one-minute-to-midnight offer only so history would show an attempt was made, only Kissinger could know. But it was far, far too late. He had already transferred all governmental responsibility to the Khmer Rouge, Sihanouk declared in a written reply to Bush's message; he would "remain until the end on the side of the Red Khmers, my allies whom I would never betray" and whose "so deserved . . . victory" must not now be frustrated.

Sihanouk was too much a realist to imagine that he would have any but a figurehead's role under the Communists; nor could he have been deluded about their frightening fanaticism. "I shall never look after the internal affairs of my country," he had told an interviewer in March. "The responsibilities of the government and of the administration of Cambodia in its entirety are and will be incumbent on the Red Khmers." Of his own role, he added: "The Red Khmer leaders have asked me to remain the head of state of Cambodia, and this until my death. These leaders have also indicated to me that I shall always be the symbol of national unity and continuity and legitmacy of the State of Cambodia. . . . I look after and shall, mostly, continue to look after foreign affairs and international relations."

In public, Sihanouk professed to believe that Khmer Rouge rule would not be unduly harsh or doctrinaire, and that only the seven or eight "main traitors" who were under sentence of death would be executed. All others associated with the Lon Nol regime would be granted amnesty, he declared, if they surrendered unconditionally to the liberation forces. Such declarations were taken seriously by some of the prince's admirers abroad, and they were endlessly repeated in Phnom Penh, where wishful thinking was now all that was left to comfort the citizens of the vanquished regime. But it is not likely that Sihanouk himself any longer believed in Khmer Rouge moderation—if he ever had. He cannot have been completely ignorant of the murders of captured Phnom Penh soldiers and officials, even petty civil servants and village schoolteachers. Nor does it seem plausible that Sihanouk did not know of the savage and violent purge of his own loyalists from the insurgent ranks, along with anyone suspected of pro-Vietnamese sympathies.

In private, it was said, the prince was deeply depressed as the Communist victory approached, even while his public statements welcomed it. But nothing could be achieved now by breaking with his Khmer Rouge allies. The country was about to be theirs whatever Sihanouk did. To accept Kissinger's eleventh-hour offer and travel to Phnom Penh would not stop the Khmer Rouge army from marching in, after which they would no doubt treat him as only another captured traitor; whatever microscopic chance he might have of moderating their rule would vanish. Accordingly, in his answer to Bush, as he explained the next day in describing the extraordinary exchange of messages, "I firmly refused to take power in Phnom Penh."

With the desperate last offer to Sihanouk, the U.S. had finally reached the end of a long, blind alley it had traveled for years of unsuccessful Cambodia diplomacy. Washington seemed never to have grasped—despite Ambassador Dean's warnings—that time was not on its side. Every time it refused to take a risk for a settlement, the administration was only assuring that it would face worse choices in the future. And in piously announcing its willingness to accept any solution reached by the Cambodians among themselves, the U.S. government was effectively abdicating all responsibility; its allies in Phnom Penh, as weak and ineffectual in this as in all other matters, had no negotiating strategy of their own, nor any other plan except to cling to their diminishing pockets of territory while waiting for the Americans to rescue them, somehow, from the dreadful trap in which they were caught.

The final plea for Sihanouk's return was a metaphor for all that had gone before: having resisted the idea when it might still have been available, the U.S. was now grasping for what had clearly become impossible. For if there was ever a chance of a Sihanouk solution, none remained in April of 1975. On the eve of their triumph, the Khmer Rouge were finally strong enough not to have to cede any part of their victory to Sihanouk or to anyone else. Nor, to Cambodia's and humanity's enduring sorrow, did they owe to anyone but themselves the right to shape the future that would follow that victory.

Even in America's final moments there, Cambodia touched a sense of shame. When the first wave of three helicopters dropped out of the sky six minutes before the scheduled L-hour onto a soccer field the evacuation planners called Landing Zone Hotel, the 90 marines aboard charged out with weapons at the ready, as if landing again on Iwo Jima or Tarawa. Instead of threatening mobs, however, they faced only a few hundred curious but perfectly calm onlookers, many of them children who stared wide-eyed at the marine rifles trained toward them and then began to smile and wave, calling out gently, "OK, bye-bye," as the evacuees raced toward the waiting helicopters.

Three hours earlier, a hand-delivered note from Ambassador Dean told Cambodian leaders that the evacuation was to begin that morning, and that any of them wishing to leave should come to the embassy. Dean drove to the prime minister's residence to deliver the message in person to Long Boret, who was one of those under death sentence by the Khmer rouge. After a hastily convened cabinet meeting, Long Boret and his fellow ministers declined the offer. So did Sirik Matak, another on the Khmer Rouge death list. Though his only post was "adviser" to the government and he thus had no official responsibilities, and though Dean personally urged him to leave, Sirik Matak chose not to join the evacuation. His answer to Dean's last message was delivered just as the first helicopters were landing:

Dear Excellency and Friend,

I thank you very sincerely for your letter and for your offer to transport me towards freedom. I cannot, alas, leave in such a cowardly fashion.

As for you and in particular for your great country, I never believed for a moment that you would have this sentiment of abandoning a people which has chosen liberty. You have refused us your protection and we can do nothing about it. You leave and my wish is that you and your country will find happiness under the sky.

But mark it well that, if I shall die here on the spot and in my country that I love, it is too bad because we all are born and must die one day. I have only committed this mistake of believing in you, the Americans.

Please accept, Excellency, my dear friend, my faithful and friendly sentiments.

Sirik Matak.

To Dean's shamed amazement, only Saukham Khoy answered the summons to the embassy—without, it turned out, having told any of his colleagues in the government that he was leaving his post.

In just over two hours, and without the slightest interference or display of hostility from the onlooking crowd, the evacuation helicopters flew 276 persons out of the threatened capital. 82 were American, 159 Khmer, and 35 of other nationalities. Many more could have gone. According to the operational plan, up to 780 passengers could have been loaded on the 36 helicopters used in the evacuation. Most of the Cambodians who left were embassy employees and their families. With others who had been semi-covertly flown out to Thailand from Pochentong by fixed-wing aircraft during the previous week, they represented all the embassy's Khmer employees except for twelve, who were offered evacuation but refused.

Also refusing evacuation were Sydney Schanberg and his Cambodian assistant, Dith Pran, with whom he had developed an extraordinarily close and intense friendship.

A driven, explosive personality, given to bursts of rage and of manic humor that were almost equal in violence, the 41-year-old Schanberg was a man of great energy and physical bravery who had been a *Times* correspondent in Asia for six years. Over that period he had come to spend more and more time in Cambodia, where the tragedy befalling a vulnerable and appealing people engaged both his professional and personal passions. Schanberg's compassion for the war's victims was matched by his anger at official corruption and callousness, both Khmer and American. His writing was rarely elegant but possessed a gritty, bristling power. His imagery was earthy and direct, conveying an unchallengeable sense of honest plainness. Over the entire course of the Indochina war, I know of no reporter who wrote more compellingly of its human tragedy.

In his dispatches, Schanberg strove—not always successfully—to maintain the impersonal tone demanded by American journalistic convention. But no one who knew him could miss his intense personal involvement with the story: an obsession, Schanberg himself called it, which kept drawing him back to Cambodia despite serious strains on himself and his marriage. When his friends and colleagues learned that Sydney had stayed to write the final chapter, though many were concerned for his safety, few of us were really surprised.

At the landing zone, a grim-faced Ambassador Dean boarded a helicopter at 10:15 A.M., carrying under his arm the folded U.S. flag that had flown over the embassy until the previous evening. Over Phnom Penh and in the skies along the helicopter's flight path toward the sea, a dozen strike aircraft and ten other support planes, including an Air Force C-130 transport serving as an airborne command post, covered the evacuation. But Khmer Rouge gunners did not zero in on the landing site until the last few moments, after all civilian evacuees were in the air and only part of the 360-man marine force remained. Just before eleven o'clock, rockets and mortar rounds began falling among the onlookers, killing a teen-aged boy and wounding another. An American corpsman bandaged the hurt youth just before leaving. The marines radioed for one of the three forward air controllers in spotter planes overhead to try to spot where the rockets were coming from, but though he made several passes the observer couldn't pinpoint the target, so no strikes were ordered. At 11:15, as the last two helicopters were taking off with the marine ground-force commander and his chief aides aboard, several more rockets fell squarely on the landing zone, just too late to cause any damage to the last departing aircraft.

An hour later, all evacuees were safely aboard ship in the Gulf, while the residences they left were being swiftly and thoroughly looted by the same Cambodian military police who had been posted there as guards.

In the few days remaining before its fall, Phnom Penh was like an eerie montage of its own memories. It was as if all the remembered scenes of the war, greatly compressed in time, were projected onto multiple screens that ringed an ever-shrinking horizon: images of great black fountains of smoke rising from burning villages and refugee encampments; of ragged, retreating soldiers; of wounded men dragging smashed limbs or lying smeared in their own blood; of unending columns of refugees on foot and in oxcarts, flowing and clotting like human lava on the hot, frightened approaches to the city.

Yet no panic or anarchy overtook the capital. "To a Westerner, the situation looks absolutely hopeless," wrote Sydney Schanberg, "and yet no sense of that has yet manifested itself in Phnom Penh. . . . The markets are busy, the lottery is continuing, the black market in gasoline is flourishing. . . ."

On the day after the U.S. evacuation, the last international flight of Air Cambodge, the civilian airline, landed at Pochentong. An American pilot flew the shrapnel-damaged DC-7 from Bangkok to rescue his Cambodian wife, making the entire round trip with only three of the plane's four engines working. Among the handful of inbound passengers was Jon Swain of the London *Sunday Times,* an adventurous 27-year-old who would be the only British reporter to cover Phnom Penh's fall. In one of those touches of fantasy that seemed to run through all Cambodian events, stewardesses poured champagne for Swain and his few fellow-passengers shortly before they landed in the midst of a rocket attack.

If such scenes were dreamlike, so were the pronouncements of the Republic's last government. On the evening of the 12th, hours after the U.S. evacuation ended, the remaining civilian and military leaders proposed, and the National Assembly quickly approved, a resolution transferring "all forms of power" to the armed forces. Administrative authority was given to a Supreme Committee of four military and three civilian members, including Prime Minister Long Boret and General Sak, who went on the radio that same evening to call on all Cambodians to "join forces against the enemy and strengthen the political and military position of our republic. . . . I would like to stress that our national armed forces have decided to try by all means to improve the military situation and ensure security for the people in Phnom Penh and in the provinces." The next day, after he was named chairman of the committee (with Long Boret as vice-chairman), Sak promised "firm action" against corruption and announced a recruiting drive for the army, while Long Boret declared courageously but implausibly, "There will be no surrender." He proposed a ceasefire, but only if the Khmer Rouge agreed to a plebiscite to decide on Cambodia's future government.

Phnom Penh's fantasies, however, were about to end. Khmer Rouge broadcasts immediately denounced the Supreme Committee as only "another traitorous organization"; after a pause on the 13th, which was also the start of the Khmer New Year, their assault strengthened. On the 14th, while the refugee stream into the city thickened until the roads were clogged with frightened, exhausted people, a defecting pilot tried to bomb the armed forces headquarters. He missed, but killed seven people and wounded about twenty others outside the command post before flying off to land his T-28 at a Communist-held airstrip in Kompong Cham Province.

The following day, the 15th, the large suburb of Takhmau south of the city fell, as did Pochentong Airport. That night a heavy artillery barrage fell on the heart of the city. Shells set fire to a crowded settlement of wooden houses built on stilts over the Bassac River near the large Monivong Bridge, not far from the Chamcar Mon Palace. Flames rushed from one house to the next so quickly that many residents burned to death before they could jump into the river for safety. After the stilts burned through and the houses collapsed, their charred corpses bobbed in the black water where survivors also swam, shouting desperately for help. All around the rim of the city other fires splashed the night's edge with red as fuel and ammunition depots and settlements were set alight.

When Phnom Penh awoke on the 16th, even the hard-line members of the Supreme Committee saw at last that further resistance was impossible. Dropping the preposterous demand for a plebiscite, the cabinet agreed at an early morning meeting to propose an immediate ceasefire followed by the immediate transfer of power to the revolutionaries. They asked only that there be no reprisals against officials and soldiers of the Phnom Penh regime. Five days earlier, in one of their last meetings before the evacuation, Ambassador Dean had proposed exactly such an appeal to Long Boret but was turned down; now the proposal, drafted by Long Boret, was sent to Sihanouk in Peking through the International Red Cross and also distributed through the French news service, Agence France Presse.

All day and all night, while rockets and shells swooshed into the city and thousands of deserting soldiers joined the bedlam of refugees thronging the streets, members of the government met to try to decide what to do next. No word came from Peking. At one point, long after midnight, they agreed to flee to Oddar Mean Chey Province in the extreme northwest, bordering on Thailand, to try to keep resisting there. At four o'clock in the morning they assembled in a garden in front of a pagoda to begin the journey, but the helicopters that were to fly them out of Phnom Penh never came.

As dawn broke on the 17th, the dispirited group returned to Long Boret's house, where they finally received Sihanouk's reply to the previous day's peace offer. It was a flat, frightening rejection. Not only would the liberation forces accept no arranged handover of power, but the membership of the Supreme Committee had been added to the seven original "traitors" on the Khmer Rouge death list. They too were "traitors who deserve hanging and should try and escape while they can," Sihanouk declared, while the only course left for government soldiers was to "raise the white flag and surrender."

Stunned, members of the government walked out of the prime minister's residence and dispersed, leaving a "strange calmness," General Sak later recalled. Only he and Long Boret were still there when an army officer arrived to report that a few helicopters were preparing to leave from the Olympic Stadium. The two leaders, each in his official car, reached the stadium shortly after eight o'clock and boarded one of the helicopters waiting there. A few minutes later, however, Long Boret's wife, two children, and his sister, along with some family friends, arrived at the landing zone, and he stepped down to join them on another helicopter. With him went his close friend, Information Minister Thong Lim Huong.

General Sak, with his wife and children, took off at eight-thirty. From the air, as they rose over the city, they could see the prime minister's party switching to still a third waiting helicopter. Whether both craft were mechanically unflyable or failed to take off for some other reason is not known. But Long Boret never left Phnom Penh. He was seen under arrest that afternoon, and shortly afterward was executed.

General Sak and his party, after stops at Kompong Thom and Siem Reap, reached the border province of Oddar Mean Chey early in the afternoon. During the day other aircraft arrived there from Kompong Som, Kampot, and Kompong Thom as well as from the capital, carrying mostly air force officers and their families. Residents of the province capital, learning that the head of the Supreme Committee was there, demanded that he be turned over to their custody. But after tense negotiations that lasted nearly the whole night, the province governor persuaded the angry civilians to let Sak and his group leave. At five o'clock on the morning of the 18th, the general and his family, along with the governor, the air force group, and some other escapers, boarded a C-123 transport at the province airport and flew safely to U Tapao air base in Thailand. The Khmer Republic was no more.

For millions of ordinary Cambodians, the fall of the Republic was a time not for fear or flight, but for grateful celebration. A "village fete" would welcome the country's liberation, Prince Sihanouk had once predicted, and briefly it seemed he was right. The privations of the present were so awful that fear of the future was submerged; no doubts about the Khmer Rouge could spoil the elated sense that peace had come at last.

In Phnom Penh, on the early morning of the 17th, white flags blossomed like flower petals. Families hung sheets or pillowcases from windows or from trees in front of their homes. Bicyclists tied strips of white cloth to their handlebars. All over the city, soldiers took the clips out of their rifles and threw them away. Near the Hotel Le Phnom, crews of armored personnel carriers parked under the flowering trees to await the surrender. As they waited, they plucked sprays of yellow blossoms and stuck them in the headlight slots of their vehicles.

At a supply depot in the middle of the city, soldiers stacked their weapons and marched out, "not despondently," a French businessman who watched the scene told Jon Swain, "but with joy and applause." Army trucks dashed through the city filled with grinning soldiers and flying white emblems tied to their radio antennas. As they passed, people in the streets clapped and cheered frantically; it was as if the goverment army was celebrating a victory, not a defeat.

In the provinces the response was the same. When news of the government's fall reached the gem-mining center of Pailin in the far west of the country, villagers beat drums and played flutes outside their houses and singers improvised songs of celebration, while flickering oil lamps were hung along the paths at night, as was traditionally done for the Khmer New Year. In Battambang, gay crowds gathered at the central market and sang and danced through the night.

The illusion of a joyous reconciliation was fostered, briefly, when a contingent of black clad soldiers marched down Phnom Penh's Monivong Boulevard early on the morning of the 17th to take the surrender of the armor and infantry soldiers near the Hotel Le Phnom. After the government troops put down their weapons, they were smilingly told to go home. Civilians nearby began embracing and crying with joy, joined by the black-uniformed arrivals. Those not too elated to notice such things, however, quickly realized that these men were too clean, too neatly dressed, and too untired to be front-line troops. In fact, they were not Khmer Rouge soldiers at all but Phnom Penh students, led by a general's son named Hem Keth Dara, whose bizarre attempt to take power before the Khmer Rouge arrived was apparently undertaken on behalf of the perpetually scheming Lon Non. In the confusion of the day Keth Dara succeeded a little later in taking control of the government radio station, announcing himself in a four-minute broadcast as head of the "Nationalist Movement." His followers he called "younger brothers" who had seized Phnom Penh in order "to allow elder brothers from outside"—presumably the Khmer Rouge—to enter the city without fighting.

By then, however, the real Khmer Rouge troops had begun marching into the capital. Far from being "elder brothers," the insurgent soldiers were overwhelmingly boys and girls in their teens. They gave the impression not of children, though, but of malevolent robots. "Grim, robotlike, brutal," wrote Sydney Schanberg of Phnom Penh's conquerors, with weapons, grenades, and rockets that "drip from them like fruit from trees."

Silent and unsmiling, the Communist soldiers filed through jubilant crowds that quickly fell quiet and fearful. Answering cheers and waves with masklike indifference, they stopped traffic, ordered drivers out of their vehicles, and corralled surrendering soldiers into frightened groups, forcing them to disrobe in the streets—a form of public disgrace that awoke a curious historical echo. Nearly fifteen years before, Khieu Samphan, who was now about to become chief of state in Communist Cambodia, had been assaulted in the street by plain-clothes police agents, stripped naked, and photographed in his humiliation—all in reprisal for his published attacks on the Sihanouk administration in his newspaper, L'Observateur.

The mood in the capital changed as if a switch had been thrown. One of those who felt elation turn to dread over the space of a couple of hours was a French priest, François Ponchaud. During ten years in Cambodia, Father Ponchaud had lived among and come to identify with peasants and the urban poor; in the war years, sickened at the corruption, callousness, and social injustice of the Lon Nol government, he sympathized with the revolution. Though he knew from refugees of acts of cruelty in the liberated zone, he still believed that Cambodia could escape its misery only with a Khmer Rouge victory. But now, as he watched the first revolutionary soldiers arrive, doubt became a physical sensation, as if "a slab of lead had suddenly fallen on the city."

Few if any government units received orders on the morning of the 17th either to surrender or to fight. While most soldiers simply waited to capitulate, there were groups that continued to resist, and here and there the sound of rifle and mortar fire mingled with the cheers for peace. One skirmish broke out near the Hotel Le Phnom, where the Red Cross hoped to establish a protected "international zone" and where hundreds of foreigners and prominent Cambodians overflowed the lobby and grounds. A teenaged government soldier, shot in the head, was carried into the hotel and treated by Red Cross doctors, but they could not save him. He died in one of the small bungalows behind the main building, near the swimming pool and the tree-shaded arbor where hotel guests used to dine.

Just before one o'clock in the afternoon, the government radio began broadcasting a message from a General Mey Si Chan, who declared himself the representative of the armed forces general staff. Instructing the soldiers to stop shooting, he invited Khmer Rouge representatives to "come to Phnom Penh city and other provincial capitals, which are open to you." A committee of officers would arrange with "brother Cambodians of the other side to achieve safety and order"—but after only a few more words, the broadcast was interrupted and another voice broke in, declaring harshly, "I hereby inform the contemptible, traitorous Lon Nol clique and all its commanders that we are not coming here for negotiations; we are entering the capital by force of arms."

Strangely, the unnamed liberation spokesman acknowledged "our younger comrades of the Nationalist Movement." But later that day, Keth Dara was seen with other Phnom Penh leaders under arrest, and Khmer Rouge leaders later indicated to foreign sympathizers that they suspected the movement—also called Monatio—was part of a CIA conspiracy to subvert and eventually overthrow the new regime. (Spoiling this plot was one of the reasons subsequently given by Deputy Prime Minister Ieng Sary for the forced evacuation of Phnom Penh.)

Though their grim cheerlessness in the hour of victory was frightening, the actions of the Khmer Rouge soldiers did not seem, at the very beginning, extraordinary. Commandeering cars, vandalizing and looting a few shops, even random shooting of people who seemed hostile or did not follow orders quickly enough—all these, if unwelcome, were certainly not unprecedented acts by conquering armies, especially armies of young and poorly educated peasant boys and girls who had been brutalized in a long war of great cruelty.

One of the first killings, which may even have been a rough attempt at mercy, seemed to suggest what grim lessons about life and death were taught on the Khmer Rouge side of the battle lines. The victim was a man of about 50, a witness later told the writers Anthony Paul and John Barron, who had been wounded by a shell during the previous night. "Although he was hit in the head, he was still alive," the witness said. "His family had brought him outside their house because they were trying to find somebody who would take him to the hospital. But at eight-fifty a Red Khmer killed him with an American AR-15 rifle. He was about eighteen and said that it was impossible to survive with the kind of head injury the man had got."

"Everyone—Cambodians and foreigners alike—thought this had to be Phnom Penh's most miserable hour after long days of fear and privation," Sydney Schanberg wrote of the Republic's fall. ". . . They looked ahead with hopeful relief to the collapse of the city, for they felt that when the Communists came and the war finally ended, at least the suffering would largely be over. All of us were wrong."

What lay ahead was much worse than some rowdiness, looting, and occasional violence in the confusion of the takeover. Schanberg himself, with Jon Swain and freelance photographer Al Rockoff, was seized by Khmer Rouge soldiers during the first hours of the "liberation" and threatened with execution. Schanberg's assistant, Dith Pran, saved their lives. Though the soldiers told him he could leave, Pran—at the risk of being shot himself—stayed to plead, argue, and cajole, and finally persuaded them not to shoot their three captives. Later, after thirteen days' internment in the French embassy, Schanberg was expelled, along with all the other foreigners who had remained in the Cambodian capital. But he was unable to smuggle Pran out and spent the next four years haunted at having failed to help the friend who saved his life. Unlike nearly every other Cambodian story, though, that one had a happy ending. In October 1979, after having survived starvation, torture, malaria, and the constant danger of instant execution if his background were discovered, Pran managed to escape to Thailand and then to rejoin Schanberg in the United States.

If Schanberg's courage in staying in Cambodia nearly cost him his life, it also enabled him to serve not just the fleeting aims of journalism but the more enduring purposes of historical truth. His reports on the Khmer Rouge takeover, filed after he and the other foreigners reached Thailand, were sufficiently backed by his own reputation for integrity and independence and by the *Time's* unmatched prestige so that the facts stood unassailable before the world's conscience, beyond any apologists' attempts to obscure or soften them.

At the moment of its victory, the Cambodian Communist movement, unlike the Vietnamese, was inexperienced and politically immature. Just five years before, it had been a tiny, ill-armed force of a few thousand men, receiving no significant help from outside and with no apparent chance of seizing power. The war had taught it to fight with increasing skill and ferocity, but not how to govern or how to win support except by pure force. Its cadres were drawn from the most backward sectors of an unsophisticated land, including members of its most despised ethnic minorities—"poor peasants," Prince Sihanouk described them, "mountain people, the inhabitants of forest regions and the most remote villages." Its soldiers were children and its leaders were driven by a blind hatred not only of their Khmer enemies but of their Vietnamese allies: the incredible regimen of forced labor they were about to impose reflected a fear-driven belief that the Cambodians must work "twice, ten times as hard as the Vietnamese people" to make Cambodia an "impregnable fortress" against Vietnamese attack.

Nor was their war against their Khmer opponents over. To the Khmer Rouge leaders waiting to emerge from their forest command post, the capture of Phnom Penh was not the end of the struggle but the beginning of a new phase, the object of which was the total transformation of Cambodian society. That transformation, moreover, was to be accomplished at a single drastic stroke. Though advised by no less prestigious a teacher than Chou En-lai that socialism should be constructed carefully and step by step— China's own attempted "Great Leap Forward," Chou reminded the Cambodians, ended in economic disaster and political disarray that took many years to repair—the Khmer revolutionaries remained fanatically determined to achieve pure Communism at once. By doing so, Khieu Samphan and his colleague Son Sen once told Prince Sihanouk, they would win for Cambodia an honored place in the history of revolution: "We will be the first nation to create a completely Communist society without wasting time on intermediate steps."

To build the new Cambodia, the old had to be done away with first. And to begin that work of extirpation, Phnom Penh's new masters would not delay even for a single day. By midday on the 17th, no more than three or four hours after the first insurgent troops entered the capital to offerings of flowers and the welcoming cheers of its population, Cambodia's calvary began. The gift of peace, thirsted for so long and so desperately and tasted so briefly, was snatched away by a faceless, pitiless force that identified itself to its victims only as "Angkar Loeu"—"Organization on High." The start of the Cambodian revolution was an act of brutality for which history, even three-quarters of the way through the most violent century humankind has ever lived, offered no exact precedent.

The revolution came to Dr. Oum Nal in a hallway of the Preah Ket Mealea Hospital, which teemed with more than 2,000 patients. He was hurrying along a corridor with his arms full of serum ampules when suddenly a single Khmer Rouge soldier appeared, ordered him to stop, and then harshly instructed him to leave the hospital—and the city.

"From now on the Angkar will attend to your injured," the soldier told him. "The American imperialists are going to bomb the city. . . . You have to take shelter outside the city." He should not take luggage, the French-trained physician was assured; he would only be gone for a night or two.

Soon more black-clad soldiers were swarming through the hospital's wards, roughly ordering everyone to leave. There were no exceptions. The limbless and the dying were turned out with everyone else into the furnacelike midday heat. The same orders were given at other hospitals, evicting thousands more sick and wounded men, women, and children into the streets. Their procession was like some mad artist's vision of cruelty. A "hallucinatory spectacle," Father Ponchaud called it, remembering one crippled patient "who had neither hands nor feet, writhing along the ground like a severed worm." Another, whose nearly severed foot dangled from the end of his leg, attached only by a strip of skin, asked the priest for shelter for the rest of the day. Helplessly Father Ponchaud told him it was impossible—feeling, as he did so, that he had lost his own humanity.

Jon Swain, who watched the train of suffering pass by the gates of the French embassy, wrote: "The Khmer Rouge army is emptying the city and its hospitals—tipping out patients like garbage into the streets. Bandaged men and women hobble by the embassy. Wives push soldier husbands on hospital beds on wheels, some with serum drips still attached. In five years of war this is the greatest caravan of human misery I have seen."

Some patients were helped by friends or family members; the less fortunate had no one. Two sick men who had no one else to assist them joined the refugee stream on a single wheeled bed which they propelled with sticks, as if poling a raft. At the main military hospital, panicked families shoved and fought at the doors trying to help their wounded sons or husbands outside, while shots sounded from inside the building and cries of pain rose from patients who had fallen to the ground and could not get up.

As the hospitals were spilling their dazed, frightened patients out the doors under the rifles of Communist soldiers, other Khmer Rouge units spread out across the city announcing to a stunned population that *everyone* must leave, and quickly. If they explained their incredible order at all, they usually gave the same reason that was given to Dr. Oum Nal: the Americans were going to bomb the city. Like Oum Nal, too, many residents were told they would not be away long and did not need to take many belongings with them. The soldiers gave an impression of lethal, inexplicable rage, shouting their instructions angrily and firing in the air. Too cowed and confused to resist, people hurried to obey, quickly packing small parcels of food and other belongings and joining the thickening swarms heading toward the suburbs.

At four minutes past two in the afternoon, an unidentified announcer again began broadcasting over Phnom Penh radio, proclaiming that the liberation forces were in control of the capital and ordering senior officials and generals of the defeated Republic "to turn themselves in immediately at the Ministry of Information to help formulate measures to restore order." By four o'clock, some 50 persons were under guard outside the building, among them Lon Non. However much despised during the war for his conniving and corruption, "le petit frère" now bore himself with considerable courage, puffing calmly on a pipe while a Khmer Rouge officer, addressing the group through a bullhorn, told them they would be dealt with "fairly."

Shortly before five, Prime Minister Long Boret arrived in a black Citroen. Sydney Schanberg and Jon Swain, only hours after being threatened with execution themselves, watched him get out, "his eyes puffy and red," Swain wrote, ". . . dazed, legs wobbling." Before leaving, Schanberg approached and grasped his hand in a wordless good-bye. Neither Long Boret nor Lon Non was seen again. A few days later, radio monitors in Thailand picked up a broadcast declaring that those members of the "traitors' committee" who had not fled the country had been beheaded.

Sirik Matak, who like Long Boret was on the death list, took refuge in the French embassy until the 20th, but was taken away when the Communists, in spite of normal diplomatic practice, refused to recognize the embassy compound as under French jurisdiction. "We are the masters in our own country, this land belongs to us," a Khmer official told Vice-Consul Jean Dyrac. "In a revolutionary war there is no such thing as extraterritoriality and no privileges." Sirik Matak too went to his execution with dignity. "I am not afraid," he declared as he was led to a flatbed truck with a few other high-ranking Cambodians to be driven off the embassy grounds. "I am ready to account for my actions." Dyrac, owing his first responsibility to the safety of the hundreds of French nationals and other foreigners, was powerless to intervene. Nor could he defy Khmer Rouge orders to expel hundreds of other Cambodians from the compound, including a number of Cambodian men married to French wives—though, by some arbitrary and unexplained rule, Cambodian women married to Frenchmen were allowed to remain. The expulsions left Dyrac, a humane man, drained and remorseful. "When we do such things," he said, with tears in his eyes, "we are no longer men."

By now, not just Phnom Penh but the newly "liberated" province capitals too were being made into ghost towns, their residents turned out onto the roads in great bewildered caravans that soon became nightmares of thirst, fever, hunger, terror, and death.

Exactly how many Cambodians were forced into the awful marches would never be known, nor would anyone ever be able to count those who died. But it was evident that the numbers were staggering. In Phnom Penh, it was estimated, there were about three million people at the end of the war, and nearly all of them were driven out of the city within a day or so of its fall. "Covering the roads like a human carpet," as Sydney Schanberg wrote, they went on foot, perhaps wheeling bicycles or motorbikes on which bundled possessions were piled. Those who owned cars that had not been seized pushed them, rather than driving, either because the gas tanks were empty or because soldiers had forbidden starting the motors. The heaving crowds were so dense that at times, people could cover only a few hundred yards an hour. Soon, young children and the old and sick began to fall from thirst or exhaustion. Some died, and their corpses lay in the fierce heat among those of soldiers who had been killed in the last hours of the fighting.

Other bodies were seen with hands tied behind their backs, evidently executed for arguing with orders or failing to obey or displeasing the implacable Khmer Rouge in some other way—perhaps just for being too well dressed, or for wearing their hair too long.

Beside the three million in the capital, somewhere between 600,000 and 750,000 people were living in other cities and towns held by the government army when the war ended. Nearly all of these were also marched into the countryside, also with great haste and brutality and with few if any exceptions for the sick or disabled or wounded. The motive was ideological: a ruthless rural egalitarianism coupled with a crazed hate for symbols and practices that came from the West. "The city is bad," a Khmer Rouge political officer explained to Father Ponchaud before he and the rest of the foreigners were driven from the French embassy to the Thai border and expelled, "for there is money in the city. People can be reformed, but not cities. By sweating to clear the land, sowing and harvesting crops, men will learn the real value of things. Man has to know that he is born from a grain of rice."

In the deserted capital the Khmer Rouge set about extirpating the physical legacy of the old society, and particularly all traces of foreign influence or control. The National Bank was blown up and millions of bank notes strewn in the streets where they could still be found years later. On the lawn of the French-built Catholic cathedral, Father Ponchaud saw heaps of books from the cathedral library and from the French Far Eastern School piled up and set afire. Also burned were books taken from private houses and from schools and other libraries. Later the cathedral itself was razed to the ground and all the bricks hauled away so no one could tell it had ever stood there.

The liberators' worst rage, however, was directed at their own people. News of terrible reprisals began to seep out across the closed borders. One incident that was corroborated by numerous refugees, including four survivors who reached Thailand separately, involved more than 300 former officers of the government army who were told, after surrendering in Battambang, that they were to be driven to Phnom Penh to welcome the returning Prince Sihanouk. In their dress uniforms, they were loaded onto six trucks and driven out of town at about 1:30 P.M. on April 23, heading down Highway 5 toward the capital. Eighteen miles farther on, however, the trucks suddenly turned down a side road toward a hill called Thippadey and the men were ordered to climb down. The trucks left and as they sat by the track, the Khmer Rouge massacred them with rifles, grenades, and mortars, leaving the bodies in red-stained heaps on the ground.

Many more massacres were reported. Not just officers but enlisted soldiers and petty government officials were murdered, sometimes with their entire families. Near Mongkol Borei, a man named Ith Thaim saw ten civil servants and their families, about 60 people in all, methodically stabbed to death on April 27 in a banana plantation. The men were killed first, then their wives, the children last. When the killings were over, Ith Thaim remembered, blood ran "like water on the grass."

After emptying the towns the Khmer Rouge made Cambodia a giant slave-labor camp, guarded by teen-aged soldiers in whom every human impulse seemed stifled except a primitive violence and an unfathomable contempt for weakness. That violence was put at the service of a leadership whose ideological rage only seemed to mount with the number of its victims. While "purifying" the population of all those associated in some way with the Lon Nol regime, the Khmer Rouge also killed those who broke their rules, or complained, or didn't work hard enough, or stole food to keep from starving, or tried to practice banned religious or folk rituals, or for numberless other reasons. When soldiers somehow discovered that one man had a pacemaker implanted in his chest, they were convinced that it was a device to call in enemy bombers—so they cut out his heart.

The Khmer Rouge even tried to kill sorrow. Weeping, said one woman after she escaped to Vietnam, was considered criticism of the regime, and informers crept under the stilts of village houses listening so they could denounce anyone heard sobbing in the night.

For each of the many thousands who died at the hands of the Khmer Rouge executioners, there were more who died of sickness or starvation. But in the empty capital of their ruined land, the leaders of Democratic Kampuchea, as they renamed the country, rebuffed all assistance offered from outside, except for some technical advisers from China. With an insanely exaggerated opinion of their own strength, the Cambodians instead nursed their fanatical hostility toward their former ally, Vietnam—a hostility that led to increasingly serious border battles and finally to a Vietnamese-led tank and infantry invasion that drove the Khmer Rouge out of Phnom Penh at the beginning of 1979, exactly four years after their own final offensive against the Republic began. In their place, the Vietnamese installed a compliant puppet regime under Heng Samrin, after which, in a last gruesome distortion of American values for geopolitical reasons, the United States gave diplomatic support to the ousted butchers.

It was an ending that contained a colossally ironic historical symmetry. Between 1970 and 1975, the United States prolonged Cambodia's war for its own purposes while remaining unforgivably careless of the human tragedy that was occurring there, only to end up having helped to bring its own worst fears to pass: the Communist conquest of Phnom Penh in a holocaust that not even the most alarmist Americans had foreseen. After 1975, the policies of the Khmer Communists made *their* greatest fear self-fulfilling. With all the immense suffering they endured and imposed, they only helped make real the image that had filled them with such violent rage. The Cambodia they left was a wasted, exhausted land that looked on the world with the face of a skull, whose only future was as a Vietnamese protectorate and whose people and culture stood at the brink of physical extinction.

The Fall

Chronology

1974

APRIL

16   Negotiations in Paris between the Saigon government and the Communists on the political provisions of the Paris agreement are suspended by the South Vietnamese delegation.

JUNE

18   A manifesto signed by 301 Catholic clergymen in South Vietnam denounces the Thieu government for corruption and authoritarian rule.

23   Meetings of the Joint Military Commission in Saigon, the agency responsible for administering the military provisions of the Paris agreement, are broken off as the result of a boycott by Communist delegates.

AUGUST

A People's Anti-Corruption Movement is formed in South Vietnam, led by a Catholic priest, the Rev. Tran Huu Thanh.

6   The U.S. House of Representatives votes to reduce military aid to Saigon to $700 million, instead of the previously authorized $1 billion.

9   President Nixon resigns.

20   The U.S. Senate, after narrowly defeating proposals for even sharper cuts, accepts the $700 million military aid appropriation.

SEPTEMBER

8   "Indictment No. 1," a document accusing Thieu and his family of various acts of corruption, is released by the new movement.

SEPTEMBER - OCTOBER

Antigovernment protests are held in Saigon.

OCTOBER

The North Vietnamese leadership approves plans for a major offensive in 1975, with the central highlands region as the "main battlefield."

8   The Provisional Revolutionary Government announces that it will no longer negotiate with the Thieu government.

30   Thieu fires three of his four corps commanders in an apparent effort to placate the anti-corruption campaign. Protesters hold the largest rally of their campaign.

31   Police violently disperse a planned anti-corruption march.

NOVEMBER

1   Thieu promises to ease restraints on the press and political parties, but insists demonstrations will not be allowed to undermine the government.

DECEMBER

13   Government garrisons come under attack in Phuoc Long Province.

1975

JANUARY

6   All of Phuoc Long, including the province capital, falls to the Communists.

8   The North Vietnamese Politburo ends a three-week review of the 1975 campaign plan. It confirms orders for a major offensive in 1975 and for the complete "liberation" of the South in 1976.

28   President Ford requests a $300 million military aid supplement for South Vietnam.

FEBRUARY 27 - MARCH 2

A U.S. congressional delegation visits Vietnam to assess aid needs.

MARCH

10   The Communist offensive opens with an attack on Ban Me Thuot.

12   Ban Me Thuot falls. An attempted counterattack fails.

14   Meeting with his commanders at Cam Ranh Bay, Thieu orders that troops be withdrawn from Pleiku and Kontum—yielding those provinces to the Communists—and brought to the coast to prepare to retake Ban Me Thuot.

16   The withdrawal from the highlands begins. It quickly turns into a panicky, disorganized flight.

19   Government forces, weakened by redeployment of the Airborne Division to the Saigon region, abandon Quang Tri Province in far northern South Vietnam.

24   Quang Ngai and Quang Tin provinces fall to the Communists.

26   The Communists capture Hue, the former imperial capital of Vietnam.

27   Chartered U.S. jets begin flying refugees out of Da Nang, South Vietnam's second largest city.

27   General Frederick C. Weyand, Army Chief of Staff, arrives in Vietnam to assess the situation for President Ford.

28   Anarchy overtakes Da Nang. U.S. ships begin boarding refugees in the Da Nang harbor.

30   Da Nang falls. 90,000 refugees are headed south in U.S. and Vietnamese ships and barges and in fishing boats.

APRIL

1   Qui Nhon, Tuy Hoa, and Nha Trang are abandoned by government forces, yielding the entire northern half of the country to the Communists.

2   The South Vietnamese Senate calls for "new leadership."

4   A U.S. Air Force plane carrying Vietnamese orphans crashes in Saigon. More than 100 children are killed.

8   A defecting South Vietnamese pilot bombs the presidential palace in Saigon.

10   President Ford asks Congress for $722 million in supplemental military aid for Saigon to "stabilize the military situation" in Vietnam.

12   The Communists demand that the U.S. "cease all its aid" to the Thieu government.

21   Thieu resigns; Vice-President Tran Van Huong is inaugurated president.

22   Huong asks for an immediate ceasefire and offers to negotiate "within the framework" of the Paris agreement. The communists reject the offer.

23   President Ford declares that the war "is finished as far as America is concerned."

28   Huong resigns; Duong Van Minh becomes president. Communist pilots in captured U.S.-built aircraft bomb Saigon's Tansonnhut Air Base.

29   A Communist artillery and rocket attack on Tansonnhut makes runways unusable. U.S. begins helicopter evacuation of 1,373 Americans and more than 6,000 Vietnamese from Saigon to Navy ships off the coast.

30   The U.S. evacuation ends. Communist tanks and infantry enter Saigon and capture the presidential palace. President Minh surrenders.

Chapter 9

"A broken sword"

Traveling again through South Vietnam in the second summer of the failed truce, I was seized by a sense of history in reverse. It was, I wrote, "as if the clocks were running backward."

In the cities and villages the American imprint was fading, not just because the GIs were gone but because a severe economic decline was rubbing away the veneer of imported prosperity. The Paris agreement seemed never to have happened. South Vietnamese soldiers were dying in battle at the rate of more than 500 a week, the worst casualty rate the government army had ever had except for the single year of 1972. In southern Quang Ngai Province, in one of the scores of war-scarred villages that lay between the coastal highway and the blue slopes of the Truong Son range, an old farmer squinted across dry brown fields as he first paused at the interpreter's unfamiliar word "ceasefire" and then, with an unintended irony that told much about what had happened to Vietnam's hopes, remembered, "Oh, yes, the time when everybody was fighting over the flags."

In Saigon there had been a few frail efforts to achieve a less warlike appearance. Some of the barbed-wire stanchions and sandbags had been removed from the sidewalks outside government offices. Sentries in their guard towers outside the Doc Lap Palace no longer wore combat fatigues but well-pressed dress uniforms. Yet when I returned to Saigon after some months on assignments elsewhere in Asia, reminders of the continuing bloodshed began before I even checked into my room at the Continental Palace Hotel. At his post on the sidewalk outside, Van Muoi, the driver of a wheezing fifteen-year-old Ford I often hired for trips to the countryside, had turned old and haggard since I had last seen him. "My son," he said, with no

Refugee boats approach U.S. ships off Cam Ranh Bay
(*U.S. Navy photo*).

295

preliminaries as he stepped forward to greet me, "has anyone told you about my son? He was killed at Ben Cat, two weeks ago." There were many days after that when I didn't see Muoi. He was sitting at home, too depressed to work.

In the hotel lobby, the smiling little concierge was at his desk, as usual, when I checked in. But a couple of days later he disappeared. He had been arrested, we learned with amazement, as a deserter. For years, while working in full view of the busiest street corner in Saigon, he had actually been in hiding from the army. The South Vietnamese seldom imprisoned deserters, even long-term ones, because there were too many of them. Sometimes they made them battlefield laborers, assigned to terribly dangerous duties but without being allowed to carry weapons, and with no benefits to their families if they were killed or wounded. Our concierge was fortunate: he was returned to duty in a safe job at the huge base at Bien Hoa. Though he was not allowed off the base, his wife and children were permitted to visit him.

Others weren't as lucky. A young woman I knew lost her brother not long after I arrived. He had overstayed his last leave by five days, telling his family he had a premonition of death. When he returned to his marine unit in Quang Tri, where he had survived the brutal fighting in 1972, he was sent as punishment to a dangerously exposed outpost—and was killed there within a week.

In the bullet-chipped villages of the central coast, where government forces had been on the offensive for most of the previous year, there was now a strong, pervasive unease. A widely-believed rumor had it that a new partition was going to be negotiated, giving a chunk of northern South Vietnam to the Communists in return for a real ceasefire. "Many people, not the wealthy but those who own some property, are selling what they own and moving south," said a local entrepreneur in Hoi An, a province capital south of Da Nang, who had heard the rumor and half-believed it. "I would like to sell my business," he added after a moment, "but I can't find anyone to buy it. If I could, I would sell." The following spring, the partition rumor would reappear with disastrous effect during the spectacular collapse of South Vietnamese resistance.

Because the government troops, receiving less U.S. aid and under orders to conserve ammunition, were using less artillery and air power, some villagers along Highway One were venturing farther into the no-man's-land that began no more than a few hundred yards from the road, braving the former free-fire zones in order to cultivate long-untilled fields. Even after the Viet Cong tax collectors had taken their share, the extra rice was still worth the added danger. At night, though, teen-aged boys were sent to more secure villages to sleep. "Otherwise," a woman explained, "the Viet Cong would come and take them away."

There was fear of their own soldiers, too, which seemed stronger and closer to the surface than I had seen it before—perhaps because poor economic conditions made the soldiers' depredations more harmful. "They are very bad," said a peasant woman bending over a few sparse rows of rice seedlings just outside some strands of rusting barbed wire behind which lay the huge expanse of the American-built Chu Lai Air Base—now almost entirely abandoned. "They rob us all the time," she added. "The people can do nothing because they have guns—we can do nothing but weep." She spoke with sadness but also with an undefeated dignity that would remain in my mind as the most notable trait of millions of ordinary Vietnamese who struggled to live in the midst of endless war and cruelty. A widow with two children, she had received no pension when her husband died, even though he was a government militiaman. The reason, she explained, was that he died of illness, not in combat. Nor had she received any compensation for being evicted from her land—the same she was now tending—when Chu Lai was built. Farmers whose land was actually in the base were paid, but hers was outside; it remained her property, but for years she could not farm it because it lay in the area cleared for defensive fire.

While the Americans were still using the base, she had worked in one of its kitchens; but since the Americans left, she had been unable to find another job. She and her children gathered and sold firewood to survive. "Our life is very hard now," she said. When we asked about the liberation front and its activities in the area, she shook her head. It was not the Communists but the ghosts, she said with a shy smile, who frightened her. "The Americans destroyed many graves when they came here," she explained. "Now there are too many ghosts. . . ."

The road across An Giang Province in the western delta, paralleling the south bank of one of the Mekong's main channels, was perhaps the most peaceful in all of South Vietnam. Along its length were no shattered villages, no outposts, and little military traffic. Guards were posted on bridges, as elsewhere in the country, but they sat in flimsy wooden shelters, not in sandbagged bunkers. Except at a very few, no one had bothered to string the customary upstream wire-and-bamboo barriers against floating mines. No one was going to blow up the bridges anyway. An Giang was the most secure province in the country. It was the home of the Hoa Hao religious sect, which fought its own private war with the Communists in the 1940s after Viet Minh assassins killed its leader, turning the sect permanently and bitterly anti-Communist. The province also had a large number of Catholic refugees from North Vietnam, who if possible were even more hostile to the Viet Cong than the Hoa Hao. As a result, the liberation front for years undertook almost no political or military activity there.

Yet if the war was distant, it still reached out for An Giang's young men. There had never been any fighting in Binh An, a Catholic hamlet, the village priest said. But he held five to seven funerals every year for hamlet youths killed in the war. This in a place with a population of only 6,000 to 7,000; if Washington, D.C., suffered proportionate casualties it would have meant 500 to 700 deaths a year. "For a while we hoped the ceasefire would mean our young men would not go away and be killed any more," one woman said. "But it has gone on just the same."

For every youth killed there were others—there was no way of knowing how many—who were in hiding, sometimes for years, from the draft.

"The only time the government soldiers come here is when they come looking for draft evaders," one villager said. "Sometimes they come just once and go away again, sometimes they come every day for one or two weeks. They might catch one or two men, sometimes none." Though many of Binh An's youths succeeded in staying out of the army, a price was still paid. "When they have to hide, they cannot leave their houses to work," a woman explained, "so it is hard for their families." A few miles farther on, in another riverbank village just across the border in Chau Doc Province, the local Hoa Hao leader agreed unhesitatingly that despite the sect's anti-Communist history and sentiment, most of the young men tried to avoid being drafted, and many did so.

"A few volunteer for the army, especially if they are very poor, but not very many," he said. "The rest—when the soldiers come and catch them, they go. When the soldiers don't come they don't go. But they can't catch them all, because there are so many." He spoke as a peasant might of some nonhuman menace—a tiger, or a typhoon. Around him, squatting on the packed earth floor of his house, other villagers nodded, murmuring their agreement.

Later I asked a Vietnamese friend if there were any disgrace in dodging the draft. She looked at me in amazement. "It's like eating," she finally answered, "it's something you do to stay alive, that's all. There's no disgrace in eating, is there?"

In the delta, as I had found elsewhere, though no dramatic changes had yet occurred on the battlefields, there was a despondent feeling that the tide was running against the government forces. In one district of Chuong Thien Province, it was said that one-third of all the Peoples Self-Defense Force members had been killed or wounded during the past year. Whether it was true or not, the fact that residents believed and repeated it was an indication of their mood. In Vinh Tuong, where I had also visited a few months after the now-forgotten truce, the orchards were still sown with Communist mines and inaccessible, and the sense of weariness and defeatism seemed far deeper than I remembered.

"Some of our boys go to the other side when they reach draft age," one of the villagers said. At times their families went with them. "If the parents are too old to work, or sick, or if they have no other sons, then they will all go to the Viet Cong. . . . No one blames them for that, the people mind their own business." As I prepared to leave, the local cabinetmaker said sadly: "I don't know about the more secure areas of the country, but here it seems it will go on like this forever. The people just live day by day. They don't think about the future."

Like a bit of alien flotsam washed up on a hostile beach, the Provisional Revolutionary Government delegation still sat in its barbed-wire-ringed compound deep inside Tansonnhut Air Base. Two days after Richard Nixon resigned the presidency of the United States, I joined my colleagues from the dwindling Saigon press corps to ride an olive-drab Vietnamese army bus out to the compound for the P.R.G.'s weekly Saturday morning press conference.

"It does not matter if there is a change of one figure in the presidency of the U.S. . . . The question of peace or war in South Vietnam depends on whether or not U.S. policies change," said Col. Vo Dong Giang, the P.R.G. spokesman. The rest of the press conference was a familiar, mind-numbing recital, the mirror image of the daily litany of Communist sins that was read each afternoon by the South Vietnamese government spokesmen downtown. "The Nguyen Van Thieu administration continues to step up its acts of war. . . . It has carried out indiscriminate bombings against populated areas inside the areas controlled by the P.R.G. . . . In two days more than 300 civilians have been killed or injured. . . . In defense of the property and lives of the population, and to preserve the Paris agreement, the liberation forces of South Vietnam and the people have dealt new punishing blows to the Nguyen Van Thieu armed forces."

It had been more than a year since I had last been at Camp Davis, but the words hadn't changed. Neither had anything else. The same photos of Liberation Front leaders still hung on the walls of the old wooden barracks where the briefings were held. The same packages of harsh North Vietnamese cigarettes and the same bottles of watery orangeade were set out on the tables.

Afterward I lingered a moment to ask Colonel Giang if his assignment hadn't become boring, since the Joint Military Commission wasn't carrying out any of the tasks it was supposed to perform. "Oh no, no, not at all," he assured me, his delegation was not bored. "We have our work, we are very busy." But what, I asked again, did he and his associates do all day?

"Oh," he replied vaguely, "we must listen to the radio, and we make our reports—we must make many reports. . . ."

To the continuing misery of war, 1974 added the hardships of an economic crisis that was comparable, in its effects, to the Great Depression of the 1930s in the United States.

Unemployment was estimated at nearly one million, about one-fifth of the civilian work force. Living costs nearly doubled in a year and a half: 65 percent inflation in 1973, 27 percent in the first six months of 1974. Since 1971, official statistics showed, real per capita production had fallen by one-fourth. U.S. embassy economists calculated that in Saigon, the average soldier or civil servant, whose wage increases since 1972 offset less than one-quarter of the rise in the cost of living, no longer earned enough for the minimum necessities of food, clothing, fuel, and housing. He could survive only if he had a second job, stole, or had another wage earner in his household. A soldier's buying power was reduced by more than a third between March 1972 and February 1974; it was estimated now at less than one-fourth what it had been in 1964.

Hardships were similar everywhere. In Da Nang, the poorest people— poor laborers and unemployed fishermen and their families—could no longer afford to boil rice, but had to cook it into a watery gruel to make it stretch further. Acute distress was reported even in the Mekong Delta, where, because it was the chief food-growing region, living standards were normally much better than in other regions of the country.

"Soldiers and low-ranking civil servants earning salaries of 20,000$VN or less per month"—about $36, at the exchange rate then in force—"do not have enough to support their families," reported the U.S. consulate-general in Can Tho, the delta headquarters. The consulate also found that "some school teachers have been seen driving pedicabs. Some wives who previously did not work now sell papers and cigarettes on the sidewalks for extra money. Soldiers and policemen drive cyclos in their off-duty hours and some RD [Rural Development] cadre work as laborers. Government services are frequently sold and absentee rates are high," with damaging results for government effectiveness: "Unwilling part-time soldiers and bureaucrats can rarely be counted upon to provide either good security or good government services." Another indication of hardship was an 11 percent decline in primary school enrollment, which fell by 126,000 students in the seventeen delta provinces. The main reason, along with poor security in some areas, was the rising cost of living, which put school fees and books beyond the reach of many villagers and also meant that more children had to find some form of casual employment to help their families survive.

The economic crisis devastated military morale. In 1973, cash allowances were substituted for soldiers' monthly rice rations, and since the cash bought less rice each month the switch amounted to a severe pay cut. Among Regional Force troops, it was estimated, a soldier's monthly salary actually supported him for only about a week. This affected "tactical performance, as well as morale," reported the U.S. Defense Attache Office, because so many men worked at other jobs and were unavailable for military duties. In February 1974, in its regular quarterly assessment of the armed forces, DAO noted that South Vietnamese commanders were

virtually unanimous in stating that no soldier can adequately support
his family on his pay and allowances. For example, a sergeant with
14 years service makes US$25 a month, not including family allow-
ance (maximum of US$9.50 for a wife and at least 4 children). The
cost to feed one person averages about 400 piastres a day, or $23 a
month. Moonlighting, theft or corruption become necessities for
survival. . . . Commanders in MR [Military Region] 1 freely admit
that they cannot keep sufficient ponchos, entrenching tools, mechanic tool kits, etc. on hand, because the soldiers, whose families are
in desperate need, sell these items on the black market to buy food.
Others commit criminal acts.

Another DAO report noted that increasingly, soldiers "leave restaurants
without paying, steal livestock, and . . . pilfer goods and money from
travelers. . . . Commanders have been able to impose only 30 days restriction, which most troops view as a respite from duty."

Though such depredations had always occurred, for interlocking reasons
they were now a worse problem than ever before. More soldiers stole
because they could not live on their pay; civilian victims resented the thefts
more because they too were suffering hardships, and commanders were
reluctant or unable to punish offending troops because there were too many
cases, or because they sympathized with their men's needs, or because many
soldiers, if unable to supplement their pay by stealing or looting, would just
desert and thus would be unavailable for duty at all. As discipline deteriorated, drug use and drunkenness increased while absence without leave or
even desertion often went unpunished.

Surveys carried out for DAO reported that 92 percent of enlisted men and
junior officers thought their pay and allowances were inadequate, 80
percent felt standard rations were insufficient, half had insufficient clothing,
and 40 percent had inadequate housing. Summarizing one set of findings, a
DAO official concluded, "It is quite clear that RVNAF [Republic of Vietnam
Armed Forces] personnel are forced to live at less than reasonable sub-
sistence levels, and that performance and mission accomplishment are
seriously affected." The "deterioration of performance . . . cannot be
permitted to continue," he added, "if RVNAF is to be considered a viable
military force."

South Vietnam's depression was related in part to the worldwide economic dislocation that followed the Arab oil embargo of late 1973 and the
consequent quadrupling of oil prices. But Vietnam's economy was already
on a downward skid, and thus the effects of the global recession were doubly
severe. Two factors contributed to the decline. One was the rice shortage of
1972, caused by poor harvests throughout Asia, which sharply increased the
price of Vietnam's staple food. The second was the U.S. troop withdrawal.
Closing American bases wiped out about 300,000 jobs while drastically
reducing what one Saigon cabinet minister wryly called "our tourist reve-

nue"—wages paid to Vietnamese workers, purchases of food and other supplies for U.S. installations, and money spent by GIs and civilians for servants, souvenirs, taxis, drinks, prostitutes, and everything else. In 1971 South Vietnam had earned about $400 million a year from the U.S. presence; by 1974, American spending had shrunk to less than $100 million.

Evidence of the depression lay in Saigon's streets, where the armies of motorbikes and racketing scooterbuses were noticeably depleted by soaring gasoline prices. The city's fleet of decrepit blue-and-cream minitaxis no longer cruised but waited for fares at curbside. Growing numbers of vendors, beggars, pimps, and whores roved the sidewalks.

From my hotel room window, I could see a perfect symbol of what had befallen the economy: the news vender whose post was in front of the popular Café Givral, opposite the old government press center where the daily news briefings were held. A couple of years earlier, when scores of American and European reporters frequented the briefings, he used to sell a full armload of the *Saigon Post* and *Pacific Stars and Stripes* every day in the briefing room, wading through the crowd handing out his papers without stopping to make change. Unerringly, he kept dozens of accounts in his head and used to settle up with us later when we passed his corner singly and he had more time. Now, most of his customers were gone. When he saw a prospective buyer, he would trot halfway up the block or dash recklessly into the Tu Do Street traffic, waving his papers anxiously over his head.

The economic crisis was a powerful element in a malaise that hung over the city like the steamy monsoon heat. "The people seem indifferent, they seem ready to bear all that happens," said the gentle, scholarly Nguyen Van Huyen, the former Senate president, when I called at his modest home at 151 Hong Thap Tu Street. "In fact the people are very angry . . . the economic situation is very difficult, but if the government had the confidence of the people it could take measures to improve matters. But there is no confidence because of corruption, because of other bad things."

We spoke in his cluttered study, under a portrait of Pope Paul VI. In retirement since resigning his Senate seat in January to protest the tactics used to pass a constitutional amendment allowing President Thieu a third term, Huyen was no longer politically active, but he remained an adviser to a group of liberal Catholic assemblymen who vainly opposed the regime's growing authoritarianism and corruption. Huyen was tired and pessimistic in the summer of 1974. In words that would later seem prophetic, he observed:

> These points on our side could lead to a very bad situation. First is the economy, second is corruption, third is the inaction of the government to improve our situation. The people don't have the essentials of life, they spend all their days just seeking their living, and naturally

they seem indifferent to politics. But I feel if the government continues this way we could have a surprise one day, a very bad surprise.

If any such worries existed in the American government, they were not publicly expressed. Instead, for most of 1974, and during the entire period when Congress was considering the 1975 aid program, Washington's official attitude was one of relentless optimism about Vietnam. Depicting the ceasefire as a relative, if not unqualified, success, administration spokesmen also characterized the Saigon government and its army as strong, confident, and effective. Far from acknowledging any erosion, Henry Kissinger spoke in one congressional hearing of "the gains for peace and stability" which it was now the U.S. objective to "consolidate." To another committee, he claimed that Saigon's military strength was sufficiently formidable to make its conquest "not an easy assignment for Hanoi."

Kissinger's colleague, Defense Secretary James Schlesinger, suggested that the Communists were being deterred by Saigon's strength from undertaking a major military effort. "At the present time," he said in June, "we do not put a high probability on an all-out offensive. . . . The armed forces of South Vietnam are giving an excellent account of themselves when there are flare-ups of hostilities. . . . To many who observed the ARVN of six or seven years ago, the account they are now giving of themselves is splendid."

Lesser officials were equally cheery. "South Vietnam is stronger militarily and politically than ever before," said Assistant Secretary of State Robert Ingersoll, "and it has excellent long-range prospects for economic self-sufficiency." Robert Nooter of AID, testifying on the administration's proposed economic assistance program, declared; "Never have I seen the present government look stronger, more competent, and more able to deal with the problems it is facing than now." The Pentagon's Dennis Doolin also brought encouraging news. "From the visits I have made to Vietnam, one quite recently, I have come away nothing but encouraged."

To another committee Doolin repeated one of Ambassador Graham Martin's pet theories that only the aging ideologues in North Vietnam's leadership were still committed to the war, and that younger "technocrats" would prove more flexible when they eventually succeeded to power in Hanoi. "I would think that there will come a point," Doolin said, "when the North Vietnamese leadership, looking at the needs of their own people as well as looking at the strength of the Republic of Vietnam, will realize that the best thing to do is to abide by the peace agreement, to have elections under international supervision, and to turn the competition into a political one, rather than a military one."

Not all his listeners were convinced. One of them, Representative Patricia Schroeder of Colorado, bluntly expressed the skepticism many felt. "I just have a feeling," she told Doolin, "you believe in the Tooth Fairy."

To deflect congressional impatience at the seemingly endless demands of the war, the administration insisted that U.S. aid would not be needed forever. While requesting $750 million in economic aid for the 1975 budget—nearly twice the 1974 program—the administration also prepared charts purporting to show that if aid continued at that level for only two or three more years, it could be ended or reduced to marginal sums after 1980. To reach that conclusion, however, projections had to be made that were transparently and ludicrously unrealistic: a sixfold increase in South Vietnam's export earnings, for instance, and a ninefold increase in aid from non-U.S. sources. No one in the administration deemed it necessary, evidently, to burden busy congressional minds with the knowledge that in the real world, neither of those assumptions appeared to have the slightest chance of coming true. In Saigon, though, where AID economists had produced the necessary charts after being told in advance what conclusions they must reach, there wasn't much pretense about them. The figures, one AID official acknowledged, didn't represent a considered forecast, but "an expression of hope."

Of all Saigon's cheerleaders in the American government, none was more indefatigable than Ambassador Martin. Vietnam's prospects were as good or even better than in the most successful Asian economies, Martin assured the Senate Foreign Relations Committee. "All the essential conditions are present in South Vietnam for an economic breakthrough along the lines achieved in Taiwan and South Korea, and in an even shorter time frame." Acknowledging temporary difficulties, Martin then pictured a national mood that would have been recognizable to few Vietnamese or foreigners familiar with conditions there. "The immediate, short-range economic picture may look unfavorable," he said, "but its very severity has, up to this point, contributed to the political unity, as all Vietnamese have tightened their belts. There has been no panic, no political unrest, but a steadfast, pervasive determination to surmount this latest obstacle to their goal of a better life, in freedom, for themselves and their children."

The author of that statement was also the author of some of the more startling episodes in modern American diplomacy.

In a service often criticized for making blandness and circumspection its chief virtues, Graham Anderson Martin was seldom circumspect, never bland. Arriving in Saigon in July 1973, a few months before his 61st birthday, he brought with him from previous ambassadorships in Thailand and Italy a reputation for controversy and abrasiveness. Partly disabled and still in pain from injuries in an automobile accident some years earlier, Martin had also suffered other personal tragedies, including the death of his adopted son, a helicopter pilot, while serving in Vietnam. Graham Martin was not one of those men softened by tragedy, however. Instead, he held his views with dogmatic passion and expressed them with a self-righteousness that sometimes verged on megalomania.

For those with a sense of history, Martin offered some striking reminders of Patrick J. Hurley, the American ambassador to China at the end of World War II who became one of the most fervent advocates of the moribund Chiang Kai-shek government, then on the brink of civil war with its Communist challengers. Hurley, wrote the historian Barbara Tuchman, "was a man whose conceit, ambition, and very vulnerable ego were wrapped up in his mission to the point of frenzy. . . . [When] he found Chinese affairs resisting his finesse, depriving him of the diplomatic success he had counted on, he could find an explanation only in a paranoid belief that he was the victim of a plot by disloyal subordinates. He did not consider that there might be a Chinese reason." Except that Graham Martin found disloyalty in the press and among other critics who he considered poisoned the mind of Congress, rather than among his subordinates, those lines could apply perfectly to him, three decades after Hurley—evidence, perhaps, that even that much time had not taught the American foreign policy bureaucracy needed lessons about Asian revolution.

Martin had a habit of issuing rather extravagant assertions of his own wisdom and trustworthiness—not realizing, apparently, that they often made him sound not persuasive but defensive and blustering. When one senator wondered about the objectivity of the embassy's reports to Washington, Martin wrote in reply:

> For more than the forty years I have spent in the service of the people of the United States the one asset I have prized most highly is a reputation for complete and total integrity. It is a deserved reputation for I have flatly refused either to equivocate or evade reporting and saying what I believed to be the exact truth. . . . This fact is too widely known to be open to serious question and will be completely evident to historians when the archives containing all my reports are finally open.

Offstage, Martin could be gracious—but he could also be intimidating. His eyes "could open an oyster," his defense attache, Maj. Gen. John Murray, once said. Despite his physical infirmities, he worked brutally long hours—but by preference with paper, not people. Seldom leaving the embassy complex, he saw very little of the country whose cause he espoused so fervently or of the huge staff that worked under him. God, one embassy aide called him: "I know he exists, but I haven't seen him." He spent little time with American representatives who worked in the countryside outside Saigon; I knew one foreign service officer who spent months as acting chief of one of the U.S. consulates-general without ever meeting the ambassador at all.

Martin habitually paid little attention to the State Department hierarchy above him, either. Instead, to the great annoyance of some of his superiors, he preferred to deal directly with the White House, even on rather trivial administrative matters. "I represent the President of the United States," he repeated at every possible opportunity—a self-concept that may contain a clue to his actions, for Martin seemingly came to regard himself as the president's word made flesh, the embodiment of Richard Nixon's and later Gerald Ford's promises not to allow South Vietnam's defeat. He did not spend long in Saigon before emerging as the truest of true believers in the South Vietnamese cause, or at least giving that appearance, whether or not it reflected his real beliefs; a "sense of theater," he once confided, was an essential part of diplomacy. One of the principal duties he imposed on himself was to answer all criticisms of the Saigon regime, which he took to be inspired by a global Communist propaganda apparatus that for efficiency, pervasiveness, and "sheer perfection of technique," he once said, "has no parallel in recorded history." From the embassy, Martin regularly cabled to Washington his own answers to Saigon's critics, whom he normally denounced as dupes or disloyal or worse. The *New York Times,* he once said, was controlled by editors "whose emotional involvement in a North Vietnamese victory is transparent." On another occasion he suggested that Senator Edward Kennedy's staff, if not Kennedy himself, represented a willing spearhead for "those whose objective it is to aid Hanoi" by reducing aid to Saigon. It does not seem to have occurred to Martin that those so accused might take offense. He found his own statements so self-evidently true, apparently, that only those with ulterior motives could fail to agree.

At times, Martin chose to debate his opponents directly, instead of going through his superiors in Washington. One of his more remarkable communications was addressed to the Reverend George W. Webber of the New York Theological Seminary, a member of an antiwar delegation that visited the Saigon embassy in January 1974. Among many other points that he made at great length (his message to the State Department recapitulating the discussions ran something like 15,000 words, enough to fill 40 or more pages of the average published novel), Martin unsuccessfully asked the group to call the Communist truce delegations in Saigon to urge acceptance of a proposed ban on indiscriminate shelling. On March 19, two months after the delegation left Saigon, a Communist mortar barrage hit a school in the Mekong Delta, and Martin promptly sent Webber a shocking set of photographs of the children who died or were terribly wounded. The attack killed 32 children, Martin wrote in an accompanying letter,

> and more than fifty others were wounded, some horribly maimed by the precise kind of weapon I begged you to use your undoubtedly

great influence with Hanoi to secure their agreement not to use. . . .
For the rest of your life, you will have to live with the unresolveable
doubt that, but for your decision not to call, these dead children
might still be alive, and these horribly maimed children might still be
whole. . . . Your responsibility for these children must rest between
you and God. But I am only an imperfect mortal and . . . I find it
impossible to either forget or forgive that, in the case of these children, when I asked you to assist in achieving the cessation of the use
of the weapons which killed and maimed them, you wouldn't even try.

An outraged Webber wrote back that he was astonished and angered at
the suggestion that his "influence" might somehow have prevented the
deaths. With his letter he returned half the photographs Martin had sent
him. The rest, he said, he would place on his office wall "until the war ends
as a tragic reminder that I share the guilt of my people. I hope you will do the
same."

If Martin's public polemics produced some embarrassment, a more serious charge against him was that within the government his reports to Washington distorted Vietnamese realities, concealing the Thieu regime's weaknesses and leaving policy makers with faulty perceptions of their ally's
strength and effectiveness. Senate investigators, after comparing reports
from U.S. province representatives with those eventually passed on to
Washington, concluded in 1974 that "the thrust of information submitted
from the field to Saigon is sometimes altered and . . , on occasion significant information is withheld altogether"—always in ways that made the
situation appear more consistent with the needs of U.S. policy. Another
congressional inquiry reported that when an embassy officer used "established State Department dissent procedures" to question the accuracy of
certain reports, Martin "responded with a personal attack on the officer's
loyalty."

Martin controlled the embassy's reporting through senior subordinates
who had the reputation of yes-men, unlikely to press information or opinions that conflicted with the ambassador's own. The result was a "closed
atmosphere" that left lower-echelon officials "stymied," one Defense
Attache Office staff member wrote, especially when anyone questioned
South Vietnamese military effectiveness. And a member of the DAO intelligence staff told a congressional inquiry after the war that because the U.S.
mission "considered itself a beleaguered camp" under threat from dissenters
in its own ranks and in the Washington bureaucracy and especially from a
"negative" press, reports that might lead to additional criticism of Saigon
were discouraged. Instead, there was a tendency "to compensate for sometimes misleading media coverage by presenting information on Vietnam in a

positive . . . light. The net result of this policy was to lull Washington level officials into a false sense of security concerning Vietnam."*

Martin responded sulphurously to suggestions that his reporting to Washington was faulty or distorted. The "verdict of dispassionate historians," he insisted, would be that he was as unfailingly right as he always said he was. If unfavorable material was excised from widely distributed reports, to prevent leaks to the press or unsympathetic members of Congress, Martin claimed that his more highly classified "back channel" messages to the White House described the situation with "all the warts showing." Some of those messages were shown to State Department examiners who conducted an extensive evaluation of the Saigon embassy in 1975, and "to some extent," one of the team said later, they were more candid than less secure messages, as Martin claimed. Still, the examiner said, the quality of information reaching Washington from Martin's staff "did concern us. . . . Normal reporting which came to the department, to the desk officers, to the assistant secretary, showed really just one side." The inspection team's overall assessment of the embassy's reports was "pretty harsh," he added, while its report sharply criticized other aspects of Martin's diplomacy and management as well. According to those familiar with its contents, the evaluation as a whole was one of the most damning ever written about a major American embassy.

It was not just his own government that Martin was accused of misleading. Some, including his defense attache, General Murray, believed he misled South Vietnam's leaders much more disastrously, by dogmatically repeating presidential promises of adequate support long after congressional

* The officer, Col. Henry A. Shockley, claimed that on several occasions, damaging information was "edited out" of intelligence reports. This is disputed by Col. William Le Gro, the DAO intelligence chief, who recalled years later that while sensitive reports were shown to Martin before being forwarded to Washington, "there wasn't any attempt to edit anything that came from the field that I know of. . . . I never felt we were being censored." DAO's reports from late 1973 on frequently stressed the loss of morale in the government army as the result of economic hardship and heavy casualties. DAO also noted from time to time, in unsparing language, such problems as corruption or social injustice in the army. If anyone was misled about the war, Le Gro thought, it wasn't because of distorted reports from Saigon but because Washington wouldn't listen. "I have the impression that policy makers at the highest level in Washington didn't want to hear, didn't want to believe what we were telling them. . . . They had no possibility of helping anyway," Le Gro told me in 1981. If there was a major distortion in DAO's reports, it was that, following the South Vietnamese reporting system, no battles were ever attributed to ceasefire violations by the government. The Vietnamese command's assumption was that whenever combat occurred, the government forces "had the right to be in the particular area. . . . and any resulting firefight was a violation attributed to enemy encroachment," said the U.S. Army's quasi-official ceasefire history—written by Colonel Le Gro—while shelling or bombing Communist targets was justified as a "response to a clear threat or to a prior violation." These assumptions led to a "certain amount of distortion," the army history acknowledged, but they were nonetheless mirrored in DAO's reports, which thus implicitly justified all actions by government forces.

approval of the administration's aid proposal was clearly in doubt, and while Murray was desperately trying to prepare the Vietnamese military command for the leaner times he saw ahead. Murray was particularly upset by the way Martin interpreted a letter President Ford sent to Nguyen Van Thieu the day after he succeeded Nixon as president. Attempting to allay Vietnamese concerns over adverse congressional votes on the aid plan, Ford wrote that the American legislative process was complicated, and he added, "Although it may take a little time, I do want to reassure you of my confidence that in the end our support will be adequate." Martin told the Vietnamese that the letter meant they would eventually get the full amount of aid the administration had proposed, a "basic contradiction," Murray told his military superiors, of his own warnings to Vietnamese commanders that they were going to have to find ways to manage with less aid.

Not surprisingly, Thieu and his colleagues believed Martin. Thieu "thought perhaps in his mind that if the U.S. ambassador in Saigon showed no visible signs of concern, the situation could not be hopeless," one associate recalled; Thieu even speculated on occasion that the administration's troubles in Congress might be "fake," for some inscrutable American reason. The South Vietnamese leaders could not easily contemplate reductions in the support they had depended on so long, and they were used to believing American assurances—just as they also believed statements by Martin and others that the aid cuts would be fatal, a belief that to some extent made the prediction self-fulfilling. Having been deceived by their ally's representative and by their own hopes, the Vietnamese were crushed when Congress voted and they finally understood that they had been wrong. The realization, a senior Vietnamese commander later wrote, had "the effect of a gigantic concussion bomb"—a shock that might have been less severe if Martin's assurances of support had been less fulsome.

By the time Vietnam's final crisis began to take shape, Martin's credibility was under serious attack from many directions. The crackpot optimism that filled his public statements was increasingly in conflict with other perceptions that South Vietnam was hard-pressed, tired, and dispirited. Martin's strident adoption of Saigon's interests and arguments as his own was raising eyebrows in Congress. One congressional visitor, Representative Donald Fraser of Minnesota, left "with the impression that the American embassy . . . perceives the interests of the Thieu government and the United States as identical," a premise, he thought, that risked "distorting the true American interest" in Vietnam. Obviously the U.S. and Saigon shared many policy goals, Fraser felt, but not all. "As long as the American embassy in Saigon proceeds in lock-step with the Thieu government, it will be difficult to discern the true nature of U.S. interests. . . . The mission of any embassy is to represent its own government to the host government. Leaving Saigon, one cannot escape the impression that to a large extent the

American embassy there is representing the government of South Vietnam."

Others in the same delegation, which visited Saigon in late February and early March of 1975, were so disturbed by their encounters with Martin that for a time they considered formally recommending his removal. "A summary of the feeling might be that Ambassador Martin's position is indistinguishable from the [Saigon] government's and that more objectivity is needed," a delegation staff aide told reporters. The idea was eventually overtaken by events. But the fact that it was even considered reinforced a feeling that Martin had become a liability, not an asset, in the administration's effort to lobby for more assistance for Vietnam.

By then time had already grown very short for the Saigon regime. In his last weeks in the South Vietnamese capital, while resistance to the Communists crumbled, Martin would add a few last bizarre paragraphs to the record of his ambassadorship, refusing until the final hours to admit that the cause he espoused so passionately, and with such evident involvement of his own ego, was lost. His show of confidence, he later implied, was part of the "theater" he had listed as among a diplomat's necessary abilities. But there remained a powerful impression that the man most successfully deceived by his stagecraft was Martin himself.

Of all Washington's misperceptions of Vietnamese realities, the most extraordinary was not the result of Martin's bowdlerizing. Instead, it was an apparently unintentional but grotesque mistake—one that led the U.S. administration to believe until late 1974, and until well after the reduced aid bills had been passed by Congress, that the level of combat in Vietnam was much lower than it actually was.

The error had to do with the truest index of war: the shedding of soldiers' blood. Among voluminous other reports, the Defense Attache Office regularly informed Washington of South Vietnamese battle deaths—a statistic, unlike the nebulous body count of claimed enemy dead, for which accurate information could be assumed to be available. But incredibly, for more than a year and a half after the ceasefire, DAO's reports of "friendly" casualties were not just wrong, but wildly so. Actual losses were about twice as high as those reported to Washington.

The error was, in effect, a bookkeeping mistake. DAO received from the Vietnamese command and passed on to Washington casualty figures that were taken from the daily operational reports of South Vietnamese units in the field. These, however, were only preliminary counts. Because of battlefield confusion, delayed messages, slow communications between administrative headquarters and hospitals, and often because of commanders' reluctance to admit heavy losses, about half of all battle casualties were listed only in later, revised reports—which DAO did *not* transmit. Unhappily, the faulty reporting coincided with the administration's political interest in claiming some degree of success for the ceasefire it had negotiated and imposed on an unwilling ally. Even the erroneous casualty totals were bad enough: nearly 20,000 South Vietnamese soldiers killed in the first eighteen months of the truce. But U.S. officials, using the extraordinary 1972 losses to make the most dramatic possible comparison, cited them to claim that the ceasefire had had a significant effect.

There had been "a substantial decrease in the level of hostilities," Henry Kissinger informed Senator Kennedy in March 1974; "for example, military casualties since the ceasefire have been about one-third the level of the casualties suffered in the years preceding the Paris agreement." Early in June, while fighting that cost thousands of casualties on both sides was blazing just north of Saigon, Kissinger was still claiming that the agreement had brought "a substantial reduction of hostilities and casualties" and that fighting was occurring only "on a relatively small scale, especially when measured against what had occurred before the signing of the Paris agreements."

The comparison was repeated by administration witnesses in numerous congressional hearings. Prepared Pentagon testimony to the armed services committees of both the Senate and House claimed that "combat deaths . . . have declined to the lowest level since 1965 and are down 75 percent compared with the rate in 1972." Ironically, that testimony was then played back as a justification for cutting aid. The Senate committee, recommending that the military aid authorization be cut from the proposed $1.45 billion to $900 million, declared that it accepted the need to keep supporting South Vietnam's armed forces, but it simply didn't believe the administration's projected requirements for equipment and munitions. "Since combat casualties have dropped by 75 percent in the past year, however, it is reasonable to expect that reductions can be made in the previous levels of military assistance."

In fact, however, no such decline in deaths had occurred. In 1973, instead of the 13,786 battle deaths reported by DAO, the South Vietnamese actually had 25,473 men killed, according to official records. This was two-thirds, not one-third, of the 1972 killed-in-action total, and was higher than for all other years except 1968, the year of the Tet offensive. In 1974 the toll was worse. For the first eight months of the year, while Congress was considering the aid legislation, Vietnamese losses were not 9,606 killed, as DAO reported and congressional committees were told, but more than twice as many: 19,375.

Eventually 1974 would be the second-worst year of the entire war for South Vietnam's armed forces, with nearly 31,000 battle deaths. If soldiers' blood was, as General Murray once said, "the gauge of war," then the ceasefire was never a partial success, as its architect Henry Kissinger and his associates claimed. From its first hours, Kissinger's peace was never anything but an illusion.

There is no reason to suppose that DAO's error was exclusively, or even significantly, responsible for congressional decisions on aid levels. Most House and Senate members, no doubt, cast their votes according to broader political judgments that would not have been changed by any single piece of new information. Yet the mistake did seem a mordant metaphor for the long record of American misconceptions in Vietnam. For years, U.S. civilian and military officials had tried to show success by reducing the war to statistics and computer tape, ignoring all its many intangibles. Now, it turned out, for the most emotionally telling statistic of all, numbers that literally meant life and death, the Americans hadn't even managed to count correctly in the first place.

The error was not corrected until October 1974, and then only by accident. A few months earlier, General Murray had begun to suspect that the casualties reported to him in daily briefings by his staff were inconsistent with other reports of understrength units, rising issues of body bags, and overflowing hospitals. Shortly before leaving Saigon in August, Murray asked the Vietnamese general staff for the official casualty records, which he then sent on to his superiors in his end-of-tour report. Those figures, which included all the battle deaths that were not reflected in DAO's earlier reports, were apparently the first accurate casualty statistics to reach Washington in the year and a half after the ceasefire. Murray never realized, however, that his figures conflicted with those being compiled by his own staff. Nor did he know of the administration's statements to Congress that the fighting was significantly reduced. ("No one ever called to my attention," Murray wrote me in 1981, "that what I was saying apparently contradicted other reporting. . . . No one testifying to Congress ever checked beforehand with me, or sent me their testimony later.")

In the Pentagon, where Murray by now had come to be regarded as an alarmist because of his incessant warnings about the effects of the aid cuts, his report was disregarded for weeks because it differed from the casualty statistics supplied through regular DAO channels. But then, by chance, a systems analyst named Thomas Thayer heard about the dispute. Thayer immediately suspected that Murray was right and the other reports were wrong, because remarkably enough, exactly the same issue had arisen much earlier in the war when for a considerable length of time the Defense Department believed that South Vietnamese forces were suffering fewer casualties than U.S. units. The erroneous figures "led one secretary of defense to believe that the Vietnamese weren't carrying their share of the load, and he criticized them harshly," according to Thayer; it was only then, in an effort to answer the criticism, that the reporting system was double-checked and the error found. When the U.S. command was dismantled after the ceasefire and replaced by the much smaller Defense Attache Office, however, the old reporting system was somehow reinstated. Thayer took one look at Murray's statistics and realized that the earlier mistake must have been repeated. He arranged for the DAO staff in Saigon to recheck its data, and it was quickly discovered that he was right. DAO's reports ever since the ceasefire had covered from America's official consciousness, like the uncaring growth of the jungle over a grave, the bones of some 25,000 dead allies.

The Aid Debate (1): "Poor man's war"

Among Vietnam's innumerable controversies, there may be none in which it is harder to disentangle truth from polemics than the question of the sufficiency of U.S. support for the South Vietnamese after the Paris agreement.

"No one knows precisely what the appropriate level of support should be," five House members declared in frustration during the summer of 1974 after listening to exhaustive testimony. Similar doubts seem to have existed in the military bureaucracy as well. "Does anyone really know how much ammunition they need?" Admiral Gayler, the U.S. Pacific commander, asked General Murray shortly before Murray's retirement. Even years afterward no categorical answer seemed possible. Perhaps South Vietnam's actual needs and capabilities weren't really relevant. When its leaders and soldiers, who had followed American guidance for so long, were told by their American associates that they couldn't defend their country with the resources now being made available, they believed—and lost.

The funding squeeze of 1974 developed in several phases. First, Congress refused to raise a legislated $1.126 billion ceiling on military aid for Saigon, while the Pentagon, anticipating a more generous budget, obligated about four-fifths of the money during the first half of the budget year. In addition, Congress specifically required that funds left over from previous budgets had to be charged against the 1974 ceiling instead of being backdated as the administration proposed. This had the effect of denying some $266 million the Pentagon planned to spend under the 1974 budget.

These decisions seemed to reflect more than just weariness with the war and with the unending demand for American support. Attitudes in Congress were also influenced by its suspicions that the administration was trying to evade legislated limits, and thus flout congressional authority, under the cloak of an impenetrably complex bookkeeping system. The Pentagon was handicapped in its presentations to Congress, acknowledged one military historian, "because seemingly no one in any Defense agency knew how much prior year money had been obligated or what supplies and equipment had already been provided." A major cause of confusion was that through Fiscal Year 1974, Vietnam aid was "service funded"—that is, commingled with funds the U.S. spent on its own armed forces, rather than administered as a separately appropriated aid program. Consequently, as a Pentagon official explained, "other than statistical estimates . . . there was no differentiation as to whether bullets shipped to South Vietnam would ultimately be expended by the U.S. army or the South Vietnamese." To make matters even murkier, assistance reached the Vietnamese through no fewer than thirteen different Pentagon accounts. "There is no question," another Defense Department official admitted to a Senate committee, "that our present reporting . . . does not measure up to the usual standards required of a reporting system."

After curtailing the planned 1974 spending, Congress turned to the proposed $1.45 billion military assistance for Fiscal Year 1975. In a series of committee and floor votes beginning in May, the House and Senate first chopped the authorization to $1 billion and then, instead of allowing even that amount to be spent, appropriated a more austere $700 million. The cuts had overwhelming support: the August 6 House vote to cut the appropriation was 233 to 157, and two weeks later in the Senate, an amendment to reduce aid still further to $550 million was beaten by only three votes. No clearer signal could have been sent that the limit of congressional patience had been reached. If the administration read the signal, however, it chose not to acknowledge it or to inform its clients in Saigon. Instead, over the next eight months it sent Congress one futile proposal after another asking more funds—none of which had any apparent chance of passing, but each one arousing Vietnamese hopes that would only turn to greater demoralization with each disappointment.

During the spring and summer of 1974, the Vietnamese had at last begun to economize. Ammunition issues were reduced. Aircraft flying hours and vehicle use were curtailed to save fuel, and so were the use and maintenance of other equipment, such as communications gear. It was ironic that the constraints were imposed just as the battlefield initiative was shifting decisively to the Communist side. In mid-1974, for the first time since the very earliest days of the ceasefire, the South Vietnamese were no longer conducting major offensive operations; just as their American support was running out, they could legitimately claim to be waging war in genuine self-defense, while the Communists were now unequivocally violating the letter and spirit of the peace agreement.

As Congress slashed aid appropriations, something close to a crisis of nerves began to overtake the South Vietnamese command. U.S. officials also were concerned—none more than General Murray.

Approaching the end not just of his tour in Saigon but of a 34-year military career, Murray was in a state of growing despondency. Murray was an emotional man with a short temper and a vinegary tongue but also with a forceful sense of decency and an appealing, uncomplicated loyalty to the Vietnamese soldiers who fought and hungered and died on their numberless battlefields. His opinions on the politics and geopolitics of the war he kept to himself; his job and commitment, he felt, was to keep those soldiers as well supplied and supported as possible. As his ability to do so diminished, his anguish mounted.

Murray's views were shaped not just by eighteen arduous months managing a military assistance program that was shrinking while the threat was growing, but also by his background and training as a logistician in an army where plentiful materiel was taken for granted. In his eyes, Congress was making a simple, immoral trade: saving American dollars by spending Vietnamese lives. He still believed that the South Vietnamese could prevail if they were given adequate support, he told the Defense Department in his last assessment from Saigon, though he also admitted that "hope hallucinates history," and nowhere more than in Vietnam. If support was not adequate, he saw only dire results. He was "apprehensive" at the Communist buildup while U.S. aid lessened, he wrote, recalling "Waterloo, 16 decades ago, where Marshal Ney 'the bravest of the brave' made a final desperate charge and ended up—in frenzied despair—beating a cannon with a broken sword."

On his way back to the U.S. and retirement, he stopped in Hawaii for a last conference with Admiral Gayler. Murray was angry and pessimistic. Aid cuts had left ARVN on a "starvation diet," he warned, and many of its officers and soldiers were beginning to think about their own safety rather than military duties. Even the loyalties of senior commanders could not be taken for granted. All Saigon's generals were veterans of previous coups d'état, Murray pointed out, and could cause a grave crisis overnight if they ever decided to challenge Thieu's leadership.

The military situation he described as precarious, particularly in the Saigon region where, he thought, one more North Vietnamese division was all it would take to tip the balance in the Communists' favor. Most ominous of all, though, were the six combat divisions Hanoi still retained in the North, an enormous danger if they were sent to the battlefield. The sum of Murray's advice to Gayler was the same as in his last assessment to the Pentagon: without adequate support, South Vietnam would lose, perhaps not right away but soon. As their conversation ended, Murray added a final admonition. "Watch those six enemy divisions in the North," he told Gayler. "Watch them like a flute player watches a cobra."

Murray's sense of danger had not yet spread very far through the military bureaucracy, apparently; at least, no inklings seemed to have reached his successor, Maj. Gen. Homer D. Smith, until he began preparing to go to Saigon. Murray was still in Hawaii when he received a phone call from Smith. "I said, 'How are things going?' " Murray remembered. "Homer said, 'I've just finished two days of briefings and Jesus Christ I feel like I've been shot at and hit.' "

It was the usual syndrome, Murray told him. "The further you get away from Washington, the closer you get to reality."

Murray's reality was, certainly, part of the truth. No one who was there could dispute that the South Vietnamese were fighting harder with fewer resources and that their morale was suffering. Silence was the evidence. No longer did the war's heart beat to the regular, spaced thump of harassing artillery fire; shells were now hoarded for actual battle. The sky no longer pulsed, as it once had, to the chopping clatter of gunships or troop-carrying helicopters. Around outposts, one began to see fresh-cut bamboo stakes instead of barbed wire; soldiers strung grenades, instead of the more costly Claymore mines, outside their positions.

Gasoline use was restricted—and with civilian prices sky-high, more of it was undoubtedly stolen and sold on the black market. In populous Binh Dinh, the U.S. province representative reported, legal sales of gasoline for civilian use dropped by two-thirds in 1974 but "surprisingly enough, there has been no appreciable decrease in traffic." Pleiku seemed to be the source of black-market gasoline, he added, noting skeptically that "the fuel leak . . . may explain the 'VC sapper attack' that destroyed fuel storages containing 5 million liters of fuel in that area." Five million liters was approximately the same as the fall in legal gasoline sales. Because of fuel shortages, tanks and armored personnel carriers sat in depots instead of being used in combat. Nearly half of all ARVN's vehicles, it was reported, were ordered put in storage.

There were other realities, though. One was that Saigon's military weaknesses were attributable to other and perhaps more important causes than the aid cuts. And another was that the effects of aid reductions were not as extreme as has since been claimed by those wishing to blame Congress exclusively for Saigon's subsequent collapse.

Aid reductions, for example, were not the only or even perhaps the main reason for the substantial decline in South Vietnam's air power. Aid-related shortages of fuel and spare parts were partly responsible for a decision to put 224 aircraft in storage—which, with approximately 300 more lost in combat or in accidents, represented a loss of about one-fourth of the air force since the ceasefire. It was also true, however, that even if funds had been unlimited, nowhere near all aircraft could have been kept in the air because there were not enough mechanics to maintain them. The Vietnamese, the

Pentagon acknowledged in March 1974, "have not yet reached the point where they can fully maintain their organic aircraft." But the chief cause for the decline of air power was the formidable buildup of Communist air defenses, which by the end of 1974 were considered "comparable to those over North Vietnam," including up to 100 surface-to-air missiles and more than 1,800 antiaircraft guns manned by 33,500 troops.

Important supply routes and bases were now so strongly defended that South Vietnamese planes did not venture over them at all, DAO reported in mid-1974: the antiaircraft threat "prohibited VNAF [Vietnam Air Force] operations over major enemy complexes," and even where planes could fly, they remained at much higher altitudes and were thus less effective in bombing or in reconnaissance. Air resupply had become far more risky, and the use of helicopters had become impossible "except under select circumstances," said a later U.S. Air Force study. Also forced out of the air over many battlefields were the Forward Air Controllers (FACs)—spotters in light aircraft directing bombers or artillery fire.

Other South Vietnamese weaknesses similarly reflected not the loss of aid but their limited ability to operate and maintain the high-technology equipment bequeathed by the Americans. For example, the Vietnamese briefly tried to use the complex sensor system with which U.S. units had monitored infiltration, but they had to quit. Their technical intelligence branch was simply unable to make the system work.

At the heart of the aid debate, however, and also its most obscure question, was the matter of ammunition. Soldiers in the field complained bitterly about reduced fire support, and anyone traveling in the countryside in 1974 could hear that artillery fire was much less than before. Communist assessments recorded the same impression: "Enemy air and artillery support has presently decreased a great deal," said one directive captured by government troops. Just how extensive the reductions were, however, and the extent to which they may have been caused by clumsy management or hoarding rather than by a genuine shortage, remains almost impossible to tell.

A frequently cited statistic was that Saigon's forces in 1974 were using only one-fourth to one-third as much ammunition as at the time of the ceasefire. What that statistic didn't show, however, was that the earlier expenditure was regarded by the Pentagon as wildly excessive, and that the bulk of the reduction was accomplished not when funding restraints began in mid-1974, but in the spring of 1973, long before the aid cuts were imposed. In June 1974, an official Defense Department document called "ARVN Ammunition Constraints" neither cited budgetary restrictions as the reason for lower munitions use nor indicated that military effectiveness was damaged:

ARVN ground ammunition issues now fluctuate between 17 and 22 per cent of the amounts issued at peak ceasefire levels. *The major reduction began in April 1973 following notification to the Vietnamese by U.S. military officials that they would have to bring ammunition down to a reasonable defensive expenditure level* (emphasis added). The Department of Defense . . . has continued to reduce consumption by careful screening of requisitions, audit, inspection, and discussions with the [Vietnamese] Joint General Staff. The Vietnamese have also helped by increasing their security precautions around ammo dumps to reduce the danger of VC sapper attacks. As a result, ammunition consumption since the first of the year [1974] has dropped down still further.

Admiral Moorer, chairman of the Joint Chiefs of Staff, also acknowledged that artillery expenditures had been "inordinate" at times and that the Americans "did place restraints on replacement allowances" to reach a reasonable rate.

What was not clear, however, was what was reasonable. Defense Department statistics were contradictory and confusing—and did *not* support assertions that there were drastic reductions in the summer and fall of 1974. Instead, Pentagon figures showed that ammunition consumption in that period was almost exactly the same as in the last few months of 1973, when there was no talk of constraints and when ARVN was conducting fairly large offensive operations in the upper delta and the coastal lowlands. Meanwhile, in apparent contradiction of the Pentagon's own officially expressed view that the peak rates had been excessive, U.S. planners continued to state that 54,000 tons a month, the amount used during the 1972 offensive, was the necessary "intensive combat rate," while the minimum "theater sustaining rate" was put at 18,000 tons a month, which was approximately the tonnage actually being used in 1974. The original military aid proposal for the year had projected a need for only 16,200 tons a month.

Complicating matters further were suspicions that the Vietnamese were actually using less ammunition than they officially reported. They were exaggerating their consumption, some Americans believed, in order to justify higher requisitions, since resupply was still theoretically bound by the "one-for-one" replacement rule in the ceasefire agreement. In May 1974, Senate investigators reported studies showing that "data being provided to the Defense Attache's Office by the South Vietnamese army did not substantiate the reported firings on which the ammunition requests were based." Uncertainties were multiplied because the Americans themselves didn't know exactly how much ammunition they had already supplied, or what remained in ARVN's depots.

Amid all these ambiguities, it was clear that there was some doubt whether all the Pentagon's assumptions were valid. And even if they were, its logic still rested on the premise that ARVN's doctrines, methods, and deployment would all remain unchanged—meaning not just very heavy use of firepower, but also maintenance of a great many isolated positions that had relatively little military value but depended on artillery (and expensive air resupply, in many cases) for their defense.

Some outposts were given up, particularly small militia positions in the Mekong Delta; the process was politely called "consolidation." The idea of a more significant strategic withdrawal was the subject of vague discussions in ARVN staff meetings during late 1974. The most extreme concept involved yielding nearly all the northern half of the country except for Da Nang and perhaps some of the other coastal cities, so that defenses could be strengthened in the more populous and prosperous regions to the south. But no detailed planning was done, and there is no evidence that any serious decision was ever approached. Instead, the idea vanished into the indecision and lack of strategy that seemed to lie, like an astronomer's black hole, at the core of the Thieu regime. Border surveillance camps, surrounded district capitals, and other outlying enclaves were regarded by Saigon as tokens of its territorial control. Giving them up could not be contemplated even though many of them had become vulnerable and defending them, as one general later acknowledged, required "a sizeable force . . . that could have been better employed in other tasks."

That force was eventually lost, piecemeal, in battles that were as hopeless as they were useless. Thousands of men and mountains of supplies were sacrificed to Thieu's inability to change policy to fit his new circumstances. As the U.S. Defense Attache Office noted in its final review of the war, "The basic defense posture remained unchanged, to maintain control of all territory the GVN [Government of Vietnam] held." That policy, DAO added, "was based primarily on the anticipated appropriation by the U.S. Congress of an additional $300 million," the amount of authorized funds that Congress had refused to appropriate. That hope was a mirage that existed only in Saigon's own wishful thoughts and in the false reassurances it received from its ally.

The truth was that nothing in ARVN's history, training, tradition, or experience prepared it for more austere methods of waging war. Nor was the leadership strong enough to change the system that had been created and nourished by American advice and wealth. A military committee was appointed to write a field manual on the tactics of "poor man's war," but its deliberations, like those on a strategic withdrawal, produced no meaningful results.

The committee members had only experienced "rich man's war," a senior Vietnamese staff officer acknowledged, and even if they had been able to imagine new tactics they saw insuperable problems in imposing any change on their soldiers. The change would be taken as evidence of weakness and would have a "profound effect on troop morale," while it would take time for units to acquire the training and endurance to walk to objectives instead of being flown by helicopter and to carry heavier unprocessed food instead of U.S.-supplied canned rations. Obviously, too, it "would prove far from easy" for soldiers who had grown used to air evacuation of casualties and lavish bombing support to return to man-packed litters or trucks for the wounded or to rely on their own mortars instead of air strikes.

Unable to imagine or enforce meaningful changes in either strategy or tactics, the South Vietnamese leaders fell back on the pipe dream that Congress would restore the funds it had cut from the aid program. Neither the administration in Washington nor the U.S. mission in Saigon counseled against that fantasy. Instead, and in spite of all apparent political realities, American officials from the president on down encouraged Vietnamese hopes. Worse, they also encouraged the Vietnamese in the conviction that without the additional funds, the war would be lost.

In May 1974, U.S. officials and the Vietnamese general staff collaborated in a joint study concluding that even with the full $1.45 billion proposed by the administration, it was questionable whether Saigon could hold against a major Communist offensive. Anything below the 1974 program of $1.126 billion "would seriously affect both the capabilities and morale" of the South Vietnamese armed forces, the study said, and if support were limited to $750 million, the government "would no longer have the capabilities to defend the entire territory under [its] control even if fighting continued at the same level" as in the previous year.

In American political discourse, such predictions are not necessarily meant to be taken literally; a degree of pardonable hyperbole is part of the tradition of Defense Department lobbying in Congress. But to the Vietnamese, the study became part of their doctrine, a basic premise of their strategy that made it even more unthinkable that aid could be denied. Different American advice might have persuaded them to examine what they *could* do with less aid: what territory might be given up, what units might be drawn from exposed or vulnerable positions. This was, after all, one of the implications of the joint study. In mid-1974 there were still space and time to try to adapt to new realities. But the Americans gave no such advice and the Vietnamese shrank from such decisions. Instead, they dithered purposelessly while telling themselves and everyone else what they *couldn't* do with $700 million. In this state of strategic paralysis, already gripped with the premonition of disaster and with no clear-eyed or useful advice from Washington, Saigon awaited the next Communist blows.

For the South Vietnamese, the August 6 House vote to cut military aid was only the first of two shocks. The second, just three days later, was the resignation of Richard Nixon.

To most Vietnamese, including both supporters and critics of the government, Nixon's departure also represented the withdrawal of American patronage from its beneficiary of so many years: President Thieu. Almost as soon as the resignation speech was broadcast, the embassy's Wolfgang

Lehmann called on Prime Minister Tran Thien Khiem to assure him, as a government communique declared, "that the United States would continue its policy of close friendship with and support for the Republic of Vietnam, including continued economic and military assistance." But few Vietnamese were convinced. "The Vietnamese consider America has been the most important supporter of Mr. Thieu, and the most enthusiastic was Mr. Nixon," said one Assembly member. "Now Mr. Nixon is gone and Mr. Kissinger, who is unfriendly to Thieu, is still there."

In Vietnamese eyes, this perception was confirmed by the new president's inability to restore the aid funds Congress had deleted from the budget. Few in Saigon, even among the most sophisticated and well-traveled, really understood the independence of the American legislature. If Congress was slashing the budget, most Vietnamese were sure, it was with the president's connivance and with the intent of signaling that Washington's mandate no longer rested with Thieu. In vain, American diplomats tried to persuade the skeptical Vietnamese that Washington's commitment was unchanged.

"The average Vietnamese, certainly the average military officer, cannot accept intellectually that the president of the United States and his secretaries of defense and state, if these men really want to give this country a supplemental military appropriation, that they can't do it," acknowledged a senior embassy officer. "They read this as the very top echelons of our government deciding that now we've got our troops out and our prisoners back, it's quite all right with us if Vietnam goes down the drain."

To the Vietnamese, President Nixon had embodied the commitment of American power to Nguyen Van Thieu. The economic crisis, battlefield setbacks, and ever deeper war-weariness had eroded Thieu's authority since the Paris agreement, but events in Washington were equally damaging. The thousand cuts of Watergate bled away not just Nixon's power but Thieu's as well. When Nixon at last stepped down, the image of his patronage fell away. It was in no way accidental that within weeks, the South Vietnamese leader was facing the most serious domestic political challenge of his presidency.

"When the glass is full . . ."

The flicker of torches illuminated the shabby, tenement-lined street in a working-class district near Saigon's Tansonnhut Airport. From atop a sound truck, a young man shouted hoarsely into a loudspeaker, "We want a president who serves the people, not a president who steals from the people!" Behind him chants rose, mingling with the eye-stinging smoke from hundreds of flaming kerosene-soaked rags: "Down with corruption! Down with dictatorship!" A life-sized effigy labeled "corruption" dangled from the back of the truck. It bore no other name, but a cigar in its mouth and a blue aviator's baseball cap on its head, both Thieu trademarks, made it instantly recognizable.

For years, no such scene would have been thinkable in Thieu's South Vietnam. But in October 1974, discontent suddenly welled up in a tide of antigovernment demonstrations. At the spearhead was the People's Anti-Corruption Movement, lead by a stocky, chain-smoking Redemptorist priest named Tran Huu Thanh.

The issue was well chosen. The government could not easily suppress the movement without seeming to condone corruption. Nor could it convincingly picture Thanh as a Communist or Communist tool. A consciously old-fashioned figure in plain black cassock and gold-rimmed glasses, the 59-year-old priest was a right-wing intellectual and anti-Communist theorist who had spent twenty years attempting to formulate an ideological counter-weapon for successive governments in Saigon. Thanh was also a regular lecturer at the South Vietnamese War College on the subject of "true anti-Communism." He taught, he later estimated, more than 3,000 officers, many of whom eventually became targets of his anti-corruption campaign.

After emerging as an unexpected protest leader, Thanh still had the mannerisms of an old-style mandarin teacher and intellectual. Speaking slowly and very formally in Vietnamese or flawless French, considering and pronouncing each word precisely through the uptilted cigarette that was invariably held between his full lips, he placed each thought carefully into a well-defined framework of theory, sometimes even snatching up a pen to illustrate his ideas with diagrams. His campaign against Thieu, he argued, was to save the country from Communism, not to undermine the war. The South Vietnamese leadership had still not learned how to form an anti-Communist society. "The French failed, then the Americans, with all their arms, failed," he explained. "And now President Thieu is failing also."

The anti-corruption movement was born in a series of seminars of Catholic lay and religious leaders during the spring of 1974, in which one of the topics was an earlier pastoral letter on corruption. After being urged by some of the participants to "do something concrete," Father Thanh drafted a manifesto for circulation among the clergy who served the potent two-million-member Catholic minority. It denounced not just corruption but the political system that shielded it, declaring that "the constitution and the law have . . . become useless adornments" and that anti-Communism was made "a spell to bind the people to silence" in the face of official abuses. "For more than 25 years," it concluded, "this anti-Communist struggle conducted only at gunpoint has proven ineffective and it will never succeed. It will only prolong the list of sufferings and casualties."

The manifesto, released June 18, was signed by 301 priests. It attracted relatively little attention at the time. But in August, joining with several liberal Catholic political figures, Father Thanh formed the nucleus of an organization, and on September 8, in Hue, he and his associates issued another document called "Indictment No. 1." In the long-suffocated Vietnamese political environment, the paper was explosive. It squarely blamed Thieu for his regime's sicknesses: "The present terrible state of corruption can exist only because the nation's leader himself has protected and initiated it. Corruption . . . robs the people down to their bones, it stabs the soldiers' backs, it undermines the national economy; and it destroys the people's strength to resist. . . . [It is] a betrayal of the people."

Listing specific charges against Thieu and members of his family, the document accused Madame Thieu of skimming profits from contributions she had raised for hospital construction; identified Thieu's brother-in-law as head of a company profiting from illegal speculation in fertilizer; charged that other Thieu relatives misappropriated funds from the government's rice-transport subsidy, causing hungry peasants in central Vietnam to eat "bulbs of banana trees and even cactuses" to keep from starving; and implied that Thieu himself, along with Prime Minister Khiem, profited from heroin smuggling. The indictment also described Thieu's real estate holdings: two houses in Saigon and a villa in Switzerland, though he had the use of at least three houses in the general staff compound, plus hundreds of acres of farmland in various places around the country. As commander-in-chief, the document asked angrily, "does he feel ashamed before his conscience when combatants are lacking rice to eat, clothes to wear and houses to live in—and whose wives sometimes have to sell their bodies in order to feed their children?"

Recalling Thieu's part in the uprising against the Diem regime, the indictment's authors called the "present rotten, dictatorial family regime" worse than the Diems'; it represented "a national disaster and a national shame, a betrayal of all those who have been sacrificing themselves for the hard, protracted struggle of our people and army for more than a quarter of a century. Is this not so?"

Three Saigon dailies, in the most serious challenge to the government's censors in years, printed the full text. Though the papers were immediately confiscated, other copies of the document were reproduced and widely distributed. The anti-corruption cause proved "so popular around the country," one of Thieu's advisers acknowledged, that in a matter of weeks it was transformed into a "vast anti-governmental crusade." The seizure of the three newspapers sparked defiance among the previously docile publishers, and a separate committee was formed to protest press censorship; other protest organizations surfaced under the auspices of leftist and Buddhist critics who had been silent for many years. A "campaign against hunger" protested economic conditions, a leftist movement for the release of political prisoners was revived, and a group associated with the An Quang pagoda— the Buddhist organization primarily responsible for the upheavals of the early 1960s—formed a group called the "National Reconciliation Force" to demand true implementation of the Paris agreement. The leader of the Buddhist group was Vu Van Mau, a cherubic-looking senator who would later be named prime minister two days before Saigon fell to the Communists. Mau and his colleagues spent more time hesitating than acting. Still, however timid, their statements represented the first time since the ceasefire that matters of war and peace were raised in South Vietnam in any terms except Thieu's.

Thieu himself seemed defensive and unsure how to respond to the growing protests. Three weeks after "Indictment No. 1" was issued, he delivered a long, rambling speech promising to crack down on corruption but giving a curiously weak answer to the accusations against himself and his family. "Let me say," he told a nationwide radio audience,

> from the time I was a lieutenant until I became president, let you, compatriots and combatants, feel free to point out to me any corrupt practice on my part, any bribe that I accepted, any time that I traded my prestige, any time I pressured people to pay me in exchange for a promotion. . . . If my relatives or my wife or children are corrupt or violate the law, let the law deal with them. I will not take up their defense or condone them. That is the answer to the charge that I am corrupt and condone corrupt elements among my relatives.

Of the specific accusations in the indictment, Thieu said not a single word.

Small, sporadic demonstrations began. One of them, in mid-October, resulted in a few broken windows at the National Assembly building on Lam Son Square. Thieu answered at first with concessions. On October 24 he dismissed four cabinet members, including his kinsman Hoang Duc Nha, who as commissioner-general for information was regarded as chiefly responsible for harsh enforcement of press censorship laws. Nguyen Duc Cuong, minister of commerce and industry, and Chau Kim Nhan, the finance minister, were sacrificed in response to complaints about the economy. The fourth man, Agriculture Minister Ton That Trinh, had been implicated in the fertilizer scandal. The following day, the defense ministry announced that 377 field-grade officers—256 majors, 101 lieutenant colonels, and 20 full colonels—would be fired for corruption, along with an unspecified number of lieutenants and captains.

The protest movement was emboldened rather than placated. It wanted general's stars, not colonel's rosettes. The demonstrations would go on,

Father Thanh declared, until there was "a change in national policy." The various opposition elements were still disunited: Buddhists and Catholics regarded each other with suspicion, and both kept their distance from overt leftists such as Mrs. Ngo Ba Thanh and the radical priest Chan Tin, who led the political-prisoner campaign. It was clear, though, that the protests had tapped a store of dissatisfaction much greater than even the organizers had realized. "All these various protest movements truly reflect the feelings of the people," said former Senate president Nguyen Van Huyen, while another politician observed: "We are not strong enough to overthrow Mr. Thieu. He still has at his disposal the police, the armed forces and the civil administration. . . . But desperate people are thinking about change, because they are so sure that with Mr. Thieu there is no hope."

On October 30, the president offered the most significant concession he had ever yielded to any political opponents, firing three of his four corps commanders. Lt. Gen. Nguyen Van Toan of II Corps, Lt. Gen. Pham Quoc Thuan of III Corps, and Lt. Gen. Nguyen Vinh Nghi of IV Corps were all relieved and assigned to lesser jobs commanding various training schools. Only the I Corps commander, Lt. Gen. Ngo Quang Truong, one of the few generals to enjoy true popular esteem for his competence and honesty, kept his post. In sacking his corps commanders Thieu for the first time struck at the very top levels of the system. But by now, even that was not enough for the protesters. The campaign "is only beginning," Father Thanh declared to his followers. If that was so, everyone in Saigon understood that only one target remained: Thieu himself.

That night, the movement held its most impressive demonstration yet, a torchlight parade that began at the Tan Chi Linh Church in suburban Saigon and wound for more than an hour through narrow streets past small shops, tenements, and the few girlie bars that still survived of the hundreds that had once catered to GIs from nearby Tansonnhut. The neighborhood was working class and predominantly Catholic. Most of its families were 1954 refugees from the North, and they contributed their sons in disproportionate numbers to elite volunteer units such as the marine and airborne divisions. The signal was unmistakable: if Thieu was losing support in Tan Chi Linh Parish, he was losing it everywhere.

The Communists drew their own conclusions from the upsurge of protests. On October 8, the Provisional Revolutionary Government announced unequivocally for the first time that it no longer would negotiate with the Thieu government, though it was committed to do so under the Paris agreement.

"As long as Nguyen Van Thieu and his gang remain in power in Saigon," the P.R.G. said, "the sabotage of the Paris agreement will go on, and it will still be impossible to achieve peace and national concord. "Thieu and his associates must be overthrown and replaced by "an administration that desires peace and national concord and is willing to implement the Paris agreement on Vietnam in a serious way," the statement declared, after which the P.R.G. would "talk with such an administration in order to arrive at a speedy settlement . . . only such an administration can engage in serious negotiations."

The statement—issued, by a historical quirk, on the second anniversary of the Communists' breakthrough proposal to Henry Kissinger in Paris agreeing for the first time to settle while Thieu remained in power—represented, in effect, the formal burial of the peace agreement. The political talks in La Celle St. Cloud near Paris had been broken off five months earlier, with neither side having significantly modified proposals that were exchanged in the first round of negotiations in the spring of 1973. Saigon offered the final version of its plan in January 1974, a proposal that differed only in inconsequential details from its earlier offers; the heart of South Vietnam's position was that an immediate election should be held as part of a process that would also include withdrawal of North Vietnamese troops from the South so the voting would be free of Hanoi's influence. The Communists had similarly not wavered in their demand that full political freedoms had to be granted first, along with establishment of an effective ceasefire and the release of all political prisoners, with elections to follow after a fairly long interval, and with the matter of armed forces in the South to be resolved only at some unspecified time after that. Their rationale was that "truly free and democratic" elections could be held only when people's democratic liberties were genuinely guaranteed, not during or immediately after a period in which Saigon police still prevented Communist political activities.

The last Communist proposal, which was also the last by either side, was embodied in a six-point plan presented on March 22, 1974, which represented no meaningful change from earlier offers. Saigon turned it down, and on April 16, four days after the fall of the long-besieged Tong Le Chan ranger base, the South Vietnamese announced suspension of the La Celle St. Cloud conference because of that and other Communist ceasefire violations. Four weeks later, the P.R.G. recalled its delegation from Paris and declared an indefinite recess in the talks. Despite subsequent appeals by the South Vietnamese, the negotiations never resumed.

In Saigon, the Joint Military Commission also lapsed into paralysis. It finally completed the disputed exchange of military war prisoners, nearly a year behind schedule and with both sides charging that the lists were incomplete. But it had resolved none of the other matters before it. During April and May 1974, wrangling resumed over the Communist delegates' treatment, and in June the Communists announced that they would boycott all future sessions.

The P.R.G.'s October 8 statement, however, was still the first formal repudiation of the promise that South Vietnam's future would be decided by negotiations between the Thieu regime and the Communists. The statement was final and incontrovertible proof of what most Vietnamese had always believed: that between those two adversaries, no issue would be settled except by force of arms.

In internal policy documents, the Communist leaders were now exhorting their cadres to abandon the "illusion of peace" to which some may have succumbed. "It was imagined that political struggles and diplomatic struggles would advance the revolution" after the Paris agreement, said a planning paper issued by the Viet Cong apparatus in Binh Dinh Province, but this had proven a false hope: "We must not delude ourselves that we can negotiate peace or national reconciliation with the Thieu clique. . . . To think of attaining peace by negotiation is to entertain an illusion. We must be prepared for violence. We can only achieve peace by defeating the enemy. . . . The entire enemy army and government must be totally expunged and the government put into the hands of the people. We should master this concept so that we will not be confused or deluded again, even if there will be conferences or the signing of another agreement in the future." Paris, evidently, was now classed as another diplomatic betrayal along with the 1954 Geneva accords and the 1946 modus vivendi with the French.

On the battlefields, the advantage in late 1974 was tilting irreversibly toward the Communists. Hanoi ordered a new phase of war, in which Communist units no longer attacked just to destroy enemy forces but also to "liberate the people and hold the land." As they did so, finding their enemy "passive and utterly weakened," their confidence grew. During the closing months of the year, they intensified pressure from one end of the country to the other. Around Hue, North Vietnamese troops battered the once-proud 1st ARVN Division so badly that at the year's end, U.S. analysts concluded it was "unlikely to be able to perform well against major initiatives by NVA units in the immediate future." In the populous coastal provinces south of Da Nang, Communist forces retook virtually all the land they had lost in the government's 1973 pacification drive. The Communists also occupied several vulnerable district capitals during August and September, gaining control of about 30,000 additional civilians in Quang Nam Province alone.

Government losses might have been lighter if evacuation were allowed from clearly indefensible positions. But for political reasons, commanders were invariably ordered not to give up any territory without a fight. As a result, defending units were left to fight battles that were often obviously hopeless from the very first shot. Some units were simply obliterated. Of the 1,000 or so men overrun at a place called Da Trach, only 174 ever returned to ARVN lines. In southwestern Quang Ngai Province, 300 to 500 men of the

70th Ranger Battalion defended an insignificant crossroads called Gia Vuc that clearly could not be held against an unexpected Communist attack. Subordinate commanders asked General Truong, the regional commander, for permission to withdraw the battalion, but were refused. When Gia Vuc fell, as expected, the only men ever accounted for were twenty rangers who happened to be picked up in the vicinity by a passing Vietnamese air force helicopter.

In the western highlands, the few remaining government enclaves fell one after another, often with most of their defenders lost. In Kontum Province, by October, only the province capital remained in government hands. Farther south, strong attacks fell on the provinces northeast and northwest of Saigon, and in the Mekong Delta, Communist forces struck heavily throughout the region in December, causing the sharpest fighting since the 1968 Tet offensive. At the end of 1974 the Viet Cong were stronger in the delta than at any time in the last five years, with uncontested control of more than 500 hamlets with about three-quarters of a million people.

The tired government army was losing men and weapons at a fearful rate. Weapons losses, a significant indicator of combat success or failure, reached unprecedented levels in 1974. According to the U.S. Defense Intelligence Agency, the South Vietnamese lost 816 crew-served weapons during the year, compared to only 384 in 1972, the year of the Easter offensive and the heaviest combat of the whole war. Soldiers lost 19,340 individual weapons in 1974, also well above the 1972 figure of 16,897. Casualties and desertion, meanwhile, left government units with manpower shortages that were serious everywhere and critical in many places. Among regular ARVN divisions, those that had been heavily engaged in combat could replace only about half their losses. Many of the replacements, including officers, were recaptured deserters or convicts freed from military jails. The 3rd Division, for instance, where average battalion strength dropped from 550 men in June to 350 at the end of December, received 60 officers who were former deserters. Among its enlisted replacements, most were ex-convicts. The same pattern existed in other divisions.

Leadership deteriorated as experienced junior officers and noncoms were killed or wounded. Morale sank. In the five northern provinces, only two of the five regular divisions were rated fully combat-effective by U.S. military analysts as 1975 began. Of the eight divisions elsewhere, three were classed as ineffective or only marginally fit for combat. Even those divisions that were considered effective were badly under strength. Regional Force and ranger units suffered similar attrition. The 360 RF mobile battalions were supposed to have 556 men each, but their actual average strength as 1974 ended was under 400. In some areas the manpower situation was worse. In Dinh Tuong Province in the upper delta, only one-third of the needed replacements were recruited in the last half of the year, and the province's militia battalions were down to half or even one-third of their normal strength.

Most of the decline reflected desertion. More than 200,000 soldiers and militiamen deserted during 1974, about one-fifth of South Vietnam's entire armed strength. In one division, the ARVN inspector- general's office found, 523 men were killed during the year and 3,328 deserted; its battalions at the end of the year averaged just 277 men each, barely half their assigned strength. Amnesties for deserters were periodically declared but accomplished little. In one province, 944 deserters turned themselves in during one amnesty; in the same period, 1,127 others deserted. In the Mekong Delta, where draft-age youths from the Khmer and Hoa Hao communities were often sheltered in pagodas, armed clashes occurred between villages and military police patrols who were trying to round up draft evaders at gunpoint.

As it awaited the more severe tests it knew would come in 1975, South Vietnam's army was a tired, dispirited, and frightened force, lacking confidence in its leaders, its future, and itself.

In Saigon, as the year drew to a close, the atmosphere of protest subsided. Police did not interfere with the big protest march near Tansonnhut on the night of October 30. But President Thieu was determined not to allow a procession planned for the following day that was more provocatively routed to the heart of the city. Early in the morning police barricaded all the streets leading away from the Tan Chi Linh Church, and they blocked Father Thanh when he tried to lead his followers toward the barricade. In the confrontation a plainclothes police agent punched him in the face, breaking his glasses and enraging the crowd. For three hours, rocks and bottles rained down on the police roadblocks; a police jeep was seized and burned. But the march did not take place.

Downtown, barbed-wire barriers were put up around the central market, the Assembly building, and other possible demonstration sites. They remained up over the November 1 National Day holiday, while Thieu, in yet another broadcast speech, promised to liberalize the press and political party laws but indicated that no more demonstrations would be tolerated.

Blaming the disorders of the past month on "underground Communist cadres," Thieu announced that dissenters would not be permitted "to propagate groundless news, to create religious divisions . . . to slander the government, to calumnify government officials, to undermine the economy." His warning and the display of force in Saigon's streets served their purpose; there were no more protest marches. Some voices continued to speak. The elders of the An Quang pagoda cautiously referred to "deep discontent" among the people, and ex-General Duong Van Minh, in his own National Day statement, declared that the Thieu regime's "impotence and corruption" had destroyed public confidence. The regime, Minh charged, "is no longer capable of putting forward any new ideas but only seeks to prolong a precarious existing situation, day after day, by means of repression, bribery, division and suppression of truth." Yet the opposition remained politically and religiously split, unable to recapture the momentum it had briefly gathered. Still, the events of September and October left a sense that the government's authority was vulnerable. "When the glass is full," said Senator Mau of the Buddhist-led National Reconciliation Force, "it takes only one drop to overflow." South Vietnam and its people were brimming with the accumulated misery of war and recession; that much was evident. Just how close the time of overflowing lay, however, no one yet knew.

The central highlands, a region of steep ridges and misty valleys etched by swift-flowing streams, comprised one-third of South Vietnam's territory but contained only about a million people, just over one-twentieth of the population. Of these, more than half were ethnically non-Vietnamese tribal people whom Westerners commonly called by the French term "montagnards," or "mountain people." The montagnards belonged to about a dozen major ethnic communities and twenty or so smaller but still distinct tribes, speaking many different dialects. They were animists, believers in sorcery, and slash-and-burn farmers who shifted their fields from year to year but not their villages, where many of them built thatched longhouses like those of the Ibans in Borneo.

The customary Vietnamese attitude toward the montagnards was one of contempt. "Moi"—"savage"—was the usual Vietnamese term for the tribal people. Assignment to the highlands was regarded by soldiers and civil servants as a form of banishment. The region was a "pseudo-Siberia" in Saigon's eyes, as one American official noted, "to which erring or incompetent (or both) officials were exiled." For their part, the highlanders feared and detested the Vietnamese as intruders and exploiters on their lands. With the connivance of corrupt or indifferent officials, tribal villages on desirable land were often forcibly relocated for "security" reasons, after which Vietnamese settlers quickly took over the abandoned areas. American officials, who hoped to win the montagnards' loyalty in the anti-Communist war, protested such practices, but usually in vain. "Encroachment of Vietnamese on recently vacated montagnard lands continues unabated with no efforts being made to stop it," said a report to the U.S. command in 1971. A year later, an American colonel who was the senior adviser to the chief of Lam Dong Province wrote him an unusually undiplomatic letter declaring that "after fourteen months as your adviser I am constantly amazed" that more montagnards did not join the Communist side. "If I were a highlander," the colonel added, "I am not sure I could continue to be loyal to a government which so poorly treats some of its citizens."

Some Vietnam theorists had long regarded the highlands as militarily expendable. The "enclave strategy" in most of its variations would have yielded all or most of the region to the Communists. Through the 1960s, however, the Americans and South Vietnamese chose instead to wage war there, trying to find and check the flow of Communist arms and troops on their way to the populous coastal regions. The war brought terrible destruction to the hill tribes' lands and their way of life. Bombing scarred the ridges and tons of chemical defoliants stripped away the vegetation from tens of thousands of acres, leaving the once green hillsides bare and brown. Two-thirds of all montagnard settlements were forcibly relocated at least once in the decade after 1961, it was estimated. Usually, when they had to move, the tribal people lost their animals, farm tools, and valuable hardwood furniture, either because they could not carry them or because they were stolen by government soldiers. By the early 1970s most of the tribal population lived in drab, ramshackle encampments huddled near the government-held towns, often with too little land to grow enough rice to feed themselves and with their comfortable, well-built longhouses a fading memory.

In the highlands war, little territory was permanently controlled by either side. The government army garrisoned the province capitals and district headquarters, where most of the people lived, and it also managed, most of the time, to keep open two road links to the rest of the country: Highway 19, which ran east from Pleiku across the jumbled ridges to reach the sea at the city of Qui Nhon; and Highway 14, which stretched south from Kontum along 160 miles of rolling, shrub-covered plateau to pass through Pleiku and picturesque Ban Me Thuot, from which another road, Highway 21, ran to the coast. Even to hold those limited positions, government forces were spread very thinly over a huge area, and as the military balance began to shift after the Paris agreement, planners in Saigon became increasingly concerned about the vulnerability of the highlands region.

Early in 1974, a routine report by the U.S. Defense Attache Office mentioned, almost in passing, the matter of the many government-held positions that were encircled by the Communists. Among the largest and most vulnerable of these enclaves, DAO's analysts wrote, was Phuoc Binh, the capital of Phuoc Long Province. "Should the Communists decide to attempt to overrun a province capital," they added, "this one might be the logical choice."

Phuoc Long lay at the southern end of the Truong Son range, tucked under the bulge of Cambodia's Mondolkiri Province. Its sparse population of fewer than 50,000 people was predominantly tribal. Though it was ethnically and economically similar to the other highland provinces, it was under the command of III Corps, the Saigon regional command, rather than under II Corps in Pleiku with the rest of the highlands. The province capital—better known to Americans who served there by its old name, Song Be—was little more than a village, with only about 8,000 residents. Though it lay only 80 miles from Saigon, it was far from any militarily or economically important communication routes. All roads leading out of the province were threatened by Communist forces, and overland convoys reached the capital only with heavily armed escort. As a result, it had relied mainly on air resupply for more than a year when, twelve days before Christmas of 1974, all of the province's outlying garrisons came under attack.

By December 26, only the province capital itself and a nearby airstrip remained in government hands, defended by militia forces and a single battalion of the 5th ARVN Division. Two C-130 transports and several other planes were shot down trying to support the beleaguered force, and thereafter frightened pilots were unwilling to drop below 10,000 feet, too high to bomb or drop supplies with any accuracy. In the first days of January, nearly 3,000 Communist artillery rounds and rockets a day crashed into government positions. Defending troops reported destroying no fewer than seventeen North Vietnamese tanks. But an equal number remained in action, firing on bunkers and buildings from point-blank range. Heavy casualties were also caused by inaccurate South Vietnamese bombing. One misaimed strike hit the province hospital, a survivor later reported, killing or wounding hundreds of patients.

Lieutenant General Du Quoc Dong, the new III Corps commander, pleaded for reinforcements, but only a token two companies of Ranger commandos were helicoptered into the battle on its very last day. Phuoc Binh fell on the 6th of January, the first province capital lost since Quang Tri 31 months before. Of the 5,400 government soldiers involved in the 24-day campaign in the province, nearly all perished or were captured. Only about 850 returned to friendly lines, along with about 3,000 civilians. Officially-sponsored protest demonstrations were held all over the country to denounce the battle as a flagrant ceasefire violation. On January 11, the United States formally protested that Phuoc Binh's capture represented "a decision by Hanoi to seek once again to impose a military solution in Vietnam" in violation of the Paris agreement. North Vietnam, Washington warned sonorously but emptily, "must accept the full consequences of its actions."

Hanoi was concerned with American deeds, however, not words. For the North Vietnamese leaders the battle was in part a test of the U.S. response to their more aggressive strategy. As they expected, there was no sign either of an American reintervention—which was barred by U.S. law in any case—or of a shift in Congress in favor of additional aid for the South. Communist officials outlined their reasoning quite explicitly. Colonel Vo Dong Giang, the Viet Cong spokesman in Saigon, told his weekly press conference that Phuoc Binh was a warning against U.S. "gunboat diplomacy," while in Hanoi, about the time of the battle, the editor of the Communist party newspaper, *Nhan Dan,* told the visiting American writer Frances Fitzgerald: "There was a theory of a 'decent interval.' According to this theory, Mr. Kissinger's 'honorable solution' to the war meant a two-year interval between the withdrawal of American troops and the fall of Thieu. Well, the two years are over."

President Thieu, decreeing three days of national mourning, vowed that the province would be retaken. But few Vietnamese believed him. Phuoc Long's loss crystallized South Vietnam's growing fears of the Communist threat and its loss of confidence in its own leadership. Rumors spread that the province was given up in some kind of secret deal with the Communists, or that the whole affair was arranged by the United States to force Thieu to resign. Even those who did not accept any of the conspiracy theories thought that Thieu's performance was vacillating and ineffective. Thieu's reputed military talent and his ability to command American power were his only claims to national leadership, in the eyes of most Vietnamese. Phuoc Long undermined both and thus represented a disastrous setback for him personally, as well as for his army and the regime.

On the same day as the fall of Phuoc Long, and with similar effects, the survivors of an 80-man militia company abandoned Nui Ba Den, the famous "Black Virgin Mountain" that rose unexpectedly out of the flat plains six miles north of Tay Ninh City. About one-fourth of the city's 100,000 people fled toward Saigon, including nearly the entire Catholic minority and most families of government and military officials. Though most returned in a few days, their flight was another symptom of the crisis of confidence that was overtaking South Vietnamese society.

Shortly after the two defeats, General Dong was relieved and replaced by Nguyen Van Toan, who had been fired from the II Corps command barely two months before in the anti-corruption campaign. However tainted, Toan had the one essential qualification to be returned to a top post: he was utterly loyal. Thieu's chronic fears of a coup d'état were heightened as his support crumbled. To forestall any conspiracy he obviously wanted III Corps, which included Saigon and the surrounding provinces, under an officer he trusted without reservation.

If South Vietnam's confidence was evaporating, the Communists' was growing. Their main-force army in the South now numbered 305,000, according to U.S. intelligence estimates, and was equipped with more than 600 armored vehicles and as many as 490 heavy artillery pieces—many more than they possesed at the time of the ceasefire, though still well short of Saigon's 1,200 to 1,400 tanks and more than 1,000 heavy guns. The

Communists had stockpiled 65,000 tons of ammunition and had extended their fuel pipeline to within 100 miles or so of Saigon. Roads through the Communist zones were so improved that a battalion could reach the Saigon region from North Vietnam in less than three weeks, riding nearly all the way on trucks. In earlier years, the same journey took more than two months.

It would later be alleged that the Communist buildup was possible because North Vietnam's allies, China and the Soviet Union, were more faithful and generous suppliers than the United States was to South Vietnam. In fact, though, American intelligence found that Russian and Chinese military aid to Hanoi dropped sharply after the Paris agreement, although economic aid increased. For a while this was advertised as a tribute to Henry Kissinger. Thanks to Kissinger's diplomatic virtuosity, Ambassador Martin commented early in 1974, Moscow and Peking had decided that "it is not to the interests of either one of them for Hanoi to have a dominant position in Southeast Asia. Therefore, they are not resupplying them with massive weapons of war as they have continuously in the past." Later in the year, though, when the administration was seeking additional aid for Saigon, those same intelligence reports became an embarrassment, since they might lead others to form the same opinion Representative McCloskey circulated to his colleagues: if both sides were receiving diminishing aid from their allies, then the only explanation for the growing Communist successes must be that "the aggressiveness, will and sense of purpose of the North, its leaders and soldiers, presently far exceed the aggressiveness, will and sense of purpose of the bulk of their South Vietnamese counterparts."

Some pressure was apparently put on the intelligence agencies to come up with different conclusions. Martin himself, in an unguarded moment, told a visitor early in 1975 that "everybody is trying to beat the intelligence community about the head and ears to increase the figures on aid to North Vietnam." Administration officials, meanwhile, began publicly chastising the intelligence analysts. The reports he was getting, complained the State Department's Philip Habib, contained "some half-baked figures" along with "six pages explaining . . . the difficulty in the methodology." After what appears to have been a good deal of bureaucratic hemming and hawing, the CIA, the Defense Intelligence Agency, and the State Department's Bureau of Intelligence and Research finally came up with a joint memorandum on the subject early in March. Their figures still showed a drop in military aid to Hanoi, which was estimated to have been $750 million in 1972, $330 million in 1973, and $400 million in 1974. Economic aid to North Vietnam from its Communist allies, however, was thought to have risen during the same period from $465 million in 1972 to $670 million the following year, reaching nearly $1.3 billion in 1974. Thus the intelligence memorandum, in an apparent effort to meet the administration's needs, stressed that if military and economic assistance were combined, the 1974 aid totals were higher than ever before.

In justifying the case for more aid to Saigon, intelligence officials were forced, in a sense, to argue backward from effect to cause instead of the other way around. U.S. support for the South must be inadequate because the South Vietnamese were having trouble holding their own, the administration's analysis held, while Soviet and Chinese backing for the North must be sufficient because the Communist forces were able, as the Defense Intelligence Agency chief, Lt. Gen. Daniel O. Graham, told one congressional committee, "to carry out a very effective military strategy." That reasoning, of course, did not address such matters as will, competence, or strategic soundness at all. The intelligence community's memorandum contained one sentence its authors may later have regretted. "Given the present military balance in the South," it said, "the GVN's forces will not be decisively defeated during the current dry season."

Still, Phuoc Binh showed a change in the relative war-making ability of the two sides. Though not the first province capital to be lost, it was the first in the entire war that could not be recaptured. Always in the past, the South Vietnamese had spent as much firepower and manpower as were needed to maintain the symbol of their control over all 44 provinces—even when, as with Quang Tri in 1972, the capitals had to be leveled before being re-occupied. Now, Saigon had no more men or resources to waste on symbols. The old axiom of the war held that the Communists, with few fixed positions to defend and with the freedom to concentrate their forces and choose where to fight, could capture nearly any objective they wanted, but that the South Vietnamese, with their air force, vastly superior firepower, mobility, and much larger army, could recapture any objective *they* wanted. That axiom was now repealed.

The loss of Phuoc Long was further proof—if any were needed—that the policy of clinging to every acre of government-held land could no longer be sustained. Talk of a strategic withdrawal was revived, partly at the instigation of a retired Australian general named P. F. Serong, who had served in Vietnam with Australian forces there and then returned after retiring as a sort of self-appointed military adviser. For months, Serong had been pressing the "truncation" concept on his friends in the South Vietnamese command; now he advised them that a withdrawal from the central highlands and all or most of the northern region of the country should be decided on no later than mid-February, in advance of the expected Communist offensive.

The rest of Serong's plan was that following a withdrawal, Saigon should propose negotiations with the Provisional Revolutionary Government for a new partition. The first offer should be to yield to the Communists everything above the 15th parallel—roughly, everything from Quang Ngai City north. If that were turned down, Serong suggested, the government should then propose partition even farther south at the 13th parallel, which crossed the country just above Ban Me Thuot. Oddly, that was also the line originally sought by the Communists at the 1954 Geneva conference before they yielded to Russian and Chinese pressure and agreed to the 17th parallel as the demarcation line.

Some senior officers were vaguely in agreement with the concept of withdrawal, if not with all the points of Serong's proposal. But again, as had also happened the preceding summer, no detailed planning was done. And Washington, disastrously, reinforced President Thieu's tendency to procrastinate. For months, a stream of military and civilian official visitors had raised Vietnamese hopes for additional funds. As General Smith, Murray's successor as defense attache, recalled, "In nearly every case when a high ranking American visited Saigon, the message was the same; to wit, every attempt would be made to secure a supplemental appropriation but no definite promises could be made. Hearing this, the Joint General Staff and other higher officers . . . believed that the chances were very good that a supplemental would be forthcoming." The Ford administration's request for a $300 million military aid supplement, sent to Congress three weeks after the Phuoc Binh battle, confirmed those hopes. If there had been any impulse in Saigon to face unpleasant facts and consider some form of retrenchment, it was now set aside while the Vietnamese leadership fell back into its comforting but wishful fantasies of an American rescue. Nor did Ford and Henry Kissinger neglect to encourage their Vietnamese allies yet again to believe that without the additional aid, they were doomed. The $300 million, the president told Congress and subsequently repeated often, was "the mimimum needed to prevent serious reversals."

Congressional leaders of both parties were said to have warned the president that it would be "extremely difficult, if not impossible," to pass the supplement. Even long-time supporters of the Vietnam effort seemed now to have had enough. Vietnam, said Senator Henry Jackson of Washington, had become a "bottomless pit," and he was not inclined to pour any more money into it. House Appropriations Committee Chairman George Mahon, like Jackson a conservative Democrat who had customarily supported funds for the war, asked skeptically: "Will we have to keep doing this, year after year, 1970's, 1980's, 1990's? Is there any end to it? Our people are sick and tired of it." Yet Ford and Kissinger continued to insist that the funds would be approved, and President Thieu—by now inaccessible to all but a tiny handful of advisers and more reluctant than ever to listen to unwelcome news—grasped at the Americans' expressed hopes to bolster his own.

In the meantime, Thieu would take no chances on renewed unrest. When Father Thanh and other oppositionists issued an "Indictment No. 2" on the first day of February, calling on him to resign, Thieu ordered nine Saigon newspapers kept off the stands for attempting to publish the document. On the night of February 2, police marched into newspaper offices, searched files, and arrested eighteen reporters and editors for alleged Communist activities. The next day, the government withdrew the licenses of five of the offending dailies.

The repression did serve to head off any revival of protest demonstrations. But it was a major blunder with respect to the U.S. Congress. When a delegation of one senator and seven representatives arrived late in February—Representative John Flynt of Georgia was the chairman—the case of the eighteen imprisoned journalists captured as much of their attention as did pleas from the Vietnamese for the $300 million supplement. The congressional tour had been organized by the White House in the hope that some doubters could be won over to support the aid request. An aide accompanying the group predicted, however, that antiwar members would use the tour to "turn the administration's gun around and blow its head off"—and so it happened, with the matter of political repression furnishing the ammunition. Representative McCloskey of California and Senator Dewey F. Bartlett of Oklahoma made headlines by demanding to see the arrested journalists, who up to that time had been held completely incommunicado, unable to see their own families or their lawyers. While the two Americans went into the prison, a Vietnamese senator—Ton That Dinh, also head of the Vietnamese Publishers Association—was kept outside. "A shame and a sorrow for our country," Dinh commented. Inside, one of the prisoners, a nineteen-year-old girl, whispered to McCloskey, "They beat us very much."

He had no way of proving or disproving her charge, McCloskey said later, but he thought the case "goes against the grain of everything Americans believe in," and that evidence of undemocratic practices made it difficult to endorse more assistance for the regime. After meeting with other dissidents, several other members of the delegation, most notably Bella Abzug of New York and Donald Fraser of Minnesota, voiced similar conclusions.

At their meeting with Thieu, several of the congressional visitors questioned him sharply—insultingly, the Vietnamese felt—about repression and other abuses, including corruption. Thieu answered politely, if stiffly, denying that his government held any political prisoners and ascribing the charges to Communist propaganda: the same answer the delegation received from Ambassador Martin. According to some of his associates, it was only after that meeting that the South Vietnamese leader began to understand that the $300 million supplement was in serious trouble. Following the U.S. delegation's departure on the evening of March 2, Thieu began thinking again about a strategic withdrawal to "lighten the ship at the top," as he once termed the idea. But, though no one in the leadership yet realized it, time had run out. If the opportunity had ever existed, it was no longer available.

Well before the Phuoc Binh battle North Vietnam's leaders had chosen the central highlands as the ground for their 1975 offensive.

At its 21st plenum in October 1973, the Communist party Central Committee had resolved that "revolutionary violence" was still the pathway to the revolution's goals, despite the Paris agreement. The following March, the Central Military Party Committee concluded, "The Vietnamese revolution may develop through various transitional stages, and it can only achieve success by way of violence with the support of political and military forces; if the war resumes on a large scale, a revolutionary war will be waged to win total victory."

The results of that meeting, which led directly to the assault in the central highlands a year later, are reported in "Great Spring Victory," an extraordinary memoir by the North Vietnamese army chief of staff, Senior Gen. Van Tien Dung.* According to Dung's account, following the March conference, the military command carefully monitored the battlefields in the South, and over the summer reported to the party that "the combat capability of our mobile main force was now altogether superior to that of the enemy's mobile regular troops, that the war had now reached its final stage and that the balance of forces had changed in our favor." In the new phase, the army and party authorities agreed, old methods of warfare and military organization no longer sufficed. "To stage large-scale annihilating battles and firmly defend the newly liberated areas, it was no longer advisable to field only independent or combined divisions," they concluded. Accordingly, divisions were grouped into corps commands for the first time, and plans were written for an unprecedented coordination of artillery, armor, and large infantry formations.

---

* Dung, the youngest member of the North Vietnamese Politburo, was Hanoi's second-ranking military leader, immediately under the famed Vo Nguyen Giap in both the army command structure and the Central Military Party Committee. He was born in 1917 in a peasant family near Hanoi and is thought to have had little formal schooling. He joined the Indochinese Communist party in the late 1930s and, like many others, was jailed in 1939, remaining in prison for about four years before escaping. During the anti-French war, he rose quickly in the Viet Minh army, becoming commander of one of its five divisions and then, as chief of staff, helping plan the Dien Bien Phu battle. After the 1954 Geneva agreement he was briefly in Saigon as a liaison officer with the original International Control Commission, but returned to North Vietnam in 1956. His memoir of the 1975 campaign was serialized in the party newspaper, *Nhan Dan*, and broadcast over Hanoi radio in installments in the spring of 1976. Detailed, personal, candid, and astonishingly free of jargon, it is unlike any other North Vietnamese account of the war. Indeed, "Great Spring Victory" may be unique among all documents produced by modern Communist movements. In contrast to Hanoi's propaganda during the war, Dung's memoir made no effort to hide the fact that the war in the South was commanded and supplied from the North and that by the 1970s, the bulk of fighting troops were regular North Vietnamese infantry rather than southern guerrillas.

Resupply efforts were expanded, on a new scale but with the Vietnamese Communists' traditional painstaking attention to preparing the battlefield. "Great quantities of material such as tanks, armored cars, missiles, long-range artillery pieces and antiaircraft guns . . . [and] hundreds of thousands of tons of materials of all types to insure powerful attacks" were sent south, while labor battalions worked "day and night" to improve infiltration routes. Arms, munitions, and troops were trucked on a 26-foot-wide, all-weather road running from Quang Tri to the edges of the Saigon plain. From the main north-south route, spurs were built running eastward toward the battlefronts. The supply system resembled "endless lengths of sturdy hemp ropes," General Dung wrote, "being daily and hourly slipped around the neck of the monster who would be strangled with one sharp yank when the order was given."

In October 1974, the Central Military Party Committee met again, this time with members of the Politburo. The meeting first tried to assess the possiblity of renewed American intervention. After the Watergate scandal, Nixon's resignation, the economic woes following the 1973 Arab oil embargo, and the sequence of congressional votes against additional U.S. aid to Saigon, the conference decided, the possibility seemed remote. "Having already withdrawn from the South, the United States could hardly jump back in," declared a resolution offered by Le Duan, the party's First Secretary, "and no matter how it might intervene, it would be unable to save the Saigon administration from collapse."

The meeting then turned to a general staff draft plan proposing the central highlands as the main battlefield for a "large-scale, widespread 1975 offensive." General Dung would assume field command, reporting to the ailing Defense Minister Giap. Underlying the plans, Dung wrote, were four assumptions:

1. The puppet troops were militarily, politically and economically weakening every day, and our forces were quite stronger than the enemy in the South.

2. The United States was facing mounting difficulties both at home and in the world, and its potential for aiding the puppets was rapidly declining.

3. We had created a chain of mutual support, had strengthened our reserve forces and material and were steadily improving our strategic and political systems.

4. The movement [in South Vietnam] to demand peace, improvement of the people's livelihood, national independence and Thieu's overthrow in various cities was gaining momentum.

After agreeing on these premises, the conference unanimously approved the general staff plan.

In early December, the top leaders of the war in the South—Pham Hung, head of COSVN and the overall party leader, and Lt. Gen. Tran Van Tra, the senior military commander—were summoned to Hanoi, along with other southern officials, to present their views. From December 18 to January 8, spanning the successful test of arms in Phuoc Long, the Politburo met to review the planned campaign once again. Party leaders did not yet anticipate total victory. "Large surprise attacks would be launched in 1975," the strategic plan stated, "creating conditions for the general offensive and uprising in 1976." But, the leadership added, "if opportunities presented themselves early or late in 1975, South Vietnam had to be liberated that year."

Even before finishing its deliberations, the leadership ordered the 316th North Vietnamese Division, then bivouacked in Nghe An Province—Ho Chi Minh's birthplace—to head for South Vietnam's central highlands. Before its departure, General Dung met with the division's cadres to tell them about the Politburo's decisions. He also read them a poem proclaiming: "In our country after 30 years of bearing arms, the moon still remains divided into halves. . . . Now is the time for us to set out together with the people of the entire country, to restore our moon to its full glory."

In military planning sessions following the Politburo meeting, the highlands campaign was given a name—"Campaign 275"—and, for the first time, a specific first objective. The chosen target was Ban Me Thuot, the most picturesque of the highlands towns, where Rhade tribesmen in brightly embroidered garments walked the streets and where Emperor Bao Dai's now-crumbling hunting lodge still stood as a reminder of more peaceful days when he and other luminaries came to hunt boar, deer, and tigers in the surrounding hills.

On February 5, General Dung—thereafter to be referred to in coded messages as "Tuan"—left Hanoi on the first leg of his journey south to take command of the campaign.

Extraordinary measures were taken to keep his trip secret. The government car that drove him to work, a Russian-built Volga, was ordered to keep making its routine two trips a day between army headquarters and the general's home. A group of soldiers who came to the house every afternoon for volleyball was instructed to continue playing as usual. Hanoi newspapers carried accounts of Dung's supposed activities in the capital. By the night of February 5, Dung had crossed the border into South Vietnam; and six days later, when the Tet festivals marked the start of the Year of the Cat, he was already in the highlands, joining an infantry detachment for the traditional holiday breakfast of glutinous rice cakes and meat pies.

In the misty, forested valleys west of Ban Me Thuot, where Dung established his headquarters, three full divisions were being assembled. They had more men, more guns, more tanks than the South Vietnamese defenders, and their leaders had more confidence. Yet the Communists were stepping into a new realm of warfare. They were masters of mobile, small-unit war; arguably, the world's best guerrillas. But they were inexperienced, even naive, when it came to seizing an important town with the intention of holding it. One agent, sent secretly to reconnoiter, reported wide-eyed to his superiors that Ban Me Thuot was "as large as Haiphong," though in fact, it had less than one-fourth the population. "We knew that Ban Me Thuot was not as large as Haiphong," Dung wrote tolerantly in his memoir, "and that it appeared larger in the eyes of our scout because it was rather large, and had many high buildings and was brightly lit by neon lamps." Even that description would have amazed the Vietnamese and the few Americans who lived there.

On the evening of February 25, Dung signed the final orders for the attack. First, though, the highlands were to be sealed off from the rest of the country. On March 4, Communist units blew up bridges and established roadblocks on Highway 19 between Pleiku and the coast. The next day other forces seized a stretch of Highway 21, which ran from Ban Me Thuot to Nha Trang and was the only other overland route out of the highlands. On March 8, soldiers of the 320th North Vietnamese Division blocked Highway 14 north of Ban Me Thuot, severing its link with Pleiku, where Maj. Gen. Pham Van Phu, the South Vietnamese II Corps commander, debated with his staff about where the next blow would fall. Though some of his subordinates wanted to reinforce Ban Me Thuot, Phu remained convinced that his own headquarters was still the Communists' principal objective. No reinforcements were sent. "Tuan," meanwhile, sent a message to Hanoi on March 9:

> We will attack Ban Me Thuot on 10 March. . . . All requirements have been met. Units are up to strength, and troops are strong and have sufficient weapons and equipment. Troop morale is high. Never before could such a powerful, concentrated attack be staged here. . . . Only books and newspapers are in short supply or arrive late. Wish you all in the Central Military Party Committee and the Political Bureau good health.

Chapter 10

Collapse

The Highlands

Most of my friends died on the road from Phu Bon down to here," the militiaman said. His voice was hoarse, exhausted, throttled with grief and humiliation. "There were many bodies on the road. Some were still alive but they had no food and no water. There was nobody to take care of them. Our commander, the lieutenant colonel, ran for his life and there was nobody in charge. . . . If we had received orders to fight— but we only tried to fight to clear the road for ourselves, we did not protect anybody. Most of the men in my battalion are still on the road. Some are dead, some are wounded, some are trying to get out through the jungle. There are more than twelve other battalions from Pleiku and Kontum and Phu Bon still left behind. They were at the back of the convoy because they never received any order to withdraw."

The date was March 26, 1975, and the great retreat from the Vietnamese highlands was exactly ten days old. That day thousands of survivors of the trek from Pleiku swarmed through Tuy Hoa, a shabby little town on the South China Sea halfway up the South Vietnamese coast. Like many other Vietnamese towns it had a huge American-built air base that now lay abandoned, its runways stretching like a beggar's arms toward the sea. A pall of anger, shame, misery, and fear hung over the mob of soldiers and refugees who milled in the dusty streets. Nor was their nightmare over. Believing they had at last reached safety, the refugees found instead that there was no military or civil organization, no help from the government, no food to buy, and no means of traveling farther. Nearly everyone, it seemed, was searching for some family member lost in one of the Communist ambushes that struck the bleeding convoy on its 135-mile journey to the coast.

"I only have two of my children here," said a wizened little infantryman, a too-large helmet slipping down over his sad, anxious eyes. "There were eight—I don't know what happened, whether they are missing or were killed. We started out together in the truck, and while we were all sitting together we were fired on. We all jumped down and ran for our lives. Since that time I have not seen my wife and children." A few steps away, an old woman wept helplessly, explaining that she could not find her 32-year-old daughter, who had been taking care of her but was then wounded and evacuated by helicopter from the convoy route. Another soldier told dully of the deaths of his brother and one of his children at the blown bridge over the Song Ba River, just ten miles from the coast, where the convoy had been blocked for five days while suffering its worst attacks. His companions described seeing hundreds of bodies floating downstream or crumpled on the banks. Some, they had heard, were deliberately massacred by machine-gun fire after trying to surrender.

Then or later, there was no way of knowing exactly how many tried to make the fearful journey. Saigon newspapers reported a quarter-million, probably an exaggeration. Cameramen who flew over the convoy guessed there were 4,000 to 5,000 vehicles and perhaps 100,000 people. Whatever the figure, only a minority reached the coast. Until the 25th, Vietnamese helicopters had been flying up to 80 missions a day to drop bread, give fire support, and evacuate the wounded. But now there were no more helicopters in the air. Those military units that somehow kept together during the march were at the head of the column and had already broken out, led by a half-dozen tanks that were the only ones of hundreds in the region to reach safety. Scores of thousands of desperate civilians and lost soldiers following behind were still trapped on the far bank of the Song Ba and were being abandoned.

In Tuy Hoa there was no one to take charge of the leaderless, frightened soldiers who had gotten that far but had lost their units. The relief troops had vanished along with the rescue helicopters. No traffic was moving south to Nha Trang, the new Military Region II headquarters, because the road had come under shellfire that morning. During the next few days it would reopen intermittently, and then it would be cut for good.

Worse, there was no one to provide food for the refugees, many of whom had eaten only leaves and roots during the last days of the march. Tuy Hoa's homes and shops were shuttered, the inhabitants gone. They had fled to Nha Trang, doubtless fearing the retreating government troops as much as the advancing Communists. The only signs of the Saigon government were banners strung uselessly over the province headquarters and over several abandoned schools, proclaiming them "collecting points" for the highlands survivors.

An angry sense of betrayal smoldered. "We don't need banners," a soldier said, "we need food." In a schoolyard crowded with refugees, a three-wheeled scooterbus lay on its side, its windshield smashed by an enraged ARVN officer after he was told there was no food at the site. Nearby a sergeant named Hoa, weaponless and wearing a ragged blue civilian shirt, pulled me aside from a cluster of refugees and asked roughly if I had brought any food, especially milk for his three-month-old daughter. When I explained I was not a relief worker but a journalist, his face tightened.

"Three day my baby no have milk," he shouted in ungrammatical but serviceable English. "Now she nearly die. If she die, I shoot." He did not say whom, but glared up at the tattered, sun-bleached banner over the school-yard gate and uttered the second most popular GI expletive. Then he spat out the most popular.

"I GI seven years," he said. "I shoot plenty VC. Now come here, no have food, no have money, no have milk for baby, no have nothing. My commanding officer go Nha Trang. I think if I stay here, I die." The baby and one other child were with him, he said. His wife and two more children were missing back along the road, and he had no idea what happened to them. Anger rose and fell in his face like a fever. As he spoke, another soldier in Ranger camouflage fatigues stood nearby, eyeing me and toying with a holstered .45 automatic pistol and a single grenade he carried clipped to his belt. He muttered something in Vietnamese.

"My friend say he no like Americans," Hoa told me, grinning malevolently. "He say if he see any American, he will shoot."

Anger at the Americans, though, was only one line in the volumes of bitterness written on the faces of the soldiers in Tuy Hoa that day. They were angry at the government that had ordered their retreat, at the generals who botched it, at their own officers who had deserted them. Above all, it seemed to me, they were angry at themselves, for being made to look like cowards, for leaving their wounded, for not just abandoning but at times robbing and terrorizing helpless civilians on the trail. The disaster was not their fault and they knew it. But the shame bit deeply just the same.

In nearly three years in Indochina I had seen defeated soldiers before, and far too many refugees. But the sensations that clung to that schoolyard I had not felt before. It took time to begin to understand the Vietnamese ethos of survival—to perceive, through the shoddiness of the regime and its lack-luster military command, the silent, cynical courage that sustained its army. Once understood, the endurance of the Vietnamese soldier was something one came to take for granted. But now it had evaporated. There was a feeling of a vital part come loose. After suffering so much for so long and for so little reward, these soldiers had now experienced a betrayal that even their remarkable resilience could not bear. Deserted by their officers and left to the terrible shambles of the road from Pleiku, they had been robbed even of the chance to redeem their pride by fighting back. It was hard to imagine what would become of the defeated, hungry, embittered, lost soldiers I saw that day. But it was impossible to believe they would ever again be an army.

The Communists' offensive in the highlands had begun just sixteen days before, on March 10. At two o'clock in the morning, by the Communist commanders' watches—three o'clock Saigon time—the first shells crashed into Ban Me Thuot and its airfield, while North Vietnamese tanks began advancing toward the city from their staging point 24 miles away. Trees surrounding the tank assembly areas had already been sawn partway through but were left standing to provide concealment until the last moment. When orders came to move, the tank crews simply knocked them down and drove off past the fallen trunks. At the Xre Poc River (also called the Krong), which crossed their line of march, ferries waited to carry tanks, artillery pieces, and other vehicles to the opposite bank.

Minutes after the bombardment began, the lights of Ban Me Thuot blinked out. Huge fires blazed at the airfield and at the ammunition dumps on the city's outskirts. General Dung's extraordinary effort to achieve surprise had been successful; for hours, the South Vietnamese commanders still did not realize they faced a major offensive. The American embassy was caught by surprise as well, with the result that its representative in Darlac Province, a 34-year-old former army lieutenant named Paul Struharik, was trapped by the Communist assault. Awakened by the first shellbursts, Struharik listened from his quarters in the U.S. AID compound as the sounds of the fighting drew closer. By 7:10 A.M., Hanoi time, North Vietnamese infantrymen were only 300 yards or so from the province headquarters. About the same time, a half-dozen Americans from Ban Me Thuot's small missionary community arrived at the AID compound. One of the group was a five-year-old girl; another was the widow of a missionary who had been kidnapped and presumed killed by Viet Cong guerrillas a dozen years earlier. Already sheltering in the compound were a young American scholar and a visiting Australian Broadcasting Commission official.

At midmorning, Struharik and the others saw the first Communist soldiers passing by on the street outside; thereafter they all remained silent except for Struharik's muffled conversations over a hand-held radio with the pilot of a circling Air America plane. Helicopters were standing by to fly in for them, the pilot radioed, but he couldn't identify the compound from the air, and Struharik didn't dare give explicit instructions because the North Vietnamese might be monitoring his transmissions. After remaining overhead nearly all day, the pilot flew off in the late afternoon, promising to be back in the morning.

It took the attackers another day and night to overrun the city's main military installations: the province headquarters, which was struck during the fighting by a misdirected South Vietnamese bomb, and the headquarters of the 23rd ARVN Division. (Though only one of the division's three regiments was operating in the area, Ban Me Thuot was its home base, and many of its officers and soldiers had their families there.) Outside the city, pockets of government soldiers held out for several more days. But at ten-thirty on the morning of the 11th, a message was received at the Communist command post: "Basically, the battle is over." Instead of the seven to ten days originally allowed by Communist planners, Ban Me Thuot had been taken in only 30 hours.

At 8:30 A.M. on the 12th, the Air America plane was back over Ban Me Thuot for the third day. The Communists had still not taken over the AID compound, but, Struharik told the pilot, it seemed the city was now liberated. When the pilot asked who was in control, Struharik answered, "The guys with the red stars." Shortly after midday, North Vietnamese soldiers finally arrived and took him and his companions prisoner. All were eventually released seven and a half months later, along with two Canadian missionaries and a CIA officer who was captured in Phan Rang some weeks later.

Also captured in Ban Me Thuot were the 23rd Division's deputy commander, Col. Vu The Quang, and the Darlac province chief, Col. Nguyen Cong Luat. The quick victory not only reinforced the Communists' confidence that they could take and hold important towns. It also disclosed something about the condition of their enemy. On the day Ban Me Thuot fell, "Tuan" dispatched a cable to "Chien"—Defense Minister Vo Nguyen Giap—reporting the success. "It appears," he added prophetically, "that morale among the enemy troops in the highlands is worsening and that they are weak and isolated."

The South Vietnamese commanders were "stunned" by Ban Me Thuot's fall, General Phu's deputy, Brig. Gen. Tran Van Cam, told Communist interrogators after he was captured. Because their families were in the fallen city, officers and soldiers of the two remaining regiments of the 23rd Division were demoralized, and many slipped away from their posts to try to find their families. More frightening to the II Corps staff was the fact that the Darlac militia, made up mainly of montagnard troops, not only did not try to defend Ban Me Thuot but in some instances defected to the Communists, turning their weapons on the ARVN garrison. The "disintegration" of the militia forces, General Cam admitted, "scared us most."*

---

* When Paul Leandri, the Agence France Presse bureau chief in Saigon, reported that montagnard troops had rebelled in Ban Me Thuot, he was summoned to the National Police headquarters to be questioned and then, as he was driving away, was shot and killed by a South Vietnamese policeman. The French government protested, and Saigon eventually apologized

Saigon could not shrug off Ban Me Thuot like the fall of Phuoc Binh two months earlier. Ban Me Thuot was larger and better known, and was also strategically important, lying, as Phuoc Binh did not, on a crucial highway—one of the only two land links between the highlands and the coast. If it remained in Communist hands, Ban Me Thuot could become a springboard for forces descending toward the sea and toward the northeastern approaches of Saigon itself. Accordingly, President Thieu ordered it retaken.

The 23rd Division's 53rd Regiment had been smashed, except for a few stragglers trying to regroup in a coffee plantation west of the town and one battalion that was still clinging to an airstrip to the east. On March 12, a helicopter airlift began to ferry the division's other two regiments, the 44th and 45th, plus a few Rangers, to a stretch of Highway 21 east of Ban Me Thuot, in a place called Phuoc An. From there, they were supposed to counterattack toward the city. But the plan didn't work. Because there were not enough helicopters, some of the troops who were supposed to take part never reached the staging area. The infantry who did land had no artillery or armored vehicles. The 23rd Division commander, Brig. Gen. Le Truong Tuong, flew to Phuoc An but promptly had himself evacuated after being superficially wounded—a cut on the face, other officers said, which should have required nothing more than a field dressing.

At Phuoc An, too, many of the division's soldiers found family members who had fled there from Ban Me Thuot. Once reunited with their wives and children, a considerable number of officers and enlisted men threw away their weapons and uniforms and headed east, away from their objective, hoping to reach safety at Nha Trang on the coast.

The airlift left only a thinned-out screen of defenders in Pleiku and Kontum, farther to the north. In Kontum, a frightened population was already beginning to flee. Prices in the markets shot up as soon as Highway 21 was blocked on March 5, and all week a growing stream of people flowed southward out of town toward Pleiku. Renting a Lambretta scooter for the journey now cost 15,000 piastres, or about $20. Truck owners were asking and getting as much as 100,000 piastres to move a family with its belongings. All over town, drivers and potential customers could be seen haggling over prices for the 25-mile trip.

Even while trying to mount their counterattack on Ban Me Thuot, the South Vietnamese commanders still did not know where the main Communist forces were, or where they were headed. General Dung, however, who later claimed to have had virtual minute-by-minute intelligence reports on

---

for Leandri's death, though it continued to deny his story. Several weeks later, however, in an admission that was hardly noticed at the time, President Thieu himself acknowledged that in neighboring Phu Bon Province, "a number of local and popular troops . . . crossed over to the enemy side."

ARVN movements, had already instructed one of his divisions to break up the counterattack. His forces far outnumbered and outgunned the frightened, confused South Vietnamese. Only a few of the attacking troops ever tried to advance toward Ban Me Thuot. After one battalion of the 45th Regiment suffered devastating casualties, the rest of the government column turned around and headed the other way, following its deserters eastward along Highway 21 toward Nha Trang.

That was the end of the 23rd Division. When its remnants were reassembled four weeks later, far to the south near Saigon, they numbered only about 1,000 men—with only twenty rifles.

On March 14, while the Ban Me Thuot counterattack was dissolving, President Thieu flew to the former U.S. logistics base at Cam Ranh Bay to confer with the II Corps commander, General Phu.

Like his commander-in-chief, Phu began his military career under the French, fighting against the Viet Minh. As a captain, he served in the siege of Dien Bien Phu and was captured there. Later, after leading the well-regarded 1st ARVN Division during the 1972 offensive, he replaced the porcine Nguyen Van Toan when the latter was fired for corruption in the fall of 1974. Phu's health was poor, and, some of his fellow generals believed, he also suffered from a disabling fear of being captured, as the result of his prison-camp experience after Dien Bien Phu.

At Cam Ranh, Phu faced Thieu; Prime Minister Khiem; Lt. Gen. Dang Van Quang, the president's security adviser; and Gen. Cao Van Vien, chief of the Joint General Staff. No aides were admitted to the room. What happened inside has been described by General Vien, by several of Phu's subordinates who were captured and interrogated by the Communists, and by others who reached the United States after the war; the different accounts contain no major inconsistencies. According to all versions of the meeting, Thieu told Phu that Ban Me Thuot must be retaken, and that he would have to use troops from Pleiku and Kontum to do so. They could not go directly overland, because Communist forces blocking the route were too strong. Instead, they would have to be brought down to the coast, then sent back up to the highlands. Implicit in these instructions, as Thieu later acknowledged, was that Pleiku and Kontum would fall to the Communists; the hope was that they could be retaken sometime in the future, after Ban Me Thuot was in government hands.

Khiem, Quang, and Vien were partly prepared for what they were hearing, since Thieu had told them two days before that some territory would be yielded in order to hold the more populous parts of the country. But Phu was hearing the idea for the first time. With more supplies, he told the president, Pleiku could be held for another month. But Thieu refused. Phu's conditions—an airlift of reinforcements and equipment—

could not be met, and the forces in both Pleiku and Kontum would have to be withdrawn.

Phu and the others listened, but no one, apparently, mustered the nerve to tell Thieu that even if the redeployment could be carried out successfully, the government forces were simply not strong enough to retake Ban Me Thuot. Vien, a colorless officer whom Thieu retained as chief of the general staff mainly because he wasn't ambitious enough to join a coup d'état (indeed, Vien had so little appetite for responsibility that he frequently asked to be reassigned as an ambassador abroad), "insinuated the riskiness" of the proposal, as he later put it, by warning Phu not to expect reinforcements. He also weakly reminded the meeting of long-ago French defeats in the region, hoping Phu would take the hint and tell Thieu the plan was impossible, or at least ask for more time to think about it. Though he later deplored the fact that Phu was not "forthright and courageous" enough to do so, Vien evidently found it impossible or imprudent to speak any more plainly himself.

The discussion then turned to the withdrawal route. Thieu asked about Highway 19, the most direct road. It was Vien who answered, again evoking the memory of French military disasters. "In the history of the Indochina war," he said, no forces had ever been able to withdraw along Highway 19 without being mauled. With the alternate road through Ban Me Thuot also impossible, the only remaining choice was a long-neglected, overgrown secondary trace that ran southeast from Pleiku to Cheo Reo, the capital of Phu Bon Province, and from there across the broken, forested ridges to meet the coast at Tuy Hoa. The road appeared on South Vietnamese maps as Highway 7-B; the distance, from Pleiku to Tuy Hoa, was 135 miles.

Highway 7-B had been unused for three years. At least three times in 1972, operations had been scheduled to clear it, using South Korean troops who were then stationed in the area. But each time the orders were cancelled because of various disagreements between the Korean commanders and the Phu Yen province chief. When the Koreans left after the Paris agreement, the plans—and the road—were forgotten. The Koreans left mines along some stretches, while the Communists mined others. Numerous bridges had been blown up and never rebuilt, or had fallen from disuse. For these very reasons, however, Phu declared, the Communists would never expect it to be used: thus Highway 7-B offered the best chance for a successful—and secret—retreat.

Before the meeting ended, Thieu issued several more orders. General Phu would choose the time for the withdrawal; the plan must be kept absolutely secret. Not even the American embassy was to be told. And the evacuation would involve only regular forces, not the provincial militia, who were predominantly montagnard tribesmen. Province chiefs and civil government officials were not to be told about the plan.

In Saigon that afternoon, General Vien, not long after coming back from Cam Ranh, met with General Smith, the U.S. defense attache. They discussed Ban Me Thuot and the general logistics situation. But Vien said not a word about the Cam Ranh meeting or about what was shortly going to occur in Kontum and Pleiku. In Pleiku, meanwhile, General Phu assembled a handful of subordinates to tell them of the withdrawal order. Only five officers were in the room, the same number that met at Cam Ranh. When one of them asked about plans to organize the evacuation of the Regional and Popular Force troops and the civilian population, Phu informed the meeting that on Thieu's orders, no such plans were to be made. Province chiefs were not to be told of the withdrawal, and the territorial troops under their command would be left where they were to screen the retreat of the regular forces.

"Let them find out about it later," Phu said. "The regional forces here consist only of highlanders. Let them return to the highlands."

Thus, after conferring with only a tiny group of officers who were too timid to argue with him, without consulting his American allies at all, and with the deliberate, cold-blooded intention of abandoning tens of thousands of his own government's soldiers, Nguyen Van Thieu reached the end of the blind alley he had traveled ever since the Paris agreement. Finally, his troops were no longer committed to defend every populated crossroads where they could manage to plant the yellow-and-red South Vietnamese flag. Had he been able to save his army by the sudden withdrawal, history might have credited Thieu with boldness and realism—with responding, however belatedly, to his changed circumstances. But it did not work out that way. Once he gave the order to retreat, it was as if he had spent all his powers of decision. All else was left to subordinates who were neither ordered nor given time to keep the withdrawal from turning into chaos. Thieu and his generals provided neither preparation nor discipline. Instead, the order to retreat from the highlands led to a sudden, catastrophic release of all the deep social and moral flaws of their regime. The sicknesses of South Vietnamese society, like agents of retribution, were about to overtake and, in only seven weeks, destroy it.

From the corps level down, few commanders bothered to assemble and organize their troops. They just collected their families and possessions and fled. Those officers who did try to lead were helpless in the breakdown of military order. The every-man-for-himself morality that had pervaded the system for years was now in command, turning the withdrawal into a desperate, doomed race for survival.

If few officers cared for their troops, even fewer gave a thought to the scores of thousands of civilians who would pour out of the abandoned provinces behind the retreating army in a great river of refugees flowing toward the sea. By venality and corruption, by refusing to reach for the slim chance of peace that might have been approached through a slightly more generous response to the Paris agreement two years before, Thieu and his colleagues had already failed their soldiers and people many times. Now those failures would come together in one of the great human tragedies of the war.

Early Saturday morning, March 15, General Phu hurriedly packed up and flew to Nha Trang. Shortly afterward, his deputy, General Cam, whom Phu had ordered the previous evening to assume overall command of the withdrawal, also flew out of Pleiku to Tuy Hoa. Neither ever returned to the highlands.

Other senior officers had left even earlier, while Phu was still in Cam Ranh. John Good, the Defense Attache Office liaison officer in Pleiku, was told on Friday that part of the II Corps headquarters staff was being shifted to Nha Trang; though Good thought it "unusual in that none of the U.S. agencies in Pleiku had been forewarned," he was not greatly alarmed. Still, since Ban Me Thuot's fall, Good had quietly arranged for some of his own Vietnamese employees and their families to move to the coast. In doing so, he was skirting instructions from the U.S. consul-general in Nha Trang, Moncrieff Spear, who feared an American evacuation would panic the Vietnamese—an issue that would arise again and again in the coming weeks.

On the 14th, however, perhaps remembering Paul Struharik in Ban Me Thuot, the consulate agreed to send special flights to take out missionaries, American civilian technicians working for the Vietnamese army and air force, and others for whom U.S. officials felt responsible.

That evening, the Vietnamese air force began its evacuation. Brigadier General Pham Ngoc Sang, commander of the 6th Air Division at Pleiku, sent his deputy to Saigon to ask for C-130 transports to fly his 6,439 airmen and their families and equipment out of the region. The request was the first clue air force commanders in Saigon had that the highlands were to be given up. Lieutenant General Tran Van Minh, the air force commander, authorized the airlift, and that night all available C-130s shuttled people and equipment from Pleiku to the air bases at Phu Cat and Phan Rang on the coast.

Missions against the enemy stopped completely as the airmen attended to evacuating themselves and their families. Some left in more or less organized fashion, but others, haphazardly learning of the withdrawal, just piled families and belongings on any available plane and joined the flight. Some pilots demanded huge bribes from civilian and military passengers who wanted to be taken along. Later, on the road to the coast, other air force officers would be shot in revenge by infuriated infantrymen.

The airlift continued on the 15th, though in worsening weather that eventually grounded the C-130s. Crowds outside the air base gates grew larger and more unruly. Special U.S. flights continued, carrying Americans and about 800 Vietnamese employees and dependents. Late that day, the consul-general finally authorized all remaining Americans to leave, and by seven o'clock, all were gone. Left on the field by the departing 6th Air Division, because of confusion and because air crews flew out earlier on transport planes, were 64 fully flyable aircraft.

As Thieu had ordered, Pleiku's civilians and administrative officials were not told of the withdrawal. Instead, sound trucks rumbled through the town that Saturday evening, warning that an attack was expected and that residents should dig bunkers and store supplies. By Sunday morning, the 16th, however, it was no longer possible to hide the fact that a general retreat was under way. A thickening stream of army trucks was flowing out of the city, loaded with those soldiers who had somehow managed to reach their units in time. Military police strung barbed-wire barricades across the road at the edge of the city to keep back civilian vehicles until all the military trucks had gone.

The barriers stayed up until late Sunday afternoon, when the police too jumped in their jeeps and drove away. Only then did the chaotic caravan of civilian cars, jeeps, buses, trucks, scooterbuses, motorbikes, and oxcarts, all jammed with people and piled high with bundles of luggage, begin to lurch down the road to the south.

Among the refugees were thousands of soldiers who had not received the withdrawal orders in time to join their units at the front of the convoy, or who deliberately stayed behind to remain with their families and pack whatever possessions they would try to take with them. Other soldiers, enraged at being abandoned, began rioting and looting. In the convoy were officials and businessmen who feared harsh treatment by the Viet Cong, ordinary Vietnamese civilians afraid of rebellion among the montagnards, and doubtless many who mindlessly joined the flight just because they saw others doing so.

Mainly, though, the column consisted of military families and others who made their living from the army. The war was Pleiku's only industry; it wasn't a city, really, but an overgrown army camp. An insignificant mountain settlement that became a small garrison town during the French war, it grew with the arrival of the Americans who made it their headquarters for the battles being fought out in the vine-tangled hills with their great misshapen outcroppings of limestone. For a decade, while it served the Americans' meals, laundered their uniforms, swept out their barracks and kitchens, and tended to their sexual wants, Pleiku grew into a muddy, ugly, military eyesore on the land, much of it built from bits of military junk. The Americans were gone, leaving only the futuristic domes and groves of antennas that stood on the surrounding ridges as monuments to the enduring American faith in war by gadgetry. The Vietnamese soldiery that remained did not offer the same opportunities as the Americans for profit and livelihood, but Pleiku still lived on the army. If the army was leaving, as was now plain, Pleiku would leave with it.

By nightfall on the 16th, huge fires were burning in the city. The main ammunition dump was ablaze, its stocks of artillery shells and bombs exploding in a terrifying roar as the refugee convoy uncoiled out of the city. There were no attacks that first night, only some robberies and rapes. Until dawn on Monday, the 17th, refugees streamed into Cheo Reo, the capital of Phu Bon Province, frightened and confused but still unwounded. Also on Monday, orders were finally given to some 3,000 Rangers to pull out of Kontum Province. The Kontum province chief, a Colonel Hung, learning of the retreat for the first time, hastily joined a Ranger unit heading for Pleiku, but was killed in an ambush on the way.

In Phu Bon, meanwhile, the retreat was suddenly becoming a nightmare. General Phu's choice of Highway 7-B had surprised the Communists, just as he expected. But once the route became apparent, General Dung ordered the 320th North Vietnamese Division—which he himself had commanded more than twenty years before against the French—to cut off the retreat. "If the enemy escapes," Dung warned the division commander, "you will be responsible." The South Vietnamese were blocked in any case by a fallen bridge just east of Cheo Reo. By the morning of the 17th, the first of General Dung's troops also reached the road in front of the convoy's line of march, and a day later, the bulk of the 320th Division was in position to flay the column from its flank.

Communist troops overran the Cheo Reo airstrip, while mutinous montagnard soldiers turned their weapons on other government units. More refugees and leaderless soldiers were crowding behind along the road from Pleiku. Even though the head of the column was under attack, those behind kept pushing forward, under a terrible, panicked compulsion not to stay still. Colonel Le Khac Ly, the II Corps chief of staff and one of the few senior officers still with the retreating army, abandoned his vehicle and began walking, under fire, toward Cheo Reo.

"I saw many old people and babies fall down on the road," he remembered, "and tanks and trucks would go over them. . . . Nobody could control anything." On the evening of the 19th, Ly, who tried valiantly but vainly to establish some order in the march, was evacuated by helicopter.

East of Cheo Reo the column moved in fitful stages, as engineers managed to put makeshift bridges across streams. As the long train of vehicles bumped down the rough, rutted road, it was lacerated by Communist machineguns and rocket-launched grenades fired from the thick underbrush at the sides of the track. Mortar shells whirred down through the arching canopy of leaves overhead. Shrapnel from the mortar bursts scythed off showers of branches that pattered down on the road and trucks with the sound of summer rain.

Frequently, Viet Cong or North Vietnamese soldiers intercepted groups of civilians. Some were allowed to pass unharmed, some were rounded up to be sent back to Pleiku, and some, according to refugee accounts, were fired on and slaughtered. With every attack, the convoy slid deeper into chaos. "Anyone who was strong enough to run fast could run for his life," a survivor said, but the weak and wounded were left behind. Demoralized and out of control, soldiers roamed up and down the route, robbing terrified civilians of their belongings. "The refugees were more afraid of the Rangers than they were of the Viet Cong," one of them remembered. Trucks crashed into each other in vain, panicky attempts to pass on the narrow, jungle-choked road. Soldiers fired on others who were trying to push toward the front of the convoy.

As the column passed into Phu Yen Province, the horror worsened. Just over the province border, after about two-thirds of the convoy had passed, Communist artillery blew up a pontoon bridge over a swift-moving stream, trapping tens of thousands of refugees and soldiers on the western bank while mortar and recoilless rifle fire poured onto them from both sides and from behind. A terrified rush to escape pushed hundreds of people into the river, where many drowned. Then Communist troops reached the riverbank and began moving about, trying to separate soldiers and military-age men from the rest of the crowd. But South Vietnamese fighter-bombers appeared overhead, dropping bombs first around the edges of the crowd and then right in the middle of it. Refugees ran, some into the river and some in both directions along the bank, and Communist soldiers opened fire on them, killing or wounding hundreds, perhaps thousands. A small handful reached a ford far downstream and crossed to continue the trek to the coast. Nearly all the rest, if they were not killed, were recaptured by the Communists.

Farther along the road, near a place called Phu Tu, another group of about a thousand people, hungry, exhausted, and frightened, refused to stop when the ARVN tanks in front of them halted. Instead, the crowd, mostly civilian families riding or pushing motorbikes, snaked around the tanks and continued on—only to run into an ambush a few miles farther on in which the entire group was shot to pieces.

As battles forced longer and longer halts, more and more families ran out of food. By the time the convoy reached the last and worst ambush on the Song Ba River, only ten miles from Tuy Hoa, many of the refugees were starving, devouring grass, roots, and leaves. Hungry, panicking soldiers were now stealing not just valuables, but the last bits of rice and bread.

At the Song Ba, a wide, shallow stream, the column had to leave Highway 7-B, paralleling the north bank, because the road had been so heavily mined by the Koreans three years before. Helicopters flew in pontoons and steel planking to build a bridge for the convoy to cross to the south bank and then turn toward the coast again. But before the bridge could be completed, thousands of trucks, jeeps, and armored vehicles reached the sandy bank in front of the crossing. There they waited under a steadily worsening rain of rockets, mortars, and artillery. Soon dozens of vehicles were on fire, sending oily black fingers of smoke into the sky. When they could, helicopter crews landed to take out the wounded. But only a small fraction could be evacuated.

On March 22, the pontoon bridge was finished at last. A first rush of people and vehicles collapsed it into the stream, but it was repaired fairly quickly, and the lacerated remnants of the convoy crossed to start the final stage of their journey, on a local road running along the south bank of the Song Ba. The road ran on top of a dike, raised above the surrounding rice fields from which Communist guerrillas fired at them. Silhouetted against the sky, vehicles were easy targets; "the guerrillas," wrote one reporter who flew over the route, "had before them what amounted to a shooting gallery." Not more than a half-mile from the road, farmers could be seen peaceably harvesting rice or tending water buffalo. But the refugees on the road remained under fire until almost within sight of Tuy Hoa.

Pursuing Communist forces closed in quickly on the Song Ba crossing. Thousands of soldiers and civilians still waiting to go over the pontoon bridge abandoned vehicles and belongings and tried to swim across under heavy rifle and machinegun fire and a constant lash of mortar bursts. Hundreds died in the stream. Those who made it walked the final ten miles to the coast through thorny scrub, arriving with feet bloody and swollen. Most of the refugees, including the many wounded, didn't make it over the river at all but stayed helplessly with the burning convoy on the far bank.

While the Pleiku convoy was making its way to the coast, smaller but no less tragic refugee streams were also flowing down from the highlands over other routes. Remnants of the 23rd Division and other survivors of the aborted Ban Me Thuot counterattack fell back down Highway 21 toward Nha Trang; joined by a paratroop brigade that was being pulled back from the north, these forces briefly halted the retreat at a place called Khanh Duong. But the position was overrun March 22, and once again the defeated government troops were on the move toward the sea.

A few other stragglers from Ban Me Thuot were making their way southward through the jungles toward the resort town of Dalat—where, as in other administrative centers in the southern highlands, officials and other civilians were fleeing even though there was no threat yet from Communist forces. Nine-tenths of Dalat's population was on the move by March 21, even though the U.S. province representative reported that "nothing of importance" had changed in the military situation. Province offices had closed, as had schools. Rumors swept the town that by agreement with the Communists, residents would be given 72 hours to evacuate. Orders from the province government to close gas stations were ignored; when they had sold their stocks to those trying to flee by car, the owners fled too. At least three days before any Communist troops arrived, all Saigon government officials were gone from Dalat, and the same happened in neighboring Quang Duc and Lam Dong provinces.

Behind the refugees, a few South Vietnamese bombers swooped down to try to blow up bridges and culverts to slow down the advancing North Vietnamese tanks. But they didn't do much damage. Nor was there much effort to destroy arms and equipment that had been left behind. Hundreds of artillery pieces and armored vehicles and mountains of ammunition and fuel were left to fall intact into Communist hands—nearly 18,000 tons of ground munitions, a month's supply, was left in depots in Ban Me Thuot, Pleiku, and Kontum.

The retreat from the highlands was the most drastic change on the Vietnamese military map in twenty years. In less than ten days, it yielded six entire provinces, a full infantry division, the equivalent of another division of Rangers, and tens of thousands more militia and support troops, along with most of their arms and equipment. It also cost Nguyen Van Thieu the confidence of his military commanders, his soldiers, and his people. After so many years of stalemate, it was almost impossible to absorb what had happened. But even before the bleeding convoy from Pleiku reached the coast, a greater catastrophe was beginning 200 miles to the north.

"We must escape"

It began, almost unnoticed, in Quang Tri. Before dawn on March 8, while General Dung's forces were preparing to attack Ban Me Thuot, other North Vietnamese units in Quang Tri launched strong probes at the battered province's defenses and against government positions in Thua Thien Province just to the south. That day and the next, some 50,000 refugees streamed out of Quang Tri toward Hue, the first in what would become the largest and most tragic refugee flight of the war.

In Saigon, President Thieu, while considering his decision to abandon the highlands, concluded that Quang Tri could not be defended either. During the second week in March, he ordered the Airborne Division shifted from the northern region back to Saigon, where it would resume its original role as strategic reserve for the capital area, which the ARVN command believed might soon come under attack—though there were also those who thought Thieu's real reason for recalling the paratroopers was to guard against a coup d'état.

General Truong, the I Corps commander, flew to Saigon to argue against the move. But the most Thieu would do was agree to put if off until the end of the month. In their meeting both men acknowledged, implicitly if not explicitly, that some of the northern region would have to be abandoned. But there seems to have been no clear decision on what area would be given up and what would be defended—an ambiguity that persisted until it was too late to save anything at all.

A few days later, after deciding to yield the highlands, Thieu changed his mind again and ordered the transfer of the Airborne Division to start immediately. On March 16, while Pleiku was emptying out, the paratroopers were pulled out of their lines west of Hue and Da Nang and began boarding ships for Saigon. One of the division's three brigades was landed at Nha Trang instead to meet the North Vietnamese rolling down from Ban Me Thuot. The other two brigades reached Saigon. Of the seven regular divisions in the northern half of the country, these would be the only major units to arrive in the South intact.

To take over the paratroopers' positions, Truong ordered the Marine division back from Quang Tri, where so many of its members died in 1972. Without the marines, the province could not be defended, and the province chief gave civilian officials permission to evacuate with their families. Most other civilians left with them. As they moved southward out of the province, the retreating marines and refugees came under sporadic shellfire but were not heavily attacked. But powerful North Vietnamese forces advanced toward the positions they had abandoned. Swarms of Communist tanks clanked southward over the sandy coastal plain, their treads throwing up great clouds of dust. On March 19, the leading units crossed the shallow Thach Han River and reoccupied the ruins of Quang Tri City without a fight.

The following day, while Hanoi ordered its II Corps to be "even more bold and agile" in northern South Vietnam, President Thieu spoke to his countrymen on the radio, admitting that the central highlands had been given up. It was the first official acknowledgment of the four-day-old retreat, although Saigon knew of it from its newspapers, which had printed dramatic accounts of the convoy to the coast. The defiance of censorship—which normally prohibited reporting any territorial loss before it was officially confirmed—was another reflection of the regime's declining authority.

Thieu, in his radio speech, indirectly confirmed Quang Tri's loss by omitting it from the list of provinces he said would be held. But he specifically denied as "false and groundless" a quickly-spreading rumor that Hue, too, was being abandoned. The remaining territory, Thieu said, would be defended "until the end." But, as Saigon had already begun to realize, Thieu was no longer in control of the events that were overtaking his army, and he and his aides seemed unable to decide whether Hue could really be defended or not. Conflicting and ambiguous messages flashed between Saigon and the commanders in the north. After meeting March 18 with Prime Minister Khiem in Da Nang and with Thieu in Saigon the following day, General Truong, the I Corps commander, believed he was to try to hold Hue. But on the evening of the 20th, the same day as Thieu's radio speech, a courier from the Joint General Staff delivered orders which Truong interpreted as directions to abandon Hue after all, though the JGS officers who drafted it later maintained they only sought to give Truong the discretion to do so if the situation worsened.

Whatever the intent of the order—and it is difficult to avoid the impression that by now nobody was really trying to make a decision but only to avoid the responsibility for one—Hue could probably not have been held in any case. The removal of the Airborne Division, the apparent strength of the advancing enemy, and the news of the debacle in the highlands cracked the morale of the ARVN troops assigned around Hue, especially in the 1st Division, whose families all lived there. On the day of Thieu's broadcast, soldiers, officials, and civilians were already in flight from Hue over the scenic Hai Van Pass to Da Nang, 50 miles to the south.

It was the confusion of Pleiku all over again. Few orders were given, fewer obeyed. No one tried to organize the evacuation of civilians, who joined the exodus after seeing troop trucks heading south or after finding government offices padlocked. As had also happened in the highlands, thousands of families were broken apart. Soldiers in Hue were being given permission to accompany their families to safety, if they bothered to ask, while others in Da Nang were being ordered back north—though trucks could not move over the refugee-choked road, and ships and barges that were to take other units by sea never left the docks. Officers had no idea where to go. "I don't even know where my wife and family are," said one, coming ashore in Da Nang. "Why should I care about my division command?

Early on Saturday, March 22, shells began to fall on the traffic heading toward Da Nang on Highway One. Later that day the road was permanently cut by the destruction of a bridge ten miles south of Hue, while the city itself came under slowly intensifying artillery and rocket fire. Most of the civilian population had already escaped. Of those who remained—no more than 10,000, it was thought, out of a population of 203,000—many flocked to the banks of the Huong Giang (Perfume) River, which flowed through Hue under the massive brick walls of its 170-year-old citadel. There, they hoped to flee on small boats to the sea and then along the coast to Da Nang.

Communist gunners that Saturday seemed to be deliberately keeping their fire away from the riverbank and the crowds of civilians there, though rockets swooshed steadily into the citadel area north of the river, where the ARVN headquarters was located. On Sunday, March 23, however, shells began falling among the refugees as the North Vietnamese tried to blow up the several bridges spanning the river in order to keep supplies or reinforcements from reaching the north bank.

That day, soldiers in Hue still thought they were going to fight to hold it. So did the 3,000 men of the 147th Marine Brigade to the north. But on the evening of the 23rd, though no Communist forces were yet threatening them, the marines were told to pull back to the coast. On the way, during the next two days, four-fifths of them were killed, wounded, or captured in numerous ambushes. All the brigade's artillery and other heavy equipment was lost. When the survivors reached the little river port of Tan My, they fought with civilians and militiamen, killing many of them, in a frantic fight for space on the jammed Vietnamese navy landing craft that were leaving for the south.

With or without orders, other government units in and around Hue melted away from their positions. The 1st Division, already depleted by casualties and by desertions as soldiers left the lines to take care of their families, "was lost as an identifiable unit," the U.S. Defense Attache Office reported. "Its decimation was so complete that no real efforts were made to reconstitute the division." Though most of the soldiers managed to escape, they destroyed almost none of the arms and equipment left behind. A colonel described leaving 37 tanks, all fueled and in running order, on the beach where he and his men boarded small boats; he had received no orders to immobilize them. Such episodes reinforced rumors that the withdrawal was prearranged, part of a secret deal between Saigon or Washington and the Communists to yield the northern provinces.

Hue was no muddy garrison town in an alien region of despised, primitive tribesmen. It was the historical and cultural heart of the country, the seat of the Vietnamese emperors for two and a half centuries after the Nguyen dynasty settled there in 1687. Located in a region of poverty but also of great natural beauty, where the slopes of the Truong Son Mountains descended very close to the sparkling South China Sea, Hue was the mandarin of Vietnamese cities, faintly scornful of Da Nang, an upstart honkytonk, and Saigon, a city of bureaucrats and businessmen built by the French and dominated by the generals and the Americans.

Foreigners who came there were often entranced by Hue and its sense of dignified grace that somehow survived from a less tawdry—if no less violent—past. Even in times when falling flares and gun flashes lit up the ridges to the west, and the crunch of bombs shook the casement window frames of its buildings, Hue had a quality of serenity, especially in the evenings when the sunset turned the river to copper and the gently rocking sampans to silhouettes from a lacquer painting. There was a "haunting attraction," wrote the journalist Don Oberdorfer, who knew Hue well, "in the slanting decorated roofs of the old palaces and shrines; the monumental tombs of the Nguyen monarchs; the sampans floating lazily on the river; the aged mandarins with wispy beards and porcelain teacups and a commission from the emperor on the wall; the echoing gongs of the pagodas, filled with gray-robed monks and nuns and youthful novices, chanting singsong prayers before a golden Buddha."

In the spring of 1975, Oberdorfer and Paul Vogle, a Vietnamese-speaking reporter for United Press International who had once taught at Hue University, were the last American correspondents to see the city before it fell. The scoop was less important to either than the chance to say farewell to affectionately remembered places, though not people, who were almost all gone when Vogle and Oberdorfer flew in aboard a U.S. helicopter on Sunday, March 23. The sampans were gone from the river; wandering in the almost empty streets, Oberdorfer thought, was like walking through Pompeii after everyone had fled but before the eruption. A few people were still in the market, where prices that had been panic-high a day earlier were now falling by the minute, as sellers decided to convert their remaining stocks into cash and seek their own escape. In a lane between the market stalls was an old man with a "thin cultivated face and wispy white beard," wearing a worn mandarin-style tunic. He looked, Oberdorfer wrote, "to be the personification of old Hue." Seated atop a small table, the old man was quietly and steadily weeping.

Of all South Vietnamese cities, Hue had the most reason to fear the Communists, who, in their 25-day occupation during the 1968 Tet offensive, executed at least 2,800 residents in the worst-known Communist atrocity of the war. Those killed included government officials, soldiers, teachers, priests, intellectuals, and other "counter-revolutionary elements," and, in the last stages, ordinary civilians who were unlucky enough to have witnessed the killings or who might identify underground Viet Cong agents who had surfaced during the occupation. Some of the victims were shot, some clubbed to death, and others apparently burned alive. Besides the 2,800 found to have been executed when mass graves were discovered in the months after the city's recapture, nearly 2,000 more Hue residents were missing after the battle and never accounted for. Though Hue had often been at odds with the Saigon government, particularly during the Buddhist uprisings of the 1960s, after 1968 it was bitterly anti-Communist. President Nixon, among many other American officials, later cited the Hue massacre as proof that the Communists would inflict a terrible bloodbath if they won the war. U.S. officials also noted with some bitterness that the massacre received relatively little public attention in America compared with another that occurred at about the same time and took only perhaps one-seventh as many lives: the killings of Vietnamese civilians by Lt. William Calley's platoon of the Americal Division in a place called My Lai.

Seven years later, the horror of the executions had hardly faded. With the North Vietnamese driving on the city again, few in Hue were willing to remain. "We could not live with the Communists," said Nguyen Gia Ung, a teacher at the famous Quoc Hoc High School, which listed Ho Chi Minh, Vo Nguyen Giap, and Ngo Dinh Diem among its alumni. "We must escape from them."

When Hue had last been evacuated in 1972, the North Vietnamese paused after seizing Quang Tri and gave the shaken government vital days to organize a defense. This year, they did not halt. On March 26, having faced almost no opposition, Communist soldiers triumphantly entered the city and planted a huge liberation flag at the citadel gate. General Dung received the news that evening in his command post in the highlands. In celebration, he lit a cigarette, a pleasure he allowed himself only at moments of great success. "When the comrades around me, including the guards, saw me smoke," he noted in his memoir, ". . . they knew that I was enthusiastic."

While Hue was emptying out, the South Vietnamese army in the rest of the five-province I Corps area was distintegrating with astonishing speed. It collapsed like a house with its timbers eaten away by termites, which has continued to look sound until the very moment it crumbles.

On Monday, March 24, Quang Tin and Quang Ngai, the two populous provinces south of Da Nang, fell in a single day. Tam Ky, the Quang Tin Province capital, was defended by two regiments of the 2nd ARVN Division, several Ranger battalions, and assorted armor and militia units. All of them dissolved after a two-hour artillery barrage before dawn. Only a handful of stragglers were left when a single North Vietnamese tank clanked into the town from the west at 9 A.M. Civilians fled the town in both directions, some north toward Da Nang and others south to the huge former U.S. air base at Chu Lai, now the 2nd Division headquarters, which stretched east from Highway One to the sea and thus offered the chance of escape by ship.

One of the refugees, a member of the lightly-armed People's Self Defense Force, was still wearing his black uniform shirt and red-and-yellow arm-band when he saw the tank arrive. Stripping off the shirt, he dove into the nearest house, stole someone's white shirt and put it on, then ran back outside, leaped on his motorbike, and raced the 40 miles to Da Nang. "I drove right by the tank," he told me that afternoon, standing with other Tam Ky refugees on a debris-strewn lot alongside the road to the Da Nang Air Base. "Nobody fired at me."

As was beginning to seem the normal pattern, higher-ranking officers were the first to run away. "The province chief fled, the soldiers fled, and I just did the same," said a minor civil servant. Much the same happened in Quang Ngai, another 40 miles to the south. As if by telepathy, every government soldier in the two provinces seemed to decide at exactly the same instant that the war was over; it was time not to fight, but to survive.

In Quang Ngai City, a few mortar shells dropped into the city during the daylight hours of the 24th. But no sounds of fighting signaled the army's sudden withdrawal after dark. The city's 70,000 people learned their defenders were leaving only when speeding trucks full of soldiers, with men sitting on the hoods and hanging from doors, suddenly began roaring through the center of town, heading in the direction of Chu Lai. Minutes after the first trucks passed, the streets were clogged with civilian vehicles as well, while many more civilians and soldiers on foot or on motorbikes set out after the army convoy. More military trucks raced through the crowd, their horns blasting. Several tanks ground along the route as well. In about a half-hour, the soldiers and fleeing civilians were gone, though shortly the streets were full again with civilians carrying bags of rice and other food from the abandoned army warehouse.

At the interrogation center a block from the province police headquarters, piles of dossiers were burning in the courtyard. The gates were open and the guard towers at the corners of the compound were empty, though a red-and-yellow government flag still hung atop one of them.

Bicycling through the nighttime crowds was a young American Mennonite, Earl Martin, who chose to remain in Quang Ngai in the hope of getting the Communists' permission to continue with the Mennonite Central Committee relief program. After five years in Vietnam, Martin spoke the language fluently. Like many other relief agency workers, he opposed U.S. policy in Vietnam and was no admirer of the Thieu government; as a pacifist he did not completely identify with the revolutionaries, either, but was relatively sympathetic to their cause. Now, as midnight approached, Martin felt "cradled in a strange peace." Quang Ngai, a revolutionary stronghold for many decades—it was the birthplace of North Vietnam's Prime Minister Pham Van Dong and General Tran Van Tra, among other leading Communists—had seen more battle over the years than nearly any other province. When its defenders fled toward Chu Lai, Martin realized, for the first time in decades, "there was no army of any kind in Quang Ngai city. We stood in a vacuum, as on an empty bridge between two kingdoms."

It was not a vacuum for long. At fifteen minutes after two o'clock in the morning, the first Communist soldiers entered the city, announcing their arrival with a volley of five AK-47 shots. "You need run no more! Peace has come to Quang Ngai," one of them told residents who came cautiously out of their houses into the darkened street to see their liberators. "But if you want to travel anywhere, feel free to go. Just carry no weapons with you!" Few tried to flee, however. Quang Ngai remained perfectly orderly. Not a single person was killed in the city's "liberation," a Communist officer told Martin the next day. The only casualty was a single Communist infantryman wounded, by a boobytrap or a mine, at the province military headquarters.

Unlike Hue, Quang Tin and Quang Ngai fell so quickly that few civilians escaped. Together, the two provinces contained 1.3 million people, double the number who had already come under Communist control in the preceding eight days. They were, with Hue, the most significant military prize the Communists had won in more than twenty years. Hardly anyone yet realized that an even more devastating triumph lay only a few days ahead.

Da Nang that Monday was choked with refugees—half a million, it was estimated, though no one really knew. They were camped at schools, at pagodas, on empty lots, huddling under flimsy poncho shelters that barely covered them and their bundled possessions. Thousands swarmed through the streets searching for missing family members or for someplace to stay, turning traffic into a bedlam of trucks, buses, jeeps, motorbikes, oxcarts, and pedestrians. Among them were many soldiers, lost and frightened but not yet mutinous.

Many of the rich or privileged were leaving for Saigon, paying three or four times the normal fare for tickets on Air Vietnam, the civilian airline. Worried depositors stood in long queues in front of banks, waiting to withdraw their savings. The atmosphere was nervous, but not yet panicky. Few Vietnamese seemed able to imagine the city falling; their worry, an airman said, was that it would become "the new demilitarized zone," subject to constant shelling. But the sense of relative safety dissolved quickly. By Wednesday, order began to break down. By Friday, the city was in an uncontrollable panic in which hundreds of people were killed not by the Communists but by their own rioting soldiers. By Sunday, four days after the loss of Hue, it was in the hands of the Communists. Da Nang was not captured; it disintegrated in its own terror. Of the 50,000 South Vietnamese soldiers stationed in and around the city, hardly any raised a rifle in its defense.

Built on a peninsula at the end of a narrow, sandy spit of land jutting into a well-protected harbor, Da Nang had been militarily important for more than 100 years. The French, who called it Tourane, began their conquest there in 1858. Even earlier, in April of 1845—130 years almost to the day before its capture by the Communists—an American naval officer named John Percival carried out what seems to have been "the first act of armed intervention by a Western power in Vietnam." Attempting to compel the release of an imprisoned French missionary, Percival seized several mandarins and held them aboard his ship, the USS *Constitution*, in Da Nang Harbor.

Like his twentieth century successors, Captain Percival was unsuccessful. The Vietnamese refused to free the missionary, and "not knowing exactly what to do with the hostages," as a French historian recorded, Percival "set them free and put out to sea." Four years later President Zachary Taylor addressed a letter of apology to "His Majesty the Magnificent King of Anam," asking the imperial court to "understand how greatly I have been grieved to hear it said, that the Captain of one of my warships had misbehaved himself, four years ago, (which I have only heard of lately, for the first time, because your country is so far from mine) by landing men from his ship in Toorong Bay and firing on your people, and killing and wounding some of them." The Vietnamese should not seek revenge, Taylor warned, but should leave the matter "forgotten and forgiven after my letter has come to your hands."

In the 1960s, Da Nang was a major logistics base for the U.S. buildup, and it was there, a decade to the month before it fell, that two U.S. Marine battalions waded ashore on March 8, 1965, ready for battle but finding none, to begin the American war. In the years that followed, Da Nang, with its big port and air base, housed more GIs than any other Vietnamese city. The inevitable consequences followed: bars, brothels, massage parlors, heroin traders, black-market stalls where stolen goods from hi-fi sets to flak jackets were displayed. With the legal and illegal livelihoods created by the huge American establishment, Da Nang's population swelled to nearly half a million, more than five times greater than in 1960. Briefly in 1973 and 1974, after the GIs were gone, the memory of an older, more pleasant city showed through the wartime tawdriness, like the faint image of an old poster under whitewash on a wall. The pimps and whores drifted away from the broad waterfront esplanade with its Chinese and Vietnamese restaurants on piers out over the lapping, muddy water. A small public-works employment program swept away the piles of garbage that had festered in the streets. But now, in a few days, Da Nang had become as overcrowded and filthy as ever.

There had been refugee invasions before, particularly in 1972 when a half-million people fled to Da Nang from the Easter offensive. Then, the city screamed with the sound of American bombers climbing off the runways day and night to strike at the Communist advance, while troop trucks and tanks rolled out of the city in long olive-drab lines and mountains of fresh munitions and supplies grew alongside the docks. This year it was different. A few South Vietnamese planes flew off the air base, but it was a puny effort compared to the American war. The soldiers stationed in the city and those streaming in from Hue and the other abandoned provinces showed no sign of taking the offensive. Like everyone else, they were simply waiting for whatever would happen next. In an amazingly short time, they were consumed by panic.

"It was incredible how quickly things fell apart," said Dennis Brown, who had spent nine months in Da Nang as the representative of the American relief agency CARE.

From the start of the refugee influx, Brown had been trying to set up an emergency program to help feed them. The food was there: 30,000 bags of rice, tagged for relief distribution, was in a Da Nang warehouse. But chaos overtook the city so fast that Brown could hardly get his program started. On Tuesday, March 25, when he went to the bank to withdraw CARE funds, he found "a tremendous mob scene, packed wall to wall, people standing on the counters." The next day the bank was locked shut. At the food warehouse the Vietnamese official in charge would no longer release the rice on Brown's signature, as had been the normal practice, but demanded payment in cash. So did the laborers who were supposed to load it on trucks to be hauled to refugee reception sites. Neither Brown nor the U.S. consulate's refugee affairs officer could find anyone at the headquarters of the city administration's refugee committee; the municipal social welfare coordinator had also disappeared.

That day in Saigon, Thieu issued an Order of the Day instructing all government units to halt the Communist advance "at all costs." Obliquely acknowledging the loss of discipline, Thieu demanded that "all combat orders must be strictly carried out. . . . All of you must be determined and strong like a fortress which the aggressors, no matter how brutal and fanatical they may be, will be unable to shake. The aggressors will be defeated in the end. I have led you through many dangerous circumstances in the past. This time, I am again by your side and, together with you, determined to fight and win!"

But the time for rallying the army had passed. Thieu's order had no more effect than his radio broadcast five days earlier. Da Nang continued to plunge into chaos. On Wednesday, rockets crashed into the air base and a nearby settlement, killing six civilians—three of them young children. Traffic jams clotted in the streets, even though more and more gas stations closed down with cardboard signs hanging from their pumps saying "het xang"— "empty." That afternoon, traffic was so bad that it took Dennis Brown three hours, instead of the normal twenty minutes, to drive across the city. Thursday morning, the few remaining police vanished and law and order disappeared completely. Looting and robberies by armed soldiers began everywhere. Outside government warehouses, some of them on fire, great heaps of looted or smashed goods lay in the streets. Drunken soldiers committed acts of senseless violence. A British relief worker watched one fling a grenade for no apparent reason at a crowd of civilians, wounding several of them.

Albert Francis, the U.S. consul-general, sent out most of his 80-man staff Wednesday on a special flight that also took out American and other foreign reporters and the families of a few high Vietnamese officials. Thursday, Francis concluded that the situation was out of control. Though shutting down the consulate might further fan the panic, he decided he could wait no longer. During the morning Dennis Brown, along with other Americans and Europeans working in Da Nang, was called to the consulate and told to prepare for evacuation. "Please, no questions," he remembered an official saying. "Just get out." After the meeting Brown returned to his office, opened the safe, and distributed his remaining cash to his ten terrified Vietnamese employees—75,000 piastres each, about $100 at the official rate but much less on the black market, where the rate was soaring higher every hour. Telling the staff they could keep or sell the office furnishings and handing over the keys to the CARE van, Brown went back to the consulate at 1 P.M.

Early in the week, before it appeared that Da Nang itself was threatened, the U.S. embassy had planned an airlift of refugees to the south, where they could be cared for more easily and where they would not impede military operations if the city were attacked. Plans called for an initial lift of about 40,000 persons and up to a quarter-million in later stages, using jumbo jets. But by the time the very first plane landed Thursday morning—a Boeing 727 tri-engined jet chartered from the World Airways Corporation of Oakland, California—the object was no longer to lighten the refugee load but to provide escape from a city that was clearly about to fall.

Vietnamese employees of the consulate and other U.S. agencies were supposed to have priority on the flights, but most of them were blocked by military police at the air base gates. The Vietnamese MPs ignored the evacuation passes given out by the consulate—crudely forged copies of which were being black-marketed at sky-high prices in the streets. Even if passengers managed to get onto the base, getting on the planes was another matter. When the first flight came in at about 9 A.M. Thursday, a large crowd waited behind the high wire fence in front of Air America's small stucco terminal. Charles Patterson, a World Airways vice-president, saw the crowd standing quietly when he first glimpsed it from the windows of the taxiing plane. But as the jet rolled to a stop, the crowd suddenly burst through the gate. When the rear loading steps were lowered, Patterson climbed down into a heaving mass of people trying to push aboard. Nearly all of them, he saw, were Vietnamese air force troops and their families, not the consular employees whom the Americans had ticketed for evacuation. Adding to the terror, though far off, were the intermittent explosions of Communist rockets landing somewhere on the base. Despite the disorder, Patterson and the crew managed to load 195 people onto the 125-seat airplane, squeezing four slim Vietnamese into each bank of three seats and putting children on the laps of adult passengers.

Al Francis, the consul-general, had been warning his embassy superiors for several days that the situation was worsening. On March 26, the day before the World Airways flights began, Francis had proposed to Col. Gavin McCurdy, the air attache, that two U.S. military helicopters be assigned to stand by for a possible evacuation of the consulate. But when McCurdy passed on the request to 7th Air Force headquarters in Thailand, he was turned down. All U.S. helicopters were committed to the anticipated Phnom Penh evacuation, he was told, and besides, using American military forces in Vietnam would skirt both U.S. law and the Paris agreement and was thus a matter of extreme sensitivity for which approval "would have to be obtained from the highest levels." No helicopters were sent, leaving only the World Airways charter flights.

Learning of the disorders at the terminal while the first flight was loading, Francis dashed to the base, where he confronted the senior Vietnamese officers who could be found, a colonel and a brigadier general. "We're trying to help," Francis told them, "but we can't unless you help keep order." If they would keep the base under control, he promised, the U.S. would see to it that air force families would be flown out of the threatened city. The two officers nodded, promising to discipline the unruly crowds. Patterson stayed to help organize the next flight while the jet took off for Nha Trang, less than an hour's flying time down the coast. As he watched it leave the runway, he doubted that the Vietnamese officers' promise could be kept, and he was right. The second flight was mobbed again. This time, Francis joined Patterson at the foot of the loading steps. The two men tried to pluck children out of the mob and hand them in so they would not be trampled. Francis pleaded frantically for order. Everyone would be flown out, he promised. But he was ignored. Airmen began hoisting their children over the side rail of the loading steps; some climbed in themselves. With 192 people on board, Francis and Patterson had to wrestle others back off the steps so the door could be closed.

When they returned for the third time, the crew taxied the plane to a far corner of the field. The tactic worked. Passengers were brought to planeside by bus and truck and everything stayed calm enough for 225 people to be jammed into the seats. But the fourth and last flight of the day, at dusk, turned dangerous again. The plane's lights were spotted, and hordes of airmen followed in jeeps and trucks as the crew moved the plane three times, looking for a safe spot to load. About 190 passengers were loaded while Patterson and the crew had their worst battle of the day with unruly air force troops at the steps.

That night, at Francis's request, Colonel McCurdy called 7th Air Force again, repeating his request for helicopters to help evacuate Da Nang. When he was turned down again, he asked desperately for a couple of C-130 transports. They wouldn't even have to land if conditions were unsafe, McCurdy said. Even if they just circled overhead, they would give "the illusion of a great number of airplanes" and ease the fears of the crowd that each flight would be the last. That request, too, was denied.

Strangely, while evacuation planes were being mobbed, Air Vietnam was still flying scheduled flights from the civilian terminal. Its planes loaded normally and in perfect order all day. Even in their fear, Da Nang's airmen were not yet bucking the graft and privilege embedded in their society.

The next morning—Good Friday—Francis and U.S. embassy officers in Saigon decided, with some misgivings, to try one more flight, the fifth of twenty called for in the initial World Airways contract. The air base commander again promised to keep order. But when the plane landed, the situation was even worse than on the day before. Crewmen used riot spray on the crowds but could not stop them, and Francis ordered the plane to take off with only 60 passengers, less than half its capacity.

After that attempt, the AID mission in Saigon ordered the airlift stopped. But Edward J. Daly, World Airways board chairman and chief executive, had other ideas.

Coming to Saigon to supervise the airlift personally, Daly ensconced himself with an entourage of secretaries and assistants in a suite at the Caravelle Hotel, where he provided some of the more bizarre moments of the war's last weeks. Hard-drinking and foul-mouthed, Daly had an unpleasant fondness for threatening physical violence. Once he drew a knife on a television correspondent who somehow displeased him, though usually he seemed to relish the attention he received from the press and cameramen. On another occasion he invited a group of newsmen, along with a roomful of other guests, to a dinner at the Caravelle's plush top-floor restaurant, but then became annoyed when some of them began chatting among themselves instead of listening to his incoherent harangue from the head table. Suddenly Daly pulled a revolver from his pocket and slammed it down next to his butter plate, announcing loudly that he would shoot the next son-of-a-bitch who interrupted him. After a moment's stunned silence, the newsmen got up and walked out.

On Saturday, March 29, without clearance from the American embassy, Daly boarded his plane and ordered it back to Da Nang. His crew loyally described it as a "humanitarian act," while angry American officials felt it was an outrageously irresponsible and harebrained bit of bravado. Whichever it was, it nearly cost Daly and his crew their lives.

From the air over Da Nang, pilot Ken Healy could see that the field was covered with people. The crew didn't know it, but the Vietnamese air force had now completely lost control of the base. It had been taken over by 1st Division troops, gripped by an uncontrollable, panicked frenzy. Healy, a veteran pilot with the face of a weatherbeaten leprechaun, had been flying supply missions to Phnom Penh, landing under rockets; as a young pilot nearly 30 years before, he had flown into besieged Nationalist outposts during the Chinese civil war. Now, he radioed the Da Nang tower. The field was under control, he was told. He would be instructed where to park, and a security detail would protect the plane while it was loading. Healy turned to his boss for a decision. Daly told him to go on in and land.

Despite the reassuring message from the tower, pandemonium broke out the minute the plane touched the runway. In vehicles and on foot, soldiers raced toward it from every direction, flinging away helmets, flak jackets, and other gear. Some threw down their weapons; others fired wild, unaimed bursts in the air.

When the plane stopped, Joe Hrezo, Daly's station manager at Clark Air Base in the Philippines, dropped off the lowered loading steps. The instant he did so, he realized it was "a goddamn mistake." Daly climbed down behind him. The two men couldn't climb back aboard before Healy had to taxi away from the mob of soldiers, so they raced on foot to the control tower. As they ran, they saw an overloaded jeep "with about twenty people hanging all over it" slam into a motorbike on the runway, sending it skidding away over the ground. Bodies, lifted into the air by the collision, thudded back down to the ground. A moment later, Hrezo saw soldiers shoot out the tires of a fire truck, piled high with uniformed men, that was rushing toward the plane.

Joe Hrezo hadn't landed in Da Nang to pick up soldiers. He wanted to fly out women, children, and other civilian refugees. He could see some, waiting on trucks in the distance. But they had not the slightest chance of reaching the plane. On the runway, he recalled that night, "all I saw was fatigue uniforms." Ken Healy, meanwhile, was zigzagging the plane down the field, trying to find a safe place to stop. But every time he halted, vehicles of all kinds came tearing toward him. A half-dozen Communist rockets, with their characteristic sound of rapidly ripping canvas, landed among the buildings to the side of the runway, but Healy had no time to worry about them. He didn't care any more about picking up refugees, either. But he would not take off without Daly and Hrezo.

Three times, while the plane was halted, hordes of desperate soldiers engulfed the still-lowered loading steps. Jan Wollett, a stewardess, stood in the door and fought helplessly with them. "What about the women and children!" she remembered screaming over and over. "What about the children!" Once, spotting a woman near the steps, Wollett reached out, grabbed her shoulders and tried to hoist her up over the heads of the mob. But a soldier on the ground seized the woman by the waist and hurled her back down. Then he crawled up the steps himself. On Thursday and Friday, soldiers charging the plane had been trying to send their families to safety. Now, even that most basic human loyalty had fractured. Men were trampling their own wives and children to get on board.

Finally, Healy managed to work the plane down by the tower, where Hrezo and Daly were waiting. As soon as they were on the steps, he began his takeoff roll. The main runway was blocked by a stalled Vietnamese A-37 jet fighter with bombs slung under the wings. So Healy used the narrower taxiway that paralleled the main strip. As he picked up speed, he could hear bursts of rifle fire. Hrezo, clinging to the still partly lowered back steps, saw enraged soldiers flinging grenades as the plane screamed past them. One blast, possibly a grenade but also possibly a collision with a parked vehicle, knocked off the inboard flap on the port wing and damaged the plane's hydraulic system.

Healy ran the full length of the runway and his wheels were on the grass before the overloaded plane finally struggled into the air. That evening, when someone asked if it had been safe to take off without knowing how badly the plane was damaged, Healy stared at the questioner in amazement for a moment and then broke into a huge laugh. "It was a damn sight safer than not taking off," he answered. Jan Wollett felt as if the nightmare had lasted for hours. In fact, they had been on the ground only about twenty minutes.

As the 727 became airborne, Daly and Hrezo were still hanging onto the loading steps, fighting to free a soldier whose leg had gotten jammed in the rail, preventing the steps from being raised. For long minutes, the two airline executives tried to extricate the terrified man. Finally they managed to haul him back inside the plane and climb back in themselves. Daly was scratched and bleeding from his back, chest, and arms. His natty safari shirt hung off his shoulders in tatters.

Healy found he could not raise his landing gear because soldiers were clinging to the struts. A backup plane—a second World Airways 727 that had flown to Da Nang but did not land there—reported seeing at least one man fall away to his death from the wheel-well. But seven others, one of them critically wounded, flew all the way to Saigon hanging from the landing gear. A larger group of 50 to 60 men were crammed in the partly open baggage hatch. In all, 330 persons had fought their way onto Ken Healy's damaged plane. Several were injured. The man who had been trapped in the steps at takeoff had a broken leg, and at least one other came aboard with gunshot wounds. On board were four women, three children, and three frightened, shaking old men. All the rest were soldiers.

Once in the air, they turned meek. Without a word they surrendered weapons and grenades. Paul Vogle of UPI, whom Daly had invited on the flight and who later wrote a first-person account that was one of the memorable news stories of Vietnam's collapse, walked down the aisle collecting armfuls of ammunition clips. "They had gone from humans to animals," Vogle wrote about the soldiers on the plane, "and now they were vegetables." Some of them even asked Jan Wollett pleadingly if there would be more flights to pick up their wives and children who had been left in Da Nang. She stared at them in amazement. "You weren't so concerned when you were getting on board, were you?" was all she could think of to say.

Healy, meanwhile, was keeping the injured aircraft in the air at 200 knots and 10,500 feet, less than half the normal speed and altitude. The backup plane circled above and beneath and radioed a report on the visible damage, while Healy wondered if he would be able to land. "The good Lord was the pilot," he said later. "I just maneuvered the controls a little bit." Two hours and 30 minutes after the near-disastrous takeoff, he touched down at Saigon's Tansonnhut Airport. South Vietnamese military police surrounded the plane as it taxied to a stop and led off the now-docile passengers, including six of those who had flown in the wheel-wells; the seventh was carried off in a stretcher. The airlift was over. Instead of 40,000 refugees, it had brought fewer than 1,200, nearly all of them soldiers or their families, to the south.

The shocked, sickened World Airways crew thought angrily of the refugees who might have been saved. "If we had had one one-hundredth of the cooperation from the refugees that we were trying to give them," said Glen Flansaas, the co-pilot, "this company could have carried out thousands of people."

Ken Healy felt sick. "I flew the first ammo flight to Phnom Penh and it looks like I've flown the last flight from Da Nang," he said that evening. "Now all I want to do is fly the next flight back to Oakland."

Among the officers and men of the Vietnamese air force's 1st Air Division at Da Nang, the last thing on anyone's mind was flying combat missions against the Communist forces approaching the city. Few sorties were flown even before discipline was lost at the air base. On the night of March 27, the division commander, Brig. Gen. Nguyen Duc Khanh, was ordered to get all his flyable planes out. But fewer than half ever took off. Approximately 180 aircraft, including 33 A-37 jet fighters, were left on the field to be captured by the Communists. Nor did most of his nearly 7,000 men escape.

As the air base dissolved in chaos, so did the city. Thursday evening, the 27th, a huge crowd collected outside the U.S. consulate on the waterfront, while CARE's Dennis Brown and other foreigners waited inside for transport out of the city. As dusk fell, the evacuees were told to slip unobtrusively out of the consulate building. They were trucked to a nearby U.S. billet whose name—the Alamo Hotel—now seemed frighteningly apt. There they spent the night listening to the hotel's large supply of rock music tapes and drinking from its ample stock of cold beer. All night, attempts to leave were frustrated by crowds of Vietnamese outside—led, Brown noticed, by the consulate's own security guards, who were determined not to let the consular staff leave without them.

About two in the morning, Brown and the others were called outside to board trucks. But before they could do so, the Vietnamese charged, "belting each other, crying and screaming." The move was called off and the evacuees trooped wearily back into the Alamo, while Al Francis and his marine guards and other security officers tried to figure out some way to get past the panicked crowd. Now that escape through the air base seemed impossible, the plan was to put the consulate's Vietnamese employees on barges at the waterfront to be taken to ships waiting offshore. But at the port, the situation was out of control. Through the night Brown heard radioed messages from Americans on the barges reporting "unbelievable panic" on shore. Every time a boat—any boat—approached the sea wall, thousands of people would surge toward the spot, trampling any who fell. As far as Brown could tell from the radio traffic, only the Americans were trying to run refugee boats. "There was no visible sign of the GVN"—Government of Vietnam—"doing anything."

A few hours before dawn, the consulate's marine security guards, a six-man detachment under Staff Sgt. Walter Sparks, drove several trucks to the Alamo to pick up the Vietnamese outside. As they moved through the dark streets, Sparks could hear Communist agents driving around in jeeps with loudspeakers, telling people not to panic and to fly Buddhist banners. "We'll be in tomorrow to restore order," the invisible voices promised.

When the trucks were loaded, they were driven to the sea wall not more than 50 yards from the consulate building, where a U.S. Military Sealift Command barge was tied up. There was no way Sparks and his small detachment could keep crowds of other refugees away. As the loading continued, the panic worsened. He saw women toss babies to people on the barge, sometimes missing and throwing the children into the black, oily water; people tried to shinny down a rope from a bollard on shore, and were sometimes caught and crushed when the barge heaved in the wash of other passing vessels or rolled under the weight of thousands of scrambling passengers. At about dawn, a Sealift Command tug began to try to push the barge out into the harbor. But the Vietnamese on shore would not cast off the line, trying instead to keep using it to climb on board. As the tug repeatedly tried to push the barge away from the wall it would swing out until the rope came taut, and then would snap back, each time jarring a few more passengers overboard. On shore, Communist shellfire was quickening and many huge fires, most of them set by looters, were burning. Finally, the rope leashing the barge to the shore snapped, and nudged by its tug, it nosed out among the hundreds of fishing boats, sampans, and other vessels milling about in the harbor. The sun was just coming up on Good Friday morning.

A couple of hours later, with the streets outside the Alamo Hotel at last relatively clear, Dennis Brown and the other evacuees walked in groups of two or three to a landing pad at a nearby compound that had been formerly occupied by the international peacekeeping force. There they were picked up by Air America helicopters that had taken off from Marble Mountain, a small military airstrip east of the city. Several dozen Vietnamese, some of them consular employees who came with American authorization but others who just walked through the compound's unguarded gate, were taken on the helicopters as well. After the short hop to Marble Mountain, the passengers transferred to an Air America C-46 transport for the flight south.

There were no mobs at the airstrip and there was enough room on the plane for everyone, but the Vietnamese were so terrified they still apparently could not believe they were safe. As Brown watched in appalled amazement, the Vietnamese stormed the plane, kicking and pummeling each other as they fought to be the first to climb on.

A few hours later in Saigon, Wolfgang Lehmann, chargé d'affaires in the absence of Ambassador Martin, was meeting with members of the American Chamber of Commerce in the South Vietnamese capital—a group neither quite as prominent nor quite as stodgy as the name suggested, whose membership ranged from staid officers of international banks and oil companies to ex-GIs running bars or one-man businesses and safari-suited adventurers operating at the margins of the law. The purpose of the meeting was for Lehmann to pass on the Vietnamese government's assurances that the rest of the country would and could be held, and to urge American businessmen to show confidence in the country's future by expanding their own enterprises and encouraging their friends and associates to invest there. Giving up the highlands and unproductive parts of the northern region was a decision forced on President Thieu by the decline in U.S. aid and by Hanoi's aggression, Lehmann told his audience, but an "aggressive defense" of the South's remaining territory was being prepared, and a display of optimism by American entrepreneurs would help Vietnamese morale.

As to South Vietnam's survival, the embassy would admit no doubt at all. Saigon might come under rocket attack, as had happened in previous offensives, Lehmann said. But he dismissed the idea of a full-scale assault. A Communist attempt to take the capital was inconceivable.

While Lehmann was delivering his pep talk and while Dennis Brown was flying from Marble Mountain toward Saigon, Paul Tracy, the senior Defense Attache Office representative in Da Nang, was aboard the Sealift Command barge in the harbor with about 6,000 refugees—one-fourth of them soldiers, Tracy estimated, many with weapons. Tracy himself carried a loaded M-16 which Al Francis had handed him at four o'clock that morning as he left the Alamo for the waterfront. He might, Francis had warned grimly, have to use it.

Waiting to load the refugees was the SS *Pioneer Contender*, a civilian American freighter of 13,532 deadweight tons that was also under charter to the Sealift Command. She had been diverted to Da Nang along with five tugs and a number of barges. About the time Tracy's barge reached her, several sampans and a Vietnamese tug jammed with refugees also found the ship, and their passengers began pouring onto the barge, fighting with those already aboard, in order to reach the ship's ladders. To get the tug to pull away, Tracy and another American climbed aboard, promising its passengers they would be loaded after the barge was empty. With two Americans on board, the refugees calmed down. Once safely away from the barge, however, Tracy and his companion slipped over the side into a sampan and then hailed a speedboat belonging to the Da Nang CIA base, which took them back to the *Contender* on the side opposite the still-crammed barge.

Already aboard the ship was Brian Barron, a blond, 35-year-old correspondent for the British Broadcasting Corporation who was one of the most courageous of all reporters in Indochina.

Barron and his cameraman, Eric Thirer, had arrived on one of the last Air Vietnam flights early the day before—Thursday, the 27th—and hitchhiked into town with a Vietnamese air force colonel, who spent the entire drive begging them to help evacuate him and his family. After checking into the two-year-old Caravelle Hotel on the waterfront, Barron hired a motorbike and drove back to the air base with Thirer to film the first of the chaotic World Airways flights. Handing the film to an Air Vietnam pilot, hoping it would reach Saigon safely, he returned to the city early in the afternoon and was astounded at the deterioration that had occurred in only a few hours. The hotel was locked and the streets were full of armed, angry soldiers. Barron and Thirer finally managed to retrieve their baggage and went to the U.S. consulate, then with other evacuees to the Alamo. Early Good Friday morning, his group went, not to the ICCS helipad where Dennis Brown had gone, but to a far end of the waterfront, where they were loaded on motor launches and taken out to the *Pioneer Contender*.

Not long after Barron boarded, the teeming barge drew alongside. The ship's crew originally planned to lower rope ladders over the side, but that idea was discarded as too dangerous. A panicky rush to the ladders could cause catastrophe. So all of the nearly 6,000 refugees filed up the ship's single gangway in a seemingly endless, tattered line uncoiling from the mass of humanity below, like a strand of yarn from a pile of wool. Miraculously, the loading stayed relatively orderly, perhaps because the passengers were so tightly packed together in the barge that none could rush the gangway even if they wanted to.

Marines from the consulate security detail—men who were kids in grade school when their older brothers waded cockily ashore to begin the American war just a few miles away and ten years and twenty days earlier—supervised the loading, carrying slung M-16s and bandoliers of clips over their civilian sport shirts. Some armed civilians, including Paul Tracy, pitched in to help. Confiscating weapons and ammunition from hundreds of soldiers, the marines helped carry babies, the sick and injured, and the elderly up the narrow ladder. Tracer rounds flew overhead from other soldiers on small boats who could not get near enough to climb onto the barge, and who fired aimless shots out of rage and frustration. When it appeared that everyone was off the barge, Sergeant Sparks of the marine detail and some of the tug crewmen climbed down for a final inspection and found two last refugees: an elderly couple, the man with a broken leg. They were "petrified," sitting so still in their shock and terror that at first Sparks thought they were dead; only when he came very close could he see that they were still alive. He helped them up to the ship, then climbed back aboard himself.

The loading lasted from mid-morning until dusk, when, with everyone finally on board, the *Contender's* crewmen anchored the barge and then cut it free from the ship. Barron watched it recede toward the flameburst of the sunset behind Da Nang. It was empty except for two dogs and an incredible litter of suitcases, sandals, bundles of clothing, sewing machines, cooking pots, bicycles and motorbikes, electric fans, and other belongings left by the refugees who now stood shoulder to shoulder on the ship's steel deck. Shortly after dark, the *Contender* steamed out of Da Nang harbor to begin the sixteen-hour journey to Cam Ranh Bay. By then a second Sealift Command vessel, the civilian-crewed navy ship USNS *Andrew Miller*, had arrived and was beginning to take aboard some 7,500 passengers from three other barges. Several more ships were on the way, including the *Contender's* sister ship, SS *Pioneer Commander*.

While the *Contender's* passengers waited to get under way, General Truong ordered a 24-hour curfew ashore, announcing that curfew violators and looters would be shot. The order had no effect. At the main ARVN supply depot, supply specialists waited for orders to destroy the huge stocks there. Under standing instructions, demolition had to be authorized by the corps command. The orders never came, even after the depot commander went personally to Truong's office and to the regional headquarters of the army logistics command, vainly seeking permission to blow up the depot. The troops guarding the depot remained at their post longer than most combat soldiers had, staying so long they finally had to escape by swimming to boats offshore. Behind them they left the depot and all its supplies, still intact. Other stocks of major equipment, including tanks and artillery pieces, were left on the docks, where they had been secretly moved days before to be shipped south. The shipment orders were cancelled when Thieu issued his "defend-to-the-death" proclamation. Later, no ships could get close enough to load without being swamped with soldiers and refugees.

At four o'clock Friday afternoon, Truong's spokesman at I Corps headquarters announced for the last time that the army would fight for Da Nang. Three hours later, the general and those who still remained of his staff left to make their way to ships offshore. By Truong's later account, he telephoned Thieu first to ask permission to yield the city but could get no clear decision, and then gave the order on his own after communications with Saigon were lost. Eventually a message reached officers aboard Vietnamese navy ships that "the order to defend Da Nang was still valid." But by then it was meaningless. Da Nang now belonged to no one except the tens of thousands of panicked, cursing soldiers in the streets.

Over the Easter weekend, while flames and smoke from burning buildings rose over the city and multicolored Buddhist banners flew in place of the Saigon flag in front of homes and shops, the flight to the sea continued. More and more fishing boats, launches, and other small craft, filled with soldiers and refugees and riding with gunwales awash in the brown river water, swarmed toward any larger vessel that seemed about to head south. Hundreds of people drowned or were crushed to death while trying to leap onto small boats from the riverfront. Many others were lost in the harbor— drowned, shot by soldiers, or dead from exposure or thirst after hours and days afloat.

At the dock area, several miles from the seething downtown sea wall, thousands more people waited on the wharves. A young man named Nguyen Hoan* had been "happy and relieved" to reach the docks late Friday afternoon with his fourteen-year-old sister and ten other family members. It seemed safe, not just because it was away from the heart of the city but because no military installations were nearby. An officer in the port administration, who was an acquaintance of Hoan's father, led the family to an office inside a huge warehouse, promising to come get them when there was a ship loading.

At ten o'clock that night, however, the warehouse was shaken by a huge explosion outside. Hoan dove for shelter under a metal desk while two more explosions, either artillery or rockets, followed. One of the blasts was no more than twenty yards away. The electric lights in the warehouse blinked out and the windows shattered, spraying glass fragments across the room. A piece of shrapnel hit Hoan's sister on the thigh, opening a wound that bled

* A pseudonym.

heavily. In the darkness he tried to pick the metal shards out of her flesh with his fingers, then bandaged the wound with a piece of cloth. Outside, the shells kept coming, the explosions marching away from the warehouse along the wharves that were packed with people. The fire was so accurate that Hoan believed the Communists must have had spotters someplace very close by. Hundreds of people, he thought, must have been killed.

The shells stopped after an hour, then began again at six the next morning. At six-thirty, Hoan decided there was no way to leave Da Nang if Communist artillerymen were determined to prevent evacuation. With his sister on his back he jogged back away from the harbor, stopping finally at an empty stretch of beach where, he thought melodramatically, he would breathe "the air of freedom" for the last time before heading back to Da Nang. But near where they stopped, a small party of Vietnamese navy officers were waiting to be picked up by a small boat to be taken to a navy ship. When it came, they took Hoan and his sister along.

Other families that had somehow stayed together earlier in the collapse were now broken apart in the frantic rush for the boats. Aboard the *Pioneer Contender*, an American teacher at Hue University, Tom Malia, found a twelve-year-old boy named Hung, whose mother was a Da Nang shop owner. They had reached the dock together and his mother lifted him into a sampan. Then a shoving crowd knocked her into the water. Hung never saw her again. When he was handed up the ship's gangway he was still clinging to a small dog and two shoulderbags containing rice, some tins of meat, and his oldest brother's high school textbooks. In a backpack he carried cooking utensils and chopsticks and the family's rice bowls, carefully wrapped in crushed paper. When Malia brought him to Saigon, Hung would not admit that his mother might have drowned, although few Vietnamese women can swim. She was coming, he kept insisting, on another ship.

Nguyen Gia Ung, the Hue high school teacher who had fled to Da Nang eight days earlier, was separated from his wife and four children on Good Friday as they tried to reach the ships. Days later Ung reached Phu Quoc Island in the Gulf of Thailand, at the very farthest point of South Vietnam from his starting place, penniless and alone.

Saturday and Sunday, the *Andrew Miller* and *Pioneer Commander* finished loading and left, while the Sealift Command tugs towed barges out of the harbor that were also packed with refugees and soldiers. The vessels' destination was Cam Ranh Bay, 250 miles to the south. Once the chief logistics port for the U.S. expeditionary force, Cam Ranh was now a ghost city of empty tin-roofed hangers, cracked, weed-grown runways, and rusting coils of barbed wire half covered with sand. It was an inhospitable place but at least it was safe, or seemed so, to group refugees there while preparations were made for their journey farther south.

Also on Easter Sunday, the *Pioneer Contender* was back off Da Nang for her second and last trip. From shortly after two in the afternoon until past nine o'clock that night, she boarded refugees from two barges and a swarm of smaller craft. Some of the refugees had been on the barges for as long as four days and were sick or terribly weak from hunger and thirst. The *Contender's* crew lowered huge cargo nets over the side to hoist refugees aboard like so many crates of pineapples. From the deck, Peter O'Loughlin of the Associated Press saw one woman, after being lowered into the ship's hold, mutely hold up a dead baby. The sailors lifted her back down to the barge so she could leave the corpse there. "It seemed better," O'Loughlin wrote, "than dropping the body over the side."

When the barges were cut loose, the ship's crew counted about 50 corpses stiffening on their steel planks. More bodies bobbed about in the dark water, torn clothes swirling about them. On shore, the crewmen could hear fighting on the city's outskirts, while conditions in the inner harbor were "chaotic." A few minutes after ten o'clock on the night of March 30, the *Contender* sailed out of the harbor. Also that day, three Sealift Command tugs left Da Nang towing barges full of refugees; their loads and the *Contender's* represented the last of approximately 34,600 people who escaped from Da Nang on American-controlled shipping.

Other refugees sailed on a bedraggled assortment of Vietnamese navy craft, two small Vietnamese coastal freighters, and various smaller vessels. Altogether, the military command in Saigon estimated, about 90,000 people reached the south by sea. About 16,000 of them were soldiers, all that now remained of the entire northern region command of nearly ten times that many men. Perhaps a million people were left in Da Nang, including hundreds who worked for the U.S. consulate and depended on American promises of evacuation, only to be left in the disintegrating city—the first, but not the last, to be thus abandoned by American officials in Vietnam.

In the hills ringing the city, some marines and a few soldiers of the 3rd ARVN Division were, in places, fighting the enemy, though mainly just to reach the coast and escape. In Da Nang itself, no fighting awaited the advancing Communist army. While the divisions of General Dung's II Corps converged from the north, northwest, southwest, and south, local guerrillas and "special action" commandos raised the liberation flag over the city hall at three o'clock Saturday afternoon. Though a Liberation Armed Forces communique claimed "complete control" of the city, there weren't enough Communist troops to take over the still-seething waterfront, where crowds boiled along the harbor's edge, spilling onto small boats in the hope of reaching larger ships farther out.

On the beaches east of the city, what remained of the Marine Division waded, swam, or floated on inflated truck tires through the surf to landing craft waiting out in the ocean. The embittered marines had retreated in relatively good order as far as the coast. But now they were firing on other soldiers and on refugees, as had other marines during the flight from Hue, to open the way for their own escape. Many marines drowned in the sea, their bodies washing back into the shallows to form sandy hummocks along with those who had been killed on the beach. Trucks and armored personnel carriers sat listing in the water, where they had stalled after frightened drivers drove them as far toward the ships as they could reach.

On Easter Sunday, General Dung's regulars arrived and restored order overnight, apparently with little difficulty and almost no casualties. By then, no doubt, much of Da Nang was ready to welcome even the North Vietnamese if it meant an end to the killing and looting. The exhausted, terrified government soldiers offered no resistance. Once escape was impossible, they were quickly and easily cowed.

On Easter Monday, another Sealift Command freighter, the SS *American Challenger*, was offshore, with orders to remain well out to sea beyond artillery range and to pick up any stragglers from fishing boats or other small craft. But there were none. The situation in Da Nang, the ship radioed back to Saigon, appeared to be "dead quiet."

Chapter **11**

"It is like an avalanche"

After Da Nang, provinces stretching along 300 miles of coastline fell like a row of porcelain vases sliding off a shelf. At their headquarters in the highlands, Communist staff officers could not redraw battle maps quickly enough to keep up with the advance of their forces.

Qui Nhon, capital of Binh Dinh Province and South Vietnam's third largest city, was evacuated on the night of March 31 as shells crashed around the province headquarters. Binh Dinh's defenders, including the 22nd ARVN Division and militia units, had been fighting hard for weeks. But now, like the troops farther north, they fought only to reach the coast and escape. In the debacle almost none of the soldiers collected their March pay, which they should have received on the last day of the month. This would seriously worsen their suffering in the refugee stream.

During the day and overnight, a few American vessels reached Qui Nhon harbor, but were kept away from shore by Vietnamese navy craft, which were shelling the city. Huge fires on shore reddened the night. An appalling confusion gripped senior commanders. Brigadier General Phan Dinh Niem, the 22nd Division commander, was said to have suffered a nervous collapse; a navy officer, Commodore Hoang Co Minh, was directed to take command of the division and the rest of the "Qui Nhon theater." But Minh, who had spent several days circling about on a small cutter while contradictory messages tumbled in on him from various headquarters, had no idea where the 22nd Division was. He didn't even know its radio frequency.

By five o'clock on the morning of April 1, Qui Nhon was in Communist hands. Later in the day the last of the American ships, the civilian-crewed navy cargo ship USNS *Greenville Victory*, sailed south; no refugees had reached her or any of the other U.S. vessels. Several thousand soldiers escaped on Vietnamese navy craft. Hardly any effort was made to destroy arms, munitions, and other supplies that were left behind. Nearly 60 aircraft were abandoned at Phu Cat Air Base, many of them flyable. ARVN supply troops managed to ship about 1,300 tons of ammunition from the Qui Nhon depot, but more than three times as much, 4,410 tons, was left and almost certainly fell intact into Communist hands.

Only hours after Qui Nhon was lost, Nha Trang, where the hapless General Phu reestablished his II Corps command after abandoning Pleiku, began to disintegrate. Two days before, Phu specifically prohibited his soldiers from moving without orders and vowed to defend what was left of his region "to the last." But shortly after noon on April 1, Phu walked out of his headquarters and left by helicopter for the airfield, from which he flew to Saigon. He told none of his subordinates except a few staff officers who saw him leave—and promptly joined him. Among those left behind was Colonel Ly, the II Corps chief of staff, who had also been left at Pleiku two weeks before. After discovering that Phu had gone, Ly went to the airfield, where air force men briefly held him hostage while demanding that Phu return. But that evening the air force abandoned the field, and Ly flew with them to the capital. By then, other officers had also deserted their troops, who began to riot and loot the city, joined by deserters and other convicts who broke out of the military prison. It was Da Nang all over again, if on a smaller scale. Armed men roamed from house to house, demanding money and valuables, while other soldiers and frightened refugees swarmed to the airfield, hoping for evacuation.

The U.S. consul-general, Moncrieff Spear, and his staff also hurriedly left Nha Trang on the afternoon of the 1st. As they prepared to go, hundreds of Vietnamese tried to climb over the whitewashed walls of the consulate compound. U.S. planes leaving from the airfield were pursued by other crowds, including soldiers who fired shots in the air. The evacuation was so chaotic that more than 100 Vietnamese consular employees, who had been promised flights to Saigon, were left behind, some of them ordered away from planeside by U.S. officials who trained rifles on them. "I'm so ashamed of the United States government," one American said, "that I'll never be able to work for them again."

What made the betrayal even worse was that it was unnecessary. Nha Trang was abandoned long before the approaching Communists were close enough to threaten it. "There was no attack on the city," said one of the last Vietnamese officers to leave. "There was not a Viet Cong to be seen anywhere"—only drunken, rioting government soldiers who looted everywhere and set great fires at the main market and elsewhere around the city. Liberation Radio announced Nha Trang's capture only on April 5, four days after the consulate was evacuated.

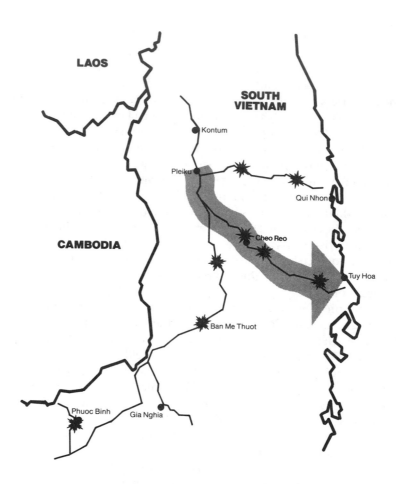

WITHDRAWAL FROM
THE CENTRAL HIGHLANDS

Shaded arrow shows convoy route from Pleiku to the coast;
blast symbol shows major Communist attacks.

Cam Ranh Bay, where Vietnamese marines coming ashore from the sealift terrorized masses of unarmed refugees and fought gun battles with other troops, was also lost before it was attacked. It was given up April 3 but not captured by the Communists until five o'clock the following afternoon. In Cam Ranh, all the equipment that had been saved from the north was lost. As a historian once wrote of another army in another war, the South Vietnamese were now losing the war faster than the Communists could win it.

From Cam Ranh, the panic raced southward to Phan Rang, the capital of President Thieu's native province. On April 3, four U.S. Navy ships carrying a battalion of U.S. Marines—the first of the evacuation task force that eventually involved nearly every American ship in the western Pacific— arrived off Phan Rang to find the waters aswarm with small boats full of refugees. The USS *Durham* lowered her accomodation ladder to begin picking them up and was quickly besieged by as many as 30 craft, bumping and scraping each other as all tried to be first alongside. Marine 2nd Lt. Patrick J. Mullin, with an interpreter and a squad of marines, boarded a landing craft and circled near the ship, trying to direct traffic. But the boats jostled so close that some were almost swamped by the wash from Mullin's craft. Somehow, almost 2,000 refugees were boarded before the *Durham*'s skipper ordered the ladder pulled up. She steamed out to sea to anchor for the night. The ship would return, Mullin's interpreter called out to those still waiting on small boats, in the morning.

As promised, the *Durham* sailed back close to shore on the morning of the 4th and began plucking more refugees from their flimsy craft. Mullin and his squad were again on the water—in a smaller ship's launch this time, so as not to endanger other boats trying to keep order. At first the loading went smoothly. But during the day more and more sampans and other small boats arrived. About 50 were still waiting to unload when, in late afternoon, *Durham*'s captain again decided to stop loading. Orders were shouted to Mullin to lead the remaining refugee boats to the USS *Blue Ridge*, the task force command ship, which was steaming about a mile away. The interpreter instructed the Vietnamese boats to follow. But when Mullin reached the *Blue Ridge*, he was told she had just received orders to sail south and could not stop to take on passengers. So he led his waterborne caravan back to the *Durham*. "They said, OK, we're pulling up the accommodation ladder," Mullin recalled later, "and we're going to take off." Mullin's orders were to get his boat away from the refugees and he and his men would be picked up after the ship was under way.

As the ladder was taken up, Mullin happened to notice a Vietnamese woman on a nearby boat holding a poncho out in front of her. She pointed at the *Durham*. But the exhausted Mullin shook his head. "And then she pulled up the poncho and there was three little kids, they couldn't have been

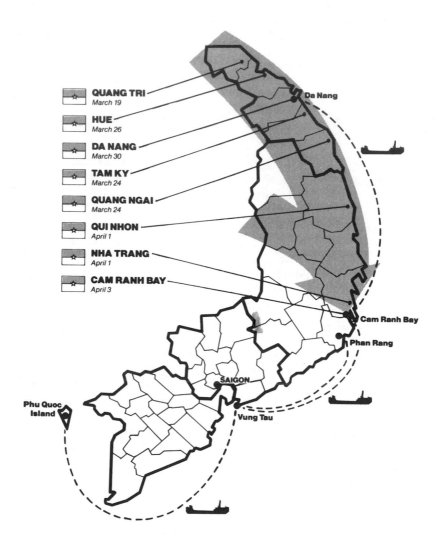

QUANG TRI
March 19

HUE
March 26

DA NANG
March 30

TAM KY
March 24

QUANG NGAI
March 24

QUI NHON
April 1

NHA TRANG
April 1

CAM RANH BAY
April 3

Da Nang

Cam Ranh Bay

Phan Rang

SAIGON

Phu Quoc
Island

Vung Tau

LOSS OF THE COAST

Principal towns and the dates they were abandoned to the
Communists are shown at left; *dotted lines* show routes of
refugee ships from the north to Phu Quoc Island.

more than one year old, one or two years old," he remembered. "She pointed to them as if she was trying to say well, how about getting these kids aboard?" The young marine had no way to help. "The captain of the ship had made a decision we had to go, so we had to go." After picking up Mullin and his men, and with 3,500 refugees aboard, the ship sailed away from shore—where, in fact, Phan Rang was under no immediate threat. Like Nha Trang and Cam Ranh, it panicked long before any Communist forces were close enough to endanger the city. The next day, in fact, an advance III Corps headquarters under Lt. Gen. Nguyen Vinh Nghi—the same general who had been fired for corruption five months before—was reestablished in Phan Rang, with a paratroop brigade, parts of the reconstituted 2nd ARVN Division, and the remnants of the 6th Air Division from Pleiku. These units held Phan Rang for nearly two more weeks until they were overwhelmed on April 16; Nghi, the air division commander, Brig. Gen. Pham Ngoc Sang, and an American observer, James Lewis, were captured there. Before the city fell, government soldiers destroyed the markers at President Thieu's family grave site.

While the *Durham* steamed south from Phan Rang, scores of other craft were heading along the coast carrying refugees from farther north. One, Vietnamese navy barge AN2801, landed at the once-chic resort of Vung Tau after an appalling nine days' journey all the way from Hue. On its steel floor, after its passengers disembarked, lay the crumpled, stiffening bodies of about 50 people, mostly women and children, dead of thirst or exposure. During the exodus, the dreadful fracturing of Vietnamese society continued. Arriving refugees told of paying up to $2 for a glass of water from profiteering fellow-countrymen at Cam Ranh and on fishing boats that came alongside the refugee craft. Sometimes a single glass would be shared by an entire family. Desperately thirsty refugees licked moisture from decks that were smeared with human waste.

The South Vietnamese government by now had no plans for the refugees except to try to keep the virus of panic away from Saigon. At Vung Tau the authorities put up barricades on the road to the capital while directing refugee ships to sail all the way to a disused prisoner-of-war camp on Phu Quoc, a stony, 30-mile-long island shaped like a pork chop which lay 22 miles west of the Vietnamese mainland in the Gulf of Thailand: the entire 700-mile length of the South Vietnamese coastline away from Da Nang.

One of the ships ordered to Phu Quoc was the 31-year-old *Greenville Victory*, with some 7,000 refugees. That was the official estimate, at any rate; Captain Raymond Iacobacci thought the actual number might have been several thousand more. Among them were hundreds of armed soldiers. Most of the passengers had been at sea since leaving Da Nang; when they boarded the 455-foot-long *Greenville Victory* from barges in Cam Ranh Bay, many hadn't eaten for days. When the ship's crew tried to serve food, starving, angry soldiers shoved women and children aside to get to the head of the food lines, or else seized food from those who had already been served. Officers ignored the crew's requests to help control the crowds. Instead, they joined enlisted men in terrorizing the unarmed civilians. The only passengers who helped were two ARVN doctors who tended the wounded and sick, and sixteen Vietnamese Red Cross workers who helped the crew distribute food.

When the ship sailed past Vung Tau, her passengers turned even more unruly. And on the morning of April 4, when she anchored off Phu Quoc, unruliness turned to mutiny.

After anchoring, Iacobacci received no messages at all from the South Vietnamese authorities on the island. The only instructions came from a Vietnamese navy patrol boat that came alongside, telling refugees through a loud-hailer that they would be taken ashore, given food and water, and then taken to the mainland by air. The boat was answered by disbelieving jeers and curses and hours passed with no sign of any landing craft. Nobody believed the authorities anyway. They had been promised refuge, food, and water at Cam Ranh and had received nothing, one of them told Iacobacci, adding, "Now they are sending us off the mainland and we do not believe they will ever send us back."

About noon, two hand-lettered signs were raised from the teeming deck, saying, "Phu Quoc no—Vung Tau." Fifteen minutes later, a delegation of passengers told Iacobacci they would kill him and blow up the ship unless he sailed immediately back to the mainland. Iacobacci agreed. "Considering the safety of the crew and passengers and the welfare of the vessel along with the possibility of this act giving similar ideas to refugees aboard the other vessels," he reported later in his official account of the incident, "the only course of action was to capitulate to their demands." Shortly, the *Greenville Victory* raised anchor and began to retrace her course around the southern tip of the Vietnamese mainland, heading for Vung Tau.

En route, the ship was bombarded with radio messages proposing that either Vietnamese navy forces or American marines from the evacuation ships board and retake control. But Iacobacci refused. Any attempt to seize the ship would result in a "violent reaction," he radioed the Sealift Command office in Saigon. Going on to Vung Tau was the safest thing to do. Events proved him right. There were no more threats after the ship left Phu Quoc and many soldiers threw rifles, grenades, and other explosives over the side—enough weaponry to convince Iacobacci that the hijackers could certainly have carried out their threat to destroy the vessel. When she landed at Vung Tau the next day, soldiers and other refugees filed peacefully off the ship. Some apologized to the crew as they left. Iacobacci's report even included a bright note. "We also became enriched by three new U.S. citizens born aboard this ship while in international waters," he wrote. The American embassy in Saigon was notified, and "the parents were presented with official birth verification papers signed by the master."

Still at Phu Quoc was the *Pioneer Contender*, whose journey was the most hellish of all of the evacuation ships.

The *Contender* had also loaded at Cam Ranh, taking on refugees from small boats all day on April 3 while a Vietnamese navy ship nearby fired at targets on shore. An answering rocket exploded only about 400 feet from the *Contender*'s stern, causing panic among the boats that were jostling for position around her. Refugees clambered from boat to boat trying to reach the ship's ladders. At least one fishing boat swamped and several of its occupants drowned. Abandoned boats drifted about, bumping into those that were still trying to reach the ship. One empty steel-hulled power boat, its engine racing in reverse and the tiller jammed to one side, raced in backward circles, pouring out smoke.

The *Contender*'s 43-man crew tried to confiscate weapons from those climbing aboard, but in the chaotic crowding the task was hopeless. Rifles, pistols, grenades, and even an M-60 machinegun were smuggled onto the ship. Just before six o'clock in the evening, after loading for ten hours, she began to steam out of the harbor. A little more than an hour later, with dusk deepening into night, she stopped alongside the USS *Frederick* to take aboard 46 marines and two Navy corpsmen under 2nd Lt. Robert E. Lee. The marines wanted to confiscate weapons, too, but in the dark, and with the decks so packed that people could hardly move, they were no more successful than the civilian seamen. During the night, as the ship steamed southward, Lee and his men heard frequent shots from the stern, where out-of-control soldiers fought and robbed civilians of whatever belongings they had managed to keep while struggling to board the ship.

The next morning, Lee's platoon tried to hand out food. But rioting soldiers rushed them, "trampling all over their kids and knocking mothers and little babies aside," remembered Lance Cpl. Robert Haines. It was the first of many food riots that would occur in the succeeding days. The marines tried to use hoses to keep water barrels filled around the deck, but Vietnamese soldiers kept slicing through the hoses and filling their own canteens. Some then sold the water, often at gunpoint, to other refugees. The marines disarmed a few soldiers but not many, and there was more shooting during the second night at sea.

At seven o'clock on the morning of the 5th, the *Contender* dropped anchor off the east coast of Phu Quoc. No one was in sight, and Capt. Edward C. Flink had no idea where he was to go or what would happen to his passengers. When his radioman tried to call Vietnamese authorities ashore, he was answered instead by another Sealift Command ship, the SS *American*

Challenger, which was anchored on the opposite side of the island along with several other vessels, including the *Contender*'s sister ship *Pioneer Commander*, the SS *Green Port*, and the civilian-crewed Navy ship USNS *Sgt. Andrew Miller*. Flink sailed around the island to join them, dropping anchor again in the western anchorage at ten-thirty in the morning under a sizzling sun. There she and her teeming, desperate cargo would remain for six horrifying days.

The Vietnamese navy officers who administered Phu Quoc seemed more worried about possible Communist infiltrators than about unloading the overcrowded ships—or perhaps they were just paralyzed, like most other Vietnamese commanders, by the events of the last few weeks. Whatever the reason, they allowed only a few hundred refugees ashore on the 5th, out of tens of thousands who were waiting. From the *Contender*, where one crewman had already collapsed from exhaustion, Flink radioed his superiors that the rest of his crew were "dead on their feet"—not surprisingly; the average age of the crews on the sealift ships was 45. At five o'clock in the afternoon, six and a half hours after she anchored, a small Vietnamese landing craft agreed to ferry some seriously ill or wounded women and small children from the *Contender*. The landing craft's crew, however, gave many of the places not to the sick or helpless but to friends or acquaintances. These were the only passengers allowed off the *Contender* that day. In the evening there was more rioting on deck when the marines tried to distribute food. Two women and five small children, by Lieutenant Lee's count, were crushed to death. Other deaths were occurring from heat exhaustion, thirst, disease, and starvation. Most who died were the very young or very old. No one could tell how many there were; most of the bodies were slipped overboard during the night.

While the few passengers to reach shore were subjected to long interrogations by the small navy detachment on the island, the *Contender*'s cargo waited again all day on the 6th. Robberies and black-market profiteering in food and water continued. No refugees at all were allowed to land from the *Contender*, and only a few hundred from the other ships. About 200 men on the *Contender*, mostly soldiers, ripped off wooden hatch covers and jumped overboard with them, hoping to float to the beach. Vietnamese navy patrol boats picked up some of them but fired at others. Lieutenant Lee saw about ten men shot in the water, while others floated into offshore currents and were swept away from the island. Much later, the *Contender*'s crew saw patrol craft heading out after them. But it was impossible to see if any were rescued.

In Saigon, where American officials only gradually learned what was happening, they urged the Vietnamese to relax security checks and land refugees more quickly. American-chartered tugs and barges were available for the disembarkation. But the Vietnamese were immovable. The situation on Phu Quoc was good, a senior Vietnamese navy officer declared blandly, with two-thirds of the refugees ashore. This, the Americans knew by now, was a lie. But, as Rear Adm. Hugh Benton cabled the evacuation ships on the evening of April 5, there were "no further actions that the U.S. or any individual could take" to change the attitudes of the Vietnamese government or navy. Benton, the representative in Saigon of Admiral Gayler, the Pacific commander, told the task force that no American-controlled craft could be used to land refugees, but that "ways must be found to provide food and water" to the shipboard refugees "or have them die while in U.S. Navy custody."

Accordingly, on the 6th, American crews on "Mike" boats from the USS *Dubuque* delivered loads of food and medicine, and later that afternoon ferried a doctor to the *Pioneer Contender*. What he found was appalling: "a viral epidemic causing high fevers, rash, nausea, vomiting and diarrhea," as an official report later put it, leading to "widespread dehydration and debilitation." There were numerous pneumonia cases and many infected wounds. In addition, half or more of the refugees had a highly contagious eye inflammation called conjunctivitis, or "pinkeye," as it was called by the marines, many of whom quickly contracted it themselves. Weeks later, the disease was still at epidemic proportions on the island.

Once again on the evening of the 6th, there was rioting when food was given out. As they had on several previous occasions, Lee's marines fired shots in the air to try to keep order. The next morning, the *Contender*'s third at anchor, word came that at last a barge would come alongside to unload her passengers. But the barge was ordered instead to sail for Saigon—empty. From the deck the desperate refugees watched it pull away. A gigantic howl of anguish arose, and the worst violence of the whole voyage broke out. Tensely, Lee gathered his marines into a single small area of the deck, so no one would be trapped in the enraged mob. Several shots were fired toward the marines but none were hit. Because of the dense crowd of innocent civilians, they did not return the fire.

On the afternoon of the 7th, Lee's exhausted marines were finally relieved by another platoon. The young lieutenant's report to his superiors was so grim that the naval task force commander again appealed to the American embassy in Saigon to arrange for the ship to be unloaded. Whether because of the embassy's intervention or not, on the 8th permission was finally given for the Sealift Command tug *Pawnee* to begin taking the *Contender*'s passengers ashore. Unloading began at nine-twenty in the morning, an hour less than three full days after the ship anchored.

It took three more days to get everyone ashore. Second Lieutenant J. Flores, commander of the platoon that had relieved Lee's, kept count as the passengers left the vessel. 16,700 left the 560-foot-long ship, he reported: an unofficial all-time record for a Sealift Command ship. (The previous mark had been set in another Asian war nearly a quarter-century before by a freighter called *Meredith Victory*, which carried about 14,000 Korean refugees). Somewhere between 200 and 400 more people on the *Contender*, most of them children, died in her purgatory of heat, violence, thirst, disease, and despair.

The Phu Quoc island commander, a navy captain named Nguyen Van Thien, had five renegade soldiers shot on the beach, two on April 5 and three more the next day, after other refugees denounced them for crimes at sea. The summary discipline worked; there were no more serious disorders after the refugees were finally ashore. But the island was desperately short of drinking water and supplies. Two weeks after the first ships unloaded, there were still just two wells working in the camp, and four dilapidated tank trucks to distribute the water. As the trucks rumbled over the potholed roads, refugees ran after them with plastic buckets or tin cans, determined to be first in line whenever the trucks stopped.

Eventually some 40,000 refugees landed on the island. About 10,000 were soldiers who were sent back to the mainland, ostensibly for reassignment to new units. A few others who had money for bribes or who were friends of the navy officers stationed there managed to leave, too. But the rest were left to await whatever would happen. The government had no time or energy or interest to spend on them. Crowded into the crumbling prison barracks with rusting tin roofs, the refugees were encircled by high barbed-wire fences dotted with searchlights, watchtowers, and black skull-and-crossbones signs with the one-word warning "Min"—"Mines." American and Australian planes flew food and some medicine into the island. But there was still not enough to eat and thirst was a constant torment. The refugees were not only living in a prison camp; they felt like prisoners.

In Hue, Da Nang, and Kontum, helicopters, transport planes, and even passenger airliners began arriving at the captured airfields from North Vietnam. They unloaded fresh troops, weapons, and ammunition. They also carried thousands of maps, newly printed by the General Staff in Hanoi. The maps were of Saigon.

It had taken the North Vietnamese leaders only two weeks from the start of the campaign to decide that it was no longer necessary to wait for 1976 to finish liberating the South. On March 24, the Politburo resolved that Saigon must be captured before the rainy season, which meant no later than early May. The next day, the North Vietnamese army's I Corps, consisting of most of the regular infantry divisions still in the North, was ordered to the front. The same day a cable went to General Dung, telling him to begin shifting his three divisions in the highlands toward Saigon. "Our plan is a big leap forward," the cable said. "We must make every effort not to lose time."

Before complying, however, Dung wanted a few more days to "attack, annihilate and disintegrate" the remaining South Vietnamese forces on the coast between Tuy Hoa and Cam Ranh. Dung was no less eager than his superiors to complete liberating the South. But he thought it would not take long to finish destroying the government army in the northern half of the country. "The enemy was now in confusion and panic and was being closely pursued by our forces," he wrote. "Our forces had sustained only marginal losses in combat; the fighting spirit of our troops had increased greatly. We were still strong logistically—only part of the ammunition earmarked for the plan had been used, and a fairly large quantity of ammunition had been seized from the enemy." But "the enemy would not disintegrate and flee if we failed to deal deadly, rapid and continuous blows." The Politburo and the Central Military Party Committee wired their assent. But, they told Dung, the campaign on the coast should be completed as quickly as possible.

The move south was the largest and most complex logistical campaign the North Vietnamese had ever tried. "Lightning speed, more lightning speed; boldness, more boldness," proclaimed signboards along the route through the highlands. In the Communist convoys were not just military vehicles but commandeered civilian trucks and buses. "The long trail of dust did not settle," General Dung recalled. Drivers switched on their headlights because of the clouds churned up by trucks ahead. Long past were the days when troops coming from the North spent three months on the trail, traveling almost all the way on foot and hiding in the daylight hours from American bombers. No longer were shells carried one at a time on the backs of soldiers or porters. Dung's I Corps would reach its jump-off line, after a journey of more than a thousand miles, in less than three weeks. The three divisions of his II Corps, meanwhile, after capturing Da Nang, headed down the coast. A dozen years before, Dung wrote in his memoirs, a single division on an exercise with only 400 trucks had gotten so snarled it could not move. Now an entire corps was moving with 2,000 vehicles, rebuilding bridges as it went. Its orders were to be in the Bien Hoa region in just eighteen days.

Spotted in the columns were pieces of booty from the previous weeks: U.S.-supplied personnel carriers and tanks, howitzers, and trucks. Captured South Vietnamese soldiers were sometimes pressed into service as drivers. But most among the great masses of government soldiers in the northern part of the country were neither forced to labor for the Communists nor even put into camps. Instead they were disarmed and given written permission to return home—even if they lived in areas still held by Saigon. Earl Martin, the young American Mennonite who remained in Quang Ngai during its "liberation" but was then ordered to travel overland to Saigon, thus gaining a unique view of the takeover, saw many "ragged bands" of defeated ARVN troops along the road, "plodding slowly and quietly toward the south." If they managed to cross the front line, such men might even have rejoined the government army. But obviously the Communists were unconcerned. Even if the defeated troops reached unoccupied territory, Martin realized, they would only further demoralize their comrades.

On April 2, General Dung and his staff left their highlands headquarters and joined the move south. The next evening he reached his new command post west of Loc Ninh, a rubber plantation town 60 miles north of Saigon. Pham Hung, the party leader in the South, was waiting for him. So was Tran Van Tra, who was soon to be named deputy commander for the final offensive. Five days later, Le Duc Tho arrived with the latest Politburo instructions, reaffirming the decision to attack Saigon before the end of the month.

Plans were drawn and redrawn. But the offensive lacked a code name. General Dung and his colleagues made a suggestion, and at seven o'clock on the evening of April 14, a reply came from Hanoi. The message was designated No. 37/TK and was signed by Le Duan. It said, "Agree that campaign for Saigon be named Ho Chi Minh campaign."

In the South Vietnamese capital, Da Nang's fall struck like the blow of an axe. The highlands and even Hue, the Saigonese knew, had long been vulnerable. But not Da Nang. It had been thought as safe as Saigon itself, and its loss with such terrifying swiftness smashed the last hopes that the army's collapse could be contained. After Da Nang, too, Saigon feared not just the Communists but its own soldiers. "Our lives are endangered by both sides," said an acquaintance of mine, a successful businesswoman who was terrified at what mutinous government troops might do to privileged Vietnamese like herself if panic enveloped Saigon. When I remarked that I thought the leaders were more to blame than the soldiers, she nodded.

"I do not blame the soldiers," she agreed. "It is corruption—I never thought much about corruption; I am a businesswoman and I accepted corruption as a way of life. But now . . ." she paused again, shaking her head. "Our people are better than this," she said finally, thinking now of the terrible shame of the men who fought so long and suffered so much with so little reward, only to end up looking to the world, to their countrymen, and to themselves, like a pack of terrified animals. My friend said again, "We are better than this."

News of more losses hammered on the traumatized nerves of the capital. Saigon did not need to wait for official announcements. In the main post office, which was now jammed every day with anxious Saigonese trying to send messages to kinsmen in the threatened provinces, a large blackboard bore a chalked list of cities for which telegrams were no longer being accepted. Each day, another province capital was added. "It is like an avalanche," said a despairing government official.

Most notable in Saigon's mood was that everyone's thoughts seemed to be only on his own personal fate. At no time in the war's last weeks was there the slightest sense of rallying to the government, even though nearly everyone dreaded a Communist victory. Extremity did not compel unity.

"No spirit of support or sacrifice has been summoned," wrote one journalist. No crowds of Saigonese collected blood or money or food for the soldiers, or helped care for the sick and wounded in the hospitals, or offered their services to the refugees. No swarms of volunteers appeared at recruiting stations. No civilians built barricades or filled sandbags or dug antitank ditches. Nor were they asked to. In its last crisis, the Saigon regime could find no reserve of will largely because it had no relation to its own people. Its leaders could conceive useless appeals to the United States for the return of the B-52s, but not to their countrymen for a common effort at survival.

Conscription continued to be an act of force imposed on an unwilling peasantry. In An Giang Province in the delta, a youth was shot in a roundup of draft dodgers in the last days of March. The next day, villagers set up a roadblock and stopped an ARVN convoy carrying other evaders and ar- rested deserters. Some jumped off the trucks and tried to run away; three were shot down by their guards.

Toward their routed soldiers and the millions of uprooted, members of the elite showed no sorrowful concern, only indifference—or fear. Only a tiny handful of senior commanders planned to stay with their troops. Brigadier General Le Minh Dao of the 18th ARVN Division, which partly redeemed the army's reputation by its courageous stand during April at Xuan Loc, was one. Major General Nguyen Khoa Nam, the delta commander, was another. In a meeting with civil servants on April 3, Nam told them that they were expected to remain in their assigned provinces and that anyone leaving without permission would be "severely dealt with." After remaining with his soldiers until after the surrender, Nam himself—according to Commu- nists accounts—committed suicide. But not many others shared his com- mitment. Like the rest of the privileged, they thought obsessively only of escape. Awaiting its end, South Vietnamese society seemed more frag- mented than ever, a recapitulation of all the weaknesses that had brought it to the brink of defeat.

Overriding all other emotions was an intense, unreasoning terror. Among Saigon's sizeable minority of northern Catholics, who had fled south after the country was divided in 1954 and who were disproportionately repre- sented (as the result of favoritism both under the French and under Ngo Dinh Diem) in the upper reaches of the army, government, and business- professional elite, many were blindly certain their entire community would be massacred. "If the U.S. had not intervened," sobbed one northerner, "the Communists would have won in 1954 and they would have killed two million people. Now we have lost two million in the war anyway, and when the Communists come they will still kill more. My wife and I are resigned to being killed. But it is our children—we want to try to save our children."

Hysteria overtook civil servants, army officers, even ordinary enlisted soldiers. It ran with particular virulence among Vietnamese who had any association with Americans. Even among those who held such menial jobs as chauffeurs or laundresses or watchmen at American installations, many were convinced beyond all argument that they would be slaughtered. Especially vulnerable were women with children by American fathers. They feared not just for themselves; the Communists, many of them were sure, would kill all the mixed-blood babies they found.

Communist terror was far from imaginary. The executions of tens of thousands of landlords and "rich peasants" after drumhead trials in North Vietnam in the mid-1950s were a fact. So was the Hue massacre. So was the long list of assassinations carried out by the Viet Cong in the South, often after torture. As bad as it was, however, the record did not suggest to a dispassionate observer that the Communists would murder children because their parents fled the North two decades before, or a mechanic just for having worked in a GI motor pool. In particular, there was no evidence that they would butcher babies of American fathers. The French army a generation before had also left a crop of war babies, including many fathered by black soldiers from France's African possessions. Mixed children, especially the half-blacks, suffered social stigma in both North and South. But it was never reported that these children had been singled out for official Communist persecution. Neither the mothers of mixed-blood babies nor many other Saigonese were dispassionate, however. For twenty years they had been taught by their leaders that the Communists represented incarnate savagery, and their terror at the approaching Communist victory was beyond any appeal to reason.

Saigon's fears were reinforced by numerous statements in Washington, which was being fed every whisper of Communist atrocities that could be collected by Ambassador Martin and his staff. Such reports—some apparently plausible, others second- or third-hand and seeming flimsy on their face—were assiduously transmitted in the belief that stories of Communist brutality might help win support in Congress for additional aid to the South Vietnamese. Some of Martin's cables were made public, including one entire series of reports that was put into the *Congressional Record* by Rep. John Ashbrook of Ohio. Embassy messages were also the basis for statements by high-ranking administration officials to congressional committees. Henry Kissinger declared that those considered "seriously endangered" in Vietnam included "all those who served in the administrative machine of the government of South Vietnam, in the various legislative bodies in the provinces, in the various police forces, [and] all those who worked for the United States in its various programs." Defense Secretary James Schlesinger gave his opinion that as many as 200,000 Vietnamese might be massacred in a Communist takeover. U.S. lawmakers repeated and sometimes embellished the bloodbath predictions. "Upwards of 170,000 South Vietnamese face death if captured," said the influential Sen. John Tower of Texas, while Rep. John Conlan of Arizona claimed on the House floor to have eyewitness reports that "the Communists are methodically slitting every throat of all Christian men, women, and children" in the villages they had captured.

With the supposed authority of American cabinet officers and members of Congress supporting them, these and similar statements were prominently headlined in Saigon newspapers, where a frightened and credulous population was ready to believe the most extreme predictions. Whether the atrocity stories had any effect on American legislators was problematic. But there was no doubt at all that they helped spread the epidemic of fear that was overtaking the South Vietnamese capital.

The city was stricken not just by terror but by grief. The losses in the north were so massive that almost everyone, it seemed, was missing some family member in the great retreat. In the telex office on Lam Son Square, on the night of the terrible last World Airways flight from Da Nang, the operator, a smiling, helpful man who had sent my dispatches for years, was weeping for his son, an air force sergeant. "Do you know if the air force was evacuated? Please find out for me," he pleaded, carefully printing the name in my notebook. In the chaos that had enveloped Da Nang it would have taken a miracle to trace one sergeant, even if he had escaped capture, but the next day I gave the name to an officer I knew at ARVN headquarters. He stared at me sardonically and put the piece of paper in a desk drawer. Days later, there was still no news.

Another acquaintance, a woman who worked in an American-owned bank, tearfully told me of a brother and three sisters who were trapped in Da Nang, where they had gone three years earlier when the family home in Quang Tri was destroyed. "They could not leave, they all have many children," she said. Nothing could have convinced her that those who stayed in their homes were almost certainly much safer than those who had tried to flee. A moment later her thoughts turned to her own fate. "Do you think they will kill everyone who has worked for Americans?" she asked, weeping—but it wasn't really a question. Like many others she knew with a dreadful and unshakable conviction that she would be murdered when the Communists came.

So much fear and grief battered the senses into exhaustion. I grew to dread encounters with Vietnamese friends. It did not seem possible to comprehend or absorb any more heartbreak. And then the final blow of that first week of April, the most grotesque of all, fell at a quarter to five on Friday afternoon, April 4, when a U.S. Air Force C-5A Galaxy transport with a cargo of 243 Vietnamese "orphans" and 62 adults tore into a rice field one and a half miles east-northeast of Saigon's Tansonnhut Airport.

"The plane took off at 4:12," the embassy's press officer read in a choked voice over the telephone. ". . . Eighteen miles out the pilot reported decompression problems and turned back to Tansonnhut. The aft pressure door failed and blew out, and in blowing out it damaged the elevators. As a result there was difficulty in controlling the rate of descent. The pilot was close to losing control when he went into his turn for the airport."

Then he did lose control. The Galaxy—247 feet 10 inches from nose to tail, 222 feet 8½ inches across the wings, the largest plane ever built—hit the ground near the Saigon River and "began to bounce and skid" across the diked paddies, breaking apart as it went. The pilot, Air Force Capt. Dennis Traynor, survived, along with about half the passengers. The rest, children and adults, were flung across the field, where they lay dead and broken in the mud amid vast untidy heaps of wreckage, luggage, and clothing. Helicopters arrived quickly from Tansonnhut, from which the smoke of the crash could easily be seen, and shuttled survivors to the nearby Seventh Day Adventist hospital. Vietnamese soldiers and civilians joined the search. Some helped, but others looted suitcases or stole money and jewelry from the bodies of the dead.

The disaster was almost too unbearable to believe. It was laden with a sense that Americans were somehow cursed in Vietnam, fated to bring only tragedy even when trying to do good. Even in their shocked sadness, though, it was doubtful that many Americans realized just how savagely ironic the Galaxy crash really was. For Operation Babylift, springing from a generous impulse on the part of Americans who were touched by the enormous tragedy, was not as uncomplicatedly humanitarian as it was imagined to be. Kindness was also a war victim. The babylift was snared in conflicting American and Vietnamese motives, in corruption and hysterical fear on one side and in well-intentioned ignorance (and not a little political posturing) on the other, even before its first flight ended in an explosion of mud, flame, and death in a Vietnamese field.

Confusion began with the fact that of the children housed by foreign adoption agencies in Saigon, many were not orphans at all in the American sense of the word. Most, though not all, were children of American fathers whose mothers gave them up because the fathers were gone and the mothers could not support them. But this was not necessarily permanent. Many mothers continued visiting their children and intended to reclaim custody if their economic circumstances improved. In normal times, if a child was offered adoption overseas, the agency staff had plenty of time to consult the mother, explaining just what was involved and giving her a chance for a considered choice whether to give up her child forever. In the frenzy of Operation Babylift, however, there was no time for anyone to think. President Ford personally and publicly ordered government agencies to "cut red tape," and as always when a presidential directive is involved, the program was put on a crash basis with everyone scrambling to carry it out as hastily as possible. Too, both American and Vietnamese officals were motivated in part by a belief that the orphan lift, by arousing sympathy for the victims of the Communist offensive, would inspire greater U.S. support for the Saigon government.

Phan Quang Dan, deputy prime minister for social welfare, wrote Prime Minister Khiem after meeting with Ambassador Martin to advise that clearance for the "orphans" to leave the country should be granted swiftly because Martin had "stressed that this evacuation along with the millions of refugees abandoning Communist-controlled zones, will help create a shift in American public opinion in favor of the Republic of Vietnam. Especially when these children land in the United States, they will be subject to television, radio and press agency coverage and the effect will be tremendous." When Dan's letter was publicized by antigovernment politicians, the American embassy issued a formal statement declaring that Ambassador Martin "has had as his overriding concern the welfare of the orphans." Yet the ballyhoo of publicity was just as he described, and in it, not many Americans were encouraged to stop and examine the rightness of what they were doing. Nor did many think of the terrible choice being forced on Vietnamese mothers, particularly those whose children were fathered by Americans, who were already caught up in an atmosphere of hysterical terror.

There were also children on Babylift planes who were not from adoption agencies at all but who were smuggled onto the flights by panicked parents, including some who were wealthy and influential, who hoped to rejoin their children later in the U.S. I learned of one such case when a friend of a friend, whom I'll call Miss Hai, came tearfully to my hotel room one afternoon to beg for help in leaving the country. She had smuggled her four-year-old half-American son onto an orphan flight and was now frantic to join him before he was given to an American family. "I did not want to do it," she wept. "But I am afraid the VC will not like American children and will kill him."

Miss Hai was fortunate. Not only did she reach the United States, but, I learned later, she was able to find and retrieve her little boy. But there was not much doubt that among the "orphans" transported in the babylift—and among those who lay crushed in the mud after the Galaxy crash—there were some, perhaps many, whose families never intended to give them up at all.

While vast public display was being made of the evacuation of Vietnamese children (President Ford—tastelessly, some thought—had himself photographed carrying a baby off one of the first flights to reach the U.S. after the Galaxy disaster), planning for a larger evacuation of Americans and endangered Vietnamese was becoming the subject of bitter and growing dispute within the U.S. government and its embassy and military mission in Saigon. The embassy's standing evacuation plan, known as CONPLAN

5060V, assumed that "the total number . . . to be evacuated from Vietnam will approximate 8,000," including no more than a few hundred Vietnamese, and that the South Vietnamese armed forces would "not interfere with the evacuation." Obviously, after Da Nang and Nha Trang, those assumptions had to be discarded. Yet drawing up a new plan proved extraordinarily difficult.

The problems reflected the fact that the different U.S. agencies involved— the embassy, the Defense Attache Office, and the evacuation task force offshore, not to mention the State and Defense departments and the White House back in Washington—all had sharply differing perceptions of the situation and of American responsibilities. The task force planners, with no other obligations in Vietnam, saw their chief mission as the safe extrication of U.S. citizens. And, like almost all military planners, they tended to try to prepare for the direst possible contingencies. Thus, they wanted substantial forces standing by to provide security, a large advance team in Saigon, landing zones designated and cleared of obstacles, and lists of evacuees prepared along with means of notifying and assembling them. From the viewpoint of those charged with having ships, aircraft, and men in the right place at the right time, these were not unreasonable proposals. But they collided with Ambassador Martin's perceptions of *his* responsibility to American policy, which was, still, to support the South Vietnamese government. Visible evidence of an impending American departure, he reasoned, could so alarm the Vietnamese leadership, army, and public that it would bring on the collapse he still hoped might be avoided.

Neither publicly nor privately would Martin deviate from the official U.S. view that the Vietnamese, if given additional aid, could stabilize the battlefields. His senior aides dutifully echoed his view. "Militarily, the North Vietnamese do not have the capability to launch an offensive against Saigon," his deputy Wolfgang Lehmann told incredulous listeners at one embassy meeting a few days after Da Nang fell. Reflecting Martin's views, the embassy opposed almost every suggestion by the evacuation task force planners. A large tamarind tree in the embassy courtyard became the symbol of Martin's intransigence. Marine pilots wanted it cut down early in April because no helicopters could land while it stood there. But Martin felt that removing the tree would announce the evacuation and panic the Vietnamese, and he would not allow that to happen until it was absolutely necessary. He and he alone would decide when the tree should be chopped down. It stood through all that followed, until only a few hours before the first evacuation helicopters landed.

The military planners found Martin's obstructionism incomprehensible and infuriating. "Criminal," one of them later called it. But Martin was not alone in refusing to admit defeat. In Washington, Henry Kissinger was also unwilling to acknowledge to others, and perhaps to himself, that all was lost in Vietnam; nor would he easily allow the American failure to be made visible by preparing for an evacuation.

General Smith, the defense attache, was caught in the middle. He was less sanguine than the ambassador about the military situation, and as early as April 1 he established an Evacuation Control Center at Tansonnhut, assigning a small team of officers to arrange for the storage of food, water, medicine, and fuel, along with auxiliary generators, bulldozers to clear landing zones, and other equipment that might be needed. After arguing to Martin that reducing the DAO staff would save money that could then be used to help rearm the South Vietnamese, Smith also won the ambassador's approval to send a number of his own and Defense Department contractor employees out of the country, so a potential evacuation would be more manageable. But Smith was not willing to go nearly as far as the task force planners in preparing for the pullout. Like Martin—but unlike the task force officers—he had an obligation to go on supporting the Vietnamese, and would do nothing he thought might damage the will of the remaining government forces to keep fighting. Thus, he too was cautious about such matters as clearing landing zones; just as with Martin's tree, Smith denied permission to chop down two tall flagpoles in front of the main DAO building. They should be left up, evacuation planners were told, for a possible final flag-lowering ceremony.

Still another perspective was that of many middle- and lower-echelon DAO and embassy officers who were haunted by the abandonment of Vietnamese employees and associates in Da Nang and Nha Trang, and who were determined that no similar betrayal would occur in Saigon. Seeking to help endangered Vietnamese friends and colleagues leave the country *before* it fell to the Communists or into such anarchy that escape would be impossible, they had to skirt both embassy policy and the South Vietnamese authorities, since almost no Vietnamese had passports or exit visas nor any chance, under extremely restrictive emigration laws, of obtaining them in time.

To this group of Americans, the embassy policy seemed a rationale for inaction until it was too late, as they believed had already been shown in Da Nang and Nha Trang. Stuart Herrington, an army captain assigned to the Joint Military Team delegation's long-dormant missing-in-action negotiations, was one of those present when Wolfgang Lehmann declared that the North Vietnamese could not attack Saigon; returning to DAO, he promptly addressed a memo to his own superior, Col. John Madison, warning, "I am convinced that if evacuation were ordered in the near future, the U.S. Mission would fail miserably in its obligation" to its Vietnamese employees.

With several other officers, Herrington was already secretly smuggling Vietnamese out of the country on Babylift flights. One woman, the wife of an American air force sergeant, flew out disguised as a Catholic nun helping to escort the children. Others were hidden in remote parts of the base and boarded flights after the Vietnamese military police had finished counting heads; in some cases, passengers on buses heading to the flight line hid under the skirts of other evacuees.

Another "underground railroad" was formed by a group of foreign service officers who were convinced that Martin would never admit South Vietnam's defeat until it was too late. On their own, these officers drew up lists of candidates for evacuation, including in-laws of present and former embassy staffers who had married Vietnamese, while preparing safe houses and covert communications links, all without the ambassador's knowledge.

U.S. intelligence officers were also concerned about their Vietnamese agents and employees, who were not only targets for Communist reprisal but also represented a security risk if captured, since they had knowledge of agents and methods that should not be divulged. Beginning about April 7, DAO officers began asking permission for "black," or covert, flights on which Vietnamese involved in U.S. intelligence activities would leave "without any of the associated U.S. or Vietnamese paperwork." Several times DAO planners were given approval "in principle." But the embassy dithered for a full ten days before any flights were actually authorized.

If the decision had been left to Martin, the delay might have been longer. The first flights were arranged after Walter Burke, head of the embassy's consular section, told the three service attaches and then General Smith that U.S. immigration authorities would accept "black" arrivals and that Smith could order the flights without waiting for specific permission from the ambassador. On the evening after his meeting with Burke, Smith called officers of the DAO's intelligence detachment to his quarters and handed them written authorization for two initial flights, which left the following day, April 18. Subsequent black flights left at the rate of about one a day, with approximately 250 passengers on each.

The disputes between Martin and those pressing for more extensive preparations bubbled over on April 11—about the same time that President Ford declared it was U.S. policy to help evacuate "those Vietnamese to whom we have a special obligation and whose lives may be endangered." The blow fell on the head of Smith's deputy, Air Force Brig. Gen. Richard Baughn, who had sent a message to the U.S. command in Thailand—known as USSAG, standing for U.S. Support Activities Group—declaring that it would be prudent to plan for "possible extreme and rapid security degradation" in Saigon. The message, which Baughn drafted with two officers from the marine evacuation force, asked for a marine security force of two rifle companies, or about 400 men, to be sent to Saigon in civilian clothes. It also proposed that 30 marine pilots be sent to augment the civilian Air America helicopter crews, so that each Air America craft would have a backup pilot.

On the basis of comments at an embassy meeting the day before, Baughn indicated in his message that the requests were agreed to by the embassy. But Martin had not assented to any such plan, and when he saw the message, he hit the ceiling. A "flash" embassy message was sent cancelling Baughn's, and the offending general was promptly relieved of his duties and hustled out of Saigon in only a few hours. Admiral Benton, Gayler's representative, replaced Baughn as DAO's chief evacuation manager.

In the next several days, official plans were revised, in accordance with President Ford's statement, to include up to 200,000 potentially endangered Vietnamese. But planning was slow and remained mired in continuing disagreements. The entire effort never escaped the tangle of cross-purposes and conflicting perspectives in which it was snarled from the start. Lines of responsibility were unclear. "Everybody thought everybody else was in charge until somebody wanted to do something," one military planner later remembered sourly, "and then somebody would disapprove it." Mutual incomprehension and mistrust among the various U.S. agencies—an ironic echo of the U.S.-Vietnamese relationship—lasted until the end. The president and his responsible cabinet officers were disastrously slow to set any clear direction. In the end, though the sailors and marines who carried out the evacuation acted with great courage and skill, those who escaped from the falling South Vietnamese capital would owe their safety more to luck and to Hanoi's deliberate forbearance than to any arm of the U.S. government.

Outside the embassy, though none of us knew the details of the intramural squabbling, many of us were also beginning to think about evacuation. After all the years of stalemate, the idea was hard to absorb. "The one ending no one could imagine in Vietnam, an outright battlefield victory for one side over the other, now seems not only possible but perhaps inevitable," I wrote the day after Da Nang fell. The next few days dissolved all remaining doubt. By the end of the first week of April, except for small enclaves at Phan Rang and Phan Thiet on the coast, two-thirds of South Vietnam's territory had been yielded to the Communists. Six of its thirteen regular divisions had vanished, along with as many more troops in Ranger, militia, air force, and support units. Losses of weapons and supplies were staggering.

The advancing North Vietnamese, by contrast, were hardly scratched. "The number killed and wounded was very small in proportion to the victories won," General Dung wrote, "and the expenditure in terms of weapons and ammunition was negligible." Since Ban Me Thuot, in fact, the Communist divisions had hardly had to fight at all except in Binh Dinh and a very few other places, or to quell the chaos left by the government's collapse. Indeed, for days at a time the North Vietnamese could not advance fast enough to stay in contact with their fleeing enemy.

One evening at a dinner party given by an embassy official for a group of correspondents, the approaching evacuation was the only topic of discussion for hours. Among those present were many who remembered similar conversations in Phnom Penh, which had so often seemed at the brink of falling to the Communists. But no such thoughts had ever before arisen in Vietnam. Afterward, as we stepped out into the humid night, one reporter with years of experience in Indochina shook his head in disbelief. "I never would have believed I'd be having this conversation in Saigon," he said. "Never."

The South Vietnamese leadership was not just shocked, but paralyzed. Official communiques were late, sparse, and usually wrong. Nobody believed them anyway. "Thieu went on the radio and said Hue would be defended to the last," a Saigonese businessman commented. "The next day Hue was abandoned. Now nobody believes what the government says." In the minds of many Vietnamese, the official silence confirmed suspicions that the truncation of the country was prearranged, by the Americans or at any rate by some force so powerful that resistance would be useless. In the bureaucracy, officials either stopped working altogether or kept mindlessly issuing routine instructions that could not be carried out. One economist was ordered to write plans for a duty-free shop at Tansonnhut; others were assigned to send reprimands to civil servants who had fled their posts in the north. The reprimands were duly written, signed, and mailed—in envelopes addressed to cities that had been occupied by the Communists for days.

The military leadership was no less inert. Ten days after the retreat from Pleiku began, Saigon still had no plans to regroup survivors or reform units that had broken apart in the withdrawal. Planning began only at the insistence of U.S. officers in the Defense Attache Office, and even then it was carried out by ARVN's Central Logistics Command without any information at all on what units had survived, where they were, how many troops they had, and what equipment was salvaged. The plan itself, when it was finally drafted, was preposterous. Predicated on a huge U.S. supplemental aid appropriation to replace not just what had been lost in the retreat but all heavy equipment lost since the Paris agreement, it proposed reequipping and reconstituting three infantry divisions by June 15—two and a half months away, though it was obvious the threat to Saigon would become critical in a matter of days, or at most a few weeks.

The Americans realized the plan was worthless, but repeated requests for a more workable proposal from the Vietnamese Joint General Staff were ignored. Finally, General Smith ordered DAO's Operations and Plans staff to draft its own plan. A few Vietnamese officers from the logistics and training commands participated, but no one from the key administrative, operations, or plans sections. The Vietnamese adopted the U.S. plan, but with one difference. Instead of attaching rebuilt battalions or regiments to still-functioning divisions, as the Americans recommended in order to simplify command problems, the Vietnamese insisted on retaining the divisional commands whose units were shattered in the north. Thus, the reconstituted units were not fully integrated with those assigned to Saigon's defenses but were deployed independently, and most were quickly destroyed a second time.

DAO and the embassy did what they could to bolster the capital's morale. When an accelerated airlift was authorized for military supplies, the embassy press office instantly released the news to Saigon newspapers. Vietnamese and foreign reporters were escorted to a normally off-limits area of Tansonnhut on April 1 to watch the first C-5A transport unload. Presumably, the embassy hoped photos of the plane in the local press would ease Saigon's crisis of nerves. The effect, however, was just the opposite. In view of the mountains of arms that had been lost, the photographs of fourteen howitzers and a few crates of shells looked, to the Saigonese, like a bitter joke.

There would not be much more. In the United States, too, the realization was setting in that the South Vietnamese government was doomed. With it, the years-long, divisive, morally confusing American debate over Vietnam was also coming to an end.

The Aid Debate (2)

The photograph showed a lone GI semi-silhouetted against a grainy background that could almost have been clouds, but was actually a distant, tree-shrouded mountainside. The soldier stood turned slightly away from the camera and just beyond the spine of a ridge, looking down at something unseen on the far side. His back was hunched a bit and his head bent forward so the line of the neck, where it tilted upward from the bulge of the shoulders into the abrupt lobed shape of his helmet, formed a perfect right angle with the barrel of the downward-slanting rifle he held in front of him. The foreground, sloping upward toward the crest of the ridge, was covered with a litter of fallen, splintered branches. And filing away from the camera in an irregular line, framing the scene, were jagged tree stumps, broken off a little higher than the height of a man, looking like roofless pillars in the ruins of some ancient temple.

In 1972 that memorable image of war, destruction, and loneliness helped win a Pulitzer Prize for a brash but brave and gifted 25-year-old photographer named David Hume Kennerly. Three years later, now the official White House photographer and good friend of President Ford and his family, Kennerly was back in Vietnam, accompanying a fact-finding team headed by the Army chief of staff and former Vietnam commander, Gen. Frederick Weyand. Arriving just as Da Nang was falling, Weyand spent most of the next week in conferences in Saigon. But Kennerly, driven by both personal and professional motives, flew north for a glimpse of the disaster. From an Air America helicopter, he photographed the refugee ships *Pioneer Contender* and *Pioneer Commander* as they steamed from Da Nang toward Cam Ranh Bay. As they flew past the *Contender*, Kennerly and the pilot saw rifle flashes wink along the decks, where angry Vietnamese soldiers were firing in their direction. The shots missed, but being fired on by "friendly" troops was unnerving.

A day or so later, Kennerly made a brief farewell visit to Phnom Penh, then only a few weeks away from its surrender to the Khmer Rouge. Images of Cambodia's last agony passed in front of his lenses: a starving baby; a woman dying of terrible shrapnel wounds in a sports arena converted into an improvised hospital; the tear-streaked face of a small girl, no more than four or five years old, looking out from the dimness of a refugee shelter while a metal dogtag glinted from a chain around her neck. Kennerly was haunted by her eyes. They conveyed something worse than fear or pain: they were vacant, without hope or terror or sadness, as if all emotion had been blown out like a candle. When he left Saigon a few days later for the long flight back to the United States, Kennerly was drained and heartsick—and certain the war was lost.

Even before the Weyand mission, President Ford had responded to South Vietnam's crisis with reflexive assurances of support. He was "determined to stand firmly behind the Republic of Vietnam at this crucial hour," he wrote privately to Thieu on March 22. "With a view to honoring the responsibilities of the United States in this situation, I . . . am consulting on an urgent basis with my advisers on actions which the situation may require and the law permit." Similar statements were made in another letter three days later, just as Hue was being abandoned to the Communists.

The messages were carefully worded not to violate the legal ban on U.S. military action in Indochina. But to a stricken Thieu, they could only mean Washington would not allow South Vietnam to fall: the fantasy he had nourished since the Paris agreement. In a sense, too, the Ford letters predetermined the outcome of the Weyand mission. They made it clear he was not to come back acknowledging defeat but, as the White House announcement said, "to inform the president about what assistance South

Vietnam needs from the United States at this crucial time." The root illusion of the administration's Vietnam policy, that weaponry and supplies were all that was needed to defeat the Communist enemy there, was still intact.

Having sent Weyand to Saigon, Ford left Washington for a golfing vacation in posh Palm Springs, California. It was not one of his presidency's more brilliant moments. Some aides winced at the imagery of the president appearing on every night's newscasts on the golf course, while other film showed graphic scenes of the human tragedy in Southeast Asia. The sense of embarrassment grew after a bizarre episode in which Ford, during a side trip, literally sprinted away from pursuing reporters at the Bakersfield airport rather than answer their shouted questions about Vietnam's collapse. The unkindest comment about the incident came at the next briefing by Ron Nessen, Ford's press secretary. "He ran," one reporter told Nessen, "almost as fast as the South Vietnamese army."

Ford was still in Palm Springs when the Weyand party returned, and it was there Dave Kennerly brought his photos, including the one of the little Cambodian girl, which eventually was hung in Nessen's White House office. "Cambodia is gone," Kennerly told the president, "and I don't care what the generals tell you; they're bullshitting you if they say that Vietnam has got more than three or four weeks left. There's no question about it. It's just not gonna last." By now, the same news was coming from intelligence agencies. A Defense Intelligence Agency estimate on April 3 declared that South Vietnam would fall in no more than 30 days. On the same day, according to later congressional testimony by CIA chief William Colby, the intelligence community as a whole reached an "authoritative judgment that Saigon's collapse was both inevitable and imminent."

U.S. policy, however, was not to be decided by intelligence estimates or by Kennerly's blunt common sense. Too many reputations and bureaucratic instincts were involved. From Saigon poured a stream of messages in Ambassador Martin's pungent if labored prose, insisting that the new, truncated South Vietnam was somehow viable. In the American military hierarchy, meanwhile, support for Saigon had become so deeply imprinted in all its bureaucratic synapses that not even imminent defeat, it seemed, could change the clichés in which it was expressed. The government's forces "are still strong and still have the spirit and capability to defeat the North Vietnamese," General Weyand told incredulous newsmen before leaving Saigon, adding that he had assured Vietnamese leaders of President Ford's "strong personal support" and his "determination to assist South Vietnam to defend itself."

Weyand was an officer of honesty and intelligence, but with his years of his own career invested in Vietnam, he was hardly a detached observer of the crisis there. As a group, senior American officers were extraordinarily unwilling to admit how badly Saigon's military leaders—men the Americans knew, or thought they did—had failed their troops and their country. (Talking about the calamitous retreats in later years, American officers often cited what they called the "family syndrome" of soldiers deserting to take care of their wives and children. Hardly ever mentioned was the fact that the army unraveled only after senior officers, beginning with a corps commander and most of his staff, deserted their troops first.) To acknowledge that South Vietnam's collapse had moral and not just material causes was painful not just because it meant years of American indoctrination and advice had failed. It also meant there was no American remedy for Vietnam's defeat, and this collided squarely with the "can do" tradition in which American military officers are schooled never to admit that any problem is insoluble.

These institutional biases were Weyand's as well. Nothing in U.S. Army doctrine or in his own sympathies made it possible for him to come to the only conclusions that were really justified by the facts: that the Saigon government's authority was irretrievably lost, its military defeat was all but certain, and there was no realistic chance that anything the United States could do would prevent it. Nor would the bureaucracy's conditioned reflexes or the administration's political needs admit such bleak truths. Instead, inescapably, Weyand's recommendations reproduced past illusions. Meeting with Ford in Palm Springs on the afternoon of April 5—by a striking coincidence, just as the symbol of an earlier failed American policy in Asia, 87-year-old Chiang Kai-shek, died in embittered exile in Taiwan—Weyand resurrected the threadbare hope that one more infusion of dollars and arms might somehow rescue American purposes in Vietnam. His report, based on a chain of illusory assumptions defying both American and Vietnamese realities, seemed a case of "can do" gone berserk.

To defend their remaining territory, Weyand told the president, the South Vietnamese needed additional equipment and supplies worth $722 million, or approximately the value of the material lost in the great retreat. As it was eventually refined and presented to Congress by the Pentagon, the resupply effort would provide 744 artillery pieces, 446 tanks and armored personnel carriers, more than 100,000 rifles, over 5,000 machineguns and 11,000 grenade launchers, about 120,000 tons of ground and air munitions, and about 12,000 trucks—an effort on a scale rivaling that of the pre-ceasefire Enhance and Enhance Plus programs. With these supplies the South Vietnamese were to equip eight infantry and Ranger divisions and another 27 independent regiments formed from existing militia units: a force that would roughly match the Communist army descending on Saigon.

Within the administration, reactions to the Weyand plan were divided. There was clearly doubt whether Saigon could hold out long enough for appreciable arms shipments to reach its army, or whether any amount of aid could save the regime. And there was not the slightest reason to think that

Congress, after refusing since January to act on the earlier $300 million request, would be any more receptive to a new proposal nearly two and a half times as large, especially when it seemed quite possible that any new arms given to Saigon would wind up being captured by the Communists anyway. An alternative to the Weyand plan would have been just to reaffirm the previous $300 million proposal. But Henry Kissinger, with his own reputation at stake as the author of the Paris agreement and chief architect of Vietnam policy since long before Ford's presidency, urged Ford to request the full $722 million. Focusing, characteristically, on the symbolism of American actions, Kissinger advocated the larger sum as the most dramatic possible sign that the administration wanted to meet its obligations to Saigon. He was also desperately anxious that if blame was to be put anywhere for the defeat, it should be on Congress.

Ford's domestic advisers, led by Robert Hartmann, disagreed. Unlike Kissinger, neither they nor the president were strongly identified with the now-failing Vietnam effort. Instead of assigning blame, they believed, the administration's purposes would be better served by reestablishing some sense of national unity as a foundation for future foreign policy decisions. The most dovish of Ford's aides was Nessen, a former combat correspondent for NBC who had been badly wounded in Vietnam. In anguish over the tragedy there, Nessen urged Ford to turn down the aid proposal altogether and to declare that since there was no assurance that anything would be achieved except to prolong Saigon's defeat, "it would be wrong for America to contribute further to the killing."

But Kissinger prevailed. Obsessively fighting the bureaucratic wars, as always, he kept all others at arms' length from the crucial White House deliberations. On April 9, the day before Ford was to announce his decision to a joint session of Congress, it was Kissinger who spent until well past midnight helping draft the speech, which largely reflected his views. Not only did Ford ask for the full $722 million military aid supplement and another $250 million for economic aid and refugee relief; he also explicitly re-vindicated Kissinger's Vietnam diplomacy, declaring that the Paris agreement had met American goals and would have been successful if it had not been "systematically violated" by Hanoi while the U.S. failed either to enforce its terms or to provide adequate support for the South.

Ford did not criticize Congress as directly as Kissinger hoped. But, despite a closing appeal for national unity, the suggestion of blame was there. And the geopolitical rationale for the aid supplement was pure Kissinger. "It has been said," Ford declared,

> that the United States is overextended; that we have too many com-
> mitments far from home; that we must reexamine what our truly vital
> interests are and shape our strategy to conform to them. I find no
> fault with this as theory, but in the real world such a course must be

pursued carefully and in close coordination with solid progress toward overall reduction in world tensions. We cannot in the meantime abandon our friends while our adversaries support and encourage theirs.

Seeming to reject any compromise, Ford insisted that the aid to Saigon "must be swift and adequate." Indecision would only invite "deeper disaster," he declared, adding, "Half-hearted action would be worse than none." He asked Congress to complete action on his proposal by April 19, only nine days away.

If any doubts lingered about Congress's mood, the response to the president's speech erased them.

Not one clap of applause greeted his appeal for more Vietnam funds. Two Democrats walked out of the chamber while he was still speaking. Even among members who had supported the war in the past, almost none endorsed the new proposal, while administration officials hardly tried to pretend it was anything but a charade. In not-for-attribution conversations with Washington reporters the day after Ford's speech, the word was put out that the White House didn't really believe the supplement would pass, or that additional arms would make a difference in Vietnam anyway. Instead, a different and cynical rationale was offered. If the South Vietnamese perceived that the U.S. was turning its back on them, officials said, they might turn their anger on the approximately 7,000 U.S. citizens still in Vietnam, explicitly or implicitly making them hostages for continued aid. The $722 million request was aimed at deflecting any such impulse. It was, in other words, a ransom payment—or, more accurately, a promissory note, since few expected the ransom would ever actually be paid.

On April 14, in an unusual White House meeting with the Senate Foreign Relations Committee, Ford himself offered the ransom argument. When several senators expressed concern for the safety of Americans in Saigon, Ford answered: "The quickest way to put them in jeopardy is not to vote the assistance money. I can't guarantee that if we say 'no more money' Thieu . . . won't do something totally irrational."

If this logic won any votes, however, it was also turned back on the White House in the form of growing pressure to begin evacuating Americans before any reprisals or blackmail could occur. Administration officials trooping to Capitol Hill to lobby for aid found themselves grilled daily on how many U.S. citizens remained in Vietnam and on what was being done to remove them. In Saigon, however, Ambassador Martin was still unwilling either to order visible reductions in the U.S. mission staff or to find ways of helping endangered Vietnamese evade strict emigration controls. Though C-141 and C-130 transports were landing at Tansonnhut day and night with supplies, most of them left empty. In the eleven days after Ford's speech to Congress, only about 2,000 Americans and roughly the same number of Vietnamese left on outbound airlift planes. A few more, but not many, departed on commercial flights, which were invariably booked full but left with few occupied seats because Vietnamese passengers were seldom able to get passports or exit visas.

On April 16, Ford declared that the embassy would begin "phasing down," and American departures speeded up somewhat. But—though the president also repeated that the U.S. had a responsibility to large numbers of Vietnamese as well as to its own citizens, and though DAO planners kept warning that waiting until the last minute for a massive evacuation was "courting disaster"—the flow of Vietnamese was still a trickle. Neither Martin nor the State Department displayed any sense of urgency. For most of April, a congressional inquiry later concluded, "there was no operative policy determining (1) how evacuations would be conducted, (2) who the U.S. should be evacuating or in what sort of priority, (3) what should be done to or for the refugees once out of Vietnam, and (4) what agency, if any, would, in fact, be responsible for the refugees once they arrived in the U.S."

As late as April 18, according to the congressional investigators, Martin told Washington he had no plans to evacuate past or present Vietnamese employees of the U.S. government. Not all the foot-dragging was Martin's, however. The State Department was just as sluggish. "Parole authority"—a waiver of normal U.S. entry visa procedures—was available during most of April only for orphans and for a few narrowly defined categories of dependents of U.S. citizens. Not until April 19 was parole broadened to include most other dependents; and "high-risk" Vietnamese, who were thought to be in danger of Communist reprisal, were not made eligible until April 25.

Relaxation of the rules for dependents helped break the logjam of Americans, too, since many U.S. citizens refused to leave Saigon unless their legal or common-law Vietnamese families could leave, too. On April 19, at an embassy meeting with General Smith and the visiting Admiral Gayler, Martin agreed to a new procedure under which Vietnamese citizens could join the U.S. airlift on the basis of a simple affidavit signed by an American sponsor declaring they were his dependents and that he would be responsible for supporting them after they left Vietnam. Having prodded Martin into approving the idea, Smith and Gayler gave him no time for second thoughts. Before leaving the embassy, they drafted the new form and arranged for it to be retyped and reproduced. The system was put into use the same afternoon. The only exceptions, at Smith's orders, were men of military age.

Airlift departures rose sharply, from a few hundred a day to several thousand. But the new system also invited abuse. In the control center at

Tansonnhut, processing officers began to notice familiar faces among the American sponsors: men who had signed affidavits for one "family" and then either slipped out of the boarding lines or left the country but returned on commercial flights to sponsor another set of dependents. Rumors flew, some of them undoubtedly true, of Americans receiving huge bribes to serve as sponsors.

What the new system did not do was ease the exit of Vietnamese who had no actual or fictional ties with an American sponsor. Employees of U.S. agencies, and others associated with the U.S. effort, remained dependent on the unauthorized actions of subordinate American officials. Some were given "certification letters" stating that they were sponsored for evacuation and subsequent asylum by a U.S. government supervisor. Though they were never officially authorized, these letters were issued by many different sections of the U.S. mission and were accepted by the airlift controllers. Other Vietnamese left with no documents at all, smuggled aboard the planes by friends in DAO or in the embassy.

Because few lower-echelon Americans had any faith either in the ambassador or in the official evacuation plan, different agencies ended up competing with each other to get their Vietnamese workers on outbound flights. Colonel Madison, head of the Joint Military Team delegation, expressed a view that was also held by many others in a cable to his Pentagon superiors: "It looks like if we don't take care of our own people nothing will be done. . . . From what we know of the official 'plan,' extraction of U.S. personnel seems workable. However unannounced extraction of U.S. personnel probably during curfew hours will negate any chance for subsequent Vietnamese extraction. These facts necessitate independent U.S. delegation action. Imperative that we get our people out now."

No mission-wide priorities for evacuating Vietnamese were set, even on paper, until the very last few days. Even then, they were applied only fitfully. With every agency acting on its own, the chance for evacuation depended not on how vulnerable someone was or how sensitive his American connection, but on how aggressive and determined his American superiors were, or how well connected with the teams actually running the control center and the airlift. Vietnamese working for military agencies and at DAO installations physically situated on the air base had the advantage. Those employed by civilian agencies far from the base were at greater risk, such as the staff of the U.S. Information Service, most of whom were eventually stranded. And Vietnamese with some legitimate or illegitimate sponsorship as dependents continued to fare much better than those who just worked for the American government, even in sensitive jobs. "Flagrant inequities" occurred, one DAO officer acknowledged in a later official report. The image was of bar-girls and corrupt officials and merchants leaving in American planes while long-time dedicated employees and other associates were left behind. It was an exaggeration—but with enough truth to taint the memory of the entire evacuation effort.

Ambassador Martin continued to block efforts to expand the exodus of Vietnamese. During mid-April, though the *Miller*, the *Greenville Victory*, and other Sealift Command ships put in at Newport, the U.S.-built dock and warehouse complex on the Saigon River just upstream from the capital, Martin would not allow any of them to board refugees before sailing. As late as April 24, he turned down a proposal by the U.S. Navy attache to load some 30,000 evacuees on the remaining ships and LSTs. When the last deep-draft vessels were ordered to leave Vietnamese waters two days later, Martin's orders were still that they must sail empty. He had "no apology whatsoever" to make for that decision, he later told congressional questioners. "Had we attempted to load those ships there was universal agreement, from those who understood Saigon, that we would have had an immediate panic situation."

Apparently, Martin was still unaware that Sealift Command officials in Saigon had defied his orders and put about 700 Vietnamese on one of the ships, SS *Green Wave*. The passengers included the Sealift Command's Vietnamese employees, the Vietnamese commander at Newport and his staff and their families, river pilots, and others who had been associated with the U.S. shipping effort. There was no panic during the loading or the ship's departure. After the deep-draft ships sailed, the LST *Boo Heung Pioneer* and several tugs and barges remained at Newport and were available to carry refugees in the final evacuation.

In Washington, meanwhile, the debate on the eleventh-hour aid proposal sputtered toward its end in an atmosphere of graceless acrimony. Stubbornly, Ford continued to insist that Saigon could stabilize the battle lines if the $722 million supplement were promptly approved. But hardly anyone else sounded as sure. When Defense Secretary Schlesinger was asked if the South Vietnamese could hold their remaining territory even with reconstituted and reequipped units, he answered, "We must recognize that the probabilities are against it . . . there is a chance." General Weyand, after an appearance before a Senate committee, sighed, "I guess because I am a general, I have trouble in saying that the military situation is irretrievable."

Two days after Ford's April 19 deadline passed, in another hearing, Weyand agreed without equivocation that the area still under Saigon's control was not defensible. "Is there any basis for your request," asked Rep. Jamie Whitten of Mississippi, "except to maintain an appearance, perhaps in the press and in the news media, when we know the end is inevitable?" "Well, sir," Weyand answered weakly, "let me say this: that sometimes the style with which we do things, or the appearance, as you say, are equally as important as substance."

Instead of the aid plan, the increasingly ill-tempered congressional debate began focusing on the expected use of U.S. military forces in an evacuation, and whether using those forces to rescue Vietnamese, as well as Americans, would violate laws against military action in Indochina. Little sympathy was expressed for any Vietnamese who were in danger, or thought they were. Instead, the antiwar bloc in the House and Senate issued preposterous warnings that the administration might somehow use an evacuation as a cover for a renewed American military intervention. To avoid that, they were ready to deny the president all but the most circumscribed chance to save some of the Vietnamese whom America had enlisted in its cause but was unable to defend and who now wanted to escape the Communist victory.

"They can do what they did in Cambodia," one Senate Democrat said grudgingly, "bring out as many as they can at the same time that they bring out Americans. But we're not going to let them go beyond that." A Pennsylvania congressman declared: "I reject absolutely the notion that we should bring several hundred thousand Vietnamese refugees to America. . . . Where will we put them? How will they live? . . . It is time we thought about our duty to the American people."

When the administration asked for a waiver of legal restrictions on military force so Vietnamese citizens could be evacuated without raising any legal questions, House liberals denounced the proposal in the most extreme, far-fetched terms. "We could bomb Cambodia and Laos and North Vietnam if the president determined that it was necessary to evacuate all foreign nationals in South Vietnam," warned Elizabeth Holtzman of New York. And the ever-combative Bella Abzug shrilled: "This legislation is just an excuse to enable the United States to remain in Vietnam and to use military force if necessary to maintain control . . . so that if we do not happen to like what happens there we can again re-engage the United States in the affairs of that country. . . . It borders on a new Gulf of Tonkin resolution."

Against the backdrop of the human catastrophe in Vietnam, Abzug and her like-minded colleagues succeeded only in sounding suspicious, mean-spirited, and bigoted. Though the long national debate on the war was obviously ending at last, its poisoning of American public life had never been more evident.

In the corridors of the White House, at President Ford's direction, photographs of state dinners and other ceremonial functions were taken down and replaced by Dave Kennerly's grim, black-and-white images of Vietnam's agony.

He wanted them hung, the president declared, so his aides would see the human face of the tragedy whenever they walked through the West Wing. For Kennerly, though, the gesture came very late. "I only wish my pictures had been hung in the White House when the war began," he wrote later, "rather than as it ended."

"A bargain whose day had passed"

As his last crisis deepened, President Thieu withdrew into a distracted silence. He gave the impression of being numbed, General Weyand told Vietnamese friends; another American in the Weyand party thought Thieu's "mind seemed to be elsewhere." Day after day, the South Vietnamese leader remained locked behind the white walls of the Doc Lap Palace, nourishing his anger at his Communist enemy and his American ally. But outside the palace grounds, where the muzzles of flak guns pointed at the sky and armored personnel carriers crouched among the flowering trees inside the spiked steel fence, virtually his entire country waited for him to resign. His generals blamed him for the bungled retreat; his soldiers cursed him; his hangers-on in the National Assembly defected in flocks. On April 2, the long-docile Senate passed a resolution blaming him for "abuse of power, corruption and social injustice" and calling for a "new leadership" in the form of a national union government. The next day, Archbishop Nguyen Van Binh suggested that the president should step down.

For the first time in years, coup rumors swept through the capital. On March 27 and again on April 4, the government announced the arrest of plotters. Among those jailed were several associates of Thieu's old rival, Nguyen Cao Ky, who admitted after the war that he and his allies were in fact tentatively planning to overthrow the regime. Ky called off the plan after receiving hints from Graham Martin that he took to mean the U.S. would back him as Thieu's replacement, which, Ky thought, would make a coup unnecessary. Instead, Martin eventually put his influence behind ex-general Duong Van Minh. If he had taken power, Ky wrote vaingloriously, he planned to turn Saigon into a Stalingrad—"a battle the world will always remember."

Meanwhile, there came a refrain of hints that if the Thieu regime were replaced, the Communists might not press their military advantage but would stop to negotiate some form of political settlement. Mrs. Nguyen Thi Binh, the Provisional Revolutionary Government's foreign minister, was quoted as saying in Algiers on April 2, "We understand that General Minh is ready to negotiate for peace and we are ready to talk with him." Minh—nicknamed Big Minh, and the leader of the 1963 revolt against the Diem regime—remained convinced that the Communists would strike a deal with him, although Mrs. Binh's reference was not endorsed by being reprinted in the Communist press, and neither she nor any other spokesman ever again publicly identified any specific person as an acceptable nego-tiating partner. Still, Communist representatives continued to invite specu-lation that peace talks might be possible if a new government came to power in Saigon. Repeated references to the Paris agreement also seemed to suggest a readiness for some of compromise. "The Provisional Revolutionary Government abides by the Paris agreement," Mrs. Binh told reporters in Kinshasha, a few days further on in her African tour, adding that the Thieu regime should be replaced by "a government which is for the application of the Paris agreement and for peace, independence, . . . and national harmony."

No one knew if such hints represented any real chance for a negotiated end to the war. Probably they did not. But if any transitory opportunity did exist, Thieu let it slip past. Like his former patron Richard Nixon in the last stages of his own political crisis the year before, the South Vietnamese leader seemed to be the last to see that the wounds to his presidency were fatal. His answer to the rising opposition came in a televised speech April 4, in which he gave no indication of resigning but instead announced that he would name a new cabinet "in order to carry on the fight." His choice for prime minister, replacing Tran Thien Khiem, was not any of the possible peace-makers but the speaker of the National Assembly, Nguyen Ba Can. Little known and little regarded, Can was chiefly reputed as a dutiful follower of Thieu in the past; clearly, he was neither a potential negotiator for peace nor a leader who could reawaken his country's devastated spirit.

The cabinet shift signaled no change in Saigon's peace policy. "Our compatriots should not doubt my stand," Thieu said, "which has remained and will remain unchanged, in the past as it is in the present and will be in the future. . . . We will never accept a coalition with the Communists. We only accept one sole peace solution: the holding of general elections as specified in the Paris agreement." Insisting that Saigon's military defeats were only temporary, Thieu put the blame everywhere but on his own actions, attributing the disaster to treachery by montagnard troops, coward-ice and defeatism in the army, the machinations of the Communist agents, and even the broadcasts of "foreign radio stations such as the BBC and the Voice of America."

Thieu's bitterest remarks, however, were directed at the United States, for failing to keep promises made when the Paris agreement was signed to provide adequate aid and to retaliate for Communist violations. "One wonders," he said derisively, "whether U.S. commitments can be trusted and whether U.S. words have any value."

Yet only the United States could provide the miracle of rescue. "We think that the world and in particular our ally, the U.S.A., now clearly realize that the Communists have launched a true general offensive," Thieu told his traumatized countrymen. If American aid continued to arrive "drop by drop . . . we will lose our land gradually to the North Vietnamese Communists until the day when we lose it all. Therefore, I hope that the American people and Congress now will see clearly the real situation . . . and the consequences of their actions over the past two years and that they will assist us in a more practical, more rapid, more efficient and more adequate manner so that we can defend our remaining territory."

On the morning of April 8, an air force pilot, 1st Lt. Nguyen Thanh Trung, took off from Bien Hoa Air Base with orders to bomb Communist positions in Binh Thuan Province, 75 miles or so to the east. Once in the air, however, Trung radioed his flight commander that he had engine problems and would have to return to base. Peeling away from the other aircraft, he headed back toward the west, alone in the sky.

In fact, there was nothing wrong with Trung's F-5E fighter-bomber. Nor did he return to Bien Hoa. Instead, he flew straight for the heart of Saigon. Just before 8:30 A.M. he put the camouflage-painted jet into a steep dive over the Doc Lap Palace, releasing two of his four bombs just before pulling out. Climbing out of the dive, he saw the bombs tumble into the palace courtyard and explode, covering the buildings with a cloud of black smoke. On a second pass he dropped his remaining bombs, but they too missed the buildings. As the explosions boomed over the hubbub of morning traffic, military police hurriedly pushed steel-and-barbed-wire barriers into place to close the streets approaching the palace. Approaching motorists were warned away by soldiers nervously waving rifles. In Lam Son Square at the city's center, pedestrians scuttled in all directions, or huddled next to building walls.

After his second pass, Lieutenant Trung still had 120 rounds of unexpended 20-mm cannon ammunition. Briefly, he considered strafing the American embassy, but decided instead to strike the Nha Be fuel storage dumps on the far side of the Saigon River. After emptying his cannons there, he streaked northward to land at the Communist-held Phuoc Long airfield, where he was welcomed, Liberation Radio announced the next day, "in an extremely warm and cordial manner." Under procedures to attract defectors by rewarding "officers, men and civil servants of the puppet armed forces and administration who acquire merits in national salvation," the broadcast added, Trung was awarded the Liberation Military Exploit Medal, Second Class, and given the rank of captain in the liberation forces.*

Less than three hours after the attack, Thieu was on the radio, announcing that "thanks to the Supreme Being's blessing," he and his family were safe and he was back at work. Subsequent broadcasts by the air force commander and other military leaders denied that the raid was part of a plot against the regime. But no reassuring announcements could prevent a deepening sense of unraveling. Like so much else in Vietnam, the raid on the palace awakened a memory of the past: in early 1962, a similar strike by disaffected pilots on Ngo Dinh Diem's residence heralded the unrest that eventually brought down the Diem regime.

There were also echoes of the Diem era within Thieu's palace, where some of his inner circle were said to be considering a maneuver similar to one planned by Diem's brother Nhu just before the two men were overthrown and murdered. Under that plan, Diem and Nhu were to leave Saigon and hand power to a figurehead group which would then, by prearrangement, call on them to make a triumphant return. The two steps of the plot were called "Bravo One" and "Bravo Two." Thieu's aides, in conceiving their version, reportedly used exactly the same code names.

While Lieutenant Trung was carrying out his raid on the palace, Communist commanders in the forests near Loc Ninh were meeting to consider the instructions Le Duc Tho had brought from Hanoi. The mood was ebullient. Tho relayed Politburo orders confirming General Dung as commander of the final campaign against Saigon. Politburo member Pham Hung, the senior southern-born Communist and long-time head of COSVN, was named chief political officer for the campaign, while Tran Van Tra and Le Duc Anh were named military deputies.

Assigned to open the attack was General Dung's IV Corps, consisting of the 7th, 341st, and 6th North Vietnamese divisions. Starting from positions in Tay Ninh and Binh Long provinces, north and northwest of Saigon, the attacking force marched in an arc looping eastward through the southern highlands, occupying Lam Dong Province and then descending on the capital's eastward approaches. By April 8 they were in position around Xuan Loc, 40 miles east of Saigon on Highway One. The next morning, after a barrage of 3,000 artillery and rocket rounds, they attacked the town.

At Xuan Loc, for the first time in many days South Vietnamese forces stood and fought. Le Minh Dao's 18th ARVN Division battled back into the burning town and continued to hold there in succeeding days, while fighting

---

* By later Communist accounts, Trung had been a secret Communist since his student days. He was said to have joined the air force at party orders and to have remained under party discipline throughout his service, which included flight training in the U.S. American intelligence officers were skeptical. They thought Trung just decided to switch sides at the last minute.

turned it into a ruin of broken masonry and unburied corpses. After weeks of easy victories, the North Vietnamese were surprised and impressed at what General Dung called "the enemy's stubbornness." South Vietnamese commanders and their American associates were elated. "We have a victory in the making," General Smith hyperbolically cabled the Joint Chiefs of Staff on the fifth day of the battle.

If Xuan Loc was a victory, however, it was only in the sense that the Warsaw ghetto uprising or the defense of Bataan or other gallant but hopeless battles were also victories. By their bravery there, South Vietnamese soldiers assured that their army would be remembered for more than just the shame of its earlier retreats. But it was too late for any acts of heroism to reverse the course of the war. Though briefly thrown off schedule, the Communist commanders soon turned the battle to their advantage, leaving just enough troops to keep Xuan Loc's defenders pinned down and to ambush reinforcements while their main assault force swept around to threaten Bien Hoa, the last major obstacle on the road to Saigon.

Though both sides suffered heavy casualties at Xuan Loc, the Communists could easily afford their losses, while Saigon's were irreplaceable. In the end, indeed, the defenders' gallantry actually assisted the North Vietnamese strategy of defeating the government's main-force units away from the capital rather than facing them in Saigon's streets. Defending Xuan Loc, the Viet Cong leader Huynh Tan Phat later declared, became one of the Thieu government's "fatal errors." Even General Dao, after his capture, told the victors he felt his men had just been used "as a shield to cover the retreat of the Americans and Mr. Thieu." When *Newsweek*'s Nicholas Proffitt managed to fly into the ruined town as the battle drew toward its inevitable close, government commanders were still calling the battle a victory. But its real meaning was expressed by a veteran militiaman who gazed over the rubble for a long moment and then told Proffitt, "We cannot afford any more 'victories' like this one."

In Saigon, the time that was paid for with blood and bones of the Xuan Loc garrison was squandered. Instead of the "fighting cabinet" Thieu promised on April 4, no cabinet at all was formed until the 14th, after ten days had been wasted in pointless, quarrelsome scheming. When the new prime minister finally announced his choices, they seemed irrelevant; the only political event Saigon waited for was Thieu's departure. But the president still gave no sign of stepping down. The new cabinet was "not a transitional government," he insisted, nor would South Vietnam's constitutional processes be set aside.

Communist statements, in tones of increasing insistence, continued to demand Thieu's removal. The hints that negotiations might follow continued. "It depends on our adversaries whether we use military measures. . . . We do not want our compatriots to die if we can obtain our objectives by other means." Mrs. Binh told two Western reporters on April 9. Within a few days, however, possibly in response to President Ford's $722 million aid proposal, the Communists began to raise the price of a possible settlement. Their previous rather vague formula had called for the United States to end "military involvement and all intervention" in South Vietnam's internal affairs; now a harsher and more specific requirement, stated by the Provisional Revolutionary Government on April 12, demanded that the U.S. must "immediately cease all its aid to the Nguyen Van Thieu clique" and remove all the aircraft and warships of the evacuation task force from Vietnamese waters. If Washington wished to remove its citizens who were illegally assisting Saigon's war effort, the P.R.G. said derisively, the liberation army would create "no difficulty or obstacle whatsoever" to their departure.

Now that they were practically in sight of the goal for which they had fought so many years and at such awful cost, it was hardly plausible that the Communists would let themselves be deflected by diplomacy. Nor was this just a common-sense judgment: by mid-April, American intelligence officers had been told by a penetration agent in COSVN that any signals seeming to invite negotiations were a deception, and that Hanoi was irrevocably committed to a military victory. But even that evidence did not end the wishful thinking that seemed to control American policy making until virtually the last hours of the war. The agent report, indeed, was suppressed for a time in the U.S. embassy—on the CIA station chief's orders, according to Ambassador Martin's later account—and was only forwarded to Washington at the indignant insistence of the officer who originally obtained it.

South Vietnam's collapse seemed to paralyze Washington intellectually just as it paralyzed Saigon politically. Like a stock speculator who cannot bear to sell at a loss, and thus helplessly watches his investment's value fall farther each day, the U.S. administration sat through the weeks of Saigon's defeat without ever summoning the imagination or will to begin detaching its own interests from Nguyen Van Thieu's. If there was ever a time when Thieu's resignation might have had enough value to be traded for some form of face-saving diplomatic arrangement, the moment was allowed to pass. Washington began contemplating his removal only after its bargaining value had vanished completely. During the retreat in the north, American ships kept arriving in place after place just too late to rescue most of the refugees and defeated soldiers they were sent to save; those ships now began to seem a metaphor for a bankrupt U.S. policy that kept rejecting choices while they were available, then vainly pursued them just as they disappeared forever.

The message ending the eight-year U.S. alliance with Thieu was delivered to the South Vietnamese leader on the morning of April 20 by one of its most passionate advocates: Ambassador Martin. He did not directly recommend that Thieu step down, Martin later told congressional investigators. But what he did say made it evident that was what the United States government now wanted. Martin began by giving Thieu the U.S. assessment that the military situation was "very grim" and that even if the remaining government units put up the best possible defense, Saigon could probably not hold out more than three weeks if Hanoi decided to assault it. Thieu asked about the prospects for a U.S. aid supplement. It would be a miracle if Congress approved it, Martin answered, but even if the miracle happened, it was too late to alter the "overwhelming" military balance against the South.

Then, although making no direct suggestion of his own, Martin outlined the reasons for Thieu to resign. The Vietnamese people blamed him for the military situation, Martin said, and neither his supporters nor his opponents believed any longer that Thieu could lead the country out of its crisis. The generals believed that resistance would be hopeless unless there were peace negotiations, and none would be possible while Thieu remained in power. In fact, Martin said, it was his opinion that if he did not leave soon, his generals would ask him to.

Thieu was still thinking about the aid bill. Would his leaving affect the vote in Congress? It might have changed some votes months earlier, Martin replied, but his resignation could no longer alter the congressional decision. Stepping aside in return for additional U.S. support was "a bargain whose day had passed." The significant question now was whether Thieu's departure could lead to negotiations and possibly avoid a final battle for Saigon. He himself didn't know if that would happen, Martin added, but most south Vietnamese seemed to think Thieu's resignation would "facilitate" peace talks.

Thieu asked if Martin was advising him to resign. No, Martin said. The decision had to be Thieu's alone, on the basis of his understanding of the situation and his concern for the people of Saigon and the country as a whole.

The conversation had lasted about an hour and a half when Thieu rose. He would do what was best for his country, he told Martin. That night, the eleven-day defense of Xuan Loc ended. With the road to Saigon blocked by strong Communist units, the survivors of the battle filtered away through jungles and rubber plantations toward the south, heading for the mass of refugees and leaderless soldiers who were crowded into the shrinking government-held enclave at Vung Tau.

The next day, April 21, while Thieu met with senior military and civilian advisers in the palace, the regime's despair was vented in an extraordinary commentary broadcast by the official Saigon radio. The world's major powers "are usually heartless and unfaithful," the commentator declared, and were abandoning the South Vietnamese to face Communism alone, just as the Hungarian insurrectionists in 1956 had been denied help against the

Russians. "Before the Communists kill us," the broadcast concluded, "each of us must kill some of them. . . . We will be stronger than the enemy when we are no longer afraid of death."

No one knew if the Communists would pause and negotiate at all. But as Martin had told Thieu, everyone—the ruling generals, the still-scheming politicians, the ordinary Saigonese in their homes and shops—was certain that they would never deal with Thieu. "Mr. Thieu is very intelligent," a national assemblyman had once said of him, "but he is a military man, and a military man is only good for waging war." Now the war was lost, and someone else had to be found to try to make peace.

Yet Thieu's reputation for stubbornness was well earned. Even on the evening of April 21, when Saigon radio broadcast that the president would speak later that night on television—announcing at the same time that the nightly curfew would begin at eight o'clock instead of nine, thus emptying the streets while he would be on the air—it was impossible to be certain that the end of the Thieu era had really arrived.

While steel shutters clanked down over shopfronts and Saigon scrambled in the warm, smoky dusk to get home before the new curfew hour, the president appeared on the television screen at exactly 7:45 P.M., seated behind a glossy-topped desk and wearing an open-necked safari shirt. Fifteen days past his 52nd birthday, he showed few physical marks of his years as wartime leader or of the catastrophe that had engulfed him in the last six weeks. His hair, black when he first came to power, was now silvered, a bit longer at the temples; his face slightly fuller, more Buddha-like than it had been, but still unlined and smooth.

He began with an odd apology for the lack of ceremony. He would have preferred, he said, to convene the National Assembly and invite the Supreme Court and other dignitaries to a formal session, instead of summoning them on short notice to a television studio. He begged his audience to excuse him for acting in a way "not fully consistent with etiquette." Then, the apology over, he hurled himself into his speech, an extraordinary, tearful harangue in which he once again blamed everyone but himself for the disaster that had overtaken his country.

Controlled at first, his voice rose as he kept speaking. His gestures grew jerkier, his sentences more disconnected and repetitive. He poured out resentment of the Americans who, he charged, forced him to sign the Paris agreement, promised to come to South Vietnam's defense if it were attacked after the ceasefire, and had then not only betrayed that promise but refused to maintain essential aid. "You have let our combatants die," Thieu raged. ". . . This is an inhumane act by an inhumane ally. Refusing to aid an ally and abandoning it is an inhumane act." Admitting that some of his officers had been cowardly, he scornfully speculated that American soldiers might have collapsed even faster had they fought, as the South Vietnamese did, with insufficient arms and munitions and air power.

For an hour he told and retold the story of his resistance to the Paris accords, Nixon's and Kissinger's threats of an aid shutoff if he did not sign, the broken promise of reintervention, the cuts in aid. Some soldiers fled without fighting in the highlands and in the north, he admitted, but even if all had fought and died, the losses in land and population would have been the same.

At last, 60 minutes after he began, eyes filling with tears and voice faltering, he announced his own decision. "Today, before both chambers of the National Assembly, before the Supreme Court, before the government, before the compatriots and before the brother and sister combatants and cadres nationwide, I declare my resignation as president." Again striking that odd note of apology for the lack of proper ceremony, he asked that his successor, the sick, half-blind Vice-President Tran Van Huong, be sworn in immediately at the close of his speech, instead of in the "solemn setting" that should have been provided.

As if unable to yield power even in the last minutes of his presidency, Thieu kept speaking for another half-hour. Even now, he offered no vision of peace, only of sustaining the war. He had been pictured as "warlike," "bellicose," and "stubborn," he said, and perhaps that image was the reason the American Congress refused to extend more aid. With his departure the aid, perhaps even B-52s, might now be forthcoming. "I think that after my resignation today, maybe tomorrow, the 300 million dollars will be raised to 722 million dollars or to more than one billion dollars and that a continuous airlift will bring in tanks and heavy artillery. Since Mr. Thieu is gone, here comes the aid, aid and more aid. I hope so. Let us wait and see whether the U.S. Congress will do so."

Weeping, at times bowing his head for long silent seconds while he struggled for self-control, Thieu vowed over and over that he had done his best for his country. "Over the past ten years, all years, months, days and hours in my life have been bad, as my horoscope forecast," he said toward the end. "As regards my fate, I can enjoy no happiness. . . . If I have some bad points and errors, I am ready to accept judgments and accusations from the compatriots. Today, as I leave my office, I ask the compatriots, combatants and cadres, together with all popular organizations and religions, to forgive those errors I have committed against the nation. . . . I am resigning but not deserting. From this moment I place myself at the service of the president, the people and the army."

After speaking exactly 90 minutes, he summoned Vice-President Huong to the rostrum, embraced him, and, head lowered, strode quickly off the stage.

Tran Van Huong, born in 1903 in the pleasant city of My Tho in the upper delta, had been a teacher; one of his students was Huynh Tan Phat, now the chairman of the Provisional Revolutionary Government. Huong had served briefly as mayor of Saigon and then spent five years as secretary-general of the Vietnamese Red Cross. Prime minister for a few months in 1964 and early 1965, he ran for president against the Thieu-Ky ticket in 1967, placing fourth, and then accepted Thieu's offer to form a government and became prime minister for the second time in 1968, serving until he was replaced by Khiem the next year. In 1971, when Ky was dropped from Thieu's un-opposed reelection slate, Huong was picked to run for vice-president. As a civilian he wielded no real power, but a slight aura of respect clung to him. He was said to be personally honest: a "sentimental symbol," one writer called him, of probity and civilian presence in the Thieu regime. In a Confucian society, his background as a teacher earned him some prestige. But he had been in poor health for a long time. At 71, he was now so crippled by rheumatism that he could not walk more than a few steps without aid. Nearly blind, he peered myopically through thick glasses that hid half his face.

Huong's inauguration took only a few minutes. Repeating the oath of office in a voice quavering with age and illness, he seemed a sad, pitiful image of the lost war. Making no proposal for peace talks in his short speech, he called only for national unity while exhorting his already-beaten soldiers to stand firm. "As long as you continue to fight," he concluded, "I will always stand by your side. . . . If one day misfortune befalls our nation, my bones will lie beside the bones of our brother combatants. I consider this my most earnest aspiration."

The Communist response was as swift and crushing as it was predictable. Barely two hours after Huong was sworn in, Liberation Radio denounced his government as the "Thieu regime without Thieu, with a cabinet of Thieu's henchmen created by him." The official North Vietnamese news agency called the change a "puppet show" and declared, "Unless Ford and Kissinger give up their neo-colonialist policy and put an end to the U.S. involvement, they will meet bitter defeat."

Hanoi issued a fuller statement early the next morning, declaring that the resignation of "the number one lackey of the U.S. imperialists" was another great triumph, but that "Thieu, Huong and their clique, as well as their masters, the Ford-Kissinger administration, have continued to manifest their extreme stubbornness. . . . Now that the U.S. imperialists' reactionary lackey regime in the South is moving toward complete collapse, the Ford administration's attempts to breathe life into this clique are futile and useless."

In their jungle command post north of Saigon, the Communist com-manders' latest orders from the Politburo, signed by Le Duan, declared that "military and political conditions are ripe for launching a general offensive against Saigon. . . . The opportunities facing us now demand that we act most quickly. By firmly seizing these great opportunities, we will surely win complete victory." On April 22, they reviewed the Ho Chi Minh campaign plan for the last time, standing over maps marked with red arrows showing the attack routes for each corps. Then General Dung and Pham Hung signed the order to put the plan into operation. There would be no negotiations. The war, now driving on Saigon's doors, would go on.

Chapter 12

"Your mission is very heavy"

In the last ten days of the war Saigon seemed like a ship that had broken loose from its anchors, drifting with no one at the helm toward something unseen but huge and frightening.

Panic and lawlessness did not erupt. Instead, the city's three million people went about their normal affairs, but with a nervous haste that gave the effect of a speeded-up film. From above, one imagined, Saigon would look like an anthill stirred by a stick, or like one of the bamboo cages, filled with the tremulous, excited flutter of birds, that hung in the live animal market off Nguyen Hue Boulevard. Along the sidewalks and alleys and in the narrow cluttered passages between market stalls, wiry pushcart men and vendors in their cone-shaped straw hats, moving with a distinctive swaying shuffle under loads slung from wooden shoulder-yokes, edged through thickening crowds of shoppers hurrying to stock up, as Saigonese had learned to do in times of danger, with rice, cooking fuel, and other supplies.

Swelling the crowds were refugees who had slipped past the government cordon outside the capital; people from the suburbs who sought the greater safety of the city center; others pursuing not safety but livelihoods that had been lost as government agencies, private businesses, and American contract firms drew back from the threatened countryside. On the wide downtown boulevards, the din of sputtering motorbikes, scooterbuses, scuttling taxis, jeeps, trucks, and buses seemed more frenzied every hour, drowning out the singsong bargaining at sidewalk stalls and the wail of popular tunes pouring out through the open doors of restaurants and coffee shops. Traffic fumes overpowered the other Saigon odors of drying fish, charcoal cooking fires, and mouldering garbage.

424

More and more hawkers appeared on the sidewalks, squatting next to ponchos on which they displayed cheap jewelry, brightly colored plastic toys, sunglasses, pens, tattered magazines, or flimsy cloth caps; or wading through the streams of people with wooden trays of bread, fruits, cut flowers, or fragrant strings of jasmine blossoms. As the 8 P.M. curfew closed in each evening, the clusters of beggars and prostitutes gathering in the hot, smoky dusk in front of downtown hotels and restaurants grew denser and more insistent; and each night, as the muffled sounds of artillery grew audible in curfew-stilled streets, there were more homeless families and ragged, lost children huddling in the litter-strewn doorways.

While the streets seethed, businesses and government offices were listless, half-empty as their occupants attended to their own escape or survival. A sense of utter aimlessness settled over the city. Even the streetcorner loud-speakers opposite the National Assembly, which for weeks had blared slogans and patriotic music, were now mostly silent, as if the government didn't know what to say any more. There was an almost physical sensation of old realities breaking apart. "In South Vietnam we have been raised to hate the Communists, just as on the other side they have been raised to hate the colonialists or the capitalists," a government official said to me on one of those dreamlike days, "but in the rest of the world there is detente, so that hatred, leading to armed conflict, has become obsolete. I have been anti-Communist all my life, but suddenly it is meaningless—everything is meaningless."

In Washington, the Ford administration at last dropped the pretense that more military aid could stop the Communist advance. The goal now, Henry Kissinger told Congress a few hours after Thieu resigned, was negotiations to avoid a battle for Saigon. Revealingly, he used the phrase "controlled solution"—the same euphemism once used about Cambodia. But Kissinger still asked for the additional funds, which he said "would be an enormous help to those of us who are attempting to bring about these controlled circumstances." As to the prospects for diplomacy, he expressed a near-categorical confidence, declaring that Thieu's exit "in all probability will lead to some form of negotiation." The same day, a Defense Intelligence Agency assessment called Saigon's prospects "grim." Communist forces could open their offensive against the South Vietnamese capital "at any time," the agency said, while the defenders' morale was low "and their leadership appears to be crumbling." How long the government could or would hold out, it concluded, "remains unclear."

The following day, President Huong proposed an immediate ceasefire, in return for which Saigon would reopen talks "on all issues within the framework of the 27th January 1973 Paris agreement," specifically including the establishment of the National Council of Reconciliation. The

REFUGEES *Facing page,* U.S. Marines keep order at bayonet point aboard the refugee ship SS *Green Port; above,* some of the nearly 17,000 refugees aboard the merchant vessel SS *Pioneer Contender* on her nightmare voyage to Phu Quoc, a barren island in the Gulf of Thailand (*U.S. Navy photos*); *immediate left,* a government soldier, with his possessions piled on a clumsy hand-drawn cart, prepares to flee the city of Hue shortly before its fall to the Communists (*photo by Don Oberdorfer*).

ESCAPE *Below,* President Ford meets with the National Security Council shortly before ordering the evacuation of Saigon (*White House photo*); *immediate right,* Ambassador Graham A. Martin is shown (*State Department photo*); *facing page, top,* Vietnamese scale the wall around the U.S. Embassy compound, seeking evacuation (*Wide World Photos*); *bottom,* because there was no room on the evacuation ships for Vietnamese helicopters from the mainland, one pilot leaped from his craft into the sea next to the USS *Blue Ridge; inset* shows crewmen pushing another helicopter over the side (*U.S. Navy photos*).

THE VICTORS *Facing page, top,* carrying the Liberation flag, Communist soldiers race up the steps of the presidential palace in Saigon on the last day of the war; *bottom,* President Duong Van Minh, wearing dark shirt and with head bowed, is led out of the palace by Communist troops. At Minh's left is Vu Van Mau, the Republic's last prime minister (*VNA photos/courtesy of Southeast Asia Resource Center*); *above,* members of the palace guard unit sit disconsolately under the weapons of Communist infantrymen, while behind them, North Vietnamese tanks are drawn up on the grounds in front of the building (*VNA/courtesy of John Spragens, Jr.*).

offer seemed stunningly unrealistic, and the Viet Cong answer was scornful. Huong's proposal "fools no one," said the Communist delegation in Saigon, "and will hardly help the Americans out of their defeat." A day later, Huong announced he would dismiss Prime Minister Can's nine-day-old "fighting cabinet" and appoint a new government to seek negotiations. And on April 25, he ordered the outgoing information minister, Brig. Gen. Phan Hoa Hiep, to try to fly to Hanoi to negotiate directly with the North Vietnamese. Hiep went to Tansonnhut to board the last of the weekly U.S. liaison flights, but was told while waiting at the flight line that Hanoi would not receive him. After several hours of confusion, the plane left without him.

The one step Huong would not take, despite the Communists' condemnation of his regime, was to resign. Rather than hand power to ex-General Duong Van Minh, he agreed only to offer Minh the post of prime minister. The two men met at the home of a mutual friend for a conversation that was full of flowery courtesy—Huong addressed Minh as "brother" and the general respectfully called him "teacher"—but empty of results. Minh demanded the presidency; Huong balked, saying that no such procedure was legally permissible. South Vietnam's "legal basis still exists," he later explained plaintively to the assembly. "The power which I possess has been granted to me by the constitution. This power is not like a handkerchief or a banknote that I can take out of my pocket, hand over to the general and tell him: Here you are. I cannot do that." Though Minh believed the Communists would negotiate if he were named president, Huong was unconvinced. "I shall believe it," he told the assembly, "only after I have proof."

The "Big Minh solution" had its believers, however. Aside from Minh's own associates, its most assiduous promoters were the French—driven, it seemed, by complex motives that included concern for their sizeable business holdings in South Vietnam and a desire to show up the Americans by successfully brokering an end to the war the U.S. had botched. Also underlying French actions, perhaps, was a semiconscious wish to validate their own supposed "civilizing mission" in their century of colonial mastery by proving that a special relationship still existed, based, the French could tell themselves, on Vietnamese gratitude for the boon of French culture. France would "do all in its power" to help settle the war, President Valéry Giscard d'Estaing's spokesman declared, while French officials theorized to reporters in Paris that the Communists were so anxious to avoid responsibility for a bloody battle in Saigon that they would accept a new coalition, even if it meant postponing complete Communist rule and reunification of the country.

In Saigon, the French ambassador, Jean-Marie Mérillon, flung himself into the political intrigues with feverish energy, apparently imagining himself, as he commented later, in the same role as the World War II Swedish diplomat who saved Paris from destruction "by staying put and negotiating with the Nazis" who wanted to set the city ablaze before its liberation by the Allies. Conferring incessantly with Saigon politicians and with Ambassador Martin (a door was cut in the wall between the adjoining U.S. and French embassy compounds so the two could meet more easily and discreetly), Mérillon kept repeating that Saigon could be spared, but only if Minh were made president. He seemed his own best listener; at any rate, the more often he told others, the more passionately he appeared to believe himself that Minh was the answer.

Hints of a "Minh solution" came also from officials of the Polish and Hungarian peacekeeping delegations who called the U.S. embassy and the CIA station regularly—"almost on an hourly basis," Martin said later—to supply "interpretations" of Hanoi's intentions. The Soviet Union, meanwhile, served as intermediary for other signals, including an extraordinary public hint to the *New York Times* Moscow bureau that the North Vietnamese did not want to attack Saigon and would hold political talks if a new South Vietnamese government were installed.

Hanoi also communicated a remarkable message to Lt. Col. Harry Summers of the Joint Military Team delegation during the liaison visit to the North Vietnamese capital on April 25—the same visit from which Saigon's would-be negotiator, General Hiep, was barred. When the flight landed in Hanoi, the customary downtown lunch was cancelled. Instead, Summer's escort, a Major Huyen, led him into an airport waiting room for a two-hour conversation that turned out be be an appeal for American understanding and even friendship, coupled with an apparent invitation to the U.S. to keep some form of diplomatic presence in Vietnam even after a Communist victory.

The Defense Attache Office staff of "military advisers" must leave, Huyen told Summers, but the Joint Military Team should remain to carry on its humanitarian work; the Americans had "done more than enough" for Saigon and had no reason for self-reproach at South Vietnam's defeat, and there was now no reason Washington and Hanoi could not establish friendly relations. When Summers replied that this would depend heavily on whether the war ended with great loss of life and atrocities, Huyen quickly assured him there would be no bloodbath. "I tell you honestly," he said with great earnestness, "there will be no reprisals—we need these people to rebuild Vietnam."

Aboard the U.S. Air Force C-130 on the return flight to Saigon, other North Vietnamese officers repeated the same message, confirming that Huyen was speaking officially and not just giving his personal views. The conversations had to do only with the U.S. presence and relations with Hanoi, not with South Vietnam's political future. But Summers thought his counterparts had inferentially indicated a willingness to negotiate, and after reading his long memorandum on the day's events, senior embassy officers apparently drew the same conclusion. Martin, for whom the thought of closing the embassy seems to have been all but unendurable, was almost ebullient. With an air of mysterious confidence, he began assuring subordinates that no complete evacuation was going to be necessary after all.

The real meaning of the signals from Moscow and from the Poles and Hungarians in Saigon remains a matter of speculation. They may have been parts of an elaborate ruse to confuse and dishearten the South Vietnamese, or they may have represented honest but mistaken impressions of Hanoi's true intentions. Henry Kissinger, on the last day of the war, professed to have believed as late as April 27 that some form of negotiated settlement was not just possible, but "highly probable." What that belief was based on, he did not say. Kissinger may have been repeating misleading signals from third parties. Or he may simply have been overstating the case—as he had done in the past, with respect to Hanoi's obligations in Cambodia and on other matters—putting too concrete a meaning on vague and ambiguous statements and giving in to his own wishful hope that somehow, a negotiated arrangement could avoid the ultimate humiliation of Americans fleeing by helicopter from Saigon's rooftops.

On April 24, the P.R.G. announced its stiffest demands so far, calling for an end to all U.S. economic as well as military aid and the withdrawal not just of the often-mentioned "military personnel disguised as civilians" but of all U.S. intelligence officers too. As for a new regime in Saigon, the P.R.G. specified it must not include anyone from the "Thieu clique," must renounce U.S. military aid and intervention in Vietnamese affairs, and must abrogate all "anti-democratic decrees" and free all political prisoners.

American diplomats professed to be encouraged, since the broadcast did not explicitly rule out talks with General Minh. But at home, President Ford was trying—at last—to write off the war. Preparing for a long-scheduled speech at Tulane University in New Orleans, Ford mused to his aide Robert Hartmann and several members of his speechwriting staff that what he really wanted to say to the students was that it was time to "think about the future, stop arguing about the past. Vietnam has been going on ever since any of them can remember," the president added. "Well, the war's over." Hartmann looked at him. "Why don't you just say that?" he asked.

Ford's first reaction was to worry if Kissinger would agree. Throughout the crisis, Kissinger had been urging him to go down "with the flags flying," while blaming Congress for the debacle. On Ford's staff, however, the feeling was growing that Kissinger's advice reflected more concern for his own reputation than for the president's. Kissinger had alienated Ford's aides by his personal style ("paranoia," Hartmann called it), his high-handed efforts to dominate foreign policy, and his unwillingness to share the spotlight with anyone else, including the president, toward whom he frequently seemed to act with infuriating condescension. If the Tulane speech displayed Ford as the master of his own policy and took Kissinger down a peg, Hartmann would not be heartbroken. No one declared the Vietnam War, he pressed Ford, "but you can declare the end of it." Ford was obviously intrigued. "See what you can come up with," he instructed Hartmann, "but don't pass it around until I decide."

Hartmann and speechwriter Milt Friedman went to work on the speech— without consulting Kissinger, though an early draft was routinely sent to the National Security Council office. Not until later, however, was the crucial passage added. It was typed into the text, in fact, aboard Air Force One en route to New Orleans. "America can regain the sense of pride that existed before Vietnam," it said. "But it cannot be achieved by refighting a war that is finished as far as America is concerned."

The Tulane field house was packed when Ford stepped to the microphones on the evening of April 23. He recalled America's humiliation at the British capture of Washington in the War of 1812 and the restoration of pride in the Battle of New Orleans; then he reached the lines on Vietnam. But hardly anyone heard the last six words. At the word "finished," a jubilant roar welled up from the 4,500 students who filled the bleachers and floor of the arena. The applause went on and on, astonishing even those aides who had urged Ford to make the declaration. It was one of those moments that seemed to crystallize the whole nation's mood. Ford's more generous instinct for what to say had been right, Kissinger's was wrong. America wanted to forget the war, not argue about the blame.

U.S. officials in Saigon were still not supposed even to breathe the word "evacuation." But the day of Ford's New Orleans speech, 488 Americans and more than 3,000 Vietnamese left Tansonnhut on U.S. airlift planes, almost ten times the daily average earlier in the month. In the six days remaining before the Tansonnhut runways were closed by Communist shellfire, about 35,000 evacuees were flown to the Philippines or Guam in American transports that rolled off the base day and night at the rate of nearly two every hour. Few of those leaving had valid travel documents or exit permits, but the Vietnamese police and air force officials who controlled the air base looked the other way in return for evacuation of their own families. As the airlift continued, more and more Vietnamese military men arrived at the processing center seeking flights for their wives or children; at times the crowds reached as many as 10,000 people. On April 25, at General Smith's request, a platoon of U.S. marines was helicoptered in from the evacuation fleet to help keep order.

That same evening, after dark, a small convoy of cars with U.S. diplomatic licenses drove past the military police checkpoint onto Tansonnhut. At the wheel of one of the cars, a large Chevrolet, was the CIA's Frank Snepp. In the back seat, awkwardly chatting about events and encounters far in the past, were the CIA station's military expert Charles Timmes and Nguyen Van Thieu. As they passed the checkpoint, Thieu, sitting in the middle of the seat with an aide on his right and Timmes on his left, ducked his head. But as usual, the guards simply waved the cars through, not even looking at the passengers. Once through the gate, the convoy headed for an unlit stretch of tarmac near the Air America terminal, across the main road from the Defense Attache Office compound. Snepp braked to a stop next to a parked U.S. C-118 transport, where Ambassador Martin waited at the boarding steps to make his farewells. The South Vietnamese leader, sleekly dressed as usual but speaking hoarsely and with tears glistening on his face, thanked Snepp briefly, then trotted up the steps into the aircraft, accompanied by aides carrying his luggage and by former Prime Minister Tran Thien Khiem. Thieu and Martin had their last conversation inside the plane. As soon as Martin had climbed back down the steps, the pilots started the motors and taxied toward the runway to take off for a destination that seemed mordantly symbolic: Taiwan, where Chiang Kai-shek's defeated Nationalist government had fled from the Chinese Communists 26 years before. His last talk with Thieu had been nothing historic, Martin told Snepp later; "just good-bye."

Not far away in another part of the sprawling air base, the remaining North Vietnamese and Viet Cong truce delegates were spending their nights digging bunkers under their barracks. Since they had no proper tools, they used fence boards and knives, and to hide their activities from the South Vietnamese military police who guarded them, they carried away the dirt inside their clothing or packed it away under the floors of their huts. In coded radio messages they urged the Communist command not to hesitate to shell the base if it became necessary. "We will dig trenches and hold on," said one message. ". . . Do not worry about us."

At dawn on April 26, North Vietnam's General Dung left Loc Ninh by car and was driven to a new command post in a wrecked house northwest of Ben Cat. His units, approaching Saigon from five directions, were now nearly in position for the final assault. That afternoon on Saigon's eastern defense line, Communist forces began advancing toward Bien Hoa and its huge air base, which, because of heavy shelling, was no longer being used by government planes. In the evening, a major artillery attack began pounding the former U.S. base at Long Binh, a few miles east of Bien Hoa. Farther around the Saigon perimeter toward the south, other Communist units heading for the capital's southeastern approaches crossed Highway 15, the route from Bien Hoa to Vung Tau which was the last land link between Saigon and the sea.

Vung Tau itself was still in government hands, defended chiefly by Vietnamese marines who had survived the evacuation from the north a month earlier. U.S. planners, anticipating a possible evacuation by sea from the coast if Saigon refugees could be transported there, had promised to take out the marines' dependents and eventually the marines themselves in return for their help in securing the Vung Tau area. In conferences over a period of several weeks with American officers who helicoptered in from Saigon, Maj. Gen. Bui The Lan, the marine commander, agreed to the plan. His men, he proposed, should control the actual embarkation points while a U.S. landing force—possibly as large as an entire brigade—held off the Communists. The reason, Lan grimly explained to his American visitors, was that U.S. rules of engagement would probably forbid American marines to shoot refugees, while his men had already carried out executions to keep order in Vung Tau and would do so again if it became necessary.

With the loss of Highway 15, an evacuation over the beach at Vung Tau, known as "Option V" in American plans, was no longer possible. But the Americans decided to keep their end of the bargain anyway. It took all day on the 26th to persuade skeptical Air Force commanders at Clark Air Base in the Philippines that the Vung Tau airstrip was still safe. But finally they agreed. The next day two C-130s landed, picked up 183 marine dependents, and flew them safely and in complete secrecy out of the country. No marine officers or enlisted men were evacuated until after Saigon surrendered three days later, according to official U.S. reports of the episode, though after the surrender, Lan and some of his men made their own way in small boats to the U.S. fleet offshore.

Meanwhile, on the 26th, the Communists discarded the last pretense that they might negotiate an end to the war. A new declaration by the Provisional Revolutionary Government dropped the concept of a new Saigon government completely. Instead, the Communists demanded that the entire South Vietnamese administration and its army and police must be abolished as agencies of "U.S. neo-colonialism." Nor did they claim any longer to be fighting to uphold the Paris agreement as a whole. Rather, they specified just three of the agreement's 23 articles: those in which the U.S. pledged not to interfere in Vietnamese affairs. As for the Third Force, its adherents no longer had any independent role to play. Instead, in a passage that seemed addressed directly to General Minh and his followers, they were called on to "see through, and in time, the pernicious scheme of the U.S. and its henchmen" and help "reduce to a minimum the sacrifices and losses of our people" by helping the revolution achieve a swift victory.

The meaning was beyond doubt: the only way to end the war now was to capitulate. But the drama being enacted in Saigon had acquired its own phantasmagoric momentum. No reality could pierce the curtain of wishful illusion behind which Huong, Minh, Martin, Mérillon, and a host of extras were preparing to play the last scenes. Driven by their multiple illusions, the play—farce or tragedy, depending on the audience—would be performed to the end.

Seeking to meet some part of the Communists' demands, Huong announced that some political prisoners would be freed and a "large number" of other cases would be reviewed, including those of the eighteen journalists whose imprisonment in February had so scandalized the visiting U.S. congressional team. But when he went before the assembly on the morning of April 26, Huong could still not bring himself to yield the presidency. Instead, he asked the assembly to decide.

His speech was full of confused contradictions. "Of course, we are lost," he acknowledged; no more American help could be expected, and without a settlement, Saigon would become "a mountain of bones and a river of blood." But he also still seemed to have fantasies of fighting on. If the assembly directed him to turn his office over to General Minh he would do so, but if not, though he would keep seeking a negotiated settlement, he would not capitulate. "The term 'negotiation' does not mean surrender," he declared at one point. "If negotiation meant surrender, why would we have to negotiate? . . . If God no longer wants Vietnam to exist, we shall die with our country, but we cannot surrender."

In response, after ten hours of debate, the assembly refused in its turn to make a decision. By a 123-to-2 vote, it merely approved a resolution to support Huong "in the mission of seeking ways and means to restore peace to South Vietnam on the basis of the Paris agreement." Another clause of the resolution empowered the president, if it became necessary, to "select his replacement to carry out the above-mentioned mission" with the assembly's consent. After thus handing the choice back to the vacillating Huong, the assembly held a moment of silent prayer for peace and for the South Vietnamese nation and people, then adjourned. Saigon's politics had always been characterized by extreme factionalism, petty quarreling, and endless intrigue leading to a paralysis the French called "immobilisme"; never did the word appear more apt than in the Republic's last three days.

Early on the morning of the 27th, as if to remind the bickering politicians that they would not wait much longer, Communist gunners sent four heavy rockets swooshing into downtown Saigon: the first attack on the capital in more than five years. Six persons died. Government forces were still falling back toward Bien Hoa, while Communist units were tightening the ring around Vung Tau, driving remnants of the 1st Airborne Brigade and the rebuilt 3rd ARVN Division out of Ba Ria at the base of the Vung Tau Peninsula. Closer to the capital on the Saigon-Vung Tau highway, Communist troops overran the town of Long Thanh. The Communist advance also continued from other directions. Highway 4 from the delta, which had been periodically cut during the preceding week, was now blocked permanently less than twenty miles southwest of Saigon, while to the north and northwest, General Dung's III Corps cut the road to Tay Ninh to seal off the 25th ARVN Division.

In the Doc Lap palace, Huong finally stopped dithering. After a last round of meetings with his advisers on the 27th, he notified the assembly that he would resign as soon as it chose his successor. Having temporized for almost a week, Huong now expressed a sense of urgency: "action must be taken," his message admonished, "as soon as possible." Senate President Tran Van Lam called the assembly into session at 6:45 that evening. After being briefed on the hopeless military situation by Defense Minister Tran Van Don, along with General Vien of the Joint General Staff and Lt. Gen. Nguyen Van Minh, the Saigon commander, the assembly began considering Huong's letter. 25 minutes after the eight o'clock curfew emptied the streets, it voted unanimously to name Duong Van Minh to the presidency to "carry out the mission of seeking ways and means to restore peace to South Vietnam."

Minh's inauguration was first scheduled for nine o'clock the next morning: Monday, April 28. But even now, he and his entourage acted as if their time was unlimited. When the hour came, Minh was still in his villa at 3 Tran Quy Cap Street, amid the hanging orchids and tropical fish tanks that had been his hobbies for many years, interviewing prospective cabinet members. During the day he sent out word of one postponement after another until, shortly before 5 P.M., he headed with his aides for the palace, just a few blocks from his home.

At the entrances to the palace grounds, the usual security procedures had been dropped. With only the most careless glances at identity cards, the military guards waved assemblymen, outgoing government officials, and journalists in through the opened steel gates. Inside, other guards directed the visitors past workmen who were repairing damage from the April 8 air raid and on into one of the large ceremonial halls, where a row of French windows along one wall stood partly open, looking out on a long balcony. Rows of seats were arranged facing a podium on which was mounted the saffron-and-red South Vietnamese national seal. On a wall behind it was a painting of Hung Vuong, the legendary founder of Vietnam's first dynasty nearly 2,900 years before Christ. Outside, the wind of an approaching thunderstorm began to stir the hot, moist air, ruffling the fronds of palm trees on the palace lawn.

President Huong, eyes hidden behind thick dark glasses, leaning heavily on a cane while an aide supported his other arm, stepped to the podium at exactly fifteen minutes past five o'clock—four hours less than a week after assuming the presidency. In a faltering voice, he declared that his age and infirmity did not permit him to lead the country in such "extremely difficult times," and that since the assembly had consented, he was no longer concerned about the legality of transferring power.

While he spoke, the first thunderclaps boomed outside the windows. The real monsoon would not begin for another six weeks or so, but such false rains were not uncommon in late April. "Mango rains," the Vietnamese sometimes called them, since they fell in the middle of the brief mango season. Times had changed, Huong was saying. "We no longer think that it is always necessary to shed blood. We no longer think that we will fight to the last combatant and the last bullet." Instead, the new president should seek peace only "without excessively undermining our country's honor." Addressing Minh directly, Huong declared: "General, your mission is very heavy. . . . Whether or not your strenuous efforts will be successful, I believe, does not depend in large measure on yourself. However, if you wholeheartedly serve the country . . . and strive to restore peace and ensure that the people can live peacefully and that the bloodshed stops, the meritorious service you render will be remembered forever by younger generations."

After speaking for ten minutes, Huong thanked his audience again, then clutched the arm of his aide and hobbled slowly and painfully away from the podium.

For a long silent moment, no one moved. Minh stayed seated, his face as blank and still as a temple image. Then one of his entourage stood, walked to the podium, and knelt down to remove the plaque with the national seal. He replaced it with another, showing the stylized outline of an apricot blossom enclosing the Chinese yin-and-yang sign, representing the two opposing but complementary forces of the universe—now meant, presumably, to symbolize Vietnamese reconciliation after so many years of division and conflict.

Minh waited, unmoving, until the new emblem was attached, then rose and walked slowly to the podium. More than eleven years had passed and an ocean of blood had soaked Vietnam's battlegrounds since he last held power. Then, he had been ousted by army officers who thought he was not waging the war against the Viet Cong vigorously enough. Now that those officers and their successors had all but lost the war, Minh was called on again to try to make peace.

Duong Van Minh was 59 years old when he became South Vietnam's leader for the second time. Nicknamed Big Minh for his six-foot height and 200-pound bulk, he also had the image of a personality often associated with large men: easygoing, folksy, not overly bright, tolerant—even indolent. "Affable . . . slow-spoken and diffident," a journalist once wrote of him; "even his supporters concede he cannot honestly be called clever or adroit. . . . He is a sort of father figure to the nation—honest, with integrity and dignity, and courageous on the battlefield. But he lacks charisma and is not considered a very competent administrator."

The impression of fumbling amiability was accepted, usually without much question, by Saigon's large community of foreign diplomats and journalists. But clearly, it was not the whole truth about Minh. Underneath an easygoing manner lay a capacity for ruthlessness. Serving as Ngo Dinh

Diem's senior military adviser was "not a job for a Boy Scout," as one journalist noted, and though Minh never admitted it, he was almost certainly the man who later issued the order to murder Diem and his brother Nhu in the revolution of 1963.*

Born in My Tho in the upper delta—where Tran Van Huong was also born twelve years earlier—Minh, like nearly all other South Vietnamese officers of his generation, began his military career in the French army. (A younger brother, Duong Van Nhut, joined the Communist side and was believed by U.S. intelligence to have become a lieutenant general in the North Vietnamese army.) Under Diem, after South Vietnam's independence, he rose quickly to major general. But he refused to convert from his Buddhist-Confucian beliefs to Catholicism, as Nguyen Van Thieu and many other ambitious officers did; nor would he join Diem's Can Lao party. Gradually falling from favor, he was assigned to a succession of posts with prestige but little real power, and he was easily recruited into the conspiracies against the regime. As leader of the 1963 coup he became a national hero, but his regime lasted only three months before being overthrown by another military faction. Minh was sent into polite exile as a "roving ambassador," with a salary, said to be $1,000 a month, paid on the understanding that he would remain out of the country. Shortly afterward he was retired with the rank of lieutenant general—later raised retroactively to full general, as part of the revision of ARVN's rank structure to conform with that of the American army.

Minh's exile ended, after protracted negotiations with the Thieu government, in the fall of 1968. Then and later, he abided in the belief that the popularity he won by overthrowing Diem remained undiminished—a belief that was unprovable, but was carefully nurtured by the clique of dissident assembly members and other followers who attached themselves to him. Nor did Minh stop thirsting to regain the power he had held so briefly. He had left the government "with the great sadness of a man who has not yet accomplished his mission," he said in 1970, "and during the past seven years . . . that sadness has grown heavier and heavier on my soul." He announced his candidacy against Thieu in 1971 but then withdrew, charging that the election would be a "farce." At that time his program explicitly opposed neutrality and coalition with the Liberation Front. But as the war ground on into the new decade, Minh—whether out of conviction, opportunism, or the influence of his entourage—began to present himself as spokesman for the Third Force between the Thieu regime and the Commu-

---

* The men who actually killed the Ngo brothers were said to be Minh's bodyguard, a Captain Nhung, and another aide, a Major Nghia. According to Tran Van Don, one of Minh's collaborators in the coup, Minh had also planned an assassination attempt against Nhu several weeks before.

nists: "all those," he once said, "who followed neither this side nor the other side and who, to this date, were never given the chance to speak their minds."

Such statements positioned him to emerge as a reconciliation leader when, as he and his followers expected, Thieu's policies failed. But South Vietnam's collapse came too quickly. By the time Minh was finally called back to the presidency, the only role remaining for him was to surrender to the advancing Communist army. There were some in the Viet Cong apparatus or among its agents, Wilfred Burchett reported, who tried at the last minute to spare Minh that humiliation. According to Burchett, Provisional Revolutionary Government officials or sympathizers arranged for a close relative of Minh's to fly from Paris to warn him against accepting the presidency. Before the flight arrived, however, the Saigon airport closed. Minh's kinsman managed to reach him by telephone from Bangkok, Burchett wrote, but too late to dissuade him.

Minh himself still believed the Communists would negotiate with him, he told the CIA's Charles Timmes a few hours before his inauguration. They needed time to develop their political apparatus in Saigon, he thought, and the southerners in the Provisional Revolutionary Government would be anxious to preserve a separate South Vietnam rather than be absorbed into a unified regime that would be dominated by Hanoi. In addition, Minh believed French influence would be helpful, while China would also prefer two separate Vietnams instead of a single more powerful nation on its southern boundary. Lastly, Minh said, the Communists knew the South Vietnamese opposed them. "They can't kill all of us," he concluded, "so it is to their interest to negotiate."

After he had waited so many years for his moment, and after he had been given such feverishly dogmatic encouragement by Mérillon and other would-be peacemakers, it was perhaps inevitable that Minh would be unable to see just how bleak his possibilities were. His acceptance speech, delivered while more thunderclaps rumbled and heavy raindrops splattered the balcony underneath the open palace windows, was unconnected to any reality. It seemed appropriate only as a last expression of the dreamlike state in which the South Vietnamese republic lived its final days.

Instead of the capitulation that was clearly no more than a few days away, Minh appeared to expect the continued existence of a non-Communist regime which, after a ceasefire, would negotiate a political settlement under the terms of the Paris agreement. Speaking in a firm voice, wearing a gray suit and dark glasses, he promised to free political prisoners and to lift restrictions on the press, while naming a liberal Catholic, my old friend and the former Senate president Nguyen Van Huyen, as his vice-president. Vu Van Mau, the head of the Buddhist-sponsored National Reconciliation Force—one of the protest groups formed to oppose Thieu the previous fall—would be prime minister. Bursts of applause greeted each name. Minh declared he would welcome "all economic and humanitarian aid" but did not mention military supplies, thus seeming to implicitly reject military assistance. Nevertheless, he ordered government soldiers not to desert or surrender but to "protect the remaining territory" until a ceasefire could be arranged. "All acts of indiscipline," he declared, "will be strictly and promptly punished."

Minh ended his twenty-minute speech with an eloquent but empty appeal to those trying to flee abroad. "This land," he said, "is our native land. . . . Remain here with your loved ones, with the tombs of your forefathers and with the altars of your ancestors. Remain here to join us and all those with good will in building a new South for our future generations—an independent, democratic, free and prosperous South where the Vietnamese will live peacefully among Vietnamese amid fraternal love."

Outside, as we gathered to watch the members of the new government drive off in a covey of official limousines, the broad flight of steps leading down from the ceremonial front entrance was slippery and glistening from the just-ended rain. Little rivulets formed in the creases of leaves and slid in silvery streams to the ground, which steamed in the damp heat. The sky was metallic, with a greenish tint. An old acquaintance, the veteran opposition deputy Tran Van Tuyen, greeted me. "Perhaps," he said wearily, "now we have some hope in this catastrophe."

Tuyen—who was later reported to have died in a Communist "re-education" camp—was wrong. Barely ten minutes after Minh stopped speaking, before I even left the palace grounds to walk the seven blocks to my hotel, Liberation Radio came on the air with a commentary that smashed the last hope for a "Minh solution." Creating a new administration in Saigon was just a scheme of the Americans, other foreigners, and their Vietnamese collaborators, the broadcast declared, "to deceive our armed forces and people, check their advance, [and] prevent the collapse of the puppet army and administration." Not just the leaders had to be changed, but the entire South Vietnamese government, including its army and police, must be dismantled. And members of the Third Force were warned, specifically and menacingly, against any acts that might delay the revolution's triumph:

It is undoubtedly culpable to take any action which may hinder the people's advance at this juncture. . . . Adherents of the Third Force must carefully ponder the Revolutionary Government's appeal, see clearly the schemes of U.S. or any other imperialism and see through the schemes of their flunkeys so as to avoid doing anything that may be harmful to the revolutionary movement, the people or the country.

. . . The only way open for the really patriotic Third Force is to join the entire people in smashing the old administration, the war machine and the repressive and coercive machinery.

Like almost everyone else in the South Vietnamese capital, I did not hear of the Communist broadcast until hours later. Like everyone else, though, I heard the message in another form: a series of enormous explosions from the direction of Tansonnhut.

The first blast came at about six-fifteen, just as I was reaching my hotel. At first I thought it was another thunderstorm. But the explosions were too evenly spaced to be thunder. A concussion wave, channeled from four miles away by some fluke of air currents and building lines, reached out invisible arms and clutched me around the ribs, compressing my lungs in a brief but infinitely menacing embrace. The detonations were answered by bursts of antiaircraft fire and then by pandemonium, as soldiers and policemen all over Saigon began blazing away blindly into the sodden clouds. On Tu Do Street, the normal evening traffic was scattering like a flock of sparrows from a thrown stone. In moments the street was empty except for a few scared pedestrians crouching in doorways or behind parked cars, wondering, like the rest of the city, what was happening. The sounds indicated an air raid. But where, and by whom, no one knew. Most Saigonese probably thought, as I did, that a coup was under way against the half-hour-old Minh government; the beginning, perhaps, of an attempt by General Ky or some other diehards to make Saigon an Asian Stalingrad.

At Tansonnhut, air controllers could not identify the attackers either. Spotting the incoming flight of A-37 fighter-bombers just as they appeared above the end of the runway, a baffled tower operator radioed, "A-37s! What group do you belong to?" One of the pilots, already diving to release his bombs, answered strangely, "These are U.S.-made aircraft." An instant later the first bombs struck. They landed among the Vietnamese air force planes parked just off the main runway. Three AC-119 gunships and several twin-engine C-47 transports were destroyed; several other aircraft were damaged.

Only a few minutes before the raid, two U.S. Air Force C-130s loaded with refugees had taken off. One of the pilots, 1st Lt. Fritz Pingle, found one of the mysterious A-37s flying off his left wing in a possible attack position. "He's coming at us, he's coming at us!" an excited crewman screamed over the intercom. Pingle, lumbering at 280 knots and just 500 feet above the Saigon River, searched for a cloud to hide in but saw none. "Just like when you needed a cop," he said later, "he wasn't there." The crew lost sight of the A-37, but Pingle didn't relax until he contacted a radar plane orbiting off the coast, who told him no one was following any more. Captain Ken Rice, piloting the other C-130, headed straight over downtown Saigon only to run into heavy fire from jittery South Vietnamese gunners on the ground. With bursts of fire coming from all directions, he climbed as steeply as he could into the thunderclouds that still hung over the city. Flying in the storm "was no fun either," he said, "but it was better than being shot at." Using radar to avoid the worst patches of weather, Rice stayed in the clouds until he reached the sea.

While the two shaken American fliers were heading toward the coast, almost 3,000 Vietnamese were crowded in the evacuation processing center at the DAO gym when the bombs struck. Captain Stu Herrington, also jumping to the quick conclusion that the strike meant an uprising against Minh, snatched a battery-powered bullhorn to warn the screaming evacuees to take cover. "Dao chanh!" he shouted: Vietnamese for "coup d'état." But it was not a coup. The strike was flown in captured aircraft by Communist pilots trained and led by Nguyen Thanh Trung, the defector who had bombed Thieu's palace. In less than three weeks, Trung had taught a small group of MIG pilots to fly the relatively simple A-37s. He and four others, in a special flight code-named "Determined to Win," took off from Phan Rang at 5:15 P.M. Saigon time, precisely as President Huong began his resignation speech. Trung led the bomb run, according to later Communist accounts, then flew rear-guard as the planes streaked back to their base, far ahead of several South Vietnamese fighters that scrambled to try to intercept them.

During the day, while Trung and his fellow pilots waited at Phan Rang for the two red flares that were their signal to take off, General Dung's infantry had rapidly been covering the last miles to the positions from which they were to open the final attack on the capital. To the southeast, the 325th North Vietnamese Division reached the town of Nhon Trach, from which its long-range 130-mm guns could fire on Tansonnhut. To the east, the final assault on Bien Hoa began, after an overnight artillery barrage. Lieutenant General Nguyen Van Toan, the South Vietnamese regional commander, had already left the III Corps headquarters in Bien Hoa and returned to Saigon; on the 28th, the rest of Toan's staff also fled. National Police units evacuated the burning city, while its defenders, including remnants of the 18th ARVN Division, were dispersed by evening into fleeing bands of survivors strung out along Highway One. Other Communist units, meanwhile, moved to cut off the two ARVN divisions guarding Saigon's northern and northwestern approaches. And to the west of the capital, an entire Communist division under Maj. Gen. Di Thien Tich spent the day hidden in the jungle, waiting for night before starting out to cross the swamps and fields that lay between its hiding place and the wide Vam Co River, which flowed past Saigon's southwestern edge. Tich's troops had been given just three days to march more than 50 miles, heading counterclockwise around the city, to start their thrust from the Vam Co.

By nightfall, as General Dung noted in his memoir, "there was no longer any safe place" for the government forces. Nor would it be safe for many more hours for the U.S. airlift. At the time Lieutenant Trung's fighter-bombers struck Tansonnhut, two inbound U.S. C-130s had been diverted and were kept circling far to the east; about 8 P.M., they were cleared to land, did so, and left again with about 360 passengers. Shortly afterward, General Smith was told that a "maximum practicable" schedule of 60 C-130 flights would be flown the following day, to take out up to 9,000 evacuees. But Tansonnhut's time had nearly run out. Only three of the planned flights would ever land in Saigon.

In the U.S. embassy courtyard, where the large tamarind tree on the parking lot still blocked any possible helicopter landing, several marines began after dark on the 28th to cut away limbs and chop partway through the trunk. But they carefully worked only on the side that could not be seen from the embassy entrance; Ambassador Martin still had not given permission for the tree to be cut down. Elsewhere in the curfew-stilled city, for greater safety from shrapnel or bursting glass, fearful Saigonese moved cots and sleeping mats out of apartment bedrooms and into hallways or stairwells, where they huddled to await whatever the morning would bring.

Chapter **13**

The Fall
of Saigon

The Americans Leave (2):
"Frequent Wind"

The last battle of the Vietnam War began at exactly two minutes before four o'clock on the morning of Tuesday, April 29.

Not long before, the last three U.S. planes to reach Saigon had finished unloading "hot cargo"—15,000-pound bombs, nicknamed Daisy Cutters—in the munitions storage area north of the Tansonnhut runways. Now, Capt. Arthur Mallano was waiting for the last of about 260 evacuees to board his C-130 for the return flight to Clark Air Base in the Philippines. A second plane had just rolled up alongside, ready to start taking on passengers. The third, piloted by Capt. Larry Wessel, was taxiing toward the boarding area from the runway.

From his cockpit seat, Mallano saw a sudden flicker in the black sky: lightning, he thought at first. Then the airfield began to explode around him. A rocket hit a fuel truck. A second swooshed into the control tower area, and another landed under the wing of Wessel's plane, rupturing a fuel tank. As fuel began pouring out onto the ground, Wessel and his crew leaped out and ran. Moments later the spilled gas caught fire, turning the damaged plane into a great red blossom of flames.

As soon as the last of his terrified passengers was aboard, Mallano lumbered down the runway with rockets slamming in on all sides. Captain Greg Chase in the second C-130 waited just long enough for Wessel and his crew to jump on, then took off right behind Mallano.

At almost the same moment, another salvo of rockets landed in the Defense Attache Office complex. One of the first rounds killed two young marines on guard outside: Lance Cpl. Darwin Judge of Marshalltown, Iowa, and Cpl. Charles McMahon, Jr., of Woburn, Massachusetts, the last American casualties in Vietnam.

Another round hit just outside General Smith's quarters, bouncing him and a dozen other sleeping officers out of bed but without injuring anyone. Nor, miraculously, was anyone wounded by a third rocket that exploded on the roof of the DAO gymnasium, where at least 1,500 evacuees were waiting for the airlift to resume. Shards of metal roofing sprayed the area but somehow missed everyone.

Soon after the first rocket bursts came the deadlier sound of General Dung's 130-mm artillery. Fired from far to the southeast and aimed with remarkable accuracy at the flight line and the runways, the shells' flight went straight over the DAO area. Rushing through the air, they sounded like high-speed trains passing on invisible rails overhead. For the next several hours, shells crashed in at the rate of nearly one every minute. In their command post near Ben Cat, meanwhile, Dung and his staff received a final message from the Politburo at 6 A.M., congratulating his forces on their advances of the last few days and urging them to proceed quickly to assault "the enemy's last den"—Saigon.

Under the bombardment, the Vietnamese air force at Tansonnhut began to disintegrate. Air crews rushed aboard transport planes and helicopters, trying to fly out of the country. Other airmen and soldiers, some firing their weapons, swarmed over the parking area and onto the runway itself, fighting to get on the departing aircraft. At least one plane crashed: a C-7 "Caribou" twin-engine transport that tried to take off on one engine but spun off the runway and burned on the grass. No firetrucks or other rescue vehicles tried to reach the blazing wreckage. An American officer who saw the crash thought most of the passengers had gotten out, but it was impossible to be sure.

By daylight, the base was in chaos. Gunnery Sgt. Vasco D. Martin, Jr., of the embassy marine guard detachment watched one overloaded helicopter try to take off near his quarters, close to a large pile of dirt. "It made two or three attempts," Martin said, "and the last attempt he swung around in a cloud of dirt and dust, and he couldn't see where he was going, and his tail blade ended up hitting the mound of dirt, and when he did that, part of the blade flew across the road and hit the building where we had been billeted." The pilots and soldiers scrambled out without bothering to shut down the motor, leaving the crippled helicopter with its main rotor blade still spinning.

Other aircraft were destroyed on the ground by shellfire and in the air by ground fire and Communist missiles, which were suddenly shown to be frighteningly close. About seven o'clock, a Vietnamese AC-119 gunship—a clumsy-looking, twin-engine plane with a stubby cigar-shaped fuselage suspended between twin tail booms, and painted flat black for night flying— was hit practically over the runway. Witnesses saw a "small thin white trail" of smoke, the trademark of the SA-7 missile, a heat-seeking weapon light enough to be carried and launched by a couple of infantrymen. The smoke trail ended in a huge explosion that virtually blotted the plane out of the sky. Amazingly, three parachutes opened, though one caught fire and fell burning to the ground.

Another C-119 was hit by a missile over Saigon and cartwheeled down in flames like a Roman candle to crash in the Chinese section of the city. Communist gunners also shot down a smaller spotter plane, apparently not with a missile but with automatic antiaircraft weapons fire, which chewed large chunks of metal off the plane and sent them spinning in the air before it finally went out of control and crashed.

On the ground, shortly after 7 A.M., airlift controllers were reporting to General Smith that the main runway was littered with jettisoned bombs and fuel tanks. A stalled F-5 fighter blocked the taxiway to the passenger-loading area, and some 40 trucks and hundreds of rioting troops were on the runway, pursuing two Vietnamese C-130s that were attempting to take off. Could U.S. planes continue using the base? Smith wanted to know. Colonel Earl Mickler, the airlift supervisor, replied that he and his subordinates did not believe so. Not only were the runways obstructed, Mickler pointed out, but the field was full of armed Vietnamese soldiers and airmen who were out of control and who would almost certainly mob·American planes just as they were already rioting to board Vietnamese aircraft. In order to continue the airlift, Mickler felt, American marines would have to take control of the entire Tansonnhut area: a major operation that would take several thousand men.

Not long after Mickler made his assessment, Lt. Gen. Tran Van Minh, the air force commander, and most of his senior staff—some 30 officers in all, carrying sidearms—marched into the DAO compound and confronted American officers there, demanding evacuation. When Smith received the message he turned to the assistant air attache, Lt. Col. Dick Mitchell, and told him to disarm the intruders. Mitchell should tell them, Smith snapped, that if they refused to give up their weapons they would be shot. Mitchell looked at his boss quizzically. "Just me?" he asked. But he went; the Vietnamese surrendered their arms without objection. "This event," as the DAO's final report pointed out, "signalled the complete loss of . . .

command and control" of the air force "and magnified the continued deterioration of an already volatile situation."

Some 2,800 Vietnamese evacuees were still waiting in the processing center, and, in response to a formal request from the new Minh government for the entire DAO staff to be withdrawn in the next 24 hours, Smith's planning team was under orders to start bus convoys at 7 A.M. to pick up all employees. But, though the artillery was slackening, Smith saw no reasonable chance for fixed-wing flights to continue. The only way he could carry out his orders was to call the helicopters from the fleet—but that was Ambassador Martin's decision, not his, and Martin, after stalling for so long, was now suddenly and passionately determined to fly out thousands of Vietnamese who would be at risk after a Communist takeover. When Smith called from Tansonnhut to report that the runways were unusable, Martin simply refused to accept his assessment. Instead, he left standing the previous night's orders for a "maximum" C-130 schedule.

In Washington, Kissinger was similiarly reluctant to believe that a final evacuation was needed. At a 45-minute meeting with the president and other national security advisers, Kissinger persuaded Ford to hold off the helicopters for the time being, in the hope that the C-130s could keep flying for at least one more day. When the meeting ended shortly after 8 P.M., Washington time, while Ford joined his wife for a late dinner—oyster cocktail, corned beef and cabbage, and black cherry gelatin, reporters were informed—his spokesman announced, "There has not been an order to evacuate Americans" from Saigon.

Also left undecided was whether the entire U.S. mission would be withdrawn or whether a reduced staff would stay to carry on relations with the Minh government or its successors. Confusing and contradictory cables flashed between Saigon and Washington and among different U.S. agencies. At one point, when the embassy was ordered to assign a reduced staff of 150 to remain, officers there had to drop all other matters to draw a list from among the 700 or so American military and government representatives in the South Vietnamese capital. At DAO meanwhile, a Pentagon message told General Smith that the Joint Military Team delegation should stay behind, as the North Vietnamese had seemed to hint they should, even if the government surrendered to the Communists. At 11:30 A.M., Col. John Madison, the head of the delegation, along with Lieutenant Colonel Summers and Capt. Stu Herrington and three enlisted aides, left DAO for the embassy. In their cars they carried rations, medical supplies and other emergency equipment, and a pile of orange banners, each imprinted with a black "4" in the center: the official JMT flag, which was supposed to confer diplomatic immunity on the delegates.

The North Vietnamese might respect the team's immunity when they came—but they weren't the problem, Herrington reflected gloomily. If the angry, defeated South Vietnamese chose to avenge their sense of betrayal on the last half-dozen uniformed Americans in the country, no truce flag was going to afford much protection.

At the embassy, though evacuating endangered Vietnamese was at last a matter of official priority, the lack of planning was suddenly alarmingly evident. There was no master list of those to leave, nor was there any reliable system for notifying, assembling, or transporting evacuees. Since almost no one except Martin still thought the fixed-wing flights could continue, embassy officers wondered how they would get Vietnamese associates out of the country even when a list was compiled. A few planners remembered the Sealift Command tugs and barges still at Newport, which could carry thousands of people down the Saigon River to the sea. But most embassy officials had no idea that there was any American-controlled shipping in Saigon at all, and there were no plans for bringing evacuees to the docks. Like much else, a barge evacuation had to be improvised by relatively junior officers.

Even where its employees were already grouped in U.S. installations, the embassy proved to have no effective method to pick them up. One hundred eighty-five Vietnamese who had been promised evacuation had been waiting since the day before in the U.S. Information Service building at No. 8 Le Qui Don Street; they would be stranded. Some 70 CIA translators and their families who were assembled in their compound were left behind, according to Frank Snepp, as were 100 or so other Vietnamese with agency connections who had gathered in the Duc Hotel, a CIA billet only a few blocks from the embassy.

At nine o'clock that morning, though Tansonnhut was still under sporadic shelling and thousands of out-of-control soldiers and airmen were roaming the base, Martin still refused to call for "Option IV"—the helicopter evacuation. Before he decided, he suddenly announced, he wanted to inspect the field himself. Leaving his flabbergasted staff behind, he strode out of the embassy into his bullet-proof limousine for the four-mile drive to Tansonnhut.

When he arrived at the DAO compound, Smith and other senior DAO officials repeated that the runways were not usable. But again, Martin would not accept their verdict. The U.S. must carry out its solemn commitment to evacuate its employees and other threatened Vietnamese, he declared, and also had to comply with its promise to withdraw the DAO staff. From Smith's office, Martin called Kissinger's White House deputy Brent Scowcroft to ask for reconfirmation of the orders to continue the C-130 flights. Scowcroft agreed, and Martin stalked out to be driven back downtown. From the embassy, shortly after he returned, he phoned Smith to read him yet another White House message directing fixed-wing flights to go on "as long as feasible."

Smith was now in the extremely unhappy position of having orders from the ambassador and the White House which he did not believe could be carried out. Nonetheless, he told his own subordinates to keep processing passengers, and several buses were actually sent to the loading ramp even though no planes were landing and shells and rockets were still falling around the flight line. Two U.S. Navy officers, Capt. H. E. Hirschy, Jr., and Lt. Cmdr. P. A. Bondi, escorted the buses and had to spend an "excruciating" 30 minutes listening to the shellbursts before they were finally ordered back to the DAO compound.

Smith, meanwhile, evidently despairing of ever persuading the ambassador, picked up the phone to call his military superior, Admiral Gayler in Hawaii. Whatever Martin or the White House thought, Smith said, there was no possibility of resuming the C-130 flights. It just could not be done.

Gayler, at least, was willing to take his word. He would call the Joint Chiefs of Staff, he promised Smith, and recommend that Option IV begin.

On the ships, waiting some 40 miles out to sea—80 nautical miles from Saigon—the pilots of three marine helicopter squadrons and ten additional air force helicopters had been waiting since dawn for orders to carry out the evacuation, poetically code-named Frequent Wind. Because of the complexities of flying from ship to ship to take on the nearly 1,000 marines of the ground security force, it would take a minimum of three hours from the time the "execute" order was received until the first evacuation helicopter reached Tansonnhut. The fliers wanted to start the operation at first light, to have the best chance of completing the evacuation before darkness multiplied its dangers. U.S. commanders at Nakhon Phanom Air Base in Thailand—headquarters of the U.S. Support Activities Group (USSAG) and 7th Air Force, the major American commands in Southeast Asia—did what they could to quicken the response time. Shortly after dawn they ordered tankers and other support planes into the air so they would be in position when needed. The airborne command post, a C-130 packed with communications gear and operating with the customary call-sign "Cricket," was on station over Saigon by 9:25 A.M. Still, when no evacuation order had been issued by mid-morning, the earliest possible time for the pullout to begin had slipped to well past noon. More than half the precious daylight hours had been squandered.

Aboard U.S.S. *Blue Ridge,* the task force flagship, marines and sailors scanned copies of the "Ridge Runner," the mimeographed news bulletin issued to the crew every day at sea. The weather forecast was not ideal. "Skies are partly cloudy to mostly cloudly with widely scattered rainshowers and isolated thundershowers," it said. "Winds are 8-14 knots. The maximum temperature will be 88 degrees with an overnight low of 81 degrees." The headline over the leading news item was more menacing: "Doomsday in Saigon Looms Closer."

Thirty-one civilian pilots employed by Air America, the celebrated "CIA airline," had volunteered to stay in Saigon to help in the evacuation. But only one of them was at the company's terminal when the attack on Tansonnhut began. Most of the rest were at their billet, an apartment building three-fifths of a mile away. Awakened by the shelling, they had assembled on the roof to watch the explosions light up the field. Air America's job was supposed to be to pick up evacuees from designated rooftops in Saigon where its lighter UH-1 "Hueys" could land but which were not strong enough or did not have the rotor clearance for the larger, heavier marine helicopters from the fleet. Until long after sunrise, however, all the pilots could do was wait on their roof and watch. The Air America buildings and loading ramp, across the road from the main DAO building, were heavily damaged by rockets and artillery rounds. The area was being peppered with rifle fire from rioting South Vietnamese soldiers. A little later, four of the company's two dozen or so helicopters were hijacked by Vietnamese pilots who flew them out to sea, in search of the evacuation fleet.

Not until 8:30 in the morning did the first Air America Huey take off. Its initial mission was to the pilots' roof, just a couple of minutes away. In three flights, altogether consuming only about fifteen minutes, 24 fliers were shuttled to the terminal, which was still receiving occasional rockets. Most were helicopter pilots, but eight were fixed-wing fliers who flew the airline's fleet of transports and courier planes—most of them World War II-vintage C-46s and C-47s. All refueling had stopped when the bombing attack occurred the evening before, so most of the aircraft were short of fuel. And, with shells still falling and the Vietnamese air force causing chaos on the runways, there was a "certain amount of hesitation about launching fixed wing planes," pilot Fred Fine commented in his diary.

Still, Air America crews were paid to be adventurous. And as a private company, the airline didn't have to wait for orders from the embassy or from Washington to decide to send its planes and personnel—except for the helicopters and crews assisting the evacuation—to safety. Two C-47s took off at about nine-thirty, and the rest left at ten-minute intervals after that. Fine's turn came at 10:45 A.M. As the last of two dozen passengers climbed onto his plane, he could see from the cockpit window that refugees were beginning to scale the high cement wall around the loading area. Quickly, once the plane's doors were closed, he taxied out from behind the Air America hangar and into a "scene of utter chaos . . . bombed and burned out planes and helicopters, others still burning, debris everywhere."

Rather than use the taxiway, which led perilously near several blazing wrecks, Fine steered alongside the civilian passenger terminal, "picking my way around scattered baggage, wrecked autos, bicycles, shell holes, you name it," before he finally reached the runway. Once in the air, he headed out to sea, then turned and followed the coast toward the southwest. But with only 500 gallons in his tanks he didn't have enough fuel to fly all the way around the Vietnamese mainland. Instead, at 8,500 feet, he "took a deep breath" and turned inland, crossing 80 miles or so of Communist-held territory in the Mekong Delta. The rest of the flight over the blue Gulf of Thailand to U Tapao air base was uneventful. But as his plane rolled to a stop on the U Tapao runway, Fine looked out and saw "about half the Vietnamese air force" parked around the southern end of the field. Saigon's surrender was still nearly a day away, but clearly, much of what remained of its air force had already abandoned the war. Among the more than 70 aircraft reaching U Tapao before the surrender were 27 F-5 jet fighters—a full squadron—several gunships, and numerous transport planes.

Not everyone who arrived in Thailand in the fleeing planes had intended to desert. Among the airmen who landed were 45 men who had had no idea that their pilots were flying out of the country; they had thought they were heading to another air base, probably in the Mekong Delta, to continue the war. Now, they frantically begged Thai and American authorities for some way to return to their families, asking for boats to sail back across the gulf or even to be taken to the Cambodian frontier so they could try to walk home. Instead, they were taken with other escaping airmen all the way to Guam, where one of them despairingly told a reporter, "Without our families, we don't want to live."

At Tansonnhut, preparations for the helicopter lift were finally completed. The flagpoles outside the DAO building were taken down and a nearby bus shelter removed, while landing zones were marked with three-foot-high letters in fluorescent orange. The last power lines and poles obstructing the landing sites were cut or bulldozed down by marine officers in the midst of the Communist artillery barrage—a risk that would have been avoided, the disgruntled marines thought, if there had been less official procrastination. If General Dung's gunners had been aiming at the DAO area, the job couldn't have been done at all. But the Communist fire was concentrated on the aircraft parking areas, fuel and munition dumps, and the runways. Its purpose, clearly, was to destroy Saigon's air force before they assaulted the capital, not to disrupt the U.S. evacuation. After the first few salvos, the Americans began to realize that the DAO area was being deliberately spared; just as they had declared publicly and promised privately through the Soviet Union, the North Vietnamese were allowing the Americans to leave unopposed—except, perhaps, by their allies.

Shortly after 9:30 A.M., a group of 40 to 50 Vietnamese air force officers and airport supervisors burst into the U.S. airlift headquarters, waving pistols. Taking three American officers hostage, they demanded to be evacuated. One of the Americans, Air Force Maj. Dale Hensley, calmly assured his captors that threats weren't needed. They would be given seats, he promised, when conditions at the field settled down. Finally one of the Vietnamese officers handed over his weapon. The others did the same, and the three Americans walked safely out of the building. To General Smith, the episode was final proof that the base was out of control. He promptly sent six marine guards to escort all other Americans out of the control center.

By now, busloads of DAO employees were arriving at the compound, while Air America helicopters were flying others from Saigon rooftops. Under the original plan, the Hueys were to ferry passengers only to Tansonnhut. But they could not refuel in the DAO compound because the one fuel truck parked there was out of order, and they could not use their own terminal because of rocket damage and sniping by South Vietnamese airmen. As a result, pilots began dropping evacuees at the embassy, instead of the air base, to save flying time and fuel. And when they did run low, the only place to go for refueling was to the evacuation ships. Though evacuation orders had not yet been issued, the Hueys began flying to the fleet—with passengers—about ten o'clock.

Among them came olive-drab Vietnamese helicopters, whose pilots followed the silver Air America craft in order to find the ships. One anxious Vietnamese nearly caused a disaster on the *Blue Ridge* when he set his Chinook down too close to a Huey that had landed a moment before. The two spinning rotor blades clanged together, and suddenly pieces of broken steel were slashing through the air. While sailors dove to the deck, the damaged Chinook swayed and almost toppled over, then rocked back upright, and its shaken passengers stepped out onto the ship.

General Smith, after his call to Admiral Gayler, called the embassy again in a last effort to convince Ambassador Martin to order Option IV. Exhausted, terribly hoarse, and looking to his staff "like a walking dead man," Martin asked if Smith were certain that fixed-wing flights could not land. He was absolutely sure, the general answered. At that, Martin relented at last. Minutes later, on the telephone to Kissinger in the White House, he asked for the helicopter evacuation to begin. Kissinger quickly called Ford in the executive mansion's residential quarters. It took Ford only a moment to agree. At 10:51 Monday night, Washington time—the same hour Tuesday morning in Saigon—the order was flashed to the U.S. headquarters in Thailand and from there to the fleet: "Execute Frequent Wind."

About the same time, Martin was informed of another decision from "the highest authority" in Washington. When the time came, all American government personnel must leave, including Colonel Madison and his Joint Military Team delegation. There would be no residual U.S. mission in Saigon, as Martin had hoped. That idea had been considered in Washington, evidently, only as long as it appeared possible that some form of independent South Vietnamese government would remain in existence to negotiate with the Communists. If the war was going to end with the North Vietnamese simply smashing into the capital, as now seemed certain, there was to be no official presence that could be taken as a signal of U.S. willingness to conduct diplomatic relations with the conquerors.

With the evacuation finally under way, the CIA's Charles Timmes left the embassy for Big Minh's villa on Tran Quy Cap Street. Timmes, a retired major general and former head of the U.S. Military Assistance Advisory Group, had known Minh since the early 1960s. Now he came to offer the general and his family a chance to leave with the American evacuation. But Minh refused. It was his "responsibility" to stay, he said; Timmes was left with the impression that Minh still expected the Communists would negotiate with him, rather than storm the city.

In the embassy courtyard, shortly before noon, security guards brought out chainsaws and axes and finally began cutting down the tamarind tree Martin had shielded for so long. In the White House, about the same time, President Ford dropped in to visit the basement situation room, where large maps showed the evacuation sites, the helicopter routes, and the tightening Communist ring around Saigon. And in Can Tho, in the Mekong Delta, where the U.S. had its last diplomatic post outside the capital, Consul-General Francis McNamara was assembling the seventeen other Americans on his staff, including a half-dozen marine guards, along with three Filipinos who worked for the large CIA base there and 294 Vietnamese, nearly all consular employees and their families. Wearing a helmet liner on which he had lettered "Commodore, Can Tho Yacht Club," McNamara loaded his charges on two small landing craft and a barge he had purchased with funds from the consulate's piastre account. Evacuating down the Bassac River to the sea, a distance of 60 nautical miles, would be safer than trying to reach Saigon or waiting for helicopters to evacuate by air, McNamara had decided. About noon, his flotilla set off from the Can Tho waterfront.

At sea, off the Vietnamese coast, marines of Battalion Landing Team 2/4—2nd Battalion, 4th Marine Regiment—lined up on the decks of the helicopter carrier USS *Okinawa* and the support ships *Peoria* and *Vancouver* to file aboard waiting helicopters. Fighter-bombers shrieked off the flight deck of the attack carrier USS *Coral Sea* at 12:15, while land-based combat and support planes also took off from Thai airfields. The first armed aircraft entered Vietnamese air space seventeen minutes later. Shortly after one, Marine Brig. Gen. Richard Carey, the landing force commander, flew from the *Blue Ridge* to Tansonnhut to await the rest of his troops.

The first wave of twelve loaded CH-53 troop-carrying helicopters lifted off the ships at 2:30 P.M., formed four Vs of three aircraft each, and headed for Saigon through a sky full of woolly clouds. Exactly 36 minutes later, the first CH-53 touched down outside the DAO building. A hot, shimmering haze hung over Saigon, thickened by smoke from the huge fires that still blazed on Tansonnhut. Visibility over the city, pilots reported, was only about a mile. It was six minutes after three o'clock on the afternoon of Evacuation Day—just over eleven hours since the first rockets smashed into the base, a little over four hours since President Ford ordered Operation Frequent Wind to begin. Only about three and a half hours of daylight remained.

First, the American radio station in Saigon was to play "I'm Dreaming of a White Christmas." Then, an announcer would say, "The temperature in Saigon is 105 degrees and rising."

That, the embassy officer had said, was how we would find out when the evacuation was on. As soon as we heard the coded signal, we were supposed to go to the closest of thirteen designated assembly points where we would be picked up and taken to Tansonnhut to be flown or helicoptered out of the country.

Coded messages. White Christmas, of all songs, in tropical Saigon's hottest month of the year. It seemed juvenile and ludicrous. I could not believe there was any way to move several thousand Americans out of the South Vietnamese capital in secrecy. Saigon's was a compact, gossipy, intensely nosy society even in normal times. Now, tens of thousands of Saigonese, from generals and cabinet ministers down to cooks and house-maids, were intently keeping track of their American acquaintances, watch-ing for the slightest sign that the evacuation was about to begin. Many Americans, perhaps most, had Vietnamese associates they were determined to take along: friends, employees, in-laws. That too guaranteed the word would spread. The "White Christmas" code might as well have been published in the newspapers. To no one's surprise, within a day or so of the embassy briefings everyone in Saigon, down to the children who sold sprays of jasmine blossoms on Tu Do Street, seemed to know about it. Occasionally, as you walked down a street, you would hear someone sibilantly call out the song's title, or even perhaps mockingly hum a few bars of the tune.

If the coded signal was ever broadcast, I never heard it. But on the morning of April 29, we needed no secret message to tell us that the evacuation was imminent. A loud knock on my room door in the old Continental Palace Hotel woke me at 6:30 A.M.—I seem to have been the only living person in Saigon who was not roused by the shellbursts at Tansonnhut. At the door was a friend, Bud Pratt of Westinghouse Broad-casting. "You better pack," Bud said. "It looks as if this may be it." Tuning their portable radios to the frequency used by the embassy's security officers, he and other correspondents had overheard transmissions that were excited and confused but still made it plain enough that Tansonnhut was under very heavy attack, that there had been marine casualties, and that no planes could land.

My other qualifications as a war correspondent may be in question, but I am always ready for a hasty exit. Thanks to a lifelong mania for unencumbered travel, I had only one suitcase, small enough to stow under an airplane seat, and a small portable typewriter. A few mementos of personal importance I had sent out with a departing friend a week or so before. It would take only a couple of minutes to pack clothes, shaving kit, notebooks, and a few other odds and ends. No need to pack the emergency supply of canned food I kept on the bottom shelf of the old-fashioned wooden wardrobe. Nor would I take the bulky combat gear purchased years before in the Saigon black market. The helmet and flak jacket could stay on their wooden pegs on the wall. With all my heart I hoped never to need, or even see, such things again.

Over rolls and coffee in the lushly planted but seedy little hotel garden, we listened to South Vietnamese bombs falling outside the city, toward the southwest. A 24-hour curfew announcement was being repeated on the radio and over the loudspeakers on Lam Son Square, but the gray-uniformed policemen in front of the National Assembly did not seem to be enforcing it; in the streets, people moved about on foot, bicycles, and motorbikes. Some were heading for the hotel lobby to look for American acquaintances. They too needed no coded broadcasts to know the evacuation was near.

After breakfast I wandered restlessly through the lobby, upstairs to a friend's room, and back down again. Most of my colleagues seemed to be doing the same. Long afterward it occurred to me that I could have gone to the telex office on Le Loi Street or tried to telephone a last story on the start of the battle for Saigon. But the last months in Cambodia and Vietnam had left me with a much-diminished professional commitment. I had come to see myself as a sort of contemptible, morbid tourist, safe by the accidents of my white face and green-covered American passport, making my living by poking about with a notebook in the lives of people whose suffering and danger were much greater than mine, and for no purpose that would be the slightest help to any of them. I could not be ungrateful for my own relative well-being and safety, much less for the circumstances that kept my wife and children from being driven from their home, broken apart and terrorized like the Vietnamese and Cambodian families I had seen streaming down so many roads filled with so much fear and grief. But I could not help, either, a growing sense of self-disgust. I felt in those weeks like a carrion crow circling over a carcass. Evacuate has the same Latin root as the word vacuum—"vacuus," meaning empty. That last morning, though still physically in Saigon, I was emotionally emptied out: in that literal sense of the word, already evacuated.

When the word came by telephone from the embassy to one of the correspondents who had volunteered as an evacuation marshal, it was a few minutes past eleven. About noon, suitcase in one hand and typewriter in the other, I left the hotel for the closest of the designated assembly sites, about three blocks away.

Under the midday sun, Saigon was at its steamiest. I felt as if I were wrapped in hot sponges. People on the street looked at me with blank eyes which I tried not to meet with mine. When I stepped off the sidewalk to cross Le Thanh Ton Street, the tarry surface, softened in the heat, clung gently to my shoes.

The pickup point was an American-leased apartment building on Gia Long Street. The door was locked, and as far as we could tell, the building was completely deserted. On the sidewalk stood about 150 people, mostly Americans or other foreigners. I thought there would be vehicles there, or at least someone with a radio to give instructions. But nobody was in charge at all, and no one knew what would happen next. More foreigners straggled toward the group, and clusters of watching Vietnamese also grew, eyeing us curiously but with no visible anger or fear. I wondered if they would stay as calm when the buses came, if they ever did. If the idea was to assemble discreetly so as not to draw a potentially panicky crowd, then something was very wrong. We might as well have announced the evacuation with movie marquee lights over our heads.

After about an hour, a young U.S. Marine captain drove up in a jeep, leading two olive-drab buses, which pulled up to the curb in front of us. The watching Vietnamese stayed where they were, staring. No one tried to crowd into the boarding lines. Neither pushing forward nor hanging back, I reached the door of one of the buses and climbed on. All the seats were already full. I went as far to the rear as I could, then put down my suitcase in the narrow aisle and sat on it. The driver was an American from DAO or the embassy, I never learned which. "I never drove one of these before," he said cheerily. "It could get bumpy, so hang on." In Vietnam, until now, just as they didn't wash their own clothes or sweep their own floors, Americans didn't drive their own buses—though our driver did fine.

There wasn't room for everyone. As we drove off in our little convoy, about 50 people were still left on the sidewalk. He would radio for another bus, our marine escort promised.

Though nobody else could conceivably squeeze aboard, we roamed inexplicably through downtown Saigon for a half-hour, evidently making a circuit of other assembly points. It seemed risky: nobody had interfered with us up to now, but if we wandered about long enough, someone might. Then our bewildering journey ended at the back gate of Ambassador Martin's residence, just a few blocks from where we started. The jammed bus was like a steam bath. After waiting for what seemed forever, we set off in convoy with several other buses toward Tansonnhut. Approaching the main gate— the only one where civilians could enter, in normal times—we heard rifle shots popping someplace in front of us. In the air, I hoped. Still, everyone ducked, or tried to. Some yards from the military police checkpoint at the gate, we stopped for several nervous minutes, then lurched into motion again and rolled through. Incredibly, through the entire day the landing force marines never took control of the checkpoint, even though it was held by only a handful of policemen. Not long after we went through, other buses were turned away and forced to head back to the American embassy, where the unanticipated crowds of evacuees became a grave and growing danger.

It was only about a half-mile from the gate to the DAO building, where our bus braked to a stop. Just as the first passengers began climbing off, the tremendous rushing noise of an incoming artillery round thundered directly overhead. All my instincts told me to hit the floor, but other passengers were too tightly packed around me. All I could do was try to retract my head between my shoulders, like a turtle. As I cringed, the shell landed with the sound of a gigantic door slamming in another room. The breath clogged in my lungs as I waited for the awful sound of falling shrapnel, but none came. We must have been just beyond the killing radius.

Still penned in my seat, soaked in sweat and fear and in unworthy thankfulness for all the other fleshy bodies between me and the bus windows, I sat paralyzed, listening for another round. Shelling is hateful not just because of the danger, I always felt, but also because it's so goddamned *humiliating;* you can't do anything but compress yourself into a tight little huddle of terror and wait, hating your own helplessness and fright. I had been under artillery fire before. But now, with the war almost over and my own reasons for being there having come to seem empty and contemptible, I found my fear almost unendurable. Not here, not now, I thought, with a spasm of hate for the war that left me shaking.

No second shell came. From the front of the bus somebody was shouting: "Keep getting off the bus! Don't stop! Get off *fast!*" That was a physical impossibility; we were too crowded. But no one panicked. Clumsily man-handling our suitcases, we climbed off in orderly fashion, then jogged into the DAO building. Inside, American officers shooed us along a series of hallways in a manner that was irresistibly remindful of sheep or cattle being driven through chutes in a slaughterhouse. Finally, we were directed to sit along one wall. A soldier moved along the line with a box, asking for weapons. I was astonished at how many of the evacuees handed over sidearms. Opposite me was a bulletin board that had on it, among other notices, a poster warning against letter bombs. "Terrorism is prevalent worldwide," it told me in large, bold type. "You could be next."

While Ambassador Martin was agonizing over whether to call for the evacuation, and while the pilots and landing force marines waited on the Navy ships farther out to sea, the Military Sealift Command freighter

Greenville Victory was riding within sight of Vung Tau on the morning of Evacuation Day.

Refugees had begun reaching the American ships the day before, on fishing boats and other small craft. One group of about 150 boarded the USNS *Sgt. Truman Kimbro* from a dilapidated Saigon ferryboat which they had bought, they told the *Kimbro*'s captain, for 46 million piastres— $20,000, at black market rates; more than $60,000 at the official exchange. About 100 refugees aboard several fishing boats and a tug reached the *Greenville Victory*, whose crew could see hundreds more boats in Vung Tau Harbor that were apparently being guarded by Vietnamese navy gunboats and not allowed to leave.

Overnight, from her anchorage three miles south of the Vung Tau sea buoy, the ship's crew could see shellfire and bomb blasts inland. By daylight on the 29th, the explosions had moved to the city itself. Splashes fountained the water along the shoreline, and shellbursts spurted in the resort area. Parts of the city were completely covered with smoke and dust. Boats from the harbor began coming alongside. As their passengers climbed onto the ship, they cut the empty boats loose and let them drift away.

As heavy firing continued on shore, Captain Iacobacci decided to move another three miles out to sea, for safety. The ship towed four fishing boats as she steamed, while flocks of others followed under their own power. No other American ships were in sight. At her new anchorage, *Greenville Victory* resumed loading. Her propeller already had one bent blade from being bumped by an abandoned boat, and security guards were posted on the stern to keep other boats away. On several occasions they fired into the water to head off craft that were closing too fast. Once, someone fired back, but there were no casualties.

Iacobacci's orders were to take on no more than 6,000 refugees. When he had done so, he pulled up his anchor and began steaming away at 5:20 P.M., with a huge flotilla of boats following in his wake. Twenty-five minutes later he was given permission to load another 2,000, and later the limit was raised again to 10,000. But as fast as his crew could take refugees aboard, more arrived in other boats. As dusk fell, the crew was using not just ladders but cargo nets and booms to lift refugees over the side. As many as twenty people were hoisted up at a time inside each net, with more hanging from the outside, including mothers frantically clutching small children with one hand while clinging to the netting with the other. Iacobacci radioed for more ships to come help, but none did.

"At 1920 hours at least 100 boats alongside with hundreds more streaming toward us," he later reported to Sealift Command authorities. "Continued loading. . . . The situation was pitiful, unbelievable and heart rending. No assistance from other ships received. At 2000 hours we just had to stop with an estimated 10,000 refugees on board and just no room for any others. 70 to 80 boats were still alongside and pleading with us to please take them. . . . We had to cut boats loose in order to get away. It's a sight that will be impressed in everyone's memory for a long time. We did our best and yet it seemed so inadequate."

Another sealift ship, SS *American Challenger*, was at Phu Quoc Island on the morning of the 29th with 8,600 refugees whom the South Vietnamese authorities had ordered there from Vung Tau. Her passengers refused to disembark at first, and Capt. Arthur Boucher ordered the hatches barred and fresh-water hoses shut off. At that, the refugees reluctantly began filing off the ship. As they did, crewmen and marines filled their water containers, or gave them five-gallon plastic jugs from their own stores. For her return voyage, *Challenger* embarked about 250 U.S. consular employees and their families who had reached Phu Quoc from the north: about 1,100 persons altogether. Another thousand or so, chosen for evacuation by U.S. officials on the island, were also taken aboard. Some had CIA affiliations; others were government officials, military commanders, or other members of the elite. The thousands of less well-placed refugees who had ridden the ship from Vung Tau were left on the island. Also near Phu Quoc was a Navy vessel, USS *Dubuque*, which had left the rest of the task force shortly after dark the previous night, with secret orders to guide and refuel Vietnamese helicopters that were fleeing not to the American fleet but to Thailand.

On the Bassac River in the Mekong Delta, meanwhile, Consul-General McNamara's little flotilla from Can Tho was trying to keep its course through a blinding rainstorm. Their escape had been threatened almost as soon as it began, when Vietnamese patrol boats fired warning shots at McNamara's landing craft, forcing him to heave to. From one of the patrol boats, the local navy commander climbed aboard, announcing he had orders to search all departing boats for military deserters or draft evaders. McNamara's heart dropped. Some of his passengers were in the prohibited categories, including men who had served as U.S. intelligence agents. But he knew the navy man: in fact, McNamara had helped his family leave the country a few days before. Now the favor was returned. Instead of searching, the Vietnamese officer simply asked if there were any deserters or draft-eligible men aboard. No, McNamara replied. Smiling, the navy man climbed back onto his own boat, waving at the Americans to proceed on down the river.

Before doing so, McNamara had all his evacuees transfer to the two landing craft and turned the slower barge over to the Vietnamese. That decision was vindicated only an hour later when the convoy came under fire from the south bank of the river. Still wearing his helmet liner, McNamara remained standing at the wheel, opening the throttle to reach maximum speed while the half-dozen marines aboard returned the fire with rifles and grenade launchers—"the last American combat action of the war," Staff Sgt.

S. B. Hasty, the detachment commander, said later. "1500 on the afternoon of 29 April. Last shots fired against the enemy."

The two boats sailed past the ambush with no damage. The narrowest, and therefore the most dangerous, part of the channel lay ahead. But the rain came at exactly the right moment, falling so heavily it curtained the boats from shore and from the view of any attackers. As they threaded their way through the islands at the river's mouth, the rain lifted. Hasty could see people approaching in small boats, perhaps hoping to be taken along. But he and his marines stood and showed their weapons, and the boats veered away.

At dusk McNamara's convoy reached the sea, only to find no ships in sight. Hasty began broadcasting the distress call "Mayday" over every radio and on every possible frequency. But for five hours, as the boats bobbed on the black swells, no one answered. The USS *Barbour County* had been dispatched to look for them, but could not find them in the darkness, and for some reason did not pick up their radio signals. At one in the morning, the two landing craft full of frightened, seasick passengers stumbled across the freighter *Pioneer Contender* and were picked up. It was lucky, Hasty thought, that there hadn't been any casualties in the firefight on the river. Anyone with serious wounds might well have died in the hours awaiting rescue.

Also heading for the sea on the evening of the 29th were the remaining Sealift Command tugs and barges from Saigon, led by the former U.S. Navy LST 117, now manned by a Korean crew and called *Boo Heung Pioneer*. The vessels left the Newport docks around noon. Though rocket and small arms fire could be heard from across the Saigon River, the major danger was not Communist gunfire but disorderly ship traffic. The tug *Chitose Maru* took more than an hour to maneuver into the channel; *Boo Heung Pioneer* had several collisions and was temporarily grounded before she finally managed to get under way.

No Saigon evacuees boarded at Newport. One or two bus convoys had started that way but could not get through the frightened crowds clogging the road. Instead, the tugs were ordered to stop at the Khanh Hoi docks on the downtown Saigon waterfront to pick up refugees before sailing on downriver. When the first tug reached the docks at about three-thirty in the afternoon, a "large, unruly crowd" was seething on shore. Strangely, however, the crowd had almost disappeared an hour or so later when a second tug, towing two barges, arrived. About 6,000 people were loaded, including those from several bus convoys that had been organized by two junior embassy officers. Conditions were so calm that someone even telephoned the embassy to ask if the convoy should wait for more evacuees, and when the barges left, between 5:15 and 5:30 P.M., they still had plenty of room.

The trip to the sea was not without drama. The *Chitose Maru* had an engine failure about nine o'clock that night; another tug, *Shibaura*, was forced aground by another vessel and remained stuck for several hours. But all the ships made it eventually: the last, *Chitose Maru*, reached international waters at six-thirty the next morning, April 30.

At Tansonnhut, after the delays and tension of the morning, the evacuation moved swiftly and smoothly once it began. The first CH-53s, with evacuees aboard, were on their way back to the fleet only six minutes after they landed in the DAO compound. A flurry of rifle shots and some grenade-launcher rounds from an ARVN housing area southwest of DAO arced up after the big helicopters. But none were hit, and later flights were directed to go out higher and on a different route. From barracks housing Vietnamese paratroopers on the far side of the landing zone, meanwhile, other soldiers sniped at groups of evacuees, wounding one small girl in the shoulder and shooting out windows in DAO buildings. U.S. Air Force security police, from a small detachment that was sent from the Philippines after the orphan-lift crash to guard against sabotage or hijackers, swapped shots with one sniper on a water tower catwalk. But the harassment was not serious enough to stop the flights. Within little more than an hour, 36 helicopters, each carrying 50 or more passengers, had flown off toward the sea.

My turn came at 3:36 P.M. After moving through the corridors a few yards at a time while evacuees were fed out through some unseen exit ahead of us, we reached the lobby of the DAO movie theater and lined up incongruously next to the popcorn machine. Abandoned suitcases littered the hallway. Twice we were waved out the door by an air force officer only to be sent back by one of the marines outside. Then we were called out a third time and directed toward a helicopter waiting with its rotor whirling on a tennis court, perhaps 200 yards away. "Run!" someone bellowed, and we galloped over.

Helicopters were landing and taking off all around, like pistons of some monstrous machine. The demented scream of their motors filled my skull. All over the landing zone marines were sprawled in firing position. Breathlessly, we scrambled aboard over the lowered rear loading-hatch. As soon as the last passenger was in, the helicopter bumped along the ground for a few yards and then rose into the air.

I didn't know it then, but to whichever western or Asian gods decided I would leave from Tansonnhut instead of the embassy, I would be grateful for the rest of my life. Whatever the other sensations and memories, at least I would not have to remember leaving Vietnam by climbing over the backs of Vietnamese human beings, as some of my friends had to do, outside the embassy wall.

Through the partly open rear hatch, as we lifted off and headed fast and low toward downtown Saigon, we could see smoke sprouting from fires around the air base. Then the jumbled red-tile roofs of the city began to spin below us as the pilot corkscrewed up through the haze to his assigned 5,500-foot altitude. About half the passengers were Vietnamese civilians, the rest mostly western newsmen and photographers. I knew many of them; some were old friends, such as Mal Browne of the *New York Times* and freelancer Ann Mariano. We must have talked, during the long, sweaty wait in DAO and the ascent over Saigon. But when I thought about it later, I could not remember exchanging a single word with anyone from the time I walked out into the noon sun from the hotel lobby. It was as if I left Vietnam for the last time in complete silence, alone.

As we climbed over the city, I tried without success not to think about the missiles in the hands of Communist infantrymen who must be very near the outskirts by now. Sitting tensely, I watched the city fade into the haze astern, while below us passed the flat green Saigon River plain, veined with waterways that glinted in the sun like polished metal ribbons riveted to the land. At four o'clock, 24 minutes after takeoff, Vung Tau slid by below the port side, and we began descending over the sea. No more missiles: you could feel the relief, like something alive and breathing, among the passengers and the now-relaxed door gunners.

At four-fifteen we felt a shudder, then the slight bump of the landing gear settling on something solid. The loading hatch was lowered and we stepped off onto a ship's fantail landing pad. The air felt warm and moist after the chilly, dry, faintly acrid air that came through the helicopter's air blowers. The huge motor was still shrieking. A navy crewman stood nearby, wearing noise suppressors that looked like oversize plastic earmuffs. I walked over and shouted the first words I remember saying during the entire journey: "What ship is this?"

He shook his head, then lifted the Mickey Mouse headset away from his ears. I shouted the question again, then bent close to hear the answer. "This is the *Mobile*," he said.

Vietnamese helicopters were heading for the fleet too, buzzing over the horizon like flights of dragonflies across a pond. Through the hum of static on the *Mobile*'s bridge radios, we could hear American pilots and navy communicators trying to talk them down:

"I have an H-1 here on my port side, looks like out about six miles if the Air America bird's trying to find him."

"Well, we were"—the Air America pilot, a twanging southern voice answering the call-sign One-three Foxtrot. "He said originally he was about ten Ks out and he was gonna turn and come inbound so that might be him."

Another ship: "I have a deck over here too if you can get him to me."

"OK, I think we better just shine some green lights out here and hope he lands."

"Yeah, I got mine going."

A moment later, the first ship calling the pilot again: "One-three Fox, this is Four Winds, looks like he might be over the destroyer now."

"Roger, saw him. We're going to run over here and check him." A pause, then: "OK, we think we've got him over here by this destroyer, we're gonna see if we can round him up and bring him over to you. Limestone?"

"Limestone's ready."

"Certainly hope this destroyer is too, 'cause it looks like he wants to land on it."

A gabble of voices: "Whatever turns him on." "Well, this thing's got a pad. . . ." "Roger, looks like he's made a touchdown, this is Four Winds." "Roger." "They don't have any room to keep him." "I think he's gonna go over the side."

Another pause, then a new American voice, young and shocked: "What a waste!"—an epitaph, it seemed, not just for the millions of dollars' worth of aircraft being pitched overboard but for the whole American experience in Vietnam, ending that day out on the wide, gentle swells of the South China Sea.

The *Mobile*, too, had a landing pad but no deck space to store helicopters. Her crew had already ditched two Hueys before we landed, and long after nightfall, at eleven o'clock, a third roared out of the darkness like a lost land bird too far out at sea. The beam of its landing light probed, then found and held the ship's fantail, met almost instantly by the answering glare of the ship's spotlights. On the fuselage, as it entered the shaft of light, we could see the Vietnamese air force insignia. The pilot hovered briefly over the stern, then dropped his skids onto the floodlit deck. The instant he had done so he cut the motor, taking no chance that he would be ordered to take off again.

Squinting in the glare of the lights, two Vietnamese airmen climbed out, and behind them a dozen men, women, and children in civilian clothes. A detail of American marines quickly surrounded them, their silhouetted figures looming bulkily next to the slim Vietnamese. After they were searched for weapons the arrivals were allowed onto the narrow steel ladder descending to the main deck. Other marines and sailors, meanwhile, after lowering the port-side safety net, ran a steel cable from one of the ship's cranes around the skids of the now-inert Huey. With crewmen pushing on the tail boom, they slid it across the flight deck, then tipped it over the side. A few sailors standing near me shook their heads unconsciously as they watched. But the waste couldn't be helped. As the craft toppled its main rotor blade snapped off, dropping like a great falling sword into the sea. Then the olive-drab fuselage struck the water. It wallowed under the lights for a moment, resembling the corpse of some huge marine beast; then filled and sank, leaving behind only a great whoosh of foam on the black skin of the sea.

It took only an hour and a half after the first helicopter wave landed in the DAO compound to fly out 2,000 evacuees. By nightfall, 3,500 more were on their way to the ships, leaving only a few hundred passengers and the landing force marines still at Tansonnhut.

Darkness brought new dangers. Pilots reported scattered antiaircraft fire along the entire flight path from the coast. At Tansonnhut, Communist rockets and artillery, which had halted during the afternoon, began falling again, though not as heavily as in the morning and still well away from the DAO buildings. A layer of smoke from numerous fires hung over the base. A violent thunderstorm grumbled, then broke. On the DAO roof, Marine Maj. David Cox and his landing zone controllers tried to talk the inbound helicopters down over soaked radios while angry Vietnamese voices broke in on their frequencies, shouting obscenities. After dark, the controllers tried to use strobe lights to guide the incoming aircraft, but pilots couldn't pick out the signals from among the blazing fires, lightning flashes, and aimlessly fired tracer rounds that streaked over the base. Finally, despite the risk that the aircraft would be visible to gunners on the ground, Cox told the pilots to flash their landing lights as they approached. Once the controllers spotted them, they could direct the aircraft to the landing zones. Conditions were still very dangerous and there was at least one near miss in the darkness, with two helicopters missing each other by no more than 50 feet. But there were no crashes, and the aircraft kept landing.

During the afternoon and evening, the Communist columns continued advancing toward the city against light resistance, while the Saigon military command virtually ceased to function. Shortly before 7 P.M., the government radio station broadcast the first and only Order of the Day by the new chief of the Joint General Staff, Lt. Gen. Vinh Loc. Admonishing his officers and soldiers against "running away like a mouse," Loc promised: "From now on, I and the commanding generals will be present among you . . . day and night." Shortly afterward, Loc boarded a helicopter for the evacuation ships. Most other senior commanders had already done the same.

At DAO, General Smith and the last of his staff, except for one civilian who stayed to help destroy communications gear, left the compound at 8 P.M. to board two CH-53s for the fleet. Then the marine landing force began leaving. General Carey flew out at 10:50 P.M. for the *Blue Ridge*. Last to leave were the demolition teams who wired the compound and its secret equipment—and barrels containing more than $3.5 million in U.S. currency—for destruction. The explosives experts blew up the secret satellite communications terminal at eleven-thirty, the main DAO building and presumably the money fifteen minutes later. As the building burned its roof buckled into a wavy, rippling shape, as if it were a collapsing tent.

At twelve minutes past midnight, as the sound of cannon fire from the approaching Communist tanks grew louder, the demolition teams boarded the last helicopters and flew off through the blackness toward the coast. Tansonnhut, and the wreckage of what was once the headquarters for an

American army of a half-million men, were left to the frightened, leaderless troops still occupying the base and to the Communists whose arrival could not be more than a few hours away.

Not far from the Tansonnhut main gate, on the road leading downtown, the bodies of Darwin Judge and Charles McMahon still lay in the mortuary of Saigon's Seventh Day Adventist Hospital. Sometime during the day, there had been an erroneous report that the remains had already been flown out; no one thought about them again.* Some $16 million in gold, the Saigon government's reserves, also remained behind, despite plans to fly it out so it would not fall into Communist hands. So did pallets of supplies that had been frantically loaded the day before at Bien Hoa and Tansonnhut: part of an estimated $2 billion worth of "serviceable assets" that would be left to Vietnam's new rulers. Still, everyone who awaited evacuation in the DAO complex got out safely—6,236 passengers, including the 816 landing force marines, in 122 evacuation sorties, despite harassing fire by ARVN soldiers, Communist rockets and shells nearby, and weather conditions that were truly terrible by evening. By any measure, the Tansonnhut evacuation, for those who managed to reach the base, was a remarkable success.

The American embassy was a different story.

The Frequent Wind operational plans filled thousands of pages. Not one of them, according to the officers who carried them out, ever called for a large-scale evacuation from the U.S. embassy in Saigon.

"A total not to exceed 100 evacuees had been anticipated from the embassy," General Carey wrote in his official after-action report. This would have included the ambassador, the embassy's marine guards, and "a small number of American citizens"—presumably, senior embassy officers whose responsibilities kept them there until the last moment. No Vietnamese evacuees were to leave from the embassy at all. Air America Hueys, not military helicopters, were supposed to take out the ambassador and his aides. The only marine aircraft called for in the final Frequent Wind plan were four twin-rotor CH-46 medium helicopters—which, unlike the heavier CH-53s, could use the embassy's rooftop pad—to fly out the embassy marines.

---

* Two other marines died in Frequent Wind, but not from Communist gunfire; they were the pilot and co-pilot of a CH-46 helicopter that crashed at sea near the USS *Hancock* after dark on the 29th. The two gunners were rescued, as were the crews of a Cobra helicopter gunship and a Navy A-7E fighter-bomber that also ditched at sea. There was at least one Vietnamese death in the crash of a Vietnamese air force T-41 trainer, which ditched during the afternoon 300 yards from the USS *Duluth*. A rescue helicopter picked up one of its passengers but could not find the other.

The bodies of Judge and McMahon were handed over by the Communists to a member of Senator Edward Kennedy's staff in February 1976.

Until late in the afternoon of Evacuation Day, neither Carey nor his deputy, Col. Wiley W. Taylor, Jr., had any idea those plans were to be changed. Then, shortly before four o'clock, word came from the embassy: somewhere between 2,000 and 3,000 people, more than half of them Vietnamese, were inside the compound, with no way to reach Tansonnhut through the increasingly chaotic streets. Among them were at least eight busloads that had been turned away at the Tansonnhut main gate or had not reached the base at all; there were also Americans and Vietnamese VIPs who had been picked up by Air America elsewhere in Saigon and flown to the embassy instead of Tansonnhut because of the refueling problem.

Major Jim Kean, the senior marine at the embassy, had more bad news. Besides the crowd inside the compound, he told Taylor, there were perhaps 3,000 more Vietnamese outside the walls trying to climb in, and his small detachment was having serious trouble keeping control.

Taylor was stunned. As commander of the landing force advance party, he had told embassy officers "at great length on a number of occasions" during the past ten days that except for a few senior officials, all evacuees had to be transported to Tansonnhut. Until the very moment he heard from Kean, Taylor thought the evacuation was going smoothly, even though later in the day than the marines would have liked. Now, he recalled later, "we had an entirely different ballgame." The complex helicopter schedules had to be suddenly revised to divert large numbers of flights "to an unsatisfactory rooftop landing zone, an unsatisfactory courtyard landing zone, to pick up personnel who we had not any idea would be in that location."

General Carey's after-action report blamed the embassy, in effect, for having no reliable estimate of the number of evacuees on the final day and "no really viable notification plan to evacuees or scheme to move them to DAO. . . . the final upshot of this planning shortfall was the huge, unexpected and ever swelling number of evacuees at the embassy, as opposed to DAO where orderly processing and evacuation was possible." The differences between the two sites were alarming. At DAO, 2,000 or more evacuees could be lifted out in an hour. At the embassy, where only one CH-46 at a time could land on the roof and the heavier CH-53s had to maneuver—also one at a time—onto the cramped parking lot, the pace would be far slower. With darkness, which was now swiftly approaching, the dangers and difficulties would be multiplied.

Carey's first move was to reinforce the security guard with three more platoons, about 130 marines, who were flown downtown between 5 and 7 P.M. to join Major Kean's beleaguered men on the compound walls where they had used boots and rifle butts to keep panicked Saigonese from climbing over. Inside the grounds, Colonel Madison, after learning that his Joint Military Team negotiators wouldn't be remaining behind after all, had taken charge of the swelling crowds. Some evacuees were waiting in the courtyard next to the parking lot, where Ambassador Martin's tree had finally been removed and the chips swept up so as not to be blown about by helicopter rotors. A larger group was in an adjacent recreation courtyard, standing or sitting on suitcases around the embassy swimming pool.

The two courtyards were separated by a structure that housed the embassy's fire trucks. A passage between them was controlled by a chain-link fence with a gate. Once the airlift began, Colonel Madison and his team were to organize passenger loads and guide them to the landing pads, while the marines would direct the helicopters and also remain in charge of protecting the compound. Until the helicopters began coming, though, Madison just wanted to keep the waiting evacuees calm. His men, including the Vietnamese-speaking Stu Herrington, moved through the crowds promising that everyone would go. Nobody, they repeated over and over, would be abandoned.

By nightfall, only a handful of helicopters had loaded and left. With the darkness came rain squalls, which helped disperse the mob outside the walls but also made flying hazardous. Communications were poor and pilots had trouble spotting the embassy; at one point, when someone set fires in barrels on the roof—either as a signal or to destroy classified documents—confusing reports reached the task force that the building was on fire. Cobra gunships, light, fast, well-armed helicopters that were circling overhead ready to meet any threat on the ground, were instead put into service as pathfinders, guiding the inbound transport craft to the landing zone.

Over the parking lot pad, to mark it for the CH-53s, a 35-mm slide projector someone found in an abandoned embassy office was mounted and turned on whenever a helicopter was descending, illuminating the pad with a sharply etched rectangle of white light. With these and other improvised ground control measures, the pilots kept landing, though not without long delays that further tautened the nerves of the evacuees waiting by the swimming pool.

Nerves were also tight in the control center at Tansonnhut, where DAO and task force officers grew increasingly exasperated at the vague, incomplete reports they were receiving from the embassy. No matter how many helicopters left, the estimate of the number of evacuees remaining never changed. It was like trying to empty a "bottomless pit," said the commander of one of the helicopter squadrons. USSAG in Thailand and Admiral Gayler's headquarters in Hawaii kept anxiously asking how many passengers were still to be flown out, and the embassy's answer, air force historians wrote, "was always the same—2,000 to go. . . . Everyone in the Evacuation Control Center believed that if the evacuation had continued for days, the estimate would have remained 2,000."

Skepticism about embassy reports reflected not just the confusion of the moment but a general distrust of Ambassador Martin, whose style the U.S.

military commanders had come to know only too well while he frustrated most of their efforts to prepare for the evacuation beforehand. Now that it was under way, some officers suspected that Martin was purposely holding back American evacuees while trying, as one officer wrote, "to evacuate the entire population of Saigon" through the embassy. The differing perspectives that had bedeviled the planning now affected the execution. Martin wanted to redeem his promise not to desert threatened Vietnamese; the military evacuation controllers, believing their first responsibility was to U.S. citizens, feared that unless someone took the decision out of the ambassador's hands, American lives—those of the evacuees and of the marine landing force and air crews—would be endangered. From those conflicting purposes came a final, and needless, tragedy.

An hour before midnight, the skies over the embassy fell quiet while all helicopters were assigned to DAO to lift out the marines there. Air crews had now spent ten or more hours flying under extremely difficult circumstances, and the task force command was worried enough about pilot fatigue and the increasingly dangerous night flying that as the heavy-lift CH-53s returned to the ships, they were ordered temporarily grounded.

General Carey did not find out about the order until he returned to the *Blue Ridge*, when he was also told the task force was considering suspension of all flights until daylight. Carey argued vehemently that the airlift should go on. His pilots could keep flying, he insisted, and by morning Saigon might be in the hands of the North Vietnamese army. And he had been assured by Martin, in a telephone conversation just before he left the DAO building, that once the helicopter flow resumed, the embassy could be cleared "in a relatively short time." Not long after midnight, the task force was told that only the ambassador and a few of his senior aides, 150 marines (actually, 173), and about 500 Vietnamese were still awaiting evacuation. The bottom of the bottomless pit, seemingly, was about to be reached at last.

There was another reason not to interrupt the airlift. The North Vietnamese for their own reasons had chosen not to oppose the evacuation, but no one knew how they might react if the flights stopped and then began again. Their forbearance would not last forever, and if it ran out, they could quickly make the evacuation untenable.

Carey won the argument. His tired pilots climbed back into their aircraft and were soon headed back to Saigon. From the air over their routes, covering fighters could see flares and artillery shells bursting like flaming flowers at Vung Tau. Fires dappled Tansonnhut, where General Dung's infantry and tanks were so close that his artillery was ordered to lift the barrage at 1 A.M., less than an hour after the last U.S. helicopters left. Ammunition dumps at Long Binh, once a major U.S. headquarters, were exploding. From the east, long snaky lines of Communist vehicles moved with their headlights on, like luminous chains reaching toward Saigon. On the city's edges, tracer rounds drew quick little exclamation marks across the night.

In the anxious crowd around the embassy swimming pool, no one knew about the argument on the *Blue Ridge*, but everyone could hear that the flights had stopped. A frightening rumor spread: after midnight, the North Vietnamese would begin shooting the helicopters down. Hoping to get on the first load, if flights resumed, people began crowding toward the gate that barred the way to the parking lot. The two young marines at the gate pushed back, then began jabbing at the crowd with rifle butts to keep them off. If the crowding grew any worse, though, the chain-link fence would not hold and the parking lot would be overrun; if that happened, no one would get out. Stu Herrington, persuading the reluctant marines to open the gate just enough for him to slip through, waded into the crowd and shouted desperately in Vietnamese that they must calm down. "No one is abandoning you," he pleaded through a battery-powered bullhorn, while hysterical evacuees shoved and battered at his legs with their suitcases. "In a little while, the helicopters will begin arriving again. But you must cooperate. . . . If you don't listen to me, no one will go."

They should abandon their suitcases, Herrington told the crowd, form a line in family groups, and back away far enough for the gate to be opened. No one obeyed. The panicked pushing worsened. In the middle of the frenzy, an American who was waiting with his Vietnamese wife keeled over with an apparent heart attack. Somehow he was extricated and carried through the gate to wait for the next flight. But then the crowd pushed in again. Herrington made no headway until finally two other members of the JMT delegation, Colonel Summers and M. Sgt. Bill Herron, came to his rescue. Linking arms, the three men managed to push the front rank of the mob back. Abruptly, in the strange manner of crowds, the panic passed. Everyone lined up docilely, and the three Americans led them through the gate and up a stairway to the roof of the fire station, from which they could see the landing zone.

When everyone was through—except for one family that chose not to come, and whom Herrington last glimpsed beginning to pick over the great mound of abandoned suitcases by the pool—the gate was closed and locked. Once inside the embassy compound, the evacuees discarded their remaining luggage and sat calmly, gazing at the sky.

Throughout the night, Ambassador Martin insisted nobody would be left behind. "Everybody in that compound is leaving—everybody," he declared in the hearing of several marines. But the information he, or someone, had sent to the fleet was inaccurate. There were not 500 Vietnamese in the embassy, as Washington and the task force believed. Herrington and his colleagues counted heads while passing the evacuees through the gate from the swimming pool area: the first time all night anyone knew exactly how many people were in the compound. The tally was 1,100, more than twice as many as had been reported. Not all were Vietnamese. A handful of Americans were in the crowd, as were about a dozen South Korean diplomats who had somehow missed their own embassy's earlier departure. Senior among them was a military officer, Brig. Gen. Rhee Dai Yong, who had formerly served as deputy commander of the 50,000-man Korean expeditionary force in Vietnam. There was also a Vietnamese-speaking German priest, who volunteered to remain until the last flight to help organize the remaining evacuees; making the same offer was a group of the embassy's Vietnamese fire fighters, wearing yellow coats and helmets.

On the *Blue Ridge,* however, General Carey was still relying on his earlier conversation with Martin and on outdated embassy reports. On that basis, Carey and the task force staff calculated that nineteen more flights would be enough to take out the 500 evacuees they believed were waiting. At seventeen minutes past two in the morning, the first four helicopters—two CH-53s and two twin-rotor CH-46s—left the fleet for the embassy, with other flights following at ten-minute intervals. By three o'clock the first aircraft reached the embassy, where Colonel Madison's team began forming passenger loads among the Vietnamese in the courtyard. Some were led inside the building and up to the roof to board the smaller CH-46s, while others were hustled onto CH-53s in the parking lot. On the task force ships and in Washington, it was assumed that the nineteen flights would complete the evacuation. A White House message to Martin was relayed by the *Blue Ridge* and also through the C-130 serving as the airborne command center, ordering him to board the last helicopter. The pilots had been briefed to pick up the last remaining Americans, they kept explaining to the marine controllers. But the marines kept putting Vietnamese evacuees aboard. In the courtyard, Madison, Herrington, and the rest of their team repeated continually to those still waiting that nobody would be stranded. They themselves, they promised, would not leave until all the Vietnamese were gone.

When the CH-53s stopped coming, about 700 evacuees had left. Ambassador Martin, looking "completely exhausted," descended to the courtyard and told Madison to assemble all the others in the parking lot and count them again. Then he turned and disappeared back into the building. A short while later, at 4:15 A.M., Madison sent word to Martin's deputy Wolfgang Lehmann: 420 people were still waiting. Just six more heavy-lift helicopters could take them all.

Lehmann's answer was a shock. There would be no more CH-53s, he told Madison. The evacuation was over, except for rooftop flights that would board only Americans. The anguished Madison reminded Lehmann that the evacuees had been promised they would not be left behind. He and his team would refuse to leave, he declared, until that promise was kept. Finally Lehmann relented, assuring Madison that the six more CH-53 flights would be provided. A few minutes later, Martin's aide Brunson McKinley came to the parking lot to confirm Lehmann's statement. Once again, as they had been doing for hours, Madison and the rest of his team walked among the remaining evacuees, promising that more helicopters would come and that no one would be abandoned.

On the fleet, however, the decision to stop the CH-53 flights was irreversible. By four-thirty, General Carey and Rear Adm. Donald Whitmire, the navy commander, realized that the limit of nineteen flights had been passed and there was still a substantial number of Americans in the embassy awaiting evacuation; meanwhile, many more Vietnamese had been flown out than the 500 the task force had thought were there, and there were still nearly that many to go. The impression of a bottomless pit was revived, and now nobody on the *Blue Ridge* was willing to trust the embassy's word that the bottom was within reach. Luck and the pilots' courage and skill had avoided casualties so far, but to keep going indefinitely was to invite disaster. In radio messages to the pilots who were still heading for the embassy, Carey issued unequivocal orders that only Americans were to be flown out from then on. And in Washington, too, it was decided that if Martin would not end the airlift as quickly as possible on his own authority, he would have to be ordered to do so. In the sky over Vietnam, an extraordinary transmission from the flying command post, in clear language, began to come over pilots' VHF radios:

> The following message is from the President of the United States and should be passed on by the first helicopter in contact with Ambassador Martin. Only 21 lifts remain. Americans only will be transported. Ambassador Martin will board the first available helicopter and that helicopter will broadcast "Tiger, Tiger, Tiger" once it is airborne and en route.

In the embassy, Major Kean, the marine commander, was told of the presidential order by a separate radio signal from the fleet. Walking to Martin's office, where the ambassador and several senior aides were waiting, Kean alerted them that Martin was to leave on the next flight.

Carey, meanwhile, had also issued orders to Capt. Gerry Berry, the commander of a CH-46 with the call-sign Lady Ace 09, that he was not to leave the embassy roof until the ambassador was aboard. When Berry's aircraft landed just before five o'clock, the marines on the roof led another load of evacuees to the pad. But Berry refused to take them. Handing a note out to one of the marines, he insisted it be sent inside to the ambassador. A few minutes later, Martin appeared. Helped by his assistant Ken Moorefield he climbed aboard. At 4:58 A.M., Lady Ace 09 rose off the pad into the dark sky and was gone. As soon as the roof was clear, a second CH-46 swooped down and boarded the rest of the senior embassy staff: the "small number of American citizens" who, the evacuation planners had believed for so long, would be the only ones flown from the embassy rooftop at all.

As the helicopters carrying Martin and his staff flew off toward the fleet, Major Kean headed downstairs to the parking lot to tell Colonel Madison that no more evacuees, except for Americans, would be taken out.

For the second time in less than an hour, Madison was stunned. Six more CH-53s had been promised, he said angrily; he wanted to take the matter up with the ambassador or Lehmann. "You can't, sir," Kean answered, pointing upward toward the roof. "They just left." In that case, Madison said calmly, he and his team would refuse to leave until everyone was evacuated, as they had promised. Kean shook his head. The airlift had ended by presidential order, he told Madison, and he was not going to disobey or risk his marines' safety by staying any longer.

For the last time, differing American perspectives were in collision. The marines' training and doctrine taught that protecting classified material and American lives was their primary responsibility; having accomplished that task, neither the landing force nor the embassy guards had any great emotional commitment to the Vietnamese who were still waiting on the parking lot. "We didn't really care at the time," one marine said later; "all we wanted to do was get out." Madison and his men, after promising so often not to abandon anyone, were devastated at having to break their word. But they had no real choice. No one wanted to disobey a presidential order. And if the marines left, staying behind would only be a useless gesture; it wouldn't save anyone. A heartsick Madison told Herrington to stay with the evacuees a few minutes longer, while the rest of the team discreetly packed their gear and made their way to the roof.

Sitting on the trunk lid of a parked car, Herrington waited until he thought the others were ready, then slipped into the embassy foyer. On the floor, lying amid heaps of litter, was a plaque honoring the marines and military police who died defending the embassy in the 1968 Tet offensive. Hours earlier, Herrington had pried it off the wall with a crowbar, planning to carry it out so it wouldn't fall into the hands of the looters or the Communists. Now he changed his mind. If the men to whom it was dedicated could see American soldiers scuttling away from 420 people they had promised to save, he thought, they would roll over in their graves.

Leaving the plaque where it lay, he ran up the stairs to the roof. A CH-46 had just landed, and Herrington, with two of the delegation's enlisted aides, scrambled on. A lone marine was the only other passenger; fifteen of those abandoned could have ridden along, if they had been able to reach the roof. It was five-thirty in the morning, April 30. The sky had lightened enough so that as the helicopter banked, Herrington could see, still waiting among the clumps of people in the courtyard below, the embassy firemen in their yellow coats and helmets. Their families had already been evacuated and were waiting aboard one of the U.S. ships, not knowing they might never see their husbands or fathers again.

Also left behind was the German priest—and the South Korean embassy group, whom everyone had completely forgotten. General Rhee, despite his diplomatic status, would not be repatriated after Saigon's surrender, but jailed by his Communist captors.

If Herrington had tried to talk, he thought, he would have wept. "I know of no word in any language," he wrote later, "that can describe the sense of shame that swept over me during that flight."

Only Major Kean's marines now remained: the embassy guard detachment, the three landing force platoons that had been flown in to reinforce them, and the helicopter controllers. The skies, after being filled so long with the clatter of engines, were quiet. All the aircraft were on their way to the ships. With daylight, people began moving again through the streets. Soon, looters were in the abandoned recreation compound, rummaging through the piles of luggage left there during the night. In the embassy courtyard, the last 420 evacuees still sat, not yet understanding that they had been deserted.

Quietly, Major Kean and M. Sgt. Juan Valdez, the head of the embassy guard unit, passed the word to marines at the gates and on the walls to slip back down into the courtyard. Once everyone was inside the compound, some of the men, as unobtrusively as possible, formed a perimeter in front of the lobby entrance. Others set up a second, tighter ring inside the first. Then the marines from the outer line pulled back through the inner one and set up a third, smaller still, so that the second perimeter could pull in in its turn. From the air the maneuver would have looked like a ripple from a stone in a pond, but shown in reverse, so the rings collapsed inward on each other instead of spreading outward.

Not until the third and last perimeter began retreating toward the lobby door did the evacuees suddenly grasp what was happening and begin racing toward the entrance, while other Vietnamese appeared atop the unguarded walls. The last few marines had to wrestle people out of the lobby before closing and barring the double door. They only managed to get the bar halfway into position before bolting for the elevators, and as the elevator door closed the men heard the bar clanging to the floor, jostled loose by the crowds pummeling on the outside of the doors.

Locking the elevators on the sixth floor, the marines filed up the stairway to the roof. From the courtyard came a tremendous crash: someone had driven a vehicle, apparently one of the embassy fire trucks, into the lobby doors, bursting them open. Once all the marines were on the roof, they blocked the door behind them with everything they could find: heavy wall lockers that had been used to store weapons and supplies; fire extinguishers on hand trucks. Marines put their personal packs on the pile. Flak jackets, too: everyone had seen weapons of all sorts lying discarded in the embassy corridors. The marines could hear people moving inside the building, where crowds of looters were growing every minute. But the improvised barricade held; no one reached the roof.

Suddenly, after all the frightened, frantic hours, there was nothing to do. Nearly an hour would pass before the first helicopters came back from the fleet. Someone sniped toward them from a nearby building, but the marines didn't return fire, just tried to stay down. The last thing they wanted was a firefight that might keep the helicopters from landing.

It was full daylight by now, bulging with the threat of heat. More rifle shots popped in the streets, which were full of aimlessly roaming soldiers. Farther off, the marines could hear the dull slams of Communist rockets falling near the city's outskirts. In the courtyard below, while looters carried their booty away from the building, a few of the abandoned evacuees were still staring up at the roof. Some, in a last desperate gesture, waved documents—letters from American sponsors, embassy identity cards, whatever papers they thought would entitle them to leave with the Americans. Occasionally, despite the sniping, a marine walked casually to the parapet so the crowd six stories down could see they had not left yet.

When the helicopters finally began coming back, the landing force marines boarded first. Sergeant Valdez and his security guards had asked to be the last to go. One by one the CH-46s bumped down, loaded, and took off. Marines tossed away radios and personal gear so that up to 24 men, instead of the usual fifteen, could climb on each aircraft.

It took nine helicopters to fly all the marines out. The last, for some reason, lagged well behind the rest. To Valdez, sitting with the very last load of eleven men, waiting for the final flight "seemed like an eternity." But he was sure it would come, and finally it did. Valdez was the last man to climb aboard. At 7:53 A.M. the helicopter lifted off the embassy roof, rose into the sky, then turned and headed eastward, toward the sun that was climbing over the independent republic of South Vietnam for the last time.

Surrender

It was a sound you used to hear sometimes in the middle of the night, long after curfew, when the South Vietnamese moved armored units through the empty Saigon streets: the roar of heavy engines, louder than any truck, and the elephantine rumble of tank treads rolling ponderously over the pavement.

Now, the sound came in full daylight. At mid-morning on April 30, in a city poised between the known and unknown, it told three million Saigonese that the future was about to begin. Instead of the red-and-yellow colors of the Saigon government, the tanks showed the Liberation star, rippling on banners that fluttered from tall radio aerials. Among the tanks rolled open trucks with wooden slats along their sides, filled with young soldiers in green uniforms and wearing sun helmets or floppy cloth hats who waved stubby AK-47 rifles and rocket-grenade launchers with projectiles like the knobs at the end of banana stalks. The roads to Saigon were open before them. No one had blown up the bridges leading into the city; there were no antitank ditches, just a few improvised barricades of sandbags and oil drums that were easily pushed aside by the advancing tanks.

Saigon waited as if in the last moments of waking from a dream. Crowds still surged at the docks, where a few small coastal freighters were still loading to sail downriver to the sea. The streets around the empty American embassy were still full of looters, though the building itself emptied out after a rumor ran through the crowd that the marines had left delayed-action charges set to explode after the helicopters were gone. No one took the plaque which Stu Herrington left on the lobby floor; Peter Arnett of the Associated Press, one of the most experienced and respected of all Vietnam correspondents, who had chosen not to evacuate with the Americans, found it in the litter and carried it back to his office.* Away from the waterfront and the embassy, though, Saigon was still. A few policemen and soldiers wandered through the streets, and families who had fled from the suburbs huddled in parks or on private lawns. But nearly everyone else stayed indoors, in their homes or perhaps in sturdier buildings where they hoped to shelter from the coming battle.

Tansonnhut was quiet too, except for the crackle of fires that still burned in the fuel and munitions dumps, sending smoke rolling up into the empty sky. At the sides of the shrapnel-scarred runways, wrecked or abandoned planes stood like hulks in a shipbreaker's yard. Near the vacant control tower was a C-130 with its back broken. The tail section was still upright but tilted backward onto the ground, pointing a torn section of fuselage upward at the sky from which its destruction had come. Helicopters lay on crushed or shattered blades like giant dead insects.

---

* Arnett hoped to return the plaque to the U.S. government. But when he and several other foreign reporters were expelled some weeks later, they were allowed only a limited amount of baggage for their personal belongings, and Arnett had no room for the heavy plaque. He left it in the AP bureau, which was subsequently taken over by the Communist authorities. What happened to the plaque is unknown.

In the Communist delegation's compound, the delegates had spent the night in the bunkers they had dug under their barracks. With them were three visitors: a Third Force delegation who had come the day before to ask if a battle for Saigon could possibly be avoided. The group consisted of Tran Ngoc Lieng, a lawyer and former political detainee; a professor named Chu Tam Luan; and Father Chan Tin, a Catholic priest belonging to the same Redemptorist order as the anti-corruption leader Father Tran Huu Thanh. All were well-known Saigon dissidents who, if not exactly under the Liberation Front's discipline, carried out activities that were almost certainly directed to some extent by Front agents. Chan Tin, who led a human rights protest movement against the Thieu regime, was perhaps the best known abroad; it was he who publicized the supposed figure of 200,000 political prisoners held by the Saigon authorities.

Mindful that Communist broadcasts since the 26th no longer called for a new Saigon administration and specifically warned the Third Force to "stand on the people's side," the three would not join the Minh government. But they agreed to visit the Communist delegation on Minh's behalf, though without official status. Late on the afternoon of the 29th, while American helicopters were still landing and taking off at DAO, the three men drove to Camp Davis. A few hours earlier, four other emissaries representing Vice-President Huyen had been turned back there by Communist guards, who dismissed them with a few bunches of bananas they had grown inside the compound and a statement that the Communist terms had been clearly enough stated on April 26, when the P.R.G. demanded dismantling the Saigon administration and army.

Perhaps because of their Front connections, Lieng, Luan, and Chan Tin were received somewhat more courteously and were admitted to the compound. But the message was the same. Orders for the attack on Saigon had already been given, the Communist spokesman Vo Dong Giang warned the group; it was up to General Minh to accept "the outcome of this great struggle of the Vietnamese people." When the three men tried to leave to deliver the message, however, Giang politely refused to allow them to go. For their own safety, since the base was under attack, he told them they should remain in the compound, in the underground bunkers. Clearly, the Communists were not now going to allow anything—not even a surrender by Minh—to prevent them from ending the war in their own fashion.

During the day, both Vice-President Huyen and the new prime minister, Vu Van Mau, made gestures attempting to meet the Communists' terms. Huyen issued a declaration calling for peace negotiations "in accordance with the spirit of the 26th April 1975 statement" of the P.R.G.; Mau promised to release all detainees and pledged the repeal of all repressive laws and reform of the police "in keeping with a truly free regime." Mau also promised "serious implementation" of the three articles of the Paris agreement requiring U.S. respect of Vietnam's national rights. Shortly afterward, Saigon radio announced the request for the closing of the Defense Attache Office.

It was too late for concessions, however. In Hanoi, the April 30 edition of the Communist party newspaper, *Nhan Dan*, was already going to press with North Vietnam's justification for the final assault: an editorial titled "Fake Peace and Independence," which denounced the "Minh-Huyen-Mau administration" for refusing to comply with the "most basic and imperative demands of the Vietnamese people at this moment. As a matter of fact," the editorial went on, "this administration is but a Thieu administration without Thieu," installed by maneuvers of "the U.S. colonial governor-general Graham Martin."

The charge was the same Hanoi had directed at Thieu's successor, Tran Van Huong. The meaning was also the same: there would be no negotiated arrangement, not even for the handing over of power. Saigon was to be "liberated" by armed force alone.

It was Duong Van Minh's fate to surrender his country not once, but twice. When his emissaries had not returned from Tansonnhut by mid-morning, he and his associates at last yielded to the inevitable. At 10:24 A.M. his slow, awkward voice began to sound on Saigon's radios. "Our policy and line consist of national reconciliation and concord to save the lives of our compatriots," he began. "I deeply believe in reconciliation among the Vietnamese so as to avoid wasting the bones and blood of the Vietnamese. For this reason, I call on all [Republic of Vietnam] soldiers to remain calm, to stop fighting and stay put. We also call on our brother combatants of the [Provisional Revolutionary Government of the Republic of South Vietnam] to stop fighting because we are waiting to meet the P.R.G.R.S.V. in order to discuss the formal handing over of power in an orderly manner, with a view to avoiding useless bloodshed." Minh's was followed by the voice of Brig. Gen. Nguyen Huu Hanh, acting chief of the Joint General Staff. Confirming Minh's ceasefire call, Hanh directed "all generals and military men of all ranks" to observe the order "absolutely."

As soon as it heard Minh's broadcast, the Army of the Republic of Vietnam began to disappear. Thousands of soldiers threw away weapons and helmets and pouches of ammunition clips and stripped off their uniforms, which they left like little olive-drab puddles in the streets. Other soldiers and officers walked out of staff offices to go home. So did policemen from the precinct houses, stopping only to siphon gasoline from police jeeps into their own motorbikes. No one stopped to blow up compromising records. At both the Joint General Staff and the National Police headquarters, the occupying Communists would find complete computerized personnel files and great sheafs of classified material, including much that identified Vietnamese who had collaborated with the CIA or other U.S. agencies.

In Lam Son Square, shortly after Minh's speech, hundreds of onlookers saw a National Police officer with the rank badges of a lieutenant colonel and a tag with the name Long sewn over his uniform shirt pocket walk slowly toward the colossally hideous soldiers' monument facing the National Assembly—a huge bronze of two charging soldiers, one crouched behind the other in an unfortunately suggestive pose that had given rise to thousands of off-color wisecracks over the years. Lieutenant Colonel Long saluted the statue, then drew his .45 automatic from its holster and shot himself in the head.

At the city's edges, soldiers left their sandbagged positions in the perimeter and began marching in long, unkempt lines back toward downtown, littering the roads behind them with discarded equipment. In the lines they left, undestroyed and unattended, hundreds of vehicles and artillery pieces.

If his own army and the rest of Saigon thought Minh had surrendered, however, the Communists chose to interpret his speech as a trick to keep their army from seizing the enemy's "last den." From the Politburo in Hanoi, an order was flashed to General Dung: "Continue the attack on Saigon." Dung relayed the directive to his units: "Continue to rapidly attack designated areas and objectives. . . . Call on enemy troops to surrender and turn in all weapons, and capture, detain and concentrate enemy officers of field grade and above. . . . Whenever the enemy resists, our troops must immediately attack and annihilate him."

Here and there, for forever private reasons of honor or despair, little knots of government soldiers did fire on the advancing Communist columns, from which a few men and tanks would then turn aside to answer the fire with an air of bored disdain, as a man might brush away a stinging insect. But acts of resistance were few. For the most part, the long files of green tanks with identifying numerals painted in white on the steel flanks of their turrets drove toward their objectives as easily as if returning from a day on the beach. Leafy clumps of palm branches, used for camouflage in the jungle, were still fastened around turrets and gunports. High above, radio aerials whipped in the sultry air. From open hatches, the tankers—in close-fitting leather helmets with earflaps, giving them the appearance of World War I aviators—stared at the shuttered buildings and at the civilians who began to line the sidewalks, waving a welcome or simply watching in silent wonder and apprehension.

The end, when it came, was an event of improbable theatricality: life imitating a propaganda film.

From Thong Nhut Avenue, where it debouched opposite the Doc Lap Palace, a dozen tanks of General Dung's II Corps roared across Cong Ly Boulevard, a few minutes after rolling by the empty, ravaged American embassy. The lead tank, No. 843, raced without slowing straight at the high steel gate in front of the palace grounds. When the tank struck, its bow rose

up for a second or two as the treads began to climb up the bars. Then the gate
buckled and tore away. The tank rocked forward again, then rushed the
several hundred feet to the bottom of the palace's front steps, firing its
cannon in the air. Just behind, Tank No. 879 also crashed through the gate,
then swerved around to point its cannon back out at the street, guarding the
rear while the rest of the tanks swarmed past onto the lawn. Their treads left
harsh brown gouges in the grass. Soldiers leaped off to cover 30 or so palace
guards, who flung down their weapons and sat in disconsolate rows next to
a driveway just to the right of the gate.

As the tanks formed a semicircle facing the steps, a lone soldier jumped
down with a Liberation flag. Waving it in violent circles over his head, and
oblivious to any possible shots from other guards inside the doors, he
sprinted across the last few feet of lawn and up the steps. As he ran, the
earflaps of his tanker's helmet jounced up and down over his shoulders. He
vanished into the building, then reappeared, a long breathless moment later,
on a second-floor balcony just above the entrance, looking down on the
lawn and the tanks below. Holding the flag in both hands he flung it from
side to side as hard as he could, as if trying to signal all the way to Hanoi that
the Ho Chi Minh campaign had ended in victory.

Inside, Minh, Mau, and their associates waited on two rows of chairs in a
reception room whose red carpet was decorated with gold embroidered
ideograms meaning "tho"—"longevity." When the first Communist soldiers burst into the room, Minh stood and said formally, "We have been
impatiently waiting for you since this morning, to hand over power." Even
now, however, he was to be denied a dignified surrender. "All power has
passed into the hands of the revolution," one of the Communist officers
replied scornfully. "The former administration has collapsed. You cannot
hand over what you no longer have."

As more truckloads of troops arrived on the lawn, a larger Liberation flag
was run up on the rooftop flagpole, to the crack of celebratory gunshots in
the air. On Saigon's clocks—still, for a while longer, an hour later than
Hanoi's—it was exactly 12:30 in the afternoon.

So little opposition met the occupying Communists that they showed no
great urgency in announcing the capitulation. Nearly three hours passed
before Minh and Mau were driven to the Saigon radio station, where Minh
broadcast his second surrender speech of the day. It was only two sentences
long. "I, the president of the Saigon administration, call on the ARVN to lay
down their arms and surrender unconditionally to the South Vietnam
Liberation Army. I hereby declare that the Saigon administration, from the
central to the local echelons, must be completely dissolved and turned over
to the P.R.G.R.S.V." Prime Minister Mau followed with an equally brief
announcement to civil servants, telling them to return to their posts to await

the orders of the revolution. And then came the voice of an unnamed spokesman for the conquerors:

"We, the representatives of the South Vietnam Liberation Forces, solemnly declare that Saigon City is completely liberated and that the unconditional surrender of Gen. Duong Van Minh, president of the Saigon administration, has been accepted." The 30-year war, at last, was over.

Quickly and with almost no fighting, the Communists took over the rest of Saigon, raising their flag over other government buildings one by one, as they were occupied. On the waterfront, swarms of defeated soldiers and other Saigonese were jammed on board several small freighters that had not yet cast off from the docks when the first jeeploads of liberation troops drove up. At the sight of the gold-starred flag moving along the shore, the passengers dejectedly but calmly filed back down the gangplanks. Looters at the American embassy and abandoned government offices melted away swiftly as more truckloads of Communist soldiers began to roll through the streets.

Obviously under orders to treat the city's residents as liberated countrymen, not vanquished enemies, the young *bo doi*—revolutionary soldiers— were courteous and diffident, smiling shyly at the civilians who ventured into the streets. As the afternoon passed without heavy fighting, the crowds swelled. Here and there, Liberation flags bloomed in windows and doorways; armed students appeared on the streets to help control traffic. A curfew was announced for six o'clock, but beyond smiling admonitions, the *bo doi* did not try to enforce it. As dusk fell, squads of them set up camp on the city's parks and lawns, building small cooking fires just as if they were still in the jungle.

Another fire that evening consumed Nguyen Ngoc Ngan's past. A former combat officer who still held an ARVN commission though he was on detached duty as a Saigon high school teacher, Ngan had spent the morning of Liberation Day with his wife and baby son among the seething crowds on the waterfront, trying vainly to reach one of the ships that might still escape. Now, he was feeding his army uniforms into the flames and leafing through a family album for other evidence connecting him to the vanquished regime. From one page he removed a photo of himself looking skinny and boyish in front of his barracks at the Thu Duc officer training school. Another, taken by a fellow cadet, showed him in uniform with his wife, just after their wedding. To the pile Ngan added the picture that had stood framed in the family living room, a formal photograph of his commissioning. For a moment, he stared at the pictures "as though they belonged to another age," then slowly dropped them into the fire.

His precautions did not serve their intended purpose. Ngan would spend years in Communist "re-education" camps before joining the fearful flight of the Boat People; after a terrible voyage he reached Malaysia, but his wife and child were lost, drowned when their unseaworthy boat broke up just off shore.

On the sea which Ngan failed to reach on Liberation Day, and which would later claim the lives of his family, other dramas of escape were still being played out. A bedraggled flotilla of 32 Vietnamese navy ships carried nearly 20,000 sailors, their families, and other refugees away from their homeland. More thousands were afloat on civilian vessels, or on small boats that were still swarming out of the sunset toward the American ships just over the horizon. The terrible moral collapse of South Vietnamese society continued. Aboard the freighter *Kimbro,* Capt. Richard Reuter, commanding the marine security detachment, watched in angry astonishment as Vietnamese officers stole milk that had been given to refugee children, then skulked off behind the deck winches to drink it. One man, in an air force major's uniform, stole a blanket from an unconscious child who was laid out on a hatch.

Two large barges teeming with refugees tied up to the *Kimbro*'s sister ship, USNS *Sgt. Andrew Miller,* on the evening of the 30th. Just as the outer barge was emptied of its passengers, a Vietnamese air force helicopter dropped out of the darkening sky and tried to land on it. The pilot had his motorbike stowed in the back and for that reason didn't want to ditch in the sea, he explained later to the ship's marine guard. But the rotor blades hit the sides of the barge and disintegrated, sending swords of steel spinning through the air just a few feet from the still-packed inboard barge. Miraculously, only one person was injured. The high sandbagged barriers built above the barges' gunwales to stop gunfire from the riverbanks stopped most of the debris, otherwise there would have been a massacre.

The *Miller*'s captain, Kurt Oltmeyer, had special cause to be dedicated to the rescue mission. Thirty-five years before, a ship captain he never met had plucked him from the Dutch coast ahead of the advancing Nazi army, and now, off Vietnam, Oltmeyer felt that he was repaying a debt. But he was so furious at the helicopter pilot for endangering the ship and hundreds of lives that he refused to let him aboard. Instead, the man was given a few canteens of water and some C-rations, then put onto a small boat and left to be picked up, presumably, by another ship.

Elsewhere around the fleet, scores of other Vietnamese helicopters were also searching for haven aboard the evacuation ships. Pilots darted for any deck they could see, ignoring all attempts to wave them off and sometimes cutting dangerously in front of U.S. helicopters that were also trying to land. No fewer than fifteen Vietnamese helicopters tried to land on the *Blue Ridge* alone. One of them came in too low and crashed into the side of the ship, sending debris flying through the air. As marines, sailors, and evacuees flattened out on the deck, the helicopter's main rotor blade, snapped off by the impact, sailed high over the ship to land with a great splash behind her stern.

Half a world away from liberated Saigon and the fear-struck sea, a visitor to Henry Kissinger's office found him saddened but philosophical. Vietnam was a great tragedy, Kissinger said. "We should never have been there at all," he added. "But now it's history."

Like the rest of the task force ships, the *Mobile* stood just off the coast while refugee boats continued to come over the western horizon. Over her bridge radios, we heard snatches of terror and flight. For hours, an intelligence officer named Khanh pleaded from somewhere out on the water to be taken aboard an American ship. Over and over, in accented but understandable English, he listed the names of advisers he had known, repeated the name and address of a sister "married with one high-ranking officer in the States," recited the units he had served with and the U.S. training courses he had attended. He even repeated, with a note of reproach that sounded clearly through the static, the telephone number on which he had tried vainly to call his American counterpart to ask for evacuation. A patient navy radioman tried to reassure him, while also gently asking him to stop tying up the ship-to-ship radio frequency. But in his exhaustion and fright Captain Khanh could not stay silent. "Sorry, sir, I am very excited, please understand, frankly I am very excited after this hell, this kind of hell trip. . . . I don't know that you people understand our case or not."

From a landing craft came another Vietnamese voice. "Please help us, we have 600 people. These are one brigade airborne, one brigade, understand?" The paratroopers. Many of them were street-tough kids from the Saigon slums who joined for much the same reasons that wild youngsters in any country find their way to the roughest units. Though brave in combat, the paratroopers were also a lot more unruly than the conscripted farm boys who filled the regular infantry divisions, and they had a well-earned reputation for thievery and careless cruelty to civilians. Now they feared vengeance. "We can't go home," said the frightened voice crackling over the radio, "we will be caught. . . . We like to go to America so now we need your help."

Through the hot days and hazy nights the boats kept coming, until by Friday, our fourth day at sea, we could see all around us the smudges of abandoned, drifting vessels, some of them on fire and sending black oily smoke into the sky. That afternoon the swarm finally ended and the task force began to move. One by one the gray ships looped eastward toward the Philippines, leaving frothy, curving wakes behind them on the glassy sea.

The *Mobile*'s orders came at dusk. The beat of her engines quickened, and the waves that had lapped lazily at her steel sides now began to hiss as she moved through the water. Just as her loudspeakers announced "Under way," two last fishing boats suddenly appeared out of the gaudy sunset. Sailors, marines, and passengers crowded the rails as the two boats raced toward our stern. They gained at first, coming close enough for us to see figures waving frenziedly from the tops of their boxy wooden wheelhouses. Then they fell away again as we picked up speed. Clearly the *Mobile* was not going to stop. But a sailor climbed to the aft rail and shooting his arms out like a boxer throwing jabs, motioned toward an LST steaming a mile or so away. As if thrust away by his reaching arms across a thousand yards of water, the two boats turned toward it.

In the falling gloom it was just possible to see the clumsy bulk of the LST slow, then stop as the smaller boats reached it and bobbed in its wake. The three shapes blurred, then were lost in the darkness. But word made its way down the rail: "They picked 'em up," and, with the sea sliding past sounding like a sigh, the *Mobile* kept heading eastward, away from Vietnam and its lost war and toward home.

In their roofless house in the jungle near Ben Cat, General Dung, Pham Hung, Le Duc Tho, and the other senior Communist commanders heard General Minh's surrender broadcast and then, in the midst of their own jubilant celebration, received a congratulatory message from the Politburo. There was also a telephoned greeting: "Congratulations to you on a great victory. Do you hear the sound of firecrackers that are exploding all over Hanoi?"

The next day, Dung and Le Duc Tho drove to Saigon over roads strewn with weapons and equipment discarded by the defeated South Vietnamese. From the Communist compound at Camp Davis, Tho sent his Politburo comrades a report in the form of a poem, which ended,

North and South are reunited under the same roof.
Uncle Ho's dream has become reality
And he will sleep in peace.
The sky today is splendid and infinitely serene.

In pursuit of that dream, Tho and the rest of the Vietnamese Communist movement had wrought one of history's most extraordinary acts of will. Their public manner, modeled on Ho Chi Minh's, was one of modest diffidence. But under the cover of that appearance, they had made themselves into men and women of almost inconceivable hardness, driven by a fierce certitude of belief in their cause and their ultimate triumph. Among the thousands of guerrilla leaders and party activists and army commanders who made the Vietnamese revolution it was rare to find any who had not survived suffering that would crush ordinary people: years in prison; more years of privation and desperate combat in which the image of victory could have been seen nowhere but in their own innermost vision; loss of family and friends to enemy shells or bombs or police stockades.

Unlike most other people, the Vietnamese Communists seemed to be consciously living in their own heroic age. "We can consider ourselves," said Tran Van Tra at the first huge Communist rally in liberated Saigon, "to be worthy of our ancestors." So immune did they seem to normal human doubt and despair and want and fear that even some of their foreign supporters, on closer acquaintance, found them chilling. The same traits that inspired his admiration also caused a "subtle fear," admitted one European sympathizer after living through the early months of the liberation; the qualities that made the revolution possible also seemed to bring its makers "to the borders of inhumanity."

In decades of struggle against superior force, the Vietnamese revolution-aries not only endured but seemingly embraced the most extraordinary sacrifices. Theirs was a spirit resembling the martyrs' passion of the early Christians. They had not only willed themselves to suffer for their cause, but exacted the same will from the entire population under their control. By a process which no scholar of human dynamics could easily explain, Ho Chi Minh and his successors made twenty million of their countrymen into a weapon as hardened as they were, able to bear the most extreme burdens of loss and private grief without ever failing to respond to their leaders' demands.

To such men and women as the Vietnamese Communists, "liberation" might mean several things—but never the freedom of the individual human consciousness to doubt, question, dissent, argue, or search for a private path to the truth. Rather, their victory must have come as a final validation of the certainties to which they were already so fanatically committed and for which they had endured so much. They had won by force of their own fierce single-mindedness; to their ungentle hands, Vietnam's future was now committed.

Chapter 14

The Limits
of Credibility

It's time we recognized," declared Ronald Reagan, "that ours was, in truth, a noble cause." His campaign advisers had not wanted him to reawaken painful Vietnam memories. But the candidate personally penciled the phrase "noble cause" into his speech, it was said, to express his strong view that the nation should not reproach itself for the Vietnam conflict. "Let us tell those who fought in that war," he added, "that we will never again ask young men to fight and possibly die in a war our government is afraid to win." The 5,000 delegates at the Veterans of Foreign Wars 1980 convention—who had earlier broken their organization's long-standing precedent to endorse the Reagan candidacy—responded, one reporter wrote, with "sustained and boisterous cheers."

At the start of a new decade, the perception that American actions in Vietnam were a worthy effort, and that they failed not because they were misconceived but only because they were not carried out resolutely enough, seemed to respond to powerful needs in American life and institutions. It was a view that protected the reputations of the political leaders who shaped and executed those actions. It soothed military professionals who could not easily contemplate their own failure to achieve more decisive results on the Vietnamese battlefields. And by placing Vietnam in the same framework of conventional patriotic values in which Americans viewed their other wars, it reassured a troubled people that they had not, after all, forfeited the special moral standing America claimed for itself among the world's nations. Shaking off Vietnam guilt seemed essential, too, to officials and commentators who feared, not wholly without reason, that a post-Vietnam reaction was preventing the United States from acting effectively in the world.

Clearly, America could not remain forever immobilized by its memories of Vietnam. But to distort those memories was to risk equal policy errors in the future, arising from the same blindnesses that produced the Vietnam failure. For what the United States really lacked in Vietnam was not persistence but understanding—that, and the flexibility to change policies that had proven bankrupt. From start to finish, American leaders remained catastrophically ignorant of Vietnamese history, culture, values, motives, and abilities. Misperceiving both its enemy and its ally and imprisoned in the myopic conviction that sheer military force could somehow overcome adverse political circumstances, Washington stumbled from one failure to the next in the continuing delusion that success was always just ahead. This ignorance and false hope were mated, in successive administrations, with bureaucratic circumstances that inhibited admission of error and made it always seem safer to keep repeating the same mistakes rather than risk the unknown perils of a different policy.

The wounds of that experience were painful enough. With the war finally over, the revisionist belief that it was lost only because of Washington's timidity, rather than for Vietnamese reasons, was the self-infliction of still another wound—a refusal to learn the lesson that had been so expensively taught.

The delusion of Vietnam policy in the Johnson administration, at least until 1968, was that increasing American military force could not just prevent defeat of an anti-Communist regime in Saigon, but could in time discourage Hanoi from supporting the revolutionary movement in the South, and thus end the conflict. The Nixon administration's delusion was more remarkable. It was that exactly the same objective could be reached while American military force was diminishing.

A good deal of evidence suggests that when Nixon and Henry Kissinger moved into the White House in January 1969, they understood that they were inheriting a failure: that the enormous military effort in Vietnam had ballooned out of all proportion to any conceivable American interest there, and that the spectacle of a huge, expensively-armed U.S. expeditionary force thrashing about in an unavailing contest with a poor, middle-sized Asian Communist state was certainly not serving any American purpose. Vietnam was making the U.S. "look like a paper tiger," Nixon is reported to have acknowledged privately in early 1968, adding his private conclusion that "there's no way to win the war. But we can't say that, of course. In fact, we have to seem to say the opposite, just to keep some degree of bargaining leverage." Henry Kissinger too, by his own later account, believed when he took office that the war was "draining our national strength and had to be liquidated."

It is less clear how squarely Nixon or Kissinger faced the corollary of their logic: if the U.S. couldn't win, then Hanoi, presumably, couldn't lose.

Kissinger left many acquaintances with the impression that he saw a Communist victory as tolerable, as long as it was suitably delayed to keep from openly humiliating the United States. Whether or not that was his real view, he certainly thought it useful for Hanoi—and Moscow—to be encouraged to believe so; the Vietnamese Communists, he evidently felt, would surely agree to a negotiated settlement once they understood that the U.S. would not actually seek to achieve its proclaimed goal of preserving a non-Communist regime in Saigon indefinitely. It would only be necessary for Hanoi to conclude, in other words, that Washington did not really mean what it said. To the administration's early offers of "serious talks," however, the North Vietnamese simply repeated their customary demands for total withdrawal of U.S. forces and removal of the Saigon "puppet administration."

Kissinger was shocked and angry at Hanoi's apparent lack of concern for American face. And he appears to have found completely unaccountable the fact that instead of saying one thing in public and something else in private, like the straightforward Americans, Ho Chi Minh and his colleagues kept saying the same unacceptable things no matter in which channel they were conveyed. Others might have considered that perhaps the Vietnamese Communists meant what they were saying. But to Kissinger, their refusal to be duplicitous was inexplicable, even suspect. It reflected a Vietnamese style of communication which, he complained in his memoirs, "was indirect and, by American standards, devious or baffling."

Whoever was being devious, Nixon and Kissinger evidently continued to believe for some months that Hanoi would agree to what they saw as a reasonable, even generous, compromise. Journalists accompanying Nixon to his Midway Island summit with Nguyen Van Thieu in June 1969 were given the impression that he had "made up his mind to do whatever he has to do in order to extricate the United States" from the war; the president's and Kissinger's appraisal, newsmen were told, was that Hanoi and the Liberation Front were "just about ready for serious negotiations." Two months after Midway, when he began his secret meetings with North Vietnamese representatives, Kissinger "still half believed that rapid progress would be made" if the Communists could be convinced of American sincerity. As late as the end of September, Nixon expressed his hope publicly. "Once the enemy recognizes that it is not going to win its objectives by waiting us out," he told a press conference, "then the enemy will negotiate and we will end this war before the end of 1970. That is the objective we have."

In part, these expectations seem to have reflected a real belief in the generosity of their own proposals. Apparently, too, Nixon and Kissinger thought the Russians and Chinese could and would deliver a Vietnam settlement in return for American consideration on other matters. Both beliefs were wrong, and rooted in a profound misreading of the adversary U.S. forces had already fought for four frustrating years. Neither the president nor his adviser had yet grasped—possibly they never did—just how intensely the Vietnamese Communists' past had led them to mistrust diplomatic arrangements. ("Never Munich again, in whatever form," North Vietnam's Pham Van Dong vowed in 1966—a comment that not only suggested Hanoi's sense that it was duped in 1946 and 1954, but was also one of those stunning ironies so abundant in the history of the Vietnam conflict, since avoiding a new Munich was also a central theme of the American involvement there.) Nor did the new American president yet understand, apparently, the full measure of the Communists' stubborn belief in their own ultimate triumph. "I think the Americans greatly underestimate the determination of the Vietnamese people," Ho Chi Minh had said, while John F. Kennedy was still in the White House and only a few thousand American soldiers had yet been sent to Vietnam. "The Vietnamese people have always shown great determination when they were faced with a foreign invader."

Neither Kennedy nor Lyndon Johnson gave enough weight to that warning; President Nixon would prove no wiser.

When it finally dawned on Nixon and Kissinger that the North Vietnamese were not interested in a compromise on terms acceptable to the U.S., their first response was to threaten redoubled military pressure.

"Measures of great consequence and force" would be taken, Nixon warned Hanoi, if there were no significant progress in the peace talks by November 1, 1969—the anniversary of Johnson's bombing halt. Pentagon planners were assigned to prepare not just for resuming the bombing but for greatly intensifying it. But Hanoi ignored the threat, and there was no consensus within the American government either in favor of reescalation or that any thinkable military step would really prove decisive. The only certain result would be domestic political storms worse than any that had already occurred, and perhaps a split in the administration itself. As his self-imposed deadline neared, Nixon allowed himself—rather easily, it seems—to be talked out of following through on his ultimatum. Putting his hopes instead on the Vietnamization concept and on the possible helpful influence of China and the Soviet Union, he let November 1 pass with no dramatic gesture. The unilateral withdrawal of American troops, which had begun after the Midway summit in June, was now an irreversible policy.

Thereafter the administration's attempt was—in Kissinger's words—"to pursue a middle course between capitulation and the seemingly endless stalemate that we had inherited." That, surely, must be one of the most astonishing purposes ever advanced for continuing a large, costly war. What could lie "between" capitulation and stalemate, after all, except a sort of slow-motion defeat? If that was the implied object of the administration's policy, moreover, it could not be acknowledged. No American government could justify the deaths of 15,000 more American soldiers for such a purpose, not to mention the far larger loss of Asian lives. Perhaps for that reason, though Nixon and Kissinger had seemed to realize before taking office that the overriding U.S. interest was extrication from the war, once in power they seemed to shrink from the logic of their own perceptions.

There were, no doubt, varied personal and institutional reasons for this. Advocating a distasteful policy from outside the government was surely easier than actually beginning to carry it out. Too, once in the White House, Nixon and Kissinger were suddenly subject to a huge array of institutional pressures arising from a self-justifying system in which numerous reputations and bureaucratic interests could only be preserved by reaffirming existing policy. The information supplied by that system, while not entirely suppressing unwelcome truths, was certainly tilted toward justifying past decisions. As the settlement they had thought they could achieve kept eluding them, Nixon's and Kissinger's attitudes toward the North Vietnamese grew more baleful; it would have taken far more forgiving personalities than theirs not to begin wishing to punish those who denied them the political triumph both men thirsted for. Nixon and Kissinger were driven, also, by anger at domestic critics—particularly those who had participated in Johnson's war policies and thus seemed, to the new administration, outrageous hypocrites. And by temporizing, the new president and his adviser changed the choices before them perhaps more quickly than they had imagined would happen. Within less than a year of taking office, they no longer had the freedom to act as if undoing the mistakes of previous administrations; instead, they were compelled to vindicate the consequences of their own actions.

When their first hopeful overtures were rebuffed by Hanoi, Nixon and Kissinger spent the rest of their first year in office not disengaging from the war but imprisoning themselves in it, just as the Johnson administration had done. By the fall of 1969, Nixon's private comments no longer admitted the war was unwinnable or predicted its swift settlement. Instead, he was telling visitors, in words that could have been Lyndon Johnson's, "I will not be the first President of the United States to lose a war."

Like Johnson, too, Nixon came to see dissenters not as honorable critics but as witting or unwitting agents of treason. His administration soon began to recapitulate its predecessor's depressing descent into an intellectual and emotional state of siege. As criticism grew, his and Kissinger's differing insecurities seemed to bond, like two chemicals, into a new compound of angry, defensive rigidity. Within the fortress of their beliefs they listened, as the writer David Halberstam observed, "only to others who were believers." All doubts, whether arising from within the government or outside, were associated with weakness or disloyalty, and rejected.

Dissenting views were banished, too, as the result of Kissinger's bureau-cratic style. Toward any possible competitors for power or influence, Kis-singer's attitude was—no other word seems adequate—pathological. Through "incessant backbiting," as speechwriter Raymond Price called it, and by every other technique he could devise, some amazingly petty, Kissinger maneuvered to keep all rivals out of foreign policy decisions. With respect to Vietnam, he was largely successful. Among those excluded, to the extent of Kissinger's considerable ability to do so, were Defense Secretary Melvin Laird and Secretary of State William Rogers, both of whom, for various reasons, hoped to reinforce Nixon's initial impulse to extricate himself and the country from the war. Instead, Laird and Rogers were largely shut out of Vietnam decision making. More than any other U.S. endeavor of such magnitude before or since, Vietnam policy in the Nixon administration came under the utter domination of only two men, who grew steadily more impervious to any perspectives that differed from their own.

If there was a single act by which the Nixon administration closed the trap on itself, it was the decision to send U.S. forces into Cambodia at the end of April 1970.

All else they had done in Indochina, Nixon and Kissinger could claim—and the American public could agree—was a matter of cleaning up someone else's mess. But Cambodia was their own. Americans knew the half-million-man army flailing about in Vietnam was not sent there by Nixon, and they seemed willing to allow him a rather generous amount of time to extricate it in some fashion that would avoid national humiliation. They did want to see it extricated, though, and sending soldiers to fight in another Indochinese nation hardly seemed like the same thing. Neither did the strident, belligerent explanations from the White House. Cambodia could not be reconciled with Nixon's promise to end the war, and that, it seemed to me, was the real reason it generated such domestic outrage.

Anger at the Cambodian offensive was answered by an equal rage in the White House against its critics. But the more Nixon and Kissinger made the war theirs, the more damaging and painful failure appeared; and the more they had to defend their actions, the more they were compelled to assert illusory achievements and unreachable goals—like Lyndon Johnson, who was driven at last to lash out at Robert Kennedy, "We are going to win this war, and in six months all you doves will be politically dead." Nixon, too, especially after Cambodia, could only vindicate his decisions with success. That need nourished both the administration's wishful hope that Hanoi would somehow prove more flexible than it sounded and that it could be pressured into giving the U.S. an acceptable settlement, and its equally wishful overestimate of Saigon's effectiveness. Nixon's and Kissinger's expectations contradicted the realities that American influence on Viet-namese events was lessening as its military effort lessened and that there was no sustainable support for stronger measures; Hanoi, meanwhile, not the U.S., still controlled the pace and course of the war while remaining single-mindedly bent not on compromise, but victory.

Unable to resolve those contradictions, Nixon began to see the source of his frustrations in American, not Vietnamese, realities. Not Hanoi but the American antiwar movement "destroyed whatever small possibility may still have existed of ending the war in 1969," he wrote in his memoirs. His critics' motives were, in effect, treasonous. "North Vietnam cannot defeat or humiliate the United States. Only Americans can do that," he declared on November 3, 1969, in the "silent majority" speech he substituted for the military blows he had threatened. In that concept lay one significant origin of the domestic abuses that would destroy his presidency: against adversaries who sought the defeat of the United States, any tactic, however extreme, could be justified.

In Indochina, meanwhile, though he carried on the war as intensely as the domestic political environment allowed, its purposes grew steadily more indistinct. Thoughts of victory—Johnson's "coonskin on the wall"—vanished in 1968, with Tet, the bombing halt, and the start of peace talks. Thereafter the definition of American objectives vanished by degrees, like Alice's Cheshire cat.

The Nixon administration first offered mutual withdrawals of U.S. and North Vietnamese forces, but then undermined its own proposal by starting to pull American troops out unilaterally. The concept of mutual withdrawal remained in the peace plans but was blurred by an ambiguous ceasefire-in-place proposal in October 1970. Subsequently, the demand for removal of North Vietnamese troops was dropped altogether. What still prevented agreement was only Hanoi's insistence on unacceptable political terms. The U.S. had no prescription of its own for a political settlement, suggesting only that the future should be decided by problematic negotiations between the Communists and Saigon.

Thus, by 1972 the specific, concrete demands of the United States on Hanoi had been reduced to exactly one: American prisoners must be returned. Beyond that, for American purposes, the U.S. asked Hanoi only for restraint—that is, that it not take advantage of American disengagement to humiliate the United States. How much restraint, and for how long, would satisfy that condition was never clear. For South Vietnam, despite the rhetoric of alliance that was customarily used, declared U.S. objectives did not even specify the indefinite survival of a non-Communist government. Washington said only that the South Vietnamese people should choose their political future freely, and not under the threat of violence. That aim accorded with American values but unhappily not with Vietnamese conditions, or with the historical experience of civil conflicts anywhere else in the world, including America's own.

   The disconnection of American objectives from Vietnamese realities was not incidental or accidental or the quirk of personality or circumstance. It was imbedded in the most fundamental strategic concepts of the nuclear age. For the overriding consideration of American actions in Vietnam was not to bring about any specific Vietnamese outcome, but to assist what had become known as "credibility," the impression that the United States was tough enough and effective enough to meet its responsibilities in the world, defend its interests, and use its nuclear weapons for those purposes if forced to that choice. Credibility was (and remains) the psychological component of the deterrence concept, which holds that the only way to avoid using nuclear arms is to possess them in enough quantity to discourage any other possessor from using them. Similarly, if the image of credibility could be sufficiently conveyed, its reality would never have to be demonstrated. Appearances, in other words, as the writer Jonathan Schell pointed out in his book *The Time of Illusion*, "were not merely important to deterrence— they were everything. If the deterrent was used, deterrence would have failed. If the image did not do its preventive work and there was a resort to action, the whole purpose of the policy would have been defeated."
   Since credibility could never be proven, the only way to establish it was to demonstrate its attributes in all other American actions in the world, while also avoiding failures or irresolution that might contradict the desired image. Thus, once U.S. forces were committed in Vietnam, the original reasons quickly lost their primacy. What became necessary for the United States was not any given set of results that could be defined as a success, but rather a display of American determination, effectiveness, and reliability as an ally. Had this not been true, the stated U.S. war aims could not have shifted so greatly during the course of the conflict. American patience was exhausted by a war whose dominant impression was of soldiers fighting again and again over the identical terrain, without advancing or retreating or winning or losing, without any apparent relationship to any other battles before or afterward, and without visible movement toward a decisive result. But that image was an accurate metaphor for the policy. The result of the war was less important to Washington than the act of fighting it.
   The U.S. intervened in Vietnam initially with ideas of defeating a Communist insurgency, containing what it then saw as a menacing and expansionist China, and disproving theories of liberation war, among other reasons. By the time the Nixon administration came to power, however, what mattered fundamentally to the U.S. leadership was not what happened to the Vietnamese, much less to the Lao or the Cambodians, but what happened to the world's—and particularly the Soviet Union's—impression of American capability and resolve. Nixon's rapprochement with the Chinese leadership made much of the war's original rationale meaningless and thus made its actual outcome a matter of even less concern to him or to the

American government. If some form of settlement on America's minimum terms could be reached, so much the better. But even if there were no settlement, or one that failed, that would not be critically damaging either, as long as the United States was not perceived to weaken.

Defining goals in Vietnam with regard to the American image elsewhere was not invented by the Nixon administration, by any means. As long ago as the beginning of 1962 the Joint Chiefs of Staff had argued for intervention on the grounds that, along with the defense of Southeast Asia from Communism, "of equal importance" was the "psychological impact that a firm position by the United States will have on the countries of the world—both free and Communist." The real trap lay in the negative of that proposition: "A United States political and/or military withdrawal . . . would have an adverse psychological impact," the Chiefs also warned, "of even greater proportion." This, when only a few more than 2,500 American soldiers had been sent to Vietnam and only a dozen or so had been killed or wounded.

Three years later, with the Johnson administration poised to commit major ground forces to the conflict, a Defense Department official, John McNaughton, wrote what would become one of the most widely quoted passages in the *Pentagon Papers*, expressing U.S. aims in percentage terms: "70%—to avoid a humiliating U.S. defeat (to our reputation as a guarantor). 20%—to keep SVN (and the adjacent) territory from Chinese hands. 10%—to permit the people of SVN to enjoy a better, freer way of life."

Thus, when Nixon declared in 1969 that defeat in Vietnam "would result in a collapse of confidence in American leadership not only in Asia but throughout the world" and would "promote recklessness in the councils of those great powers who have not yet abandoned their goals of world conquest," he was not being at all inconsistent with previous American reasoning. The difference, though, was that by then all *other* goals of the intervention were vanishing. Thoughts of victory had evaporated, and nearly all specific demands on Hanoi were about to do the same.

Too, the more global-minded Nixon and Kissinger spun the credibility concept much farther from any local or regional circumstances than Johnson had. Though he was aware of more distant interests, Johnson normally focused on the classic assumptions of the domino theory: a failure of American resolve in Vietnam would endanger Thailand or Malaysia or, at a slightly greater distance, Indonesia and the Philippines. Nixon's and Kissinger's was a sort of super-domino theory. If America proved ineffectual in Vietnam, they thought, it would also be weakened—a "pitiful helpless giant"—in the Middle East, in strategic arms talks, everywhere on the globe, in fact, where important U.S. interests existed. Vietnam was part of a strategy in which everything was linked to the Soviet-American nuclear confrontation, and thus everything was also linked to everything else. The war there was limited, but to the extent that it was fought for the purpose of nuclear credibility, the stakes were unlimited. Vietnam was indivisible from preventing World III and saving the entire world, including the U.S., from possible nuclear blackmail and Communist totalitarianism. As Jonathan Schell put it, "the aim of upholding American credibility superseded any conclusions drawn from a simple accounting of tangible gains and tangible losses" in Vietnam.

Such an accounting would probably have dictated to most Americans— perhaps even Nixon and Kissinger—a policy of cutting losses and withdrawing. But, as Schell wrote, "The tangible objectives of limited war had been completely eclipsed by the psychological objective. The war had become an effort directed entirely toward building up a certain image by force of arms. It had become a piece of pure theatre."

For men who prided themselves on realism, Nixon and Kissinger were remarkably myopic about a world that was, inevitably, messier in reality than in strategists' theorizing. The issues of nuclear survival and their own balance-of-power design filled their vision so completely that they seemed not to grasp that other nations had other priorities. They acted as if they expected lesser nations to subordinate their own interests to superpower needs, on the ground that the safety of the entire world must override any narrow national goal.

The loss of superpower control, Nixon and Kissinger believed, was dangerous—as was explicitly spelled out by Kissinger when, speaking not of Southeast Asia but of the Mideast, he referred to the danger created when "two groups of countries with intense local rivalries . . . [are] backed by major countries, but not fully under the control of the major countries confronting each other." This, Kissinger said, "is the sort of situation that produced World War I." If world order was menaced when local rival states were "not fully under the control" of the major powers to whom they were allied, it followed that the superpowers were not only entitled but obliged to assert that control: the United States over nations under its influence and the Soviet Union over those in the Soviet orbit, in the name of the greater good of nuclear peace.

Obviously, this reasoning is not completely groundless, any more than is the concept of nuclear credibility. Regional disputes do raise the threat of possible superpower conflict. But Nixon and Kissinger characteristically saw *only* the Soviet-American dimension of all international issues. All other aspects were blotted out. On their mental map, the rest of the countries on the globe became blank spots, without individual character or history or motive, as lacking in feature and distinctive shape as squares on a chessboard.

Thus, though for years Vietnam preoccupied U.S. policy makers more than almost any other issue, the real Vietnam with all its particularities was hardly seen at all through Washington's lenses. The Vietnamese reasons for the conflict were irrelevant because they fell outside the circular logic of the American effort: the reason Americans had to prevail was because American troops and prestige were committed to doing so. Vietnam was vital because we had declared it vital, not for any attributes of its own. We were there, in a nutshell, because we were there. The war could have been anywhere else in the world and nearly all the issues and arguments, as far as Nixon and Kissinger were concerned, would have been the same. Their perspective almost demanded disregard of Vietnamese realities, in fact, for the Vietnamese circumstances so clearly failed to justify the size or cost of the American effort there. Rather than proceeding from an assessment of the actual events and the possible advantages or disadvantages of our intervention, American policy was stagecraft. Vietnam was an abstraction. And so, in the end, was the settlement that capped four excruciating years of Henry Kissinger's diplomacy.

The Paris agreement settled nothing but the issue of American involvement. The issue over which the war was fought—who would rule South Vietnam—was not resolved at all, but left to be negotiated along with other matters that all Vietnamese on both sides knew were not really negotiable. Even Secretary of State Rogers acknowledged that the political half of the agreement was "ambiguous, but deliberately ambiguous. We never pretended that it was definite and if we had attempted to work it out we would still be fighting."

The agreement was another illusion, detached from Vietnamese reality. Nor was it ever clear what Nixon or Kissinger really thought would be its outcome, except that presumably they believed it would meet their minimum condition of avoiding a clear American humiliation. The peace, in other words, was exactly what Schell called the war: a piece of theater, in which Vietnamese actors were expected to follow a script written not to resolve the conflict that was ravaging their country, but to make an American failure look like a success and thus preserve America's reputation elsewhere in the world.

After the Paris agreement, a last chance to detach America's interests from the ambitions and abilities of its Vietnamese client was squandered.

For the American public, it seems clear, disengagement had been the chief objective of the long and frustrating negotiations. The agreement disengaged American troops, to be sure. But for reasons that may have reflected sheer bureaucratic inertia as much as any process of conscious decision, the U.S. did not disengage its policy or its interests or its prestige from the conflict. Very quickly, the American leadership placed its commitment to the Saigon government above its commitment to the agreement. Once American troops were withdrawn and American prisoners recovered, Washington accepted the Thieu regime's perspectives as its own. These were an ultra-suspicious and grudging attitude toward the agreement, a fanatical unwillingness to take any but the most trivial risks in carrying it out, and a determination to inflict the most violent possible reprisals for any violation. All these quickly became U.S. attitudes as well. Both Vietnamese sides violated the truce; that was plain to anyone who bothered to look. But the U.S. supported Saigon virtually regardless of the circumstances, and thus quickly lost any standing to claim that its actions were taken impartially in defense of the agreement. South Vietnamese acts and policies remained all but indistinguishable from those that preceded the ceasefire, and so did American expressions of support.

There is no evidence of any serious American effort to restrain Thieu even from obvious violations of the ceasefire. At every opportunity, indeed, the administration expressed eagerness to supply the needed weapons and war materiel for Thieu to carry out his policies. And as the alliance was quickly recreated after Paris, so were all the American mistakes of the past. American support continued to serve Saigon's leaders as a substitute for the support of their own people. American policy makers continued to underestimate the determination and capabilities of the Communists, and to exaggerate the effectiveness and resolve of their ally. Military considerations continued to blot out all others. And U.S. aims were more beset by contradictions than ever. At the heart of the American effort, a fundamental distortion grew between the need to support a major war in Vietnam and the need—which became greater as domestic scandal embattled the Nixon White House—to speak of it in the past tense at home, since his "structure of peace" was Nixon's chief argument against impeachment.

The contradiction grew too between American goals and American influence on events. "Limited means to achieve excessive ends," said the authors of the *Pentagon Papers*, was "the old dilemma of the U.S. involvement dating from the Kennedy era." Now, with all U.S. military forces removed and legally prohibited from returning, the means were more limited than ever. But the objective of American policy did not change. As it became clear the Paris accords had not created peace after all, U.S. actions seemed to promise only endless violence. And they began to convey a morally obtuse willingness to spend Asian lives forever for nothing more than a vague concept of American prestige.

In the confusion of its own purposes, the U.S. became a hostage to Thieu's. Those, at least, were clear: victory over the Communists and the establishment of Saigon's authority over all South Vietnamese and all parts of the country. But those objectives had not been achieved by a half-million American soldiers supported by a huge fleet of American warplanes; they were still unattainable; and they commanded no support in the United States public and Congress. If Americans could be persuaded to invest any more effort and resources at all in Indochina, which was doubtful, it could only have been on the basis of upholding the compromise that was supposed to have been achieved, not to win the war for Nguyen Van Thieu. But the Nixon administration, seeming to see no distinction between those two objectives, was unable to sustain support for either.

After South Vietnam's defeat, Nixon and Kissinger, in their memoirs and other public statements, found no fault with their own policies or perceptions. Nor did they yet acknowledge Vietnamese causes for Vietnamese events. Instead, their views remained consistent with Nixon's long-ago assertion that only Americans could defeat or humiliate the United States in Vietnam.

"Congress refused to fulfill our obligations," Nixon wrote, and this "tragic and irresponsible action" was entirely to blame for the loss of the war, the human tragedies associated with the defeat, and the subsequent brutalities inflicted on their own people by the Vietnamese and Cambodian Communists. Kissinger, professing to believe that "the agreement could have worked," ascribed its failure not to any flaws of its own but to the "collapse of executive authority as a result of Watergate."

The specific charges against Congress are two: it undercut the Paris agreement by refusing to allow its enforcement by U.S. bombing, and it undermined South Vietnam's forces by reducing U.S. material support. There is no dispute that both these things happened, but the assertion that they were responsible for Saigon's defeat remains hypothetical, since no one knows what would have happened if bombing had not been prohibited, if Congress had funded military aid at the levels requested by the executive branch, or if Watergate had not weakened the Nixon presidency. Obviously such questions are not susceptible to proof or disproof. But because lingering attitudes on these matters still affect American policy choices years later, they are worth examining further.

First, bombing. To Nixon, as he later declared in his memoirs, U.S. air power was "the means to enforce the Vietnam peace agreement." Kissinger's view was the same. Yet that belief rests on the same fallacy that marked the start of the U.S. intervention all the way back at the beginning of 1965: that bombing could intimidate the North Vietnamese into giving up their war in the South. For eight years, the U.S. carried out the heaviest bombing in the history of warfare without ever convincingly demonstrating that it could achieve that purpose. Those who argue that bombing, or the threat of it, would have been any more effective in 1973 must bear a heavy, and probably impossible, burden of proof. The evidence against them is more than hypothetical, since bombing of considerable intensity did go on after the ceasefire, for a month in Laos and more than six months in Cambodia, much of it aimed at North Vietnamese supply routes and logistical bases, just as before the agreement. There is not a scrap of evidence that Hanoi's actions or intentions were in any way altered by those strikes, except that they may have perceived the bombing as evidence of American bad faith and thus as additional reason to disregard the peace agreement.

If Nixon and Kissinger really thought, when they signed the agreement, that it could be enforced by American bombers, then they were not just subscribing to a highly questionable air-power myth, but were also deceiving themselves, it seems to me, about the limits of public and congressional tolerance at home. They would have had to assume, as one American diplomat speculated to me years afterward, that "a sense of responsibility for the ceasefire" would supplant the overwhelming American desire to be done with the war, and that the sense of relief at the ceasefire would also recognize an obligation to retaliate for its violation.

Perhaps. But only a month before the ceasefire, congressional outrage at the Christmas bombing had convinced the administration that the war would be ended by legislation if it were not settled quickly. And trying to conceive what actually would have happened, in any attempt at retaliation, raises questions the air-power cultists usually do not address: How much bombing? Where? For how long? With what losses? And with how many new POWs, whose return would then have to become either the subject of another negotiation or the aim of another open-ended war?

No thinkable answers to these questions make it imaginable that bombing could have been resumed without an immediate and irresistible domestic reaction against reinvolvement—certainly not bombing on a scale significant enough (if there was such a scale) to influence Hanoi.

As to the effects of Watergate, similarly, one can only guess. But it is hard to avoid the conclusion that bombing would have been politically out of the question with or without a domestic crisis in the Nixon administration. For a time, in fact, Watergate may even have had the opposite effect. It seemed to me, in the spring and early summer of 1973, that the air campaign in Cambodia might have become a major controversy much earlier if the attention of Congress and the press had not been consumed by the Senate Watergate hearings. In any event, Congress was clearly running out of patience with the war long before Watergate was a significant issue. And the immediate cause of the ban on further military action in Indochina was not the domestic scandal but the administration's uncompromising and incomprehensible refusal to stop the Cambodian bombing before Congress acted. By forcing a showdown on what was arguably the least effective and least justified bombing of the entire war, the administration lost its last freedom of military action. If bombing was really a weapon to enforce the peace, which is doubtful, Nixon and Kissinger to a large extent knocked it out of their own hands.

With respect to U.S. support for South Vietnam's armed forces, the facts are explained, to the best of my ability, in an earlier chapter of this book. They show, I believe, that as to the real needs and the adequacy of American material supply, there are ambiguities that will probably never be resolved. Saigon's forces did suffer significant logistical shortages in the last year of the war, but those shortages were not as crippling as was later alleged in the effort to blame Congress exclusively for the defeat, and material shortages were obviously not the only or even necessarily the chief cause of the Saigon regime's military and political deterioration. The psychological damage of the aid cuts was almost certainly greater than the real. To a military and bureaucratic elite that gravely lacked self-confidence, the cuts were a symbolic act of American abandonment, a blow from which the South Vietnamese leadership never recovered. And it was the leaders, not the soldiers, who collapsed. By 1975, to be sure, ARVN soldiers were depressed and demoralized by economic hardship and by what they perceived as the loss of U.S. support, embodied first in the departure of American troops and then in the reduction of military aid. But the army did not collapse in its foxholes, or for lack of supplies. It disintegrated when its senior officers—the class of South Vietnamese society that had virtually monopolized the material and political rewards of the American alliance—deserted it.

Material shortages, in other words, may explain the decision to give up the central highlands. But they cannot explain why, once that decision was made, ranking commanders fled before their troops—a pattern that was repeated, with only a few honorable exceptions, as defenses unraveled in the rest of the country. "Those who were supposed to lead the South Vietnamese army failed in their task," a former Saigon diplomat said, and the ex-CIA official Douglas Blaufarb wrote that the "panic" of the Vietnamese leadership at the decline of U.S. support was "caused, one can only surmise, by the realization of the Vietnamese officer corps that it was really not up to its job. In the final analysis, those who had played out the charade had never been fooled by it." Only the Americans, Blaufarb added, were deceived, "and deceived largely as a result of their own blindness to the political realities of a land where they had lived and worked for so many years without learning the most elementary truths of the scene about them."

There is another question to be addressed: What would have been the result if the administration's aid proposals had prevailed?

I know of no assessment suggesting that even with the full amounts requested by the executive, South Vietnam could have done any more than preserve the battlefield deadlock for another year, after which the whole exhausting American debate would have to be replayed yet again—and in a presidential election year, at that. If there was a "failure" caused by congressional actions, there was certainly no clear corresponding "success" that could have been achieved under the administration's plans. Washington offered only a prescription for continuing the slaughter; just as for many years in the past, its policies held no promise of changing the war's fundamental reality that in order to prevail, the Communists had only to endure.

As I reexamined these matters after an interval of seven years, one memory was persistent. It was of a scene during the congressional tour early in 1975—the same visit that is said to have persuaded Thieu that he could expect no additional U.S. aid, and thus perhaps helped precipitate the decision to abandon the highlands.

It was the delegation's last day in Vietnam and its members (except for Rep. John Murtha of Pennsylvania, who told his colleagues he was afraid he wouldn't be able to control his feelings) were driven to the Communist compound at Tansonnhut to confront the North Vietnamese and Viet Cong on the matter of missing-in-action Americans. As television cameras whirred, few in the American group resisted the chance to perform. Senator Dewey Bartlett of Oklahoma theatrically waved a POW bracelet with the name of Air Force Capt. Clifford Fieszel of Tulsa, shot down in 1968. "When I go back to Oklahoma," Bartlett boomed, "what am I going to tell his wife?"

The Communists as always had their own performance to put on, however. When it was their turn in front of the cameras they were not interested in the Americans' agenda; for them, it was a chance to present their view of the "general situation," including Washington's and Saigon's many misdeeds and the consequent need to remove the Thieu government.

In increasingly testy mutual frustration, the two groups talked past each other. It was, someone said, like a match between two boxers in different rings, each sparring furiously with the air. The encounter seemed a metaphor for the huge gap in experience and comprehension that had always lain between Americans and Vietnamese. With all their posturing, the congressional visitors also reflected their background in the American political traditions of give-and-take, and they were genuinely outraged and astonished when their hosts insisted on bringing up other more intractable issues instead of responding to the single humanitarian matter of the missing-in-action. The Americans grew increasingly enraged, though perhaps not entirely aware of what was happening—which was that they were being made the studio audience in a Communist propaganda production. Ostentatiously, most of the Americans stopped listening to the harangue, and as far as I could tell none were paying attention when the North Vietnamese spokesman, a Colonel Bao, commented in passing on the broader issue they had come from Washington to examine: supplemental aid for South Vietnam.

"Hundreds of billions of dollars and a half-million United States troops have failed to subdue the Vietnamese people," Colonel Bao said. "$300 million more to Saigon can in no way change the situation." One didn't have to accept that the Vietnamese people and the Communist movement were synonymous. But it was hard not to feel that the colonel's second sentence was no more than simple truth. How quickly the end would come no one then knew. But most Vietnamese on both sides, I think, already realized what only the Americans did not yet see: that the time of American influence on Vietnamese events was running out.

It remains to ask, was there another way? The Nixon administration's critics owe somewhat more sympathy than was usually expressed at the time for the choices facing the new American president at the start of 1969.

He was not responsible for the huge American army in Vietnam or for the commitment it represented to the anti-Communist Vietnamese, who believed the U.S. was their only protection. He and Kissinger are probably right in believing that an abrupt, unilateral exit of U.S. forces at the beginning of their term would have led to chaos and tragedy from which all but the most committed leftist ideologues in the American peace movement would have recoiled. Nixon's critics are just plain wrong in contending, as some did and still do, that the terms reached four years later were available in 1969. They were not, and remained out of reach until October 1972, when Le Duc Tho for the first time offered a settlement without the removal of Nguyen Van Thieu. The policies of the first Nixon term were dictated by choices so narrow that I believe much the same course would have been followed even if Hubert Humphrey or some other moderate-to-liberal Democrat had been elected president in 1968. The circumstances simply did not seem to offer any other feasible policy than to withdraw American forces, but cautiously enough so the South Vietnamese did not completely collapse in their wake. That is what Nixon and Kissinger did, for all their belligerent rhetoric. If they could not keep emotionally detached enough to sustain a realistic view of what could ultimately be achieved in Vietnam, it was a failing to which few political leaders could have remained immune.

There is one great exception to that judgment, however, and that concerns Cambodia. The decision to make war there, unlike most others in Nixon's first term, was avoidable. It did not follow from choices made in the past. It offered significant but temporary tactical advantages at the price—which Nixon and Kissinger refused to see—of attaching the United States to a new, disastrously unprepared client, at a time when the public mood at home would not tolerate any new entanglements. Cambodia complicated all the political and diplomatic problems of the war; it forced the U.S. from 1970 on to try to find a way out of not one conflict but two, which soon put diverging demands on American policy. Ultimately Cambodia was also an important factor in the breakdown of the Paris accords. The U.S. intervention there was a military, political, strategic, and moral catastrophe for which only Richard Nixon and Henry Kissinger, not the acts of past administrations, could be held responsible.

As to the decisions of the second Nixon term, it is true, as Kissinger once wrote in a different context, that "missed opportunities unfortunately can never be proven." Yet the events following the Paris agreement leave a sense of wasted chances. Only the most insensitive or ideologically committed among American antiwar critics could feel that the U.S. had no obligation to those in Vietnam who had come to depend on American protection. But that obligation did not have to be interpreted as it was. Instead, Washington could have seen that the task of U.S. diplomacy after Paris was to force Nguyen Van Thieu to face his new realities. It took no great wisdom in 1973 to perceive that Congress would not fund Saigon's war forever. Both for South Vietnamese and American purposes it would be essential for the Vietnamese to conserve their resources, even if they had to forgo some opportunities on the battlefield. And it would also be essential that Thieu be seen in the U.S. as willing to take some risks for peace.

Had the U.S. perceived these realities more squarely it could have maintained its own standards, instead of accepting Thieu's, for measuring compliance with the ceasefire. And it could have encouraged him to decide much earlier that it was better to defend some of his territory adequately than to try to defend all of it inadequately. Giving up marginal positions much earlier, and forgoing some of the major offensive campaigns of 1973 and early 1974, might well have saved Thieu from the disastrous withdrawal he was compelled to attempt in 1975. And less grudging attitudes toward the Paris agreement might have preserved the U.S. support for which Saigon would risk nothing until it was far too late.

Instead of guiding Thieu to greater realism, however, the U.S. nourished his fantasies of support in pursuit of an unattainable victory. In doing so, Nixon and Kissinger repeatedly promised aid that could not be delivered; having disregarded Vietnamese realities, they were compelled by their own logic to disregard the nature of their own democracy as well. Different American decisions might not have changed the war's outcome, but they might have lessened the tragedy. Nixon's and Kissinger's did neither. Their failure was inevitable. The price was paid not just in Vietnamese lives but in damage to American institutions—and to the American credibility they had sought, above all else, to preserve.

On the second day of July 1976, while Americans were preparing to celebrate the Bicentennial Independence Day, Vietnamese radios broadcast the voice of Kissinger's old negotiating opponent Xuan Thuy, presenting a series of resolutions to the newly elected National Assembly in Hanoi:

"(1) Vietnam is an independent, unified and socialist country and is named the Socialist Republic of Vietnam.

"(2) The national flag of the Socialist Republic of Vietnam is a red flag with a five-pointed gold star in the middle.

"(3) The national emblem of the Socialist Republic of Vietnam is round in shape, has a red ground with ears of rice framing a five-pointed gold star in the middle and with half a cogwheel and the words 'Socialist Republic of Vietnam' at the bottom.

''(4) The capital of the Socialist Republic of Vietnam is Hanoi.

''(5) The national anthem of the Socialist Republic of Vietnam is the song 'Tien Quan Ca' ('March of the Army').''

After the resolutions were read, Politburo member Hoang Van Hoan asked for a show of hands to approve them. They were adopted unanimously. There followed a series of other votes for a committee to draft a new constitution and for the organization and membership of the new government. And then listeners heard the quavering voice of 87-year-old President Ton Duc Thang. After presenting Prime Minister Pham Van Dong to the Assembly, the aging Thang intoned:

''The Government of the Socialist Republic of Vietnam hereby replaces the Government of the Democratic Republic of Vietnam and the Provisional Revolutionary Government of the Republic of South Vietnam.''

Mingled with the earth of unified Vietnam—in the red dirt of the Saigon plain, in the muck of the Mekong tributaries and the countless canals of the delta, among the boulders clinging to remote mountainsides and the roots that writhed around them, in bomb craters or graves scooped from the pebbled coast—were the ashes of numberless cremated villages and the bones of perhaps two million human beings. Shot, crushed, burned to death, shredded by bombs or shellfire; soldiers and civilians, adults and children; just how many, in three decades of fighting, would never be exactly counted. As after all wars, it was for the victors to state the purpose: the achievement, at last, of national unity and independence. What those abstractions might have meant to the dead, no one could ask, or know.

Notes

A Comment on Sources

An invaluable source for this book was the series of quarterly assessments of the Republic of Vietnam Armed Forces (RVNAF) prepared by the U.S. Defense Attache Office in Saigon between October 1973 and June 1975. In the Notes, these are cited as DAO Assessments or, in the case of the last in the series, DAO Final Assessment. These reports, each containing several hundred pages, summarize the operations of every major South Vietnamese unit during each reporting period and thus provide a basic tactical history of the war, while also giving innumerable other details of South Vietnamese military affairs and assessments of Communist military actions and apparent intentions. The Final Assessment, compiled after South Vietnam's surrender, contains significant material on the planning and execution of the American evacuation of Saigon, including the written recollections of the Defense Attache and a number of other U.S. military officers and civilian officials who were associated with that event. Except for a few brief passages still deemed sensitive, all of these reports are now declassified and available to researchers at the U.S. Army Center of Military History in Washington.

A second basic source for military events in 1973–75 is Col. William E. Le Gro's *Vietnam from Ceasefire to Capitulation.* Colonel Le Gro was DAO's chief intelligence officer and prepared this history for the Center of Military History with the use of his own notes and files and DAO situation reports, intelligence summaries, message files, and other official records.

Colonel Le Gro's work is one of a series produced by the center and called the Indochina Monographs. All the other volumes in the series were written not by Americans but by former high-ranking South Vietnamese, Cambodian, or Lao military officers. These authors were also given access to official U.S. records while preparing their studies, which deal with various aspects of the Indochina conflict from a perspective that was rarely considered or appreciated by Americans during the war. A number of them are cited in this book.

Also on file at the Center of Military History are the regular monthly or biweekly situation reports by U.S. representatives in South Vietnam's provincial headquarters and the "Quarterly Regional Assessments of Community Security and Local Government," which were prepared by the four U.S. consulates-general in South Vietnam. Due to various organizational rearrangements, the province situation reports appear under several different titles, but for the sake of simplicity they are cited uniformly in the Notes as Province Reports. They comment on security issues, local government and political affairs, economic developments, and numerous other matters.

Along with the regular situation reports are various others, including end-of-tour reports by American officials and assessments that were prepared on specific topics. These are cited in the Notes by full title but are not listed separately in the Bibliography.

Tape recorded interviews from the Marine Corps Oral History Collection furnished a mass of vivid and significant detail on the voyages of refugee ships and on the Saigon and Phnom Penh evacuations. In the Notes, these are cited as USMC Interviews, followed by the number corresponding to the appropriate entry in the Oral History name index and by the respondent's name. These tapes are available through the Marine Corps Historical Center in Washington. The center also made available written transcripts of interviews with several members of the embassy and consular marine security guard detachments. These are unnumbered but are identified in the Notes by the names of the respondents.

In those parts of the book having to do with the fall of Cambodia, there are a number of references to a series called "Khmer Reports." These were weekly situation reports sent to the State Department from the U.S. embassy in Phnom Penh. Those reports for the period March 4 through April 8, 1975, summarizing military and political developments as the Khmer Republic approached its final collapse, have been declassified and are included in the Declassified Documents Reference System of the Carrollton Press. (The appropriate entry numbers for the Carrollton *Quarterly Catalogue* are given in the Bibliography.)

Beside these government records, there is another category of sources that can be considered semiofficial. Examples are the long three-part account of the Saigon evacuation in the *Marine Corps Gazette*, written by the marine ground force commander, and the published history of the U.S. delegation to the Joint Military Commission in Saigon, written by the delegation's official historian. In that they closely parallel official documents and were based on official reports prepared by the same authors, these have the nature of official accounts. I have indicated in the Bibliography which sources are of this type.

A brief explanation of the use of Communist source material may also be useful to the reader. Communist documents, statements, and broadcasts are cited from a large variety of sources, including the official Vietnamese and Chinese news agencies; the

English-language *Vietnam Courier* and the pictorial magazine *Vietnam*, both published in Hanoi; the *Peking Review* and the Hong Kong-based Communist newspaper *Ta Kung Pao*; translations from two radio-monitoring services, the U.S. Foreign Broadcast Information Service and the British Broadcasting Corporation's Summary of World Broadcasts; and translations by the U.S. mission in Saigon that were distributed in either of two publications, *Vietnam Documents and Research Notes* or *Principal Reports from Communist Sources*, or in some cases were reproduced and distributed as separate handouts.

In all cases, the source cited in this book is that actually used, which may not be the original source. For example, a commentary may have originated as an editorial in the Communist party newspaper, *Nhan Dan*, but if I used the version distributed by the Vietnam News Agency, the citation in the Notes will be to VNA. If for any reason a document's origin is pertinent, it is made clear either in the text or by including the full title in the citation. Since most Communist statements and commentaries were carried in all print and broadcast media, and often in the media of other Communist countries as well, a researcher will not necessarily have to track down the precise source cited here in order to find a specific statement. Normally it will also exist, though perhaps with some slight variations in translation, in the files of any of the official Communist news agencies or in the reports for the appropriate dates of the Foreign Broadcast Information Service or the Summary of World Broadcasts.

Part 3 of the Bibliography lists all congressional documents that are cited in the Notes. These are grouped by committee and then numbered in chronological order. In the Notes, for the sake of brevity, only the committee name and the appropriate number are given; thus a reader will have to refer to the Bibliography to find the actual name of the hearing or report cited.

There are no citations in the Notes for speeches or press conferences by the president, his national security adviser, or the secretary of state. These can easily be found in contemporary news accounts or in such widely accessible reference works as the *Weekly Compilation of Presidential Documents* or the *Department of State Bulletin*.

The following abbreviations are used in the Notes:

DAO —Defense Attache Office
DPSA —Deputy Province Senior Adviser
FBIS —Foreign Broadcast Information Service
JCS —Joint Chiefs of Staff
NCNA—New China News Agency (Peking)
PSA —Province Senior Adviser
SWB —Summary of World Broadcasts
VNA —Vietnam News Agency (Hanoi)

Chapter 1.
"THIS WAR WILL NEVER END"
Page
8. Nolde letter: *New York Times*, Jan. 29, 1973.
9. Thieu speech: FBIS, Jan. 29, 1973.
11. "Initiated a new war": Province Report, Lam Dong, Jan. 1973.
11. Trang Bang incident, ceasefire at Quang Tri: *New York Times*, Jan. 29, 1973; also Shaplen, "Letter from Vietnam," Feb. 24, 1973, p. 106.
12. "War appeared": *Time*, Feb. 12, 1973.
13. "War of aggression": "Appeal of South Vietnam N.F.L. Central Committee and R.S.V.N. P.R.G.," NCNA, Jan. 28, 1973.
13. "Our children": Isaacs, *No Peace*, p. 166.

Chapter 2.
THE PARIS AGREEMENT

17. "Our northern armed forces": "Document Analyzing the Twentieth VWP [Vietnam Workers Party] Central Committee Plenum Resolution," in U.S. Embassy, Saigon, *Principal Reports*, no. 11, Aug. 10, 1972, p. 11.
17. Exempt classes called up: Jenkins, *Giap and the Seventh Son*, p. 2.
17. Entire regiment surrendered: Turley and Wells, "Easter Invasion," p. 22; Truong, *Easter Offensive*, p. 30.
17. "No longer developing": *Vietnam Courier* (Hanoi), July, 1972.
17. "Fell short": Porter, *Peace Denied*, p. 297.
18. Tran Van Tra comment: Reuter, Mar. 16, 1973.
18n. Sorties against the North: House Judiciary Committee [1], pp. 97–98.
18n. "Questions cannot be ignored": House Armed Services Committee [1], p. 47.
18. Considered calling off the summit: Nixon, *RN*, pp. 600–602.
19. Air power reinforced: Doglione et al., *Air Power*, pp. 15–30.
19. Troops in Thailand: House Foreign Affairs Committee [1], p. 47.
20. "Air defense tasks": "Document Analyzing the Twentieth VWP Central Committee Plenum Resolution," pp. 11–12.
20. "Serious escalation": Porter, *Peace Denied*, pp. 112–13.
20–21. *Nhan Dan* commentaries: VNA, May 18 and 20 and June 2, 1972; *Vietnam Courier* (Hanoi), Sept. 1972.
20–21n. Vietnamese felt betrayed: Isaacs, *No Peace*, p. 173; Fall, *Two Vietnams*, p. 196, and *Vietnam Witness*, p. 72; *Pentagon Papers*, House Armed Services Committee ed., bk. 1, pt. 3–C, pp. 1–2, 19, 22, 33; Burchett, *At the Barricades*, pp. 180–84; Lancaster, "Power Politics at Gene-

va," pp. 125–44; Turner, *Vietnamese Communism*, pp. 89–93.
23. "Ample evidence": Collins, *South Vietnamese Army*, p. 122.
24. "We did not change our views": House Select Committee on Intelligence [1], pt. 5, pp. 1657–58.
24. Johnson's question: *Pentagon Papers*, New York Times ed., p. 567.
26. "It had become a symbol": Truong, *Easter Offensive*, p. 67; marine casualties, p. 71; "dogs ate pebbles," p. 167.
26. 200 fighter-bombers: Turley and Wells, "Easter Invasion," p. 29.
27n. Desertions: Khuyen, *The RVNAF*, pp. 151–52; 'RVNAF Desertion Rates," *Southeast Asia Analysis Report*, June-July, 1971, p. 12.
28. "Nonaggression treaty": Kissinger, *White House Years*, p. 1063; China would not be "enmeshed," p. 1052.
28. Chinese reassured Hanoi: *China News Analysis* (Hong Kong), Dec. 17, 1971, p. 1.
29. Not a word appeared: Hedrick Smith, *The Russians*, pp. 349–50.
30. "Attentive attitude": Kissinger, *White House Years*, p. 1303.
30. Le Duc Tho sketch: *New York Times*, Jan. 24, 1973; U.S. Embassy, Saigon, *Vietnam Documents*, no. 114, pt. 1, July 1973, pp. 26–28.
31. Nixon predicted: Nixon, *RN*, p. 390.
31. "Too egotistical": Kissinger, *Years of Upheaval*, p. 26.
31. "Miserable little country": Kissinger, *White House Years*, p. 1120.
31. "Third-class peasant state": Kalb and Kalb, *Kissinger*, p. 68.
32. Kissinger describes Nixon: Kissinger, *White House Years*, p. 1329.
32. Nixon's version: Nixon, *RN*, p. 721.
32. Pham Van Dong speech: VNA, Feb. 4, 1972.
33. "About as positive": Kissinger, *White House Years*, p. 1313.
33–34. Hanoi changed signals: VNA, Aug. 31 and Sept. 1, 1972; P.R.G. statement, ibid., Sept. 11, 1972.
34. Next meeting "decisive": Kissinger, *White House Years*, p. 1337; Hanoi promised "constructive spirit," p. 1340.
34. Saigon's anxiety: Baltimore *Sun*, Sept. 29 and 30, Oct. 6, 1972.
35. "Unfulfillable" demand: Kissinger, *White House Years*, p. 1314; U.S. "did not pursue," p. 1315; possible amphibious landings, p. 1324; "infuriating style," p. 1323; "Vietnamese opaqueness," p. 1326; Haig's report, p. 1339.
35–36. Hanoi's draft, timetable agreed: "Statement of D.R.V.N. Government on State of Negotiations," VNA, Oct. 26, 1972.

36–37. "We have done it": Kissinger, *White House Years,* p. 1345; advised Thieu to seize territory, pp. 1350, 1357; two matters remained unresolved, p. 1355; proposed texts transmitted, p. 1365; aides were hopeful, p. 1366.

37. Both sides "agreed to be responsible": VNA, Nov. 2, 1972.

37. Like a lumberjack: Sheehan, *Arabs, Israelis, and Kissinger,* p. 203.

37. Giap remarked: Dommen, *Conflict in Laos,* p. 44.

38. "Clashes with our allies": Kissinger, "Vietnam Negotiations," p. 225n.

39. Kissinger produced an English copy: Don, *Endless War,* pp. 201–2; Hinh, *Vietnamization and the Ceasefire,* p. 117; Szulc, "Behind the Ceasefire Agreement," p. 55. This was also confirmed to the author by one of the participants in the meeting.

39. "Like a professor": Goodman, *Lost Peace,* p. 132.

39. Typewritten document: Hinh, *Vietnamization and the Ceasefire,* p. 118.

39–40. Nixon's message to Dong: Nixon, *RN,* p. 695.

40. Hanoi accepted American formulations: Kissinger, *White House Years,* p. 1380.

40. "Satisfied all points": "Statement of D.R.V.N. Government on State of Negotiations," VNA, Oct. 26, 1972; Kissinger, *White House Years,* p. 1388.

41. Proposals of May and October, 1971: Kissinger, *White House Years,* pp. 1488–90.

42. "Dependent on the U.S. for policies": Khuyen, *The RVNAF,* p. 385.

42. "No matter how well-intentioned": Hinh and Tho, *South Vietnamese Society,* pp. 70, 168.

43. "Were you to find the agreement": Nixon, *RN,* p. 700; Nixon had already instructed, p. 697; also Kissinger, *White House Years,* pp. 1377, 1382.

43. "Everyone is tired": Thien, "Light at the Tunnel's End?" p. 35.

44. Thieu rejects agreement: Don, *Endless War,* pp. 208–9; Fallaci, *Interview With History,* pp. 50–56; Kissinger, *White House Years,* pp. 1385–87.

44. "Difficulties in Saigon": Kissinger, *White House Years,* pp. 1388–89; Nixon rejects bombing halt, pp. 1389–90; last meeting with Thieu, pp. 1390–91.

45. Broadcast from Hanoi: "Statement of D.R.V.N. Government on State of Negotiations," VNA, Oct. 26, 1972.

46. Lodge cable: *Pentagon Papers, New York Times* ed., p. 209.

46. Thieu's statements: Baltimore *Sun,* Oct. 29 and Nov. 1, 1972.

47. "Thieu owes his existence": VNA, Nov. 2, 1972.

47–48. Enhance and Enhance Plus: Records supplied by the Defense Department to Rep. Paul N. McCloskey, Jr., of California—made available to the author by Rep. McCloskey—show the following major items shipped in the Enhance programs:

ENHANCE (May–October 1972)

39 175-mm guns (3 battalions)
120 M48A3 tanks
37 CH-47 helicopters
32 UH-1H helicopters
2 F-5E jet fighters
5 F-5A jet fighters
48 A-37 jet fighters
23 AC-119K fixed-wing gunships
12 C-119G maritime patrol aircraft
14 RC-47 photo reconnaissance planes
23 EC-47 electronic reconnaissance planes
28 C-7 transport planes
100 TOW antitank weapons
32 twin-mounted 40-mm antiaircraft guns
96 quad-mounted .50 caliber machineguns
3 high-speed endurance cutters
4 fast patrol craft

ENHANCE PLUS (October–November 1972)

28 A-1 fighters
90 A-37 jet fighters
116 F-5A jet fighters
32 C-130 transport planes
277 UH-1H helicopters
72 M48A3 tanks
117 M-113 armored personnel carriers
8 M-706 armored cars
44 105-mm howitzers
12 155-mm howitzers
1,302 2½-ton trucks
424 5-ton dumptrucks

Figures that are approximately the same but not identical are in Le Gro, *Ceasefire to Capitulation,* p. 17.

48. Equipment of Korean divisions: Senate Foreign Relations Committee [8], p. 8.

48. "Memorandum of Understanding": Dillard, *Sixty Days,* p. 69; American negotiators' attitude, pp. 60–61, 176.

48. "If we had been giving": Goodman, *Lost Peace,* p. 147.

49. Bui Diem comment: Hosmer, Kellen, and Jenkins, *Fall of South Vietnam,* p. 33.

49. Air force inventory: Momyer, *Vietnamese Air Force,* p. 61; "beyond their ability," pp. 55–56.

49. $1,000 a week: *New York Times,* Feb. 25, 1974.

49–50. Nixon's Nov. 14 message: *New York Times,* May 1, 1975.

50. South Vietnamese proposal "preposterous": Kissinger, *White House Years,* p. 1417.

50. Le Duc Tho statement: NCNA, Nov. 19, 1972.

50. Hanoi's spokesman: Reuter, Dec. 17, 1972; handshake with a butler, ibid., Dec. 11, 1972.
50. Duc delivered a letter: Don, *Endless War,* p. 215.
50. "Face reality": Nixon, *RN,* p. 724.
50–51. Thieu's speech: FBIS, Dec. 12, 1972.
51. Nov. 5 Liberation Front declaration: U.S. Embassy, Saigon, *Principal Reports,* no. 19, Nov. 10, 1972, pp. 10–11.
51. Giai Phong agency declared: NCNA, Nov. 19, 1972.
51. "Legitimate demand": VNA, Dec. 13, 1972.
51. "Without delay and without change": Reuter, Dec. 17, 1972.
52. Decree Law 020: State Department translation. Summarized in U.S. embassy telegram Saigon 5239, Apr. 22, 1974.
52. Criminal charges against detainees: letter from Ray A. Meyer, U.S. embassy, to Jerry M. Tinker, staff consultant, Senate Judiciary Subcommittee; in *Congressional Record,* June 4, 1973, p. 17842.
52. P.R.G. propaganda: NCNA, Dec. 4 and 15, 1972; *Vietnam Courier* (Hanoi), Dec. 1972.
52. 20,000 arrests: *Far Eastern Economic Review,* Dec. 23, 1972.
52. Embassy officer reported: Meyer to Tinker.
53. "A mere scheme": VNA, Dec. 17, 1972.
53. Vietnamese were stalling: Kissinger, *White House Years,* p. 1440.
54–56, 55n. Bombs began falling: McCarthy and Allison, *Linebacker II,* pp. 42–43; "your target," p. 50; "targets in a shooting gallery," p. 59; Maj. Ashley's mission, pp. 59–64; Dec. 29 raids, pp. 124–25; "a long four minutes," p. 47; "don't drop," p. 50; first B-52 loss, pp. 33–35; "no sweat" orders were changed, p. 30.
54. Hanoi evacuations: U.S. Embassy, Saigon, *Principal Reports,* no. 21, Dec. 11, 1972, p. 16, and no. 22, Dec. 21, 1972, p. 7; Burchett, *Grasshoppers and Elephants,* p. 163.
55. Aircraft losses: House Appropriations Committee [2], p. 5.
55n. First B-52 mission: Kritt, "B-52 Arc Light Operations," p. 149.
55. "War by tantrum": Nixon, *RN,* p. 738. The columnist was James Reston.
55. 1,000 fighter-bomber sorties: Van Staaveren, "Air War against North Vietnam," p. 98
56. Embassies damaged, Polish ship hit: Reuter, Dec. 20 and 22, 1972; *Facts on File,* Dec. 24–31, 1972, p. 1033.
56. Bach Mai hospital: VNA, Dec. 23, 1972; *Vietnam Courier* (Hanoi), Feb. 1973.
56. "Several thousand feet away": House Appropriations Committee [2], p. 40; Adm. Moorer comment, p. 51.

56. Civilian deaths: *Vietnam Courier* (Hanoi), Mar. 1973; Burchett, *Grasshoppers and Elephants,* pp. 166–67.
56–57. International reactions: *Newsweek,* Jan. 8, 1973; *Time,* Jan. 1 and 8, 1973; *New York Times,* Dec. 29, 1972; Reuter, Dec. 20, 22, and 29, 1972.
57. Hamburg casualties: Majdalany, *Fall of Fortress Europe,* p. 253. After British-American raids on Hamburg in July 1943, German authorities listed 30,482 persons known dead, 17,372 missing and presumed dead, and 900,000 homeless.
57. Senator Scott comment: *Facts on File,* Dec. 17–23, 1972, p. 1013.
58. Adm. Moorer claimed: House Appropriations Committee [2], p. 16.
58. "Preferably with your cooperation": Nixon, *RN,* p. 737.
58–59. Nixon's Jan. 5 letter: *New York Times,* May 1, 1975.
59. Jan. 16 letter: Nixon, *RN,* pp. 749–50.
59. Nixon demanded "positive" answer: Hosmer, Kellen, and Jenkins, *Fall of South Vietnam,* p. 30; also Kissinger, *White House Years,* pp. 1469–70.
60. "Kissinger promised me": Reuter, Feb. 1, 1975.
60. Tran Van Lam recalled: Warner, *Certain Victory,* p. 5.
63. "The most arduous problem": NCNA, May 13, 1972.
64. Burchett account: Burchett, *Grasshoppers and Elephants,* pp. 161–62.
65. A-37s replaced A-1s: "Defense Rebuttal of Rep. Aspin Claim Re Aircraft to SVN," Secretary of Defense message to DAO Saigon, 141358Z, June 1974.
65. U.S. promised to withdraw civilians: State Department, "Interpretations of the Agreement," p. 332.
65. 74 dead Americans returned: Baltimore *Sun,* July 22, 1981.
65–66. Prisoner exchanges: "Note of the Ministry of Foreign Affairs of the Republic of Vietnam Concerning the Exchange of Prisoners: Saigon, March 12, 1974," in *Vietnam Foreign Affairs Review,* no. 2, 1974, p. 64; also "ICCS Accomplishments," an unclassified U.S. embassy memorandum of June 26, 1974.
66. State Department's legal interpretation: State Department, "Interpretations of the Agreement," p. 332.
68. "An agreement in principle": ibid., p. 329.
68. Le Duan on "transitional phases": Turner, *Vietnamese Communism,* p. 262; "a time for us to advance," p. 271.
69. Nixon "vacillated": Zumwalt, *On Watch,* p. 399. The comment is attributed to Alexander Haig.

69. Kissinger met with Burchett: Burchett, *At the Barricades*, pp. 277–78.
69. Kissinger told Chou En-lai: Szulc, "Behind the Ceasefire Agreement," p. 44.
70. "The agony of four years": Kissinger, *White House Years*, p. 1470.

Chapter 3.
CEASEFIRE

71. Civilians killed, houses destroyed in Tay Ninh: Province Report, Tay Ninh, Jan. 1973.
78. Sa Huynh battle: Le Gro, *Ceasefire to Capitulation*, p. 25; hamlets seized, pp. 26, 31.
79. Situation reports: Province Reports, Gia Dinh, Phu Yen, Lam Dong, Chuong Thien, Jan. 1973.
79. "Higher than 1972": DAO Assessment, 4th Quarter FY1973, chap. 2, p. 1.
80. Infiltration charges: *New York Times*, Mar. 14, 1973; Shaplen, "Letter from Indochina," June 2, 1973, p. 44
80. "Not later than the 27th": Le Gro, *Ceasefire to Capitulation*, p. 31.
80. Classified report: General Accounting Office, *Stronger Controls Needed*, pp. 37, 41.
80–81. "Because of the Communists": FBIS, Jan. 30, 1973.
81. "Fascist militarist forces": U.S. Embassy, Saigon, *Principal Reports*, no. 26, Feb. 23, 1973, p. 7.
81. "Not to break the deadlock": Shaplen, "Letter from Indochina," June 2, 1973, p. 46.
81. Saigon's, Communist peace plans: Texts are in Porter, *Vietnam: Definitive Documentation*, 2:629–33.
81. Communist rationale: D.R.V.N. Foreign Ministry, "One Year of Implementation of the Paris Agreement on Vietnam," in FBIS Supplement no. 5, Feb. 4, 1974.
82–83. Directive just before the ceasefire: COSVN Directive 02/CT/73, "On Policies Related to the Political Settlement and Ceasefire," Jan. 19, 1973; in U.S. Embassy, Saigon, *Vietnam Documents*, no. 113, June 1973, pp. 9, 12, 14–15.
82–83. Dong's report: U.S. Embassy, Saigon, *Principal Reports*, no. 27, Feb. 27, 1973, pp. 5, 15, 17–18.
83. 80 civilians killed in Hong Ngu: Le Gro, *Ceasefire to Capitulation*, p. 45; "Communist activities in the delta," p. 35.
83–84. "Not fully assessed": COSVN Directive 03/CT/73, Mar. 1973, in Porter, *Vietnam: Definitive Documentation*, 2:617–20.
84. "End of the second war": Le Gro, *Ceasefire to Capitulation*, p. 32.
84. 6,600 killed: DAO Assessment, 2nd Quarter FY1975, chap. 2, pp. 32–33.

86, 86n. "Attempts to eliminate": ibid., 4th Quarter FY1973, chap. 1, p. 9; 1st Division "far from effective," chap. 5, p. 14.
86n. Airborne casualties: Le Gro, *Ceasefire to Capitulation*, p. 61.
87. "Permissive environment": Momyer, *Vietnamese Air Force*, p. 63.
92. P.O.W. exchanges: "Press Communique of the Republic of Vietnam Military Delegation to the Two-Party Joint Military Commission," March 26, 1974; in *Vietnam Foreign Affairs Review*, no. 2, 1974, p. 68. Slightly different figures are in "ICCS Accomplishments."
92. "Humane and lenient policy": VNA, Mar. 4, 1973.
93–96. Weyand warned: Dillard, *Sixty Days*, p. 17; sites proposed for Communist teams, p. 115; Ban Me Thuot incident, pp. 117–18; U.S. proposed to Saigon, pp. 45–46; "an impossible task," pp. 177–78.
97. "Im cho coi sao" and "I Can't Control Shit": Herrington, "Third Indochina War," p. 89.
98. Sharp, Gauvin comments: *International Perspectives* (Ottawa), May–June 1973, pp. 14–15 and 16–17.

Chapter 4.
"AN ARMY WITH A COUNTRY"

102–3. "Soldiers in ARVN": letter from Claudia A. Krich, codirector, American Friends Service Committee, Quang Ngai Province, Feb. 26, 1975, to Rep. Paul N. McCloskey, Jr. and Sen. Dewey F. Bartlett. Made available to the author by Rep. McCloskey.
103. Police "in mortal fear": "Advisory Team 16 Policy Papers" (Quang Tin Province), tab A, no. 4, Mar. 22, 1972.
103. ARVN officers chosen: Lung, *Strategy and Tactics*, p. 90.
103. Not dependent on salaries: DAO Assessment, 4th Quarter FY1974, chap. 12, p. 6.
103. Officers' origins: Collins, *South Vietnamese Army*, p. 76.
103. "Government of 'them' ": Blaufarb, *Counterinsurgency Era*, p. 272.
103–4. "Traditional remote attitude": "Assessment of Local Government Services in Military Region I," U.S. Consulate-general, Da Nang, June 18, 1974.
104–5. "ARVN a political cabal": Blaufarb, *Counterinsurgency Era*, p. 245; Americans "were convinced," p. 277; "when a regime relies," pp. 303–4.
105. "Like a planet": Dinh, "Vietnam 1974," p. 441.

106. "Not a massive police operation": *New York Times*, Aug. 18, 1974.

106. Statistic publicized by Chan Tin: House Foreign Affairs Committee [4], pp. 113–20.

106. Martin insisted: Graham A. Martin letter to Sen. George S. McGovern, in *Congressional Record*, Aug. 2, 1974, p. 26593; Senate Foreign Relations Committee [7], p. 416.

106. "There are political prisoners": House Foreign Affairs Committee [3], pp. 58, 60.

106–7. Law against "pro-Communist neutralism": House Government Operations Committee [3], p. 205.

107. An Tri procedures: Decree Law 020/72, State Department translation; also U.S. embassy Airgram A-107, June 1973.

107. American attitude: "An Analysis of Province Security Committees," n.d. Supplied by Rep. McCloskey.

107. Military court procedures: *New York Times*, Aug. 18, 19, 20, 1974.

107. Trials "far from fair": Lung, *Strategy and Tactics*, p. 46.

108. "Torture was employed": Blaufarb, *Counterinsurgency Era*, p. 213.

108. Quakers reported: *Congressional Record*, June 4, 1973, p. 17845.

108. "Security forces are penetrated": CIA, "Stocktaking in Indochina," p. 8.

108. 20,000 "eliminations": House Government Operations Committee [3], p. 183.

108. "Thought of by geniuses": Santoli, *Everything We Had*, p. 200.

108. "Marginally effective": "Phoenix," *Southeast Asia Analysis Report*, June–July 1971, p. 1; most were not party members, p. 3.

108. State Department officer's assessment: Cooper, "Phung Hoang Program."

109. 90 percent of eliminations were battle casualties: House Government Operations Committee [3], p. 206; Blaufarb, *Counterinsurgency Era*, p. 275.

109. "The most fundamental problem": Province Report, An Giang, Jan. 1973.

110. Customs a "cesspool": House Government Operations Committee [4], p. 11.

110. Going rate to avoid the draft: Lewy, *America in Vietnam*, p. 201.

110. Price list: "Observation of PSA Vinh Binh," memo for Depcords M.R. IV, Oct. 27, 1972.

110–11. "Pilots are robbers": Herrington, "Third Indochina War," p. 173; Military Security Service report, p. 71.

111–12. Similar cases in Navy: Le Gro, *Ceasefire to Capitulation*, pp. 71–72.

112. "Selling positions is commonplacc": DAO Assessment, 2nd Quarter FY1974, chap. 12, p. 15; "cronyism," ibid., 4th Quarter FY1973, chap.

5, p. 53; 20,000 were paying bribes, ibid., 4th Quarter FY1974, chap. 12, p. 20.

112. Senate investigators' report: Senate Foreign Relations Committee [8], p. 5.

112. "Flower soldiers" in Delta: Hosmer, Kellen, and Jenkins, *Fall of South Vietnam*, p. 120.

112. "House leaks": Herrington, "Third Indochina War," p. 69.

112–13. Gen. Quang's wife: Westmoreland, *Soldier Reports*, pp. 243–44.

113. Penalty caused "a sensation": Khuyen, *The RVNAF*, p. 359.

114–15. Thieu's early life: *Current Biography Yearbook* 1968, pp. 397–400; Fallaci, *Interview With History*, p. 70; *New York Times*, Oct. 25, 1972 and Apr. 21, 1975; Sully, *We the Vietnamese*, p. 175.

115–16. Generals "the most important institution": U.S. embassy telegram Saigon 4312, June 21, 1965, DDRS No. (79)455C.

116. 1967 elections: Joiner, *Politics of Massacre*, p. 149.

116–17. "Thousands of farm boys": Grant, "Vietnam without GI's," p. 21.

117. "A young man entering ARVN": End of Tour Report, DPSA Vinh Binh, Aug. 19, 1971.

117. "Bombing, defoliation": Parker, "Vietnam: War That Won't End," p. 360.

117. "Minimal supplies of rice": Young, "Political Attitudes in Binh Duong."

117. 50,000 Communists "rallied": Hinh, *Vietnamization and the Ceasefire*, p. 86.

117. Statistics showed; "virtually disappeared": "A GVN People's Army," *Southeast Asia Analysis Report*, Aug.–Oct. 1971, p. 7.

117–18. "Threat is containable," "raiding parties": Thompson, "Successful End to the War," p. 460; "a degree of security," p. 462.

118. "The war is settled": Heinl, "Vietnam War Has Been Won."

118. "Lower level VC": End of Tour Report, DPSA Vinh Binh, Aug. 19, 1971.

118. "Numerical losses": MAC-V, Directorate of Intelligence, "Big Mack Evaluation," pp. 6–7.

118. "Communists chose not to contest": CIA, "Stocktaking in Indochina," pp. 13–14.

119. "Topsy-turvey": Young, "Political Attitudes in Binh Duong."

119–20. "Half-hearted democracy": Hinh and Tho, *Vietnamese Society*, p. 166.

120. Government tried cadre concept: Blaufarb, *Counterinsurgency Era*, pp. 225–31.

120. "Vietnamese in the street": *Pentagon Papers*, House Armed Services Committee ed., bk. 7, IV.C.9.(b), p. 59.

121. Thieu worried the Americans would overthrow him: Hosmer, Kellen, and Jenkins, *Fall of South Vietnam*, pp. 69, 81.

121. "Not giving up real estate": Momyer, *Vietnamese Air Force*, p. 58.

Chapter 5.
THE AMERICANS LEAVE (1)

125. Truck loaded with coffins: *Far Eastern Economic Review*, Apr. 9, 1973.
125. "UUUU": Cincinnatus, *Self-Destruction*, p. 44.
126. "Tactical mobility, devastating firepower": *Logistics Review, U.S. Army Vietnam*, pp. I–9, I–10.
126. U.S. and Communist munitions expenditure: Defense Department fact sheet. Made available to the author by Rep. McCloskey.
126n. "Where the enemy might be"; 1966 study: Enthoven and Smith, *How Much Is Enough?* pp. 305–6.
126n. Gen. Mildren comment; army's study observed: Ott, *Field Artillery*, pp. 187–88.
126. 56-to-1 ratio in 1974: McCloskey, "North Vietnam-South Vietnam Confrontation," p. 6777.
126–27. "An opponent that walked": Komer, "Bureaucracy Does Its Thing," p. 48.
127. "Ineptitude at the top": Cincinnatus, *Self-Destruction*, p. 10; Samson's body count, p. 86.
127. Generals were polled: Kinnard, *War Managers*, pp. 74–75.
127. "Battalions raised the figures": Enthoven and Smith, *How Much Is Enough?* p. 295.
127. Americans added to ARVN claims: Defense Department fact sheet.
127. Estimate of 180,000 enemy out of action: Le Gro, *Ceasefire to Capitulation*, p. 18.
128. "You never defeated us": Harry Summers, *On Strategy*, p. 1.
128. "Mirror image": Cincinnatus, *Self-Destruction*, p. 31.
128. "Road-bound, over-motorized": Fall, *Two Vietnams*, p. 325.
128. "Not until 1959": Collins, *South Vietnamese Army*, p. 12.
129. Word for word translations: Khuyen, *The RVNAF*, pp. 210–11.
129. Vietnamese developed no doctrines: Hinh and Tho, *Vietnamese Society*, p. 60; "habits of a rich man's army," p. 59.
129. "They have no leadership": Shaplen, "Letter from Saigon," Apr. 14, 1975, p. 127.
129. ARVN didn't carry mortars: Hinh, *Vietnamization and the Ceasefire*, p. 93.
129. "We have created": Completion of Tour Report, PSA Quang Tin, June 10, 1972.
129. No adjustments in training: Lung, *Strategy and Tactics*, p. 58.
130. Manpower statistics: Khuyen, *The RVNAF*, p. 40.
130. "Cannot continue": "A GVN People's Army," *Southeast Asia Analysis Report*, Aug.–Oct.

1971, p. 9; $3 billion needed, "even this level," pp. 6, 8.
130. Rand study: Jenkins, *People's Army*, pp. 2, 7–8.
131. "Friendly cooperation": "Accounting for the Missing and Dead," briefing paper, U.S. delegation, Four-Party Joint Military Team.
131. U.S. protest: Note to North Vietnam, July 29, 1973, in House Select Committee on Missing Persons [1], pt. 5, p. 178.
132. "Of course we have": Herrington, "Third Indochina War," p. 91.
132. Americans felt a precedent was set: "Accounting for the Missing and Dead."
132. Binh Chanh incident: *New York Times*, Dec. 16 and 17, 1973.
133. Secret message from Nixon: House International Relations Committee [3], p. 25; Kissinger handed a document, pp. 5, 57.
133. Pham Van Dong reply to Nixon: VNA, May 22, 1977.
134. Agreement on "principles, functions": Text is in Porter, *Vietnam: Definitive Documentation*, 2:623.
134. "Objectives, not obligations": House Foreign Affairs Committee [1], p. 10; also State Department, "Interpretations of the Agreement," p 329.
134. Written understandings: Kissinger, *White House Years*, pp. 1495–96.
134–35. "Another condition": House Select Committee on Missing Persons [2], p. 116; also see Porter, "Kissinger's Double-Cross."
135. "Because of difficulties": McCauley, "Operation End Sweep, " p. 22.
135–36. Bombing considered: Kissinger, *Years of Upheaval*, pp. 315–26.
135–36. Sen. Cotton comments: Senate Appropriations Committee [1], pp. 1996–97.
137. Minesweeping task force: McCauley, "Operation End Sweep," p. 22.
137. "Performance on Article 20 was essential": telegram from Maurice Williams to Secretary of State, June 18, 1973; in Porter, *Vietnam: Definitive Documentation*, 2:638.
137. Joint Military Team continued: "Accounting for the Missing and Dead."
138. "We stand with you"; Nixon-Thieu communique: *New York Times*, Apr. 4, 1973.
138. Nixon's private assurances; celebration on Thieu's plane: Hosmer, Kellen, and Jenkins, *Fall of South Vietnam*, p. 38.
138–39. Procedures to request air strikes: ibid., pp. 40–41; also Khuyen, *The RVNAF*, pp. 386–87; Le Gro, *Ceasefire to Capitulation*, p. 62; Lung, *Strategy and Tactics*, p. 62; also confirmed to the author by Maj. Gen. John E. Murray, former Defense Attache.

139. "Our leaders believed": Khuyen, *The RVNAF*, p. 387.
140. U.S. officers remonstrated: Dillard, *Sixty Days*, pp. 40–41, 45; "more active support," p. 183.
140. Firing faster than munitions plants could manufacture: Senate Foreign Relations Committee [6], p. 33.
140. U.S. formally notified the Vietnamese: "ARVN Ammunition Constraints," Defense Department document, in Senate Foreign Relations Committee [7], p. 217.
140. "We could detect no evidence": Senate Foreign Relations Committee [8], p. 47.
141. "Enemy actions have been defensive"; ARVN "expanded control"; "aggressive ARVN actions": DAO Assessment, 4th Quarter FY1973, chap. 1, p. 9.
141–42. Military actions described: Le Gro, *Ceasefire to Capitulation*, pp. 54–55, 58, 64–67, 76–77, 97–98. Also Herrington, "Third Indochina War," p. 87; DAO Assessment, 2nd Quarter FY1974, chap. 2, pp. 4, 8, 29.
142–43. Nobel prizes: *New York Times*, Oct. 17, 19, 20, 24, 1973; "like a dictionary," ibid., Jan. 17, 1975.
143. "Revolutionary violence": Dung, "Great Spring Victory," p. 1.
143–44. Orders to Communist units; Bien Hoa attack: *New York Times*, Oct. 21, Nov. 5 and 7, 1973
144. Thieu's speech: FBIS, Jan. 4, 1974.
144. South Vietnam's military gains; "have been exemplary": Senate Armed Services Committee [3], pp. 1880–81; also Senate Foreign Relations Committee [8], p. 4; Frelinghuysen, *Vietnam— Changing Crucible*, p. 4.
144–45. Martin's cable: Full text is in Le Gro, *Ceasefire to Capitulation*, pp. 81–82.
145. "Hanoi has developed": DAO Assessment, 1st Quarter FY1974, chap. 1, p. 1; Gen. Murray's appraisal, ibid., 2nd Quarter FY1974, Foreword.
145–46. Murray complained: Le Gro, *Ceasefire to Capitulation*, p. 82; "near disastrous," p. 81; Tri Phap and Parrot's Beak offensives, pp. 67, 89–95.

Chapter 6.
LAOS: THE KINGDOM OF LANE-XANG

153. "America has ended": Lao Presse, Feb. 9, 1973.
155. "Foreign countries do not care": Dommen, *Conflict in Laos*, p. 186.
156. "Profound insignificance": *Wall Street Journal*, Aug. 14, 1973.
156–57. "Neither a geographic nor an ethnic unit": Halpern, *Government in Laos*, p. 2.

156. Economic statistics: U.S. Aid mission, *Facts on Foreign Aid*, pp. 86–92.
156. Rice was sacred: Roberts, et al., *Area Handbook*, p. 219.
157. "Not learned to kill": Galbraith, *Ambassador's Journal*, p. 93.
157. "Delightful qualities": Zasloff, *Pathet Lao*, p. 42.
158. "Puritanism of the Vietnamese": Langer and Zasloff, "Revolution in Laos," p. 151.
159. "Fish eat ants, ants eat fish": Zasloff, *Pathet Lao*, p. 72.
159. "Communists believe": CIA, "Stocktaking in Indochina," p. 26.
159. Joint Chiefs of Staff recommendation: House Government Operations Committee [1], p. 8; Dommen, *Conflict in Laos*, p. 98.
159–60. "In their most optimistic": Senate Foreign Relations Committee [3], p. 21.
160. First air strikes: Senate Foreign Relations Committee [1], p. 370.
160. Five missions a week: Westmoreland, *Soldier Reports*, p. 110.
160. "Air power now used": *Pentagon Papers*, New York Times ed., p. 623.
160–61. "There is a temptation": Thayer, "War Without Fronts," pp. 824–26.
161. Bombing statistics: House Judiciary Committee [1], pp. 90–103.
161–62. "Black is predominant": *Far Eastern Economic Review*, Jan. 8, 1972.
162. "Aren't any villages": Senate Judiciary Committee [2], p. 2.
162. "Like a test range": *Congressional Record*, Apr. 28, 1972, p. 14917.
162. "There wasn't a night"; "never saw the sun": *Christian Science Monitor*, Mar. 14, 1970.
162. Reports cited by Senate investigators: Senate Judiciary Committee [1], p. 29.
162. Draft animals in Xieng Khouang: *Far Eastern Economic Review*, Dec. 23, 1977.
162. "We could work only at night": Strock, "Laotian Tragedy," p. 13.
162. "Planes came like birds": Project Air War, *Air War*, p. 32.
162. Dr. Weldon comment: Garrett, "Hmong of Laos," p. 111.
162. Officials guessed the death rate was higher: Senate Judiciary Committee [1], p. 27; Strock, "Laotian Tragedy," p. 13.
163. "Principal shortcoming": Senate Foreign Relations Committee [1], p. 371.
163. "Your chief of staff": Halberstam, *Best and Brightest*, pp. 110–11.
163. "Outclass the LPLA": Zasloff, *Pathet Lao*, p. 92.
163. "More effective": Zasloff, "Laos 1972," p. 75; "reflected decay," p. 67.

164. "U.S. strategic aims": Girling, "Nixon's Algeria", pp. 541–42.
165. Electronic war: Weiss, "Battle for Ho Chi Minh Trail"; Harvey, "Air War Vietnam"; Dickson, *Electronic Battlefield*, pp. 32–38, 83–89, 113.
165. "Comparable to the Gurkhas": Dommen, *Conflict in Laos*, p. 5.
166. "They say we like to fight": Garrett, "Hmong of Laos," pp. 86–87.
166–67. Long Pot story: Everingham, "Destruction of Meo Villages."
167. Vang Pao's practice confirmed: *Washington Post*, Aug. 31 and Sept. 5, 1971; Blaufarb, *Counterinsurgency Era*, p. 154.
167. Origins of Meo army: Sananikone, *Lao Army*, p. 78; Shackley, *Third Option*, p. 122.
167. "Splendid fighting men": *Pentagon Papers*, New York Times ed., p. 134.
168. Tribal conflicts were usually settled: Stillman, *Minority Policies*, p. 1.
168. "No help to your case": Woodruff, "Meo of Laos," pt. 2.
168. "Do you see any obligation?": Senate Foreign Relations Committee [1], p. 519.
168. "Losses over the past year": CIA, "Stocktaking in Indochina," p. 28.
168–69. "Most of the young men"; "shows something": Rickenbach manuscript.
169. Vang Pao talked of resettling: Woodruff, "Meo of Laos," pt. 3; Senate Foreign Relations Committee [1], p. 501.
169. Irregulars' strength dropped: Senate Foreign Relations Committee [4], p. 18; casualties, p. 21.
169. Malaria was "hyperendemic": Senate Judiciary Committee [5], pt. 3, p. 57.
169–70. 21,000 Thai troops in Laos: Senate Foreign Relations Committee [6], p. 15.
170. Souvanna's letter: Reuter, July 6, 1972.
170. Pathet Lao's five points: "Statement of the Central Committee of the Lao Patriotic Front," Mar. 9, 1970; in Gettleman, et al., eds., *Conflict in Indochina*, pp. 328–30.
170. Souphanouvong chided Souvanna: VNA, Aug. 31, 1972.
171. Souvanna kept Gandhi's works: Van Praagh, "Laos Still Lives," p. 26.
171. Souvanna believed: Sananikone, *Lao Army*, p. 149.
172. "We come to Vientiane": VNA, Oct. 29, 1972.
172. "Guarantee foreign supporters": Dommen, "Toward Negotiations," p. 41.
172. U.S. slowed down 1964 negotiations: *Pentagon Papers*, Gravel ed. 3:197.
173. Delegations "met as equals": Brown and Zasloff, "Politics of Reconciliation," p. 260.
173. Laos publicly asked the U.S.: Reuter, Dec. 4, 1972.

173. 8,900 bombing sorties: *Congressional Record*, May 9, 1973, p. 14991.
174. Dean "frequently urged": Sananikone, *Lao Army*, pp. 149–50.
174. "Unpleasant surprises": Senate Foreign Relations Committee [6], p. 12.
177. "PL proposed neutralization": Brown and Zasloff, "Politics of Reconciliation," p. 262.
178. "See you next war": *New York Times*, Feb. 23, 1973.
179. "We have fought the bombers": ibid., Feb. 24, 1973.
180. Casualties dropped: Senate Foreign Relations Committee [6], p. 12.
180. "Meeting engagements": Brown and Zasloff, "Laos 1974," p. 175.
181. Savang Vatthana's prediction: Dommen, *Conflict in Laos*, p. 392n.
181. 20,000 incarcerated: Brown and Zasloff, *Communist Indochina*, p. 103.

Chapter 7.
CAMBODIA: "THE LAND IS BROKEN"

192. "Living standards are low": Hickey, "War in Cambodia," p. 53.
192. Fish "abundant": *Henri Mouhot's Diary*, p.113.
192. "Khmer farmers ate well": Jeffrey Millington, U.S. AID mission, Phnom Penh, "Refugees in the Khmer Republic," in Senate Judiciary Committee [5], pt. 1, p. 55.
192. "Eaters of Khmer earth": Shaplen, *Time Out of Hand*, p. 308.
193. "Middle-aged dandy": Bloodworth, *Eye for the Dragon*, p. 102.
193. "Prince charming": Lancaster, "Decline of Sihanouk," pp. 53–54.
193. "Intelligent but flighty": Nixon, *RN*, p. 125.
193. "Incorrigible assassins": Sihanouk, *War and Hope*, p. 147.
193–94. Cambodia must accommodate: Laura Summers, "Cambodia: Model of the Nixon Doctrine," p. 254.
194. "Our interests": Leifer, "Peace and War in Cambodia," p. 71.
194. Secret raids: Defense Department, "Operations in Cambodia and Laos," pp. 29–31.
194. Abrams proposal: House Judiciary Committee [1], p. 51.
194. Joint Chiefs proposal: JCS memorandum, Mar. 13, 1969.
194. "Deliberate test": Nixon, *RN*, p. 380.
195. Menu raids: Defense Department, "Operations in Cambodia and Laos," pp. 5–18; House Judiciary Committee [1], p. 6; Shawcross, *Sideshow*, pp. 28–31; also, Senate Armed Services Committee [1].

195. Joint Chiefs proposed another strike: JCS memorandum, Apr. 9, 1969.

195. 16 percent of all missions; Gen. Wheeler comment: JCS memorandum, "Recapitulation of Menu Program," Feb. 4, 1970.

195. Adm. Moorer comment: JCS memorandum, Oct. 7, 1969.

195. Sihanouk earlier complained: Hughes, "Cambodia," p. 8.

195. "Offensive spirit": Pike, "Cambodia's War," p. 18.

195–96. "No confirmed shipments": JCS memorandum, "Assessment of Menu Operations," Mar. 14, 1970.

196. "A few thousand peasants": Bennett, "Cambodian Diary," p. 395.

196. "Cambodian attitude has hardened": JCS memorandum, "Recapitulation of Menu Program," Feb. 4, 1970.

196. "Something appears": JCS memorandum, "Assessment of Menu Operations," Mar. 14, 1970.

197. "VC/NVA under orders": Sak, *Khmer Republic,* p. 63.

198. Sihanouk's decline: Milton Osborne, *Politics and Power,* pp. 6–7, 72–79, 92; Laura Summers, "Cambodia: Model of the Nixon Doctrine," p. 252.

198. Lon Nol on recovering lost provinces: Gerard Brisse, intro. to Sihanouk, *War and Hope,* p. xxix.

198. Sirik Matak inspired aggressive policy: Milton Osborne, *Politics and Power,* p. 111.

199. Sihanouk announces National United Front: "Message to Compatriots and Solemn Declaration by Cambodian Head of State," Mar. 23, 1970; in *Peking Review,* Mar. 27, 1970.

199. "I am not a Communist": Sihanouk, "Future of Cambodia," pp. 5, 10.

199. "Barely lifted a finger": Kissinger, *White House Years,* p. 474; "weeks before," p. 467; "began plunging," p. 505; "gradually and reluctantly," p. 470.

200. South Vietnamese attacks: Senate Foreign Relations Committee [2], pp. 1–2; Hinh, *Vietnamization and the Ceasefire,* p. 65; *New York Times,* Mar. 26, 28, 29, 1970.

200. Directive to Communist units: Tho, *Cambodian Incursion,* p. 95; Vietnamese began attacking, p. 153.

200. "North Vietnamese would be reluctant": Amos, "Military Elements," p. 221.

200. "Intelligence community identified": "The War in Cambodia," *Southeast Asia Analysis Report,* Jan.–Feb. 1971, p. 2.

201. Chinese emissaries: Sak, *Khmer Republic,* p. 15; also Girling, "Nixon's Algeria," p. 532; *Year-*book on International Communist Affairs, 1971 ed., p. 538, and 1975 ed., p. 305.

201–2. Joint Chiefs' comments: JCS memoranda, Apr. 2, 7, and 14, 1970.

202. Khmer approached embassy; "requests for air strikes": Amos, "Military Elements," pp. 212, 207.

202. Secret flights by Ky: Sak, *Khmer Republic,* p. 80.

202–3. Thieu secretly authorized: Tho, *Cambodian Incursion,* p. 36; first penetration, p. 44; U.S. actions in support, pp. 113–14.

203. First American assistance: Senate Foreign Relations Committee [2], pp. 11–12; Tho, *Cambodian Incursion,* p. 32.

203. "Nodis Khmer": Amos, "Military Elements," p. 216; civilians on the working group warned, p. 220.

204. "Do not believe he is going to survive": Kissinger, *White House Years,* p. 516.

204. "Temporary disruption": CIA, "North Vietnamese Intentions," p. 13.

.04. Decisions taken without military advice: Westmoreland, *Soldier Reports,* p. 389.

204. Mahon-Laird exchange: House Appropriations Committee [1], pp. 800, 806.

205. "New government is weak": *Washington Post,* May 31, 1970.

205. "Bulk of the Communist forces": CIA, "North Vietnamese Intentions," pp. 30–33.

205. Douglas Pike concluded: Pike, "Cambodia's War," pp. 27–28.

205. "Liberation is the work of the Khmer": "Statement of the D.R.V.N. Government on the Present Patriotic Struggle of the Cambodian People," Mar. 25, 1970; in *Peking Review,* Apr. 3, 1970, p. 19.

205–6. "Within four months": "The War in Cambodia," *Southeast Asia Analysis Report,* Mar.–Apr. 1971, p. 46.

206. Vietnamese organized a Khmer liberation movement: David Brown, "Exporting Insurgency," pp. 126–34.

206. Growth of Cambodian insurgents: Sak, *Khmer Republic,* p. 27.

206–7. "It is normal": Sim Var, "Restoring Peace," pp. 164–65.

207. Official cable to Lon Nol not delivered; "it was the practice not to tell": Amos, "Military Elements," p. 231; Lon Nol didn't believe Nixon's deadline, p. 227.

207–8. No details communicated to Cambodians on the invasion: Sak, *Khmer Republic,* p. 82; Chenla II debacle, pp. 74–79.

208–9. "The government of the Khmer Republic": "Conclusion and Recommendation of Appropriations Committee Delegation Visiting

Southeast Asian Nations—January 1973," in Senate Appropriations Committee [2], appendix 5, p. 1461.

209. War's effect on education: Whitaker et al., *Area Handbook*, p. 114; hospitals destroyed, p. 89.

209. Mataxis comment: Knight News Service, May 5, 1980.

209–10. Laos and Cambodia "are victims": Senate Foreign Relations Committee [4], pp. 37–38.

211–12. Tho-Kissinger exchanges: Kissinger, *White House Years*, pp. 1495–96, 1465.

212. U.S. negotiators' unilateral statement: State Department, "Presidential Authority."

212. Legal rationale: State Department, "Interpretations of the Agreement," p. 329.

213. Lon Nol speech: FBIS, Jan. 29, 1973.

213. "Not the kind of offer": Senate Foreign Relations Committee [6], p. 22.

214. "The problem of each Indochinese country": "Joint Communique on Samdech Norodom Sihanouk's Visit to D.R.V.N.," VNA, Oct. 28, 1972.

214. "Never compromise"; New Year's message: FBIS, Jan. 4 and Jan. 3, 1973.

214–15. "Our friends told us": Senate Foreign Relations Committee [9], p. 651.

215. "So-called ceasefire": FBIS, Jan. 31, 1973.

215. "No compromise is possible": Statement of Royal Government of National Union of Cambodia, in Senate Foreign Relations Committee [9], p. 652.

215. "No question of signing agreements": *Far Eastern Economic Review*, Feb. 12, 1973.

215. Sihanouk offered to meet Kissinger: Fallaci, "Sihanouk," pp. 26, 31.

215. "When we speak of negotiating": *Peking Review*, Apr. 20, 1973, p. 11.

216. "Absolutely not under the guidance": Ith Sarin, "Nine Months," p. 39.

216. "Sabotage the Khmer Rouge": Sihanouk, *War and Hope*, pp. 10–11; "Clear out of Cambodia," p. 22.

217. "Mortal hate": Ith Sarin, "Nine Months," p. 39.

217. Bombing tonnages: House Judiciary Committee [1], pp. 90–103.

217. No land that did not contain human habitation: William Harben letter to Thomas Enders, in appendix, Kissinger, *Years of Upheaval*, p. 1225.

217–18. Schanberg account: *New York Times*, May 24, 1973.

218. "FANK was grossly inadequate": Defense Department, "Selected Comparisons in Cambodia—1973 and 1974," in Senate Appropriations Committee [3], p. 1107.

218–19. Infantrymen marched into Phnom Penh

for their pay: *Far Eastern Economic Review*, May 21, 1973; Reuter, May 15, 1973.

219. Formal agreement with the U.S.; U.S. withheld $4 million; six officers reprimanded: Senate Appropriations Committee [2], pp. 1079–83.

219. "Your allegations are true": Senate Appropriations Committee [1], p. 2006.

219. "B-52s are killing": Harben letter to Enders, p. 1226.

219. 65,000 "nonexistent personnel": House Appropriations Committee [5], pt. 1, p. 1223.

220. Cambodian food consumption: Hickey, "War in Cambodia," p. 59.

220–21. "Performance has been impressive": Senate Judiciary Committee [2], p. 72.

221–22. Swank comments: General Accounting Office, "Problems in the Khmer Republic," p. 89; Cambodia's war victims budget, p. 94; drug shortage "extreme," p. 99.

221–22. "Vast majority are self-sufficient": Senate Judiciary Committee [4], p. 10; "Khmer government takes pride," p. 3; O'Connor statement on pharmaceutical supplies, p. 25; Cambodian request for drugs and Red Cross reply, pp. 17–18.

222. "Patients writhing": State Department, "Cambodia: Assessment of Humanitarian Needs," p. 7894.

222–23. Robert Nooter testimony: Senate Judiciary Committee [5], pt. 1, pp. 31–32, 36–38.

223. "Small amounts of assistance to families in camps": House Foreign Affairs Committee [2], pp. 5–6.

223. "Tourism to Angkor Wat": House Appropriations Committee [3], p. 1389.

223. U.S. refugee relief grants: Senate Judiciary Committee [5], pt. 1, p. 33.

223. Economic aid totals: House Appropriations Committee [5], pt. 3, p. 72.

224. Prewar rice harvests: International Monetary Fund, "Cambodian Economic Situation," p. 115.

224. Economy devastated: U.N. Economic Commission for Asia, *Economic Survey 1973*, pt. 2, pp. 147–48, 152; House Foreign Affairs Committee [7], p. 7; AID mission to Phnom Penh, *Economic Data Book.*.

224. Rising malnutrition reported in 1971: General Accounting Office, "Problems in the Khmer Republic," p. 97.

226–27. Rogers presented a legal memorandum: State Department, "Presidential Authority."

227. "If you look at Article 20": Senate Appropriations Committee [1], p. 2068.

227. Richardson statement: *Congressional Record*, May 7, 1973, p. 14615.

227. Buzhardt testimony: House Armed Services Committee [2], pp. 15–16.

228. Strikes in February and March against "lines of communication into South Vietnam": Senate Foreign Relations Committee [5], p. 1.
228. "As far as B-52 efforts are concerned": Senate Appropriations Committee [1], p. 2012.
228. "To interdict the flow": House Foreign Affairs Committee [2], p. 85.
229. Neak Luong accident: *New York Times,* Aug. 9, 12, and 24, 1973.
230. "Attitude in the embassy": Batchelder and Quinlan, "Eagle Pull," p. 53.
230. Draft law "badly applied": *New York Times,* Aug. 4, 1973.
230. 10,000 insurgents killed: Senate Appropriations Committee [2], p. 1102.
231. "Slashed and clubbed": Hughes, *End of Sukarno,* p. 175.
231. "Ridding the soil": Shaplen, *Time Out of Hand,* p. 124.
232. "Traditional literature": Milton Osborne, "Reflections," p. 5.
232. Friezes at Angkor Wat: Burchett, *Second Indochina War,* pp. 19–20.
232. Cambodian intelligence report: State Department, "Cambodia: Can the Vietnamese Export Insurgency?"
232–33. Cadres trained in submissiveness: Ith Sarin, "Bureaus of the Khmer Rouge," pp. 46, 48.
233. Farmer could never be "progressive": Laura Summers, "Cambodia: Model of the Nixon Doctrine," p. 254.
233. "Tightening control": Quinn, "Political Change," p. 9; brutality "limited," p. 22.
233. "No real hatreds": *New York Times,* Feb. 6, 1973.
233. "Decided to accelerate": Carney, *Communist Party Power,* p. 21.
233–34. "All vestiges": Quinn, "Political Change," p. 11; Buddhist practice, other folkways forbidden, p. 15; "terror escalated," p. 23.
234. Government soldiers advanced: *Far Eastern Economic Review,* Aug. 20, 1973.
234. "It was quiet enough": *New York Times,* Aug. 17, 1973.
234. "Major efforts were thwarted": State Department, "Summary of Negotiating Efforts."
234–36. Kissinger's account of "major effort": Kissinger, *Years of Upheaval,* pp. 344, 351–69.
235. Schlesinger comment: Senate Appropriations Committee [2], p. 1288.
236. Sihanouk: "It is too late": Reuter, July 5, 1973.
236–37. Long Boret proposal: FBIS, July 9, 1973.
236n. Sihanouk told guests: ibid., Jan. 22, 1973.
237. Sihanouk "formally excluded": ibid., Jan. 22, 1973.
237. "Sihanouk ousted for good": ibid., Jan. 9, 1973.

237. Kissinger regarded Lon Nol as a bargaining chip: Kissinger, *Years of Upheaval,* p. 346.
238. "Mean and despicable": Sihanouk, "Forty-third Message to the Khmer Nation," NCNA, July 16, 1973.
238. Insurgent's war aims: "Declaration of the N.U.F.C. to Friendly Countries and Peoples," NCNA, July 25, 1973.
238. "We do not need him"; "if you use his name": Kirk, "Revolution and Violence," p. 218.
238. Sihanouk appealed to foreign powers: Sihanouk, "Forty-third Message."
238. Sihanouk cabled Mansfield: Reuter, Aug. 11, 1973.
239. Ieng Sary statement: *China Mail* (Hong Kong), Sept. 11, 1973.
239. "Khmer Rouge do not love me": Fallaci, "Sihanouk," p. 32.
239. "They are pure patriots": *South China Morning Post* (Hong Kong), July 23, 1973.
239. "They kill people": Kirk, "Revolution and Violence," pp. 222–23; murders at Oudong, p. 216.
239. "A traditional and state religion": "Declaration to Friendly Countries."
240. Religious books burned in the temples: "Sihanouk in the Khmer Rouge Shadow," *Asian Analysis,* July, 1974.

Chapter 8.
FALL OF THE KHMER REPUBLIC

242. Final siege began: Reuter, Jan. 1, 1975.
243. Gen. Graham comment: House Appropriations Committee [7], p. 29.
243. Gen. Fish comment: House Appropriations Committee [5], pt. 3, p. 11.
245. Dock workers hid grain: *New York Times,* Dec. 17, 1974.
245–46. Hospital conditions: Indochina Operational Group of the Red Cross, "Circular no. 14"; State Department, "Cambodia: Assessment of Humanitarian Needs"; memorandum to Thomas Olmsted, U.S. AID mission, Phnom Penh, from Dr. John E. Kennedy, 1974.
248. Battalions had 100 men: House Foreign Affairs Committee [7], p. 2.
248. One replacement for three men lost: House International Relations Committee, [1], pt. 2, p. 330.
248. "Lop-lop certificate": *New York Times,* Dec. 17, 1974.
249. 3,500 deserted: U.S. embassy, "Khmer Report—March 18, 1975."
250–51. Health, malnutrition problems: State Department, "Cambodia: Assessment of Humanitarian Needs."
251–52. Rice distribution system: Senate Foreign Relations Committee [10], pp. 5, 154–55; House International Relations Committee [1], pt. 2, pp.

270–71, 275; House Foreign Affairs Committee [7], p. 10; U.S. embassy, "Khmer Report—Apr. 1, 1975."

254. Government casualties: House International Relations Committee [1], pt. 2, p. 330.

255. 7,000 civilian casualties a month: Senate Judiciary Committee [7], p. 78.

255. "Enemy is writhing": SWB FE/4856, Mar. 17, 1975.

255. Funding problems: House Appropriations Committee [5], pt. 3, p. 43; House International Relations Committee [4], pp. 624–25.

255. Reports that the Cambodians should conserve: Senate Foreign Relations Committee [7], pp. 258–59.

255. "FANK depend on firepower": fact sheet prepared for congressional delegation, Feb. 28, 1975. Made available to the author by Rep. Fenwick.

257. "Where is the Khmer Republic?": House Appropriations Committee [5], pt. 1, pp. 1277–78.

259–60. Dean's efforts: House International Relations Committee [1], pt. 4, pp. 622–23, 629, 636, 639, 647; House Foreign Affairs Committee [6], p. 20; Shawcross, Sideshow, pp. 325–28.

259. Martin's view: notes made available by Rep. McCloskey: also Snepp, Decent Interval, p. 97.

260. Lon Nol proposed negotiations: FBIS, July 9, 1974.

260. Ford administration proposals: State Department, "Summary of Negotiating Efforts."

260–61. Fenwick comment: Senate Foreign Relations Committee [10], p. 75.

262. "Lack of coordination": U.S. embassy, "Khmer Report—March 25, 1975."

265–66. Lon Nol's departure: Washington Post, Apr. 2, 1975; Time and Newsweek, Apr. 14, 1975; notes given to the author by Paul Brinkley-Rogers, then Newsweek's correspondent in Phnom Penh.

266. Eleven-minute statement: SWB FE/4868, Apr. 3, 1975.

266–67. Asian ambassadors stepped in; Cambodians asked Lon Nol to leave: Brinkley-Rogers notes; Sak, Khmer Republic, p. 160.

267. Half-million dollars promised: House International Relations Committee [4], pt. 4, p. 647.

267n. Schanberg report: New York Times, Apr. 17, 1975.

267–68. Sihanouk statement: NCNA, Apr. 1, 1975.

268. Saukham Khoy comments: Brinkley-Rogers notes.

268. 160 men made their way; dance halls and theaters closed; soldiers airlifted from Kompong Scila: U.S. embassy, "Khmer Report—Apr. 8, 1975."

268. Howitzers, shells lost at Neak Luong: Sak, Khmer Republic, p. 156.

268. Cannibalism episode: A cameraman who saw and photographed this incident described it to the author. Also, Washington Post, Apr. 6, 1975.

269. Quarter-million refugees in Battambang: U.S. embassy, "Khmer Report—Apr. 1, 1975."

269. Province governor sold supplies: Shawcross, Sideshow, p. 326.

269. "Empty holes": Time, Apr. 7, 1975.

269. Saukham Khoy asked: SWB FE/4869, Apr. 4, 1975.

269. Dean proposed evacuation: USMC interview 6040 (Col. S. H. Batchelder).

269. 80 or 90 rounds: Batchelder and Quinlan, "Eagle Pull," p. 58.

270. Schlesinger comment: House Foreign Affairs Committee [5], p. 73.

270. Opinion polls: Time, Mar. 24, 1975.

270. Mahon comment: Congressional Quarterly Weekly Report, Mar. 1, 1975, p. 433.

270. Intelligence estimates: Senate Foreign Relations Committee [11], p. 23; Snepp, Decent Interval, p. 154.

271. "Not a sacrificial lamb": New York Times, Mar. 19, 1975.

271. McCloskey comments: Senate Foreign Relations Committee [10], pp. 48, 64; Sen. Scott comment, p. 68.

272. Senate committee majority and minority reports: Senate Foreign Relations Committee [11], pp. 6–10, 22–25.

273. "The U.S. led Cambodia": Washington Post, Apr. 12, 1975.

273–74. Evacuation preparations: Defense Department, "Chronology—Eagle Pull"; Batchelder and Quinlan, "Eagle Pull," pp. 58–60; USMC interviews 6040 (Batchelder) and 6132 (Lt. Col. Curtis G. Lawson).

274. U.S. offer to Sihanouk: Reuter, Apr. 12, 1975; New York Times, Apr. 13, 1975; Shawcross, Sideshow, pp. 360–61.

274. Sihanouk comments: Far Eastern Economic Review, Mar. 28, 1975; SWB FE/4862, Mar. 24, 1975.

275. Sihanouk depressed: Shawcross, Sideshow, pp. 343, 349.

275–78. Evacuation of Phnom Penh: Defense Department, "Chronology—Eagle Pull"; Batchelder and Quinlan, "Eagle Pull," pp. 58–60; USMC interview 6040 (Batchelder); New York Times and Baltimore Sun, Apr. 13, 1975; Newsweek and Time, Apr. 21, 1975.

276. Dean told Cambodian leaders; Sirik Matak's answer: House International Relations Committee [1], pt. 4, pp. 626–27; all Khmer employees except for twelve, p. 667.

276. Saukham Khoy did not tell colleagues: Sak, Khmer Republic, p. 163.

277. Schanberg's obsession: Schanberg, "Death and Life."

278. "To a westerner"; stewardesses poured champagne: *New York Times,* Apr. 14, 1975.
278. National Assembly resolution, Sak comments, Khmer Rouge denounced: SWB FE/4877–79, Apr. 14–16, 1975.
279. Long Boret: "no surrender": *New York Times,* Apr. 14, 1975.
279. Defecting pilot; Takhmau and Pochentong fall: Sak, *Khmer Republic,* pp. 166–67; SWB FE/4878 and 4880, Apr. 15 and 17, 1975; Baltimore *Sun,* Apr. 16, 1975.
279. Settlement catches fire: *Sunday Times* (London), Apr. 20, 1975.
279. Ceasefire proposed: Sak, *Khmer Republic,* pp. 167–68; *Time,* Apr. 28, 1975; *New York Times,* Apr. 17, 1975.
279. Dean had proposed: *New York Times,* Apr. 14, 1975.
279–80. Government tries to flee; Sak's escape: Sak, *Khmer Republic,* pp. 168–71.
280. Sihanouk rejects ceasefire: Baltimore *Sun,* Apr. 17, 1975.
280–88. Phnom Penh falls: Vignettes of the Khmer Rouge takeover and the expulsion of Phnom Penh's people are based primarily on Ponchaud, *Cambodia Year Zero,* pp. 4–32; Barron and Paul, *Peace with Horror,* pp. 3–36; Schanberg, "Death and Life," and Schanberg's long account in the *New York Times,* May 9, 1975; and Jon Swain's account in the *Sunday Times* (London), May 11, 1975.
281. Keth Dara broadcast: SWB FE/4881, Apr. 18, 1975.
282. Khieu Samphan assaulted: Laura Summers, intro. to Khieu Sampham, *Cambodia's Economy,* p. 9.
282–83. Gen. Mey Si Chan broadcast: SWB FE/4881, Apr. 18, 1975.
283. Khmer Rouge suspected the CIA: Hildebrand and Porter, "Politics of Food," p. 21.
284–85. "Poor peasants": Sihanouk, *War and Hope,* p. 27; "ten times as hard," p. 46; Chou En-lai's advice; "we will be the first," p. 86.
285. Dr. Oum Nal account: *Le Figaro* (Paris) Feb. 11, 1977, trans. Casimir C. Petraitis, in House International Relations Committee [2], p. 59.
286. An unidentified announcer: SWB FE/4881, Apr. 18, 1975.
286. Beheadings announced: Baltimore *Sun,*, Apr. 20, 1975.
287. Population estimates: Hildebrand and Porter, "Politics of Food," pp. 2, 13; Ponchaud, *Cambodia Year Zero,* p. 20; W. J. Sampson letter to the *Economist* (London) Mar. 26, 1977, in House International Relations Committee [2], p. 55.
Sampson was an economist and statistician who worked with the Khmer Republic's central statistical office. His letter estimated that in Au-

gust 1974 600,000 people were living in government-held cities and towns outside Phnom Penh. Barron and Paul list these population estimates: Battambang, 200,000; Svay Rieng, 130,000; Kompong Chhnang, 60,000; Kompong Speu, 60,000; Kompong Cham, 40,000; Pailin, 40,000; Siem Reap, 50,000; Pursat, 40,000; Kampot, 40,000; Takeo, 40,000; Kompong Som, 25,000; Poipet, 20,000; Sisophon, 15,000, for a total of 760,000 (*Peace with Horror,* p. 36n).
288. National bank blown up, cathedral razed: Laurie, "Cambodia: Five Years Later"; Gornicki, "Asian Holocaust."
288. Battambang massacre: Ponchaud, *Cambodia Year Zero,* pp. 41–43; Barron and Paul, *Peace with Horror,* pp. 65–68, 70.
288. Ith Thaim account: Barron and Paul, *Peace with Horror,* pp. 82–84.
288–89. Soldiers discovered a pacemaker: Emerson, "Mass Murder in Cambodia."
289. Weeping was considered criticism: Burchett, *At the Barricades,* p. 5.
289. Thousands who died: Statistics on the Cambodian holocaust are little more than guesses. But it clearly was one of the great manmade catastrophes of history, on a scale with the destruction of European Jews in World War II or the communal slaughters in Hindu-Muslim violence when India was partitioned in 1947. The enormous loss of life in Cambodia was particularly anguishing, however, because it was inflicted on a population that was relatively small to begin with.

Most demographers estimated Cambodia's 1970 population at slightly over 7 million. In 1980, according to a research paper published by the U.S. Central Intelligence Agency—based, its authors acknowledged, on "highly speculative" assumptions—the population was estimated at between 4.7 and 5.5 million, with 5.2 million the "most likely" figure. This meant a decline, through deaths, migration, and a decrease in fertility, of one-fifth to one-third of the prewar population. The CIA analysts estimated 600,000 to 700,000 war-related deaths between 1970 and the Khmer Rouge takeover in April 1975—nearly 10 percent of the population. Under the Khmer Rouge, from April 1975 to January 1979 the population was believed to have fallen between 1.2 and 1.8 million. A further drop of 700,000, the CIA calculated, occurred in the first year of the Vietnamese-sponsored Heng Samrin regime.

At the time of the Vietnamese invasion, Cambodia's rural economy was at the point of total collapse, under the accumulated strains of the past and the impact of still another war and another massive uprooting of the population. For the second half of 1979, the CIA study derived a statistic as grim as it was astonishing: "A conservative estimate is that for every Kampuchean born during July–December 1979, ten died" (*Kampuchea: A Demographic Catastrophe*, pp. 1–2, 5–6).

Chapter 9.
''A BROKEN SWORD''

300. Unemployment estimated: *American Aid and Vietnam Economy*, p. 2; Senate Armed Services Committee [5], p. 6; House Foreign Affairs Committee [5], p. 252.

300. Soldier's buying power: DAO Assessment, 4th Quarter FY1973, chap. 10, p. 23; Frelinghuysen, *Changing Crucible*, p. 9.

300. Da Nang's poorest: U.S. Consulate-general, Da Nang, "Quarterly Regional Assessment," Dec. 20, 1974.

300. "Soldiers and civil servants": U.S. Consulate-general, Can Tho, "Quarterly Regional Assessment," June 20, 1974.

300–301. Cash substituted for the rice ration: DAO Assessment, 4th Quarter FY1973, chap. 5, p. 53; "tactical performance," chap. 9, p. 7; "virtually unanimous," ibid., 2nd Quarter FY1974, chap. 12, pp. 15–16; "leave restaurants," ibid., 3rd Quarter FY1974, chap. 12, p. 14; survey results, ibid., 1st Quarter FY1975, chap. 12, p. 4.

301. "RVNAF personnel are forced": cited in Herrington, "Third Indochina War," p. 174.

301–2. Effects of U.S. withdrawal: *American Aid and Vietnam Economy*, pp. 6–7; Senate Armed Services Committee [5], p. 6.

303. "Gains for peace": House Foreign Affairs Committee [5], p. 4; Schlesinger statement, p. 58; Ingersoll statement, p. 249.

303. "Not an easy assignment": Senate Appropriations Committee [3], p. 1318.

303. "Never have I seen": Senate Foreign Relations Committee [7], p. 90.

303. "From the visits I have made": Senate Armed Services Committee [3], p. 1881.

303. Doolin's exchange with Schroeder: House Armed Services Committee [4], p. 917.

304. Martin's testimony: Senate Foreign Relations Committee [7], pp. 386–89.

305. Hurley's "conceit, ambition, and ego": Tuchman, *Practicing History*, pp. 196, 198.

305. "For more than 40 years": Senate Foreign Relations Committee [7], p. 383.

305. "I know he exists": *New York Times*, Jan. 17, 1974.

306. "I represent the president": House International Relations Committee [1], pt. 3, p. 582; "a sense of theater," p. 549.

306. "Sheer perfection": U.S. embassy, Saigon, "Memoranda of Conversations," p. 9917.

306–7. *New York Times* was controlled: Senate Foreign Relations Committee [7], p. 385; exchange with Webber, pp. 425–28.

306. Kennedy's staff a spearhead: *Congressional Record*, Apr. 2, 1974, p. 9144.

307. "The thrust of information": Senate Foreign Relations Committee [8], pp. 13–14.

307. "Established dissent procedures": "The American Embassy in Saigon," draft statement prepared for Rep. Donald Fraser, probably March 1975.

The draft was in files made available by Rep. McCloskey, who was, with Fraser, a member of a congressional delegation that visited Saigon in late February and early March 1975. In response to an inquiry, Fraser wrote the author on Jan. 6, 1981; "I am sure it was written by one of my staff and it does accurately reflect my views after the Saigon trip."

307. "Closed atmosphere": Herrington, "Third Indochina War," p. 235.

307–8. "A beleaguered camp": House Select Committee on Intelligence [1], pp. 1658–59.

308n. Vietnamese command's assumptions: Le Gro, *Ceasefire to Capitulation*, p. 41.

308. "Verdict of dispassionate historians": House International Relations Committee [1], pt. 3, p. 535.

308–9. Gen. Murray's views: typed manuscript; Gen. Murray's summary of a meeting with Adm. Gayler, the Pacific commander, in Hawaii, Aug. 20, 1974.

309. "Effect of a concussion bomb": Khuyen, *The RVNAF*, p. 286.

309–10. Fraser's impression: "The American Embassy in Saigon" (*see* note to p. 307).

310–13. Casualty statistics: Thayer, "War without Fronts," pp. 939, 849.

The faulty reporting is reflected in DAO's quarterly assessments, which throughout 1974 showed weekly totals of "friendly" deaths and also gave cumulative totals that were derived by adding the week-by-week figures. On Feb. 1, 1975, a new DAO assessment contained a revised chart showing new statistics for each month back to January 1973. These figures, attributed to the ARVN adjutant general, were about twice those reported earlier (DAO Assessment, 2nd Quarter FY1975, chap. 2, pp. 32–33). The discrepancy between initial casualty reports and later, revised records is confirmed in Khuyen, *The RVNAF*, p. 118, and in notes supplied by the former ARVN intelligence chief, who also pointed out that the adjutant general's records "should be considered the most reliable . . . because they were regarded by ARVN as official documents for budget, financial and payroll planning, justification and control."

311. Kissinger told Kennedy: letter to Sen. Kennedy, Mar. 25, 1974; in *Congressional Record*, Apr. 1, 1974, p. 9035.

311. "Substantial reduction"; "a relatively small

scale": House Foreign Affairs Committee [5], pp. 4, 12.

311. Pentagon testimony: Senate Armed Services Committee [3], p. 1875; House Armed Services Committee [4], p. 895.

311. "Since casualties have dropped": Senate Armed Services Committee [4], p. 163.

313. "No one knows precisely": House Appropriations Committee [6], p. 162.

313. "Does anyone know how much they need?": Gen. Murray's notes (*see* note to pp. 308–9).

313. Four-fifths of the money: House Armed Services Committee [4], p. 919.

314. "No one in any Defense agency": Le Gro, *Ceasefire to Capitulation*, p. 84.

314. "Other than statistical": House Appropriations Committee [7], p. 5.

314. "There is no question": Senate Armed Services Committee [2], p. 67.

315. Murray's last assessment: DAO Assessment, 4th Quarter FY1974, foreword.

315–16. Conference with Gayler; phone call from Smith: Gen. Murray's notes (*see* note to pp. 308–9).

316. "Surprisingly enough": Province Report, Binh Dinh, Jan. 25, 1975.

316. 224 aircraft stored: DAO Assessment, 2nd Quarter FY1975, chap. 4, p. 4.

316. 300 planes lost: Defense Department, "Fact Sheet on Aircraft Losses," supplied by Rep. McCloskey.

317. "Not reached the point": House Armed Services Committee [3], p. 53.

317. "Comparable to North Vietnam": Momyer, *Vietnamese Air Force*, p. 63; helicopters and FACs forced out of the air, pp. 65–66.

317. 100 missiles, 1,800 antiaircraft guns: Defense Department, "Fact Sheet on Air Defense," supplied by Rep. McCloskey.

317. "Prohibited VNAF": DAO Assessment, 4th Quarter FY1974, chap. 1, p. 9.

317. Tried to use sensor system: Hinh, *Vietnamization and the Ceasefire*, p. 74.

317. "Enemy air and artillery": "COSVN Directive 08," U.S. embassy translation, p. 10.

318. "Ground ammunition issues": Defense Department, "ARVN Ammunition Constraints," in Senate Foreign Relations Committee [7], p. 217.

318. Expenditures "inordinate": House Appropriations Committee [4], p. 483.

318. Defense Department statistics: A chart supplied by the Defense Department to the Senate Armed Services Committee in early 1974 showed these monthly figures for short tons of ammunition expended:

Feb. 1973	77,900	May	11,200
Mar.	31,100	June	14,800
April	11,400	July	10,400

Aug.	15,900	Nov.	18,300
Sept.	14,600	Dec.	16,800
Oct.	19,000	Jan. 1974	18,600

A classified fact sheet called "GVN Ground Ammunition Situation" that was supplied to congressional visitors to Saigon in February 1975 reported that 131,000 tons were consumed between July 1, 1974, and January 31, 1975, an average of about 18,700 tons a month—the same as in late 1973 and substantially higher than in the period April–September 1973. The same pattern can be derived from the regular quarterly reports of the Defense Attache Office, which listed artillery expenditures in rounds for each week in each region. These reports show that 1973 averages were about 39,000 rounds a week in April and May and rose to more than 65,000 rounds a week in November and December. In 1974, the DAO records show that South Vietnam fired about 76,000 rounds a week during May and June and slightly more than 63,000 rounds a week in September, October, and November— *after* severe cutbacks were supposed to have taken place. It was the 1975 fact sheet that defined the "intensive" and "sustaining" rates used by U.S. planners. It also declared that the "critical" stockpile level was considered to be two months' supply at the intensive rate plus another 18,000 tons as a cushion, or 126,000 tons altogether. Under the trimmed-back 1975 program, the fact sheet showed, scheduled shipments would be about 30 percent under the supposed minimum of 18,000 tons a month, and thus ARVN would have to deplete its stocks to below the critical mark well before mid-1975. Much later, however, the Pentagon reported that when South Vietnam fell the Communists were estimated to have captured 130,000 tons of ammunition—which, if true, means the critical level was still maintained. (Senate Armed Services Committee [2], p. 106; Defense Department fact sheet, "GVN Ground Ammunition Situation," supplied to the author by Rep. Fenwick; DAO Assessment, 1st Quarter FY1974, chap. 2, pp. 27–33; ibid., 2nd Quarter FY1974, chap. 2, pp. 49–63; ibid., 4th Quarter FY1974, chap. 2, pp. 33–39; ibid., 2nd Quarter FY1975, chap. 2, pp. 26–29. The Pentagon estimate of 130,000 tons of munitions captured was reported by Reuter, Nov. 8, 1976.)

318. "Data being provided": Senate Foreign Relations Committee [8], p. 22; also Snepp, *Decent Interval*, pp. 95, 103.

319. Discussions of withdrawal: House International Relations Committee [1], pt. 3, pp. 538–39; Momyer, *Vietnamese Air Force*, p. 59; Snepp, *Decent Interval*, pp. 109–10; Lung, *Strategy and Tactics*, p. 61; Hosmer, Kellen, and Jenkins, *Fall of South Vietnam*, pp. 111–13.

319. "A sizable force": Hinh, *Vietnamization and the Ceasefire*, p. 161.

319. "The basic posture": DAO Final Assessment, chap. 1, p. 3.

319–20. Committee on "poor man's war": Lung, *Strategy and Tactics*, pp. 59–60.

320. U.S.-Vietnamese joint study: Khuyen, *The RVNAF*, pp. 282–85.

324. Thieu's speech: SWB FE/4722, Oct. 7, 1974.

325–26. P.R.G. statement: NCNA, Oct. 10, 1974.

326. Last Communist proposal: "Statement on Achieving Peace and National Concord in South Vietnam," Mar. 22, 1974; in *Ta Kung Pao* (Hong Kong), Mar. 28, 1974.

326. Suspension of Paris talks: *New York Times*, Apr. 16 and May 14, 1974.

327. Communist planning paper: "Resolution of the Third [Binh Dinh] Province Party Conference," U.S. embassy translation, pp. 14–15.

327. "Liberate the people": Dung, "Great Spring Victory," p. 3; "passive and weakened," p. 4.

327–28. 1st division "unlikely to perform": DAO Assessment, 2nd Quarter FY1975, chap. 5, pp. 14–15; Communists gained in Quang Nam, ibid., 1st Quarter FY1975, chap. 2, p. 1; Da Trach battle, chap. 2, p. 17; rangers survived Gia Vuc, chap. 2, p. 18.

328. Commanders asked to withdraw from Gia Vuc: Le Gro, *Ceasefire to Capitulation*, p. 124; enclaves fell in western highlands, pp. 112–13, 122–23; attacks near Saigon, pp. 135–36; Delta fighting, pp. 143–44.

328. Communists controlled 500 hamlets: U.S. embassy airgram A–009, Feb. 8, 1975.

328. Weapons losses: Defense Department charts, "Friendly Crew-served Weapons Lost in South Vietnam" and "Friendly Individual Weapons Lost in South Vietnam," supplied by Rep. McCloskey.

328. Battalion strength in 3rd Division: Hinh, *Vietnamization and the Ceasefire*, p. 178.

328. Officers were former deserters: DAO Assessment, 2nd Quarter FY1975, chap. 5, p. 15; divisions were rated, chap. 2, pp. 14–18; RF mobile battalions, chap. 9, pp. 1–2.

328. Recruitment in Dinh Tuong: Province Reports, Dinh Tuong and My Tho City, Jan. 25, 1975.

329. Desertions: DAO Final Assessment, chap. 12, p. 2; Province Report, Ba Xuyen, Feb. 8, 1975.

329. Armed clashes: Province Reports, Kien Hoa, Feb. 8, 1975, and Vinh Binh, Feb. 22, 1975.

330. Montagnard life: Hickey, "Aspects of Hill Tribe Life," pp. 757, 765; McAlister, "Mountain Minorities," p. 777; Harvey Smith et al., *Area Handbook*, pp. 73–74; Buttinger, *Dragon Defiant*, p. 16.

330. "Pseudo-Siberia": Completion of Tour Report, PSA Khanh Hoa, Nov. 1972.

330. "Encroachment continues": MACCORDS, "Military Region II Overview," May 1971.

330–31. "After fourteen months": Letter from PSA to chief of Lam Dong Province, May 15, 1972.

331. Too little land to grow rice: General Accounting Office, "Follow-up Review of Refugees," p. 141.

331. "Should the Communists decide": DAO Assessment, 2nd Quarter FY1974, chap. 1, pp. 16–17.

332. Fall of Phuoc Binh: DAO Assessment, 2nd Quarter FY1975, chap. 2, p. 10; Le Gro, *Ceasefire to Capitulation*, pp. 136–37; Momyer, *Vietnamese Air Force*, p. 71; Reuter, Jan. 8, 1975.

332. Tanks destroyed: U.S. embassy telegram Saigon 1236, Jan. 31, 1975.

332. Hospital bombed: *New York Times*, Feb. 2, 1975.

333. "Gunboat diplomacy": Reuter, Jan. 11, 1975.

333. "There was a theory": Fitzgerald, "Journey to North Vietnam," p. 118.

333. Nui Ba Den abandoned; Gen. Dong relieved: Le Gro, *Ceasefire to Capitulation*, pp. 135–36, 142; also Province Report, Tay Ninh, Jan. 14, 1975.

333–34. Communist buildup: DAO Final Assessment, chap. 1, p. 1; Le Gro, *Ceasefire to Capitulation*, p. 145; House Appropriations Committee [7], pp. 9–12; Defense Department confidential fact sheet, "Vietnam Order of Battle Figures"; McCloskey, "North-South Confrontation," pp. 6676–77; Senate Armed Services Committee [5], pp. 3–4; State Department, "Report on Vietnam Situation," Jan. 23, 1975; Ministry of Foreign Affairs, Republic of Vietnam, "Two Years of Implementation of the Paris Agreement," Jan. 1975, p. 28.

334. Martin's comment: U.S. embassy, Saigon, "Memoranda of Conversations," p. 9921.

334. "Aggressiveness, will": McCloskey, "North-South Confrontation," p. 6778.

334. "Everybody is trying to beat": Rep. McCloskey's notes on a meeting with Ambassador Martin; supplied by Rep. McCloskey.

334–35. Habib comment: House Appropriations Committee [7], p. 89; Gen. Graham comment, p. 14.

334–35. Joint memorandum on aid to Hanoi: CIA, DIA, and Bureau of Intelligence and Research, "Communist Military and Economic Aid to North Vietnam," pp. 3–4.

335–36. Serong's plan: Warner, *Certain Victory*, pp. 13–14.

336. "In nearly every case": DAO Final Assessment, chap. 16–B, p. 1.

336. "Difficult, if not impossible": *New York Times*, Jan. 29, 1975.

336. "Bottomless pit": ibid., Jan. 24, 1975.

336. "Will we have to keep doing this?": House Appropriations Committee [7], p. 46.

337. Thieu began to understand; "lighten the ship": Hosmer, Kellen, and Jenkins, *Fall of South Vietnam*, pp. 179, 111; Herrington, "Third Indochina War," p. 225.

338–41. "Revolutionary violence": Dung, "Great Spring Victory," p. 1; "Revolution may develop" and "combat capability," p. 2; "great quantities" and "hemp ropes," p. 3; "having already withdrawn," p. 6; four assumptions, p. 5; "large surprise attacks," p. 8; Dung read a poem, p. 10; "campaign 275," p. 9; Dung left Hanoi, secrecy measures, p. 13; Tet breakfast, p. 17; "as large as Haiphong," p. 19; final orders, p. 20; "we will attack," p. 27.

338n. Dung's background: U.S. Embassy, Saigon, *Vietnam Documents*, no. 114, pp. 35–36.

341. Phu debated with his staff: Le Gro, *Ceasefire to Capitulation*, p. 150; Hosmer, Kellen, and Jenkins, *Fall of South Vietnam*, pp. 169–71; "Talking with Former Puppet Officers," p. 8.

Chapter 10.
COLLAPSE

345–46. Battle of Ban Me Thuot: Dung, "Great Spring Victory," pp. 28–32; Le Gro, *Ceasefire to Capitulation*, p. 150; DAO Final Assessment, chap. 1, pp. 10–11; Hosmer, Kellen, and Jenkins, *Fall of South Vietnam*, pp. 169–71.

345. Struharik was trapped: House Select Committee on Missing Persons [1], pt. 2, pp. 24–25.

345–46. Missionaries arrived: Miller, *Captured!*, pp. 16–18, 22–25; "guys with the red stars," p. 28.

346. Commanders "stunned": "Talking with Former Puppet Officers," p. 8.

346–47n. "A number of local troops": SWB FE/4871, Apr. 7, 1975.

347–48 Counterattack fails: DAO Final Assessment, chap. 1, p. 11, and chap. 5, p. 18; Le Gro, *Ceasefire to Capitulation*, pp. 151–52; Hosmer, Kellen, and Jenkins, *Fall of South Vietnam*, pp. 171–74.

347. Flight from Kontum: Province Report, Kontum, Mar. 11, 1975.

347. Minute-by-minute intelligence: Dung, "Great Spring Victory," p. 35.

348. Only 1,000 men: Le Gro, *Ceasefire to Capitulation*, p. 173.

348–50. Meeting at Cam Ranh Bay; Phu told subordinates: Vien, *Leadership*, p. 141; Vien and Khuyen, *Reflections on the War*, pp. 128–29; Khuyen, *The RVNAF*, p. 389; Hosmer, Kellen, and Jenkins, *Fall of South Vietnam*, pp. 182–88; Dung, "Great Spring Victory," pp. 45–46; DAO Final Assessment, chap. 16–B, pp. 2–3; "Talking with Former Puppet Officers," p. 8; Snepp, *Decent Interval*, pp. 192–95; speech by Thieu, SWB FE/4885, Apr. 23, 1975.

349. Plans to clear Highway 7–B: Province Report, Phu Yen, Jan. 1973.

351. Phu and Cam left Pleiku: Vien, *Leadership*, p. 143; Hosmer, Kellen, and Jenkins, *Fall of South Vietnam*, p. 189.

351. John Good arranges evacuation: DAO Final Assessment, chap. 15, pp. 10–11.

351–52. Air Force evacuates: Momyer, *Vietnamese Air Force*, pp. 74–75; DAO Final Assessment, chap. 6, p. 3.

353. Rangers ordered to pull out of Kontum: Viet, *Leadership*, p. 143.

353. "If the enemy escapes": Dung, "Great Spring Victory," p. 44.

353. "Many old people and babies": Hosmer, Kellen, and Jenkins, *Fall of South Vietnam*, p. 192.

354. "More afraid of the Rangers": Butterfield, "How South Vietnam Died," p. 34.

354. Bombing incident, ambush at Phu Tu: U.S. embassy telegram Saigon 4808, Apr. 11, 1975.

354–55. Song Ba crossing: Vien, *Leadership*, p. 145; Le Gro, *Ceasefire to Capitulation*, pp. 153–54.

355. "Shooting gallery": *Christian Science Monitor*, Mar. 27, 1975.

355. Khanh Duong overrun: Le Gro, *Ceasefire to Capitulation*, p. 163.

355–56. Dalat evacuated: Province Report, Tuyen Duc, Mar. 25, 1975; U.S. embassy telegram Saigon 2510, Apr. 15, 1975.

356. 18,000 tons of munitions left in depots: DAO Final Assessment, chap. 5, p. 28.

356. 50,000 refugees streamed out: Province Report, Quang Tri, Mar. 10, 1975.

356–57. Airborne division shifted: DAO Final Assessment, chap. 1, p. 8, and chap. 16–B, pp. 3–4; Le Gro, *Ceasefire to Capitulation*, p. 156; Hosmer, Kellen, and Jenkins, *Fall of South Vietnam*, pp. 177–78, 209–10.

357. "Bold and agile": Dung, "Great Spring Victory," p. 48.

357–58. Thieu spoke on the radio: SWB FE/4860, Mar. 21, 1975.

357–58. Indecision about defense of Hue: Le Gro, *Ceasefire to Capitulation*, p. 158; Hosmer, Kellen, and Jenkins, *Fall of South Vietnam*, pp. 214–17; Khuyen, *The RVNAF*, p. 389.

358. "Don't know where my wife and family are": *New York Times*, Mar. 27, 1975.

359. Marines pulled back: DAO Final Assessment, chap. 8, p. 1 and chap. 15, p. 4; 1st division "lost," chap. 5, p. 15.

359. 37 tanks on the beach: *Washington Post*, Apr. 7, 1975.

360. "Haunting attraction": Oberdorfer, *Tet!* p. 202.

360. Oberdorfer's last visit to Hue: *Washington Post,* Mar. 30, 1975.
360. Hue massacre: Oberdorfer, *Tet!* pp. 210–34; Pike, *Viet-Cong Strategy,* pp. 43–64.
361. Dung lit a cigarette: Dung, "Great Spring Victory," p. 49.
362–63. Quang Ngai "liberation": Martin, *Reaching the Other Side,* pp. 88–92, 99.
363–64. "First armed intervention": Lam, *Vietnamese Response to Intervention,* p. 4; Buttinger, *Smaller Dragon,* p. 391.
364. President Taylor's apology: Dinh, "Catholics in Vietnam," p. 35.
365. Thieu's Order of the Day: SWB FE/4865, Mar. 27, 1975.
367. Francis requested helicopters: DAO Final Assessment, chap. 15, pp. 12–13.
368. McCurdy called 7th Air Force again: ibid., chap. 15, pp. 13–14.
370–71. Vogle account: UPI, Mar. 29, 1975. *See* Dawson, *55 Days,* pp. 182–84.
371. Planes ordered out: Momyer, *Vietnamese Air Force,* p. 76.
372. Sparks account: USMC History Division interview transcript, S./Sgt. W.W. Sparks.
373. Lehmann met with Chamber of Commerce: Dawson, *55 Days,* pp. 171–72.
373–74. Tracy account: DAO Final Assessment, chap. 15, pp. 9–10.
375. Sparks found two last refugees: USMC History Division, interview transcript (Sparks).
375. Other ships arrive: Military Sealift Command, Far East, "Sealift Evacuation History," pp. 1–3.
375. Demolition never ordered: DAO Final Assessment, chap. 5, p. 25.
376. Truong telephoned Thieu: Hosmer, Kellen, and Jenkins, *Fall of South Vietnam,* pp. 222–23.
376. Buddhist flags: *New York Times,* May 4, 1975.
376–77. "Nguyen Hoan" account: "Hoan" described his experiences to Don Oberdorfer, who made his notes available to the author. The narrator's name is not completely clear in the notes and for that reason a pseudonym is used.
377. 12-year-old named Hung: *Christian Science Monitor,* Apr. 8, 1975.
378. "It seemed better": *Washington Post,* Mar. 30, 1975.
378. Crew counted corpses: *Pioneer Contender,* "Refugee Ops Report."
378. Escapes on U.S.-controlled ships: Military Sealift Command, Far East, "Sealift Evacuation History," p. 3.
378. 16,000 soldiers reached the south: DAO Final Assessment, chap. 2, p. 2.
378. Liberation flag was raised: "Peoples Liberation Armed Forces Communique," Mar. 30, 1975; Dung, "Great Spring Victory," p. 51.

378–79. Marines swam to landing craft: DAO Final Assessment, chap. 8, p. 1; *Washington Post,* Apr. 7, 1975; *Pacific Stars and Stripes* (Tokyo), Apr. 3, 1975.

Chapter 11.
"IT IS LIKE AN AVALANCHE"

380. Could not redraw maps: Dung, "Great Spring Victory," p. 56.
380. U.S. ships at Qui Nhon: Military Sealift Command, Far East, "Sealift Evacuation History," p. 4; *Greenville Victory,* "Refugee Evacuation."
380. Minh was directed: U.S. Naval Historical Center interview transcript, Commodore Hoang Co Minh; also Vietnam Press, Apr. 1, 1975.
380. Qui Nhon in Communist hands: SWB FE/4868, Apr. 3, 1975.
381. Aircraft, ammunition losses: DAO Final Assessment, chap. 6, p. 31, and chap. 5, pp. 27–28; Le Gro, *Ceasefire to Capitulation,* p. 163.
381. Phu vowed to defend: SWB FE/4867, Apr. 2, 1975.
381. Phu and staff flew out: Hosmer, Kellen, and Jenkins, *Fall of South Vietnam,* p. 203; DAO Final Assessment, chap. 16–B, p. 7.
381. Riots began; consulate evacuation: *Washington Post,* Apr. 2, 1975; Martin, *Reaching the Other Side,* p. 231.
381. "So ashamed": *Newsweek,* Apr. 14, 1975.
381. "No attack": *Christian Science Monitor,* Apr. 3, 1975.
381. Nha Trang's capture announced: SWB FE/4871, Apr. 7, 1975; Cam Ranh captured, ibid., FE/4872, Apr. 8, 1975.
383. Marines terrorized: *Pioneer Contender,* 'Refugee Ops Report'; *New York Times,* Apr. 2, 1975; *Time,* Apr. 14, 1975.
383. All equipment was lost: DAO Final Assessment, chap. 16–B, p. 8.
383. A historian wrote: Ryan, *A Bridge Too Far,* p. 59.
383–85. U.S. ships at Phan Rang: Military Sealift Command, Far East, "Sealift Evacuation History," pp. 6–7; USMC Interview 6097 (1st Lt. Patrick J. Mullin); USS *Durham,* "Command History for 1975," enclosure 1, p. 5.
385. Barge AN2801: *New York Times,* Apr. 7, 1975.
385–90. Voyages of *Greenville Victory* and *Pioneer Contender:* Military Sealift Command, Far East, "Sealift Evacuation History," pp. 6–7; *Greenville Victory,* "Refugee Evacuation"; *Pioneer Contender,* "Refugee Ops Report"; MSC Office Saigon Residual, "Activities of MSCOV"; 1/4th Marines Post-Exercise Report, "Amphibious Evacuation RVN"; USMC interview 6099 (L. Cpl. Robert Haines); *Sealift,* June, July, Oct., and Dec. 1975.
390–92. Planes unloaded: Dung, "Great Spring

Victory," p. 65; Politburo resolved to capture Saigon, pp. 56–57; cable to Dung, p. 57; "enemy
was in confusion," p. 53; "enemy would not disintegrate," p. 52; Politburo assented, p. 58;
"lightning speed," "long trail of dust," p. 64; exercise with 400 trucks, p. 66; captured soldiers
used as drivers, p. 68; Dung left the highlands, p.
67; new command post west of Loc Ninh, p. 71;
Tho arrived with instructions, p. 73; message
37/TK, p. 77.

391. "Ragged bands": Martin, *Reaching the Other
Side*, p. 229.

393. "No spirit of support": *Time*, Apr. 21, 1975.

393. An Giang incident: Province Report, An
Giang, Apr. 5, 1975.

393. Nam told civil servants to remain: Province
Report, Kien Phong, Apr. 5, 1975.

393. Nam's suicide reported: Terzani, *Giai Phong!*
p. 182; Burchett, *Grasshoppers and Elephants*,
p. 66.

394. Martin's cables: *Congressional Record*, Apr.
24, 1975, pp. 11825–26; House Armed Services
Committee [5], pp. 1787–91.

394. Kissinger declared: Senate Appropriations
Committee [4], pp. 35–36.

394. Schlesinger's opinion: *New York Times*, Apr.
16, 1975; "Upwards of 170,000," ibid., Apr. 10,
1975.

395. "Slitting every throat": *Congressional Record*,
Apr. 23, 1975, p. 11539.

397. Dan's letter: Baltimore *Sun*, Apr. 7, 1975.

397–98. Evacuation plan assumed: DAO Final
Assessment, chap. 16–H, p. 1.

398. "North Vietnamese do not have the capability": Herrington, "Third Indochina War," pp.
272–73.

398. Tree in the courtyard: USMC interview
6042 (Lt. Col. Harper L. Bohr, Jr.).

399. Smith's preparations: DAO Final Assessment, chap. 16–B, pp. 9–10, chap. 16–E, pp.
1–4, and chap. 16–F, pp. 1–2; Tobin, Laehr, and
Hilgenberg, *Last Flight*, pp. 27–29.

399. DAO flagpoles: USMC interview 6133 (Col.
Wiley W. Taylor, Jr.).

399. "I am convinced": Herrington, "Third Indochina War," p. 274; smuggled Vietnamese
onto Babylift flights, pp. 256–58.

400. "Underground railroad": Snepp, *Decent
Interval*, pp. 295–96; Kennerly, *Shooter*, p. 173.

400. "Black flights": DAO Final Assessment,
chap. 16–G, p. 1; Tobin, Laehr, and Hilgenberg,
Last Flight, p. 43.

400–401. Baughn's message: USMC interview
6045 (Lt. Col. Herbert G. Fischer).

401. Plans revised: DAO Final Assessment, chap.
16–C, p. 5.

401. "Everybody thought": USMC interview
6043 (Maj. David E. Cox).

401. "The number killed": Dung, "Great Spring
Victory," p. 62.

402. Duty-free shop: Butterfield, "How South
Vietnam Died," p. 40.

402. Reprimands to civil servants: *New York
Times*, Apr. 15, 1975.

402–3. Plans to reconstitute units: DAO Final
Assessment, chap. 5, pp. 33–35, 50–51; Le Gro,
Ceasefire to Capitulation, pp. 172–73.

404. Kennerly's photographs: Kennerly, *Shooter*,
pp. 170–73.

404. Ford's letters to Thieu: Nessen, *Sure Looks
Different*, p. 107; "almost as fast as the Vietnamese army," p. 97.

405. "Cambodia is gone": Ford, *Time to Heal*,
p. 253.

405. Defense Intelligence estimate: Le Gro, *Ceasefire to Capitulation*, p. 171.

405. "Authoritative judgment": House Select
Committee on Intelligence [1], p. 1695.

406. Weyand plan: Ford, *Time to Heal*, p. 253;
House Appropriations Committee [8], p. 3; House
International Relations Committee [1], pt. 2, pp.
473–77.

407. Domestic advisers disagreed; Kissinger
helped draft: *Time*, Apr. 14 and 21, 1975.

407. Nessen urged: Nessen, *Sure Looks Different*,
p. 101.

408. Not-for-attribution conversations: Baltimore
Sun, Apr. 12, 1975; *Time*, Apr. 21, 1975.

408. "The quickest way": Nessen, *Sure Looks
Different*, p. 105.

409. Only 2,000 Americans: DAO Final Assessment, chap. 16–E, p. 3; "courting disaster,"
chap. 16–C, p. 6.

409. "No operative policy": House International
Relations Committee [1], pt. 3, p. 616; Martin
told Washington, p. 619; parole authority
widened, p. 544.

409. Martin agreed to a new procedure: DAO
Final Assessment, chap. 16–B, p. 12.

410. Processing officers noticed: Tobin, Laehr,
and Hilgenberg, *Last Flight*, p. 67; House International Relations Committee [1], pt. 3, p. 591.

410. "Certification letters": Tobin, Laehr, and
Hilgenberg, *Last Flight*, p. 63.

410. Madison's cable: Herrington, "Third Indochina War," p. 288.

410–11. "Flagrant inequities": DAO Final Assessment, chap. 16–C, p. 15; Navy attache's proposal, chap. 16–C, p. 18.

411. "No apology": House International Relations Committee [1], pt. 3, p. 581.

411. Vietnamese on SS *Green Wave*: MSC Office
Saigon Residual, "Activities of MSCOV."

411. "We must recognize": Baltimore *Sun*, Apr.
16, 1975; "Because I am a general," ibid., Apr.
18, 1975.

411. "Is there any basis?": House Appropriations
Committee [8], p. 10.

412. "They can do": *Time*, Apr. 28, 1975.

412. "I reject": *Congressional Record*, Apr. 22,

1975, p. 11287; "We could bomb," p. 11265; "legislation just an excuse," p. 11268.

412–13. "I only wish": Kennerly, *Shooter*, p. 174.

413. Ky admitted: Ky, *Twenty Years*, pp. 203–21.

414. "We understand that General Minh": *New York Times*, Apr. 3, 1975.

414. "The Provisional Revolutionary Government": SWB FE/4871, Apr. 7, 1975; Thieu speech, ibid.

415–16. Bombing of palace: Dung, "Great Spring Victory," p. 82; SWB FE/4873, FE/4874, FE/4875, and FE/4881, Apr. 9, 10, 11, and 18, 1975; *Time*, Apr. 21, 1975.

416n. American intelligence was skeptical: Snepp, *Decent Interval*, p. 316.

416. "Bravo One" plan: Shaplen, "Letter from Saigon," Apr. 21, 1975, p. 138.

416–17. Politburo orders: Dung, "Great Spring Victory," p. 73; attack on Xuan Loc, pp. 79–80; "stubbornness," p. 80.

417. "We have a victory": Le Gro, *Ceasefire to Capitulation*, p. 174.

417. Huynh Tan Phat declared: Burchett, *Grasshoppers and Elephants*, p. 33.

417. Gen. Dao told the victors: "Talking with Former Puppet Officers," p. 10.

417. "We cannot afford": *Newsweek*, Apr. 28, 1975.

417. "Not a transitional government": SWB FE/4879, Apr. 16, 1975.

417–18. "Depends on our adversaries": *Washington Post*, Apr. 10, 1975.

418. "Immediately cease all aid": VNA, Apr. 13, 1975.

418–19. A penetration agent in COSVN: Snepp, *Decent Interval*, pp. 366–68; House International Relations Committee [1], pt. 3, p. 583; Martin's meeting with Thieu, pp. 546–47, 599.

419–22. "Heartless and unfaithful": SWB FE/4885, Apr. 23, 1975; Thieu and Huong speeches and Communist reactions, ibid.

422. "Sentimental symbol": Pond, "Vietnamese Politics," p. 5.

423. "Conditions are ripe": Dung, "Great Spring Victory," p. 104.

Chapter 12.
"YOUR MISSION IS VERY HEAVY"

425. Kissinger told Congress: House Appropriations Committee [8], pp. 29–30, 33.

425. Defense Intelligence assessment: "Defense Intelligence Notice Summary 150–75," DIA message 220714Z, Apr. 1975.

425. Huong proposed ceasefire: Ministry of Foreign Affairs, Republic of Vietnam, "Note to the Signatories of the Act of the International Conference on Vietnam," Apr. 23, 1975.

432. Hiep went to Tansonnhut: Herrington, "Third Indochina War," pp. 309–10.

432. "Legal basis still exists": SWB FE/4889, Apr. 28, 1975.

432. "All in its power": Baltimore *Sun*, Apr. 22, 1975.

432. French officials theorized: *Far Eastern Economic Review*, May 2, 1975.

432–33. Mérillon imagined: Terzani, *Giai Phong!* p. 24.

433. Mérillon conferred; "Minh solution" hinted: ibid., p. 23; House International Relations Committee [1], pt. 3, pp. 599, 609; Don, *Endless War*, pp. 247–49; Hosmer, Kellen, and Jenkins, *Fall of South Vietnam*, p. 246; Snepp, *Decent Interval*, pp. 324–25; *New York Times*, Apr. 19 and 24, 1975.

433. Hanoi's message to Col. Summers: Herrington, "Third Indochina War," pp. 311–14.

434. Martin assured subordinates: Snepp, *Decent Interval*, p. 448; *Christian Science Monitor*, May 6, 1975.

434. P.R.G. announced its demands: SWB FE/4887, Apr. 25, 1975.

434–35. Ford mused to Hartmann; Hartmann drafted speech: Hartmann, *Palace Politics*, p. 321; Kissinger's "paranoia," p. 329.

434. "With flags flying": Ford, *Time to Heal*, pp. 253–54.

435. Crucial passage typed on Air Force One: Nessen, *Sure Looks Different*, p. 108.

435–36. 488 Americans and 3,000 Vietnamese: DAO Final Assessment, chap. 16–E, p. 3; crowds reached 10,000, chap. 16–F, p. 4; Smith requested marines, chap. 16–B, p. 13; Thieu's departure, chap. 16–E, p. 14, and Snepp, *Decent Interval*, pp. 435–37.

436. Communist delegates dug bunkers: Dung, "Great Spring Victory," p. 85; Dung left Loc Ninh, p. 107.

436. Communists advanced toward Bien Hoa, crossed Highway 15: Le Gro, *Ceasefire to Capitulation*, p. 177.

436. Artillery attack on Long Binh: "Intelligence Summary 75–117B," USSAG message 270350Z Apr. 1975.

437. Gen. Lan proposed; marine dependents evacuated from Vung Tau: DAO Final Assessment, chap. 8, p. 3, and chap. 16–C, pp. 18–19; Tobin, Laehr, and Hilgenberg, *Last Flight*, pp. 68–69; USMC interview 6045 (Fischer).

437. New declaration by P.R.G.: VNA, Apr. 26, 1975.

438. Prisoners freed; Huong's speech; Assembly resolution: SWB FE/4889, Apr. 28, 1975.

438. "Immobilisme": Shaplen, "Letter from Saigon," Apr. 21, 1975, p. 127.

438. Military developments on the 27th: DAO Final Assessment, chap. 2, p. 5, and chap. 5, pp. 14–15; "Spot Report," USSAG message 270930Z

Apr. 1975; Le Gro, *Ceasefire to Capitulation*, p. 177; Dung, "Great Spring Victory," p. 108; SWB FE/4890, Apr. 29, 1975.

439–40. Huong notified; Assembly named Minh: SWB FE/4890, Apr. 29, 1975; Huong's resignation speech, ibid., FE/4891, Apr. 30, 1975.

440. "Affable, slow-spoken": *Far Eastern Economic Review*, Jan. 29, 1973.

441. "Not a job for a Boy Scout": Buckley, "Is This Written?" p. 93.

441n. Diem's killers: Don, *Endless War*, pp. 102, 112.

441. Minh biographical sketch: Reuter, Nov. 24, 1970; *Far Eastern Economic Review*, May 2, 1975; *Time*, May 5, 1975.

441. "Great sadness": *Far Eastern Economic Review*, Nov. 21, 1970.

442. "Neither this side nor the other": *New York Times*, Feb. 27, 1973.

442. Minh's kinsman flew from Paris: Burchett, *Grasshoppers and Elephants*, p. 39.

442. Minh still believed: Timmes, "Vietnam Summary," pt. 2, pp. 28–29.

442–43. Minh's speech: SWB FE/4890, Apr. 29, 1975.

443. Tuyen's death reported: Toai, "Lament for Vietnam," p. 69.

443–44. Liberation Radio commentary: SWB FE/4891, Apr. 30, 1975.

444. "What group do you belong to?" VNA, May 8, 1975.

444. Three gunships destroyed: DAO Final Assessment, chap. 16–E, p. 14.

444–45. Pingle, Rice accounts: Tobin, Laehr, and Hilgenberg, *Last Flight*, pp. 71–72.

445. "Dao chanh!": Herrington, "Third Indochina War," p. 326.

445. Pilots trained and led by Trung: VNA, May 8, 1975.

445–46. 325th Division reached Nhon Trach: Dung, "Great Spring Victory," p. 111; "no safe place," p. 109.

445. Bien Hoa abandoned: "Intelligence Summary 75–118B," USSAG message 281130Z Apr. 1975.

445. Division hid in the jungle: Burchett, *Grasshoppers and Elephants*, pp. 38–39, 48.

446. Two C-130s cleared to land: DAO Final Assessment, chap. 16–E, p. 15; 60 flights scheduled, chap. 16–B, p, 13; Defense Department, "Chronology—Frequent Wind"; Tobin, Laehr, and Hilgenberg, *Last Flight*, p. 73.

446. Marines began to saw through tree: USMC interview 6043 (Cox).

Chapter 13.
THE FALL OF SAIGON

447–50. Attack on Tansonnhut; Vietnamese air force disintegrates: DAO Final Assessment, chap.

16–B, pp. 13–14, and chap. 16–E, pp. 15–16; Tobin, Laehr, and Hilgenberg, *Last Flight*, pp. 76–79, 81–82, and 85–87; Herrington, "Third Indochina War," pp. 327–32; USMC interview transcript, Gy. Sgt. Vasco D. Martin, Jr.; USMC interview 6043 (Cox).

448. Politburo message: Dung, "Great Spring Victory," p. 110.

450. Formal request from Minh: SWB FE/4891, Apr. 30, 1975.

450. Bus convoys ordered: DAO Final Assessment, chap. 16–A, p. 3; Tobin, Laehr, and Hilgenberg, *Last Flight*, pp. 84–85.

450. Smith called from Tansonnhut: DAO Final Assessment, chap. 16–B, p. 14.

450. Ford met with advisers: Baltimore *Sun*, Apr. 29 and 30, 1975; Nessen, *Sure Looks Different*, p. 109.

450. A reduced staff of 150: Snepp, *Decent Interval*, p. 483.

450–51. Joint Military Team delegation to remain: Herrington, "Third Indochina War," pp. 332–34.

451. Lack of planning: Snepp, *Decent Interval*, pp. 473–504; CIA translators and others left behind, pp. 512–13, 567.

451. U.S.I.S. employees stranded: Dawson, *55 Days*, pp. 2, 329–30, 337, 344–45.

451. Martin arrived at DAO: DAO Final Assessment, chap. 16–E, p. 16; Homer Smith, "Forty-Five Days," p. 15.

452. "Excruciating" 30 minutes: Hirschy and Bondi, "Final Hours."

452. Smith called Gayler: DAO Final Assessment, chap. 16–B, p. 15; Defense Department, "Chronology—Frequent Wind."

452. Minimum of three hours: Carey and Quinlan, "Frequent Wind," pt. 3, p. 37.

452. Support planes in the air: Defense Department, "Chronology—Frequent Wind."

453. Air America pilots volunteered: DAO Final Assessment, chap. 16–D, p. 14; only one was at the terminal, chap. 16–B, p. 15.

453–54. Fliers were shuttled; Fine's dairy: Robbins, *Air America*, pp. 282–84.

454. Aircraft reaching U Tapao: PROVMAG 39 "Command Chronology for 19 April to 30 April," tab PP.

454. 45 airmen had no idea: *Washington Post*, May 4, 1975.

454. Preparations for the helicopter lift: USMC interview 6043 (Cox).

454–55. Three Americans taken hostage: DAO Final Assessment, chap. 16–E, pp. 16–17; Hueys could not refuel, chap. 16–B, p. 15; Tobin, Laehr, and Hilgenberg, *Last Flight*, pp. 87–88.

455. Nearly a disaster on the *Blue Ridge*: *Newsweek*, May 12, 1975.

455. Smith called the embassy: DAO Final Assessment, chap. 16–B, p. 15.

455. "Like a dead man": Snepp, *Decent Interval,* p. 498.

455. Kissinger called Ford: Nessen, *Sure Looks Different,* p. 109.

455. Order was flashed: Defense Department, "Chronology—Frequent Wind."

455. All U.S. government personnel must leave: DAO Final Assessment, chap. 16–A, p. 3; Herrington, "Third Indochina War," p. 335.

456. Chainsaws and axes: ibid.; Snepp, *Decent Interval,* p. 501.

456. McNamara's flotilla: USMC interview transcript, S. Sgt. S. B. Hasty; House International Relations Committee [1], pt. 3, pp. 593–94.

456. Marines lined up: Carey and Quinlan, "Frequent Wind," pt. 3, p. 38.

456. Fighters took off: Defense Department, "Chronology—Frequent Wind."

456–57. First wave of helicopters: Carey and Quinlan, "Frequent Wind," pt. 3, pp. 39–40; 9th MAB "Command Chronology," pt. 2, p. 4; 9th MAB "After Action Report."

461. A dilapidated ferryboat: *Sealift,* June 1975, p. 9; USMC Interview 6048 (Capt. Richard L. Reuter).

461–62. *Greenville Victory* loads refugees: Military Sealift Command, Far East, "Sealift Evacuation History," pp. 13–15.

462. *American Challenger* at Phu Quoc: ibid., pp. 12, 16; *Sealift,* June 1975, p. 8; USMC interview 6061 (Capt. M. T. Mallick).

462. *Dubuque* also at Phu Quoc: USS *Dubuque,* "Command History for 1975," p. 3; USMC interview 6068 (Gy. Sgt. John O. Cohen).

462–63. McNamara's voyage: USMC interview transcript, S. Sgt. S. B. Hasty; CTF76 "After Action Report."

463–64. Tugs and barges sailed from Saigon: DAO Final Assessment, chap. 16–D, p. 19; Military Sealift Command, Far East, "Sealift Evacuation History," p. 13; MSC Office Saigon Residual, "Activities of MSCOV."

464. Flurry of shots; snipers: Tobin, Laehr, and Hilgenberg, *Last Flight,* pp. 97–98.

464. 36 helicopters had left: Defense Department, "Chronology—Frequent Wind."

467. 5,500 evacuated by nightfall: ibid.

467. Antiaircraft along the flight path: PROVMAG 39 "Command Chronology for 19 April to 30 April," tab LL.

467. Soaked radios; Cox told pilots: USMC interview 6043 (Cox).

467. Near collision: Tobin, Laehr, and Hilgenberg, *Last Flight,* p. 101.

467. Loc's Order of the Day: SWB FE/4891, Apr. 30, 1975.

467. Smith left: DAO Final Assessment, chap. 16–B, p. 16.

467. Carey flew out; sound of cannon fire: 9th MAB "After Action Report."

467. Demolition teams: Tobin, Laehr, and Hilgenberg, *Last Flight,* pp. 104–6; DAO Final Assessment, chap. 16, p. A–4.

468. Erroneous report on bodies: House Appropriations Committee [9], p. 631; $16 million in gold, p. 654; "serviceable assets," p. 650.

468n. Two other marines died: PROVMAG 39 "Command Chronology for 19 April to 30 April," pt. 7.

468n. Navy fighter-bomber ditched: Defense Department, "Chronology—Frequent Wind."

468n. Vietnamese T-41 ditched: report by commanding officer, USS *Duluth.*

468n. Bodies returned: *New York Times,* Feb. 23, 1976.

468. Tansonnhut evacuation statistics: Defense Department, "Chronology—Frequent Wind."

468. "A total not to exceed": 9th MAB "After Action Report."

468. The only marine aircraft: Carey and Quinlan, "Frequent Wind," pt. 3, p. 39.

469. Word came from the embassy: USMC interview 6133 (Col. W. W. Taylor, Jr.); 9th MAB "Command Chronology," pt. 2, p. 5.

469. Eight busloads: Herrington, "Third Indochina War," p. 341.

469. "No viable plan": Carey's first move: 9th MAB "After Action Report."

469–70. Col. Madison had taken charge: Herrington, "Third Indochina War," pp. 336–44; slide projector used, p. 349.

470. Poor communications: ibid., p. 350; USMC interview 6046 (1st Lt. J. J. Martinoli).

470. Reports that the building was on fire; Cobras used as pathfinders: Carey and Quinlan, "Frequent Wind," pt. 3, p. 43.

470–71. "Bottomless pit"; "entire population of Saigon": Herrington, "Third Indochina War," p. 365.

470. "Always the same—2,000 to go": Tobin, Laehr, and Hilgenberg, *Last Flight,* p. 106.

471. Carey argued: Carey and Quinlan, "Frequent Wind," pt. 3, pp. 43–44.

471. 500 Vietnamese still waiting: RLT–4 "Command Chronology," pt. 3, p. 22; Defense Department, "Chronology—Frequent Wind."

471. Fighters could see flares: Tobin, Laehr, and Hilgenberg, *Last Flight,* pp. 101, 111.

471. Dung's artillery was ordered: Dung, "Great Spring Victory," p. 113.

471. Dumps at Long Binh exploding: Snepp, *Decent Interval,* p. 548.

471–72. Vehicles with headlights on: *Washington Post,* May 1, 1975.

472. People began crowding: Herrington, "Third Indochina War," pp. 352–56.

472. Martin insisted: USMC interview 6046 (Martinoli).

472–73. Herrington counted heads: Herrington, "Third Indochina War," p. 356.

473. Nineteen more flights; White House message: Carey and Quinlan, "Frequent Wind," pt. 3, p. 44; 9th MAB "Command Chronology," pt. 3, pp. 5–6; PROVMAG 39 "Command Chronology for 19 April to 30 April," tab F; CTF76 "After Action Report."

473. Pilots had been briefed: USMC interview 6046 (Martinoli).

473–74. Martin descended; Madison's exchange with Lehmann; McKinley confirmed: Herrington, "Third Indochina War," p. 358.

474. 19-flight limit had been passed: 9th MAB "Command Chronology," pt. 3, p. 6; Carey issued orders, ibid.

474. "The following message": Tobin, Laehr, and Hilgenberg, *Last Flight*, p. 111.

474. Martin's departure: Carey and Quinlan, "Frequent Wind," pt. 3, p. 44; Snepp, *Decent Interval*, pp. 558–59; USMC interview 6046 (Martinoli); PROVMAG 39 "Command Chronology for 19 April to 30 April," tab G.

475–76. Madison's exchange with Kean; Herrington's departure: Herrington, "Third Indochina War," pp. 358–62.

476. Gen. Rhee jailed: Dawson, *55 Days*, p. 353; Snepp, *Decent Interval*, p. 560.

476–77. Evacuation ends: USMC interview transcript, M. Sgt. Juan J. Valdez; Valdez, "The Last to Leave"; USMC interview 6046 (Martinoli).

478–79. Embassy emptied out: Terzani, *Giai Phong!* p. 84; Third Force delegation, pp. 78–79; Dung, "Great Spring Victory," p. 114.

479–80. Huyen and Mau statements; *Nhan Dan* editorial; Minh and Hanh broadcasts: SWB FE/4891 and FE/4892, Apr. 30 and May 1, 1975.

480. Soldiers stripped: Terzani, *Giai Phong!* p. 87; *Washington Post*, May 11, 1975.

480. Police siphoned gas: Dawson, *55 Days*, p. 9.

480. Communists found computerized files: Dung, "Great Spring Victory," p. 118.

481. Police colonel's suicide: Dawson, *55 Days*, pp. 7–8; Terzani, *Giai Phong!* p. 87.

481. "Continue the attack": Dung, "Great Spring Victory," p. 118.

481–82. Capture of Doc Lap palace: "Saigon, the Historic Hours," *Vietnam Courier*, May 1975, pp. 3–4; *Vietnam* (Hanoi), no. 201, 1975, pp. 4–5. This description is also based on the film of the scene made by Neil Davis, one of the bravest and most skillful of all Vietnam war cameramen.

482–83. Second surrender speech: SWB FE/4892, May 1, 1975.

483. Passengers filed off ships: *New York Times*, May 1, 1975.

483. *Bo doi* built cooking fires: Terzani, *Giai Phong!* p. 101.

483–84. Nguyen Ngoc Ngan burned photos: Ngan, *Will of Heaven*, p. 8.

484. 32 Vietnamese navy ships: "Data for Operation New Life," enclosure 3.

484. Officers stole milk: USMC interview 6048 (Reuter).

484. Helicopter incident: on *Miller:* Military Sealift Command, Far East, "Sealift Evacuation History," p. 16; USMC interview 6066 (Capt. Edward R. Palmquist); Amphibious Evacuation Security Force "Command Chronology," pt. 2, p. 2.

484–85. Helicopters tried to land on *Blue Ridge:* CTF76 "After Action Report"; *Update* supplement (*Blue Ridge* shipboard magazine), April 1975.

485. A visitor to Kissinger's office: Stoessinger, *Anguish of Power*, p. 77.

486. "Do you hear firecrackers?": Dung, "Great Spring Victory," p. 120.

486. Tho's poem: Terzani, *Giai Phong!* p. 113.

487. "Worthy of our ancestors": VNA, May 7, 1975.

487. "Subtle fear": Terzani, *Giai Phong!* p. 160.

Chapter 14.
THE LIMITS OF CREDIBILITY

488. Reagan's VFW speech: Cannon, *Reagan*, p. 271; *Baltimore Sun*, Aug. 19, 1980.

489. "A paper tiger": Whalen, *Falling Flag*, pp. 131, 137.

489. "Draining our strength": Kissinger, *White House Years*, p. 235.

490. Kissinger left the impression: Landau, *Uses of Power*, pp. 158–63, 180–83; Stoessinger, *Anguish of Power*, p. 50.

490. "Indirect and devious": Kissinger, *White House Years*, p. 259; "still half believed," p. 279.

490. "Made up his mind": John Osborne, *Nixon Watch*, pp. 176–77.

491. "Never Munich again": Fall, *Last Reflections*, p. 161.

491. "Americans underestimate": Fall, *Viet-Nam Witness*, p. 105.

491. "Measures of great consequence": Nixon, *RN*, p. 394.

491. Plans to intensify bombing: Kissinger, *White House Years*, pp. 284–85; "middle course," p. 288.

492. "I will not be the first": Nixon, *RN*, p. 400.

492. "Only to others": Halberstam, *Best and Brightest*, p. 807.

493. "Backbiting": Price, *With Nixon*, p. 306.

493. "We are going to win": Shannon, *Heir Apparent*, p. 121.

494. "Destroyed whatever possibility": Nixon, *RN*, p. 403.

495. "Not merely important": Schell, *Time of Illusion*, p. 354.

496. Joint Chiefs argued: *Pentagon Papers*, Gravel ed., 2:663.

496. McNaughton memo: *Pentagon Papers, New York Times* ed., p. 432.

497. "Aim of upholding credibility": Schell, *Time of Illusion,* pp. 362–63.

497. "Two groups of countries": Landau, *Uses of Power,* p. 123.

498. Rogers comment: House Foreign Affairs Committee [1], p. 36.

499. "Limited means": *Pentagon Papers, New York Times* ed., p. 536.

500. "Congress refused": Nixon, *RN,* p. 889; "the means to enforce," p. 887.

500. "Could have worked": Kissinger, *White House Years,* p. 1470.

500. Kissinger's view on bombing: Kissinger, *Years of Upheaval,* pp. 320–27.

502. "Panic" of the Vietnamese leadership: Blaufarb, *Counterinsurgency Era,* pp. 304–5.

504–5. "Missed opportunities": Kissinger, *Years of Upheaval,* p. 1029.

505–6. Reunification proceedings in Hanoi: SWB FE/5251, July 5, 1976.

Bibliography

This bibliography contains only works cited in the text.

Bracketed numbers following names of congressional committees refer to the documents listed in part 3 (Congressional Hearings and Reports). These are grouped by committee, then numbered in chronological order.

1. GENERAL

American Aid and Vietnam Economy. Office of the [South Vietnamese] Deputy Prime Minister in charge of Economic Development. Saigon, March 1975.

Amos, Harry O. "Military Elements of the U.S. Embassy, Phnom Penh, 18 March 1970 to 30 June 1970." Appendix C in Tho, *Cambodian Incursion.*

Barron, John, and Anthony Paul. *Peace with Horror.* London: Hodder & Staughton, 1977. Also published in the United States under the title *Murder of a Gentle Land.*

Batchelder, Sydney H., Jr., and D. A. Quinlan. "Operation Eagle Pull." *Marine Corps Gazette,* May 1976. Colonel Batchelder was the marine ground force commander for the evacuation of Phnom Penh. This account is based on official military records.

Bennett, Joseph. "A Cambodian Diary." *Hudson Review,* Autumn 1971, pp. 388–418.

Berger, Carl, ed. *The United States Air Force in Southeast Asia, 1961–1973.* Washington, D.C.: Office of Air Force History, 1977.

Blaufarb, Douglas S. *The Counterinsurgency Era: U.S. Doctrine and Performance, 1950 to the Present.* New York: Free Press, 1977.

Bloodworth, Dennis. *An Eye for the Dragon.* London: Secker & Warburg, 1970.

Brown, David E. "Exporting Insurgency: The Communists in Cambodia." In *Indochina in Conflict,* pp. 125–35. *See* Zasloff and Goodman 1972.

Brown, MacAlister, and Joseph J. Zasloff. "The Pathet Lao and the Politics of Reconciliation in Laos, 1973–1974." In *Communism in Indochina,* pp. 259–82. *See* Zasloff and Brown 1975.

———. "Laos 1974: Coalition Government Shoots the Rapids." *Asian Survey,* February 1975, pp. 174–83.

Buckley, Tom. "Is This Written in the Stars? See It Through with Nguyen Van Thieu." *New York Times Magazine*, September 26, 1971.

Burchett, Wilfred. *At the Barricades*, New York: Times Books, 1981.

———. *Grasshoppers and Elephants: Why Vietnam Fell*. New York: Urizen Books, 1977.

———. *The Second Indochina War: Cambodia and Laos*. New York: International Publishers, 1970.

Butterfield, Fox. "How South Vietnam Died—by the Stab in the Front." *New York Times Magazine*, May 25, 1975.

Buttinger, Joseph. *A Dragon Defiant: A Short History of Vietnam*. New York: Praeger, 1972.

———. *The Smaller Dragon*. New York: Praeger, 1958.

Cannon, Lou. *Reagan*. New York: Putnam, 1982.

Carey, Richard E., and D.A. Quinlan. "Frequent Wind." *Marine Corps Gazette*, February, March, and April 1976. General Carey was commander of the marine ground security force in the evacuation of Saigon. This detailed account is based on military records.

Carney, Timothy Michael. *Communist Party Power in Kampuchea (Cambodia): Documents and Discussion*. Data Paper no. 106. Southeast Asia Program, Department of Asian Studies, Cornell University, Ithaca, N.Y., January 1977.

Cincinnatus [Cecil B. Currey]. *Self-Destruction: The Disintegration and Decay of the United States Army during the Vietnam Era*. New York: Norton, 1981.

Collins, James Lawton, Jr. *The Development and Training of the South Vietnamese Army, 1950–1972*. Vietnam Studies Series. Washington, D.C.: Department of the Army, 1975.

Cooper, Wayne L. "The Phung Hoang Program in IV CTZ—A Personal Assessment." Can Tho, South Vietnam, February 1970. Typescript.

Dawson, Alan. *55 Days: The Fall of South Vietnam*. Englewood Cliffs, N.J.: Prentice-Hall, 1977.

Dickson, Paul. *The Electronic Battlefield*. Bloomington: Indiana University Press, 1976.

Dillard, Walter Scott. *Sixty Days to Peace: Implementing the Paris Peace Accords, Vietnam 1973*. Washington, D.C.: National Defense University Press, 1982. Colonel Dillard was the official historian of the U.S. delegation to the Four-Party Joint Military Commission and subsequently wrote the delegation's "Final Report." This published history of the commission's activities was written from that report and other official records, including the delegation's message file. The "Final Report" itself was still classified in early 1983.

Dinh, Tran Van. "Catholics in Vietnam." *Worldview*, November 1972.

———. "Vietnam 1974: A Revolution Unfulfilled." *Pacific Community*, April 1974.

Doglione, John A., et al. *Air Power and the 1972 Spring Offensive*. U.S. Air Force Southeast Asia Monograph Series, vol. 2, monograph 3. Washington, D.C.: U.S. Government Printing Office, 1976.

Dommen, Arthur J. *Conflict in Laos: The Politics of Neutralization*. Rev. ed. New York: Praeger, 1971.

———. "Toward Negotiations in Laos." *Asian Survey*, January 1971, pp. 41–50.

Don, Tran Van. *Our Endless War*. San Rafael, Calif.: Presidio Press, 1978.

Dung, Van Tieng. "Great Spring Victory." Translated by Foreign Broadcast Information Service. FBIS supplement 38, June 7, 1976, and supplement 42, July 7, 1976.

Emerson, Gloria. "U.S. Helped to Legitimize Mass Murder in Cambodia." Independent News Alliance, January 13, 1981.

Enthoven, Alain P., and K. Wayne Smith. *How Much Is Enough? Shaping the Defense Program, 1961–1969.* New York: Harper & Row, 1971.

Everingham, John. "The Planned Destruction of Meo Villages in Laos." September 1971. Typescript.

Fall, Bernard B. *Last Reflections on a War.* Garden City, N.Y.: Doubleday, 1967.

————. *The Two Vietnams: A Political and Military Analysis.* Rev. ed. New York: Praeger, 1964.

————. *Vietnam Witness, 1953–1966.* London: Pall Mall Press, 1966.

Fallaci, Oriana. *Interview with History.* Translated by John Shepley. New York: Liveright, 1976.

————. "Sihanouk: The Man We May Have to Settle For in Cambodia." *New York Times Magazine,* August 12, 1973.

Fitzgerald, Frances. "Journey to North Vietnam." *New Yorker,* April 28, 1975, pp. 96–119.

Ford, Gerald R. *A Time to Heal.* New York: Harper & Row, 1979.

Frelinghuysen, Peter. *Vietnam—A Changing Crucible,* U.S. House of Representatives. Report 93–1196. July 15, 1974.

Galbraith, John Kenneth, *Ambassador's Journal.* Boston: Houghton Mifflin, 1969.

Garrett, W. E. "The Hmong of Laos: No Place to Run." *National Geographic,* January 1974, pp. 78–111.

Gettleman, Marvin, ed. *Vietnam: History, Documents, and Opinions on a Major World Crisis.* Harmondsworth, Middlesex: Penguin Books, 1966.

Gettleman, Marvin, Susan Gettleman, Lawrence Kaplan, and Carol Kaplan, eds. *Conflict in Indochina.* New York: Random House, 1970.

Girling, J. L. S. "Nixon's Algeria—Doctrine and Disengagement in Indochina." *Pacific Affairs,* Winter 1971–72, pp. 527–44.

Goodman, Allan E. *The Lost Peace: America's Search for a Negotiated Settlement of the Vietnam War.* Stanford, Calif.: Hoover Institution, 1978.

Gornicki, Wieslaw. "An Asian Holocaust." Baltimore *Sun,* April 15, 1979.

Grant, Zalin B. "Vietnam without GI's." *New Republic,* May 19, 1973.

Halberstam, David. *The Best and the Brightest.* New York: Random House, 1972.

Halpern, Joel M. *Government, Politics, and Social Structure in Laos: A Study of Tradition and Innovation.* Southeast Asia Studies Monograph Series no. 4. Yale University, New Haven, 1964.

Hartmann, Robert T. *Palace Politics: An Inside Account of the Ford Years.* New York: McGraw-Hill, 1980.

Harvey, Frank "Air War Vietnam—1972." *Worldview,* March 1972.

Heinl, Robert D., Jr. "On Basis of Pacification, Vietnam War Has Been Won." *Armed Forces Journal,* February 1972.

Herrington, Stuart A. "The Third Indochina War, 1973–1975: A Personal Perspective." Thesis, May 1980. Published as *Peace with Honor: An American Report on Vietnam, 1973–1975.* Novato, Calif.: Presidio Press, 1983.

Hickey, Gerald C. "Some Aspects of Hill Tribe Life in Vietnam." In *Southeast Asian Tribes,* vol. 2, pp. 745–69. *See* Kunstadter 1967.

————. "The War in Cambodia: Focus on Some of the Internal Forces Involved." Santa Monica, Calif.: Rand Corporation, September 1, 1970. Internal note.

Hildebrand, G. C., and Gareth Porter. *The Politics of Food: Starvation and Agricultural*

Revolution in Cambodia. Washington, D.C.: Indochina Resource Center, September 1975.

Hinh, Nguyen Duy. *Vietnamization and the Ceasefire.* Indochina Monograph Series. Washington, D.C.: U.S. Army Center of Military History, 1980. The Indochina Monographs are a series of papers written following the war by high-ranking Vietnamese, Cambodian, and Lao officers who succeeded in reaching the United States. The papers were commissioned by the U.S. Army, and the authors were given access to U.S. military records while preparing them.

Hinh, Nguyen Duy, and Tran Dinh Tho. *The South Vietnamese Society.* Indochina Monograph Series. Washington, D.C.: U.S. Army Center of Military History, 1980.

Hirschy, H. E., Jr., and P. A. Bondi. "The Final Hours." *Supply Corps Newsletter* (U.S. Navy Supply Corps), June–July 1975.

Hosmer, Stephen T., Konrad Kellen, and Brian M. Jenkins. *The Fall of South Vietnam: Statements by Vietnamese Military and Civilian Leaders.* New York: Crane, Russak, 1980.

Hughes, John. "Cambodia." *Atlantic Monthly,* February 1969, pp. 4–12.

———. *The End of Sukarno.* London: Angus & Robertson, 1968.

Indochina Operational Group of the Red Cross. "Circular No. 14." In House International Relations Committee [1], pt. 2, pp. 480–86.

International Monetary Fund. "Report on Cambodian Economic Situation." In House Government Operations Committee [2], pp. 81–120.

Isaacs, Harold R. *No Peace for Asia.* Cambridge, Mass.: MIT Press, 1967.

Ith Sarin. "Nine Months with the Maquis" and "Life in the Bureaus of the Khmer Rouge," from *Sranaoh Pralung Khmer (Regrets for the Khmer Soul).* Translated by U.S. embassy, Phnom Penh. In *Communist Party Power in Kampuchea. See* Carney 1977.

Jenkins, Brian M. *Giap and the Seventh Son.* Paper P-4851. Santa Monica, Calif.: Rand Corporation, September 1972.

———. *A People's Army for South Vietnam: A Vietnamese Solution.* Report R-897-ARPA. Santa Monica, Calif.: Rand Corporation, November 1971.

Joiner, Charles A. *The Politics of Massacre: Political Processes in South Vietnam.* Philadelphia: Temple University Press, 1974.

Kalb, Marvin, and Bernard Kalb. *Kissinger.* Boston: Little, Brown, 1974.

Kennerly, David Hume. *Shooter.* New York: Newsweek Books, 1979.

Khieu Samphan. *Cambodia's Economy and Industrial Development.* Translated by Laura Summers. Data Paper no. 111. Southeast Asia Program, Department of Asian Studies, Cornell University, Ithaca, N.Y., 1979.

Khuyen, Dong Van. *The RVNAF.* Indochina Monograph Series, Washington, D.C.: U.S. Army Center of Military History, 1980.

Kinnard, Douglas. *The War Managers.* Hanover, N.H.: University Press of New England, 1977.

Kirk, Donald. "Revolution and Political Violence in Cambodia, 1970–1974." In *Communism in Indochina,* pp. 215–30. *See* Zasloff and Brown 1975.

Kissinger, Henry. "The Vietnam Negotiations." *Foreign Affairs,* January 1969, pp. 211–34.

———. *White House Years.* Boston: Little, Brown, 1979.

———. *Years of Upheaval.* Boston: Little, Brown, 1982.

Komer, Robert W. *Bureaucracy Does Its Thing: Institutional Constraints on U.S.-GVN Performance in Vietnam.* Report R-967-ARPA. Santa Monica, Calif.: Rand Corporation, August 1972.

Kritt, Robert R. "B-52 Arc Light Operations." In *U.S. Air Force in Southeast Asia,* pp. 149–67. *See* Berger 1977.

Kunstadter, Peter, ed. *Southeast Asian Tribes, Minorities, and Nations.* Princeton: Princeton University Press, 1967.

Ky, Nguyen Cao. *Twenty Years and Twenty Days.* New York: Stein & Day. 1976.

Lam, Truong Buu. *Patterns of Vietnamese Response to Foreign Intervention: 1858–1900.* Southeast Asia Studies Monograph Series no. 11. Yale University, New Haven, 1967.

Lancaster, Donald. "The Decline of Prince Sihanouk's Regime." In *Indochina in Conflict,* pp. 47–55. *See* Zasloff and Goodman 1972.

––––––. "Power Politics at the Geneva Conference 1954." In *Vietnam: History, Documents, and Opinions,* pp. 125–44. *See* Gettleman 1966.

Landau, David. *Kissinger: The Uses of Power,* Boston: Houghton Mifflin, 1972.

Langer, P. F., and Joseph J. Zasloff. *Revolution in Laos: The North Vietnamese and the Pathet Lao.* Memorandum 5935-ARPA. Santa Monica, Calif.: Rand Corporation, September 1969.

Laurie, Jim. "Cambodia: Five Years Later." *The Correspondent.* Foreign Correspondents Club of Hong Kong, April 1980.

Le Gro, William E. *Vietnam from Ceasefire to Capitulation.* Indochina Monograph Series. Washington, D.C.: U.S. Army Center of Military History, 1981.

Leifer, Michael. "Peace and War in Cambodia." *Southeast Asia,* Winter-Spring 1971, pp. 59–73.

Lewy, Guenter. *America in Vietnam.* New York: Oxford University Press, 1978.

Lung, Hoang Ngoc. *Strategy and Tactics.* Indochina Monograph Series. Washington, D.C.: U.S. Army Center of Military History, 1980.

Majdalany, Fred. *The Fall of Fortress Europe.* Garden City, N.Y.: Doubleday, 1968.

Martin, Earl S. *Reaching the Other Side.* New York: Crown, 1978.

McAlister, John T., Jr. "Mountain Minorities and the Viet Minh: A Key to the Indochina War." In *Southeast Asian Tribes,* vol. 2, pp. 771–844. *See* Kunstadter 1967.

McCarthy, James R. and George B. Allison. *Linebacker II: A View from the Rock.* U.S. Air Force Southeast Asia Monograph Series, vol. 6, monograph 8. Air War College, Maxwell Air Force Base, Ala., 1979.

McCauley, Brian. "Operation End Sweep." Annapolis: *U.S. Naval Institute Proceedings,* March 1974. Admiral McCauley was the commander of the task force assigned to clear mines from North Vietnamese waters following the 1973 peace agreement.

McCloskey, Paul N., Jr. "The North Vietnam-South Vietnam Confrontation." Report on Vietnam Fact-finding Trip, February 24 to March 3, 1975. In *Congressional Record,* March 14, 1975, pp. 6775–79.

Miller, Carolyn Paine. *Captured!* Chappaqua, N.Y.: Christian Herald Books, 1977.

Momyer, William W. *The Vietnamese Air Force, 1951–1975, An Analysis of its Role in Combat.* U.S. Air Force Southeast Asia Monograph Series, vol. 3, monograph 4. Washington, D.C.: U.S. Government Printing Office, 1975.

Mouhot, Henri. *Henri Mouhot's Diary: Travels in the Central Parts of Siam, Cambodia, and Laos during the Years 1858–1861.* Abridged and edited by Christopher Pym. Singapore: Oxford University Press, 1966.

Nessen, Ron. *It Sure Looks Different from the Inside.* Chicago: Playboy Press, 1978.

Ngan, Nguyen Ngoc. (with E. E. Richey). *The Will of Heaven: A Story of One Vietnamese and the End of His World.* New York: Dutton, 1982.

Nixon, Richard. *RN: The Memoirs of Richard Nixon.* New York: Grosset & Dunlap, 1978.

Oberdorfer, Don. *Tet!* Garden City, N.Y.: Doubleday, 1971.

Osborne, John. *The Nixon Watch.* New York: Liveright, 1970.

Osborne, Milton. *Politics and Power in Cambodia: The Sihanouk Years.* Camberwell, Australia: Longman, 1973.

————. "Reflections on the Cambodian Tragedy." *Pacific Community,* October 1976.

Ott, David Ewing. *Field Artillery, 1954–1973.* Vietnam Studies Series. Washington, D.C.: Department of the Army, 1975.

Parker, Maynard. "Vietnam: The War That Won't End." *Foreign Affairs,* January 1975, pp. 352–74.

Pentagon Papers. Gravel ed. Boston: Beacon Press, 1971.

Pentagon Papers. House Armed Services Committee version (complete).

Pentagon Papers. *New York Times* ed. Toronto: Bantam Books, 1971.

Pike, Douglas. "Cambodia's War." *Southeast Asian Perspectives,* March 1971, pp. 1–48.

————. *The Viet-Cong Strategy of Terror.* Saigon: U.S. embassy, February 1970.

Ponchaud, François. *Cambodia Year Zero.* Translated by Nancy Amphoux. New York: Holt, Rinehart & Winston, 1978.

Pond, Elizabeth. "South Vietnamese Politics and the American Withdrawal." In *Indochina in Conflict,* pp. 1–24. *See* Zasloff and Goodman, 1972.

Porter, D. Gareth. "Kissinger's Double-Cross for Peace: The Broken Promise to Hanoi." *Nation,* April 30, 1977.

————. *A Peace Denied: The United States, Vietnam, and the Paris Agreement.* Bloomington: Indiana University Press, 1975.

————, ed. *Vietnam: The Definitive Documentation of Human Decisions.* Stanfordville, N.Y.: Earl M. Coleman Enterprises, 1979.

Price, Raymond. *With Nixon.* New York: Viking Press, 1977.

Project Air War and Indochina Resource Center. *Air War: The Third Indochina War.* Washington, D.C., March 1972.

Quinn, Kenneth. "Political Change in Wartime: The Khmer Krahom Revolution in Southern Cambodia, 1970–1974." *Naval War College Review,* Spring 1976, pp. 3–31.

Rickenbach, Ron. Untitled typed manuscript on Long Cheng, Laos. March 5, 1971.

Robbins, Christopher. *Air America.* New York: Putnam, 1979.

Roberts, T. D., et al. *Area Handbook for Laos.* Washington, D.C.: U.S. Government Printing Office, June 1967.

Ryan, Cornelius. *A Bridge Too Far.* New York: Simon & Schuster, 1974.

"Saigon, the Historic Hours." *Vietnam Courier* (Hanoi), May 1975.

Sak Sutsakhan. *The Khmer Republic at War and the Final Collapse*. Indochina Monograph Series. Washington, D.C.: U.S. Army Center of Military History, 1980.

Sananikone, Oudone. *The Royal Lao Army and U.S. Army Advice and Support*. Indochina Monograph Series. Washington, D.C.: U.S. Army Center of Military History, 1981.

Santoli, Al. *Everything We Had: An Oral History of the Vietnam War by Thirty-three American Soldiers Who Fought It*. New York: Random House, 1981.

Schanberg, Sydney. "The Death and Life of Dith Pran." *New York Times Magazine*, January 20, 1980.

Schell, Jonathan. *The Time of Illusion*. New York: Knopf, 1976.

Shackley, Theodore. *The Third Option: An American View of Counterinsurgency Operations*. New York: Reader's Digest Press, 1981.

Shannon, William V. *The Heir Apparent: Robert Kennedy and the Struggle for Power*. New York: Macmillan, 1967.

Shaplen, Robert. "Letter from Vietnam." *New Yorker*, February 24, 1973, pp. 100–111.

———. "Letter from Indochina." *New Yorker*, June 2, 1973, pp. 40–60.

———. "Letter from Saigon." *New Yorker*, April 21, 1975, pp. 124–38.

———. *Time Out of Hand: Revolution and Reaction in Southeast Asia*. New York: Harper & Row, 1969.

Shawcross, William. *Sideshow: Kissinger, Nixon, and the Destruction of Cambodia*. New York: Simon & Schuster, 1979.

Sheehan, Edward R. F. *The Arabs, Israelis, and Kissinger: A Secret History of American Diplomacy in the Middle East*. New York: Reader's Digest Press, 1976.

Sihanouk, Norodom. "The Future of Cambodia." *Foreign Affairs*, October 1970, pp. 1–10.

———. *War and Hope: The Case for Cambodia*. Translated by Mary Feeney. New York: Pantheon Books, 1980.

Sim Var. "Restoring Peace to Cambodia." *Pacific Community*, October 1970.

Smith, Harvey H., et al. *Area Handbook for South Vietnam*. Washington, D.C.: U.S. Government Printing Office, April 1967.

Smith, Hedrick. *The Russians*. New York: Quadrangle Books, 1976.

Smith, Homer D. "The Final Forty-five Days of Vietnam." Personal account. In only slightly different form this also appears as chapter 16-B in the DAO Final Assessment.

Snepp, Frank. *Decent Interval*. New York: Random House, 1977.

Stillman, Arthur D. *Notes on Minority Policies in Laos*. Edited by Robert L. Solomon. Paper P-4381. Santa Monica, Calif.: Rand Corporation, May 1970.

Stoessinger, John G. *Henry Kissinger: The Anguish of Power*. New York: Norton, 1976.

Strock, Carl. "Laotian Tragedy: The Long March." *New Republic*, May 9, 1970.

Sully, Francois, ed. *We the Vietnamese: Voices from Vietnam*. New York: Praeger, 1971.

Summers, Harry G., Jr. *On Strategy: A Critical Analysis of the Vietnam War*. Novato, Calif.: Presidio Press, 1982.

Summers, Laura. "Cambodia: Model of the Nixon Doctrine." *Current History*, December 1973.

Szulc, Tad. "Behind the Vietnam Ceasefire Agreement." *Foreign Policy,* Summer 1974, pp. 21–69.

"Talking With Former Puppet Officers." *Vietnam Courier* (Hanoi), August 1975.

Terzani, Tiziano. *Giai Phong! The Fall and Liberation of Saigon.* Translated by John Shepley. New York: St. Martin's Press, 1976.

Thayer, Thomas C. "How to Analyze a War without Fronts: Vietnam, 1965–1972." *Journal of Defense Research, Series B: Tactical Warfare,* Fall 1975. This was a classified journal produced and distributed within the Defense Department.

Thien, Ton That. "Vietnam: Light at the Tunnel's End?" *Orientations* (Hong Kong), January 1971, pp. 35–39.

Tho, Tran Dinh. *The Cambodian Incursion.* Indochina Monograph Series. Washington, D.C.: U.S. Army Center of Military History, 1979.

Thompson, Sir Robert. "A Successful End to the War in Vietnam." *Pacific Community,* April 1971.

Timmes, Charles. "Vietnam Summary: Military Operations after the Ceasefire Agreement." *Military Review,* August and September 1976.

Toai, Doan Van. "A Lament for Vietnam." *New York Times Magazine,* March 28, 1981.

Tobin, Thomas G., Arthur E. Laehr, and John F. Hilgenberg. *Last Flight from Saigon.* U.S. Air Force Southeast Asia Monograph Series, vol. 4, monograph 6. Washington, D.C.: U.S. Government Printing Office, 1978.

Truong, Ngo Quang. *The Easter Offensive of 1972.* Indochina Monograph Series. Washington, D.C.: U.S. Army Center of Military History, 1980.

Tuchman, Barbara W. *Practicing History.* New York: Knopf, 1981.

Turley, G. H., and M. R. Wells. "Easter Invasion 1972." *Marine Corps Gazette,* March 1973.

Turner, Robert F. *Vietnamese Communism: Its Origins and Development.* Stanford, Calif.: Hoover Institution, 1975.

United Nations Economic Commission for Asia and the Far East. *Economic Survey of Asia and the Far East, 1973.* Preliminary draft by ECAFE Secretariat, Bangkok, January 25 and February 6, 1974.

Valdez, Juan J., interviewed by Tom Bartlett. "The Last to Leave." *Leatherneck,* September 1975.

Van Praagh, David. "Laos Still Lives in the Shadow of Indochina's Larger Conflict." *International Perspectives* (Ottawa), July-August 1973, pp. 26–30.

Van Staaveren, Jacob. "The Air War against North Vietnam." In *U.S. Air Force in Southeast Asia,* pp. 69–99. *See* Berger 1977.

Vien, Cao Van. *Leadership.* Indochina Monograph Series, Washington, D.C.: U.S. Army Center of Military History, 1981.

Vien, Cao Van, and Dong Van Khuyen. *Reflections on the Vietnam War.* Indochina Monograph Series. Washington, D.C.: U.S. Army Center of Military History, 1980.

Warner, Denis. *Certain Victory: How Hanoi Won the War.* Kansas City: Sheed Andrews & McMeel, 1977 and 1978.

Weiss, George, "Battle for Control of the Ho Chi Minh Trail." *Armed Forces Journal,* February 15, 1971.

Westmoreland, William C. *A Soldier Reports.* Garden City, N.Y.: Doubleday, 1976.

Whalen, Richard J. *Catch the Falling Flag: A Republican's Challenge to His Party*. Boston: Houghton Mifflin, 1972.

Whitaker, Donald P., et al. *Area Handbook for the Khmer Republic (Cambodia)*. Washington, D.C.: U.S. Government Printing Office, 1973.

Woodruff, John E. "The Meo of Laos." Baltimore *Sun*, February 21, 22, and 23, 1971.

Yearbook on International Communist Affairs. Stanford, Calif.: Hoover Institution, 1971 and 1975 eds.

Young, Steve. "Political Attitudes and Organizations in Binh Duong." March 1, 1970. Typescript.

Zasloff, Joseph J. "Laos 1972: The War, Politics, and Peace Negotiations." *Asian Survey*, January 1973, pp. 60–75.

―――――. *The Pathet Lao: Leadership and Organization*. Lexington, Mass.: D. C. Heath, 1973.

Zasloff, Joseph, J., and MacAlister Brown, eds. *Communism in Indochina: New Perspectives*. Lexington, Mass.: Lexington Books, 1975.

―――――. *Communist Indochina and U.S. Foreign Policy: Postwar Realities*. Boulder, Colo.: Westview Press, 1978.

Zasloff, Joseph J., and Allan E. Goodman, eds. *Indochina in Conflict*. Lexington, Mass.: Lexington Books, 1972.

Zumwalt, Elmo R., Jr. *On Watch*. New York: Quadrangle Books, 1976.

2. U.S. GOVERNMENT DOCUMENTS AND RECORDS

Some of the military records listed below were made available to the author from various private files. Most of them, however, can be found on file at the U.S. Army Center of Military History, the Marine Corps Historical Center, or the Naval Historical Center, all in Washington, D.C. The initials *DDRS* following an entry mean that the document is included in the Declassified Documents Reference System of the Carrollton Press. The numbers following the initials represent the year and entry number in Carrollton's *Quarterly Catalogue*.

CENTRAL INTELLIGENCE AGENCY

"Stocktaking in Indochina." Office of National Estimates. April 17, 1970. DDRS (77) 270C.

"North Vietnamese Intentions in Indochina." Special National Intelligence Estimate 14.3–1–70 (draft), June 26, 1970. DDRS (80)32A.

"Communist Military and Economic Aid to North Vietnam, 1970–1974." Joint memorandum prepared by CIA and DIA [Defense Intelligence Agency] and concurred in by Bureau of Intelligence and Research, Department of State. March 5, 1975.

Kampuchea: A Demographic Catastrophe. National Foreign Assessment Center. May 1980.

DEPARTMENT OF DEFENSE

"Report on Selected Air and Ground Operations in Cambodia and Laos." September 10, 1973.

"Chronology of Significant Events—Operation Frequent Wind" and "Chronology of Significant Events—Operation Eagle Pull." In memorandum from Vice Adm. Harry D. Train II, Director, Joint Staff, for the Assistant Secretary of Defense (Public Affairs). August 25, 1975. These are cited in the source notes as "Chronology —Frequent Wind" and Chronology—Eagle Pull."

Southeast Asia Analysis Report. Classified journal produced by the Office of the Assistant Secretary of Defense for Systems Analysis.

ARMY

The Logistics Review, U.S. Army Vietnam, 1965–1969. U.S. Army Logistics Management Center, n.d.

DEFENSE ATTACHE OFFICE, SAIGON

DAO Quarterly Assessments and Final Assessment, October 1973-June 1975.

"Accounting for the Missing and Dead." Briefing paper, U.S. Delegation, Four-Party Joint Military Team. February 28, 1975.

JOINT CHIEFS OF STAFF

Memoranda to the Secretary of Defense concerning Operation Menu, March 13, 1969, through April 14, 1970. DDRS (79)385B through 401A. Included in this series are "Recapitulation of the Menu Program," February 4, 1970, DDRS (79)396C, and "Assessment of Menu Operations," March 14, 1970, DDRS (79)399A. In the Notes, these are cited as JCS Memoranda.

MARINE CORPS

"Amphibious Evacuation RVN." Post-exercise report from Commanding Officer, 1st Battalion, 4th Marine Regiment, to Commanding General, III Marine Amphibious Force. April 30, 1975.

9th MAB (9th Marine Amphibious Brigade). "Frequent Wind After Action Report." CTG79.1 Message 021510Z May 1975. Appears as tab E, PROVMAG 39 "Command Chronology" for May 1–12, 1975; also in DAO Final Assessment, chap. 16-H, pp. 2–17.

RLT-4 (Regimental Landing Team 4, 9th Marine Amphibious Brigade). "Command Chronology 27 March to 30 April 1975." May 13, 1975.

PROVMAG 39 (Provisional Marine Aircraft Group 39). "Command Chronology for Period 19 April to 30 April 1975" and "Command Chronology for Period 1 May to 12 May 1975." May 17, 1975. Attachments include After Action Reports by 9th MAB and Task Force 76, extracts from various Defense Intelligence Agency and USSAG intelligence reports, and messages transmitted during the execution of Operation Frequent Wind.

9th MAB. "Command Chronology 26 March to 30 April 1975." May 19, 1975.

Amphibious Evacuation Security Group. "Command Chronology." Appears as annex F, 9th MAB "Command Chronology."

Marine Corps Oral History Collection. Tape recorded interviews. Oral History Section, Marine Corps Historical Center, Washington, D.C.

Transcripts, interviews with marine security guards. Oral History Section, Marine Corps Historical Center, Washington, D.C.

MILITARY ASSISTANCE COMMAND-VIETNAM

"Big Mack Evaluation: Field Research in Binh Duong and Chuong Thien Provinces." MAC-V Strategic Research & Analysis Division, Directorate of Intelligence Production. 1970.

"Military Region II Overview." MACCORDS (Civil Operations and Rural Development Support). May 1971.

NAVY

"Refugee Evacuation: Report 1–75." From Master, USNS *Greenville Victory*, to Commander, Military Sealift Command Far East. April 9, 1975.

"Refugee Ops Weekly Report." SS *Pioneer Contender*. April 11, 1975.

Task Force 76. "Frequent Wind After Action Report." CTF 76 Message 020344Z May 1975. Appears as tab D, PROVMAG 39 "Command Chronology" for May 1–12, 1975.

"Chronological Data for Operation New Life 26 April 1975–5 July 1975." Operational Archives Branch, Naval Historical Center.

Report by Commanding Officer, USS *Duluth* (LPD-6) to Commanding Officer, Amphibious Squadron 5. June 4, 1975.

"Activities of MSCOV During the Vietnam Evacuation." Memorandum from Acting Chief, MSC Office Saigon Residual, to Commander, Military Sealift Command Far East. June 27, 1975.

"Vietnam Sealift Evacuation History." Report by Commander, Military Sealift Command Far East, to Military Sealift Command. July 24, 1975.

Transcript, interview with Commodore Hoang Co Minh. Operational Archives Branch, Naval Historical Center. Interview conducted September 8 and 18, 1975.

USS *Durham* (LKA 114). Command History for Calendar Year 1975. February 26, 1976.

USS *Dubuque* (LPD-8). Command History for Period 1 January 1975 to 31 December 1975. May 14, 1976.

GENERAL ACCOUNTING OFFICE

"Problems in the Khmer Republic (Cambodia) concerning War Victims, Civilian Health, and War-related Casualties." Report B-169832, February 2, 1972. In Senate Judiciary Committee [3], pp. 83–112.

"Follow-up Review of Refugees, War Casualties, Civilian Health, and Social Welfare Programs in South Vietnam." In Senate Judiciary Committee [6], pp. 132–55.

Stronger Controls Needed over Major Types of U.S. Equipment Provided to the Republic of Vietnam Armed Forces. Report B-159451. December 18, 1974.

DEPARTMENT OF STATE

"Cambodia: Can the Vietnamese Communists Export Insurgency?" Bureau of Intelligence and Research. September 25, 1970. DDRS (80)179C.

"Interpretations of the Agreement on Ending the War and Restoring Peace in Vietnam." Briefing paper by State Department legal adviser. In Senate Judiciary Committee [8], pp. 327–33.

"Presidential Authority to Continue U.S. Air Combat Operations in Cambodia." April 30, 1973. In *Department of State Bulletin*, May 21, 1973, pp. 652–53; also *Congressional Record*, May 16, 1973, pp. 15996–97.

"Summary of Negotiating Efforts on Cambodia." March 4, 1975.

"Cambodia: An Assessment of Humanitarian Needs and Relief Efforts." Inspector General for Foreign Assistance. In *Congressional Record*, March 20, 1975, pp. 7891–94.

AGENCY FOR INTERNATIONAL DEVELOPMENT

Economic Data Book. AID Mission to Phnom Penh. April 28, 1974.

Facts on Foreign Aid to Laos. AID Mission to Laos. Vientiane. 197–.

U.S. EMBASSY, PHNOM PENH

"Khmer Reports." Weekly situation reports, March 4 through April 8, 1975. DDRS (80)182B through 184C.

U.S. EMBASSY, SAIGON

"Memoranda of Conversations on Jan. 16, 17 & 18, 1974, between Ambassador Martin, Embassy Officers, and a Group of American Citizens Visiting Vietnam." In *Congressional Record*, April 4, 1974, pp. 9915–24.

"ICCS Accomplishments." Memorandum, June 26, 1974.

Principal Reports from Communist Sources. A publication of the U.S. Information Service in Saigon, containing translations and analyses of material from the Vietnamese Communist press.

Vietnam Documents and Research Notes. An embassy publication containing translations of Communist documents, including internal documents captured by U.S. or allied forces, and analytical commentary on various political, military, or organizational aspects of the Vietnamese Communist movement.

3. CONGRESSIONAL HEARINGS AND REPORTS

HOUSE OF REPRESENTATIVES

APPROPRIATIONS COMMITTEE

1. *Department of Defense Appropriations for 1971.* Pt. 6, "U.S. Operations in Cambodia," May 4, 1970.

2. *Department of Defense Appropriations—Bombing of North Vietnam.* January 9 and 18, 1973.

3. *Foreign Assistance and Related Agencies Appropriations for 1974.* Pt. 2, "Indochina Postwar Reconstruction Assistance," July 18, 1973.

4. *Department of Defense Appropriation for 1975.* Pt. 1, January 9, February 13 and 26–28, March 5–6, 1974.

5. *Foreign Assistance and Related Agencies Appropriations for 1975.* Pt. 1, "Military Assistance," June 5, 1974; Pt. 3, "Budget Amendment for Military Assistance to Cambodia," February 3, 1975.
6. *Department of Defense Appropriation Bill, 1975.* H. Rept. 93–1255, August 1, 1974.
7. *Department of Defense Appropriations—Oversight of Fiscal Year 1975 Military Assistance to Vietnam.* January 30 and February 3, 1975.
8. *Emergency Supplemental Appropriations for Assistance to the Republic of South Vietnam for Fiscal Year 1975.* April 21, 1975.
9. *Department of Defense Appropriation for 1976.* Pt. 3, "South Vietnam Equipment Remaining and Cost of Evacuation," May 12, 1975.

ARMED SERVICES COMMITTEE

1. *Unauthorized Bombing of Military Targets in North Vietnam.* Report by the Investigating Subcommittee. December 15, 1972.
2. *Full Committee Consideration of Privileged Resolution H. Res. 379, Concerning Certain Military Actions in Cambodia and Laos.* May 8, 1973.
3. *Hearing on H.R. 12565—Supplemental Authorization for FY1974.* March 18 and 19, 1974.
4. *Hearings on Military Posture and H.R. 12564, Department of Defense Authorization for Appropriations for Fiscal Year 1975.* Pt. 1, February 7, 13–14, 19, 21–22, 28, and March 1, 4–6, 11, 14, 26, 1974.
5. *Hearings on Military Posture and H.R. 3689 [H.R. 6674], Department of Defense Authorization for Appropriations for Fiscal Year 1976.* Pt. 1, February 18–19, 21, 24, 26; March 3, 10–11, 13, 19–20; April 14, 17, 21–22, and May 6, 1975.

FOREIGN AFFAIRS COMMITTEE

1. *Situation in Indochina.* February 8 and March 6, 1973.
2. *U.S. Policy and Programs in Cambodia.* May 9–10, June 6–7, 1973.
3. *The Treatment of Political Prisoners in South Vietnam by the Government of the Republic of Vietnam.* September 13, 1973.
4. *Political Prisoners in South Vietnam and the Philippines,* May 1 and June 5, 1974.
5. *Fiscal Year 1975 Foreign Assistance Request.* June 4–5, 11–13, 18–20, 26, and July 1–2, 10–11, 1974.
6. *U.S. Aid to Indochina.* Report of a staff survey team to South Vietnam, Cambodia, and Laos. July 25, 1974.
7. *Military and Economic Situation in Cambodia.* Report of a staff survey. Confidential Committee Print. March 13, 1975.

GOVERNMENT OPERATIONS COMMITTEE

1. *U.S. Aid Operations in Laos.* 7th Report to 86th Congress. June 15, 1959.
2. *Economy and Efficiency of U.S. Aid Programs in Laos and Cambodia.* July 12, 1971.
3. *U.S. Assistance Programs in Vietnam.* July 15–16, 19, 21, and August 2, 1971.
4. *U.S. Assistance Programs in Vietnam.* H. Rept. 92–1610. October 17, 1972.

SELECT COMMITTEE ON INTELLIGENCE

1. *U.S. Intelligence Agencies and Activities: Risks and Control of Foreign Intelligence.* Pt. 5, November 4, 6, and December 2–3, 9–12, 17, 1975.

INTERNATIONAL RELATIONS COMMITTEE

1. *The Vietnam-Cambodia Emergency, 1975.* Pt. 1, "Vietnam Evacuation and Humanitarian Assistance," April 9, 15–16, 18, and May 7–8, 1975. Pt. 2, "The Vietnam-Cambodia Debate," March 6, 11–13, and April 14, 1975. Pt. 3, "Vietnam Evacuation: Testimony of Ambassador Graham A. Martin," January 27, 1976. Pt. 4, "Cambodia Evacuation: Testimony of Ambassador John Gunther Dean," May 5, 1976.
2. *Human Rights in Cambodia.* May 3, 1977.
3. *U.S. Aid to North Vietnam.* July 19, 1977.

JUDICIARY COMMITTEE

1. *Bombing of Cambodia.* Book 11, Statement of Information and Hearings, Presidential Impeachment Investigation. 1974.

SELECT COMMITTEE ON MISSING PERSONS IN SOUTHEAST ASIA

1. *Americans Missing in Southeast Asia.* Pt. 2, November 5, 11–12, 19, and December 17, 1975; Pt 5, June 13 and 25, July 21, September 21, 1976.
2. *Americans Missing in Southeast Asia.* Final report. H. Rept. 94–1764. December 13, 1976.

SENATE

APPROPRIATIONS COMMITTEE

1. *Second Supplemental Appropriations for FY1973.* Pt. 2, "Department of Defense," May 7, 1973.
2. *Foreign Assistance and Related Programs Appropriations FY1974.* Pt. 2, "Aid Program for Cambodia," June 11, 1973; "Foreign Military Assistance Program," July 24, 1973, and Appendix.
3. *Foreign Assistance and Related Programs Appropriations FY1975.* "Security Assistance Programs," June 25, 1974, and "Department of State," July 24, 1974.
4. *Emergency Military Assistance and Economic and Humanitarian Aid to South Vietnam.* April 15, 1975.

ARMED SERVICES COMMITTEE

1. *Bombing in Cambodia.* July 16, 23, 25–26, 30, and August 7–9, 1973.
2. *Military Procurement Supplemental—Fiscal Year 1974.* March 12 and 19, 1974.
3. *Fiscal Year 1975 Authorization for Military Procurement.* Pt. 4, "MASF," April 9, 1974.
4. *Authorizing Appropriations for Fiscal Year 1975 for Military Procurement.* S. Rept. 93–884. May 29, 1974.
5. *Vietnam Aid—The Painful Options.* Report by Sen. Sam Nunn. February 12, 1975.

FOREIGN RELATIONS COMMITTEE

1. *U.S. Security Agreements and Commitments Abroad.* Pt. 2, "Kingdom of Laos," October 20–22, 1969.
2. *Cambodia: May 1970.* Staff report. June 7, 1970.
3. *Laos: April 1971.* Staff report. August 3, 1971.
4. *Thailand, Laos, and Cambodia: January 1972.* Staff report. May 8, 1972.

5. *U.S. Air Operations in Cambodia.* Staff report. April 27, 1973.
6. *Thailand, Laos, Cambodia, and Vietnam: April 1973.* Staff report. June 11, 1973.
7. *Foreign Assistance Authorization.* June 7, 21, 26, July 24–25, 1974.
8. *Vietnam: May 1974.* Staff report. August 5, 1974.
9. *Background Information Relating to Southeast Asia and Vietnam.* 7th ed. rev. December 1974.
10. *Supplemental Assistance to Cambodia.* February 24 and March 6, 1975.
11. *Supplemental Assistance for Cambodia.* S. Rept. 94–54. March 21, 1975.

JUDICIARY COMMITTEE

1. *Refugee and Civilian War Casualty Problems in Indochina.* Staff report. September 28, 1970.
2. *War-Related Civilian Problems in Indochina.* Pt. 2, "Laos and Cambodia," April 21–22, 1971.
3. *War Victims in Indochina.* GAO reports for the Subcommittee to Investigate Problems Connected with Refugees and Escapees. May 3, 1972.
4. *Problems of War Victims in Indochina.* Pt. 2, "Cambodia and Laos," May 9, 1972.
5. *Relief and Rehabilitation of War Victims in Indochina.* Pt. 1, "Crisis in Cambodia," April 16, 1973; Pt. 3, "North Vietnam and Laos," July 31, 1973.
6. *Humanitarian Problems in Indochina.* July 18, 1974.
7. *Humanitarian Problems in South Vietnam and Cambodia: Two Years after the Ceasefire.* Study Mission report. January 27, 1975.
8. *Congressional Oversights of Executive Agreements—1975.* May 13–15 and July 25, 1975.

4. BROADCAST TRANSLATION AND MONITORING SERVICES

Foreign Broadcast Information Service (FBIS). U.S. Central Intelligence Agency. "Daily Report, Asia-Pacific" and supplements.
Summary of World Broadcasts (SWB). British Broadcasting Corporation. 2nd ser. pt. 3: "The Far East."

Index